SHAKER LITERATURE
A Bibliography

SHAKER LITERATURE
A Bibliography

Compiled & Annotated by MARY L. RICHMOND

IN TWO VOLUMES

VOLUME I. BY THE SHAKERS

Published by SHAKER COMMUNITY, INC.
Hancock, Massachusetts
and distributed by the
UNIVERSITY PRESS OF NEW ENGLAND
Hanover, New Hampshire
1977

IN MEMORY
OF
Eldress Catherine Allen
Elder Alonzo Giles Hollister
Eldress Emma B. King
Wallace Hugh Cathcart
John Patterson MacLean
Edward Brockway Wight
The pioneers whose remarkable foresight assured
the preservation of Shaker printed materials in the
collections that made this bibliography possible.

CONTENTS

VOLUME I. BY THE SHAKERS

VOLUME II. ABOUT THE SHAKERS

FOREWORD

by John W. Chandler

The large collection of literature recorded and annotated in this bibliography has to do with a movement whose all-inclusive membership throughout its two centuries on American soil embraced only about 20,000 persons. The Shakers now alive, fewer than a dozen, are at the end of a movement which, at its zenith in the second third of the nineteenth century, included no more than 6,000 members. Who were these people, and why, despite their relatively small number, have they inspired such a consuming interest for so long a period?

Although the American Shaker movement dates from the migration to America by Mother Ann Lee and some of her followers in 1774, its traceable roots extend back to southeastern France in the last two decades of the seventeenth century.

With the revocation of the Edict of Nantes in 1685, the French Protestants lost the guarantee of tolerance and safety they had enjoyed since 1598. The ensuing years witnessed mass migrations by the Huguenots as well as armed conflict between some Protestant groups and the Catholic forces that controlled France. One of the most serious conflicts involved the Protestant peasants of Cévennes called Camisards, a millenarian group best known for their dramatic prophetic utterances and attendant vivid bodily manifestations of spirit possession.

Some of these Camisard Prophets took refuge in England in 1706 after their military defeat in France in 1705. In England they continued to proclaim the imminence of the millennium, which was to be ushered in by the destruction of organized churches and other enemies of the Lord. The Prophets became the center of great excitement in England, where they stirred brutal opposition among the defenders of the conventional faiths and inspired fierce loyalty among their new English converts. Once it had been successfully transplanted to England, however, the prophetic movement proved to be remarkably hardy and persistent.

The Prophets, both French and English, exhibited a number of identifying traits: ecstatic religious experience marked by seizures and trembling; obsession with millennial prophecies and computations; hostility to all organized ecclesiastical structures, Protestant and Catholic; and special appeal to the poor working-class people, both rural and urban.

By Shaker accounts their movement can be traced to an important link with the Prophets in the form of a religious society formed by James and Jane Wardley in 1747 in Bolton, near Manchester, England. The Wardleys had been Quakers but came to embrace the millennial teachings of the Prophets. The Wardleys and their followers combined the Prophets' forms of worship with the old Quaker forms. While in silent meditation they would begin to tremble, and the trembling often led to agitated shouts, violent shaking, singing, and fulminations against sin. The name Shakers or Shaking Quakers originated from these worship sessions led by the Wardleys.

The religious society the Wardleys began would probably have remained obscure if it had not attracted Ann Lee, who joined in September 1758, at the age of twenty-three. She had endured a miserable childhood as a laborer in a Manchester cotton mill. Later, following her marriage in 1762 to Abraham Stanley, she had witnessed the deaths of her four infant children. According to Shaker sources, while serving a sentence in the Manchester jail in 1770 for profaning the Sabbath, she had a vision that was to supply the principal Shaker tenet, celibacy. The vision revealed that the sin of Adam and Eve was sexual intercourse and that sexual lust was the root cause of the various expressions of human depravity.

"Mother Ann," as she now came to be called, reported that another vision had directed her to America, where, she was promised, the millennial church would be established. She and eight of her most ardent followers landed in New York City in August 1774. A vanguard of the group proceeded to Niskayuna (Watervliet), near Albany, where they bought land. Ann Lee's husband, Abraham Stanley, abandoned her late in 1775, and she left New York City to join her followers in Watervliet the following spring.

When Mother Ann died in September 1784, three years before the formation of the communities that would institutionalize the Shaker devotion to celibacy and common ownership of property, the center of the movement shifted from Watervliet to nearby New Lebanon, where the organization of the first community got under way in September 1787. With the death of Mother Ann and the beginning of the communities, Shakerism passed from its earlier dependence on charismatic leadership to assume the institutional characteristics that were to stabilize and define the movement for the remainder of its history.

The New Lebanon settlement served as the mother church and model for subsequent Shaker communities, and the "ministries" (composed of the elders, male and female) of the various communities deferred to the authority of the New Lebanon or Central Ministry. The Shakers capitalized on the religious excitement and curiosity associated with frontier revivals. By 1826 the United Society of Believers in Christ's Second Appearing, popularly known as the Shakers, encompassed nineteen communities or separate societies, each containing from one hundred to six hundred members. These communities were made up of families (Church Family, South Family, etc.), each of which was an economically independent unit. The movement reached its peak strength in the East by the middle of the nineteenth century, by which time Shaker fortunes had already begun to decline in the West and the South.

In the nineteenth century Shakerism acquired stability and regularity in its social organization, liturgical forms, and theological doctrines. The dances lost their earlier spontaneity and became formalized; spirit-inspired utterances diminished in frequency and importance as Shaker exegetes and historians developed and emphasized a corpus of literature which attempted to square the main tenets of their faith with the Bible, and which set down the life and teachings of Mother Ann Lee.

Whereas the eighteenth-century Shakers adopted the Prophets' policy of hostility to the established churches, in the nineteenth century alienation gave way initially to competition and debate and eventually to accommodation. In competing with the established Protestant bodies for the allegiance of the evangelized frontier crowds, the Shakers engaged in discussions of questions of church history and theology. Such discussions led to a greater authority for the Bible among nineteenth-century Shakers than it had enjoyed in the times of the Wardleys and Mother Ann Lee.

The organization of Shakers into classes or orders facilitated intellectual and economic commerce with the outside world. The church order, consisting of carefully screened adults who had forever renounced title to all personal property, constituted the spiritual elite, and from their ranks the elders were selected. The junior order consisted of those who still held title to their property, even though they lived celibate lives in the religious community and permitted the community the use of their property. The novitiate order consisted of members who continued to live in families and to own and use private property, but who accepted the spiritual guidance of the Shakers. The latter two orders served as a link with the outside world and helped to buffer members of the church order against communication with the larger society.

Following the Civil War the Shakers, whose pacifism had created many problems for them during that conflict (as well as during the American Revolution), developed more and more interest in the burgeoning technology and intellectual ferment of the larger society. Shaker artisans, for example, began to read books and pamphlets that related to their crafts.

It was above all Elder Frederick W. Evans who granted a kind of legitimacy to the non-Shaker world which earlier Shakers had been unwilling to concede. To Mother Ann Lee and her early successors, James Whittaker and Joseph Meacham, the redeemed society of Shakers would coexist with a much larger society whose organization and behavior were based on a fundamental acceptance of lust and its progency of vices—greed, violence, deceit, and the like. But Evans, who dominated the Shaker scene from 1861 to 1892, perceived many of the forces and movements in the larger society as intimations and adumbrations of the same spirit and truth whose most pristine expression was Shakerism. And the purpose of Evans's extensive correspondence, writings, and lectures was to establish rapport between Shakerism and kindred movements.

The softening of Shaker sectarian opposition to the dominant culture was symptomatic of the incipient demise of the movement. In one of the most thoughtful and original interpretations of Shakerism (*The American Shakers: From Neo-Christianity to Presocialism,* translated from the French and edited by John K. Savacool, Amherst: University of Massachusetts Press, 1971), Henri Desroche contends that the movement lost its historical thrust and direction because of failure to resolve its ambivalent character as both a late expression of Protestant left-wing sectarianism and an early expression of socialism. According to Desroche, neither expression gained dominance.

It is pertinent to point out, however, that English Shakerism was spawned among urban industrial workers who knew the devastating effects on family life of the new conditions imposed by factory labor, but with its relocation to America, Shakerism became a religion of farmers and artisans from small-town and frontier areas. In this new setting its doctrines did not develop the social criticism that might have emerged if it had remained in the industrial centers of England. Shaped by agrarian and frontier conditions, American Shakerism, in fact, went into rapid eclipse as the forces of industrialization following the Civil War began to influence it. Its economic base was severely affected by the inability of its craftsmen to compete with the mass-produced commodities of the factories.

How then does one explain the current revival of popular and scholarly interest in the Shakers? Part of the answer has to do with longevity. The movement has lasted longer than any similar venture and has proved to be more durable and stable than most national societies.

The alienated character of so much of modern work has stimulated a special interest in Shaker industries and craftsmanship. An incredible number of articles on Shaker furniture have appeared; many are replete with photographs and even do-it-yourself diagrams. Several prosperous businesses are responding to the growing demand for kits and finished reproductions of Shaker furniture.

The Shakers attract interest chiefly, however, because they were concerned with issues that are once again the focal points of a vast amount of social unrest and private questioning. Just as industrialization weakened the family by curtailing its economic function, so today the nuclear family has come under new questioning because of a multiplicity of developments, many of which dispute the traditional belief that sexual activity, procreation, the family structure, and child-rearing are indissolubly bound together. Those who perceive the extended family as superior to the nuclear family as a locus for emotional and moral development and fulfillment are understandably curious about the communal family organization of the Shakers. Similarly, the Shaker denial of private ownership in favor of communal property attracts those who believe individual ownership to be a root cause of social injustice.

Another feature of Shaker theology and social organization which is attuned to a central theme of current social reform is the role of women as equals of men. To her followers Mother Ann Lee was the female incarnation of the Christ, just as Jesus of Nazareth was the male incarnation. Consistent with this central theological tenet, the Shakers maintained a careful balance of the sexes in the composition of the boards of Elders and Eldresses who ruled the communal families.

Because the issues that concerned the Shakers and to which they developed institutional answers are fundamental questions that will continue to trouble and challenge mankind, the place of the Shakers in history is secure and important. The bibliographic references recorded and described here will make access to these fascinating and sturdy people immeasurably easier.

The invaluable work of scholarship represented by this collection of bibliographic data is the product of five years of devoted and thorough work by Mary L. Richmond. Her sleuthing for remote and obscure materials has been imaginative and painstaking. Her lucid and concise annotations are informed by extensive first-hand acquaintance with the materials, sympathetic interest in Shaker people, and mature scholarly judgment. The flood of new publications about the Shakers will almost certainly continue, but Mrs. Richmond's bibliography should serve as a basic, indispensable work.

John W. Chandler

Williams College
Williamstown, Massachusetts

INTRODUCTION

In its simplest form bibliography concerns itself with the how and when and why and where and whence of books. Bibliographies . . . are intended as tools for the scholar, weapons for the bookseller, and armor for the collector.—A. Edward Newton, *Bibliography and Pseudo-Bibliography.*

It is not too much to say that no bibliography, however scholarly in conception and however meticulous in execution is either complete or free from error.—John Carter, *Taste and Technique in Book-Collecting.*

The Shakers became a new interest in my life in 1937 soon after my arrival in Williamstown, Massachusetts, only a short driving distance from both Hancock Shaker Village in Massachusetts and the Shaker community at Mount Lebanon, New York. I visited both communities which were at that time no longer the neatly efficient, thriving agricultural enterprises so much commented upon by nineteenth-century visitors. Some cultivation by hired hands was in progress at Hancock and a few hand-made pincushions, jellies, and Shaker boxes and baskets were for sale at the store. The Shakers were pleasant, some even jolly, but one was left with the impression of a once flourishing undertaking very slowly running down, with only the elderly left to carry on the Shaker way of life. There were at Mount Lebanon perhaps twenty-five members beyond their prime, but Robert Wagan's chair business was still being carried on by Eldress Sarah Collins and chairs could still be ordered. My most vivid memory of this visit is of Eldress Sarah finishing chairs by hand-rubbing and the serenity of her quiet pleasure in her work. Those gnarled arthritic hands were still active in spite of the handicaps age had brought. Here was the picture of the dignity of labor and the Shaker ethic "Hands to Work and Hearts to God," and I have always regretted that I did not have a camera to record this scene.

I was eager to learn more about the Shakers but discovered that *Shakerism; Its Meaning and Message,* by Anna White and Leila S. Taylor (Columbus, Ohio, 1904), then the most recent work on the history of the sect, was out of print. Fortunately, the Wight collection at the Williams College Library offered a rich resource of Shaker publications and the examination of this collection convinced me that there was need of a new Shaker bibliography. Many of the works in the collection had not been recorded in John P. MacLean's *A Bibliography of Shaker Literature* (Columbus, 1905). Since my professional training and experience had fitted me for just such work, I went happily about assembling Shaker references. Then I learned that someone else was busy at the same task. Reluctantly, I laid aside my project, little dreaming that over thirty years later there still would be no new Shaker bibliography and that I would find myself again assembling references. In 1937 it was my wish that a new Shaker bibliography would make accessible those materials which might attract an American historian to undertake a history of the Shakers written in the perspective of American history. Hopefully, the present bibliography may accomplish this purpose.*

In the interval at least nine different new Shaker bibliographies have been undertaken and aborted after varying lengths of time and for various reasons. The need for a new Shaker bibliography was recognized as early as 1912 when Wallace H. Cathcart, soon to become Director of the Western Reserve Historical Society, Cleveland, Ohio, had accumulated a large number of Shaker items not included in MacLean's *Bibliography*. He wrote to Eldress Catherine Allen of the Mount Lebanon Shaker Society, August 28, 1912, "When I get out in future years the large Bibliography of the Collection, I am going to have your portrait and Eldress Harriet's [Bullard] as frontispieces." (a.l.s. Western Reserve Historical Society.) Cathcart was the best qualified person to undertake the new Shaker bibliography, since he had succeeded in building the largest collection of Shakeriana anywhere, and a new Shaker bibliography would have been its natural corollary. Cathcart's collection was cataloged meticulously, but for reasons unknown his bibliography never materialized.

The purchase of Hancock Shaker Village by Shaker Community, Inc., in 1960 and the restoration plans projected for the Village reactivated my interest in the Shakers. In May 1967 Mrs. Lawrence K. Miller, President, Shaker Community, Inc., suggested that I compile a Shaker bibliography. Previous commitments and other reasons prevented any serious work before February 1968. In the intervening time Shaker references were accumulated, a history of the Shaker periodical *The Manifesto* (and its precursors) and *The Day-Star* were written, and background reading, especially about Shaker antecedents, was accomplished.

ORGANIZATION. Initially this Bibliography was projected roughly as an updated parallel of J. P. MacLean's *Bibliography,* and would therefore have included only unannotated primary printed materials (excluding newspaper accounts). As hundreds of references accumulated, however, questions were encountered. The question of what really constituted primary printed materials where the Shakers are concerned caused a reconsideration of the original intention. Another consideration was the still accelerating interest in all aspects of Shaker life and beliefs reflected in the torrent of words published about these peculiar people, their religion, history, communal life, culture, architecture, craftsmanship, and industries. Among these works were many contributions that extended knowledge about the Shakers, and research

* The name "Shaker" was originally a mocking epithet derived from the shaking that possessed members of this religious sect while under the stress of spiritual exaltation during their meetings. The Shakers ignored the formerly derisive intent and referred to themselves generally as Shakers (or Believers). Many different names are encountered in the titles of Shaker publications and in formal communications: The United Society of Believers in Christ's Second Appearing, Church of Christ's Second Appearing, The United Society of Believers, the United Society of Shakers, The Believers, The United Society, The Society of Shakers, The Millennial Church, The Aletheians, and Church of Christ (Shaker). The name "Shaking Quakers," widely used in the nineteenth century, is a misnomer. In this bibliography the name "Shaker" is used throughout.

would undoubtedly uncover many more. It was therefore decided to enlarge the Bibliography and to organize the printed materials into two parts (now published as two volumes): By the Shakers, and About the Shakers—each volume to be divided into a section recording books (parts of books, and pamphlets) and another section devoted to periodical articles. Consequently, it was necessary to back up and record the secondary items that had been found while searching for primary materials. The legal cases compiled by Gerard C. Wertkin were added as a section now at the end of Volume I. When about two thousand entries had been completed and organized in two parts, the accumulation was shown to several colleagues. It became apparent from the questions asked that annotations should be added if the bibliography were to enjoy wide usefulness and to offer essential information for those who were un-informed about the Shakers. Adding annotations involved backtracking again to re-examine items already recorded; annotations were added for any title not self-explanatory, and in some instances the annotations provide considerable information.

Nearly five years were spent in the compilation, verification, and examination of the over four thousand entries in the present bibliography, examination of perhaps a thousand items that were discarded, and examination of many works that are cited only in the annotations. The entries include nearly two centuries of Shaker publica-tions and attest the unflagging interest in the Shakers as shown in the works about them which cover the same time span. The body of materials recorded and described is intended to be comprehensive and to represent the wide spectrum of Shaker printed materials and the published works written about the Shakers.

The two volumes of this Bibliography approximate the conventional division of primary and secondary materials, with some qualifications. Shaker printed materials do not lend themselves to such neat categories or to a strict interpretation of what may be conventionally considered to be proper primary materials. Delimitation of the materials to be included in Volume I and Volume II involved many borderline cases. The question of what constitutes Shaker membership needed clarification.

If Shaker membership were construed to include only bona fide Shaker Covenant members, it would lead oddly to the exclusion of the father of Shaker literature, Richard McNemar, who was expelled, among other reasons, because he had not signed the Shaker Covenant at Union Village, Ohio. McNemar's position was anomalous. He expended so much time and effort persuading western Shakers to sign Shaker Covenants that, apparently through some oversight, he neglected to sign the covenant at his home, Union Village. Charles Lane, an Englishman, presents the other extreme. Lane established his residence in the Shaker community at Harvard, Massachusetts, after the failure of Bronson Alcott's Fruitlands community, and in-dentured his young son to the Shakers. Lane's relation to the Shakers remains ambiguous. He never signed the Covenant, but he did live among the Shakers long enough to reverse his opinion of some Shaker practices and to regret the indenture of his son. John Whitbey never signed the Covenant but lived among the Shakers at Pleasant Hill, Kentucky, seven years before he was expelled. Among other borderline cases are J. M. Peebles, often referred to as an "associative" member, and Cyrus Teed (*pseudonym* Koresh) who was made a member at Mount Lebanon; but neither one lived as a Shaker.*

The Universalist minister John P. MacLean made frequent visits to Shaker communities in search of Shaker manuscripts and printed publications, but his interests were those of a bookman, historian, and friend. Although he stated that he had been made a member of four different Shaker Societies, there is no indication that he showed any personal interest in Shaker religious beliefs or their communal life. On the contrary, MacLean clearly pointed out that he had "studiously avoided the discussion of doctrinal theories, because it would have been superfluous and no tangible results would have been derived therefrom." He urged those who were interested in Shaker religious beliefs to communicate directly with the Shakers or to consult their standard works (*Shakers of Ohio,* Columbus, Ohio, 1907, p. 9).

Such ambiguities were resolved by adopting in Volume I a broad interpretation of Shaker membership which allows for a wider inclusion of materials interpreted here to be Shaker publications. Persons who have lived among the Shakers for a considerable period whether as Covenant, novitiate, or probationary members are considered to be Shaker authors because they have experienced at firsthand the Shaker way of life, and their writings derive from this experience. It should be recognized, however, that the Shakers themselves might well have employed a narrower interpretation. After several visits to the Shakers at Harvard, Massachusetts, Ralph Waldo Emerson commented: "It is true that a community cannot be truly seen from the outside. If deep sympathy exists, what seems interference, is not, being justified by the heart of the suffering party" (*Journals and Miscellaneous Notebooks,* Cambridge, Belknap Press of Harvard University Press, 1971, IX, 1843–1847, p. 162). Volume I also embraces works printed by the Shakers; works issued with Shaker authorization; works written by Shaker apostates and by those who were expelled; and a few works published before the authors joined the Shakers. Other works conventionally considered to be primary—state and national documents, patents, legal documents, etc.—are likewise included in Volume I. The writings of John P. MacLean are *not* included in Volume I because they are clearly historical, bibliographical, or descriptive and are not concerned with Shaker religious beliefs and practices or the Shaker communal way of life. Shaker printed materials omitted from Volume I include all printed labels, display posters for Shaker products, packaging materials, business forms and letterheads, school attendance records and merit award forms, and other fugitive materials, as well as newspaper accounts. Shaker manuscripts are omitted but are occasionally cited in the annotations.

The works contained in Volume II, About the Shakers, comprise publications about Shaker beliefs, history and practices, pacifism, music, art, dancing, design, architecture, craftsmanship, agriculture, industries, communitarianism, anti-Shaker

* The Western Reserve Historical Society, Cleveland, Ohio, maintains a Shaker membership file of more than 16,000 names, but many Shakers are unaccounted for except in Shaker manuscripts that are widely dispersed; many manuscripts in all likelihood were destroyed.

tracts by non-Shakers, and in addition works of poetry, drama, and fiction in which Shakers appear or Shaker settings are utilized. These entries cover books, parts of books and pamphlets, and periodical articles which were published before 1973. (A Supplement of 1973-1974 items has been added.) Travelers' and visitors' accounts are also included in Volume II. Many of these accounts are valuable firsthand observations made by serious and informed observers such as those recorded by Robert Owen's party and the accounts of John Finch, Frederika Bremer, Harriet Martineau, Harriot Kezia Hunt, Hepworth Dixon, Marianne Finch, Benson Lossing, Charles Nordhoff, the anonymous writer of *Letters from Kentucky,* and others. On the other hand, among the thousands of nineteenth-century visitors to the Shakers, relatively few were interested in anything except the Sunday meetings, which they attended in droves to view the spectacle, particularly the dancing. Visiting the Shakers at New Lebanon, New York, was considered to be part of any sojourn at Lebanon Springs, a flourishing spa and resort frequented in the late eighteenth and nineteenth centuries by visitors from all parts of the United States and abroad. This Shaker visit was advertised as an added tourist attraction included in a long weekend package offered by the Hudson River Railroad and the Hudson and Berkshire Railroad Stage. Earlier it was part of an excursion offered by the Hudson River Steamboat Company. Similar casual visits took place at the other Shaker communities. The accounts written by such visitors are for the most part repetitious and prejudiced reactions to an unorthodox form of religion and are of little value as firsthand observations of the Shaker way of life. Nevertheless they are of interest in recording visitors' reaction to the Shakers and have been included in Volume II.

The voluminous literature about the Camisards, French and English Prophets described in the Foreword as Shaker antecedents, has not been included in this Bibliography. The similarities of beliefs and practices of these groups with those of the Shakers are evident, and the Shakers themselves have testified to an undefined connection, but this area remains largely unexplored in scholarly Shaker studies, and a direct relationship has not been documented. The best account is found in John Symonds, *Thomas Brown and the Angels* (London, Hutchinson, 1961). Henri Desroche, *The American Shakers,* translated by John K. Savacool (Amherst, Mass., University of Massachusetts Press, 1971), discusses the marked resemblances between the Camisards and the Shakers. References to the Girlingites, followers of Mother Mary Anne Girling (1864-1886), often called English Shakers, Hampshire Shakers, or Shakers of New Forest, have been omitted because no relationship existed between them and the American Shakers, followers of Mother Ann Lee. References to the American Indians of the Northwest identified as Indian Shakers or Puget Sound Shakers have not been included except where a possible relationship to the American Shakers is explored and discussed. Book reviews have been omitted in Volume II, except for a few nineteenth-century reviews that contain a reprinted account of the Shakers taken from the book being reviewed.

COLLECTORS AND COLLECTIONS. All serious scholars concerned with the Shakers owe a debt of gratitude to the pioneers who built the Shaker collections available in public institutions, and this Shaker bibliography is dedicated to them. Most of these collections were built in the first part of the twentieth century and were the result of the efforts of John Patterson MacLean, who first recognized the importance of preserving Shaker manuscripts and printed materials. MacLean's interest in the Shakers was aroused in the last years of the nineteenth century during an investigation of the Ohio mounds near the abandoned Shaker community at North Union (now Shaker Heights). He visited the western Shaker communities, where he established friendships with the old Shakers, who freely offered firsthand information about their past, furnished him with Shaker publications and manuscripts, and often called attention to long-forgotten publications. Later his collecting activities were expanded to include the eastern Shakers, with one of whom, Elder Alonzo Hollister, he enjoyed a fast friendship. Elder Alonzo encouraged and aided his search for Shaker materials. At that time Hollister was a member of the Ministry at Mount Lebanon, the parent body and seat of spiritual authority. After MacLean's great find of 1907 (*see* no. 2418, below) of the cache of Richard McNemar's publications at Union Village, Ohio, Hollister wrote to Brother Harlan at the same place, February 3, 1908, rejecting any Shaker claim on these materials (a.l.s. Berkshire Athenaeum, Pittsfield, Mass.). "I believe that he [MacLean] is in good work & am glad if he prosperd. I doubt if the pecuniary reward will any more than compensate him for the labor he has performed without money or price. Whatever money value the books may have, he has been the agent of its discovery & the creater (under the higher unseen power), of the demand." Hollister also accorded MacLean the credit for arousing public interest in Shaker literature and continued, "He has distributed a great deal without pay, that was lying around idle in our garrets & storerooms."

MacLean's genuine interest in Shaker history is evident in his many publications, but more important were his collecting interests and his activities in the dispersion of Shaker printed materials. Bookselling activities were carried on largely by mail, and sales were promoted by issuing catalogs as additional items became available. MacLean supplemented these enterprises by an extensive correspondence in a barely legible hand with librarians and collectors. The choicest items were always offered first to the Library of Congress, where he later placed his own private collection. His *Bibliography of Shaker Literature* has served librarians and collectors since 1905 as the most complete Shaker bibliography. Hollister described it in the letter quoted above as "a laborious & elaborate production, that must have required considerable correspondence."

The largest collection of Shakeriana is owned by The Western Reserve Historical Society, Cleveland, Ohio. It was assembled by Wallace H. Cathcart, with the invaluable assistance of Eldress Catherine Allen of the Shaker community at Mount Lebanon, New York.* When Cathcart became the first fulltime Director of the Western

---

* I am indebted to James W. Gilreath who has courteously allowed the use of information in his unpublished paper "Wallace Cathcart, Catherine Allen and the Formation of the Shaker Library." See also no. 3242.

Reserve Historical Society, there were only nine or ten Shaker items in the library, but he regarded the former Shaker community at nearby North Union as part of Western Reserve history and an area that came under the institution's collection policy. He was a knowledgeable bookman; his collecting skills had been developed and refined since early high school days. At the time Cathcart undertook collecting Shaker materials, he was aware that the finest collection of Shakeriana was owned by the Library of Congress and that MacLean offered the rarest items to that institution, and also that Eldress Catherine contributed some of the items because she thought that "as a national center things of special value would find the most fitting place" (a.l.s. to W. H. Cathcart, Nov. 19, 1911, Western Reserve Historical Society). Cathcart went about collecting intrepidly on his own and addressed his first inquiry to Elder Alonzo Hollister. This was an unfortunate approach because of Hollister's advanced age and his fast friendship with MacLean, but worse, in introducing himself Cathcart used the name of Joseph Slingerland, a western Shaker Elder who was then persona non grata. The inquiry brought meager results, and a year later he wrote again. The second letter came to the attention of Eldress Catherine Allen of the Mount Lebanon Ministry because of the death of Elder Alonzo in August 1911. Her reply was cordial but not encouraging; Cathcart was referred to MacLean, to whom she had recently sent many large packages of books in accordance with Hollister's desire. Although MacLean had been a former librarian of the Society, he chose not to cooperate in the building of its Shaker collection. A wary but friendly competition existed between him and Cathcart, interspersed with occasional boasting when either acquired an especially choice item.

Cathcart persisted and continued his correspondence with Catherine Allen, and as her responses grew friendlier, more Shaker items were sent to him. A warm friendship developed as she gradually became aware of Cathcart's genuine and unselfish interest in building the best Shaker collection in any public institution. The Society had not provided funds for this enthusiasm of Cathcart's, and, as his interest expanded to include all Shakerdom, his personal outlay became considerable. Moreover, he was meticulous in the preservation, treatment, and cataloging accorded each item acquired. He had a specially designed and engraved bookplate made by William F. Hopson of Boston for the collection. It shows the Mount Lebanon meeting house in a natural setting, with Shakers in the road. The portraits of Elder Alonzo G. Hollister and Eldress M. Catherine Allen are on either side of the bookplate. Eldress Catherine was presented with a specially bound and interleaved copy of MacLean's *Bibliography* in which Cathcart had indicated the items already acquired and those that he knew were needed to complete the collection. The inscription, dated October 16, 1911, signified that he now considered her to be a partner in his undertaking.

When Cathcart visited the Library of Congress and inspected its Shaker collection, he wrote to Eldress Catherine, perhaps not ingenuously, "that the collection had not been touched to put it into shape" [i.e. cataloged]. Her reaction was not immediate, but she soon informed Cathcart that he would now have first choice of all rare and printed items, and that they would be sent directly to him, but that the business arrangement previously planned with MacLean would be kept. She continued, "Both your high motives and fine methods in preserving records of worth dispose us to glean closer among our treasured stores that you may have sufficient data for connected history so far as we will be able to furnish." This welcome news enabled Cathcart to push his endeavors into new areas. Thereafter, Eldress Catherine Allen acted as intermediary between Cathcart and the other communities, and she wrote letters of introduction to the leading elders and eldresses so that he might obtain their cooperation with her approval.

As the collecting proceeded, Cathcart became convinced that much was yet to be found, and he urged Eldress Catherine to investigate as she traveled to other Shaker communities. Among other things he wrote that the early western Shakers Benjamin Seth Youngs and Freegift Wells had returned to the Watervliet, New York, Shakers and that their effects must surely be at that community. Eldress Catherine visited Watervliet in August 1912 and wrote, "Yesterday, a cupboard from which the key had long been lost was opened from the back and I have found a few treasures." Indeed she had: among them were the original manuscript of *The Testimony of Christ's Second Appearing* and an author's autographed first edition of the same work (Lebanon, Ohio, 1808) with the inscription "Miami Country, Ohio, Dec. 1808" (a.l.s. Western Reserve Historical Society).

The Shaker collection at the Western Reserve Historical Society had surpassed that of the Library of Congress in printed materials during the short period 1911–13 and would soon surpass it in the number of manuscripts. Because it is the best and largest Shaker collection, it has naturally attracted many gifts from other sources. Even MacLean came to recognize that "nowhere else had the Shaker material received such care in preservation methods and in making it accessible to students" (a.l.s. Catherine Allen to William W. Wight, May 14, 1918, Williams College Library, Williamstown, Mass.). Eldress Catherine remained alert to items of interest to Cathcart, and their correspondence continued in the same warm vein until her death in 1922.

Eldress Catherine, importuned by many others for Shaker materials, made substantial contributions to holdings in the following institutions: New York State Library, Albany; Public Library, Schenectady, N.Y.; the State Library, Hartford, Conn.; Berkshire Athenaeum, Pittsfield, Mass.; Garrett Theological Seminary, Evanston, Ill.; the American Society for Psychical Research, New York; and the Connecticut Valley Historical Society, Springfield, Mass.

The Edward Brockway Wight Shaker Collection at Williams College, Williamstown, Massachusetts, represents a distinguished example of undergraduate collecting. The bulk of the Wight Collection was assembled between 1903 and 1907, but it was not presented to the College until 1931. Wight had an interest in the Shakers before entering Williams and shortly thereafter visited the community at Mount Lebanon, New York, armed with a letter of introduction from a Williamstown inhabitant who was a friend of Eldress Anna White. Some years later Eldress Catherine Allen described Wight at this time as a young man "who manifested an unusual interest in sociological efforts and who was making a thorough study of Shakerism and for that purpose was very persevering in collecting Shaker literature" (a.l.s. Catherine Allen to Wm. W. Wight, May 14, 1918, Williams College Library). He made frequent trips to nearby Hancock Shaker Village, not only to acquire Shaker literature but also to observe and discuss with the Shakers their religious and communal lives and to draft a plan of the entire Village and buildings to be used in a long term paper. The Shakers were often his hosts during his travels about New York and New England. He enjoyed their cordial hospitality at various communities where he was encouraged to learn more about Shaker history and practices and was sometimes told to help himself to whatever publications he needed. A number of the items in his collection bear the marks of former Shaker ownership. He has described seeing cupboards and trunks of Shaker books and pamphlets that had been unopened for fifty years. Some items were acquired from MacLean, with whom he exchanged duplicates, and some of the scarce apostates' accounts were acquired in the area bookshops. After he was graduated from Williams College, he left his collection with his father in Milwaukee while he went to his first job in Bremerton, Washington.

William Ward Wight, the father, was an enthusiastic bookman who had originated the plan whereby Milwaukee could acquire the beginnings of a public library by having the Young Men's Association turn over to the city its 10,000 volumes. He initiated a correspondence in 1909 with Elder Alonzo Hollister in an effort to purchase Shaker items to add to his son's collection. He received several Shaker publications from Hollister, but some of the lacks were western Shaker printing and for these he turned to MacLean, who supplied most of the lacunae. After the collection was presented to the College, further additions were made. The printed items in the Wight Collection rank after the Cathcart Collection at The Western Reserve Historical Society, but the collection lacks the extensive ephemera collected by Cathcart. The few Wight manuscripts in no way compare in either number or importance with the thousands of Shaker manuscripts in the Historical Society's collection.

The wide-ranging collecting activities of the late Edward Deming Andrews and Faith Andrews included Shaker furniture of every variety, textiles, artifacts, spirit drawings, manuscripts, and printed materials. The Andrewses lived near the Hancock, Massachusetts, and New Lebanon, New York, Shakers, where they were frequent visitors, but they also visited the Shakers in other communities. They bought widely from the Shakers, beginning very modestly in the early 1920's, and during more than forty years built enviable collections in almost every area of Shaker interest. (See the catalog *Shaker; Furniture and Objects from the . . . Andrews Collections Commemorating the Bicentenary of the American Shakers,* Washington, D.C., Published for the Renwick Gallery of the National Collection of Fine Arts by the Smithsonian Press, 1973). The Andrews Collection of Manuscripts and printed materials is reflected in their many books and articles recorded in this Bibliography. For some time in the late 1950's the collection was part of the library holdings of Yale University, but in 1969 the Andrews Collection was dedicated as part of the library at the Henry Francis DuPont Winterthur Museum, Wilmington, Delaware. Although the collection was not cataloged at that time, this compiler was allowed to examine and record the printed materials.

Elder Otis Sawyer, a nineteenth-century member of the Sabbathday Lake community and Bishop of the Maine communities, was the exception to the Shaker lack of concern for the preservation of Shaker manuscripts and publications described above. Elder Otis assiduously preserved archival records and other manuscripts and printed materials at both the Sabbathday Lake and Alfred communities. This interest is reflected in the 1883 description by Aurelia Mace of Sabbathday Lake in *The Aletheia* (Farmington, Me., 1907): "I visited a library containing a copy of each book published by this Order since it was founded. It consists of one hundred and seventy-five volumes, with their revised editions. These books have been collected and numbered, and the library set in order for the reception of other books that may be published." Elder Otis used a printed bookplate to identify items in the collection. After his death in 1884 the collection was enhanced by the Shakers charged with administering the collection. Additions to it have been made by gift and purchase as items became available. Unfortunately, the valuable body of materials in the collection at Alfred was lost in 1902 in a fire that destroyed the dwelling house and the meeting house.

The Emma B. King Library, Shaker Museum, Old Chatham, New York, commemorates the Eldress responsible for the 1961 addition of printed and manuscript materials that enabled the library to take its place among the best working Shaker collections. The founder, John S. Williams, had become interested in 1935 in collecting and preserving Shaker furniture, tools, and workshop equipment. As he collected these artifacts he also began to accumulate Shaker manuscripts and publications. Considerable new material became available to him with the closing of the Mount Lebanon, New York, Shaker community in 1947. The intention of the ruling eldership, relocated at Canterbury, New Hampshire, was that manuscript and printed materials be sent to The Western Reserve Historical Society, but Williams persuaded them that the materials should not leave the East and offered to buy the collection for his museum. For some time Eldress Emma King had been fearful that a fire might destroy the materials remaining at Canterbury. The Shakers had valid reasons for fearing fire; every Shaker community at one time or another had suffered severe losses from devastating fires. In 1961 Mr. Williams again offered to buy the materials and was allowed to do so with the proviso that the collection be housed in a fireproof or at least a strongly fire-resistant building. He agreed to erect such a building which was dedicated in 1962 and now houses the library of printed and manuscript materials. Subsequent additions to this collection have been made by purchase as items became available.

Over thirty collections of Shakeriana are listed alphabetically by state in *A Guide to Shaker Museums and Libraries* published by the Shaker Museum Foundation, Inc., Old Chatham, New York. This list is revised biennially and contains addresses and visiting hours, and in some instances indicates areas of strength in the collections.

SHAKER MANUSCRIPTS. The range of printed materials by and about the Shakers is impressive, but serious research on the Shakers must eventually involve the use of manuscripts that are not within the scope of this bibliography. Unfortunately, no census of Shaker manuscripts exists.

A surprising variety and quantity of manuscript records were kept in the separate families of each Shaker community by elders and eldresses, trustees, by the Ministry at Mount Lebanon, and others. These manuscripts comprise journals, account books, diaries, accounts of travel and of visits to other Shaker communities, covenants, matters concerning discipline, legal matters, correspondence, and records of membership and deaths. In addition there are the original manuscripts of Shaker publications; accounts of dreams and visions written mostly during the period of manifestations, 1837–1847; Shaker music; records concerning a single activity, such as farm or orchard journals; and account books for industries carried on by individual families—seeds, herbs, chairs, baskets, weaving, tanning, animal husbandry, and others.

During the years preceding the dissolution of a community the remaining Shakers were often aged and discouraged and showed little concern for the preservation of publications and the archival records in the community's possession. J. P. MacLean has commented that "A wise edict went forth from the New Lebanon Ministry that full records of the different communities should be kept ... But nowhere, either directly or indirectly, do I find an injunction that such records shall be preserved." He continues that from the "inception of Shakerism in the West, Union Village has been the chief and ruling community. It would be supposed that the principal center would guard all archives with care ... It is positively known that some of these records have been purposely burned ... There were pamphlets published, but afterwards forgotten and no attempt made to preserve a copy" ("The Watervliet, Ohio, Shaker Community," in his *Shakers of Ohio,* Columbus, Ohio, 1907, pp. 192–93). Much later, Eldress Catherine Allen described how she tried to sharpen the historical awareness of the eastern Shakers. "[I] have been able to materially change the attitude of some [Shakers] concerned through the reading of your [Cathcart] letters with the thought that as an Order of people—a link in the chain of evolution ... our history belongs to the nation and to the world, and it is our bounden duty to use every reasonable means of having it preserved and perpetuated." She wrote later that "much has been destroyed for so many are surprised that I find value in much they considered of no account" (a.l.s. Catherine Allen to W. H. Cathcart, Feb. 1, 1912; Aug. 20, 1912, Western Reserve Historical Society, Cleveland, Ohio). In the absence of a census of Shaker manuscripts, and because of the disappearance of manuscripts and the wide dispersion of remaining manuscripts among institutional and private libraries, the researcher has no way of anticipating where particular manuscripts will be located, or indeed if they exist. It was customary among the Shakers to make multiple copies. Consequently, copies of the same manuscript may be present in several collections. Manuscripts of individual communities will be found scattered among several libraries, and it is not unusual for manuscripts to be unidentified by either author or title.

The *National Union Catalog of Manuscript Collections* currently being published by the Library of Congress (Washington, D.C., 1959 to date) locates a few Shaker manuscripts, and as publication progresses, it is hoped that more and more Shaker manuscripts will be recorded and described. The Cathcart Collection of Shaker Manuscripts relates to twenty Eastern and Western communities and covers the period 1782–1940. *A Guide to Shaker Manuscripts in the Library of the Western Reserve Historical Society with an Inventory of Its Photographs,* by Kermit J. Pike (Cleveland, Ohio, 1974) contains 10,581 items and also 1876 volumes of Shaker manuscripts. *The Catalogue of the Emma B. King Library of the Shaker Museum* compiled under the direction of Robert F. W. Meader (Old Chatham, N.Y., 1970), pp. 51–61, lists the manuscripts in that collection. The Edward Deming Andrews Collection at the Henry Francis Du Pont Winterthur Museum contains many Shaker manuscripts, seventy-two of which are listed in E. D. Andrews, *The Community Industries of the Shakers* (Albany, N.Y., 1932. New York State Museum *Bulletin* no. 323), pp. 301–307; others are referred to in "A Note on Sources," in his *The People Called Shakers* (New York, Dover Publication, Inc., 1963), pp. 293–338. The large collection of Shaker manuscripts in the Manuscript Division of the Library of Congress consists preponderantly of manuscripts from western communities and includes manuscripts of Richard McNemar. Over one hundred manuscripts from the Shaker communities at Watervliet and Mt. Lebanon, New York, are owned by the New York Public Library. A sizable collection of manuscripts of the eastern Shaker communities is to be found in the New York State Library, Albany. A large representative collection of Shaker manuscripts and printed materials is in the library of the still active community at Sabbathday Lake, Maine. The Fruitlands Museums Library, Harvard, Massachusetts, has a good representative collection of manuscripts pertaining to the Shaker communities of Harvard and Shirley, Mass. The Ohio Historical Society, Columbus, has available a mimeographed list of the Shaker manuscripts in its collection, which originated for the most part in the communities of North Union and Watervliet, Ohio. The Filson Club, Louisville, Kentucky, has many Shaker manuscripts of the Shaker community at Pleasant Hill, Kentucky, and these are supplemented by the collection at Shakertown at Pleasant Hill. A sizable collection of Shaker manuscripts, mostly those of South Union, is owned by the Kentucky Library, Western Kentucky University, Bowling Green. Smaller Shaker manuscript collections are found in the Berkshire Athenaeum, Pittsfield, Massachusetts; Wight Collection, Williams College Library, Williamstown, Massachusetts; Hancock Shaker Village, Pittsfield, Massachusetts; New Hampshire Historical Society, Concord; Connecticut State Library, Hartford; Harrodsburg Historical Society, Harrodsburg, Kentucky; and The American Society for Psychical Research, New York City. The descriptions of Shaker manuscript collections in "Preservation of Shaker Historic Materials," by Charles C. Adams, in New York State Museum *Bulletin* no. 323 (Albany, New York, 1941), pp. 123–28, are still useful.

PREVIOUS SHAKER BIBLIOGRAPHIES. The earliest bibliography of Shaker publications was contained in Charles Nordhoff's *Communistic Societies of the United*

States . . . (New York, Harper, 1875), pp. 421–28, nos. 1–72, where the works of Shaker apostates were included. "List of Works in the New York Public Library," published in the New York Public Library, *Bulletin,* Vol. 8 (Nov. 1904), pp. 550–59, contained Shaker publications along with a few works about the Shakers. John P. MacLean's *Bibliography of Shaker Literature* . . . (Columbus, Ohio, For the Author by F. J. Heer, 1905) contains 548 entries, including some manuscripts and works about the Shakers, but the contents are preponderantly Shaker publications. It was the first bibliography of Shaker literature that could be considered a full representation of Shaker publications at the time it was published, and it has remained the standard bibliography of the Shakers for seventy years. The introductory essay, pp. 3–20, devoted primarily to early western Shaker publishing and printing, is a valuable source of information. More recent compilations of library collections include "Shaker Literature in the Grosvenor Library, A Bibliography," compiled by Esther C. Winter, Grosvenor Library, *Bulletin,* Vol. 22 (June 1946), pp. 116–19. Some works about the Shakers are included among the 388 entries. This compilation was revised by Joanna S. Ellett and published under the title "Shaker Literature in the Rare Book Room of the Buffalo and Erie Public Library" (Buffalo, New York, 1967); it contains 274 entries representing only Shaker publications. *Catalogue of the Emma B. King Library of the Shaker Museum,* referred to above, contains 319 entries for Shaker printed publications, pp. 5–50, and maps and photographs, p. 62. "A Bibliography of Shaker Periodical Literature," compiled by David Proper, *Shaker Quarterly,* Vol. 4 (Winter 1964), pp. 130–42; Vol. 5 (Spring 1965), pp. 26–32, includes about 300 periodical articles and more than 40 newspaper accounts. The entries are listed by title and arranged chronologically. "Addenda," including newspaper articles, and "Corrigenda" were published in Volume 5 (Winter 1965), pp. 141–44; Vol. 8 (Winter 1968), pp. 107–10; Vol. 10 (Winter 1970), 138–40; and Vol. 13 (Spring 1973), pp. 33–36.

The section on the Shakers in Charles Haywood's *Bibliography of North American Folklore* (New York, Greenberg [1951]), pp. 726–32, contains basic Shaker works, publications by Shaker apostates, and works about the Shakers. A bibliographical essay on various aspects of the Shakers and Shakerism is contained in Arthur E. Bestor's *Backwoods Utopias* . . . (Philadelphia, University of Pennsylvania Press, 1950), pp. 255–58. Similar bibliographical information is found in Donald D. Egbert and Stow Persons, eds., *Socialism and American Life* (Princeton, Princeton University Press, 1952, 2 vols.). Volume 2, "Bibliography: Descriptive and Critical," compiled by T. D. Seymour Bassett, contains references to Shakerism, Shakers, their crafts, music, etc., pp. 11, 114–21, and 444–57, and further references are available in the index.

ENTRY FORMS. The entries in Volumes I and II of this Bibliography represent Shaker publications and works about the Shakers published through 1972. (Addenda and 1973–1974 Reprints and Supplement were added later.) Entries beginning with names spelled "Mc" are entered as if the names were spelled out "Mac." The entries are numbered consecutively throughout; a few unnumbered information entries have been included and are easily identified as such. Cross references in the annotations are given by entry number and lead to related materials.

Individual entries within each part and subsection are given under the author's name, which is found enclosed within square brackets in those cases where the name has been supplied by the compiler. When the authorship of an entry cannot be reasonably attributed, the entry has been made under the title of the work. Entries have been made under corporate authors or under form entries where such treatment is appropriate. Repetition of an author's name is shown by an author ditto (a three-em line: ———) which is placed before all titles and editions that follow the first entry under the author's name. Works by a single author are followed by the works in which the author has collaborated as a joint author (see the entries under Calvin Green, nos. 732–745). Pseudonymous works are entered under the author's name when it has been identified, and a cross reference is made from the pseudonym. Rewritten, revised, or enlarged works of an author are entered under the name of the original author. A few groups of related materials in Volume I have been kept together under category headings (Almanacs, Catalogs, etc.) listed in the Table of Contents. Such category designations are followed by explanatory notes, and the entries under each category heading are arranged in alphabetical order.

Individual entries throughout the Bibliography contain, in addition to the author's name, the title of the work; titles supplied by the compiler are set in square brackets. In some instances long titles are shortened by the use of ellipses (...) where the omission does not affect the meaning of the title. Repetition of an identical title is indicated by the use of a title ditto (a five-em line: ————).

Sometimes identical repetitions in the first part of a long title are indicated in the same manner. In works that do not contain a title page the title has been taken from the cover title and so indicated before the collation (see below). The titles of periodical articles are enclosed within quotation marks. Editions other than the first, are given when indicated on the title page or on the cover title. Imprints are given in full, if ascertainable: place of publication:* publisher or printer, and date of publica-

---

* Users of the Bibliography may sometimes be confused when Shaker communities are referred to by more than one name. For example, the name New Lebanon, New York, was changed to Mount Lebanon when the post office was established in 1861. The site of the Watervliet, New York, Shaker community was formerly known as Niskayuna, an Indian name with variant spellings. Shakers, New York, was often used as the post office address. Since 1895, the community has been included in the township of Colonie. The original community at Sodus Bay, New York, was moved to Groveland (sometimes referred to as Sonyea) in 1837–38.

Publications often carried post office addresses. For example, the Canterbury community used the addresses Shaker Village and East Canterbury, New Hampshire; the Enfield, New Hampshire, community was also addressed Shaker Village. The Harvard and Shirley communities used South Groton and Ayer (Groton Junction), Massachusetts; Tyringham used the address South Lee, Massachusetts. Since part of the Hancock community was located in West Pittsfield, Massachusetts, this address was sometimes used as well as Stearnsville, Pittsfield, and Shaker Village, Massachusetts. Shaker Station and Thompsonville, Connecticut, were addresses of the Enfield, Connecticut, Shakers. The Sabbathday Lake community had the post office address West Gloucester, Maine,

tion.* When the imprint or any item of the imprint has been supplied, it is placed within square brackets.

In Volume I the total number of pages of a book is given, as represented by the last numbered page, or the total number of volumes. When the last numbered page includes the cover title, it is indicated by the comma that follows "cover title" in the collation; otherwise, "cover title" is followed by a period. Pages, if preceding the text, not accounted for by the last numbered page are indicated as p. l. or p. ll. (preliminary leaf, leaves); unnumbered pages are indicated by placing the appropriate numbers within square brackets. It has seldom been necessary to indicate irregularities by describing gatherings. Surprisingly few variants were found in Shaker publications except for the unsolved enigmas of Richard McNemar's printing (*see* pp. 122-23). In Volume II only the last numbered page of a book (or the total number of volumes) is given. Arabic numerals are given in all entries for periodical articles (roman numerals have been converted, when necessary), and the inclusive pages of an article are given. Illustrations are indicated, but not in great detail. The height of a work is given to the nearest half centimeter. Both the height and width of broadsides are given to the nearest half centimeter. No measurements are given for works in Volume II.

Although broadsides might be considered a distinct category, they have not been separated from other formats because many Shaker publications were issued both as broadsides and as small leaflets or pamphlets. The isolation of broadsides would have necessitated one more section in the bibliography, and no real purpose would have been served by separating identical texts in this way. Broadsides are so identified only when printed on the recto (right-hand side) of a sheet. If printed text appears also on the verso, the item is described as [2] pp.

Annotations follow bibliographical entries. If the title indicates the contents of a work, it has not always been considered necessary to add an annotation. In many instances, however, annotations are given in some detail when the information is considered to be of importance; in other entries a short reference has been considered sufficient.

------

although New Gloucester is found on some publications. In 1890 the address was changed to Sabbathday Lake, to be replaced in 1955 by Sabbathday Lake, Poland Spring. South Union often used Russellville, Kentucky, and Union Village used Lebanon, Ohio, as post office addresses.

* Somewhat less than half of the entries in Volume I were printed by the Shakers. Most of the remaining entries were printed by job printers or in commercial printing establishments, but many do not carry any imprint. In the early Shaker communities it was not uncommon to find printing presses operated by printers who were Shakers. In 1818 John Dunlavy's *The Manifesto*, a book of 520 pages, was printed at Pleasant Hill, Kentucky, on Shaker-made paper and was bound in the community. At Hancock, Massachusetts, Josiah Tallcott, Jr., printed *Millennial Praises* in 1812 and 1813. Presses were active at one time or another at Pleasant Hill, Kentucky; Union Village, North Union, and Watervliet, Ohio; Mount Lebanon and Watervliet, New York; Harvard, Massachusetts; and Sabbathday Lake, Maine, where the printing of small items has been undertaken again recently. At Canterbury, New Hampshire, substantial Shaker works were printed after 1842, and the Shaker periodical *The Manifesto* was printed there from 1887 through 1899. No study of Shaker printing has ever been published.

The entries in Volume I, By the Shakers, conclude with a shortened reference to other standard bibliographies where the work is recorded (see pp. xxxvii–xxxviii), followed by symbols which represent libraries that own the work (see pp. xxxix–xlv). These symbols are not intended to comprise an exhaustive list of the libraries where the item may be found, but where possible do represent a wide geographical distribution. The presence of a single symbol indicates the only library where the item was located. The considerable holdings of the Shaker Library, Sabbathday Lake, Maine, are not included because this collection was not available to the compiler; its holdings are not represented in the National Union Catalog. The holdings given represent libraries indicated on the cards in the National Union Catalog at the Library of Congress (as of 1970 and 1971), unless the number of libraries exceeds twenty-five. In addition, some holdings for libraries that do not report to the National Union Catalog have been included. It was considered unnecessary to give the library holdings for the entries in Volume II.

ACKNOWLEDGMENTS. I have been the fortunate recipient of generous cooperation from many persons interested in the compilation of this Shaker bibliography. In the Shaker spirit of sharing, persons sometimes previously unknown to me have generously volunteered whatever knowledge or material they possessed in the hope that it might help to portray the vitality and diversity of the religious communal lives of the Shakers. This extensive cooperation has enabled the compiler to examine practically all of the entries in this bibliography, or to examine photocopies supplied from several sources. In some instances a few trusted colleagues have acted as surrogates and have verified or completed references.

I am most grateful to the late Eldress Marguerite Frost and to Eldress Gertrude Soule, whose friendly advice and benevolent best wishes for the success of the Shaker Bibliography were a great encouragement, and to Eldress Bertha Lindsay and Sister Miriam Wall, who have kindly and patiently answered several inquiries.

In a special category I am greatly indebted to the Shaker Community, Inc., Pittsfield, Massachusetts, and in particular to its President, Mrs. Lawrence K. Miller, for her many kindnesses and for the initial grant for Volume I; for the expense of office equipment and supplies, telephone calls, photocopies, and the extensive travel involved in visits to more than fifty libraries in search of Shaker printed materials; and in addition for later support that covered most of the costs of preparing the final manuscript. Volume II is the compiler's contribution to Shaker studies. The copyright is held by Shaker Community, Inc.

An unusual debt of gratitude is owed Lawrence E. Wikander, Librarian of Williams College, Williamstown, Massachusetts, who not only provided an office for four years but also offered unlimited access to the Wight Shaker Collection and numerous other courtesies. I also wish to express my gratitude to the Williams Library staff for friendly and unfailing cooperation in meeting my often bizarre requests. In particular, I thank Nancy G. McFadyen, Assistant to the Librarian, for uncanny ingenuity in producing obscure titles on interlibrary loans; to Mary McInerney, Catalog Librarian, and Marie Pistorius, Cataloger, for helpful advice and reassurance;

to Juanita Terry, formerly Reference Librarian, Sarah C. McFarland, Reference Librarian, Anne H. Fitz, Circulation Librarian, and Isabella E. Welch, formerly Acquisitions Librarian, for various kindnesses; Judy Jane Jones for her painstaking efforts which produced excellent photocopies; and Donald E. Cary, former Assistant Librarian, for checking the alphabetizing throughout the bibliography.

An almost identical debt of gratitude is owed Meredith B. Colket, Jr., Director, The Western Reserve Historical Society, Cleveland, Ohio, and to Kermit J. Pike, Chief Librarian, both of whom offered every facility during my many visits to the Cathcart Collection in that institution. Special thanks go to Jack Large, Jr., Archives and Publications, whose solicitous attention for my welfare away from home eased the way; to Virginia G. Hawley, General Reference Supervisor, for many kindnesses extending over a long period; and to Anthony W. C. Phelps, Assistant Librarian. The basis of Volume I of this bibliography was compiled at Williams College and at this institution. The first work involved recording, collating, and describing every Shaker item in the Wight Collection. These records were compared individually with Shaker items in the Cathcart Collection in an attempt to discover variants. The procedure necessitated a month's time on the first visit to the Cathcart Collection, where Shaker references were amplified very considerably on later visits and some scarce items in Volume II were added.

It is with the greatest pleasure that I acknowledge appreciation and indebtedness to a formidable list of individuals who contributed freely in various ways to the accuracy and completeness of this Bibliography: to Gerard C. Wertkin, Counselor at Law, New York City, whose conscientious and prolonged pursuit of clues produced especially for this Bibliography the first compilation of legal cases involving the Shakers. To A. Donald Emerich, Old Chatham, New York, whose knowledgeable and enthusiastic encouragement really got the Bibliography under way initially, and for other contributions and courtesies. To Eugene M. Dodd, former Curator of Hancock Shaker Village, Pittsfield, Massachusetts, for his sustained interest and encouragement throughout the preparation of the Bibliography, his alertness in bringing current publications to my attention, and for innumerable other kindnesses. To Wilma Stein Davis, Camp Springs, Maryland, who upon learning of the preparation of this bibliography, spontaneously sent the notebook containing more than 150 entries of her Shaker bibliography compiled in the 1940's and also for her unique interleaved copy of J. P. MacLean's *Bibliography of Shaker Literature* which Wallace H. Cathcart presented to Eldress Catherine Allen in 1911, and for searching records in the U.S. Copyright Office. To George J. Finney, Alexandria, Virginia, whose long-standing scholarly knowledge of the Shakers was freely shared with me, for volunteering his accumulated references toward a Shaker bibliography undertaken in the late 1930's, and for his assiduous and trustworthy verification of references available in the Library of Congress, the National Archives, and the U.S. Copyright Office. To William Henry Harrison, Director, Fruitlands Museums, Harvard, Massachusetts, for his courteous and intelligent cooperation during several visits that included the unbounded and friendly hospitality of both him and his wife, Clio. To Julia Neal, former Director of the Kentucky Library, Western Kentucky University, Bowling Green, whose knowledge of the western Shakers clarified several questions, and for her warm and pleasant cooperation and gracious hospitality, including that of her Library staff, whose high morale brought a glow of pleasure. To Wyllis E. Wright, former Librarian of Williams College, who generously contributed the accumulated references for his Shaker bibliography undertaken in the late 1940's. To H. Richard Archer, Custodian, Chapin Library, Williams College, for many courtesies. To Robert F. W. Meader, Director, Shaker Museum, Old Chatham, New York, whose generous cooperation and trust allowed unsupervised use of the Shaker collection, and who never was content to answer a telephone inquiry without later sending photocopies to document the information. To Professor Elmer Ray Pearson, Institute of Design of the Illinois Institute of Technology, Chicago, whose knowledge of the Shakers was brought to bear upon many questions, for his generosity in allowing me to compare my list of Shaker patents with the list he had compiled, and for furnishing many photographs of Shaker publications. To James W. Gilreath, graduate student, Case Western Reserve University, Cleveland, Ohio, for allowing the use of a prepublication copy of "Wallace Cathcart, Catherine Allen and the Formation of the Shaker Library," for enthusiastic cooperation, including the verification of information, and for his pursuit of my clues to sometimes nonexistent Shaker publications. To Professor Walter Brumm, Saint Mary's College, Notre Dame, Indiana, who recorded the Shaker holdings of the Dayton and Montgomery County Public Library and of the Cincinnati Public Library, and who also kindly allowed the use of several photocopies of materials on the western Shakers. To Peter Smyrl, graduate student, Princeton Theological Seminary, Princeton, New Jersey, who spontaneously recorded and sent to me a list of the Seminary's Shaker holdings. To Sandra G. Brown, Rare Book Bibliographer, George Arents Research Library, Syracuse University, Syracuse, New York, who furnished copies of the catalog cards of the Shaker items in that Collection. To Julian P. Boyd, Editor of The Thomas Jefferson Papers currently being published by the Princeton University Press, Princeton, New Jersey, for having the Jefferson Papers searched in an attempt to verify Jefferson's often cited quotation about *The Testimony of Christ's Second Appearing* and Jefferson's purported ownership of this work (see no. 1471). To F. Gerald Ham for assistance in establishing Barnabas Bates's authorship of *The Peculiarities of the Shakers,* for advice about Abram Van Vleet's *Account of the Conduct of the Shakers,* and also for allowing me to read and take notes on his unpublished Doctoral Dissertation, "Shakerism in the Old West," University of Kentucky, 1962. To Mrs. Harold Goddard, Keeper of Books, Merrimack Valley Textile Museum, North Andover, Massachusetts, who kindly furnished references about Shaker textiles in her library. To John Ott, Director, Hancock Shaker Village, Pittsfield, Massachusetts, for innumerable kindnesses. To Mr. and Mrs. John Parker Carr, Enfield, New Hampshire, who courteously allowed me to check the Shaker collection of the late Clarice Carr. To Williams College Professors John K. Savacool, who verified and completed references in the Bibliothèque Nationale; Don Gifford, who read parts of the manuscript and made perceptive suggestions; Benjamin W. Labaree, who made many beneficial suggestions about changes made in the copy-edited manuscript; and Nicholas Fersen and Laszlo Versenyi, who translated Russian and Hungarian texts about the Shakers. To Thomas Swain, Woodbine, New Jersey, who volunteered to lend his records of the Shaker holdings in the libraries of the Philadelphia area. To John S. Wondolowski, Atlantic Community College, Mays Landing, New Jersey, who volunteered to lend the Shaker references for his doctoral dissertation in progress, Ball State University, Muncie, Indiana. To T. D. Seymour Bassett, Curator, Wilbur Collection, University of Vermont, Burlington, for wise counsel in the initial planning of the Bibliography. To Stanley Clarke Wyllie, Dayton Collection, Dayton and Montgomery County Public Library, Dayton, Ohio, for his courtesy in supplying a photocopy of William J. Hamilton's unpublished typescript of the "Tentative Bibliography of Books, Leaflets, Broadsides ascribed to Richard McNemar." To Professor C. William Miller, Temple University, Philadelphia, Pennsylvania; Professor Rollo G. Silver, Boston, Massachusetts; Roger P. Bristol, University of Virginia, Charlottesville; Richard Anders, American Antiquarian Society, Worcester, Massachusetts; and George J. Finney, Alexandria, Virginia—for their helpful suggestions and efforts toward the identification of the still unidentified *A Concise Statement* (no. 1007, below). Others who have offered helpful information or courtesies are Robert E. Eshleman, Franklin Public Library, Franklin, Ohio; Arlen H. Benning, Old Chatham, New York; Gladys Cook, Bucknell University, Lewisburg, Pennsylvania; Ronald D. Emery, Darrow School, New Lebanon, New York; Charles Lothridge, New York City; the late Mrs. Herman J. Nord and Frank A. Myers, Shaker Historical Society, Cleveland, Ohio; Mrs. Phyllis Shimko, Aurora, Oregon; and Brother Thomas Whitaker, St. Mark's Monastery, South Union, Kentucky.

I wish to thank the following librarians who offered both routine and special cooperation which sometimes involved the expenditure of time and effort. The institutions are identified by the symbols in parentheses (see pp. xxxix–xlv). Marjorie Gray Wynne (CtY), Helen B. Uhrich (CtY–D), Dudley Ball (DLC), Frank H. Sommer (DeWint), Riley Handy (KyBgW), James R. Bentley (KyLoF), James C. Thomas and Edward S. Nickels (KySP), Leo and Helen Flaherty (M), Mrs. Evelyn Vradenburgh (MBC), Richard J. Wolfe (MBCo), Barbara M. Hill (MBP), Mrs. Harriette Williams (MH–BA), Violet S. Durgin (MNF), Robert G. Newman and Mrs. Janet M. Edwards (MPB), Mary M. Ritchie (MSaE), Marcus McCorison and Mary Brown (MWA), Robert Volz (MeB), Mrs. David Astor (MeHi), Mrs. Mildred Ledden, Darrell P. Welch, and James Corsaro (N), Charles C. Willard and James S. Irvine (NjPT), James J. Heslin (NHi), Virginia Close and Kenneth C. Cramer (NhD), Mrs. Elmer S. Forman (OCHP), Walter W. Curley (OCl), Yeatman Anderson, III (ODa), Marian H. Bates (OHi), Hazel Spencer Phillips (OLeWHi), Mrs. Lillian Tonkin (PPL), Jane A. Rittenhouse (PSC-Hi), and John H. Stanley (RPB). Visits to other libraries were made as a member of the public, identifying neither myself nor the Shaker Bibliographical project. It was an illuminating experience—the discovery of how perfunctory some large library public services have become in the pressures of the 1970's.

I am indebted to Jacquelin M. Clermont, who typed a large portion of the final manuscript, and to Eileen Sprague, who faithfully completed it.

In memory of Alden Johnson, former President and founder of Barre Publishers, I wish to express deep gratitude for his intelligent and quick understanding of bibliographical problems and for his enthusiastic acceptance of the Shaker Bibliography for publication long before submission of the final manuscript in 1972. Unfortunately, his untimely death delayed publication for over three years. To Barre editor, Jon Beckman, my gratitude for his cooperative understanding of problems, including those of copy editing. To David Horne of The University Press of New England for helpful criticisms and for expediting the publication of the Bibliography.

A very special debt is owed Donald E. Richmond, whose interest, enthusiasm, and encouragement have been invaluable. His support in every phase of this compilation includes thousands of miles of driving, miles of leg work, checking numerous library card catalogs, deciphering manuscripts and microfilms, and proofreading the final manuscript.

The many persons who have contributed in one way or another are in no way responsible for inaccuracies that may be discovered; that responsibility rests with the compiler.

Wallace H. Cathcart's remarkable collection of Shakeriana long ago made evident the need for a more complete bibliography than was available. After more than sixty years this need has now been fulfilled. Meanwhile the accelerating interest in all aspects of Shaker life had increased the scope of the problem, extending the Bibliography to more than four thousand entries. These entries and the annotations have considerably expanded information concerning many areas of Shaker activities and show the wide-ranging interest in the Shakers. In the process of gathering this information new questions have arisen which provide interesting and fruitful topics for further research. Inevitably, omissions will be discovered, but unless this bibliography serves as a nucleus of information about the Shakers which will stimulate the gathering of additional relevant information and the correction of existing information, it will not have served its full purpose.

Mary L. Richmond

Williamstown, Massachusetts

SYMBOLS & ABBREVIATIONS

Symbols used in the entry forms are as follows:

——	denotes the repetition of an author's name.
———	denotes the repetition of all or part of the title.
—— ———	denotes the repetition of both an author's name and all or part of the title.
[——]	Information enclosed in square brackets has been supplied by the compiler. Brackets are also used for corrections and interpolations in quotations.
[——]	author's name has been supplied by the compiler.
[———]	title has been supplied by the compiler.
. . .	denotes the omission of less than one sentence from a quotation, title, etc.
. . . .	denotes an omission of one sentence or more from a quotation, title, etc. More than four points duplicates a series of points in the original.
*	with library location symbol indicates ownership of the copy described.
/	indicates line ending in poetry, title, etc.
Add.	Addenda
a.l.s.	autograph letter, signed.
a.n.s.	autograph note, signed.
c.	copyright.
ca.	(*circa*), about, approximately.
cf.	compare.
col.	column.
comp.	compiler, compiled.
ed.	edition, editor, edited.
ex rel.	at the information of, by the relation; used in law cases.
et seq.	(*et sequentes*) and the following pages, entries.
f., ff.	following page, pages; entry, entries.
fac.	facsimile.
fig.	figure.
front.	frontispiece.
ftn.	footnote.
i.e.	that is.
ibid.	(*ibidem*), in the same place.
illus.	illustration(s), illustrated.
in re	in the matter of, in the affair of, concerning; used in law cases.
inc.	incomplete.
incl.	including, included.
l., ll.	leaf, leaves.
ms., mss.	manuscript, manuscripts.
N.B.	(*nota bene*), note well; take notice.
n., nn.	note, notes.

n.d.	no date of publication.
n.p.	no place of publication.
n.s.	new series.
no., nos.	number, numbers.
opp.	opposite.
p.l., p.ll.	preliminary leaf, leaves.
pl., pls.	plate, plates.
passim	here and there (in place of specific pages where references are scattered).
port., ports.	portrait, portraits.
pseud.	pseudonym.
pt., pts.	part, parts.
Rep.	Reprint.
s., ser.	series.
sic	so, thus; indicates that quoted material is literal, an erroneous date, etc. Occasionally [!] is used.
Supp.	Supplement.
trans.	translator, translated.
unp.	unpaged.
v., vs.	(*versus*) against.
vol., vols.	volume, volumes.

SHORTENED REFERENCES

Evans   Evans, Charles. *American Bibliography; A Chronological Dictionary of all Books, Pamphlets and Periodical Publications Printed in the United States of America.* (Chicago, 1903–1959, 14 vols.). Vol. 1 (1639) – Vol. 12 (1799 letter N); Vol. 13 (1799–1800), completed by Clifford K. Shipton; Vol. 14, Index, compiled by Roger Pattrell Bristol.

The information in Evans' entries should be supplemented by the corrections and more recent bibliographical findings found in Clifford K. Shipton and James E. Mooney, *National Index of American Imprints through 1800. The Short-title Evans.* (Worcester, Mass. American Antiquarian Society and Barre Publishers, 1969, 2 vols.).

McCorison   McCorison, Marcus H. *Vermont Imprints 1778–1820* (Worcester, Mass. American Antiquarian Society, 1963).

MacLean   MacLean, John Patterson. *A Bibliography of Shaker Literature with an Introductory Study of the Writings and Publications Pertaining to Ohio Believers.* (Franklin, Ohio, Printed for the Author by Fred J. Heer, 1905, 71 pp.) Cited in annotations: MacLean, *Bibliography.*

Sabin   Sabin, Joseph. *Bibliotheca Americana. A Dictionary of Books Relating to America, from its Discovery to the Present Time.* Begun by Joseph Sabin, Continued by Wilberforce Eames, and Completed by R. W. G. Vail, for the Bibliographical Society of America. (New York, 1868–1936, 29 vols.)

Shaw   Shaw, Ralph R. and Richard H. Shoemaker, compilers. *American Bibliography. A Preliminary Checklist for 1801–1819.* (New York, Scarecrow Press, 1958–1963, 19 vols.) Continued by Richard H. Shoemaker, Compiler, *A Checklist of American Imprints, 1820–1829.* (New York, Scarecrow Press, Inc., 1964–1971, 9 vols.)

Continued by Gayle Cooper, Compiler, *A Checklist of American Imprints, 1830.* (Methuen, N.J., Scarecrow Press, Inc., 1972, 1 vol.)

Streeter   Parke-Bernet Galleries, Inc. *The Celebrated Collection of Americana Formed by the Late Thomas Winthrop Streeter.* (New York, Parke-Bernet Galleries, Inc., 1966–1969, 7 vols. and Index).

Green, Calvin. "Biographic Memoir of the Life and Experience of Calvin Green. Designed as his Testimony of the Goodness and the Blessed Effects of the Gospel System Established in this Great Day of Christ's Second Appearing ... ms. copy made by Alonzo Hollister. 3 vols. Copy 2, Western Reserve Historical Society, Cleveland, Ohio. Cited in annotations: Green, "Biographic Memoir."

Ham, F. Gerald. "Shakerism in the Old West." Unpublished Ph.D. Dissertation, University of Kentucky, 1962. viii, 323 [1] numb. 1. Cited in annotations: F. G. Ham, "Shakerism in the Old West."

Hamilton, William J. "Tentative Bibliography of Books, Leaflets, Broadsides, ascribed to Richard McNemar, 'Eleazar Wright,' as Author, Compiler, Editor, or Printer . . ." Unpublished typescript, 16 ll., 1954. Cited in annotations: Hamilton, "Tentative Bibliography."

MacLean, John Patterson. *A Sketch of the Life and Labors of Richard McNemar.* (Franklin, O., Printed for the Author by the Franklin Chronicle, 1905, 67 pp.) Cited in annotations: MacLean, *Life.*

Other references cited in annotations contain adequate information for identification.

LIBRARY LOCATION SYMBOLS

The library symbols used to indicate ownership of the publications in Volume I, By the Shakers, are those assigned to libraries in *Symbols of American Libraries Used in the National Union Catalog of the Library of Congress.* (10th ed., Washington, D.C., 1969) and the National Union Catalog itself, including its published volumes through June 1973. A location symbol followed by an asterisk indicates ownership of the copy described. Symbols for a few libraries not included in the National Union Catalog have been assigned in accordance with the same principles; thus MPH represents Massachusetts, Pittsfield, Hancock Shaker Village. Library ownership symbols used by Evans, Sabin, MacLean, and others have been changed to conform with the National Union catalog symbols. The list of locations is fairly comprehensive, but it has not been feasible to indicate the holdings of all libraries that may own Shaker publications. Private collections are not identified. Ownership of the publications in Volume II, About the Shakers, has not been indicated.

ALABAMA
AU	University of Alabama, University.

CALIFORNIA
CBBD	Berkeley Baptist Divinity School.
CBDP	Church Divinity School of the Pacific, Berkeley.
CHi	California Historical Society, San Francisco.
CLamB	Biola Library, La Mirada.
CSmH	Henry E. Huntington Library, San Marino.
CSt	Stanford University, Palo Alto.
CU	University of California, Berkeley.
CU–SB	University of California, Santa Barbara.

COLORADO
CoD	Denver Public Library.
CoDB	Bibliographical Center for Research, Rocky Mountain Region, Inc., Denver.
CoDU	University of Denver.
CoU	University of Colorado, Boulder.

CONNECTICUT
Ct	Connecticut State Library, Hartford.
CtHC	Hartford Seminary Foundation.
CtHT–W	Trinity College, Watkinson Library, Hartford.
CtHi	Connecticut Historical Society, Hartford.
CtW	Wesleyan University, Middletown.
CtY	Yale University, New Haven.
CtY–D	——, Divinity School.

DISTRICT OF COLUMBIA
DLC	U.S. Library of Congress.
DNAL	U.S. National Agricultural Library.
DNLM	U.S. National Library of Medicine, Bethesda, Maryland.

DELAWARE
DeWint	Henry Francis DuPont Winterthur Museum, Winterthur.

FLORIDA
FMU	University of Miami, Coral Gables.
FTaSU	Florida State University, Tallahassee.

GEORGIA
GU	University of Georgia, Athens.

ILLINOIS
ICJ	John Crerar Library, Chicago.
ICN	Newberry Library, Chicago.
ICMe	Meadville Theological School, Chicago.
ICRL	Center for Research Libraries, Chicago.
ICU	University of Chicago.
ICarbS	Southern Illinois University, Carbondale.
IEG	Garrett Theological Seminary, Evanston.
IEN	Northwestern University, Evanston.
IU	University of Illinois, Urbana.

IOWA
Ia-HA	Iowa State Department of History and Archives, Des Moines.
IaU	University of Iowa, Iowa City.

INDIANA
In	Indiana State Library, Indianapolis.
InHi	Indiana Historical Society, Indianapolis.
InI	Indianapolis-Marion County Public Library.
InU	Indiana University, Bloomington.

KANSAS
K	Kansas State Library, Topeka.
KEmT	Kansas State Teachers College, Emporia.
KHi	Kansas State Historical Society, Topeka.
KU	University of Kansas, Lawrence.

KENTUCKY
KyBgW	Western Kentucky State University, Bowling Green.
KyHi	Kentucky Historical Society, Frankfort.
KyLo	Louisville Free Public Library.
KyLoF	Filson Club, Louisville.
KyLx	Lexington Public Library.
KyLxCB	Lexington Theological Seminary.
KyLxT	Transylvania College, Lexington.

KySP	Shakertown at Pleasant Hill.
KyU	University of Kentucky, Lexington.
KyWAT	Asbury Theological Seminary, Wilmore.

LOUISIANA

| LU | Louisiana State University, Baton Rouge. |

MASSACHUSETTS

M	Massachusetts State Library, Boston.
MA	Amherst College, Amherst.
MB	Boston Public Library.
MBAt	Boston Athenaeum.
MBAU	American Unitarian Association, Boston.
MBC	American Congregational Association, Boston.
MBCo	Countway Library of Medicine (Harvard-Boston Medical Libraries), Boston.
MBSpnea	Society for the Preservation of New England Antiquities, Boston.
MBrZ	Zion Research Library, Brookline.
MH	Harvard University, Cambridge. (Represents Central Collection of College Library and smaller miscellaneous libraries).
MH–AH	—— Andover-Harvard Theological Library.
MH–BA	—— Graduate School of Business Administration.
MH–L	—— Law School.
MH–P	—— Peabody Museum.
MHarF	Fruitlands Museums, Harvard.
MHi	Massachusetts Historical Society, Boston.
MMHi	Milton Historical Society.
MMeT	Tufts University, Medford.
MNF	Forbes Library, Northampton.
MNtcA	Andover Newton Theological School, Newton Center.
MPB	Berkshire Athenaeum, Pittsfield.
MPH	Hancock Shaker Village, Pittsfield.
MPeaHi	Peabody Historical Society.
MSaE	Essex Institute, Salem.
MSo	Public Library of the City of Somerville.
MU	University of Massachusetts, Amherst.
MWA	American Antiquarian Society, Worcester.
MWiW	Williams College, Williamstown.

MARYLAND

| MdBE | Enoch Pratt Free Library, Baltimore. |
| MdBP | Peabody Institute, Baltimore. |

MAINE

Me	Maine State Library, Augusta.
MeB	Bowdoin College, Brunswick.
MeBaT	Bangor Theological Seminary.
MeHi	Maine Historical Society, Portland.

MeP   Portland Public Library.
MeU   University of Maine, Orono.

MICHIGAN
MiD   Detroit Public Library.
MiDW   Wayne State University, Detroit.
MiU   University of Michigan, Ann Arbor.
MiU–C   —— William L. Clements Library.

MINNESOTA
MnDu   Duluth Public Library.
MnU   University of Minnesota, Minneapolis.

MISSOURI
MoU   University of Missouri, Columbia.

MISSISSIPPI
MsU   University of Mississippi, University.

NEW YORK
N   New York State Library, Albany.
N–L   New York State Law Library, Albany.
NB   Brooklyn Public Library.
NBLiHi   Long Island Historical Society, Brooklyn.
NBP   Pratt Institute, Brooklyn.
NBuG   Grosvenor Reference Division, Buffalo and Erie County Public Library,
                   Buffalo.
NBuU   State University of New York at Buffalo.
NCH   Hamilton College, Clinton.
NCooHi   New York State Historical Association, Cooperstown.
NCoxHi   Greene County Historical Society, Inc., Coxsackie.
NHi   New-York Historical Society, New York.
NIC   Cornell University, Ithaca.
NN   New York Public Library.
NNC   Columbia University, New York.
NNG   General Theological Seminary of the Protestant Episcopal Church, New
                   York.
NNNAM   New York Academy of Medicine.
NNUT   Union Theological Seminary, New York.
NOC   Shaker Museum, Old Chatham.
NPV   Vassar College, Poughkeepsie.
NRAB   Samuel Colgate Baptist Historical Library of the American Baptist
                   Historical Society, Rochester.
NRCR   Colgate-Rochester Divinity School, Rochester.
NRHi   Rochester Historical Society.
NRU   University of Rochester.

| NSchU | Union College, Schenectady. |
| NSyU | Syracuse University. |

NORTH CAROLINA

NcA–S	Pack Memorial Public Library, Sondley Reference Library, Asheville.
NcD	Duke University, Durham.
NcMHi	Historical Foundation of the Presbyterian and Reformed Churches, Montreat.
NcU	University of North Carolina, Chapel Hill.

NEW HAMPSHIRE

Nh	New Hampshire State Library, Concord.
NhD	Dartmouth College, Hanover.
NhDo	Dover Public Library.
NhHi	New Hampshire Historical Society, Concord.
NhM	Manchester City Library.
NhU	University of New Hampshire, Durham.

NEW JERSEY

NjMD	Drew University, Madison.
NjNbS	Gardner A. Sage Library, Theological Seminary, New Brunswick.
NjP	Princeton University.
NjPT	Princeton Theological Seminary.
NjR	Rutgers—The State University, New Brunswick.

OHIO

O	Ohio State Library, Columbus.
OC	Public Library of Cincinnati and Hamilton County, Cincinnati.
OCH	Hebrew Union College, Jewish Institute of Religion, Cincinnati.
OCHP	Cincinnati Historical Society.
OCU	University of Cincinnati.
OCl	Cleveland Public Library.
OClJC	John Carroll University, Cleveland.
OClW	Case Western Reserve University, Cleveland.
OClWHi	Western Reserve Historical Society, Cleveland.
OCo	Columbus Public Library.
ODa	Dayton and Montgomery County Public Library, Dayton.
OFH	Rutherford B. Hayes Library, Fremont.
OGK	Kenyon College, Gambier.
OHi	Ohio State Historical Society, Columbus.
OKentU	Kent State University, Kent.
OLeWHi	Warren County Historical Society, Lebanon.
OO	Oberlin College.
OOxM	Miami University, Oxford.
OU	Ohio State University, Columbus.
OWoC	College of Wooster.

OREGON

OrP   Library Association of Portland.

PENNSYLVANIA

PBa	Academy of the New Church, Bryn Athyn.
PCC	Crozer Theological Seminary, Chester.
PHC	Haverford College.
PHatU	Union Library Company, Hatboro.
PHi	Historical Society of Pennsylvania, Philadelphia.
PLT	Lancaster Theological Seminary of the United Church of Christ.
PMA	Allegheny College, Meadville.
PP	Free Library, Philadelphia.
PPAmP	American Philosophical Society, Philadelphia.
PPB	Philadelphia Bar Association.
PPC	College of Physicians of Philadelphia.
PPD	Drexel Institute of Technology, Philadelphia.
PPDrop	Dropsie College for Hebrew and Cognate Learning, Philadelphia.
PPL	Library Company of Philadelphia.
PPLT	Lutheran Theological Seminary, Krauth Memorial Library, Philadelphia.
PPLas	LaSalle College, Philadelphia.
PPPD	Philadelphia Divinity School.
PPPrHi	Presbyterian Historical Society, Philadelphia.
PPULC	Union Library Catalogue of the Philadelphia Metropolitan Area.
PPWa	Wagner Free Institute of Science, Philadelphia.
PPeSchw	Schwenckfelder Historical Library, Pennsburg.
PPiPT	Pittsburgh Theological Seminary.
PPiU	University of Pittsburgh.
PSC	Swarthmore College, Swarthmore.
PSC-Hi	Friends Historical Library, Swarthmore.
PSt	Pennsylvania State University, University Park.
PU	University of Pennsylvania, Philadelphia.
PWcHi	Chester County Historical Society, West Chester.

RHODE ISLAND

RHi	Rhode Island Historical Society, Providence.
RP	Providence Public Library.
RPB	Brown University, Providence.
RPJCB	John Carter Brown Library, Providence.

TENNESSEE

TNJ-R   Joint University Libraries, Vanderbilt School of Religion, Nashville.

TEXAS

TxDaM	Southern Methodist University, Dallas.
TxFTC	Texas Christian University, Forth Worth.

TxU   University of Texas, Austin.

UTAH
UPB   Brigham Young University, Provo.

VIRGINIA
Vi   Virginia State Library, Richmond.
ViU   University of Virginia, Charlottesville.
ViW   College of William and Mary, Williamsburg.

VERMONT
VtHi   Vermont Historical Society, Montpelier.
VtMiM   Middlebury College.

WISCONSIN
WHi   State Historical Society, Madison.

WASHINGTON
Wa   Washington State Library, Olympia.
WaU   University of Washington, Seattle.

SHAKER COMMUNITIES

		Founded	Disbanded
1	Alfred, Maine	1793	1931
2	Canterbury, New Hampshire	1792	Still active
3	Enfield, Connecticut	1790	1917
4	Enfield, New Hampshire	1793	1918–1923
5	Groveland, New York	1836	1892
	(Known also as Sonyea)		
6	Hancock, Massachusetts	1790	1960
7	Harvard, Massachusetts	1791	1919
8	Mount Lebanon, New York	1787	1947
	(New Lebanon until 1861)		
9	North Union, Ohio	1822	1889
10	Pleasant Hill, Kentucky	1806	1910
11	Sabbathday Lake, Maine	1794	Still active
12	Shirley, Massachusetts	1793	1908
13	South Union, Kentucky	1807	1922
14	Tyringham, Massachusetts	1792	1875
15	Union Village, Ohio	1805	1910
16	Watervliet, New York	1787	1938
17	Watervliet, Ohio	1806	1910
18	Whitewater, Ohio	1824–1825	1907

SHORT-LIVED COMMUNITIES

	Founded	Disbanded
*Gorham, Maine	1804	1819
*Savoy, Massachusetts	1817	1825
*Sodus Bay, New York	1826	1836
(Moved to Groveland, No. 5 above)		
*West Union (Busro), Indiana	1810	1827
(Abandoned during Indian troubles 1812–1814)		
*White Oak, Georgia	1898	1902
*Narcoossee, Florida	1896	ca. 1911

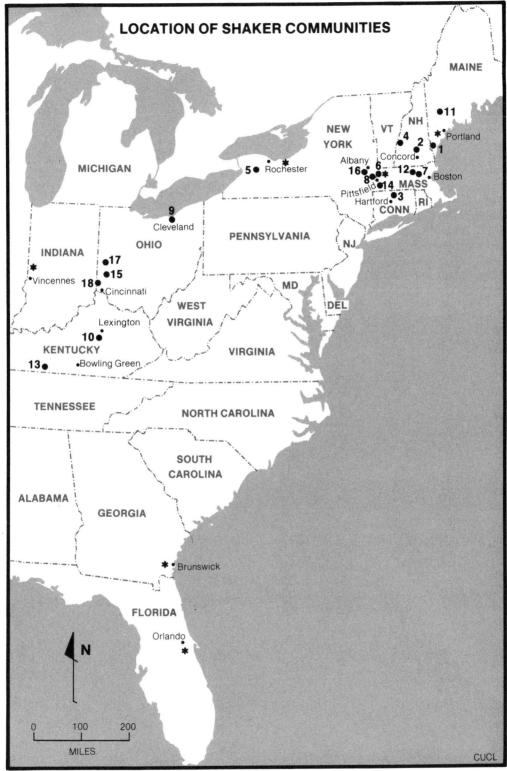

LOCATION OF SHAKER COMMUNITIES

MAINE

MICHIGAN

NEW YORK

●11

VT

NH

●4

●2

Albany

Concord

●1 Portland

16●

●6

8

12●

7

Rochester

5●

Pittsfield

14

MASS

Boston

Hartford

●3

CONN

RI

9

Cleveland

PENNSYLVANIA

NJ

OHIO

●17

INDIANA

●15

MD

Vincennes

18●

Cincinnati

DEL

WEST VIRGINIA

Lexington

10●

VIRGINIA

KENTUCKY

13●

Bowling Green

TENNESSEE

NORTH CAROLINA

SOUTH CAROLINA

ALABAMA

GEORGIA

Brunswick

FLORIDA

Orlando

N

0   100   200

MILES

CUCL

From: Robert F.W. Meader, *Illustrated Guide to Shaker Furniture*, (N.Y.: Dover, 1972).

Books, Pamphlets, Broadsides

A

A.B.B. *See* B., A. B., no. **60**.

1 Accompanying this Letter, are . . . . Copies of a Book, Written by a Member of the United Society (called Shakers,) at New Lebanon, Columbia County and State of New York. This Book was written by Divine Inspiration, and Printed by the Society, Agreeable to the Command of the Almighty. And we are Required by the Lord God of Heaven and Earth, to Present . . . . Copies of this Book to the . . . . [New Lebanon, N.Y.: 1843?]. Broadside. 21½ X 18½ cm.

A blank form to accompany the copies of Philemon Stewart's *A Holy, Sacred and Divine Roll and Book* (1843) which were presented to the world by order of the Ministry. Recipients are requested "to acknowledge receipt of the books by letter (in the English language)." *See* no. **1340**.
MWiW*.

Account of Some of the Proceedings of the Legislatures of . . . Kentucky and New-Hampshire. 1828, &c. *See* [McNemar, Richard]. *Investigator* . . . 1846, no. **927**.

2 An Acrostic. [n.p., n.d.]. Broadside. 14 X 8½ cm.

Poem of four stanzas beginning: Blessed Mother, Heavenly Parent, we adore thy holy name. First letter of the first word of each line forms "Blessed Mother Anna Lee," when read vertically.
OClWHi*.

3 ADAMS, MARY ELIZABETH. Satan's Last Ingenious Attempt to Lower the Moral Standard. [n.p., n.d.]. Broadside. 42 X 11½ cm.

An allegorical poem, signed: *Mary Elizabeth Adams.*
OClWHi*.

4 An Address to the State of Ohio, Protesting against a certain Clause of the Militia Law, Enacted by the Legislature, at their Last Session; and Shewing the Inconsistency of Military Power Interfering with Persons or Property Consecrated to the Pious and Benevolent Purposes of the Gospel. By Order of the United Society, Called Shakers. . . . Lebanon, Ohio: Printed at the Office of the Farmer, by George Smith, March, 1818. Cover title, 24 pp. 18½ cm.

Introductory note signed: *In behalf of the society, Richard M'Nemar, Calvin Morrell, Union Village, March 30, 1818*, p. [2]. The Shakers were protesting against the provision in the militia law that "Stewards . . . trustees or elders of any connected or associated society, whose property is all vested in common stock, shall be bound for, each and every member thereof, who is liable to do military duty," and all properties of such bodies "shall be held liable and bound for the payment of any fines assessed by the provisions of this act." The Shakers claim that because of "prejudice and persecution on account of their faith and manners, as a religious community," "many schemes have been devised to deprive" them of their rights and privileges, and that the militia law was enacted "for the purpose of disannulling our church covenant."
MacLean 110. Sabin 97881. Shaw 45693.
CSmH, DLC, MWA, NOC*, OCHP, OClWHi, ODa.

5 Advice to Children on Behavior at Table [poem]. [n.p., 18-]. Broadside. 26½ X 20½ cm.

Poem, 96 lines, begins: First, in the morning when you rise,/ Give thanks to God who well supplies/ Our various wants, and gives us food . . . Old Chatham, N.Y.: 196-? Reprinted by the Shaker Museum Foundation. Broadside. 28 X 20 cm. *See also Red Book*, 125 (August 1965), 64; *New York Folklore Quarterly*, 1 (1945), 233-36. *See also* nos. **119-125**. Authorship has sometimes been attributed to Daniel Offord.
MacLean 116. DLC, MHarF*, N, OClWHi.

6 Agreement. This is to certify that —— of —— County of —— State of —— have placed —— in the care of the Society of Shakers at East Canterbury, N.H., by agreement with ——

Trustee of the society. Should —— fail to give satisfaction to —— Shaker friends, —— agree again to be responsible for —— and release the society from all obligation. —— also agree not to interfere with the government of the —— nor claim any compensation for services —— may render while —— remain. In consideration for —— board and education, —— promise to pay $—— per month, the first payment to be made —— 190——. [Canterbury, N.H.: 190-?]. Broadside. 26½ X 20 cm.

> Also contains blank spaces for the signatures of parties involved and witnesses. *See also* nos. 835, 836, and 1375.
> OClWHi*.

7 Albany County, to Wit. At a Court Martial held for the Trial of Delinquents in the 136th Regiment of Infantry, at the House of Jonas Yearsley, on the 17th day of November, in the Year 1828 ... [Albany, N.Y.: 1828]. Broadside. 32 X 19½ cm.

> Affidavit blank for exemption from military duty in the form of a certificate of residence in another state. Affirms membership in the United Society of Believers, commonly called Shakers, and that in accordance with the signer's religious faith and principles he is "averse to bearing arms or performing militia duty or commuting therefor ..." Consequently, his residence has been changed to the Shaker community at Hancock, Mass., and the member is no longer subject to militia duty in New York state." *See also* no. 1650.
> OClWHi*.

8 "Albert Gallatin [Secretary of the Treasury] to Jared Mansfield, Surveyor General, Cincinnati, March 10, 1812." In C. E. Carter, ed., *Territorial Papers of the United States.* Washington, D.C.: Government Printing Office, 1934-62. VIII:171.

> Sale of the tract of land requested by the Shakers at West Union (Busro), Ind., cannot take place until the surveys of all private claims have been completed. Requests information about the progress of the surveys. *See* no. 1190.

9 ALLEN, MINNIE CATHERINE. Biographical Sketch of Daniel Fraser of the Shaker Com-

munity of Mt. Lebanon, Columbia County, N.Y., by Catharine Allen ... Albany, N.Y.: Weed, Parsons & Company, Printers, 1890. 38 pp. 19 cm.

> Several variations of Eldress Catherine Allen's name appear on her works: Minnie Catherine, M. Catherine, Catherine. Catherine is also found spelled "Catharine," and Mary Catherine Allen is found in some library entries. Many of her letters have been examined by the compiler; all were signed: *Catherine Allen.*
> MacLean 118. CtY, DLC, MH, MHarF, MPB, MPH, MWA, MWiW*, MiU-C, NBuG, NN, NOC, NSyU, Nh, NjPT, OClWHi, ODa, OHi.

10 —— A Century of Communism; The History of the People Known as Shakers, by M. Catherine Allen ... Pittsfield, Mass.: Press of Eagle Publishing Co., 1902. Cover title. 15[1] pp. 15 cm.

> Second edition of no. 11, with minor changes in the text. The word "strangers" is misprinted "strangeas," p. [1] at end (back cover).
> MacLean 120. MH, MHarF, MPA, MPB, MWA, MWiW*, NHi, NN, NNG, NOC, O, OClWHi.

11 —— A Full Century of Communism. The History of the Alethians, Formerly Called Shakers, by M. Catherine Allen ... Pittsfield, Mass.: Press of Eagle Publishing Co., 1897. Cover title. 16 pp. 12½ cm.

> MacLean 119. CSmH, CtY, MH, MHarF, MPB, MWiW*, MeHi, NBuG, NN, NOC, NSyU, NjPT, OClWHi, OHi, WHi.

12 —— Manna. A Shakeress on the Subject. [Mt. Lebanon, N.Y.: n.d.]. Broadside. 33½ X 7½ cm.

> Signed: *Catharine Allen.*
> CtY, MHarF, MWiW*, NBuG, NN, OClWHi.

13 —— —— [n.p., n.d.] Broadside. 19½ X 7 cm. Printed from a different setting of type.
> OClWHi*.

14 —— —— 4 pp. 17 cm.

> In an undated a.l.s., Eldress Catherine Allen to Wallace H. Cathcart [ca. 1913], in the Western Reserve Historical Society, the author explains the reasons for the scarcity of this item. "*Manna* really did exist. I am responsible for its no longer existing. It was handed me—perhaps several hundred in the

bunch ... Having already a few left in the long column [broadside] I thought these need not be kept." She explains that it was written very hurriedly for an evening meeting and during a busy day, and also that she "could see no reason why it was printed at all." Moreover, "it was printed without revision" and without her knowledge. "I did not at all admire Elder Frederick's [Evans] judgment in that, although I loved him very much."
MacLean 121 (credits NN, OHi, and WHi).

15 —— The Mirror of Truth. A Vision. Catherine Allen. Mount Lebanon, N.Y.: The Lebanon Press, [1890?]. Cover title. [4] pp. 14 cm. (Lebanon leaves. Faith series, no. 1.)
MacLean 122. DLC, ICN, MHarF, MPB, MPH, MWiW*, NBuG, NN, NOC, NjPT, OC, OCl, OClWHi.

16 —— Questions of the Day. Catharine Allen. [Mt. Lebanon, N.Y.: 188–?]. Caption title, 6 pp. 13½ cm.
Discussion of international peace, women's suffrage, single tax, free trade. Appeared in *The Manifesto* 22 (December 1892), 269–73.
MacLean 123. DLC, MHarF, MWiW*, NN, OC, WHi.

17 —— Shaker Life and Ideals. Address before the International Council of Women, Toledo, Ohio. By M. Catherine Allen ... [Mt. Lebanon, N.Y.: 1906]. Cover title. 14 pp. 15 cm.
Printed also in the *15th Annual Executive Report* of the International Council of Women (1906), pp. 185–91. *See also* nos. 34–37.
MHarF, MWiW*, NN, NNC, NOC, NPV, OClWHi.

18 ALLIBACO, W. W. The Philosophic and Scientific Ultimatum Written in the Constitution and Laws of Universe by the Omnipotent Hand of Divine Intelligence and Spread before All Mankind in the Universal Language of Organic Mind and Matter, Cause and Effect for the Guide of Nations and the Promotion of Human Happiness Copied and Read from the Divine Original .... New York: Published by the Author, 1864. 420 pp. 19½ cm.
Author's autograph presentation note on the flyleaf of the Berkshire Athenaeum (Pittsfield, Mass.) copy indicates that the author was a Shaker (probably a seceder). "Presented ... by the author to his brethren and sisters of the United Society of Believers." The work treats religious and quasi-philosophical communications from the deity.
DLC, M, MB, MH, MPB*, NN, PPPD.

ALMANACS

Although the so-called Shaker almanacs were published by Andrew Judson White, they are included here because they were published with the Mt. Lebanon, N.Y., Shakers' cooperation and approval, and much of the copy was furnished by these Shakers. Manuscript letters, business records, etc., in the Emma B. King Library, Shaker Museum, Old Chatham, N.Y., reveal that the Shakers—in particular the trustee, Benjamin Gates—were in large part responsible for the extraordinary success of A. J. White's widespread wholesale medicine and drug business. In 1875 White was operating a small medicine business under primitive conditions in New York when he was visited by Benjamin Gates, who gave him several Shaker formulas, including that for Shaker Extract of Roots. At this time the money necessary for the expansion of White's business and advertising was advanced by Gates acting for the Shakers; other advances were made later. When White encountered English sales resistance, Gates traveled to London to assist in introducing and promoting the sale of Shaker Extract of Roots, later known as Mother Seigel's Syrup. The introduction, promotion, and merchandising of Shaker Extract was so successful that fifty to seventy persons were soon kept busy at Mt. Lebanon, N.Y., supplying the English market. Meanwhile, White's business in the United States continued to expand as a result of his assiduous and novel promotion of Shaker medicines (*see* advertisement, *Shaker Manifesto*, June 1879). The almanacs were the vehicles for glowing testimonials for White's medicines and were intended for his numerous retail agents to distribute among their customers. The blank space, headed "Presented by" on the almanac covers, provided for the addition of the agent's name and address. White supplied the rubber stamps for this purpose. Retail agents operated on credit; orders were paid for only after the medicines had been sold. Sales were stimulated by the award of a variety of premiums, the values of which were proportional to the number of sales. White died in England in 1898, but as late as 1902 Mt. Lebanon records show large shipments of "White's medicine" being sent to London. Specific citations to the manuscript sources have been omitted here as a courtesy to Robert F. W. Meader, Director, Shaker Museum, Old Chatham, N.Y., who kindly allowed the use of this material even though he had in preparation a documented history of the successful business relationship of the Mt. Lebanon, N.Y., Shakers with Andrew Judson White. *See also* nos. 327-35 and 2262.

19 The Story of the Shakers and Some of Their Favorite Cooking Recipes. Calendar for 1882 ... [New York: A. J. White, 1881]. Cover title. [36] pp. illus. 20 cm.

"The Story of the Shakers," by Henry Vincent (no. 1407), pp. [4, 6], is followed by a letter from Mary Carr. Woman's portrait, front cover, recto, "A Likeness of the Baroness Burdett Couts," and back cover, verso, which has also a blank space headed "Presented by." The illustrations have no relation to the Shakers, but Shaker recipes are scattered throughout. Testimonials for Shaker Extract of Roots, Shaker Family Pills, Shaker Soothing Plasters extend to p. [30]. "Ups and Downs of Life," pp. [31-34]. CtHi, MBC, MiU-C, NOC*, OClWHi.

20 ——— Calendar for 1882-83. [New York: A. J. White, 1882]. Cover title, [32] pp. illus. 20 cm.

The calendar covers June 1882 through May 1883. Contains excerpts from Shaker publications, Shaker recipes, testimonials for Shaker medicines, jokes, conundrums, stories, etc. KyU, MHarF, MWiW*, MeHi, N, OClWHi, OHi.

21 New and Favorite Cooking Receipts of the Shakers and Illustrated Almanac for 1883. The Story of an Accidental Discovery. [New York: A. J. White, 1882]. Cover title. [36] pp. illus. 20 cm.

The accidental discovery concerns the successful methods employed in the introduction, promotion, and merchandising of Shaker Extract of Roots and Mother Seigel's Curative Syrup in England. "During the past four years upwards of fifteen millions of bottles have been sold through the London

office of Mr. White." Portrait of seated woman (Mother Seigel?), front cover, recto. Portrait of "Leon Gambetta, the great French Statesman. Died January 1st, 1883," back cover, verso. "The Art of Making Money," pp. [2, 4, 6]. The illustrations are mostly humorous, with four portraits. Shaker recipes are scattered throughout. NN, NOC*.

22 ——— Illustrated Almanac for '83 & '84. The Story of an Accidental Discovery. [New York: A.J. White, 1883]. Cover title. [36] pp. illus. 20 cm.

Calendar for April 1883 – March 1884. The account of the discovery of Mother Seigel's Syrup appears to be fictitious in view of information in the manuscript records in the Shaker Museum, Old Chatham, N.Y. MacLean 500. MH, MWiW*, MeHi, MiU-C, NN.

23 Shaker Almanac. 1884. [New York: A. J. White, 1883]. Cover title. 32 pp. illus. 20 cm.

Running title: Shaker Family Almanac. Colored covers show Mother Seigel (?), front cover, recto; Statue of Liberty, back cover, verso. Illustrations: "Shaker Church Mt. Lebanon, N.Y.," p. 18; "Group of Shakers, Mt. Lebanon, N.Y.," p. 20; "Shaker Dwelling House, Mt. Lebanon, N.Y.," p. 26. Other illustrations have no relation to the Shakers. MB, MHarF, MeHi, N, NOC, NSyU, OClWHi*.

24 Shaker Almanac. 1885. The Joys and Sorrows of a Poor Old Man. [New York: A. J. White, 1884]. Cover title. 32 pp. illus. 20 cm.

Contains "a series of illustrations, showing the various and painstaking processes of manufacture of world-famous Shaker Extract of Roots, or Mother Seigel's Syrup—made by the Shakers, of Mt. Lebanon, N.Y.—From the crushing of the crude material to the shipping out." The artist's presence was recorded, "An artist from New York comes to take views for illustrating Dr. White's medical almanac." Entry for July 1, 1884, p. 48, Anna Dodson, "Journal," Vol. 3, 1883–85, ms., Shaker Museum Library, Old Chatham, N.Y. MB, MHarF, MWiW*, MeHi, N, NN, NOC, OClWHi.

25 Shaker Almanac. 1886. The Mystery Explained. [New York: A. J. White, 1885]. Cover title. 32 pp. illus. 20 cm.

The mystery involves a dramatic cure and is followed by an account of the discovery of Mother Seigel's Curative Syrup. Colored illustrated covers: front cover, recto (Mother Seigel?); "The Money Makers of America," with portraits, back cover, verso. A variant back cover, verso, is entirely blank. Five illustrations of procedures in the preparation of Shaker herbal medicines are repeated from the 1885 *Almanac*. Other illustrations are portraits of prominent men: Wm. H. Vanderbilt, Samuel J. Tilden, Leland Stanford, etc. CSmH, MBC, MHarF, MPB, MWiW*, MiU–C, N, NOC, OClWHi.

26 Almanac, 1887. The Peaceful Life of the Shakers. [New York: A. J. White, 1886]. Cover title. 34 pp. illus. 15½ cm.

Colored decorative covers. Young child with flowers, front cover, recto. Mary F. Carr's letter (*See also* no. 143), pp. 1–2; information about the Shakers, pp. 2, 3, 5, followed by the story of the discovery of Mother Seigel's Curative Syrup. Part of this item was published without the almanac designation in the title. *See* no. 140. NN, NOC, OClWHi*.

27 The 100th Anniversary of the Founding of a Community. Almanac for 1888. [New York: A. J. White, 1887]. Cover title. 32 pp. illus. 15½ cm.

Running title: Among the Mountains. General information about the Shakers by an unidentified author, pp. 1–8; bits of information about the Shakers are scattered throughout the testimonials, etc. Nine illustrations of the procedures in the preparation of Shaker herbal medicines are repeated from the 1885

Almanac. Alonzo Hollister at the vacuum pan, back cover, verso. CSmH, MB, MWiW*, NOC.

28 Shaker Family Almanac. 1888. Containing Portraits of 12 Millionaires. [New York: A. J. White, 1887]. Cover title. 32 pp. ports. 15½ cm.

Running title: Shaker Extract of Roots. The text and illustrations are different from those in no. 27 and have no relation to the Shakers. An a.l.s. Alonzo Hollister to William Ward Wight, December 1909, in the Williams College Library, states, "I send you my only copy. We had no hand in publishing it." "Discovery" begins on the front cover, verso, and continues on the even-numbered pages through p. 24 and pp. 25–29. It is the history of the discovery of Mother Seigel's Curative Syrup, or Shaker Extract of Roots. MacLean 124. DLC, MPB, MWiW*, OClWHi.

29 How the Shakers Cook and the Noted Cooks of the Country. [Shaker Almanac, 1889]. [New York: A. J. White, 1888]. Cover title. 48 pp. illus. 15½ cm.

The cover title does not identify this as a Shaker almanac, but a calendar for 1889 is included. It contains the same information as other almanacs. "How the Shakers Cook, and How They Live," a letter dated at Cincinnati, June 30, 1888, signed: *Margaret*, begins on the front cover, verso, and continues on the even-numbered pages through p. 12. Information about the portraits of chefs who served wealthy U.S. citizens (August Belmont, Whitelaw Reid, etc.), the salaries they commanded, and recipes are scattered throughout, including the back cover, verso. *See* no. 335. DLC, MWA, MWiW*, MiU–C, NN, NOC.

30 ———. [Shaker Almanac, 1889]. [New York: A. J. White, 1888]. Cover title, 48 pp. illus. 15½ cm.

The type has been reset with slight differences in the text. The most easily identifiable difference occurs on the back cover, verso, where the last word, "tips," has been enclosed within quotation marks. *See also* no. 335. NOC*.

31 Shaker Almanac. 1891. [New York: A. J.

White, 1890]. Cover title. 32 pp. illus. 19½ cm.
Running title: Shaker Family Almanac. Front
cover, recto, shows a little girl with snowballs;
verso, "Planets Regarded as Morning and Evening Stars, 1891"; back cover, verso, shows an
unidentified landscape cut. Miscellaneous bits
of information are interspersed among testimonials for A. J. White's medicines.
DLC, KyBgW, NN, NOC, OClWHi*.

32 Shaker Almanac. 1892. [New York: A. J.
White, 1891]. Cover title. 32 pp. illus. 19½ cm.
The miscellaneous illustrations have no rela-
tion to the text or to the Shakers. The text
contains jokes, advertisements for Shaker
medicines, particularly Shaker Extract of
Roots, etc.
N*.

---

33 American Museum ... Every Day and
Erening [sic] this Week, Commencing Monday,
Sept. 28th [1846]. Magnificent Performances
... Greatest Novelties and Attractions in Exis-
tence ... Shaking Quakers! Composed of Three
Beautiful Ladies and Gentlemen, who Have
Recently Seceded from the Society at Cante-
bury [sic] N.H. ... In the Full Shaker Costume!
And Will Introduce a Great Variety of Singing,
Dancing, Whirling and Shaking, Peculiar to
These People. During these Exhibitions Miss
Willard, a Beautiful Lady Will Whirl Round with
the Velocity of a Top!! [New York:] Apple-
gate's Steam Press, [1846]. Broadside. 44½ X
16½ cm. illus.
The names of the performers are given in no.
2535. Here they appear with "Col. Claffin,
the Celebrated and Most Interesting Dwarf,"
a living orangutan, and a monster serpent,
followed at the end by a balloon ascension.
A woodcut, signed: Strong, depicts six
Shakers dancing in Shaker costume. This
playbill does not itemize the Shaker part of
the program.
Private collection.

34 The American Shakers. [n.p., n.d.]. Cover
title. [3] pp. 23½ cm.
This appears to be a later edition of nos. 35
and 36, with slight textual changes, which
lacks subtitle and the section "Government."

E. C. Fales [Shaker List] (no. 2108), item
582, identifies this as "Compiled by Eldress
Marguerite Frost." Maine Auction Service
Gallery, Auction (no. 971), item 29, attrib-
utes authorship to Minnie Catherine Allen,
with imprint: [East Canterbury, N.H.: 195-?].
See also no. 17.
MPB*, NOC.

35 The American Shakers; A Celibate, Religious
Community. [n.p., n.d.]. Caption title. [4] pp.
15½ cm.
A brief outline of the faith. Intended for
distribution to visitors. Printed on white
glazed paper.
MHarF, MPB, MWiW*, NSyU, OClWHi.

36 ——— [n.p., n.d.]. Caption title. [4] pp.
13 cm.
Different type and setting, printed on off-
white matte paper. Slight changes in text
from no. 35.
NWiW*, OClWHi.

37 ——— [Sabbathday Lake, Me.: Published by
the Shakers, n.d.]. Postcard. 14 X 9 cm.
Condensed version of nos. 35 and 36. Copies
were printed in black ink, and in brown ink
with different settings of type. See also Add.
nos. 37a and 37b.
MHarF, MWiW*.

38 [AMERY, GEORGE B.]. Correspondence.
Water Baptism. Is Dancing as Worship Authorized
by the Scriptures? Marriage. Was Ann Lee a
Divine Teacher? [n.p., 1887?]. Caption title.
8 pp. 21 cm.
Correspondence between Elder G. W. B——,
H——, Ind., June 1st, 1877, and Geo. B.
Amery, Whitewater Village, O., June 1877.
MWiW*.

39 ANDERSON, MARTHA JANE. The Bird-
craze [poem]. [Mt. Lebanon, N.Y.?: n.d.].
Broadside. 30 X 10½ cm.
Protests use of feathers in women's costumes,
especially hats.
MacLean 126. DLC, MH, MPB, MWiW*, NN,
OClWHi, WHi.

40 ——— Peaceful Victory [hymn]. [Mt.

Lebanon, N.Y.?: 190-?]. Broadside. 19 × 13 cm.
An introductory note, signed: *Daniel Offord*, says in part, "In the early days of the agitation for arbitration, the following hymn was composed by one of the inspired poets of the Shaker order." This printing may have been in connection with the Peace Conference, August 31, 1905. The hymn was originally printed with the music in the *Shaker Manifesto* 8 (Nov. 8, 1878), 286-87, under Martha Anderson's name.
DLC, MPB, MWiW*, NBuG, NOC, OClWHi.

41 —— Social Life and Vegetarianism. Mt. Lebanon, N.Y.: [Chicago, Guiding Star Printing House], 1893. 27 pp. 12½ cm.
"Written for the 'Herald of Health'." "Health Notes from Mount Lebanon," pp. 3-16, reprinted from *The Manifesto* 22 (March, May 1892), 92-94, 100-101; "Common Sense Recipes," pp. 17-24; "Table Monitor," pp. 25-27.
MacLean 127. CSmH, CtY, DLC, MHarF, MPB, MWA, MWiW*, MiU-C, NBuG, NN, NOC, NSyU, NjPT, OClWHi, OO, WHi.

42 —— Vice. [Mt. Lebanon, N.Y.?: 189-?]. Caption title. 7 pp. 13½ cm.
Contains also: "Intemperance," by Lucy S. Bowers (from *The Manifesto* 20 (December 1890), 273-75). *Vice* appeared in *The Manifesto* 19 (June 1889), 25-27.
MacLean 128. MPB, MWA, MWiW*, NBuG, NN, OClWHi.

43 [ANDERSON, MARTHA JANE], and Others. Social Gathering Dialogue, Between Six Sisters [Margaret Pattison, Ann Offord, Martha Anderson, Charlotte Byrdsall, Melissa Soule, Margaret Cleveland] of the North Family of Shakers, Mt. Lebanon, Columbia County, N.Y. Albany, N.Y.: Weed, Parsons & Company, Printers, 1873. 18 pp. 18½ cm.
In the form of a conversation among the six sisters. Appeared in *Shaker and Shakeress* 3 (March, April 1873), 22-23, 30-32, with the title, "Dialogue. The Gospel Work—Its Present and Future Increase," where it was stated that "It was expressly prepared by the sisters for the Social Gathering of the three families of the Novitiate Order at Mr. Leba-

non, held in the pine grove in Canaan, September 1872." The "music sung in connection with the dialogue," printed in *Shaker and Shakeress* 3:32, is omitted here. Authorship is attributed by MacLean to Charlotte Byrdsall and Martha J. Anderson, and by the British Museum to Margaret Pattison. Martha J. Anderson, a "vigorous author" among the Shakers, appears to be the most likely among the group. This annual festival, held on a hill that rose from the shores of Queechy Lake, has been described by Sister A. Rosetta Stephens in "A Social Gathering," *Peg Board* (no. 3522), Vol. 4 (1936), 57, 59.
MacLean 446. CtY, MHarF, MPB, MWA, MWiW*, MiU-C, N, NN, NSyU, NjPT, OClWHi, OHi, PPL, WHi.

44 ANDREWS, A. W. K. . . . The Identification of Israel. Chicago: Guiding Star Publ. House, 1888. Cover title. 26 pp. 18 cm.
At head of title: Koreshan. Published by the official publishing house of the Koreshan Unity. *See* nos. 652 and 1361.
NN, OClWHi*, OO (28 pp.).

45 ANDREWS, W. WATSON. Communism. [n.p., n.d.]. Caption title. 7 pp. 13½ cm.
Reprinted from *The Shaker*, 2 (October 1872), 75-76, where the author is given as Watson Andrews. Contains also: "Unselfish Interest" [by] Martha J. Anderson (from *The Manifesto*, 18 (February 1888), 31-32); "The Two Fires" [by] Oliver Prentiss.
MacLean 129. MPB, MWA, MWiW*, NBuG, NN, OHi, OClWHi.

46 Ann Lee. A Sketch of Her History and Character. [n.p., n.d.]. Broadside in 2 columns. 60 × 20½ cm.
From the *American Socialist*, 2 (1876), 137, 145, where it appeared as editorials in 2 successive issues with the statement that it was "drawn entirely from Shaker books." Reprinted in *The Shaker*, 7 (July 1877), 51-52.
OClWHi*.

47 The Ann Lee Cottage in Shaker Village Will Open June 15th under the Management of the Shakers. [Mt. Lebanon, N.Y.: 19-?]. Broadside. 7 × 11½ cm.

Signed: *Emma J. Neale.* An advertisement for summer visitors which points out the modern conveniences, excellent table, and beautiful situation. Inquiries to be addressed to Emma J. Neale, Mount Lebanon, Columbia Co., N.Y.
NOC, OClWHi*.

48 Anthony's Standard Business Directory and Reference Book of Pittsfield, 1903–04. Representing the Progressive and Up-to-date Business Firms of Pittsfield and Selected Towns in Berkshire County Who Want Your Trade ... [Natick, Mass.:] Anthony Publ. Co., 1904. 76 pp. 25½ cm.

> Shaker advertisements and listings: pp. 11, 24, "Ira R. Lawson wholesale dealer in flour, grain, meal, feed, etc. Agent for the Shaker swifts. A reel for winding and doubling yarn," p. 29; Shaker School, Mt. Lebanon, N.Y. p. 76; Shaker Mills, West Stockbridge, Mass. Back cover, Shaker cloaks. Clarissa Jacobs, Maker, Mt. Lebanon, N.Y. Paragraph about the Shakers, p. 3.
> OClWHi*.

AN ANTIQUARIAN [pseud.]. *See* [Hinman, Royal Ralph], *comp.*, no. 776.

49 ATHERTON, SIMON T. and ELIJAH MYRICK. [Communications]. In U.S. Commissioner of Patents, *Report for 1853, Pt. II, Agriculture.* (33rd Cong., 1st Sess., Sen. Exec. Doc. 27), pp. 10, 89–90, 109, 171, 269, 280–81, 290, 294, 300–301.

> Written in response to a circular from the Commissioner of Patents requesting agricultural information. Cattle, land improvement, corn (Indian), potatoes, apples, pears, plums, cherries, and grapes as grown at the Shaker community, Harvard, Mass., are described.
> CtY, DLC, KyU, MWA, MWiW*, N, NN, NhD, OC.

AURELIA [pseud.]. *See* Mace, Aurelia Gay, no. 881 ff.

50 Authorized Rules of the Shaker Community. Given for the Protection and Guidance of the Members in the Several Societies. Mt. Lebanon,

N.Y.: [Printed at Shaker Village [Canterbury], N.H.], 1894. 16 pp. 17½ cm.

> A manuscript note on one of the Western Reserve Historical Society copies states that this was arranged and printed by H. C. Blinn. An advertisement, *The Manifesto*, 24 (December 1894), recto, back cover, carries the statement, "The religious basis of the ORDER must be a foundation resting on the principle of righteousness, which principle is God. This should rule the life of the individual for the protection of his own soul, for the peace of the family and as an evidence of his upright standing before the world." A manuscript note found in one of the copies examined by Wilma Stein Davis states in part, "It is order that all carless [*sic*] or wilful violation of these orders shall be confest as a sin. No soul can travel or progress in our gospel with sin wilfully covered from the Witnesses of truth, or the Elders who are faithful to their trust, & without such Elders, no family or Society of Alethian Believers can prosper." *See also* nos. **1356, 1615, 1641** and **1766.**
> MacLean 130. CtY, KyBgW, MB, MH, MHarF, MPB, MWA, MWiW*, MeHi, N, NBuG, NN, NOC, NSyU, NhD, NjPT, O, OCl, OClWHi, ODa, OHi, PPULC.

51 AVERY, GILES BUSHNELL. Autobiography by Elder Giles B. Avery, of Mount Lebanon, N.Y. [written in 1880]. Also an Account of the Funeral Service which was Held at Watervliet, N.Y., December 30, 1890; Together with Testimonials of Respect from his Many Friends. East Canterbury, N.H.: 1891. 34 pp. music. 23½ cm.

> Cover title: Translated. Elder, Giles B. Avery. Mount Lebanon, N.Y. 1890. "An Account ..." was prepared by Anna White, according to L. S. Taylor, no. 1359, p. 71; attributed to Anna White by MacLean.
> MacLean 132. CoDB, DLC, KyU, MHarF, MPB, MPH, MU, MWA, MWiW*, MiU, NBuG, NN, NHi, NOC, NSyU, NhD, NjPT, O, OClWHi, OHi, WHi.

52 —— [Communication, dated Dec. 11th, 1850]. In U.S. Comm. of Patents, *Report for 1850, Pt. II, Agriculture.* (31st Cong. 2d Sess.,

House Exec. Doc., 32), pp. 426–29.
    Written in response to a circular from the
Patent Commissioner requesting agricultural
information. Wheat, corn, oats, barley, rye,
butter and cheese making, fertilizers, cattle,
sheep, and wool growing at the New Lebanon Shaker community are described.
CtY, DLC, KyU, MWA, MWiW*, NN, NhD,
OC.

53 —— [Communication, dated January 15th,
1850]. In U.S. Commissioner of Patents, *Report
for 1849, Pt. II, Agriculture.* (31st Cong., 1st
Sess., House Exec. Doc. 20), pp. 99–103.
    Written in response to a circular from the
Patent Commissioner requesting agricultural
information. Oats, rye, barley, maize, hay,
root crops, butter, sheep, hogs, fertilizer,
mulching, and precipitation at the New
Lebanon, N.Y., Shaker community are described.
CtY, DLC, KyU, MWA, MWiW*, N, NN,
NhD, OC.

54 —— The New Creation. [Mt. Lebanon,
N.Y.: 189–?]. Caption title. 8 pp. 13½ cm.
    Reprinted from *The Manifesto* 19 (June
1889), 28–30. Contains also: "Unpardonable
Sin" by F. W. Evans (from *Shaker Manifesto*
9 (September 1879), 197–98); "The Future
Life" by F. W. Evans (from *The Manifesto*
14 (February 1884), 39–41); "Government"
by Martha J. Anderson (from *The Manifesto*
14 (June 1884), 125–26).
MWiW*, N, NN, OClWHi.

55 —— A Sermon ... Delivered in Church at
Shaker Village, Mer. Co., N.H., July 1, 1877.
Canterbury, N.H.: Shaker Village, [1877].
Caption title. 4 pp. 21 cm.
CtY-D, MPB, NOC, NjPT, OClWHi*.

56 [——]. Sketches of "Shakers and Shakerism."
Synopsis of Theology of United Society of
Believers in Christ's Second Appearing. Albany:
Weed, Parsons and Company, Printers, 1883.
Cover title. 35 pp. illus. 19 cm.
    Contains also: A Shaker's Answer to the Oft-
repeated Question, "What Would Become of
the World if All Should Become Shakers?"

by R. W. Pelham (no. **1183**), pp. 21–35.
Electroplate engraved views of 6 Shaker
communities, including Harvord [sic], Mass.,
on front cover, and Shirley, Mass., on verso
of back cover.
MacLean 133. CtHi, CtY, MB, MH-P,
MHarF, MHi, MPB, MSaE, MWA, MWiW*,
MiD, MiU, NBuG, N, NN, NOC, NjPT,
OClWHi, ODa, PU, RHi.

57 —— ———— Albany: Weed, Parsons and
Company, Printers, 1884. Cover title, 50, [2]
pp. illus. 19 cm.
    Avery's name appears as author on the front
cover of this edition. Also contains: "Ann
Lee" by Andrew Jackson Davis, pp. 27–30
(*see* no. **2034** ff.); "A Shaker's Answer" by
R. W. Pelham, pp. 31–46; "An Open Letter,
to All Reformers ..." by G. B. Avery, pp.
48–50; post office addresses of 17 Shaker
societies, p. [2] at end; views of 14 Shaker
communities, including Mt. Lebanon, on
verso of back cover.
MacLean 134. CSmH, CtHi, CtY-D, DLC,
ICJ, ICN, KyU, MB, MBAt, MBC, MH,
MH-P, MHarF, MPB, MWA, MWiW*, MeHi,
MiU, MiU-C, N, NBuG, NN, NNG, NOC,
NRCR, NSyU, NhD, NjMD, NjPT, OCl,
OClWHi, OHi, OO, PCC, PPULC, PPWa,
PSC, PU, RPJCB, WHi.

58 —— Spiritual Life. [Published at Shaker
Village, Mer. Co., N.H., 1888?]. Caption title.
4 pp. 22 cm.
    Also contains: "My Brother, my Sister and
Mother" by Henry Blinn. *Spiritual Life* is
reprinted from *The Manifesto* 18 (November
1888), 241–43.
MacLean 135. DLC, MPB, MWiW*, NBuG,
NjPT, NN, OClWHi.

59 —— To Our Brethren and Sisters who Find
it Some Difficulty to Raise the Necessary Funds
to Subscribe for their Annual Quota of the
Shaker Manifesto ... [Watervliet, N.Y.: 187–?].
Broadside. 23½ × 12 cm.
    A circular pertaining to an offer of Grover
and Baker Sewing Machines at a special low
price for large numbers of new subscriptions
to the *Shaker Manifesto.*
OClWHi*.

B

60 B., A. B. Shakerism, "the Possibility of the Race." Being Letters of A. B. B. and Elder F. W. Evans. [Watervliet, N.Y.:] Office of the Shaker, 1872. Cover title. 14 pp. 13 cm.
  MacLean 290. DLC, MHarF, MPB, MPH, MWiW*, N, NBuG, NN, OClWHi, ODa.

61 BAILEY, LUTHER. [Communications]. In U.S. Commissioner of Patents, *Report for 1853, Pt. II, Agriculture.* (33d Cong., 1st Sess., Sen. Exec. Doc. 27), pp. 16, 86, 145, 178, 273.
  Written in response to a circular from the Patent Commissioner requesting agricultural information. Cattle, fertilizer, wheat, sweet potatoes, and apples at the Shaker community, North Union, O., are described.
  CtY, DLC, KyU, MWA, MWiW*, N, NN, NhD, OC.

62 BAKER, W. ... New Zealand Letter. [Pittsfield, Mass.?: 1884?]. Broadside. 29 × 8 cm.
  At head of title: From the *Pittsfield Sun.* A letter of inquiry about Shaker tenets addressed to Elder F. W. Evans from W. Baker, Sen'r, Watchmaker, Gore, Otago, New Zealand, dated: Jan. 1884. Elder Evans's reply, no. 594. Reprinted in *The Manifesto* 14 (October 1884), 229-30.
  MacLean 137. CtY, MPB, MWiW*, NN, OClWHi, OHi, WHi.

63 [BARKER, RUTH MILDRED]. Greetings to You from the Society of American Shakers ... [Sabbathday Lake, Me.:] 1937. Broadside. 18½ × 15½ cm.
  Brief outline of beliefs and request for patronage. *See also* no. 1496.
  MWiW*, NOC.

64 BASTING, LOUIS. Christianity. West Pittsfield, Mass.: [Printed at East Canterbury, N.H., 1891]. Cover title. 8 pp. 14½ cm.
  Reprinted from *The Manifesto* 21 (March 1891), 68-70.
  MacLean 138. CtY, DLC, MPB, MWA, MWiW*, MeHi, NN, NOC, OClWHi.

65 BATES, ISSACHAR. New Songs, on Different Subjects. Composed by Issachar Bates ... Salem, New-York: Printed by Henry Dodd, 1800. 16 pp. 17½ cm.
  Eight songs which are religious meditations, essentially balladic and elegiac. They were written and published before Issachar Bates was converted to Shakerism in August 1801, and have not previously been credited to him in Shaker references. No mention of this publication occurs in the manuscript account of his "Life and Experiences," which is available in 3 printed versions. (*See* nos. **66, 1501,** and **1503.**) The information here about Bates' early life depends upon Elder Henry Blinn's version in *The Manifesto* 14 (August-October 1884). Bates was a fifer with the Revolutionary forces and claimed that "he could sing about every song that was generally known, whether civil, military, sacred, or profane." Thomas Brown, *An Account of the People Called Shakers* [no. **114**], p. 349, characterized Bates as having "but little literary information but somewhat of a poetical genius." This collection shows abundant evidence of Bates' authorship, and the contents parallel the known facts of his life at this period. The place names coincide with his removal, accompanied by his large family, in 1786 from Massachusetts to the state of New York. Soon thereafter, he joined the Baptists, and in 1791 was licensed by them to preach, which he did until he joined the Shakers. Bates became an influential Shaker whose preaching talents quickened the spread of Shakerism in the early nineteenth century. A few months after conversion he "was sent, in company with Benjamin Youngs, to preach the testimony of Believers" to Vermont and New Hampshire where many converts were attracted to Shakerism. Bates and Youngs, along with John Meacham, were chosen for the historic mission of planting Shakerism in

the West at the time of the Kentucky Revival. Their spectacular success culminated in the establishment of seven Shaker communities in Kentucky, Ohio, and Indiana. *See also* no. 3517. Contents: I, "The Author's Trials" (to the tune of "Major André"), pp. 3–6; II, "The Hunter's Midnight Prayer" [the author composed this song near Schroon Lake, where he encamped for a night], pp. 6–8; III, "A Prospect of Lake Schroon, Composed on its Banks," pp. 8–10; IV, "The Harvest," pp. 10–11; V, "The Author's Soliloquy, Composed on a Sabbath Day Morning, being on a Journey," pp. 11–12; VI, "Composed on the Death of Mr. Isaac Orcutt, who was Killed by the Fall of a Tree, in Hartford, State of New-York," pp. 12–14; VII, "The Newlight's Hymn. Composed by a Youth, and Transposed, with some Additions by the Author," pp. 14–15; VIII, "Composed on the Late Sickness in Hartford, State of New-York," pp. 15–16.
Evans 36909. MWA*, NN, NHi.

66 —— The Revolutionary War and Issachar Bates. Old Chatham, N.Y.: Shaker Museum Foundation, 1960. Cover title. [14] pp. 21 cm.
Excerpted from a copy of Bates' manuscript autobiography in the Shaker Museum Library, Old Chatham, N.Y. For other versions *see* nos. 1501 and 1503.

67 BATES, PAULINA. The Divine Book of Holy and Eternal Wisdom, Revealing the Word of God; Out of Whose Mouth Goeth A Sharp Sword . . . Written by Paulina Bates . . . Including Other Illustrations and Testimonies. Arranged and Prepared for the Press at New Lebanon, N.Y. . . . . Published by the United Society called "Shakers." Canterbury, N.H.: 1849. 2 vols. in 1, paged continuously, xxii, 696 pp. 21½ cm.
Preface signed: Seth Y. Wells. Calvin Green, Editors. Title page, vol. 2, p. 375, varies slightly. "Errata," p. 696. Also issued in "thin paper." This book is a product of the intense preoccupation with spiritualism at this period. The contents were received by inspiration through the instrumentality of a member of the Watervliet, N.Y., Shaker community who "wrote whatever the Angel of God dictated." The Appendix, pp. 659–96, contains testimonies of various divine and heavenly witnesses in the sacred truth. Later, this book was suppressed along with no. 1340. This series of inspired communications was copied by Elder Joseph Hodgson, but "were without order or arrangement for a book." Seth Y. Wells and Calvin Green edited and "arranged it in Chapter and verse & added Titles," and "prepared the work in such a manner, and in such language as to be understood by natural people." Publication was delayed "owing to its Testimony against slavery and its liability to stir up persecution in a Slave state," Calvin Green, "Biographic Memoir," pp. 632–36. In order that an edition of 2500 copies might be printed by the Shakers at Canterbury, N.H., it was necessary to purchase a Tuft's press, inking machine, and additional type. *See In Memoriam*, H. C. Blinn (no. 830), p. 31. Daryl Chase, "The Early Shakers" (unpubl. dissertation, University of Chicago, 1936), l. 176, characterizes this work as "Perhaps the most pretentious of all the inspired Shaker writings." MacLean 5. Sabin 79704. CSmH, CoDU, CtHi, CtY, DeWint, DLC, ICJ, KyBgW, KySP, KyU, MB, MHarF, MPB, MU, MWA, MWiW*, MeHi, MiU, N, NBuG, NHi, NIC, NN, NNC, NOC, NRCR, NSyU, NhD, NjMD, O, OC, OCl, OClWHi, ODa, OHi, OO, OOxM, PPC, PPL, PPULC, UPB, WHi.

68 BAXTER, GEORGE H. A Cluster of Thought Flashes. [n.p.], 1908. Cover title. 16 pp. 15½ cm.
The contents are mostly aphorisms and epigrams.
MH-AH, MHarF*, MPB, MWA, NBuG, OClWHi.

69 BEAR, HENRY B. Henry B. Bear's Advent Experience. [Whitewater Village, Harrison O.: n.d.]. 10 pp. 23 cm.
Bear was a disillusioned Millerite who joined the Shaker community at Whitewater, Ohio.
MWA, OClWHi*.

70 —— A Scientific Demonstration of the Prophecies of Daniel and St. John. Preston, Ohio: Alexander Smith, Printer,

[189–?]. Cover title. 13 pp. 13½ cm.
MacLean 139. DLC, MHarF, MWiW*, NN,
OClWHi (proof sheets), WHi.

71 —— Scientific Demonstration of Theology,
Prophecy and Revelation. [Preston, O.:] 1896.
Cover title, [1], 48 pp. 18 cm.
Caption title: A scientific investigation of
theology.
NOC*, NSyU, OClWHi, OHi (ms. correc-
tions), WHi.

72 —— ——— Preston, Hamilton Co.,
Ohio: 1900. Cover title. [1], 56 pp. 18 cm.
MacLean 140. CtY, DLC, ICN, MH, MPB,
MWA, MWiW*, MiU–C, N, NBuG, NHi, NN,
NjPT, OClWHi, OO, WHi.

73 The Believer's Appeal. [n.p., n.d.]. Broad-
side in 2 columns. 20 × 16 cm.
Poem of 11 numbered stanzas beginning:
Man in his first creation/ As he was made
upright,—you know/ While in that situation./
He walked in the light—you know .... This
appears to be Richard McNemar's printing.
OClWHi*.

74 BENNETT, DE ROBIGNE MORTIMER.
The World's Sages, Thinkers, and Reformers,
Being Biographical Sketches ... 2d ed. Revised
and Enlarged. New York: Liberal and Scientific
Publ. House, 1876. 1075 pp. 23½ cm.
Life and beliefs of D. M. Bennett, pp. 1060–
75. Recollections of his Shaker life, New
Lebanon, pp. 1061–64. Bennett joined the
Shakers at 14 years of age and was put to
work in the seed gardens at the New Lebanon, N.Y., community. Later he transferred
to the medical department where he developed a knowledge of medical herbs and roots,
etc., and was eventually appointed physician
to the society. He seceded in 1846, married,
and eventually became an advocate for
liberalism in religion. His education with the
Shakers enabled him to establish a successful
career in proprietary and other medicines in
the Middle West, but following several unsuccessful investments, he became active as a
freethinker, publisher, and pamphleteer in
New York City. Bennett received national
notoriety because of his arrest and imprison-

ment as a result of a charge brought against
him by Anthony Comstock for sending so-
called indecent matter through the mails.
Frederick W. Evans' letter to the New York
Tribune protesting the conviction and imprisonment of Bennett as a "church and state
persecution" was reprinted in *The Manifesto*,
9 (August 1879), 181–82. D. M. Bennett's
letter from Ludlow Street jail, N.Y., expressing
gratitude to Evans, was reprinted in the same
issue, p. 183. For G. B. Avery's letter of protest addressed to President Rutherford B.
Hayes, *see* no. **1490**. This work was originally
published with the title, *The World's Sages,
Infidels, and Thinkers* ... (1876), where it is
stated, pp. 926–29, that James M. Peebles
"constantly urged upon Spiritualists the
recognition of the Shaker Brotherhood and
on many occasions has brought them to the
front in a conspicuous manner. With reserva-
tions he [Peebles] accepts their social and
communistic principles ..."
DLC*, MH, OClWHi.

75 BENNETT, DE ROBIGNE and G. H.
HUMPHREY. Christianity and Infidelity; Or, The
Humphrey–Bennett Discussion ... Conducted in
the Columns of the Truth Seeker, Commencing
April 7, 1877, Closing Sept. 29, 1877 ... New
York: D. M. Bennett, Liberal and Scientific
Publishing House, 1877. 533 pp. 19 cm.
"Sketch of [the life of] D. M. Bennet," pp.
ix-xv, signed: *D.M.B.* In 1873 Bennett launched
the radical monthly *The Truth Seeker*, and be-
gan publication of books and pamphlets expressing
liberal and freethinkers' views. *See also* no. 74.
CtY, DLC*, IU, IaU, MH, OO.

76 Biblical Recitation. [Canterbury] Shaker
Village, Mer. Co., N.H.: [1885?]. Caption title.
4pp. music. 24 cm.
"The following recitation was given before
the Brethren and Sisters of the Church family."
"Duty to God," with words and music reprinted from *The Manifesto* 14 (June 1884),
141–43. "Information for Inquirers," p. 4,
reprinted from *The Manifesto* 15 (January
1885), 25. This text varies slightly from that
of separate publications. *See* no. **837**. Paragraph 6: Parents that become members ...
7: "No corporal punishment is approved ..."

MacLean 141. DLC, MPB, MWiW*, OClWHi.

77 A Biography of the Life and Tragical Death of Elder Caleb M. Dyer, Together with the Poem and Eulogies at his Funeral, July 21, 1863. Manchester, N.H.: American Steam Printing Works of Gage, Moore & Co., 1863. 16 pp. 21 cm.

Caleb Dyer, son of Mary Dyer (no. 530 ff), was taken to the Enfield, N.H., Shaker community by his father, Joseph (no. 525 ff), when he was 13 years of age. He became a popular, successful first trustee, and initiated greatly expanded building and business programs which eventually involved the Shakers in more worldly commerce than proved to be wise. After he was shot by a disgruntled father, Thomas Weir, a Civil War veteran, whose children had been placed with the Shakers, Dyer's unorthodox accounting records cost the Shakers thousands of dollars. *See* M. Melcher, *Shaker Adventure* (no. 2451), p. 233. MacLean 142. ICN, MWA, MWiW*, MiD, N, NN, Nh, NhD, NjPT, OClWHi, RPB.

78 BISHOP, EBENEZER. Farewell Address of Elder Ebenezer Bishop, of New Lebanon, to the Inhabitants of Zion. Written at the Holy Mount, Dec. 29, 1842. Canterbury, N.H.: 1850. 15 pp. 13½ cm.

"Nearly seven years ago, Holy Mother Wisdom, thro' one of her instruments, required Elder Ebenezer to leave, in writing, his testimony and experience in the work of God, and his faith concerning the late out-pouring of the spirit of God, throughout every branch of Zion"–"Introduction," p. [3], which is signed: *Rufus Bishop. Holy Mount. Nov. 1, 1849.* End of text, p. 15, is signed: *Ebenezer Bishop, Holy Mount, Dec. 29, 1842.* Elder Ebenezer Bishop died Oct. 9, 1849. This message was delivered through an "instrument" after his death. MacLean 143. CSmH, DLC, ICN, MPB, MWA, MWiW*, NBuG, NN, NOC, NSyU, NjPT, OClWHi, OOxM.

79 [BISHOP, RUFUS and SETH Y. WELLS]. A Circular Epistle. The Ministry of Elders of the Church, to All Those Living and Faithful Witnesses of the Truth, Whose Early Faith in the Gospel Gave Them the Privilege of a Personal Acquaintance with Our Ever Blessed Mother and Elders. [To Accompany *Testimonies* ...]. [Hancock, Mass.: J. Talcott & J. Deming, 1816]. Caption title, 3 pp. 17½ cm.

At end of text: New Lebanon, April 15th, 1816. The same type and paper were used to print *Testimonies* (no. 80). Because of the lapse of time and "want of personal interviews ... it has been extremely difficult to be so correct, in many particulars, as the nature of such a work requires." It is probable "that the time will come when a new more perfect edition will be called for." A request is addressed to those who were personally acquainted with "first witnesses" to communicate anything "of sufficient importance which may be of service in correcting and improving the work." Presumably, the improvements were to be incorporated in a new edition, no. 81. A copy of this circular was included in copies of the *Testimonies*, no. 80. Shaw 38918. MWiW*, OClWHi.

80 [——], *eds.* Testimonies of the Life, Character, Revelations and Doctrines of Our Ever Blessed Mother Ann Lee, and the Elders with Her; through whom the Word of Eternal Life was Opened in this Day of Christ's Second Appearing: Collected from Living Witnesses, by Order of the Ministry, in Union with the Church .... Hancock [Mass.]: Printed by J. Tallcott & J. Deming, Junrs., 1816. xi, 405 [1] pp. 18 cm.

"Errata," verso p. 405. "Entitled 'Mother's Sayings,' the *Testimonies* were collected in 1812, by Elder Rufus Bishop ... It was edited by Seth Y. Wells," White and Taylor [no. 1447], pp. 322–23. MacLean, *Bibliography*, p. 32: "This book was used solely by the elders, and was sometimes called the 'Secret Book of the Elders'." Many of these testimonies were scattered through the account of the early history of the Shakers and Ann Lee, and differ from the testimonies in no. 1421. Both were written to counteract those reports intended "to vilify and calumniate the characters of the *First Witnesses* and especially that of Mother Ann Lee." The Shaker Museum (Old Chatham, N.Y.) copy contains Alonzo G. Hollister's a.n.s., "Only 20 copies of this edition printed under Mother Lucy's ministration." Hollister wrote the same information to William

Ward Wight in an a.l.s., Dec. 16, 1909, now in the Williams College Library, Williamstown, Mass.
MacLean 99. Sabin 102602. Shaw 38921. DLC, KySP, MPB, MWA, MWiW*, NN, NOC, NjPT, OClWHi.

81 [——] ——— Testimonies of the Life, Character, Revelations, and Doctrines of Mother Ann Lee and the Elders with Her, through Whom the Word of Eternal Life was Opened in this Day, of Christ's Second Appearing, Collected from Living Witnesses, in Union with the Church . . . . Second Edition. Albany, N.Y.: Weed, Parsons & Co., Printers, 1888. ix, 302 pp. 21 cm.
Often cited by the binder's title, Precepts of Mother Ann Lee and the Elders. The revision of this edition is generally attributed to Giles Avery. Cf. A. White and L. S. Taylor, *Shakerism* (no. 1447), p. 323. MacLean 100. Sabin 102602. CBBD, CtY, DLC, ICJ, InU, KySP, KyU, MPB, MWiW*, N, NBuG, NN, NNG, NOC, NSyU, NcD, NjPT, O, OCH, OClWHi, ODa, OHi, PCC, PPL, PPULC, WHi.

82 [——] ——— (Reprint). New York: AMS Press, 1973.

83 BLAKE, EDWARD U. The Sacred, Solemn and Sealed Roll Opened and Read by the Mighty Angel. Mount Lebanon [N.Y.]: Feb. 2d 1843. Broadside. 28 × 21 cm.
John Large, Jr., courteously reported that he found this item (trimmed) in the Western Reserve Historical Society in Volume VII of a set of financial records of the Groveland, N.Y., Shaker community. *See also* no. 1261. OClWHi*.

84 BLAKEMAN, ELISHA D'ALEMBERT. Two Hundred Poetical Riddles. For the Instruction and Amusement of Children and Youth. By E. D. Blakeman. New York: D. M. Bennett, 1875. 42 pp. 15½ cm.
Copyright 1874, "By Elisha D. Blakeman." "Blakeman's Two Hundred Poetical Riddles," pp. [3]-34; "Answers to Blakeman's Two Hundred Riddles," pp. [35]-42. Advertisements, [6] pp., at end. Both the author and the publisher were former members of the Church Family at the Mt. Lebanon Shaker

community, *See* no. 74. Blakeman seceded in 1872. His name is listed in D. M. Bennett's *A Truth Seeker Around the World* (N.Y. [1882]. 4 vols.), among more than 500 persons who contributed toward the costs of Bennett's trip in 1881 as a delegate to the Freethinkers' Congress in Brussels. DLC, NN*.

85 [——] The Youth's Guide in Zion and Holy Mother's Promises. Given by Inspiration at New Lebanon, N.Y., January 5, 1842. Canterbury, N.H.: 1842. 35 [1] pp. 16½ cm.
MacLean attributes this to Elisha D. Blakeman. Cf., Note, p. [3], "The following is a communication from Holy Mother Wisdom to the Elders of the First Order, at Holy Mount of God, brought by a holy and swiftwinged angel, belonging to the fifth band of the angels of love at Holy Selon ... given to be inscribed on paper by the hand of mortal clay Sabbath morn Nov. 1841." This was not intended to circulate in the "outside world." Excerpts were reprinted in the New Hampshire *Report of the Examination* . . . . No. 1071. MacLean 478. CSmH, DLC, MHarF, MPB, MPH, MWA, MWiW*, MeB, MiU, N, NBuG, NN, NOC, NSyU, NhD, NjPT, O, OClWHi, OHi, PHi, PPULC, WHi.

86 [——] ——— [Reprint, copyright by the United Society, [1963]. 30, [1] p. 21½ cm. (Mother's work series, No. 1.)
Enlarged facsimile title page of 1842 edition. This is reprinted from the *Shaker Quarterly* 3 (Spring, Summer 1963), 18–36, 64–72. MPH, MWA, MWiW*, NOC.

87 BLANCHARD, GROVE B. Experience. [n.p., 183–?]. Broadside. 15 × 9 cm. (trimmed). Signed: *Composed by Elder Grove Blanchard, Nov. 9, 1831*. A hymn of 8 stanzas, beginning: Come hearken dear companions, and I will just relate./ How I have been progressing, on from my youthful state/ . . . . MWiW*.

88 —— ——— [n.p., n.d.]. Broadside. 19 × 11 cm. With 2 lines of manuscript music in Shaker letter notation. OClWHi*.

89 —— ———— [n.p., n.d.]. Broadside.
20 X 11 cm. Printed on yellow paper.
OClWHi*.

90 BLINN, HENRY CLAY. Advent of the
Christ in Man and Woman. [East Canterbury,
N.H.: 1896]. Cover title. 16 pp. music. 23 cm.
Words and music for "Infinite Love" and
"Spirit World," pp. 14-15. Advertisements
for Shaker publications, p. 16.
MacLean 144. CtY, DLC, ICN, KySP,
MB, MHarF, MPB, MPH, MWA, MWiW*,
MiU-C, N, NBuG, NN, NOC, NRCR, NSyU,
Nh, NhD, O, OClWHi, OHi, WHi.

—— Brief Account of Shakers and Shakerism.
See nos. 107-109.

91 —— A Christian Community. East Canterbury, N.H.: [1897]. Cover title. 16 pp. illus.
23 cm.
An informally written description of Shakerism and Shaker life reprinted from The
Manifesto 27 (February, March, April, May
1897), 17-21, 33-36, 49-53, 65-68. Electroplate engraved frontispiece, "East Canterbury, N.H.," shows many of the buildings in
this Shaker village.
MacLean 145. CtY-D, DLC, InU, MHarF,
MPB, MWA, MWiW*, N, NBuG, NN, NOC,
NSyU, OClWHi, WHi, WaU.

92 —— ———— By Henry C. Blinn of the
Canterbury Shakers. East Canterbury, N.H.:
[n.d.]. Cover title. 16 pp. illus. 23½ cm.
The text differs slightly, and the typeface
and typography differ. The frontispiece has
been replaced by a photograph which shows
the same view of the village.
MPH, MeHi, MWA, N, NOC, OClWHi*.

93 [——], comp. A Collection of Hymns and
Anthems Adapted to Public Worship. Published
by the Shakers .... East Canterbury, N.H.: 1892.
[2], iv, [blank leaf], 144 pp. music, 23½ cm.
Cover title: Hymns and Anthems for the
Hour of Worship. Preface signed: H. C. B.,
where it is stated that this collection is in a
more convenient form than that found in
The Manifesto where the hymns and anthems
appeared originally (over a 14-year period).

"All that were stereotyped in pamphlet size"
are collected here. The typography varies as a
result of these hymns and anthems having been
printed at various times and places. Words and
music mostly written in 4-part harmony. Conventional notation.
MacLean 12. CBDP, CtHC, CtY, DLC, DeWint,
IU, MPB, MWiW*, MeHi, MiU, N, NBuG, NcD,
NN, NRCR, OClWHi, ODa, OHi, OLeWHi, OU,
PCC, PPULC, RPB, WHi.

94 [——], comp. A Concise Catechism, Contain-
ing the Most Important Events Recorded in the
Bible. Also a Short Sketch of the Lives of our
First Elders and Parents, Mother Ann, Father
William & Father James. Shaker Village, Canter-
bury, N.H.: 1850. 40 pp. 14 cm.
Cover title: A Concise Shaker Catechism.
Preface signed: H. C. B. Poem, "Sin of Waste-
fulness," on verso, back cover.
MacLean 197. CSmH, DLC, MPB, MWiW*,
N, NBuG, NN, NOC, NSyU, NjPT, OClWHi.

95 [——], comp. Dew Drops of Wisdom.
Canterbury, N.H.: Printed by H. C. Blinn, 1852.
125 pp. 4½ X 3½ cm.
Note in Ethel Peacock's autograph in MHarF
copy: "They printed just a few of these."
Religious Aphorisms for each day of the year.
The smallest book printed by the Shakers.
MHarF*, NOC, OClWHi.

[——] From the Shakers. See no. 715.

96 [——] The Life and Gospel Experience of
Mother Ann Lee ... Canterbury, N.H.: Published
by the Shakers, [1882?]. Cover title. 24 pp.
17½ cm.
"Prefatory" signed: H. C. Blinn, Canterbury,
N.H. An advertisement for this work occurs
on the back cover of The Manifesto, January
1883.
MacLean 146. DLC, KyU, MHarF, MPB,
MPH, MU, MWA, MWiW*, MeB, MiD, MiU-C,
NBuG, NN, Nh, O, OClWHi, OHi.

97 [——] ———— [1883]. Cover title. 24 pp.
17½ cm.
"Prefatory" signed: Henry C. Blinn. Canterbury, Mer. Co., N.H., 1883. "Mother Ann Lee"
on the title page is printed in a larger type size

and different typeface. The replacement of
many broken types throughout the text indicates that this is a second, revised printing.
DLC, MPH, MWiW*, NBuG, NN.

98 —— ———— 1889. *See, Shaker Quarterly,*
3 (Fall 1963), 103.
   Listed as "(Not in MacLean)." *See also*
   "List of Works in the New York Public
   Library Relating to the Shakers," N.Y.P.L.,
   Bulletin, 8 (November 1904), 555, where a
   24-page copy is dated: [1890], no. **3488**. No
   copy located.

99 —— ———— East Canterbury, N.H.: The
Shakers, [1901]. 264 pp. 19 cm.
   "Prefatory" dated: 1901; authorship is
   acknowledged on the title page. Essentially
   the same account, printed under Blinn's name
   in *The Manifesto,* Vols. 16–18 (April 1886–
   July 1888), is headed by the statement,
   "Published expressly for the several com-
   munities of Believers in 1816. Rewritten by
   Henry Blinn." This greatly expands the
   material in the earlier pamphlets.
   MacLean 6. CBBD, CSmH, CtY-D, DLC,
   DeWint, MH, MHarF, MPB, MWiW*, MiU-C,
   N, NBuG, NN, NOC, NjPT, OClWHi, OHi,
   OLeWHi, PPULC, TNJ-R, UPB.

100 [——], *comp.* A Little Instructor. Canterbury, N.H.: Printed by H. C. Blinn, 1849. 128 pp.
5½ X 4½ cm.
   MacLean 61 identifies this as "Smallest
   Shaker book," but *see* no. **95**. "It is with
   pleasure that we present to our little readers
   these few choice pieces, selected from among
   many; hoping they will be the means of doing
   some good to those who are willing to receive instruction in the days of their youth
   ..." Preface. Contains short sermons with
   Biblical paraphrases, etc.
   NOC*.

101 ——, *ed.* The Manifestation of Spiritualism
Among the Shakers 1837–1847. East Canter-
bury, N.H.: 1899. [2], 101 pp. 18 cm.
   Cover title: Spiritualism Among the Shakers.
   Includes written accounts by Shakers who
   received visions and spirit messages, some of

which have been published in the *Progressive
Thinker.*
MacLean 147. AU, CSmH, DLC, KySP,
MHarF, MPB, MWA, MWiW*, MeB, MiU, N,
NBuG, NN, Nh, NhD, NjPT, O, OC, OClWHi,
ODa, OHi, WHi.

102 [——], *comp.* A Sacred Repository of
Anthems and Hymns, for Devotional Worship
and Praise .... Canterbury, N.H.: 1852. xiii,
[blank leaf], 222, [1] pp. music. 20 cm.
   Preface signed: *H. C. B.* Blinn explains that
   many of the anthems and hymns were communicated "by the holy gift of inspiration."
   Words with music, written in Shaker letter
   notation employing the letters "a" to "g,"
   which is explained. "Errata" p. [1] at end.
   Blinn states in his "Autobiographical Notes,"
   In Memoriam (no. **830**), p. 33, that he
   printed this book and continues: "This was
   the first attempt at publishing a work having
   the hymns set to music. As the Believers at
   this time had no music type, and as their
   system was quite unlike that of the world at
   large, we were obliged to have a font cast for
   our special use. This involved considerable
   expense; but after exercising extreme patience,
   I brought out a book of 220 pages." Clearly,
   Elder Henry also set the music type. While
   this is the first use of printed Shaker notation
   in a hymnal, I. N. Youngs made and set Shaker
   music type earlier in *A Short Abridgment*
   (New Lebanon, N.Y., 1843), *see* no. **1479**.
   Printed music in Shaker notation also occurs
   in R. Haskell's *Musical Expositor* (New York,
   1847), no. **771**. Moreover, several hymns with
   the music in Shaker letter notation appeared
   in Vols. 11 and 12 of *The Day-Star,* 1846–47,
   no. **494**. "Errata" [1] p. at end.
   MacLean 88 (attributed to Marcia Hastings
   and Henry C. Blinn). CtY, DLC, IU, KyBgW,
   MH, MPB, MPH, MWiW* (24 pp.), MeHi,
   MiU, NBuG, NN, NOC, NSyU, OClWHi, OHi,
   WHi.

103 [——] What Shall I Do to Be a Shaker?
[East Canterbury, N.H.: 1885?]. Caption title.
[2] pp. 22½ cm.
   A letter of Giles Avery dated: Sept. 1885,
   The Manifesto 16 (January 1886), 20,

acknowledges receipt of this circular and *Information for Inquirers* (no. 837), and states that "They are neatly printed and fully satisfactory." This may have been written to replace the broadside version by Henry Cummings who seceded in 1881 and married. MacLean 467. MHarF, MHi, MPB, MWiW*, MiU–C, NBuG, NN, NOC, OClWHi.

The Blue Laws of New Haven Colony. *See* [Hinman, Royal Ralph], no. 776.

104 [BOLTON, AQUILA MASSIE]. Some Lines in Verse about Shakers. Not Published by Authority of the Society so Called .... New York: William Taylor & Co. [Edward O. Jenkins, Printer], 1846. 56 pp. 23½ cm.
MacLean attributes this to A. M. Bolton. Bolton, "the Eagle," continues his controversy with members of the Union Village community. Includes "Lines by Charlotte Cushman," pp. 53–54, and "Answer" [by H. L. Eads], pp. 54–56. *See also* nos. 491 and 546.
MacLean 447. Sabin 79720. CtW, CtY, DLC, ICN, MB, MH, MPB, MSaE, MU, MWA, MWiW*, MeHi, N, NBuG, NHi, NN, NSyU, OClWHi, OOxM, PPL, RPB, WHi.

105 —— The Whore of Babylon Unmasked; Or, a Cure for Orthodoxy; Being a Letter Addressed to Richard Mott, of New York .... Philadelphia: 1827. Cover title. 36 pp. 17½ cm.
A letter written in verse and dated, Union Village, 31st Aug., 1827. Bolton defends Shakerism and censures Quakerism. Later, Bolton was expelled from the Union Village Shaker community for advocating unorthodox ideas.
MacLean 148. Shaw 28214. DLC, ICN, MPB, MWiW*, NBuG, NN, OClWHi, PHC, PPULC.

106 [BOWERS, LUCY S.]. Concise Statements Concerning the Life and Religious Views of the Shakers. North Family, Mt. Lebanon, Columbia Co., N.Y. [Mt. Lebanon, N.Y.: 1895?]. 21 [2] pp. 13½ cm.
"This little tract containing a brief citation of the religious views, customs and regulations of the 'United Society of Believers' ... has

been written with the hope of answering collectively, the questions most frequently asked by strangers ... Being designed to enclose with letters, brevity becomes a necessity." "A List of Publications," p. [1] at end, lists Shaker publications as late as 1895. "Post Office Address of the Several Communities," p. [2] at end, includes Narcoossee, Osceola Co., Florida. *See also* no. 1438.
MacLean 198. DLC, MB, MHarF, MPB, MWA, MWiW*, MeB, MeHi, MiU–C, N, NBuG, NHi, NN, NNC, NSyU, OClWHi, PHC, PPULC, WHi.

107 [Brief Account of Shakers and Shakerism]. Beloved Friends, We Have Published a Pamphlet of 16 pp.—"*A Brief Account of Shakers and Shakerism*" ... a Select Piece of Music is Printed on Every Alternate Page. Shaker Village, [Canterbury] Mer. Co., N.H.: 1875. Broadside. 23½ × 15 cm.
Signed: *H. C. Blinn.* Dated: July 22, 1875. "We are also publishing some sheet music ... have now on hand the following: 'Star of Hope,' 'Morning Dawn,' 'More Love,' 'Happy Land,' 'The Call,' 'True Inspiration'. Also some leaflets of four pages each, containing Hymns and Select Pieces, arranged expressly for public use ... We shall print only a limited supply of the above leaflets for the benefit of our society. We extend this offer to others, so desiring, may secure a few copies. Those receiving the leaflets, may at any time bind them in pamphlet form ..."
OClWHi*.

108 Brief Account of Shakers and Shakerism. Several Pages of Shaker Music Are also Added that Have Never Before Been Published. Canterbury, Printed in Shaker Village, Mer. Co., N.H.: [1875]. Cover title. 16 pp. music. 15 × 19 cm.
Includes 9 hymns printed on the even-numbered pages and back cover, verso, with the music printed in conventional notation and scored for the treble clef, airs only. "Now published for the first time," p. 1. The dates of publication supplied by MacLean, no. 149, [1850?], and Sabin 79694, [184–?], are much too early because the effective change from Shaker letter notation to conventional

or modern notation was made in 1871 (*see* annotation, no. 975). "More Love" is printed from the same type setting (except the decorative type border) as is shown in the illustration in E. D. Andrews, *Gift to be Simple* (no. 1764), opp. p. 84, where it is identified as an example of the Canterbury leaflet songs "of the early 1870's."
MacLean 149. Sabin 79694. ICN, MB, MPB, MWA, MWiW*, NN, OClWHi, RPB.

109 —— [1876?]. Cover title. 20 pp. music. 15 X 19 cm.
A later edition. The statement on p. 1 has been changed to read "This pamphlet is published." Includes 9 hymns; five are repeated from no. 108. Eight of the hymns are printed with music scored for the treble clef only, but "The Prayer," repeated here on pp. 18–19, has been scored for 4-part singing, printed with both the treble and bass clefs. "The Prayer" is printed from the same type setting as is found in *The Shaker*, 6 (May 1876), 33. The verso of the back cover carries an advertisement, "Shaker Sheet Music," which lists 13 hymns, 3 of which were printed in no. 108.
ICN, KyU, MB, MHarF, MPB, MWiW*, NBuG, OClWHi, RPB.

110 BRIGGS, NICHOLAS A. God,——Dual. [East Canterbury, N.H.?: n.d.]. Caption title. 7 pp. 13½ cm.
Contains also "The Second Eve" by Ruth Webster, Union Village, Ohio.
MacLean 157. KyU, MPB, MWiW*, NN, NOC, NSyU, NjPT, OClWHi, WHi.

111 BROWN, GRACE ADA. Sister Corinne. Written by Sister Grace Ada Brown. In Memory of Sister Corinne Bishop, Who Passed to Her Spirit Home, Dec. 3, 1929. [n.p., n.d.]. Cover title. [3] pp. 8½ X 14 cm.
Poem of 6 stanzas. Unsigned manuscript note on the New York State Library copy, "Printed by the nuns for Sarah Collins." Shaker Museum (Old Chatham, N.Y.) copy has imprint: [New York, Lew Ney, 1929].
N, NOC*.

112 —— Song and Story . . . . Pittsfield

[Mass.]: The Eagle Publishing Co., 1902. vii, 188 pp. 21 cm.
A collection of poems written by a member of the North Family, Mt. Lebanon, N.Y. Many of these poems deal with non-Shaker subjects.
MacLean 8. DLC, MHarF, MPB, MWiW*, NBuG, NN, NOC, NSyU, OClWHi, OHi, WHi.

113 —— Under the Sheet; A Recital of Facts. [Mt. Lebanon, N.Y.: Shaker Press, 1900?]. Cover title. [7] pp. 15½ cm.
"Reprinted from The Arena."
MacLean 158. DLC, MHarF, MPB, MWiW*, NBuG, NN, NjPT, OClWHi.

114 BROWN, THOMAS. An Account of the People Called Shakers: Their Faith, Doctrines, and Practice, Exemplified in the Life, Conversations, and Experience of the Author during the Time He Belonged to the Society. To Which is Affixed a History of Their Rise and Progress to the Present Day . . . . Troy [N.Y.]: Printed by Parker and Bliss, Sold at the Troy Bookstore; By Webster and Skinners, Albany; and by S. Wood, New-York, 1812. 372 pp. 18 cm.
A 1-page extract from a favorable review in *Port Folio* n.s. [3d], 8 (1812), 329–43, is tipped in following title page in some copies. "Errata," p. ix; "Subscribers' Names," pp. [x]–xii; "Appendix," pp. [363]–72, contains Shaker hymns. Thomas Brown attended many Shaker meetings, confessed his sins to the elders, and made several long visits with the Watervliet and New Lebanon Shakers, but because of disagreements over Shaker doctrine apparently he never became a covenant member in residence. Brown's offer to have his manuscript examined by the Shaker Ministry before publication was declined. This account is generally considered to be a seceder's moderate appraisal of Shakerism at that time. It attracted wide attention in the U.S. and abroad, and other contemporary accounts were based upon it. *See also* nos. 1418, 2761, and 2656, 2827. The Shakers disapproved of this *Account* and denied that Brown was a Shaker. Richard McNemar stated that Brown's "pretentions of having been a member of our Society are unfounded," and that his history

was "false and pretentious" *The Other Side of the Question* (no. 946), p. 148. As late as Dec. 6, 1909, Alonzo G. Hollister referred to it as "garbage" and advised William Ward Wight, "If you have Thomas Brown's History of the Shakers—you had better burn it. It contains lies of seceders" a.l.s. Williams College Library, Williamstown, Mass. Thomas Jefferson ordered Thomas Brown's book from a Philadelphia bookseller, and it was part of his library when sold to the Library of Congress in 1815, U.S. Library of Congress, *Catalogue of the Library of Thomas Jefferson* . . . (Washington, D.C., 1952–59. 5 vols.), II, 187, no. 1707. For Brown's intention of publishing a new edition, *see* no. 1418. There was no new edition, perhaps because Thomas Brown was occupied with the publication of the second edition of *The Ethereal Physician, or, Medical Electricity Revived* . . . (Albany: Printed for the Author, by G. J. Loomis & Co., 1817–1823. 2 vols.), Add. 115b. MacLean 9. Sabin 8567. Shaw 24952. CSmH, CtHC, CtHi, CtY, DeWint, DLC, FTaSU, ICRL, KyBgW, KyU, MB, MBC, MHarF, MHi, MPB, MPH, MSaE, MWA, MWiW*, MeB, MiU, N, NBuG, NHi, NN, NNC, NNG, NSyU, NhD, NjMD, NjPT, NjR, O, OC, OCl, OClWHi, PHC, PHi, PPL, RPB, WHi.

115 —— ———— (Reprint). Communal Societies in America, 1st series. New York: AMS Press, Inc., 1972.

116 —— "The Shakers." In Israel D. Rupp's *He pasa ekklesia* (Philadelphia, 1844), no. 2656, pp. 656–62.

A brief history of the sect and its religious tenets.

117 BROWNSON, HANNAH. The Christian Spiritual, or Heavenly Manna. Lowell, Mass.: S. J. Varney, Printer, [n.d.]. Broadside. 23½ × 18 cm.

Signed at end: Caleb B. Page, Lowell, Mass. A poem of 8 stanzas of 8 lines each. The text closely follows her "Spiritual Cake." Apparently, this is a later, enlarged version with a new title. At head of poem: "The foregoing lines were composed by Hannah Brownson, of Canterbury, N.H., a sister of the connec-

tion of believers usually called Shakers, by reason of a report that was in circulation, that they put a kind of seed into their bread or cake that so bewitched people joining them, that they never desired to leave." MBSpnea*.

118 [——] Spiritual Cake. [n.p., n.d.]. Broadside. 19 × 16½ cm.

Poem of 7 stanzas of 8 lines each. Note at end: "The foregoing hymn was composed by Hannah Brownson, a Shakeress, in consequence of a story being circulated that the Shakers put some kind of seed into their cakes" which made those who partook of it wish to remain among them. Facsimile reprint, Sabbathday Lake, Me. [1970?]. NOC*.

119 [——] Table Monitor. Gather up the Fragments that Remain, that Nothing be Lost.— Christ. Shaker Village, [Canterbury, N.H.]: 1830?. Broadside in 2 columns. 25½ × 16 cm.

Poem of 8 stanzas. It is generally attributed to Hannah Brownson. At end of text: "Shaker Home, 1830," with "Visitor's [!] Dining Room" printed in a break in the double rule border. A manuscript note on the copy at Western Reserve Historical Society (Cleveland, O.), states that this was "Republished at Mt. Lebanon, 1903." The *Table Monitor* was an outgrowth of a manuscript set of rudimentary rules for behavior and manners at table, *see* E. D. Andrews, *People Called Shakers* (no. 1767), pp. 182–85. The poem was presented to guests in an effort to prevent wasteful habits. "On being seated at the table, a printed sheet was handed to the guest which at first might be mistaken for a bill of fare, but inspection proved to be an injunction to take upon the plate only what was to be eaten." "From this comes the expression, 'To Shaker your plate,' full of homely and pertinent truth" C. E. Robinson, *A Concise History of the United Society* (no. 1249), p. 117. *See also* no. 1357. Table Monitors are often printed on heavy stock, sometimes glazed, and sometimes with 2 holes punched at the top.

It is not possible to identify MacLean 453 because inadequate information is given. DeWint, MWiW*, NOC, OClWHi.

120 [——] ——— [n.p., n.d.]. Broadside.
17½ X 9½ cm.
At head of title: The following lines were
composed in consequence of the prevailing,
prodigal custom of leaving a variety of food
on the plate, after eating.
OClWHi*.

121 [——] ——— [n.p., n.d.]. Broadside
in 2 columns. 25 X 16 cm.
"Visitors' Eating-Room, Shaker Village" is
printed in a break in the double rule border
at the foot. Reprinted in C. Nordhoff, *The
Communistic Societies of the United States*
(no. 2517), p. 169, and in W. A. Hinds,
American Communities (no. 2242), among
the illustrations preceding the title page.

122 [——] ——— [n.p., n.d.]. Broadside
in 2 columns. 25½ X 18 cm.
Poem with 8 numbered stanzas. The ornamental type border and printing appear to
be a Canterbury, N.H., product.
MWiW*, OClWHi.

123 [——] ——— Canterbury, N.H.:
Shakers' Press, [n.d.]. Broadside in 2 columns.
25 X 20 cm.
At head of title: Shakers'. Shakers' Press,
Canterbury, N.H., is printed in a break in
the ornamental type border at the foot of
the card.
MPB, OClWHi*.

124 —— ——— By Hannah Bronson [sic].
Gather up the Fragments that Nothing be Lost.
—Christ. Shaker Village, Canterbury, N.H.:
[n.d.]. Broadside. 22 X 16½ cm.
A poem of 7 numbered stanzas. This is the
only *Table Monitor* which includes Hannah
Bronson's [i.e., Brownson's] name, although
this poem has been generally attributed to
her. It is printed here with slight differences
in text and punctuation, and the 5th stanza
has been omitted, i.e., Tho' Heaven has
bless'd us/ With plenty of food:/ Bread,
butter, and honey,/ And all that is good;/
We loathe to see mixtures/ Where gentle

folks dine,/ Which scarcely look fit/ For
poultry or swine./
MWiW*, N, OClWHi.

125 [——] Table Monitor of the Shakers at
Mt. Lebanon, N.Y. "Gather up the Fragments
that Remain, that Nothing may be Lost."—
Christ. Mt. Lebanon, [N.Y.]: 1868. Broadside
in 2 columns. 27½ X 21½ cm.
Poem of 8 numbered stanzas. At end of text:
Copied by Elizabeth R. Avery, Mt. Lebanon,
Shaker Village, June, 1868.
MB, MWiW*, MiU–C, OClWHi.

126 [BUCKINGHAM, DAVID AUSTIN]. . . .
Perpetual Calendar. New Lebanon, N.Y.: Printed
by E.[lisha] D. B.[lakeman.], [187–?]. Broadside. 24½ X 15 cm.
This ingenious calendar is followed by instructions for finding the day, week, or month at
any given date, and a 4-line verse. It is printed
within an ornamental type border on yellow
paper. Note in what appears to be Eldress
Catherine Allen's autograph, "By Eld. D. A.
Buckingham." Blakeman, the printer, seceded
from the Shakers, Mt. Lebanon, N.Y., in 1872,
which should date this item 1870 or 1871.
OClWHi*.

127 [BULLARD, HARRIET]. The Outrage at
the Watervliet [N.Y.] Shaker Settlement.
[Albany, N.Y.: 1872]. Broadside. 33½ X 7½ cm.
"From the Albany Argus," signed: *Harriet.*
Letter addressed: Dear Eldress Antoinette,
and dated: Shakers (Albany County) November, 1872. Concerns two disastrous fires within
one week at the Watervliet Shaker community.
OClWHi*.

128 BURNETT, MICAJAH. [Communication].
In U.S. Commissioner of Patents, *Report for
1853, Pt. II, Agriculture.* (33rd Cong., 1st Sess.,
Sen. Exec. Doc. 27), pp. 8, 23–25, 29–30, 40,
51–52, 80, 107, 131–32, 160, 170, 205, 214,
262, 279, 284, 288, 293, 295–96, 299, 314, 320.
Written in response to a circular from the
Patent Commissioner requesting agricultural
information. Cattle, dairying and dairy cows,
horses, mules, sheep, hogs, fertilizer, corn,
wheat, oats, potatoes, hemp, clover, apples,

pears, peaches, plums, cherries, quince, grapes, strawberries, and raspberries at the Shaker community, Pleasant Hill, Ky., are described.

CtY, DLC, KyU, MWA, MWIW*, N, NN, NhD, OC.

129 BUSH, BELLE (i.e., Arabella). The Artist and the Angel. [Shirley, Mass.: 1903?].

No copy has been located. This entry is made up from a notice in the *Banner of Light,* Apr. 11, 1903, p. 5, soliciting orders for the poem, which is described as a leaflet. Miss Bush states that her health is impaired and that her "temporal needs are such that no manna from heaven has yet been able to meet them." She is to be addressed at Shirley, Mass. This plea indicates that Belle Bush had not yet joined the Shakers. In an article about Dr. Arthur Franklin Ewell, mathematics teacher, Mt. Lebanon community, *Peg Board* 4 (June 1936), pp. 77, 78, by Richard Randolph Miller, Sister Emma Neale is quoted as saying that Dr. Ewell came to Mt. Lebanon from Shirley, Mass., with the three Bush sisters, founders of Belvidere Seminary. Only two names are given: Belle Bush and Harriet, wife of Dr. Ewell. All were spiritualists. Belle Bush's death at Mt. Lebanon North Family, July 5, 1914, is recorded in a manuscript North Family "Journal, 1910–1914," Emma B. King Library (Old Chatham, N.Y.). The name is given as Arabella Bush in the extensive file of Shaker membership at Western Reserve Historical Society.

130 —— The Blessed Life. [n.p., n.d.]. Broadside. 23½ × 9 cm. (Mt. Lebanon Love Leaflet, No. 5.)

A poem of 5 stanzas of varying lengths. The Library of Congress treats the name Belle Bush as a pseudonym; here it is considered

to be a shortened form of the author's name, Arabella Bush.

NOC*.

131 —— . . . The Clock of Gold. By Belle Bush. Respectfully Dedicated to Her Majesty Queen Victoria. [New York: Press of Frank L. Hamilton, 1884?]. 12 pp. 25½ cm.

At head of title: In Memory of H.R.H. Leopold, Duke of Albany. Leopold George Duncan Albert, Duke of Albany, the fourth and youngest son of Queen Victoria, died March 28, 1884. The date of publication is therefore assumed to be 1884 or later.

NBuG*.

132 —— October. Nature's mood betraying;/ Then these wasted forms/ Rent by force of winds or storms/ Fall, no use portraying. [n.p., n.d.]. [2] pp. 13½ × 5½ cm.

Signed: *Belle Bush, Shirley, Mass.* [Later of Mt. Lebanon]. Poem of 11 stanzas, 6 lines each. This title is taken from the National Union Catalog, Library of Congress.

OClWHi*.

133 —— To a Dear Sister on Her Birthday [poem]. Shirley, Mass.: January 31, 1905. Cover title. [2] pp. 9 × 23 cm.

NOC*, NSyU.

134 —— Voices of the Morning. By Belle Bush . . . Philadelphia: J. B. Lippincott & Co., 1865. 270 pp. 16½ cm.

Collection of poems about the Civil War, previously printed in 23 newspapers and magazines, including *Godey's, Graham's, Saturday Evening Post,* etc.

DLC*, NBuG, NN, OU, PPL, PPULC.

135 —— —— 2d ed. Boston: Wallace Spooner, [c1904]. 270 pp.

CtY, NN, RPB*.

C

136 Call to Zion. City of Peace. True Heirs of Heaven. [n.p., n.d.]. Broadside in 2 columns. 13½ × 18 cm.

Three hyms without music, tipped in following p. 194 of *A Collection of Millennial Hymns* (no. **467**) in the Williams College copy (Williamstown, Mass.). Another Williams College copy printed on pink paper has been pasted inside a Shaker box as a lining paper. Last line reads: And life eternal. MWiW*, OClWHi.

137 CALVER, AMELIA J. Every-day Biography. Containing a Collection of Brief Biographies Arranged for Every Day in the Year, as a Book of Reference for the Teacher, Student, Chautauquan and Home Circles. New York: Fowler & Wells Co., 1889. 378 [6] pp. 19½ cm.
  Advertisements [6] pp. at end.
  MacLean 10. CtY, DLC, MWiW*, NN, NNUT, NOC, NSyU, OClWHi, OHi, PP, PPLaS, PPULC, ViU.

138 —— ——— ... [Publisher's advertising circular with excerpts from reviews]. New York: Fowler & Wells Co., [1889]. [2] pp. 24 cm.
  Advertised as a book of reference for the teacher, student, Chautauquan and home circles, with an analytical and classified index for ready use.
  OClWHi*.

139 CARR, BURTON W. Gleanings of Religion, Or a Compilation Containing the Natural History of Man—A True Account of the Different Sects in the Religious World ... Lexington, Ky.: Printed by Joseph G. Norwood, 1829. 300 pp.
  "Shakers, or Shaking Quakers," pp. 212-70, is a long account reprinted from J. Woods, Shakerism Unmasked, no. 1463. Carr states that his personal knowledge of the Shakers is limited to Union Village, O., in 1828.
  Shaw 38074. CSmH, DLC, KyBgW, KyLo, KyLxT, KyU, NN, TNJ-R.

140 [CARR, MARY FRANCES]. Life among the Shakers. New York: Wemple & Company [Printers?], [188-?]. Cover title. 35 pp. illus. 13 cm.
  Colored illustrated covers. Child with umbrella, front cover, recto. "Sunday at Mount Lebanon. Strangers Coming to the Shaker Meeting," verso, back cover, with space for an agent's name to be added. Contents include "The Following Account of a Visit to the Shaker Settlement is from Mary F. Carr ...", pp. 2-5, reprinted from The Shaker 1

(January 1871), 6, See also no. 143; general material on the Shakers, pp. 5-9; history of "Mother Seigel's Curative Syrup" now manufactured by the Shakers of Mt. Lebanon, and known as Shaker Extract of Roots, or Curative Syrup, pp. 9-26; testimonial letters for Shaker Extract, many addressed to A. J. White. The latest is dated Oct. 27, 1880. "The Oldest and the Youngest Shakers" and "The Shaker School Children," black-and-white cuts, pp. 3, 7. A. J. White's address, 54 Warren Street, N.Y., dates this pamphlet 1885 or later.
  MPH, MWiW*, N, NHi, NSyU, OClWHi, OHi.

141 —— ——— [New York?: 188-?]. Cover title. 35 pp. illus. 13 cm.
  Colored illustrated covers differ from no. 140, but the contents are identical. Front cover, recto, shows a woman (Mother Seigel?) seated with a book in her lap. A blank space below, headed "Presented by," provides for an agent's name and address to be added.
  MHarF, NSyU*.

142 —— ——— [New York?: 188-?]. Caption title. 8 pp. illus. 27½ X 20 cm.
  Same text, black-and-white cuts, and testimonials (usually addressed to Mr. A. J. White) as no. 140. Portrait of Mother Seigel (?), p. [1]. A list of druggists who handle Shaker Extract of Roots, or Curative Syrup, p. 8.
  MWA, OClWHi*.

143 [——] The Peaceful Life of the Shakers. [n.p., 188-?]. Caption title. 16 [4] pp. illus. 14½ cm.
  Contents: Letter from Mary Francis [!] Carr of Mount Holly City, N.J., pp. 1-4, with the same text as her Life Among the Shakers, no. 140; "Few Know about the Shakers of Mt. Lebanon," pp. 5-6; advertisements for Shaker medicines follow. See also no. 26.
  MHarF, MPH*, MWA, N, NBuG (8 pp.), NSyU, OClWHi.

144 [——] Shakers; A Correspondence between Mary F. C[arr] of Mount Holly City, and a Shaker Sister Sarah L[ucas], of Union

Village. Ed. by R. W. Pelham, Union Village, Ohio. [Union Village, O.?:] 1868. Cover title. 24 pp. 16½ cm.

> Contains: "To the Reader," p. [2], and liberal extracts from Mary Carr's "Visit to the Shaker Settlement," with three of her letters and two replies from Sarah Lucas. Mary's final letter acknowledges satisfaction with the answers to her questions about Shaker beliefs and practices. "Visit to the Shaker Settlement," reprinted in *The Shaker* 1 (January 1871), 6, is signed: *Mary Frances Carr;* Sarah's first reply reprinted, *The Shaker,* 2 (Oct. 1872), 78-79. The last line of page 16 contains a misprint and an omission of words.
>
> CtY, DLC, MB, MH, MHarF, MPB, MPH, MWA, MWiW*, NOC, NjPT, OClWHi, OHi, OU.

145 —— —— Cincinnati, O.: P. T. Schultz, Printer, 1869. Cover title. 23 [1] pp. illus. 15 cm.

> "Family Dwelling," electroplate illustration signed: *Ferguson, Albany,* shows the Mt. Lebanon Church Family dwelling and Ministry shop. Some copies lack this illus-

tration and have only a blank page at end. MacLean 405, 406? MPB, MPH, MSE, MWA, MWiW*, N, NHi, NBuG, NN, NOC, NSyU, NjMD, NjPT, O, OC, OClWHi, ODa, OHi, OOxM, PPL, WHi.

146 —— —— Springfield, Mass.: Samuel Bowles & Company, Printers, 1870. Cover title. 23 pp. 15 cm.

> MacLean 407. DLC, ICN, InU, KyBgW, MBC, MHarF, MWiW*, N, NOC, NjP.

147 CARTER, RHODA T. Gathered Harvest, 1903. Concord, N.H.: Rumford Press, 1903. 80 pp. port. 18½ cm.

> "Short Sketch of My Shaker Experience," pp. 5-8.
>
> DLC, MHarF*, NIC, NN.

148 —— The Journey of Life. Concord, N.H.: Rumford Printing Co., 1905. 96 pp. front. (port.). 19 cm.

> Autobiography and poems. Reminiscences of her life with the Shakers at Enfield, N.H., where the author lived from the age of 9 to 45 years.
>
> DLC, MWA, MWiW*, NN, OClWHi.

CATALOGS, BROADSIDES, ADVERTISING FLYERS, ETC.

Unquestionably, more of these ephemeral Shaker publications existed than are recorded here, although those listed below are the result of a fairly widespread search in an effort to show a representation of the full range of Shaker industries. Representation of the industries pursued in some communities is inadequate. North Union, Ohio, industries are completely unrepresented and those of some other communities are represented by only one product. The varied industries of the western Shaker communities are described in F. G. Ham's unpublished Ph.D. dissertation, "Shakerism in the Old West" (U. of Ky., 1962), where it is stated (p. 240) that "Throughout the 1850's Pleasant Hill's seed pedlars brought home $4500 annually" and that "North Union fenced off its seed gardens in 1853 when they entered 'the business on a large scale'." Furthermore, "It was only a step from seed gardening . . . to raising medicinal herbs," and "Pleasant Hill, South and North Union all had physic gardens and processed herbs for sale." In addition to the more usual Shaker industries, Pleasant Hill was famous for the high quality of its livestock, whose sales brought as much as $6000 annually before the Civil War. The gristmills and sawmills of the Mill Family at North Union "were great sources of income. The saw-mill turned out lumber, and vessels of various kinds that met with a ready and profitable sale" (J. P. MacLean, "Rise, Progress, and Extinction of the Society at Cleveland, Ohio," in his *Shakers of Ohio* [no. 2410], p. 135). It would be surprising if printed catalogs, broadsides, price lists, etc. were not issued in connection with any of these successful industries. Although devoted primarily to the industries of Mt. Lebanon, N.Y., E. D. Andrews, *Community Industries of the Shakers* (no. 1759) includes relevant information about the industries of the other eastern communities. Andrews gives a full description and discussion of Shaker industries, which is profusely illustrated and extensively documented with manuscript sources, but few printed catalogs, etc., are cited. The discovery of some items below was fortuitous. The only copy of the *Rural Register and Almanac* for 1876 (no. **261**) was not encountered until the final manuscript was in preparation. Some of the seed lists were discovered by rummaging through uncataloged materials in libraries; others were found hanging on museum walls. A small degree of clairvoyance would have benefited the search for these materials in library card catalogs, where they are to be found entered under the names of Shaker trustees, Shaker communities, cover titles, arbitrarily shortened titles, etc. (Entries below are taken from the title pages, if present.) It is hoped that the list below will create an awareness of the lacks in this area, that it will in turn provoke further searches, and that eventually a complete compilation of the catalogs, etc. of the many Shaker industries may be achieved through some cooperative enterprise. Advertisements in periodicals and newspapers, labels (printed on packages or mounted on bottles), as well as packaging materials, letterheads, business cards, invoices (unless they contain a printed list of seeds, etc.), colored lithographed display posters, and the large labels mounted on Shaker seed boxes have been omitted as unsuitable for inclusion in this bibliography. The items below are arranged by Shaker community and subject.

ALFRED, ME. Fancy Goods

149 Catalog of Fancy Goods made at Shaker Village, Alfred, York County, Maine. Fannie C. Casey, Trustee and General Manager. [n.p.], 1908. 10 pp. illus. 13½ × 19½ cm.
"Thirty-two distinct types of goods made from woven poplar wood are illustrated ... Other handicrafts listed are oval carriers, hand brushes, the famous Shaker sweaters, knee warmers, leggings, and bed socks," etc. T. E. Johnson, "Random Notes," Maine Library Association *Bulletin*, 22 (February 1961), 20. MHarF, MPH*, MeHi, MiU–C, NBuG.

150 ——— (Reprint). Sabbathday Lake, Me.: The United Society, 1971. (Hands to Work Series, No. 1.)

ALFRED, ME. Medicinal Herbs

151 Catalogue of Medical Plants, Prepared in the United Society, Alfred, Maine. [n.p., n.d.]. Broadside in 2 columns. 32 × 17 cm.
A list of 82 medicinal herbs with "Price per Paper." The highest price is 33¢ for Rose flowers; "Belladona" and "Popy flowers" are 25¢. Among the lowest priced are "Raspberry leaves" and "Roman wormwood" at 8¢, with "Sumach berries" at 5¢. MiU–C, OClWHi*.

ALFRED, ME. Seeds

152 Catalogue of Garden Seeds, Raised by the

United Society, at Alfred, Maine. Sold by Nathan Freeman ... 184 . Among which are the following: [n.p., 184–?]. Broadside in 2 columns.
This entry is made from a reprinted broadside, Sister R. Mildred Barker, "History of the 'Holy Land' —Alfred, Maine," Pt. II, *Shaker Quarterly*, 3 (Winter 1963), p. [117]. This is a list of 47 varieties of seeds, mostly vegetable, in "Papers at 6¢." The partial date "184 " in the title has been altered in ink to "1850." Information about other Alfred industries is found on pp. 112–18, in the article cited above.

153 Garden Seeds, Raised at Alfred, Me. & sold by John Wooley.... [n.p., 182–?]. Broadside in 2 columns. 14 × 17½ cm.
At head of title: Alfred, Maine, 182 . The last digit has been supplied in ink for "1821." A list of 23 varieties of seeds, mostly vegetable, with the prices in ink. This is a completed order for $11.78.
OClWHi*, OHi.

CANTERBURY, N.H. Clothing (including "Dorothy" Cloaks)

154 Catalogue. Canterbury Shakers, Manufacturers of "Dorothy Cloaks," All-wool Sweaters and Fancy Goods. East Canterbury, N.H.: [n.d.]. Cover title. [8] pp. illus. 15½ cm.
Priced catalog with illustrations of the front and back views of the cloak. Orders are to be addressed to Hart & Shepard, East Canterbury, N.H. Hamamelis (extract of witch hazel) price

list, p. [8], directs patrons to address orders to Arthur Bruce, East Canterbury, N.H. The Shaker floor-length, hooded cloaks made at Canterbury are generally thought to have been named the "Dorothy" cloak as a special tribute to the beloved and widely respected Eldress Dorothy Durgin.
NOC*, OClWHi.

155 Canterbury Shakers, Manufacturers of "Dorothy" Cloaks, Men's All-wool Sweaters, Fancy Goods and Medicines. East Canterbury, N.H.: [n.d.]. Cover title. [8] pp. illus. 17½ cm.
Priced catalog showing the side and back views of the cloak. Medicines, p. [8], directs patrons to address orders to Arthur Bruce, East Canterbury, N.H. For other items, orders are to be sent to Hart & Shepard, East Canterbury, N.H. The copy at the Shaker Museum Library, Old Chatham, N.Y., has a ms. note on the cover, "2nd edition."
NOC*, OClWHi.

156 ——— 16 cm.
Contains slight differences in the items listed and in their arrangement. The copy at the Shaker Museum Library, Old Chatham, N.Y., has a ms. note on cover, "3rd edition."
NOC*, OClWHi.

157 Catalogue of Goods Manufactured by the Canterbury Shakers. [East Canterbury, N.H.: n.d.]. [6] pp. (sheet folded). illus. 14½ cm.
Fancy goods, infants' wear, poplar baskets, "Dorothy" cloaks, with photographs showing front and back views.
NOC, NhHi*.

158 Catalogue of Goods Manufactured by the Shakers, East Canterbury, N.H.:[n.d.]. 6 pp. (sheet folded). illus. 11½ cm.
Shaker Museum Library, Old Chatham, N.Y. copy has ms. note on cover, "1st edition."
NOC*.

159 [The "Dorothy" Cloak]. [East Canterbury, N.H.: n.d.]. [4] pp. illus. 20½ cm.
Title is taken from p. [2]. Order blank with instructions for taking proper measurements, p. [3]. Includes photographs showing front, back, and 2 side views of the cloak, and

the registered trademark for "The Dorothy."
OClWHi*.

160 [———] [3] pp. 15 cm.
The cloak is not illustrated; only the trademark is reproduced on the cover. p. [3], verso blank.
OClWHi*.

161 ... The "Dorothy" Shaker Cloak Supplies a Long-felt Want for Auto, Carriage, Street or Ocean Travel, or, in Pastel Shades for Evening Wear ... [n.p., n.d.]. Cover title. [4] pp. illus. 14½ cm.
Order blank showing front, side, and back views of the cloak.
OClWHi*.

162 General Rule for Shaping Knit Drawers, as Made for Sale in the Church at Canterbury ... [East Canterbury, N.H.: n.d.]. Broadside. 18 × 15 cm.
Private collection.

163 Hart & Shepard, Manufacturers of Athletic and Fancy Goods. Holiday Goods a Specialty. East Canterbury, N.H.: [n.d.]. Cover title. [8] pp. 17½ cm.
Medicines, and Hamamelis, p. [6].
NOC*.

164 Retail Price of All-Wool Sweaters Manufactured by the Canterbury Shakers. [East Canterbury, N.H.: 1920?]. [4] pp. 21 cm.
The sweaters are available in "navy blue, Dartmouth green, gray, white, and maroon." Address the "Canterbury Shakers, East Canterbury, N.H." The copy in the Library, Shaker Museum, Old Chatham, N.Y., has ms. note on the front cover, "1920."
NhHi, NOC*.

165 Retail Price of Sweaters and Coat Sweaters, January 1910. East Canterbury, N.H.: Canterbury Shakers, 1910. [4] pp. 15½ cm.
Includes wholesale prices of sweaters and coat sweaters.
NOC, OClWHi*.

166 A Rule for Knitting Common Size Feetings. [Canterbury, N.H.: n.d.]. Broadside. 15 × 14 cm.
Private collection.

CANTERBURY, N.H. Medicinal Herbs, Etc.

167 Catalogue of Medicinal Plants and Vegetable Medicines. Prepared in the United Society, Canterbury, N.H. ... Orders to be Directed to T. Corbett, Shaker Village, Merrimack Co., N.H. Printed at Shaker Village: 1835. Cover title. 16 pp. 15½ cm.

> A list of common and botanical names (according to Eaton), and the price per lb., pp. 1-8. Advertisements and testimonials of Shaker medicines, pp. 9-16.
> MHarF, NOC*.

168 ———— ... Prepared in the United Society of "Shakers," Merrimack County, N.H. [Printed at Canterbury, N.H.: n.d.]. Broadside. 46 X 30½ cm.

> Lists over 200 herbs, barks, etc., under the common and botanical names. Prices are not included, but blank spaces allow for the prices to be added in ink. At end: Orders to be Directed to [blank space to be filled in]. Reprinted in *Historical New Hampshire,* 8 (March 1952), 18.
> NhHi*.

169 Catalogue of Medicinal Plants and Vegetable Medicines, to which is Annexed their most Prominent Medical Properties. Prepared in the United Society, Canterbury, N.H. ... Orders to be Directed to Thomas Corbett, Shaker Village, Merrimack Co., N.H. Printed at Canterbury, N.H.: 1847. Cover title. 8 pp. illus. 17½ cm.

> Common names and prices per lb. are printed in single columns, pp. 2-8. Cut of a beehive appears on the front cover, recto; "Agents in Boston" and an advertisement for "Reimproved Rocking Trusses," with illustration, back cover, verso.
> NOC*.

170 ———— Orders to be Directed to David Parker, Shaker Village, Merrimack Co., N.H. Printed at Canterbury, N.H.: 1848. Cover title. 8 pp. 17 cm.

> Common and botanical names, and price per lb. are printed in 2 columns. "The botanical names are from Eaton's Manual of Botany."
> NhD, NOC, OClWHi*.

171 ———— Orders to be directed to Thomas Corbett, Shaker Village, Merrimack, N.H. Printed at Canterbury, N.H.: 1848. Cover title, 8, 8 pp. 17 cm.

> Pages 1-8 (first sequence) are printed on blue paper; text is identical with no. 170. Pages 1-8 (second sequence) consist of advertisements for Compound Concentrated Syrup of Sarsaparilla, etc., with testimonials. A copy at the Shaker Museum Library, Old Chatham, N.Y., has "Orders to be Directed to David Parker."
> NOC*.

172 ———— Orders to be Directed to James Kaime, Shaker Village, Merrimack Co., N.H. Printed at Canterbury, N.H.: 1854. Cover title, 8 pp. 17 cm.

> The text is unchanged from no. 170, but it is reset, and there are some changes in prices, advertisements, etc.
> NOC, OClWHi*.

CANTERBURY, N.H. Medicines

173 Corbett's Shaker Compound Syrup of Sarsaparilla. Shaker Village, Mer. Co., N.H.: [n.d.]. Caption title. [2] pp. illus. 28 cm.

> At head of title, "Shaker Village, Mer. Co., N.H.," a cut showing part of the community and buildings. The attributes of this product are described as follows: "Medicine good for chronic inflammation of the digestive organs, dyspepsia, jaundice, weakness and sourness of the Stomach, Rheumatism, Salt Rheum, Secondary Syphilis, functional disorders of the liver, chronic eruption of the skin; and all scrofulous diseases." Maynard & Noyes, Boston, Mass., agents for U.S. and Canada. A chart of the metric system, p. [2].
> DLC, NOC, OClWHi*.

174 ———— [Shaker Village, Merrimack Co., N.H.: 1850]. Caption title. [3] pp. 26 cm.

> Signed: *With Respect, David Parker, Trustee in Behalf of the Society: Thomas Corbett, Physician.* This edition is directed to the medical profession. "We are desirous that it be more generally introduced to the 'Medical Faculty' and with pleasure take this method to bring it to their notice, assuring them that a strict adherence to the Formula will be

observed . . ." Those who wish to carry it on their circuits, it will be furnished in gallon jugs at $5.00, "with the written signature of Thomas Corbett" on each jug. Brown's Fluid Extract of Valerian is similarly described. Both medicines are supported by the testimonials of many physicians. OClWHi*.

175 Corbett's Shakers' Compound of Wild Cherry Pectoral Syrup. Prepared by the Canterbury Shakers, Shaker Village, N.H. [Trademark] Registered Feb. 9, 1886. No. 4722. (U.S. Pat. Off., Ann. *Report of the Comm.*, 1886, p. 407). N*, OCl.

176 Corbett's Shaker Vegetable Family Pills . . . [n.p., n.d.]. Broadside. 24 × 9 cm.
    The testimonials include those for Corbett's Shaker Compound Wild Cherry Pectoral Syrup, with that for Corbett's Shaker Dyspepsia Cure printed at the end. NOC*.

177 Esteemed Friends [Letter], Dr. Corbett's Compound Concentrated Syrup of Sarsaparilla is an Old and Well Tried . . . [n.p., n.d.]. Broadside. 9 × 10 cm.
    "This medicine is prepared by the Society of Shakers in Shaker Village, Mer. Co., N.H." Signed: *Benj. H. Smith, Trustee.* OClWHi*.

178 Jarabe Compuesto y Concentrada de Zarzaparrilla de Corbett de la Compañía de Shakers. Manufacturado en el Pueblo de Shaker, Departamento de Merrimack, New Hampshire. Con una onza puro hidriodato de potazo [i.e., iodide of potassium] á doce Botellas. [n.p., n.d.]. Caption title. 11 pp. illus. 20½ cm.
    Spanish translation of advertisements and testimonials from the *Shakers' Manual* (no. 181) for Corbett's Shaker Sarsaparilla, Brown's Fluid Extract of Valerian, and other medicines. NOC*.

179 Shaker Medicines, Shaker Knit Goods and Religious Publications: Also a Variety of Fancy Articles. East Canterbury, N.H.: [1893?]. Cover title, [8] pp. illus. 14½ cm.

"Shaker Village, East Canterbury, N.H.," a cut showing part of the community and buildings. Orders for fancy goods, beeswax, turkey feather fans, pincushions, etc., to be sent to Hart & Shepard; orders for medicines to be sent to Arthur Bruce; those for publications to be sent to H. C. Blinn. MacLean 182. DLC, MWiW*, NOC, OClWHi.

180 Shaker Sarsaparilla Lozenges. Made by the Canterbury Society of Shakers, Shaker Village, N.H. [Trademark] Registered Feb. 9, 1886. No. 4721.
    N*, OCl.

181 The Shakers' Manual. Shaker Village, Merrimack Co.: [Electro-stereotyped at the Boston Stereotype Foundry], 1851. Caption title, 11[1] pp. illus. 24 cm.
    Signed: *In behalf of the Society, David Parker, Trustee.* Advertising circular with testimonials for Corbett's Shaker Compound Concentrated Syrup of Sarsaparilla, Brown's Shaker Fluid Extract of English Valerian. Includes reproductions of the medals awarded to both medicines in 1850 by the Massachusetts Charitable Mechanic Association, Boston, Mass. MacLean 180. DLC, MiU-C, NBuG, NN, NOC, OClWHi*.

182 ——— Shaker Village, Merrimack Co., N.H.: [Electro-stereotyped at the Boston Stereotype Foundry], 1852. Caption title, 23 [1] pp. illus. 24 cm.
    MHarF, MPB, MWiW (inc.), MiU-C, OClWHi*.

183 The Shakers' Manual. Corbett's Shaker Syrup of Sarsaparilla . . . . [n.p., n.d.]. Cover title. 16 pp. 22½ cm.
    Signed: *In behalf of the Society, Nicholas A. Briggs, Joseph Woods, Trustees.* "Shaker Village, Merrimack County, New Hampshire, where [it] is manufactured,'. illustration, on front cover. General information about the Shakers, pp. 3, 5, 7, "Useful Recipes," pp. 9, 11. Medal award, 1850, for the sarsaparilla is reproduced p. 4, as is the new medal awarded November 1878 at the 47th exhibition of the American Institute, New York. Otherwise the contents are similar to earlier *Manuals*.

MacLean 181? (J. S. Kaime and B. H. Smith, Trustees). DLC, MWiW*, NOC.

184 ——— Concord, N.H.: E.D. Green & Co., 1879. Cover title. 16 pp. illus. 22½ cm.
This is a different printing with a variation in the advertisements; the information about the Shakers is shorter than the foregoing undated *Manual*, and the number of testimonials has been increased.
NOC*.

185 Superfine Flour of Slippery Elm (ulmus fulva). Prepared in the United Society, called "Shakers," at Canterbury, Merrimack Co., N.H. [n.p., n.d.]. Broadside. 18½ X 12½ cm.
MBCo*.

186 Superfine Flour of Slippery or Red Elm (ulmus fulva). This Flour when taken Internally, is Applicable to a [word missing] Important Uses .... Prepared at the United Society, Canterbury, N.H. [n.p., n.d.]. Broadside. 19½ X 19½ cm.
OClWHi* (mutilated copy).

CANTERBURY, N.H. Seeds

187 Garden Seeds. Raised at Canterbury, New Hampshire 181[0] and Sold by [Francis Winkley]. [n.p., 181-?]. Broadside in 2 columns. 19½ X 15½ cm.
The zero in the date 1810 and the name Francis Winkley have been supplied in ink. This is a complete order totaling $20.87, with the amounts and prices in ink, and a ms. note on the verso, "F. Winkley's Bill 1810 Seeds." It is a combination order form and list of 22 varieties of seeds, mostly vegetable. The first column lists seeds by the ounce, the second by papers.
MH-BA*.

CANTERBURY, N.H. Trusses

188 Re-improved Rocking Trusses. Single, Double, and Umbilical Trusses: Adapted to all Ages and Sexes; For the Relief and Permanent Cure of Hernia, or Rupture; Invented, Manufactured, Applied and Sold in the United Society of Shakers, in Canterbury, N.H. [n.p.,

n.d.]. Caption title, 11[1] pp. illus. 17½ cm.
Testimonials are dated 1838 and 1839, and it is stated that the Society has manufactured trusses "for more than 30 years." Instructions and illustrations for use are included. Orders to be addressed to "Thomas Corbett, Shaker Village, N.H."
NhHi, NOC*.

CANTERBURY, N.H. Washing Machines

189 Improved Shaker Washing Machine; Designed Particularly for Hospitals, Hotels, Laundries, &c. Patented January 26, 1858, by David Parker, Shaker Village, N.H. Manufactured and for Sale by the United Society of Shakers, at Shaker Village, N.H. Also, Improved Hydro-extractor, Recipes for Making Soap, &c. Concord [N.H.]: Steam Printing Works of McFarland & Jenks, 1859. 24 pp. illus. 23 cm.
Cover title: Improved Washing Machine ... Introductory information on p. 6, signed: *David Parker, Robert Shepard, Trustees.* "Making Soap," by Dr. Buttolph, pp. [22]-23. Includes directions for installing and using the machine. The patent, no. 19181, was granted January 26, 1858, to "Nicholas Bennet of New Lebanon, assignor to David Parker, of Shaker Village, New Hampshire" no. 1138. An engraved plate and "Explanation of the Plate" precedes the title page.
MacLean 160. DLC, MWiW*, NBuG, OClWHi.

190 ——— Patented May 23, 1859, in Great Britain, Ireland, etc. Manufactured and for Sale by the United Society of Shakers, at Shaker Village, New Hampshire. Also, An Improved Hydro-extractor or Wringer, and a Newly Constructed Mangle, Operated by a Screw. Concord, N.H.: McFarland & Jenks, 1862. 31 pp.
MacLean 161. NN, NOC*, OClWHi.

191 ——— Manufactured and for Sale by the United Society of Shakers, at Shaker Village, N.H. Also, a Newly Constructed Mangle, Operated by a Screw. [Concord, N.H.: McFarland & Jenks, 1870?]. 8, [3] pp. 22½ cm.
Patent notice on verso, title page. Introductory information on p. 4, signed: *J. S. Kaime, Trustee, Successor to David Parker.* A list of 25 institutions using the machine, p. [1], at end.

MacLean 163. MWiW*, OClWHi.

192 ——— Concord, N.H.: Charles C. Pearson & Company, Printers, 1876. Cover title, 22 [1] pp. illus. 22½ cm.

The text is the same as no. 191, with 2 illustrations and testimonials added. Reset with type of different size and face. Introductory information on p. 6, signed: *N. A. Briggs, B. H. Smith, Trustees.*
MWiW*, OClWHi.

193 ——— Concord, N.H.: Charles C. Pearson & Company, Printers, 1877. 28 [1] pp. illus. 22½ cm.

A notice of the Philadelphia Centennial award, 1876, tipped in following title page, also carries the statement, "Patented July 23, 1877," i.e., Patent No. 193802 granted to "Nicholas Briggs and Elijah Knowles, Shaker Village, N.H., assignors to said Briggs." *See* no. 1141. Changes in the text include the announcement, "We now build four sizes: —eight tubs, six tubs, four tubs, and three tubs" p. [2]. "Shaker Laundry Soap .... We have at last, at considerable expense, obtained a most invaluable Soap Formula," p. [25]. Cuts of the Centennial medal, back cover, verso.
MacLean 162. MPB, MSaE, MWiW*, NBuG, NN, NOC, OClWHi.

ENFIELD, CONN. Medicinal Herbs

194 Catalogue of Medicinal Plants, Barks, Roots, Seeds and Flowers, with their Therapeutic Qualities and Botanical Names. Also, Pure Vegetable Extracts, and Shaker Garden Seeds, Raised, Prepared and Put Up in the Most Careful Manner, by the United Society of Shakers, Enfield, Conn. All Orders Addressed to Jefferson White, Thompsonville, Conn., Wholesale Agent for the Shaker Society, will meet Prompt Attention. First Established in 1802, being the Oldest Seed Establishment in the United States. Hartford [Conn.]: Elihu Geer, Stationer and Steam Printer, 1854. Cover title. 24 pp. 19 cm.

This catalog bears a strong resemblance to the Mt. Lebanon *Catalogue*, no. 286. "To our Patrons," front cover, verso, has been adapted, but several sentences are identical as are other parts of the text. The lists of medicinal herbs, extracts, etc., vary. "A Catalogue of Garden Seeds," pp. 18–20. "Catalogue of Flower Seeds," back cover, recto; back cover, verso, is blank. Most of the text of "Supplementary," pp. 20–23, is identical.
MWiW*, WHi.

195 Fresh Herbs, Raised, Gathered, and Put Up by the United Society ... Shakers ... Enfield, Conn. Address Jefferson White (Seedsman and Herb Agent) Thompsonville, P.O., Conn. (on or before July annually.) Pressed and Neatly Put Up in Packages, from 1 oz. to 1 lb. each as Ordered. [n.p., 185–?]. Broadside in 3 columns. 49 × 39 cm.

About 300 items are listed under the common names and the botanical equivalents with prices and properties, with 18 extracts at the end. The copy described here is a filled-in order made out to Dr. N. J. Middleton, Norwich, Conn., dated in ink, March 25, 1857.
OClWHi*, MPH (55½ × 43 cm.).

ENFIELD, CONN. Seeds

196 Catalogue of Flower Seeds, Cultivated by the United Society—Shakers—Enfield, Conn. Address Jefferson White, Thompsonville P.O., Conn. Hartford, Conn.: Elihu Geer, [n.d.]. Broadside in 2 columns. 29 × 23 cm.

A list of 96 varieties of flower seeds giving the common names and the scientific equivalents, with prices not indicated. "We spare no expense in procuring every desirable variety ... that can be obtained ... and as all have been raised under our inspection, we do not hesitate in warranting them fresh and genuine."
MPB, OClWHi*.

197 Garden Seeds, Fresh and Genuine, Raised by the United Society (Shakers), Enfield, Conn. Jefferson White, Thompsonville P.O., Conn. Seedsman and Agent. For Sale [blank space for name to be supplied]. [Hartford, Conn.: Elihu Geer, n.d.]. Broadside in 2 columns. 34½ × 22½ cm.

List of 109 varieties of vegetable seeds followed by 5 herb seeds, all without prices.

Blank columns allow spaces for the amounts and prices to be filled in.
OClWHi*.

198 ———— Raised by the United Society, — Shakers, Enfield, Conn. Address Nathan Damon, Thompsonville, Conn., Seedsman and Agent. For Sale [blank for name to be supplied]. [Hartford: Elihu Geer, n.d.]. Broadside in 2 columns. 33 × 21½ cm.

A list of 130 varieties of vegetable seeds, followed by 9 herb seeds, all without prices. Blank columns allow for the amounts and prices to be filled in. At the end: a 3½-line note about other Shaker products includes "Herbs used for Medicinal Purposes put up in pressed packages of one-eighth of a pound to one pound each." OClWHi*.

199 ———— Raised by the United Society — Shakers—Enfield, Conn. Address Jefferson White, Thompsonville P.O., Connecticut (on or before July annually), Seedsman and Agent. For Sale [blank space for name to be supplied]. Hartford: Elihu Geer, [n.d.]. Broadside in 3 columns. 49 × 31½ cm.

List of 210 varieties of vegetable seeds, followed by 15 herb seeds, and 10 grass seeds— available in "papers," without indication of prices. At end: "N.B. Some seeds such as cannot be successfully raised in this climate, are procured from the best sources. Herbs for Medicinal Purposes, put up in pressed packages from one ounce to one pound each." OClWHi*.

200 ———— For Sale by David Young, Seedsman, Americus, Geo.[rgia]. [Hartford, Conn.: Elihu Geer, n.d.]. Broadside in 3 columns. 49 × 31½ cm.

A few items differ from those in the foregoing list. Chinese Sugar Cane has been added to "Grass Seeds," which are sold "By the Pound or Bushel." The ornamental type borders are identical. MPB, OClWHi*.

201 ———— [same title as no. 199] —Enfield, Conn. Address Nathan Damon, Thompsonville, Ct., on or before July annually. Seedsman and Agent. For Sale by [blank for name to be supplied]. [Hartford, Conn.: Elihu Geer, n.d.]. Broadside in 3 columns. 41½ × 28½ cm.

A list of 222 varieties of vegetable seeds, followed by 17 herb seeds and 11 grass seeds. This list is set in smaller type than the two foregoing lists and printed within a different ornamental type border. OClWHi*.

202 ———— For Sale by Clark, George & Co., Seedsmen and Druggists, Mobile, Alabama. [Hartford, Conn.: Elihu Geer, n.d.]. Broadside in 3 columns. 41½ × 28½ cm.

This list is identical with the foregoing list, but is printed within a different ornamental type border. OClWHi*.

203 Garden Seeds, Raised at Enfield, (Conn.) For Sale by [blank space for name to be supplied]. [n.p., n.d.]. Broadside. 45½ × 16½ cm.

A list of 46 varieties of seeds, mostly vegetable, available in "papers," with prices (all but 2 items are 6¢) and blank columns for the amounts to be added. This appears to be a much earlier seed list than others recorded above. OClWHi*.

The Gardener's Manual, Published for Earl Jepherson, Enfield, Conn. (Albany, N.Y., 1835) and "By Earl Jepherson" (Hartford, 185–?). *See* Crosman, Charles F., *The Gardener's Manual*, nos. 483 and 487.

ENFIELD, N.H. Medicinal Herbs

204 Catalogue of Medicinal Plants and Vegetable Medicines to which is Annexed their most Prominent Medical Properties. Prepared in the United Society, at Enfield, N.H. Orders to be Directed to Hiram C. Baker, Shaker Village, Enfield, N.H. Concord, N.H.: From L. L. Mower's Printing Engine, [186–?]. Cover title, 7 pp. 19 cm. DeWint*.

ENFIELD, N.H. Medicines

205 Brown's Shaker Pure Extract of English

Valerian. [n.p., n.d.]. [4] pp. 23 cm.
Advertising circular. "In 1874 they were
doing a business of $30,000 in seeds and
$4,000 in distilled valerian ..." M. F.
Melcher, "... The New Enfield Shakers,"
Shaker Quarterly, 1 (Fall 1961), 96.
N, OClWHi*.

206 ——— (valeriana officinalis) ... Prepared
by the United Society of Shakers, for Sale by
all Druggists, Price 25 cents per Bottle. Orders
to be addressed to McKesson & Robbins, Sole
Agents, New York. [n.p., n.d.]. Cover title.
24 pp. 16 cm.
Medal awarded to Fluid Extract of Valerian
at the 6th Exhibition of the Mechanics Association, Boston, 1850, reproduced on the
front cover. The latest testimonial is dated
1879.
N*, OClWHi.

207 Facts Concerning Brown's Shaker Pure
Fluid Extract of English Valerian. ("valeriana
officinalis") made at Enfield, N.H. ... [Enfield,
N.H.: n.d.]. Cover title. 24 pp. 11½ cm.
MacLean 159 (26 pp.). NOC*.

208 Shaker Medicines, Approved by the Regu-
lar Faculty. Compound Syrups, Extracts, Pills,
&c. Prepared in the Society of Shakers, by
Jerub Dyer, Enfield, N.H. Boston [Mass.]:
Devereux & Co., [n.d.]. Broadside. 35 × 29½ cm.
The broadside reprints the labels used on
bottles of Shaker Family Cough Syrup ...
Arnikate of Tannin, Alternative Syrup, Com-
pound Concentrate Decoction of Rumex,
Vegetable Pills, Shakers' Pure Extract of
English Valerian, and Extract of Dandelion.
MHarF(photocopy)*, NHi.

HANCOCK, MASS. Cloaks

209 Information Concerning the Well Known
Shaker Cloaks, [n.p., n.d.]. Cover title, [3] pp.
illus. 15½ cm.
Information about ready-to-wear cloaks and
instructions for taking measurements for
special orders, signed: *Sophia Helfrich, West
Pittsfield,* [*Hancock*], *Mass.* Photograph
showing the back of the cloak with hood
and cape, p. [2]. Elder Henry Blinn visited

the Second Family of the Hancock community, August 15, 1898, and noted in his
diary, "Eldress Sophia Helfrich invited us to
call and see the cloaks that they were making.
Visitors to the Village call at this place to see
the goods and make purchases." *The Manifesto*, 28 (October 1898), 149.
MacLean 169. MWiW*, NN.

210 ——— [n.p., n.d.]. Broadside. 20½ × 12½ cm.
"Sophia Helfrich, Maker of Shaker cloaks" at
the head of the order form which has blank
spaces for supplying measurements.
OClWHi*.

211 Ready Made Shaker Cloaks. [n.p., n.d.].
Broadside. illus. 15½ × 16½ cm.
Photograph of back view of the cloak showing
hood and cape.
OClWHi*.

HANCOCK, MASS. Seeds

212 ... Catalogue of Garden Seeds, Raised and
Sold by the United Society, Pittsfield, Berkshire
Co., Mass. [n.p., 183-?]. Broadside in 2 columns.
32½ × 21½ cm.
At head of title: 183 . The date 1836 has
been completed in ink. Above the date, "J. H.
Pierson Esq. Ramapo" (Rockland Co., N.Y.),
has been noted in ink. At end: All Orders to
be Directed to Stearnsville Post Office. Justice
Brewster [supplied in ink] Agent. This is a
filled order for $51.30. The list contains 71
varieties of seeds, mostly vegetable, at 6¢ each.
MH-BA*.

213 ——— [n.p., 183-?]. Broadside in 2 columns.
This entry has been made from a facsimile
shown in P. W. Gates, *The Farmer's Age*,
1815-1860 (N.Y.: Holt, Rinehart and Winston,
1960. 2 vols.), II: fol. p. 300. This is a different
printing from the foregoing list, with slight
changes in the varieties of seeds. The date,
1839, at the head of title, and the name, *Jos.
Patten*, have been supplied in ink.
NCooHi*.

214 Garden Seeds, Raised at Hancock, and Put
Up in Papers, with the Retail Price Printed on
them, For Sale by [blank space for name to be

supplied]. Among which are the Following:
[n.p., 1813?]. Broadside. 35 × 15 cm.

List of thirty-five varieties of seeds, mostly
vegetable, with printed prices, 4¢–13¢. A
m.s. notation on the verso, "Bill of Garden
Seeds April 1813." The name of the Shaker
who handled this order for $19.41 is lacking.
MH–BA*.

215 Garden Seeds Raised at Hancock, Berkshire Co., (Mass.) and Put Up in Papers, with
the Retail Price Printed on them: For Sale, By
[blank space for name to be supplied] Among
which are the Following: [n.p., 1819?]. Broadside. 35 × 14 cm.

List of 49 varieties of seeds, mostly vegetable. A ms. notation, "Ramapo Works [?]
April 1819," near the top, and on the verso,
"Jno. Wright (Shaker) Bill Garden Seeds—
send in the fall of 1819," along with a note
addressed: "Friend Pierson," and signed:
"J. W." This note explains that "White Onion
and Lettuce ... were cut short this season
so that it was not possible for us to answer
your demand." This is a filled order for
$50.76.
MH–BA*, MHarF, MPH.

216 ———— [n.p., 1819?]. Broadside. 38 × 15½
cm.

"Garden Seeds" in the title is printed in a
semicircle. "All orders to be directed to
Pittsfield Post-Office" is printed vertically
along the price column at right. A list of 53
varieties of seeds, mostly vegetable with
prices in "papers" at 4¢–12½¢. It is a filled
order for $51.54 with a ms. note on verso,
"Shakers Bill Garden Seeds in the fall of
1819." Another copy in the Library of the
Harvard Graduate School of Business Administration has a ms. note with date, May
1823.
MH–BA*.

217 ———— [n.p., 1824?]. Broadside. 38 × 15
cm.

"Garden Seeds" in the title is printed in a
semicircle, and a long type-ornament precedes the list of 51 varieties of seeds. *"Mer-
chants and others, who wish to purchase
Seeds, are requested to forward their Orders*

*by the 4th of July preceding the time of sale,
Directed to [John Wright] Pittsfield, Berkshire Co., Ms.,"* printed vertically, along the
price column at right. The name "John
Wright" has been supplied in ink, and a ms.
note on verso gives the date 1824. This is a
completed order for $42.08.
MH–BA*.

218 Garden Seeds, Raised at Hancock, Berkshire County, Massachusetts. And Neatly Put
Up in Papers, having the Name and Retailing
Price of the Seed Printed on them, and the
Letters D. G. For Sale By [blank for name to be
supplied]. [n.p., 1826?]. Broadside in 2 columns.
33 × 20 cm.

After "By" in the title, "J. G. Pierson Brothers" has been supplied in ink. At end, *"Mer-
chants and others who wish to purchase
Seeds, are requested to forward their Orders
by the 4th. of July, preceding the time of
sale, Directed to [Wm. Deming,* supplied in
ink] *Pittsfield, Berkshire Co. Ms."* The letters "D. G." in the title are the initials of
Daniel Goodrich. A list of 58 varieties of
seeds; the completed order totals $59.85. A
ms. notation on verso has the date "fall of
1826."
MH–BA*.

219 ———— [n.p., 1827-28?]. Broadside in 2
columns. 33 × 22 cm.

This list is almost identical with the foregoing list, except that winter butter squash
has been omitted and Scotch kale added.
The date, "March 1828," with the Shaker's
name, "Wm. Deming", occurs in a ms. note
on verso, where the filled order for $49.97
is identified as that of J. H. Pierson, Ramapo,
New York. Other copies of this broadside in
the Harvard Graduate School of Business
Administration have the ms. dates "July
1830" and "Nov. 1830," and "Jos. Patten."
MH–BA*.

HARVARD, MASS. Medicinal Herbs

220 Catalogue of Herbs, Roots, Barks, Extracts, Ointments, Powdered Articles, &c.,
&c. Prepared in the United Society, Harvard,
Mass. ... Orders to be Directed to Simon T.
Atherton, South Groton, Mass. Boston: H. L.

Devereux & Co., Printers, 1851. Cover title. 8 pp. 17½ cm.

  MacLean 483. DLC, MHi, MWA*, OClWHi.

221 Catalogue of Herbs, Roots, Barks, Powdered Articles, &c., &c. Prepared in the United Society, Harvard, Mass. ... Orders addressed to Simon T. Atherton, South Groton, Mass. will meet with Prompt Attention. Boston, Mass.: Cross & Freeman, Printers, 1853. Cover title. 8 pp. 17 cm.

  "N.B. For Botanical names we have relied on Prof. Gray's Botany," p. [1]. Common and scientific names with the prices per lb. Agents in Boston listed on back cover, verso. MHarF.

222 ——— Boston: J.E. Farwell & Co., Printers, 1854. Cover title. 8 pp. 17½ cm.

  Etc. replaces &c., &c. in the title of no. 221. Agents in Boston listed on back cover, verso. In the Williams College copy (Williamstown, Mass.) the prices have been altered in ink. "N.B. The Botanical names have been revised by Prof. Gray, Harvard College, Mass.," front cover, verso. Asa Gray's relation with the Harvard Shaker community has never been clarified, but A. H. Dupree refers to Gray's visiting this Shaker community "to get medical herbs for Sir William Hooker's museum" (Kew Gardens, now the Royal Botanic Gardens), *Asa Gray 1810–1888* (Cambridge, Mass., 1959), p. 222. In a letter dated August 3, 1853, Gray advised Sir William, "I will endeavor to get some account of Shakerdom for you. They are a queer people indeed," *Letters,* Ed. by Jane L. Gray (Boston, 1893, 2 vols.), II:401. MHarF, MWiW*.

223 ——— Boston: J. E. Farwell & Co., Printers, 1856. Cover title. 1 p. l., 14 pp. 17½ cm.

  In the title "&c." is printed "&G." Page [2] is misnumbered "4." The products are pressed in cakes, 4 X 8 inches square, about 1¼ inches thick. "Herbs and Flowers are pressed in half-pound cakes, and two cakes in each paper, neatly done up and labelled with their common and Botanical names." Ounce papers are provided for the retail trade. "Synonyms," pp. 10–13, lists the

common name equivalents. Boston and other agents listed, p. 14.
MHarF, MWiW*.

224 ——— Boston: Printed by Evans & Company, 1857. Cover title. 16 pp. 17½ cm.
MWiW*, OClWHi.

225 ——— Boston: Printed by Fred Rogers, 1860. Cover title. 16 pp. 18 cm.

  At top of title, a ms. note, "Wm Davidson Corrected April 22, 1862. Not to be sent off," in the Williams College (Williamstown, Mass.) copy. Corrections in prices are made in ink. MWiW*, OClWHi, WHi.

226 ——— Boston: C. C. P. Moody, Printer, 1868, Cover title. 15 [1] pp. 17½ cm.
MHarF, MWiW*, OClWHi.

227 ——— &c. Prepared in the United Society, Harvard, Mass. Post Office Address, S. T. Atherton, Ayer (formerly Groton Junction), Mass. 187 . [n.p., 1875?]. Broadside in 3 columns. 34½ X 21½ cm. (trimmed).

  Lists over 200 medicinal herbs with the prices per lb. At the end 8 sweet herbs are listed by the can, with prices per dozen.
MWiW*.

228 Catalogue of Medicinal Plants, and Vegetable Medicines, to which is Annexed their most Prominent Medical Properties. Prepared in the United Society, Harvard, Mass. ... Orders to be Directed to [blank space for name to be supplied] Harvard, Mass. Boston: J. Howe's Sheet Anchor Press, 1845. Cover title. 8 pp. 17 cm.

  The autograph of *S. T. Atherton* has been supplied in ink in the space provided. The imprint date has been altered in ink to *1847,* and the prices have been altered in ink. "The botanical names are from Eaton's Manual of Botany, last edition," p. 8. Lists nearly 200 medicinal herbs, with 8 "Sweet Herbs in Canisters," and 13 "Extracts," p. 7. The common names, botanical names, prices per lb., and properties are given for each item. MacLean 484. MHi, MWiW*.

229 ——— Boston: H. L. Devereux, Printer, 1849. Cover title. 8 pp. 16½ cm.

Atherton's name has been inked out and replaced by *L. D. Grosvenor, South Groton.*
MWA*.

230 Catalogue of Roots, Herbs, Barks,
Powdered Articles, &c. Prepared in the United
Society, Harvard Mass. Orders Addressed to
Simon T. Atherton, Groton Junction . . .
Boston: C. H. Shepard, Printer, 1873. Cover
title. 15 [1] pp. 18 cm.

> Lists 211 medicinal herbs, pp. [5]–10, with
> common names, prices per lb., botanical
> names, and properties. "Synonyms," pp. 12–
> 15. Unnumbered page at end lists dealers
> that act as agents for Shaker herbs in Boston
> and Salem, Mass., and Providence, R.I.
> MacLean 176. DLC, MHarF, MWA, MWiW*,
> N, OClWHi.

231 Reduced Price List. Catalogue of Herbs,
Roots, Barks, Powdered Articles, Rosewater,
Etc. Prepared in the United Society, Harvard,
Mass. Post Office Address: John Whitely, Suc-
cessor to S. T. Atherton, Ayer, Mass. [n.p.,
1889?]. Cover title, 7 pp. 19 X 8½ cm.

> Portrait of S. T. Atherton on cover title;
> cut of the Church Family, Harvard Shaker
> Village, back cover, verso, shows the com-
> munity and buildings. "Shaker Herbs," p.
> [2], states that "Medicinal Herbs, Roots and
> Compounds were first prepared for the
> market by the United Society (called
> Shakers) in Harvard, Mass.," and that much
> of the success "is due to the intelligence and
> strict integrity of the late Simon T. Ather-
> ton," who died Oct. 1, 1888. Over 200 medi-
> cinal herbs, etc., are listed under the com-
> mon names, with the prices per lb.
> MacLean 175. MHarF, MWA, MWiW*, NN,
> OClWHi.

232 Reduced Price List. Herbs, Roots, Barks,
Powdered Articles, Etc., Prepared in the United
Society, Harvard, Mass. Post Office Address,
S. T. Atherton, Ayer (formerly Groton Junc-
tion), Mass. 188 . [n.p., 188–?]. Broadside in
3 columns. 34 X 22 cm.

> Over 200 items are listed under the common
> names, with prices per lb. Fruitlands Museums
> (Harvard, Mass.) has one copy with the date,

1883, in ms. on verso; another copy has ms.
date, *1884*.
MHarF*, N, OClWHi.

233 Shaker Herbs. [n.p., n.d.]. Broadside. illus.
18½ X 12½ cm.

> A general statement about the Harvard herb
> industry and its success which is due to Simon
> T. Atherton, with a portrait of Atherton.
> Signed: *E. Myrick, Trustee, Successor to the
> late Simon T. Atherton, P.O. Address, Ayer,
> Mass.*
> MWiW*.

HARVARD, MASS. Miscellaneous

234 Catalogue of Fruit Trees, Etc., Raised in the
Shaker Nursery, Harvard, Mass. Post Office Ad-
dress. Elijah Myrick, South Groton, Mass.
Boston: Geo. C. Rand & Ayer, Prs., [n.d.].
Cover title, [5] pp. illus. 19 cm.

> Twenty-one varieties of apple and 16 varie-
> ties of cherry trees are listed with remarks,
> but prices are not given. Individual sections
> are devoted to grapes, currants, the Mountain
> Seedling Gooseberry (illustrated), and the
> Lawton Blackberry.
> MH–BA*, OClWHi.

235 Shaker Medicinal Spring Water. This Water
is a Cure for Bright's Disease of the Kidneys,
Stone in the Bladder and Kidneys, Liver Complaint, Dropsy . . . Boston, Mass.: [1881?].
Cover title. 16 pp. illus. 14½ cm.

> History, testimonials (latest dated, April 25,
> 1881). State Assayer's analysis of the water
> (dated, Nov. 15th, 1880) marketed by the
> Harvard Society. The Shaker Medicinal Spring
> "lies in the heart of a forest, about a mile
> from the Village of Harvard Community, near
> Ayer, Mass." The title illustration shows a
> Shaker brother holding a goblet in his hand.
> "The Rural Home," advertisement and illus-
> tration, back cover, verso, shows the North
> Family Dwelling House built under Elder
> August Grosvenor's direction. It proved to be
> an expensive and unsuccessful undertaking
> and was later leased and used as a summer
> hotel.
> MWiW*, MeHi.

236 —— Boston: Shaker Agency, [n.d.]. [4] pp. illus. 14½ cm.

An advertising folder found also as a broadside (unfolded), with the measurements given as 14½ X 18 cm.
MPH*, MiU-C, NBuG, NOC.

237 Whitcomb, Faith, Medicine Co., *Boston, Mass.* ... The History of the Shakers. [Boston?: 1881?]. Cover title, 16 pp. illus. 21½ cm.

At head of title: Illustrated. Short text interspersed with advertisements for Faith Whitcomb's Shaker Liniment, Balsam Bitters, Pills, etc. The illustrations show Faith Whitcomb in Shaker costume, the herb garden at Harvard, Mass., the Rural Home, the New Lebanon, N.Y., Meeting House, etc. The latest date found in the testimonials is March 7, 1881.
MB, MHarF*, NSyU ([12] pp.), OClWHi.

MT. LEBANON (formerly New Lebanon), N.Y.
Chairs

238 Catalogue and Price List of Shakers' Chairs. Pittsfield, Mass.: Press of Geo. T. Denny, [187-?], 15 [1] pp. illus. 14 cm.

Cover title: Illustrated Catalogue and Price List of Shakers' Chairs. Manufactured by the Society of Shakers. R. M. Wagan & Co., Mount Lebanon, N.Y. "Directions for Ordering Chairs," p. [2]; "Introduction," pp. [3]-5; engraved illustrations of chairs in sets, Nos. 0-7, with prices for each size, signed: *Ferguson, Albany*, pp. 6-11 (the same plates were used in all other chair catalogs); chair cushions and foot benches, pp. 12-13; prices for chair frames, "worsted lace seats," etc., pp. 14-15; chair measurements, p. [16]. The text extends through the back cover, recto, where "Colors of Braid and Plush used in our Chairs and Cushions" are identified by numbers and letters. "We were awarded a Diploma and Medal at the Centennial Exhibition for combining in our chairs, Strength, Sprightliness, and Modest Beauty," p. 13. This statement dates this catalog after 1876. The Shaker trademark, an armless rocker, is illustrated on the back cover, verso, with a warning about counterfeits. There are no advertisements. A greatly enlarged reproduction of this catalog, with the title page omitted, is included in R. F. W. Meader, *Illustrated Guide to Shaker Furniture* (no. 2449), following p. 128.
MacLean 167 (18 pp.). MPB, MWiW*, N, NOC.

239 —————— [Canaan, N.Y.?:] Canaan Printing Co., [n.d.]. 16 pp. illus. 13 cm.

Cover title: Illustrated Catalogue and Price List of Shakers' Chairs. Manufactured by the Society of Shakers. R. M. Wagan & Co., Mount Lebanon, N.Y. The contents and arrangement of this catalog vary only slightly from that printed by Denny, no. 238.
MacLean 168. MWiW*, N.

240 Centennial Illustrated Catalogue and Price List of the Shakers' Chairs, Foot Benches, Floor Mats, Etc. Manufactured and Sold by the Shakers, at Mt. Lebanon, Columbia Co., N.Y. Also Containing Several Pieces of Shaker Music. Albany [N.Y.]: Weed, Parsons & Co., Printers, 1876. 31 [1], [11] pp. illus. 17½ cm.

Issued in connection with the exhibit of Shaker chairs in the main building of the Centennial Exhibition, Philadelphia, 1876, but no mention of the chair award is made. Attention is called to "several manufacturers of chairs who have made and introduced in the market an imitation of our own style of chairs, which they sell for Shaker chairs," and reassurance is given that "All Chairs of our make will have a Gold Transfer Trade Mark attached to them, and none others are Shakers' Chairs." The illustrations include 5 full-page cuts of exhibition buildings. The chairs are illustrated individually with text descriptions, and in the usual sets, Nos. 0-7. Shaker music occurs on pp. 24, 26, 28, 30, and [1] following. Advertisements of authorized dealers for Shaker chairs, etc., pp. [1-10] of the last number sequence. Advertisement for Shaker chairs, front cover, verso; for the Shaker green corn cutter, back cover, recto; for *The Shaker* (no. 982), back cover, verso.
MacLean 166. DLC, MWA, MWiW*, NOC, OClWHi, PHi, RPB.

241 FIELD, MARSHALL & COMPANY. Chairs and Rockers Manufactured by the Society of

Shakers at Mount Lebanon, N.Y. Chicago:
Marshall Field & Co., [n.d.]. 16 pp. illus.
9½ × 15 cm.

> The illustrations of various styles of Shaker
> chairs in sets, sizes, Nos. 0–7, are printed
> from the same plates used in the catalogs
> published by the Shakers at Mt. Lebanon,
> N.Y. This catalog was probably published
> after 1876 because Marshall Field did not
> advertise as an authorized dealer in the *Cen-*
> *tennial Catalogue*, no. 240, above. E. Ray
> Pearson, Chicago, Ill., owns a Marshall Field
> refund slip for Shaker chairs which is dated
> Feb. 28, 1884. The cover of this catalog is
> maroon-colored heavy flock paper.
> NOC*.

242 Illustrated Catalogue and Price List of
Shakers' Chairs, Manufactured by the Society
of Shakers. R. M. Wagan & Co., Mount Lebanon,
N.Y. [Pittsfield, Mass.: Press of Geo. T. Denny,
n.d.]. Cover title, 15 [1] pp. illus. 14 cm.

> Half title: Catalogue and Price List of Shakers'
> Chairs. The printer's name, Geo. T. Denny,
> appears on the back cover, verso. With the
> exception of a slightly longer "Introduction,"
> pp. [3]–5, the contents are essentially like the
> other chair catalog, no. 238, printed by
> Denny. The decorative type borders at the
> top and bottom of the cover title are new.
> N*.

243 ——— Facsimile reprint. [Pittsfield, Mass.:
Eagle Printing and Binding Co., 1972].

> An unknown number of this facsimile was
> privately printed. Originally, the catalog
> carried no indication that it was a facsimile
> reproduction, but sometime later the identi-
> fication, "Reprinted 1972," was stamped on
> copies. Copies that may not have been
> stamped with this identification are most
> easily identified by the metal staples which
> have been pierced through the terra-cotta-
> colored cover. The original catalog was hand-
> sewn and tipped into the cover. Also, a
> manuscript notation, "Old time pieces," ap-
> pears at the top of the half title.
> MPH, NOC*.

244 An Illustrated Catalogue and Price-list of
the Shakers' Chairs. Manufactured by the

Society of Shakers. Mount Lebanon, N.Y.:
R. M. Wagan & Co., [n.d.]. Cover title.
15 pp. illus. 14½ cm.

> Issued without title page. The statement
> about the Shaker chair award at the Phila-
> delphia Centennial, 1876, appears at the
> foot of p. 11. "Directions for Ordering
> Chairs," p. [12]. Oval wooden boxes, Nos.
> 1–7, are illustrated with the prices per dozen
> and by the nest, p. [13]. Lewis & Conger
> advertisement, verso of p. 15; advertisement
> for Green Corn Cutter, back cover, recto.
> The front cover, verso, of the copy described
> here has an illustration of the Shaker armless
> rocker. Some copies with the same cover title
> and collation have an advertisement for
> Charles Jones, N.Y., importer of house fur-
> nishings, front cover, verso.
> MWiW*, NOC, OClWHi, WHi.

245 ——— Mount Lebanon, N.Y.: R. M. Wagan,
[n.d.]. Cover title. 16 pp. illus. 14½ cm.

> The statement of the Shaker chair award at
> the Philadelphia Centennial, 1876, appears at
> the end of "Directions for Ordering Chairs,"
> front cover, verso, and also at the foot of
> p. 3. Illustrations of individual chairs, pp.
> [9–13]. Advertisement for Lewis & Conger,
> N.Y., as a "Depot for Shaker Chairs," back
> cover, recto, and the Shaker trademark, an
> armless rocker, with the usual counterfeit
> notice, back cover, verso.
> MPB, MWA, MWiW*, NHi, NOC, OClWHi.

246 ——— Facsimile reprint. Newton, Mass.:
Emporium Publications, 1971.
> MPH*, NOC.

247 An Illustrated Catalogue and Price List of
the Shakers' Chairs, Foot Benches, Floor Mats,
Etc. Manufactured and Sold by the Shakers, at
Mt. Lebanon, Columbia Co., N.Y. Lebanon
Springs, N.Y.: B. F. Reynolds, Book, Card, and
Job Printer, 1875. 11 [2] pp. illus. 13 cm.

> Cover title lacks "Manufactured and Sold by
> the Shakers ..." Full-page engraving of the Mt.
> Lebanon chair factory building, p. [2]. "Ad-
> dress R. M. Wagan, Mount Lebanon, N.Y.," p. [3].
> MWiW*, KyBgW.

248 Illustrated Catalogue of Shaker Chairs,

Foot Benches, Floor Mats, etc. Mt. Lebanon, Columbia County, N.Y. Albany: Weed, Parsons & Co., 1874. 29 pp. 16 pp.

> This entry is taken from MacLean's *Bibliography*. No copy has been examined. MacLean 165. PPL.

249 Price List of Shakers Chairs. Manufactured in the United Society, New Lebanon, Columbia Co., N.Y. For the Year 185 . [n.p., 185-?]. Broadside. 22½ × 16 cm.

> Signed: *Jessie Lewis. D. C. Brainard.* This is the earliest price list of Shaker chairs that has been found. It includes rocking, dining, easy, and kitchen chairs of various sizes, and children's chairs, with the prices supplied in manuscript. Prices are also given for splint and tape seats, cushions, and "Button joint Tilts." George O. Donnell's patent (no. 1145) for a "metallic ferrule, ball, and foot piece" ("tilter") was granted Mar. 2, 1852, but no mention of the patent occurs in this broadside. The date of publication may have been any time in the 1850s since the blank space for the year to be added is not filled in. OClWHi*.

MT. LEBANON (formerly New Lebanon), N.Y. Gardening and Seeds

250 ... Bought of Levi Shaw. [Mt. Lebanon, N.Y.: 188-?]. Broadside in 2 columns. 30 × 23 cm.

> At head of title: Mt. Lebanon, N.Y. . . . . 188 . A list of varieties of pea, bean, beet, carrot, turnip, onion, and corn seeds available in packages, but without any indication of the prices. OClWHi*.

251 Brainard's Shaker Catalogue and Amateur's Guide to the Flower and Vegetable Garden. D. C. Brainard, Mount Lebanon, New York: Albany, Weed, Parsons & Company, Printers, 1874. iv, 96 pp. illus. 23 cm.

> Introductory information includes instructions on soil preparation, culture and treatment of flower seeds, etc. Notes under most entries include directions for culture. The contents are based upon the earlier *Gardener's Manual* by C. F. Crosman (nos. 482-87). Later catalogs which bear a strong resem-

blance to Crosman's *Manual* appear below. N, NOC (inc.), OClWHi*.

252 Catalogue of Choice Vegetable Seeds. Shaker Seed Co. D. M. Mount Lebanon, N.Y.: [n.d.]. Broadside. 22 × 54 cm.

> The initials in the title are David Meacham's. Meacham was appointed senior trustee in 1791, but his initials continued to be used for many years after his death in 1826. MPB*.

253 Descriptive Catalogue of Vegetable Seeds Raised at New Lebanon, N.Y., with Directions for their Cultivation. All Orders should be Directed to D. C. Brainard, Mount Lebanon, N.Y.: [n.p.] Chickering & Axtell, Steam Printers, 1870. Cover title. 19 pp. 21½ cm.

> "Special Description of Various Kinds of Vegetables, with Notice of New Varieties," pp. 15-18. NOC*.

254 ——— New York: Lange, Little & Hillman, 1873. Cover title. 23 pp. illus. 22½ cm.

> NOC.

255 For Sale by Shaker Seed Co., Mount Lebanon, N.Y. Read the Verdict! Cleveland's Alaska Pea ... Sold only under the Seal of the Originators. [n.p., n.d.]. Cover title. [6] pp. 28 cm.

> Description of the pea, with testimonials from growers. Prices are by the bushel, quart, pint, and packet. Private collection.

256 Fresh Garden Seeds. A General Assortment of such as are in Common Use, Lately Received from the Quakers' [sic]. [n.p., 1814]. Broadside in 2 columns. 25½ × 16 cm.

> At end; Hartford, March 14th, 1814. Over forty varieties of seeds are listed, without price, or any indication of the amounts, i.e., papers, ounces, or pounds. MPH (photocopy)*.

257 "Garden Seeds Warranted Fresh and Genuine, Raised by the United Society of Shakers. Strattan and Warner, Sole Agents," in *Annual Herbalist's Catalogue of Medicinal Plants...* (New York: n.d., 48 pp.), pp. [46]-48.

"Shaker Sieves" are included in the reference above. This catalog published by Stratton & Warner, Wholesale Herbalists, N.Y., bears a strong resemblance to Shaker medicinal catalogs, but the word "Shaker" does not appear except as shown in this reference.
MWiW*.

Gardener's Manual. *See* Crosman, Charles F., no. 482 ff.

258 Grape. A New and Choice Variety. Early Northern Mus[cadine]. The Subscriber has Thought Proper to Change the Name to Roy[al]. N[ew Lebanon, Shaker] Village, Columbia Co., N.Y.: [n.d.]. Broadside. illus.

The title is taken from a mutilated copy; brackets indicate the parts that are illegible; no size has been given because the edges are destroyed. It is an advertising handbill (with a cut of a bunch of grapes) for the Royal, Burton's Early August, and Sage's Mammoth grapes – superior to Isabella and Catawba grapes.
MPH*.

259 Just Received. A New Assortment of Choice Garden Seeds, Raised and Put up in the Best Manner by the United Society of Shakers, at New-Lebanon, Columbia County, New-York, and ... Marked with the Letters D. M. For Sale [blank space to be filled in]. Albany, N.Y.: Van Benthuysen, Printers, [n.d.] Broadside. 29 X 22 cm.
OClWHi*.

260 New Tomato "Livingston's Beauty." Shaker Seed Company, Wholesale and Retail Dealers in Garden Seeds. Mt. Lebanon, N.Y.: Buffalo, Clay and Richmond, [n.d.]. Broadside. illus. 23 X 15 cm.

Advertising flyer with a description, growing habits, the price per packet for seeds, and a bright red colored cut of the tomato.
OClWHi*.

261 Rural Register and Almanac for 1876 from D. C. Brainard, Mount Lebanon, N.Y. For the Southern and Middle States. Albany [N.Y.]: Weed, Parsons & Company, Printers, 1876. Cover title. 63 pp. illus. 22 cm.

At head of title: For Gratuitous Distribution. The first half of the contents depend in large part upon the earlier *Gardener's Manual* by Charles F. Crosman, nos. 482–487. "Introduction to Annual Catalogue of Vegetable Seeds Raised at Mount Lebanon," pp. 2–3. "We issue annually Brainard's splendid Illustrated Catalogue and Amateur Guide to the Flower and Vegetable Garden ..." p. 4. The price, 25¢, was credited on orders over $1.00. List of seeds with illustrations and directions for cultivation, pp. 6–35; "Medical and Sweet Herbs," p. 36; "The Hot-bed," p. 37; "A calendar indicating the proper sowing times for different crops raised in the southern and middle states," pp. 38–61.
NOC*.

262 The Shaker Seed Co.'s Annual Price List for Market Gardeners. Pittsfield, Mass.: Eagle Job Print., 1886. Cover title. [4] pp. 28½ cm.
Only vegetable seeds are listed.
MacLean 183. DLC, MPB, MWA, MWiW*, N, NBuG, OClWHi.

263 Shaker Seed Co.'s Special Price List of Vegetables and Other Seeds for Grangers. [Mt. Lebanon, N.Y.: n.d.]. [4] pp. 41 X 29 cm.
"Our Annual Price List for Grangers," includes vegetable, herb, and some flower seeds, priced by the pound and by the ounce. "We are the growers and producers of most of the seeds we sell."
Private collection.

264 ——— of Vegetables and Other Seeds for Market Gardeners. Mt. Lebanon, N.Y.: Shaker Seed Co., [1888?]. [4] pp. 29 cm.
Prices for seeds are given by the pound and by the ounce. We "have added to our list of last season a great number of new and choice varieties." The text refers to this list as "Our Annual Price List for Market Gardeners."
OClWHi*.

265 Shaker Seed Co.'s Wholesale Price List of Garden Seeds. January 1st, 1885. Shaker Seed Co., Mt. Lebanon, Columbia Co., N.Y. If you Want a Splendid Garden, Plant Shaker Seeds; They are the Best. Pittsfield [Mass.]: Berkshire County Eagle Print., [1884]. 14 [1] pp. 18½ cm.

Terms: Accounts are payable June 1st 1885 and subsequent purchases payable on Dec. 1st.
MPB, MWiW*.

266 ——— Jan. 1st, 1886. Shaker Seed Co., Mt. Lebanon, Pittsfield, Mass.: Berkshire County Eagle, [1885]. Cover title. 13 [2] pp. illus. 18 cm.

Advertisement, "Shakers Early Sweet Corn," front cover, verso. Colored advertisement for Livingston's Beauty Tomato, back cover, verso. This publication is printed on yellow paper and lists only vegetable seeds.
MPB*.

267 ——— January 1st, 1887. [n.p., 1886]. 23[3] pp. illus. 18 cm.

Errata slip tipped in preceding the title page, and also "Errata" at end p. [3]. Advertisement for Shakers' Early Sweet Corn, front cover, verso; advertisement for Cleveland's Alaskan Pea, back cover, recto. Colored advertisement for Livingston's Beauty Tomato, back cover, verso. Printed on yellow paper. With the exception of a few melon and herb seeds, only vegetable seeds are listed.
MPB*.

268 Shaker Seed Co.'s Wholesale Price List of Seeds, Grown and for Sale by the Shaker Seed Co., Mt. Lebanon, N.Y. For Dealers Only. [n.p., 1887]. Caption title. [4] pp. illus. 35 X 16½ cm.

At head of title: Established 1794. January 1st, 1888. Lists about 300 vegetable and herb seeds (sweet, pot, and medicinal), available by the pound or packet, with quarter and half bushels at the bushel rate.
MPB, MWA, MWiW, OClWHi*.

269 [Shakers' Annual Catalogue of Vegetable Seeds and Rural Register. Mt. Lebanon, N.Y.] [n.p., 1874]. pp. 25-56.

This entry is taken from the *Catalogue of the Emma B. King Library*, Shaker Museum (Old Chatham, N.Y., 1970), item 80. The catalog is incomplete and lacks the title page, but R. F. W. Meader, Director, reports that a comparison with the *Rural Register* above, reveals that "it is almost certainly D. C.

Brainard's work, and probably Weed, Parsons & Co.'s printing."
NOC*.

270 Shakers' Catalogue and Amateur's Guide to the Flower and Vegetable Garden. Charles Sizer, Mount Lebanon, N.Y., Albany, N.Y.: Weed, Parsons & Co., 1875. 84 pp. illus. 23 cm.

Introductory information includes instructions on soil preparation and treatment of seeds. Vegetable seeds, pp. 54-83, includes annotations on culture of seeds, under most of the seed entries.
NOC*.

271 Shakers' Descriptive and Illustrated Annual Catalogue and Amateur's Guide to the Flower and Vegetable Garden. Mount Lebanon, N.Y. Established 1795. Mount Lebanon, N.Y.: Washington Jones, Book and Job Printer, 1882. 84 pp. illus. 23 cm.

The title indicates that this is the 18th edition.
MacLean 177. DLC*.

272 ——— Mt. Lebanon: Printing Press of the United Society [Washington Jones, Book and Job Printer], 1883. 84 pp. illus. 23 cm.

The title page indicates that this is the "Twelfth Edition," but *see* no. 275.
DLC*.

273 Shaker Seed Co. [n.p., 1886]. 76 [1] pp. illus. 23½ cm.

Cover title: Illustrated Catalogue of the Shaker Seed Co., Mt. Lebanon, N.Y. Laid in: Addressed envelope for ordering Shaker seeds. Vegetables and flowers are illustrated with line cuts which accompany the descriptions. The covers are highly decorated.
OClWHi*.

274 ——— Mount Lebanon, N.Y.: 1888. 98 pp. illus. 23½ cm.

Cover title: Illustrated Catalogue of the Shaker Seed Co., Mt. Lebanon, New York. The front cover is printed in brown ink on bright yellow paper. Advertisement for Livingston's Beauty Tomato in color, front cover, verso. Vegetables and flowers are illustrated with line cuts, accompanied by full

descriptions and prices. "Novelties," pp. 57–67, printed on pink paper, includes only vegetable seeds. "Our Premium List," p. 7, offers atomizers, armed Shaker rockers of various sizes, etc., as premiums for orders of various amounts.
MacLean 178. DLC, MPB, MWA, MWiW*, N, NN, OClWHi.

275 Shakers' Descriptive and Illustrated Catalogue and Amateur's Guide to the Flower and Vegetable Garden. From Charles Sizer. Mt. Lebanon, N.Y.: Mount Lebanon Printing Press of the United Society of Shakers [Washington Jones, Book and Job Printer], 1876. 84 pp. illus. 23½ cm.
At head of title: Established 1795. "Twelfth Edition" appears at the foot of the title page, cf. no. 272. Jones used the Shaker Press of the Mt. Lebanon Center Family.
DLC*, MPB, MPH (cover only).

276 Shakers' Descriptive and Illustrated Catalogue of Flower and Vegetable Seeds for 1881. Address D. C. Brainard Ag't, Mount Lebanon, N.Y. [Rochester, N.Y.: Rochester Dem. and Chron. Print.], 1881. 60 pp. illus. 25½ cm.
Cover title: Shakers' Annual Catalogue and Price-list of Flower and Vegetable Seeds. The cover is printed in brown ink on bright yellow paper. The introductory information, pp. [2–4], describes the proper preparation of the soil and cultivation of seeds, including the hot-bed method with instructions for its preparation. Each vegetable and flower is shown in a line cut. Laid In: An envelope addressed to D. C. Brainard, Mount Lebanon, Columbia County, N.Y. Also an order blank, [4] pp. (sheet folded), and "Shaker Garden Seeds" (broadside 25½ × 20 cm.), which is a list of seeds in the catalog.
N, OClWHi*.

277 ——— From William Anderson, Mount Lebanon, N.Y. Mt. Lebanon, N.Y.: Printing Press of Washington Jones, Book and Job Printer, 1881. 84 pp. illus. 22½ cm.
At head of title: Sixteenth Edition. Printed in gold on a royal blue heavily decorated cover. Contains culture and other instruc-

tions for raising flowers and vegetables.
N*, OClWHi.

278 Shakers' Garden Seeds, Raised at New Lebanon, Columbia Co., N.Y. [n.p., n.d.]. Broadside in 2 columns. 35 × 21 cm.
At end: N.B. Orders should be forwarded . . . addressed to Peter H. Long, Agent for the Society. "The following are selected from the numerous varieties of culinary vegetables, as most useful, choice, and best calculated to repay the expense of cultivation . . ." "Papers at 6¢."
NOC*.

279 ——— [Albany, N.Y.: Van Benthuysen, 184–?]. Broadside in 2 columns. 34½ × 23 cm.
At end: N.B. Orders should be forwarded . . . addressed to Edward Fowler, Agent for the Society. This shows very little variation from the preceding broadside, including the price of 6¢ per paper of seeds. Both broadsides date after 1843. E. D. Andrews quotes an entry from a ms. "Journal of Garden Accounts Commencing July 27, 1840, New Lebanon Church Family" for "1843 – Feb. 24. – We have concluded to have the prices of all seeds at 6 cents . . ." *Community Industries of the Shakers* (no. 1759), pp. 77, and 303, No. 19.
OClWHi*.

280 Shakers' Genuine Garden Seeds. From New Lebanon (Columbia County), N.Y. Post Office Address, William Anderson, Mount Lebanon, Columbia County, N.Y. Albany: Weed, Parsons & Co., Printers, [188–?]. Broadside in 6 columns. illus. 32 × 59 cm.
Printed on yellow-gold paper with cuts which depict 21 of the vegetables. Lists 95 varieties of seeds, mostly vegetables, with prices by the paper.
MPB, MWiW, OClWHi*.

MT. LEBANON (formerly New Lebanon), N.Y.
Medicinal Herbs

281 Annual Catalogue of Herbs, Medicinal Plants, with their Therapeutic Qualities and Botanical Names; Also Extracts, Ointments,

Essential Oils, Double Distilled and Fragrant Waters, Raised, Prepared and Put Up in the Neatest Style, and Most Careful Manner, at the Botanic Garden, New Lebanon, Columbia County, N.Y. [n.p., n.d.]. 12 pp. 20½ cm.

"Catalogue of Garden Seeds, Sold by ...." p. 2. "The Botanical names [are] from Eaton's Manual of Botany, last edition." NOC*.

282 ... Bought of Charles F. Crosman, Agent for the United Society, New Lebanon, N.Y. The Following Medicinal and Vegetable Medicines. [n.p., 1838]. Caption title. [3] pp. 37 X 14 cm.

At head of title: New-Lebanon .... 18 . The copy described here is a partially filled-in order for D. Miller & Co., with the date *Nov. 20, 1838* supplied in ink. This list contains more than 170 herbs, barks, roots, etc., under the common names with the prices per lb., pp. [1–2]. Extracts, ointments, double distilled and fragrant waters, snuff, and syrups of liverwort, sarsaparilla, black cohosh, etc., are listed, p. [3], with the prices. OClWHi*.

283 Catalogue of Medicinal Plants and Vegetable Medicines, Prepared in the United Society, New-Lebanon, N.Y. ... Orders to be Directed to New-Lebanon, N.Y. Albany: Printed by Hoffman and White, 1836. 8 pp. 15½ cm.

"Students of Botany and others, can be supplied with Herbariums containing a large collection of specimens of our indigenous plants and cultivated exotics; arranged according to the Linnean System with correct labels. Prices reasonable," p. 8. The catalog lists common names and botanical names with the prices per pound. The botanical names are from Eaton's *Manual of Botany*. OClWHi*.

284 ———— To which is Affixed their most Prominent Medical Properties. Prepared in the United Society, New Lebanon, N.Y. ... Orders to be Directed to [blank for name to be supplied] New Lebanon, N.Y. Albany: Printed by Packard and Van Benthuysen, 1837. Cover title. 8 pp. 16 cm.
OClWHi*.

285 ———— New York: New Franklin Printing Office, 1841. Cover title. 12 pp. 17½ cm. NOC*.

286 Catalogue of Medicinal Plants, Barks, Roots, Seeds, Flowers and Select Powders, with their Therapeutic Qualities and Botanical Names. Also Ointments, Waters, &c. Raised, Prepared, and Put Up in the most Careful Manner, by the United Society of Shakers, at New Lebanon, N.Y. ... For Sale by W. A. Leckler, 71 Maiden Lane, New York. E. B. Hyde & Co., [n.p., n.d.]. 24 pp. 16½ cm.

"Supplementary," pp. 20–23, gives a general discussion and history of herbs and materia medica.
MHarF*, NCooHi, NCoxHi.

287 ———— with their Therapeutic Qualities and Botanical Names; Also, Pure Vegetable Extracts, Prepared in Vacuo; Ointments, Inspissated Juices, Essential Oils, Double Distilled and Fragrant Waters &c., &c., Raised, Prepared and Put Up in the Most Careful Manner by the United Society of Shakers at New Lebanon, N.Y. ... Orders Addressed to Edward Fowler will meet with Prompt Attention. Albany: Van Benthuysen, Printer, 1851. Cover title, 34 pp. 16 cm.

CSmH, DLC, MiU–C, NCooHi, NN, NOC*, PPULC, RPB.

288 ———— Orders Addressed to Edward Fowler ... Albany: Van Benthuysen, 1860. Cover title, 35 pp. (blank page follows). 17½ cm.

In some copies, otherwise identical, the name Edward Fowler has been omitted following "Orders Addressed to" in the title, and the resulting blank space provides for the substitution of another name. In an OClWHi copy the name Benjamin Gates has been substituted. Since the growing and processing of herbs has become profitable, others have engaged in the trade who are "destitute of the knowledge of the details of the business [and have] employed seceders from this society, who had become acquainted with their manner of preparation and who very properly adopted their improvements, and with them the very euphonious title 'Shaker Herbs' for their advertisements," p. 34, followed by a disclaimer. Testimonials, dated 1850 and 1851, are printed on the back cover, verso. MacLean 171? MPB, MWiW*, NN, OClWHi.

289 ———— Orders Addressed to Edward Fowler ... Albany: Van Benthuysen, Printer, [n.d.]. Cover title. 34 pp. (blank leaf follows). 17½ cm.

The contents are almost identical with no. 288 but are printed from a different setting of type. Some copies omit the name Edward Fowler in the title.
MacLean 172 (1862?). MPB, MPH, MWiW*, NhD, OClWHi.

290 ———— Orders Addressed to [blank space for name to be supplied] will Meet with Prompt Attention ... Albany: Van Benthuysen, Printer, [n.d.]. Cover title. 32 pp. 17½ cm.

It is stated in "To our Patrons," front cover, verso, that "We have made, and are now making, heavy expenditures in buildings, machinery, and very complete accommodations and fixtures for drying, powdering," and that orders will be filled promptly. "Hereafter, all our extracts will be finished in vacuo; thereby obviating the evils produced by high temperatures." "For the generic and specific names, we have relied on Gray's *Botany of the Northern United States*" (1st ed., 1848). The testimonials on the back cover are dated 1850 and 1851, which dates these improvements after 1851.
MWiW*, OClWHi.

291 ———— Orders Addressed to [blank space for name to be supplied] will Meet with Prompt Attention ... New Lebanon, N.Y.: W. H. Hill, Printer, [n.d.]. 23 pp. (followed by a blank page). 18 cm.

The text varies from the catalogs above, and "Supplementary" at the end is omitted. One "&c.," in the title is omitted. "Fonda and Bagley, Wholesale Druggists, Albany, N.Y.," is stamped on back cover, verso.
MacLean 174 (1866). DLC, MWiW*, RPB.

Catalogue of Medicinal Plants ... 1873 and 1875. *See* Druggist's Hand-book, no. 293.

292 Catalogue of Shaker Herbs, Roots and Medicinal Plants ... Raised, Manufactured and

Put Up by the Shakers of New Lebanon ... New York: 1848. 10 pp.

This entry is taken from Alex Berman, "An Unpublished Letter ...," no. 3076, p. 463, ftn. 10.
NNNAM*.

293 Druggist's Hand-book of Pure Botanic Preparations, &c. Sold by the Society of Shakers, Mt. Lebanon, N.Y. Albany, N.Y.: Weed, Parsons & Company, Printers, 1873. vi, 58 pp. 17½ cm.

Cover title: Catalogue of Medicinal Plants, Barks, Roots, Seeds, Flowers & Select Powders, with their Therapeutic Qualities & Botanical Names .... The title page is misleading. Actually the cover title varies only slightly from those of earlier Mt. Lebanon catalogs, but this enlarged publication is directed to druggists. "In the commencement of the New Lebanon establishment, most of the native remedies offered in the market were collected by persons destitute of necessary botanical information and ignorant of the proper season of collecting, and the correct manner of preparation; but who gathered such simples as were in general use ... But these, from exposure to atmospheric influences, and being tied up in loose bundles were generally worthless." The employment of seceders in business firms and the spurious use of "Shaker Herbs" in advertisements is described, and the trade is assured that improvements in Mt. Lebanon gardens and apparatus are being made "to meet the progressive demands of the age," and that the Shakers intend "to sustain the character and estimation they have long enjoyed." Medicinal herbs are listed, pp. 1–46, under popular names, followed by the botanical names with full indications of illnesses and conditions in which the herb will be efficacious. "A Catalogue of Garden Seeds ..." back cover, verso.
MiU–C, MWA*, OClWHi.

294 ———— Albany, N.Y.: Weed, Parsons & Company, 1875. vi, 58 pp. 17½ cm.
MWiW*, OClWHi.

295 ... Price List Adopted January 1st, 1919. Shaker Medical Department, Mount Lebanon, Columbia County, N.Y. [n.p., 1918]. Broadside. 8½ × 14 cm.

Prices for various quantities of Norwood's Tincture Veratrum Viride are included, cf. no. 1096. "Trade supplied by Williams Mfg. Co., 118 St. Clair Ave., Cleveland, Ohio." OClWHi*.

296 Prices of Fluid Extracts, Manufactured by the Shakers, Mount Lebanon, N.Y. [n.p., 1867]. Caption title. [3] pp. 25½ cm.
Lists about 180 fluid extracts of herbs, barks, roots, etc., in 2 columns under common names, followed by botanical names with prices for 1 lb. and 5 lb. bottles, pp. [1-2]. About 60 solid extracts are listed under the botanical names, followed by the common names and prices for 1 oz. to 4-lb. glass or earthenware jars, p. [3]. OClWHi*.

297 ——— 1868. [3] pp. 25½ cm.
At head of title: Corrected to January 1, 1868. OClWHi*.

298 Revised Prices Current of Pure Medicinal Extracts, Prepared by the Shakers, Mount Lebanon, Columbia County, N.Y. Benjamin Gates. [n.p., n.d.]. Cover title. [4] pp. 20½ cm.
S. D. Brown, Agent, 49 Warren St., N.Y., p. [3]. MPH*.

299 Shakers' Fluid Extracts, Prepared by the Society of Shakers, Mount Lebanon, N.Y. Albany: Printed by C. Van Benthuysen, [n.d.]. Cover title. [8] pp. 10 cm.
"We offer to the public the following new preparations, Pearls of Ether, Pearls of Chloroform, Pearls of Turpentine." MPH*, MWA, NOC, OClWHi.

300 ... Shakers' Price List of Medicinal Preparations, Mount Lebanon, Columbia Co., N.Y. Herbs, Roots, Barks, and Powders, Net Prices. Fluid and Solid Extracts, Discount According to the Amount Purchased. [n.p., 1874]. Caption title. [4] pp. 27½ cm.
At head of title: April 1st, 1874. At end, p. [3], "All Orders Should be Addressed to Edward Fowler ..." MWA*.

301 ——— [n.p., 1874]. [4] pp. 27½ cm.
At head of title: May 1st, 1874. MWA, NOC*.

302 Shakers' Wholesale Price List. Of Medicinal Herbs, Roots, &c., &c. Nett [!] Prices Cash. To Wholesale Dealers Only. Corrected March 1872. Mount Lebanon, N.Y. [n.p., 1872]. Broadside in 5 columns. 34 X 22 cm. MPB*, OClWHi.

303 ——— Corrected to June 1872. To Wholesale Dealers Only. Mount Lebanon, N.Y. [n.p., n.d.]. Broadside in 5 columns. 35 X 21 cm.
"Orders should be Addressed to Edward Fowler." MWiW, N (Edward Fowler's name omitted), OClWHi*.

MT. LEBANON (formerly New Lebanon), N.Y.
Medicines

304 Asthma. What is it? It is a Chronic Paroxysmal and Intermittent Disease Of Respiration ... The Asthma Cure is Manufactured Exclusively by the Shakers. [Mt. Lebanon, N.Y.: 1884?]. [2] pp. 22 cm.
At end, p. [1]: Address D. C. Brainard, Mount Lebanon, Columbia Co., N.Y. Testimonials for the Shaker Asthma Cure, p. [2], dated 1883. Private collection.

305 Compound Concentrated Syrup of Sarsaparilla, Prepared Directly by B. Hinckley, Physician of the United Society of Shakers, New Lebanon, N.Y. [New Lebanon, N.Y.: 185-?]. [2] pp. 35 cm.
Signed: *Edward Fowler, Agent.* Testimonials for and general information about the syrup. The latest testimonial is dated Jan. 4, 1856. MPB, MWiW*, OClWHi.

306 Digestive Pills, for Indigestion or Dyspepsia, Sourness of the Stomach, Loss of Appetite and Liver Complaints. Prepared in the United Society, New-Lebanon, Columbia Co., N.Y. [n.p., n.d.]. Broadside. 20½ X 16½ cm.
The recipe for making the pills and directions for use are on each package. OClWHi*.

307 The Improved Vegetable Renovating Pills, A
Powerful but Safe and Efficient Cathartic, and
Valuable Family Medicine...Prepared in the Unit-
ed Society of Shakers, New-Lebanon, N.Y. [New
York:] J. W. Kelley, [n.d.]. Broadside. 30 × 25 cm.
    At head of title: For Sale Here. Printed on
    green paper.
    MPB*, OClWHi.

308 New Cure for Consumption; the Pthisis
Eradicator. Prepared by the Shakers, New-
Lebanon, N.Y. For Sale Here. [n.p., n.d.].
Broadside. 49½ × 60 cm.
    OClWHi*.

309 Seven Barks [Manufactured by the United
Society of Shakers, Mt. Lebanon, N.Y.]. [n.p.,
n.d.] 32 pp. 13 cm.
    Often called Brown's Seven Barks, this medi-
    cine was made by the Shakers exclusively
    for Dr. Lyman Brown of New York under
    business arrangements similar to those al-
    ready established with A. J. White (see
    ALMANACS). Seven Barks was introduced
    late in the 19th Century, and as late as 1909
    large shipments were being sent to London
    as shown in ms. records in the Library of
    the Shaker Museum, Old Chatham, N.Y.
    OClWHi*.

310 ——— [n.p., 191–?]. [8] pp. 15 cm.
    OClWHi*.

311 ... Shaker Asthma Cure. [Mt. Lebanon,
N.Y.?: n.d.]. Broadside. 21½ × 13 cm.
    At head of title: The following Rules should
    be Strictly Observed ... At end: Address,
    D. C. Brainard, Columbia County, N.Y.
    MPH*.

312 Shaker Cough Syrup. [n.p., n.d.]. Broadside. 26 × 17 cm.
    "This is not a patent medicine, nor a secret
    remedy, and we make no secret of its compo-
    sition. The basis of this preparation is wild
    cherry bark ..."
    OClWHi*.

313 Shaker Hair Restorer. [n.p., n.d.]. Broadside. 24 × 15 cm.
    OClWHi*.

314 ——— Restores Gray Hair to its Original
Color, Beauty, Softness. [n.p., n.d.]. Caption
title, [4] pp. 20½ cm.
    At the foot of p. [1]: Address, D. C.
    Brainard. Most of the testimonials are dated
    1885, but the latest is dated May 1886.
    "The well-known Society of Shakers, located
    at Mount Lebanon, N.Y., U.S.A., has, for a
    century past been engaged in the cultivation
    of medicinal herbs and in the preparation of
    various essences, extracts, and compounds,
    that are largely used in medical practice and
    by the public at large. The Society takes great
    pleasure in informing the public that they
    have added a Hair Restorative to their al-
    ready long list of preparations ... Gray hair
    may be honorable, But the natural color is
    preferable." Includes an advertisement for
    the Shaker Asthma Cure, with testimonials,
    p. [4].
    OClWHi*.

315 ——— Prepared by the Society of Shakers,
Mount Lebanon, Columbia County, N.Y., U.S.A.
Address D. C. Brainard ... Albany, N.Y.: Burdick
& Taylor, Printers, [1889?]. Cover title. [4] pp.
23½ cm.
    The latest testimonial is dated February 1889.
    Advertisements for the Shaker Asthma Cure,
    with testimonials, p. [4].
    Private collection.

316 Shaker Preparation. The Genius of Beauty!
Toilet Prize and Sufferer's Panacea, or Imperial
Rose Balm. Prepared only by the Shaker Society,
New Lebanon, Columbia Co., N.Y. [n.p., n.d.].
Broadside. 23½ × 15 cm.
    At end: Address Thomas Estes or Rufus
    Crossman, New Lebanon ... "Unequalled for
    cleaning the Teeth, Healing Sore or Spongy
    gums ... curing Pimples, Tetters, Ringworms,
    Salt Rheum ... Cure of Chapped Hands ....
    This article is excellent for Cleaning Kid
    Gloves ..."
    NOC*.

317 ——— [n.p., n.d.]. Broadside. 31½ × 25 cm.
    At head of title: For Sale Here.
    MiU–C*.

318 ... The Shaker Vegetable Remedy. Pre-

pared by the Society of Shakers, Mount Lebanon, Col., Co., N.Y. [n.p., n.d.]. Broadside. 24 × 14 cm.

> Address: D. C. Brainard, Mount Lebanon, N.Y. "Cures sick headache, constipation, torpid liver, etc., by removing the cause through natural channels . . ."
> MPB, MPH*.

319 . . . Shaker's Pure Lemon Syrup, Prepared from Positively Pure and Doubly-refined White Sugar . . . . Manufactured by the Shaker Society, New Lebanon, Columbia Co., N.Y. [n.p., n.d.]. Broadside.

> At head of title: For Sale Here. An advertising flyer for "hotels, refreshment saloons, and private families." This description was made from a photograph. The size appears to be about 28 × 24 cm.
> Private collection.

320 Shaker's Rose Cream. Will Remove Freckles, Pimples, Moth Patches and Sun Burn . . . Manufactured by Mt. Lebanon Shakers North Family, New York. [n.p., n.d.]. Broadside. 9½ × 6½ cm.

> Private collection.

321 Shaker's Tooth Ache Pellets. Always Ready and Convenient. [n.p., n.d.]. 18½ × 13½ cm.

> Trademark for this Shaker product registered June 30, 1906, no. 2354.
> OClWHi*.

322 Testimonials. [New Lebanon, N.Y.: 185-?]. Broadside. 24½ × 18 cm.

> Signed: *Edward Fowler, Agent, New Lebanon, N.Y.* At head of title: Wholesale Agents, Wilson Fairbanks & Co., No. 45, Hanover St., Boston. Testimonials for Shaker "extracts prepared in vacuo" at the New Lebanon, N.Y. Society. The testimonials are signed by J. H. Salisbury, M.D., New York State Chemist (Apr. 4, 1853); H. H. Childs, M.D., President, Berkshire Medical Society (Dec. 20, 1850); William Clough, M.D., Pittsfield, Mass. (Jan. 21, 1851). Includes an undated quotation from a letter written by "Professor Hosford of Harvard University."
> OClWHi*.

323 Testimonials in Favor of the Shaker

Asthma Cure. [n.p., 1884?]. [2] pp. 25 cm.

> Signed: *D. C. Brainard, Mount Lebanon . . .* Latest testimonials are dated 1883. These are supposed to have been inserted in the orders billed by D. C. Brainard.
> NOC*.

Therapeutical Powers and Properties of Veratrum Viride. *See* [Norwood, Leslie C.], no. 1096 ff.

324 To Druggists, Apothecaries, and All Others Dealing in or Using Medicinal Extracts Prepared by the Shakers. Having Dissolved my Relations with the Society of Shakers at New Lebanon, I Consider it Due to the Public . . . [n.p., 1860?]. Broadside. 30 × 23½ cm.

> A ms. note on the Western Reserve Historical Society copy (Cleveland, O.) is addressed: *Giles B. Avery,* and signed: *James Long,* who joined the Shakers at New Lebanon in Sept. 1830, and seceded Sept. 1860. This statement is intended to be facetious.
> OClWHi*.

325 . . . To the Drug Trade of the Dominion of Canada. Montreal: 1885. Broadside. 26 × 20 cm.

> Signed: *Benjamin Gates,* Trustee for the Society of Shakers, and dated at Montreal, January 27th, 1885. At head of title: Office of A. J. White Limited, Branch: 67 St. James Street, Montreal. This is an announcement that "proceedings at law were taken by the Shakers charging the said firm [Smith Bros.] with fraudulently using and stating without authorization in their pamphlet that this medicine [Shaker Blood Syrup] was prepared by the Shakers." The suit claimed damages and provided that registration of the trademark for Shaker Blood Syrup be cancelled. The Shakers withdrew their action after Smith Bros. signed a declaration on Jan. 24, 1885, admitting that their marketing, advertising, and trademark had not been authorized by the Shakers and were consequently fraudulent. Damages were not paid because Smith Bros. became insolvent shortly after the Shaker legal action was taken. It was further stated that "The Shakers of Mount Lebanon are the only persons authorized by

law to prepare and sell Shaker Extract of
Roots ... and 'Mother Seigel's Curative
Syrup' and that the only persons authorized
to deal in said Shaker medicines is the firm
of A. J. White." *See also ALMANACS.*
NOC*.

326 Vegetable Pulmonary Pills. Improved
Renovating Pills ... Prepared in the United Society, New-Lebanon, N.Y. [n.p., n.d.]. Broadside in 2 columns. 21 X 25 cm.
MPB, OClWHi*.

MT. LEBANON (formerly New Lebanon), N.Y.
Medicines – A. J. White Publications

327 The Donkey Puzzle. [New York: 1895].
Cover title. 32 pp. illus. 14 cm.
An illustration on the front cover depicts a
bearded man steadying a child astride a
donkey. The solutions for "The Donkey
Puzzle," p. 32, and the "A & B Puzzle," back
cover, verso, "will be wrapped with every 25
cent bottle of Shaker Digestive Cordial."
"For Sale by All Druggists and by A. J.
White, General Agent, 30 Reade St., New
York," back cover, recto. "Life Among the
Shakers," by Mary Frances Carr, pp. 1–3.
Otherwise the contents are advertisements
and testimonials for Shaker Digestive Cordial,
pp. 3–23, with the latest testimonial dated
Mar. 29th 1895, and advertisements and
testimonials for Laxol, which is not a Shaker
product, pp. 23–30. For other A. J. White
publications and information, *see ALMANACS.*
Private collection.

328 A Gift Worth Preserving, Printed on Per-
fumed Paper. Take one Home. The Fragrance is
Delightful. Presented by [blank space for agent's
name]. [New York: A. J. White, 187–?]. Cover
title, 16 pp. illus. 15 cm.
Undated testimonials for Shaker Extract of
Roots with descriptions of the illnesses in
which its use is indicated. Illustrations show
"The Stealthy Approach of Disease," and
"Dr. White and his Wife together with their
Blooming, Healthy, and Interesting Child-
ren." This pamphlet was supplied in quantity
and free of charge to A. J. White's agents.
NOC*, OClWHi.

329 "Look on This Picture [woman's portrait]
and on This [woman's portrait]. How We Shall
Look When We Grow Old." [New York: A. J.
White, 1890?]. Cover title. 32 pp. illus. 15 cm.
Advertisement and testimonials for Shaker
Family Pills, Shaker Soothing Plasters, etc.,
and descriptions of physical ailments which
have been cured (improved) by Shaker Extract of Roots, which also arrests the aging
process. Fourteen pairs of portraits show the
effects of aging: "As She (or he) Now Appears" and "As She (or he) Will Appear when
She (or he) is Old." The latest testimonial is
dated 1889.
N, NOC, OClWHi*.

330 One Agent in a Place. [New York: A. J.
White, 187–?]. [4] pp. illus. 24 cm.
An advertising flyer intended to attract new
agents to introduce medicines distributed by
A. J. White. Throughout the text the integrity
and merit of Shaker products are emphasized.
The generous terms offered to agents include
a rubber stamp with the agent's name and
address, free advertising pamphlets, and a
variety of premiums for increased sales.
NOC*, OClWHi.

331 Seven Times Nine are Sixty-three. [New
York: 188–?]. 32 pp. illus. 15 cm.
The title is from the front cover, verso; bare-
foot child standing with her arms pressed
against a wall, front cover, recto. Woman is
described and pictured by decades, from
babyhood to 100 years of age, with "7X8"
labelled "decline of life," and "7X9" labelled
"old age." Advertisements and testimonials
for Mother Seigel's Syrup (Extract of Roots)
which will arrest the signs of old age.
MPB*.

332 Shaker Family Pills Cure Sick Headache.
New York: A. J. White, [n.d.]. Cover title,
[2] pp. 20 cm.
"For constipation, sluggish liver, and the im-
mediate symptoms and effects of biliousness."
Private collection.

333 Shaker Soothing Plasters. Good for Back-
ache. New York: A. J. White, [n.d.]. [2] pp.
illus. 12½ X 8 cm.

Small advertising flyer showing colored picture of a little girl, p. [1]; account of the curative properties, p. [2], "lumbago, muscular rheumatism, all pain and lameness in any part of the body, and for every ailment in which an external application is desirable and valuable."
NOC*.

334 Thomas A. Edison as He now Appears. [And] as He Will Appear When He is Old. [New York: A. J. White, 1889?]. 32 pp. illus. 15½ cm.

Contemporary portraits of Edison and other prominent persons, and altered portraits which depict the changes that will occur in old age. Among its therapeutic values, Shaker Extract of Roots (Seigel's Syrup) will arrest the aging process and increase longevity. "The health and vigor of the Shakers has furnished proof of its secret power." The latest testimonial is dated March 20th, 1889. KySP, NOC*.

335 Vanderbilt's Candy Church: The Kings of the Kitchen. [New York: A. J. White, 1889]. Cover title. 32 pp. ports. 15 cm.

Includes short biographies and portraits of professional chefs (New York), Shaker recipes, advertisements and testimonials for Seigel's Syrup (Extract of Roots). The latest testimonial is dated Nov. 1888. Facsimile of ms. sworn statement, back cover, verso: "We hereby certify that *Shaker Extract of Roots,* or *Seigel's Curative Syrup,* Sold by A. J. White, 168 Duane Street, New York; is Manufactured, Bottled & Wrapped at the Laboratory of the Shaker Community at Mount Lebanon, Columbia Co., N.Y." Signed: *Trustees, Benjamin Gates, Robert Valentine.* Sworn statement, 31st Jan. 1889, is notarized by J. Henry Cox, Notary Public. Contains a calendar for 1889; this item may be another version of White's *Almanac* for 1889, *see* no. 29.
MeHi*, MWiW.

MT. LEBANON (formerly New Lebanon), N.Y.
Miscellaneous

336 Analysis, Artesian Well Water of Mt. Leba-

non, N.Y. by Professor S. C. Chandler, Union College, N.Y. [n.p., n.d.]. Broadside card. 14 X 19 cm.
Describes the chemical content of the water. N, OClWHi*.

337 Directions for Setting and Using Corn Cutting Machine. [n.p., 187-?]. Broadside. 30 X 12½ cm.

An engraved illustration of the machine, signed: *Ferguson, Albany,* precedes title. The instructions are numbered, 1st-9th. OClWHi*.

338 Fancy Oval Covered Wooden Boxes. [n.p., n.d.]. 4 pp.
This entry was furnished by Syracuse University Library. The publication includes Shakers' upholstered chairs without arms; Shakers' upholstered chairs with arms, and rockers; directions for ordering chairs. NSyU*.

339 Green Corn Cutting Machine. Patented Feb. 23rd 1875. By Wm. J. Potter, Mt. Lebanon, N.Y. [n.p., 1876]. [4] pp. 14½ cm.

This advertising folder, circulated at the Philadelphia Centennial, 1876, includes instructions for use, description, etc. "The price of the machine is $200.00 delivered on the cars." Inquiries to be addressed to R. M. Wagan, or Wm. J. Potter, Mount Lebanon ... OClWHi*.

340 Honey. Soul of Flowers to Sweeten the Soul of Man. Shakers North Family. Mt. Lebanon, Columbia Co., N.Y.: [19- -]. Cover title, [4] pp. 18 cm.

Price list of extracted and comb honey. W. H. Cathcart's ms. note on the Western Reserve Historical Society (Cleveland, O.) copy gives the information that the Art Nouveau cover "was designed by Brother Peter Neagoe, a Roumanian living at the North Family, Mount Lebanon, N.Y. in 1906." MPB, MWA, MWiW*, OClWHi.

341 Levi Shaw, Manufacturer of and Wholesale Dealer in Shaker Carpet and Rug Whips ... [Mt. Lebanon, N.Y.?: 1902?]. Broadside. illus. 25 X 16 cm.
MWiW*.

342 Levi Shaw, Manufacturer of Wire and
Rattan Goods, Mt. Lebanon, N.Y.: 1903.
Broadside. illus. 25 × 19 cm.
   Reproduction of a typewritten letter, dated
   1/20/1902, corrected in ink to *1903*.
   MWiW*.

343 Products of Intelligence and Diligence.
Shakers Church Family. Mount Lebanon, Col.
Co., N.Y.: [1908]. Cover title. 16, [1] pp.
illus. 18 cm.
   Priced catalog of Shaker-made articles includ-
   ing hoods, cloaks, bags, dolls, boxes, etc.
   The cover is modified Art Nouveau designed
   by Peter Neagoe, a Roumanian living in the
   North Family at Mt. Lebanon.
   KyBgW, MPB, N, NBuG, NOC, OClWHi*,
   PPULC.

344 .... Shaker Carpet and Rug Beaters. [n.p.,
n.d.]. Broadside. 24 × 15 cm.
   At end: North Family Shakers, Mount Lebanon, New York. Daniel Offord, Agent. A
   corrugated spring-wire beater, coppered
   spring-wire loop beater, and rattan beater
   are described and illustrated. Patent No.
   613120, granted October 25, 1898, to
   Charles M. Comstock, Windsor, N.Y., was
   assigned to Levi Shaw; Comstock went to
   Mt. Lebanon to instruct the Shakers in the
   manufacture of the wire carpet beater and
   other wire products.
   OClWHi*.

345 The Shaker Cloak. [Mt. Lebanon, N.Y.:
n.d.]. [2] 11. illus. 17½ cm.
   A form letter with blank spaces for the name
   of the addressee and the date. A cover photograph shows front and back views of the
   Shaker cloak. A label showing the front and
   back views of the floor-length Shaker cloak
   with attached hood was registered (U.S.
   Patent Office) under the name, E. J. Neale &
   Co., Mt. Lebanon, N.Y., Nov. 26, 1901. No.
   37336. The fancy silk-ribbon bookmarks
   used to advertise the Shaker cloak and the
   silk labels sewn into the garment have not
   been included in the bibliography.
   MPB, MWiW*, N, NOC, OClWHi.

Pleasant Hill, Ky. Medicines

346 Pure Reliable Medicines! Manufactured
and for Sale by the Shakers, Pleasant Hill, Ky.
[n.p.] Reynolds & Pierce, Printers, [1877].
   This entry is made from a photograph found
   on the February panel of the 1972 calendar
   published by Shakertown at Pleasant Hill,
   Ky., *see* no. 2746.
   KySP*.

347 Shakers' Aromatic Elixir of Malt. [Louis-
ville, Ky.: 1888–?]. Broadside. 19½ × 13 cm.
   Advertising broadside. "Manufactured ex-
   clusively by the Shakers, at Pleasant Hill,
   Mercer Co., Ky., under the supervision of
   R. B. Rupe, M.D., Pharmacist." Orders are
   to be addressed to E. S. Sutton, General
   Agent, Louisville, Ky. The manufacture of
   malt elixir, 1880–1883, was a short-lived
   enterprise. Sutton marketed the product
   successfully, but lack of profits caused the
   Shakers to abandon the undertaking, F. G.
   Ham, "Pleasant Hill ... 1805–1910" (M.A.
   Thesis, U. of Ky., 1955), 244–45.
   KySP*.

*SABBATHDAY LAKE, ME. (formerly New
Gloucester, including Poland Hill).* Fancy Goods

348 Catalog of Fancy Goods. The Shaker Cloak
and many other Articles, made at Shaker Vil-
lage, Sabbathday Lake, Cumberland County,
Maine. [Poland, Me.: Printed at Ye Chipman
Printery, 1907]. 18 [1] pp. illus. 14 cm.
   MiU–C, OClWHi*.

349 ———— [n.p.], 1910. illus. 14 cm.
   OClWHi*.

350 For Sale the Celebrated Shaker Goods. A
Great Variety of Ladies' Basket Work, Pin
Cushions, Needle Books ... [Sabbathday Lake,
Me.: 1883]. Broadside. 27½ × 19 cm.
   Signed: *Otis Sawyer. Continental House* and
   Aug. 15, 1883 have been supplied in ink.
   Private collection.

351 Price List of Goods Manufactured and for

Sale. Sabbathday Lake, Maine: [n.d.]. [3] pp.
15½ cm.
   Includes handkerchief boxes, knitted goods,
   notions, wooden oval carriers, etc.
   Private collection.

352 The Shaker Cloak. Sabbathday Lake, Me.:
[191-?]. Broadside. 14 × 13 cm.
   Signed: *Lizzie M. Noyes, Sabbathday Lake,
   Me.* Includes prices and a list of the measure-
   ments to be sent with orders.
   Private collection.

*SABBATHDAY LAKE, ME. (formerly New
Gloucester, including Poland Hill).* Fruit Plants

353 A New Grape! Stewart's New Seedling
Grape! [n.p., 1855]. Broadside. illus. 29½ × 23
cm.
   At end: P. Stewart, West Gloucester, Cumberland County, Me. "This is the first season
   that I have suffered a root, or slip of this
   grape to go out of my garden." Special
   prices are announced for purchasers who
   sign bonds "to the amount of $50, to keep
   it entirely in their own hands for 4 years to
   come." An advertising handbill with a cut of
   a bunch of grapes, and testimonials reprinted
   from newspapers. This broadside is reprinted
   in D. C. Smith, "William A. Drew and the
   Maine Shakers," *Shaker Quarterly,* 7 (Spring
   1967), opp. p. 30 (no. **1299**), where the date
   1855 is assigned. *See also* nos. **773** and **970**.
   Private collection.

354 Premium Wine Grape! At N.Y. State Fair,
Albany, October, 1859. To All Interested in
Growing the Grape either for Wine or for the
Table .... P. Stewart, Producer, Isaiah Wentworth, as General Agent for the Eastern States.
Post Office Address, West Gloucester, Cumberland County, Maine. Portland [Me.]: Tucker,
Caloric Power Job Printer, [1859]. Broadside.
illus. 52½ × 30 cm.
   Advertising flyer for the Northern Muscadine Grape and the Mountain Seedling Gooseberry, a new variety. A cut of a bunch of
   grapes, shown on its side with the stem facing
   the left margin, is referred to as "a facsimile."
   Private collection.

355 ———— To All Interested in the Growing of
the Grape for Wine or the Table. Portland [Me.]:
David Tucker, Job Printer, [1859]. Broadside.
illus.
   At end: Address P. Stewart, Producer, Post
   Office Address, West Gloucester, Cumberland
   County, Maine. Advertising handbill for the
   Northern Muscadine Grape with cut of a
   bunch of grapes and directions for planting,
   training, and pruning; also advertises the
   Mountain Seedling Gooseberry with cut of
   gooseberries and directions for setting and
   training. This entry has been made from a
   microprint which did not include the size.
   It appears to be slightly longer than no. **354**
   and very much wider.
   Private collection.

356 Strawberries! The Mammoth King, 12 or 14
of the Berries often Weighing a Pound, said by
Horticulturists Generally to be the Largest
Strawberry in the World, Called the Austin Seed-
ling .... Portland, Me.: David Tucker, Printer,
1861. Broadside. 30 × 23 cm.
   At end, signed: *P. Stewart, West Gloucester,
   Cumberland Co., Me., Poland, August 30th,
   1861.* Directions for preparing the soil and
   the cultivation of the strawberry are given.
   This strawberry "originated by the Society of
   Shakers near Albany, N.Y." The lower half of
   the handbill advertises, "Roots also, of the
   Genuine Muscadine Grape."
   OClWHi*.

357 ———— Address P. Stewart, West Gloucester,
Cumberland Co., Poland May 9th, 1862. Port-
land [Me.]: David Tucker, Job Printer, [1862].
Broadside. 30 × 24 cm.
   Printed on mauve colored paper.
   OClWHi*.

*SABBATHDAY LAKE, ME. (formerly New
Gloucester, incl. Poland Hill).* Medicinal
Herbs, Medicines, Etc.

358 Catalogue of Herbs, Roots, Barks, Powdered Articles, &c., Prepared in the United Society, New Gloucester, Maine. Orders Addressed to
Charles Vining, West Gloucester, Maine, will meet
with Prompt Attention. Portland [Me.]: B.
Thurston, Printer, 1864. 15 pp. 22½ cm.

This is the Society's "first printed catalogue of herbs, roots, barks, and powders," *Shaker Quarterly*, 2 (Spring 1962), 39. Charles Vining is given as author, *ibid.*, 11 (Winter 1971), 175. "N.B. The Botanical names have been revised by Prof. Gray of Harvard College, Mass.," p. [3]. Common names are given for 211 herbs, etc., with the botanical names, properties, and prices per lb., pp. [5]-10, with 4 sweet herbs available in cannisters, p. [11], and "Synonyms" (common name equivalents), pp. [12]-15.
MacLean 164. DLC, MPB, MWiW*, NBuG, NN, NOC.

359 ——— (Reprint). Sabbathday Lake, Me.: United Society, 1972. (Hands to Work Series, No. 2).

360 Catalogue of Medicinal Plants Prepared in the United Society of "Shakers." New Gloucester, Cumberland County, Maine: [n.d.]. Broadside in 2 columns. 35½ × 15½ cm.
A list of 83 herbs with common names and prices per paper. Saffron sells at 60¢; other prices are from 8¢ to 33¢.
OClWHi*.

361 Poland Mineral Springs. Medicinal Water from the Newly Discovered Springs on Poland Hill, Maine. [n.p., n.d.]. Broadside. 54 × 33 cm.
"N.B. This medicine alone, or in combination with these waters can only be had of the subscriber, who is now located in the Society of Shakers, on Poland Hill, Maine ..." Orders, etc., should be addressed to P. Stewart, West Gloucester, Cumberland County, Maine. This is an advertising broadside which describes a cure for scrofula, cholera morbus, rheumatism, healthy secretion of the kidneys and liver, and other physical complaints. *See also* no. 2626 ff.
Private collection.

362 The Shaker Tamar Laxative. [n.p., 1884?]. Caption title, [4] pp. 20½ cm.
"The West Gloucester Society are the only *Shakers* who make the Shaker Tamar Laxative, and all others bearing the name of *Shakers* are not genuine." Address William Dumont, Trustee of Shaker Society, West

Gloucester, Me. This is an advertising flyer with testimonials; the latest is dated: Dec. 13, 1883. The history and formula for this medicine are found in "The Tamar Fruit Compound ..." by Frances Carr, *Shaker Quarterly*, 2 (Spring 1962), 39-41.
Private collection.

363 The Shaker Tamar Laxative, A Fruit Lozenge ... Put up by Shaker Society, West Gloucester, Me. H. Chandler, Agent. [n.p., 189-?]. [4] pp. 13 × 7 cm.
An advertising novelty (2 cards joined with a metal holder) which includes "A Perpetual Gregorian Calendar commencing Oct. 15, 1852, and continuing indefinitely."
Private collection.

364 The Shaker Tamar Laxative for Constipation. Price List ... H. Chandler, West Gloucester, Me. [n.p., 189-?]. Broadside. 7½ × 14½ cm.
Private collection.

SABBATHDAY LAKE, ME. (formerly New Gloucester, incl. Poland Hill). Miscellaneous

365 Get the Best Mower. The Improved Shakers' Maine Mower for Ease of Draft, Durability, Perfection, and Beauty of Execution .... Manufactured by the United Society of Shakers, West Gloucester, Me. Hewitt Chandler, Trustee. By Whom all Orders will be Promptly Filled. A. Briggs, Travelling Agent. West Gloucester: June 1866. Broadside. illus. 24½ × 19½ cm.
Illustrated with a cut of the mower. Recommendations for the mower are dated 1865. The patent was granted August 22, 1865, *see* no. 1142.
Private collection.

366 ... The Improved Shakers' Maine Mower! .... Manufactured by the United Society of Shakers, West Gloucester, Me. Hewitt Chandler, Trustee. By whom all Orders will be Promptly filled. A. Briggs, Travelling Agent. Portland [Me.]: Tucker Printers, 1866. Broadside. illus. 24½ × 19½ cm.
OClWHi*.

367 Wool Carding. For the Convenience of Farmers and the Public in General the Under-

signed Gives Notice that He Is Prepared to Card Wool This Season in the Shakers' New Mill .... West Gloucester, Shaker Village: 1856. Broadside. 29½ X 24½ cm.

> Signed: *Ranson Gilman. Shaker Village, West Gloucester, June 1856.*
> Private collection.

SHIRLEY, MASS. Seeds

368 Garden Seeds Raised at Shirley, Massachusetts, and Sold by [blank space for name to be supplied] among which are the Following: [n.p., 180–?]. Broadside in 2 columns. 21½ X 18½ cm.

> An unpriced list of 27 varieties of seeds (including 5 herbs) with the seeds for sale by the ounce in the first column and by "papers" in the second column. The copy described here is a completed order for $11.70, with the individual prices supplied in ink. The name *Oliver Burt* has been supplied in ink in the title and a ms. note on the verso has date *Oct. 27th* (29th?), but a mutilation has obscured the year. This appears to be an earlier printing than the following seed broadside.
> MPB*.

369 ──── [n.p., 181–?]. Broadside in 2 columns. 21½ X 17½ cm. (trimmed).

> This is a different printing than the foregoing seed list. It lists 28 varieties of seeds (including 5 herbs). "Tunip (turnip) Raddish" and "Salmon Raddish" have replaced "Raddish" in the foregoing list. The name *Oliver Burt* has been supplied in ink in the title, and ms. note on verso is dated *1810 March 2. Received payment for the within of H. Masters & Son.* The Williams College copy (Williamstown, Mass.) has ms. note on verso dated *Feb. 11th* [?] *1811.*
> MHarF*, MWiW.

370 ──── and Sold by 182– . [blank space for the name to be supplied]. Among which are the Following: [n.p., 182–?]. Broadside in 2 columns. 18½ X 15 cm.

> A list of 29 varieties of seeds (including 4 herbs) for sale in "Papers"; the prices to be supplied in ink. The date in the title has been completed: 1826.
> OClWHi*.

371 ──── and Sold by 183–. [blank space for name to be supplied]. Among which are the Following: [n.p.], Carter Andrews, & Co. Print., [183–.]. Broadside in 2 columns. 21½ X 17½ cm.

> A list of 33 varieties of seeds (including 3 herbs) for sale in "Papers"; the prices to be supplied in ink. "For Augustus Haven Ludlow," ms. note at top.
> OClWHi*.

372 Garden Seeds, Fresh and Genuine, Raised and Put Up by the United Society. Shirley Village, Mass. Boston: Franklin Printing House, [1855]. Broadside in 2 columns. 26 X 17½ cm.

> "Orders Addressed to Jonas Nutting ... will be punctually attended to." A list of 43 varieties of seeds, mostly vegetable. The date has been completed: 1855. Printed on heavy stock blue paper.
> OClWHi*.

373 ──── Fitchburg, Mass.: [186–?]. Broadside in 2 columns. 25 X 19½ cm.

> The date in the title has been filled in: 1865. Printed on thin white paper.
> OClWHi*.

SOUTH UNION, KY. Livestock and Poultry

374 Poultry! ... The Improved Light Brahmas and Partridge Cochin Fowls. [n.p., n.d.]. Broadside. 20½ X 12½ cm.

> Signed: *Jane Cowan, South Union, Ky. December 1876.* A priced list of fowls for sale.
> OClWHi*.

375 Sale Catalogue of the Centre-House Herd of Thoroughbred Durham Cattle, the Property of the United Society of Shakers at South Union, Ky. 1882. [n.p., n.d.]. 1 p.l., 19 pp. illus. 23 cm.

> Cover title: Annual Sale Catalogue of Shorthorns. Bred by the Shakers, South Union, Ky. "The animals are all bred by the Shakers, and are either recorded or eligible for record in the American Herd Book" (no. 1741). Includes

23 lots of cattle, Cotswold sheep, Poland China and Berkshire hogs, Light Brahmas, Plymouth Rock, Partridge Cochin chickens, and Shaker garden seeds. "Address H. L. Eads, South Union, Logan County, Ky." OClWHi*.

376 Shakers' Farm Annual. South Union, Ky.: 1885. 32 pp. illus. 19 cm.

This publication was described in *The Manifesto*, 15 (September 1885), 214, as having "a long list of choice Kitchen, Garden Seeds. A notice of one hundred head of Pure Bred, registered Short Horns, from five to eighteen months old. A chapter on Shaker Preserves ... notice of brooms ... An extended account of Improved Breeds of Poultry they have for sale, is clearly set forth in an illustrated article ... Orders addressed to H. L. Eads, Trustee."
MacLean 179. DLC, KyU, NOC*, OClWHi.

377 Shakers, South Union, Ky. Breeders of Choice Light Brahmas, also, Partridge Cochins of First Quality. Having by Experience Learned that these two Varieties make the Best Returns of any known. Price of Eggs for Hatching Follows ... Louisville, Ky.: Courier-Journal Print., [1877]. [2] pp. 21½ cm.

Description of Brahma breeding stock, verso.
MiU-C, OClWHi*.

SOUTH UNION, KY. Miscellaneous

378 Fulling Mill. The Society Called Shakers, in Logan County, Ky. Continue Their Fulling Mill in Operation. Their Customers ... Russellville, Ky.: Printed at the Office of the Weekly Messenger, 1815. Broadside. 20 cm.

Signed: *John McComb, Sam'l G. Whyte, agents. South Union, Jasper Springs, September 12th, 1815.* Lists the stores where customers may leave cloth and find printed instructions for its preparation, *see* no. 379. The mill opened January 1815. The Western Reserve Historical Society (Cleveland, O.) copy has not been cut away from the *Instructions* ... (no. 379), and together they measure 51½ X 23 cm. in one sheet.
Shaw 35910. DLC, KyBgW*, OClWHi.

379 ... Instructions for the Information and Benefit of Domestic Manufacturers in Woolen Cloths. Russellville, Ky.: Printed at the Office of the Weekly Messenger, 1815. Broadside in 2 columns. 20 X 17 cm.

At head of title: Public Utility, at end: South Union, Logan County, Sept. 12, 1815. Detailed instructions for the preparation of wool and cloth to be dressed at the Shaker fulling mill. This was printed on a sheet with *Fulling Mill* (no. 378). Western Reserve Historical Society (Cleveland, O.) copy is intact. Together they measure 51½ X 23 cm.
KyBgW*, NOC, OClWHi.

380 Shaker Sash Balance, Patented by S. J. Russell, July 16, 1872. Improved and Perfected with Cord-holder Attachment, Feb'y 1, 1875 .... [n.p., 1875?]. Broadside. illus. 35 X 21 cm.

Includes instructions for operating the balance, with illustration showing the sash balance and cord. At end: "Good agents wanted, for further particulars, samples, etc., address, S. J. Russell, So. Union." *See also* no. 1163.
NOC*.

381 Shakers' Cholera Remedy! Made and Put Up by the United Society of Shakers at South Union .... [n.p., n.d.]. Broadside. 46½ X 31½ cm.

"The remedy was discovered by Dr. J. P. Holmes, deceased, late member of the Royal College of Surgeons, London ... from whom we obtained the formula." A statement of the efficacy of this remedy in the London epidemics is signed: *J. P. Holmes, M.D.* "Orders by mail will receive prompt attention. Address Pearcifield & McGown, South Union, Ky." OClWHi*.

SOUTH UNION, KY. Seeds

382 Catalogue of Garden Seeds. Cultivated by the Shakers at South Union, Ky. Bowling Green, Ky.: Gazette Print., 1884. Cover title, [4] pp. 21½ cm.

Orders are to be mailed to H. L. Eads, South Union, Ky. Order Blank for dealers, p. [4].
NOC*, OClWHi.

383 ———— From the Shakers at South Union, Ky.

Crop of 1873. [n.p., 1873]. Broadside. 32 ✕ 13½ cm.

A list of 48 varieties of vegetable seeds. "Terms Cash.—5 cents per paper. The seed will be shipped by express C.O.D. freight pre-paid unless otherwise ordered. Address U. E. Johns, South Union, Ky." OClWHi*.

384 ——— From U.E. Johns. South Union, Ky. Crop of 1872. [n.p., 1872]. Broadside. 32 ✕ 14 cm.

A list of 51 varieties of vegetable seeds. OClWHi*.

385 ——— Grown by the Shakers at South Union, Ky. Crop of 1875. [n.p., 1875]. Broadside. 34 ✕ 13½ cm.

A list of 45 varieties of vegetable seeds, preceded by "Number of Papers in Assorted Box," and at end, "300—Total Number of Papers." This list itemizes the contents of a Shaker compartmentalized display seed box sold to storekeepers. OClWHi*.

386 ——— Grown by the Shakers at South Union, Ky., For the Spring of 1877. [n.p., 1877?]. Broadside. 32 ✕ 13 cm.

A list of 48 varieties of vegetable seeds, intended for Shaker seed display boxes. The amounts and varieties vary somewhat from the foregoing list. OClWHi*.

387 Catalogue of Shaker Garden Seeds. Grown at South Union, Ky. Crop of 1867. [n.p., 1867]. Broadside in 2 columns. 37 ✕ 26 cm.

A list of 67 varieties of vegetable seeds. Orders to be addressed to U. E. Johns, South Union, Ky. KyBgW, MHarF, OClWHi*.

388 ——— Crop of 1868. [n.p., 1868]. Broadside in 2 columns. 35 ✕ 21½ cm.

A list of 65 varieties of vegetable seeds. OClWHi*.

389 ——— Crop of 1869. [n.p., 1869]. Broadside in 2 columns. 35 ✕ 21½ cm.

A list of 67 varieties of vegetable seeds. OClWHi*.

390 ——— Crop of 1870. [n.p., 1870]. Broadside in 2 columns. 35 ✕ 21½ cm.

A list of 61 varieties of vegetable seeds. Statement near the end includes the information that "South Union Seed Gardens ... have been in successful operation for about half a century." OClWHi*.

391 ——— Crop of 1871. [n.p., 1871]. Broadside in 2 columns. 35 ✕ 21½ cm.

A list of 58 varieties of vegetable seeds. MiU–C, OClWHi*.

392 Garden Seed. Crop of 1856. Cultivated by the Shakers, at South-Union, Ky. [n.p., 1856]. Broadside. 30 ✕ 11½ cm.

A list of 38 varieties of vegetable seeds, preceded by "No. of Papers." The printed total is "150 Papers," intended for a Shaker compartmentalized display seed box for storekeepers. At end, "Orders for Garden Seeds or Sweet Meats" [sic] should be directed to John M'Lean, South-Union, Logan County, Ky." OClWHi*.

393 ——— Crop of 1858. Cultivated by the Shakers, at South-Union, Ky. [n.p., 1858]. Broadside. 31½ ✕ 11½ cm.

A list of 44 varieties of vegetable seeds intended for Shaker seed display box. OClWHi*.

394 ——— Crop of 1861. Cultivated by the Shakers, at South-Union, Ky. [n.p., 1861]. Broadside. 29½ ✕ 11½ cm.

A list of 34 varieties of vegetable seeds, intended for Shaker seed display boxes. No directions or name given for addressing orders. OClWHi*.

395 ——— Crop of 1853. Grown by the Shakers, at South-Union, Ky., [n.p., 1853]. Broadside. 31 ✕ 11½ cm.

A list of 42 varieties of vegetable seeds. At end, "N.B. Orders ... should be forwarded to South Union, Ky. As early as the first or middle of October. John M'Lean, Agent." OClWHi*.

396 Garden Seed. Grown by the Shakers, at South Union, Ky. Crop of 1866. [n.p., 1866]. Broadside. 34½ × 13 cm.
  A list of 46 varieties of vegetable seeds. At end, "Address U. E. Johns, South Union, Ky." OClWHi*.

397 ――――― Crop of 1868. [n.p., 1868]. Broadside. 34½ × 15 cm.
  A list of 47 varieties of vegetable seeds. OClWHi*.

398 ――――― Crop of 1869. [n.p., 1869]. Broadside. 31½ × 13 cm.
  A list of 43 varieties of vegetable seeds. OClWHi*.

399 ――――― Crop of 1870. [n.p., 1870]. Broadside in 2 columns. 34½ × 13½ cm.
  A list of 48 varieties of vegetable seeds. MiU-C, OClWHi*.

400 ――――― Crop of 1871. [n.p., 1871]. Broadside. 36½ × 12½ cm.
  A list of 56 varieties of vegetable seeds. MiU-C*.

401 ――――― Crop of 1850. Raised at South Union, Ky. [n.p., 1849]. Broadside. 31 × 12 cm.
  A list of 38 varieties of vegetable seeds. OClWHi*.

402 ――――― Raised at South Union, Ky. [n.p., 18-?]. Broadside. 31 × 9½ cm.
  An undated list of 34 varieties of vegetable seeds which appears to be the earliest South Union seed list that has been located. OClWHi*.

403 Garden Seeds. Crop of 1872. [n.p., 1872]. Broadside. 32 × 13½ cm.
  A list of 48 varieties of vegetable seeds. OClWHi*.

404 Crop of 1873. [n.p., 1873]. Broadside. 32 × 13½ cm.

A list of 41 varieties of vegetable seeds. OClWHi*.

405 Just Received, a New Assortment of Choice Garden Seeds, Raised and Put Up in the Best Manner by the United Society of Shakers, at South Union, Jasper Valley, Logan County, Ky., and Marked with the Name, and the Retail Price of the Seeds, and the Letters E.M.S.U. For Sale [blank space for name to be supplied]. Bowling Green, Ky.: Gazette (?) and Advertiser Office, [n.d.]. Broadside. 18½ × 26 cm.
  An advertising broadside or handbill. The letters in the title are the initials of Eli McLean, South Union. OClWHi*.

406 Shakers' Catalogue of Garden Seeds, Grown at South Union, Ky. Crop of 1866. [n.p., 1866]. Broadside. 30½ × 19 cm.
  A list of 62 varieties of vegetable seeds. MHarF, OClWHi*.

407 ――――― Crop of 1876. [n.p., 1876]. Broadside 32½ × 19 cm.
  A list of 45 varieties of vegetable seeds. Orders to be addressed to U. E. Johns, South Union, Ky. OClWHi*.

TYRINGHAM, MASS. Seeds

408 Catalogue of Garden Seeds, Raised by the United Society of Shakers in Tyringham, Berkshire County, Mass. Lee, Mass.: French and Royce, Printers, 185 . Broadside in 2 columns. 32 × 20 cm.
  A list of 67 varieties of seeds, mostly vegetable, for sale in "papers." At end, "All Orders for Seeds to be Directed to South Lee Post-Office ... to Willard Johnson, Agent." MHarF*.

409 Seeds. Garden Seeds, Raised at Tyringham, Berkshire County, Mass. And Put Up in Papers with the Retailing Prices of the Seeds on them. For Sale by [blank space for name to be supplied] Among which are the Following:– [n.p., 182-?]. Broadside. 31 × 10½ cm.
  A list of 26 varieties of seeds priced from 4¢ to 12¢. The copy described here is a com-

pleted order for $7.00 with credit for seeds returned. A ms. notation is signed: *Freeman Stanley, May 1826.* A photograph of this list is found opp. p. 38 in M. F. Sommer, *Shaker Seed Industry,* no. 2790.
NOC, OClWHi*.

UNION VILLAGE, O. Medicinal Herbs, Etc.

410 Annual Wholesale Catalogue, of Herbs, Medical Plants; Also Extracts, Essential Oils, Double Distilled and Fragrant Waters. Prepared, and for Sale by the United Society of Shakers, at Union Village .... Orders addressed to Peter Boyd, Union Village, near Lebanon, Ohio, will meet with prompt Attention. Union Village, Ohio: Printed by G. H. Vandever, 1850. 11 [1] pp. 18 cm.

The text of the cover title and title page is identical. An alphabetical list of over 250 medicinal herbs, etc., under the common names, followed by the prices per lb., and the botanical names, pp. [3]-8; extracts, inspissated juices, essential oils, pulverized sweet herbs, etc., pp. 10-11; testimonials for "Compound Fluid Extract of Sarsaparilla," p. [1], at end. "The common names in the Catalogue are such as are in use in the Cities of Cincinnati, St. Louis, Louisville, New Orleans, &c. The Botanical names are from Eaton's *Manual of Botany,* Griffith's *Medical Botany,* and Rafinesque's *Medical Flora."*
CSmH, DLC, MH, MPB, MWA, MWiW*, NBuG, NOC, OHi, OCHP, OClWHi, WHi.

411 ———— Printed at Union Village, Warren County, Ohio: 1856.

No copy has been located. Western Reserve Historical Society has a trial pull of the cover which indicates that an 1856 edition was printed. It is possible, however, that only the cover of an earlier edition was replaced by one of a later date.

412 Catalogue of Medical Plants, Extracts, Essential Oils, Etc. Prepared and for Sale by the United Society of Shakers, at Union Village, O. [Lebanon, O.?: n.d.]. [4] pp. 20½ cm.

A list of about 175 medicinal herbs and 18 extracts, etc. Orders are to be directed to:

A. Babbitt, Lebanon P.O. [Shaker Box], Warren County, Ohio.
MWA, OClWHi*.

413 Catalogue of Medical Plants, and Extracts; to which are Affixed their most Prominent Medical Properties. Also Essential Oils, and Double Distilled Fragrant Waters. Prepared and for Sale by the United Society of Shakers at Union Village, Ohio ... Union Village, O.: Day Star Print., Jan. 1847. 8 pp. 20½ cm.

"Orders addressed to Peter Boyd, Union Village, Lebanon Post Office, Ohio, will meet with prompt attention." J. P. MacLean states that "The botanical catalogues of 1847 and 1850 were printed" on Richard McNemar's Press, *Life* (no. 2411), p. 61.
OClWHi*.

UNION VILLAGE, O. Medicines

414 A Brief History of the Shaker Community of Union Village, O. [Lebanon, O.?: 188-?]. Caption title. 8 pp. illus. 23 cm.

Authorship has been attributed to Peter Boyd and also to Charles Sumner, who is reputed to have read this work first as a lecture. A short history of the Union Village Shaker community is followed by a discussion of the merits of The Shakers' Extract of Sarsaparilla. A notarized unanimous endorsement by the Lebanon, O., Medical Society, Oct. 29, 1849, testifies to "the purity of the Pharmaceutical preparations of the Shakers ... especially the extracts of the narcotic plants and of sarsaparilla." The caption under the portrait of Peter Boyd, p. [1], describes him as "82 years a Shaker." Electroplate illustrations show several buildings of the Union Village community.
N, OClWHi*.

415 Howe, S. D. & Co. Dr. S.[tewart] D. Howe's Shaker Extract Compound Sarsaparilla. Cincinnati, O.: Stereotyped by A. C. James, [185-?]. Cover title. [4] pp. illus. 27 cm.

Advertising leaflet, signed at end: *S. D. Howe & Co., Proprietors, No. 1, College Hall, Cincinnati.* The bust of a Shaker brother is shown on the cover title, and a Shaker brother is shown holding a sarsaparilla bottle, back

cover, verso. A testimonial, signed: *D. M. Bennett (Mar. 1, 1849)*, states that this is the same recipe as that used by the Shakers in New York and New Hampshire. Bennett, formerly physician to the New Lebanon, N.Y., Society, seceded in 1846 (*see* no. 74), and it may be fairly assumed that he furnished Dr. Howe with the formula for Howe's "Shaker Sarsaparilla." *See* annotation no. 419 for the Shakers' precaution against such deceptions.
NOC*.

416 The Influence of the Shaker Doctor [Dr. Louis Turner]. [n.p., 1849]. 10 pp. illus. 23½ cm.
Advertising circular for medicines made by the Shakers at Union Village, Ohio.
NOC, OClWHi*.

417 The Influence of the Shaker Doctor, Dr. Zusser. St. Louis, Mo.: [n.d.]. 8 pp. illus. 25½ cm.
OClWHi*.

418 Shaker Cough Syrup. [n.p., n.d.]. Broadside. 25½ × 16 cm.
"The Extract is made with cold alcohol ... Besides the Wild Cherry, squills, and Seneca Snake-root are the leading ingredients of Shaker Cough Syrup. Rhubarb is also added ... Morphia and Antimony, in very small proportions, are the remaining constituents." Nothing in the printed text of this broadside indicates that the cough syrup was made at Union Village, O., but this designation has been supplied in ink in a space at the end.
MWiW*, OClWHi.

419 Shaker Sarsaparilla. [Union Village, O.?: n.d.]. Broadside. 28 × 26 cm.
A statement about the quality, ingredients, and diseases which this medicine will benefit. "It is well known, that the general character of the Extract of Sarsaparilla now in the market, is deficient in quality ... To prevent imposition we have procured a mould for bottles, lettered as follows: 'Shaker Sarsaparilla, prepared by the United Society, at Union Village, Ohio, P. Boyd, Agent. All prepared at Union Village bears the <u>facsimile</u>

signature of Peter Boyd'." *See also* no. 2759.
DLC, MWiW*, OClWHi.

420 The Welcome Letter. Illustrated Monthly Published for the United Society of Shakers Union Village, Warren Co., Ohio. St. Louis, Mo.: Welcome Letter Publishing Co., [1890?]. 16 pp. illus. 18 cm.
Case history of a miraculous cure with Shaker Wonder Drug, pp. 1–2; short account of Shaker history, with portraits, pp. 3–5; jokes, homely sayings, anecdotes scattered through advertisements and testimonials for Shaker medicines marketed by Dr. Louis Turner, Shaker Medicine Co., 1533 Franklin St., St. Louis, Mo. Calendar for 1891, back cover, verso.
OClWHi*.

UNION VILLAGE, O. Miscellaneous

421 Catalogue of Short Horn Cattle, Owned by the Shakers at Union Village, Warren Co., Ohio. To be Sold on the Fair Grounds, at Lebanon, Ohio, on Thursday, October 13, 1859. Commencing at 10 O'clock A.M. ... Union Village, Ohio: [1859]. 18 pp. illus. 24 cm.
"Terms of the sale. A credit of six months, without interest, or of fifteen months, with interest at six percent; notes with approved security required. A discount of eight percent on cash payments," from the title page. *See also* no. 1741.
DLC*.

422 Shaker Community Wines. A Treatise on Pure Wines and its Beneficial Uses. Shaker Community Wine Growers, Wm. G. Ayer, Assistant Trustee, Union Village, Ohio. Vineyards on the Shores of Lake Erie ... Established 1805. [n.p., n.d.]. Cover title. [11] pp. illus. 17½ cm.
"Shaker wines are medicinal wines. They are for medicinal purposes ... Above all things they are not incentives to drunkeness."
DLC, OClWHi*.

WATERVLIET (formerly Niskayuna), N.Y. Medicinal Herbs

423 Catalogue of Herbs, Medicinal Plants, and Vegetable Medicines, with their Theapeutic [sic]

Qualities and Botanical Names; Also, Extracts, Ointments, Essential Oils, Double Distilled and Fragrant Waters; With a List of Garden Seeds .... Raised, Prepared and Put Up in the most Careful Manner, by the United Society of Shakers, Watervliet, N.Y. Orders to be Directed to Buckingham and Copley, Post Office, Albany, N.Y. Albany: Printed at the Office of the Evening Atlas, 1845. 11 pp. 18½ cm.

The text of the cover title and title page are identical. "Catalogue," pp. [3]-6, lists about 165 medicinal herbs and 4 culinary herbs; 28 extracts and 4 ointments, p. 7; advertisements for Shaker medicines, pp. 8-9; "Garden Seeds," p. 11. List of agents, back cover, verso. MWiW*, NBuG, OClWHi.

424 —— Fragrant Waters. Raised, Prepared, and Put Up in the most Careful Manner, by the United Society of Shakers. Watervliet, N.Y. Orders to be Directed to Buckingham and Copley, Albany, Post Office, N.Y. New York: Piercy and Hovel, Printers, 1847. Cover title. 7 [1] pp. 18½ cm.
OClWHi*.

425 —— Raised, Prepared and Put Up in the most Careful Manner, by the United Society of Shakers, Watervliet (near Albany,) N.Y. Orders to be Directed to Chauncey Copley, Albany P.O., N.Y. Albany: Printed by Charles Van Benthuysen, 1850. 11 pp. 17 cm.

"Theapeutic" has been corrected in the title. A quotation on the title page has been omitted. A cut of growing flowers is signed: *Anderson.* An area of the verso of the back cover is blank to provide for the names of agents to be supplied. MWiW*, OClWHi.

426 Catalogue of Medicinal Plants and Vegetable Medicines, Prepared in the United Society, Watervliet, N.Y. [quotation]. Orders to be Directed to [blank for name to be supplied] Watervliet, N.Y. Albany, N.Y.: Printed by Packard and Van Benthuysen, 1830. Cover title. 8 pp. 17 cm.

The quotation in the title reads: Why send to Europe's distant shores/ For plants which grow at our own doors? "The common names in this catalogue are such as are in general

use in the cities of New York, Albany, Troy, &c. The Botanical names are from Eaton's Manual of Botany, last edition." OClWHi*.

427 —— Prepared in the United Society, Watervliet, N.Y. [quotation]. Orders to be Directed to [blank for name to be supplied] Watervliet, N.Y. Hudson [N.Y.]: Printed by Ashbel Stoddard, 1833. Cover title. 8 pp. 17 cm.

"Catalogue," pp. [3]-6, lists 137 medicinal herbs under common names, with prices per lb. and the botanical names, 12 extracts, and 4 ointments. Advertisements for Shaker medicines, pp. 6-8. The quotation in the title is followed by a cut of a basket of flowers in some copies. A variant cover on the copy at the American Antiquarian Society (Worcester, Mass.) lacks the quotation, and the cut shows 2 gazebos, a garden, trees, etc. DeWint, MWA, N, OClWHi*.

428 —— and Vegetable Medicines, To which is affixed their most Prominent Medical Properties. Prepared in the United Society, Watervliet, N.Y. ... Orders to be Directed to [blank for name to be supplied] Watervliet, N.Y. Albany: Printed by Packard and Van Benthuysen, 1837. Cover title. 8 pp. 16 cm.

"Catalogue," pp. [2]-5, lists over 160 medicinal herbs, 15 extracts, and 4 ointments; advertisements for Shaker medicines and simples, pp. 6-8. Advertisement for the agents, A. B. & D. Sands, Wholesale Druggists, N.Y. back cover, verso. MPH, MWA, MWiW*, MiU-C, OClWHi.

429 —— Albany [N.Y.]: Printed by C. Van Benthuysen and Co., 1843. Cover title. 12 pp. 18 cm.
OClWHi*.

430 Catalogue of Medicinal Plants, Barks, Roots, Seeds and Flowers, with their Therapeutic and Botanical Names. Also, Pure Vegetable Extracts, and Shaker Garden Seeds, Raised, Prepared, and Put Up in the most Careful Manner, by the United Society of Shakers, Watervliet (near Albany,) N.Y. All Orders Addressed to Chauncey Miller, Shaker Village,

(Albany P.O.), N.Y. [n.p., n.d.]. Cover title.
22 pp. 18½ cm.

"To our Patrons, p. [1], "In presenting a
new edition of our Catalogue, we ... are
now making, heavy expenditures in buildings,
machinery, and very complete accommodations and fixtures for drying and preparing
the various articles in the following Catalogue ..." "For the generic and specific
names, we have relied on Gray's *Botany of
the Northern United States*, — adopting
those common names best known among
druggists, herbalists, and botanic physicians."
The list of medicinal herbs, etc., has been
increased to nearly 300, other products have
been increased accordingly, and "Synonyms"
(common name equivalents) have been
added, pp. 17–21. A statement, p. 13, signed:
Chauncey Miller, refers to thirty years of experience which should date this catalog in
the 1850's or 1860's.
MHarF, MWA, MWiW*, OClWHi, WHi.

WATERVLIET (formerly Niskayuna), N.Y.
Medicines

431 Cephalic Pills for Periodical and Nervous
Headache, Chronic Lameness, and Nervous
Debility. Watervliet, N.Y.: [n.d.]. [2] pp.
23½ cm.

Advertising flyer that includes Vegetable
Bilious Pills, p. [2].
OClWHi*.

432 For the Eyes and Ears the Shaker Eye and
Ear Balm. [n.p., n.d.]. Broadside. 28 X 35 cm.

"For all derangements by Inflammation;
Dimness of vision weakness from any cause;
Soft Cataracts gradually vanish ... All
Ophthalmic affections cured ... Deafness
from whatever cause dispelled."
Private collection.

433 Laurus Eye Water. For the Cure of Acute
and Chronic Inflammations of the Eyes, and
Morbid Weakness of Sight. [Watervliet, N.Y.:
n.d.]. Broadside. 21½ X 12½ cm.

Advertising flyer with directions for dosage.
N*.

434 Rose Balm for the Eyes. ... Prepared by

Shaker Sisters. Address Bullard & Ayres, Shakers,
N.Y. [Watervliet, N.Y.: 187-?]. Broadside. 29 X
36 cm.

"For inflammation of the eyes from whatever
cause; weak eyes of clergymen, students,
printers, clerks ... Rose Balm is a specific for
all ophthalmic affections."
OClWHi*.

435 Syrup of Liverwort, Hepatica Triloba, a
New, Safe, and Valuable Medicine for Coughs,
Spitting of Blood, and Consumption. Prepared
in the United Society. — D.M. Watervliet, N.Y.
[n.p., n.d.]. Broadside. 13 X 18½ cm.
OClWHi*.

436 Wonderful Discovery! Spiritene ... for the
Relief and Cure of Piles ... George P. Price,
Shakers [i.e., Watervliet], Albany, N.Y.: [n.d.].
Broadside. 22 X 15½ cm.

"This medicine is prepared by the 'Shakers'
who were the discoverers, and are the manufacturers of this marvelous and thorough
remedy." With prices and "Directions for
Using."
OClWHi*.

WATERVLIET (formerly Niskayuna), N.Y.
Seeds, Plants, Etc.

437 ... Bought of Chauncy [i.e., Chauncey]
Miller. No Seed Warranted and no Damages
Allowed above the Price of the Seeds when Sold.
[n.p., 187-]. Broadside in 2 columns. 41 X 28
cm.

At head of title: Shakers, Albany Co., N.Y.
187-. An unpriced list of about 120 varieties
of seeds, mostly vegetable, sold by the pound
or bushel.
OClWHi*.

438 ... Bought of Philip Smith. N.B. While We
Exercise the Greatest Care to have all Seeds
Pure and Reliable, it is Hereby Agreed ... that
We do Not Warrant Same, and are Not in any
Respect Liable or Responsible for Seeds Sold by
Us, for any Damage Arising from any Failure
thereof in any Respect. [n.p., 188-]. Broadside
in 2 columns. 37 X 28 cm. (trimmed).

At head of title: Shakers, Albany Co., N.Y.
188-. This copy is a partially filled order,

with the date filled in for February 26, 1881. The list is almost identical with the foregoing. MWiW*.

439 ———— 38 X 28 cm. (trimmed).
At head of title: Shakers, Albany Co., N.Y. 188-. A partially filled order made out to John Higgins and Co., which lacks precise date. The list is almost identical with the two foregoing lists.
Private Collection.

440 The Great Austin Shaker Seedling Strawberry is Believed to be the Largest Strawberry in the World. All orders addressed to Chauncy [i.e., Chauncey] Miller, Shaker Trustee, Albany, N.Y. [n.p., 186-?]. Broadside. 25 X 20 cm.
"This remarkable strawberry originated at our settlement in Watervliet, N.Y. four years ago." An announcement is made that plants will be exhibited at various eastern locations. *See also* no. **356.**
OClWHi*.

441 ———— Address Chauncy [i.e., Chauncey] Miller, Albany, N.Y., Shaker Trustee; or, Wm. S. Carpenter, 468 Pearl Street, New York. [n.p., n.d.]. Broadside. 25 X 20 cm.
The text and printing are identical with the foregoing, except for statement regarding orders.
OClWHi*.

442 List of Garden Seeds Raised by the Society of Shakers, near Albany, N.Y. Orders Addressed to Chauncy [i.e., Chauncey] Miller, Shakers, Albany, N.Y., Dealer in Brooms, Brushes, Prepared Sweet Corn, Medical Herbs, Roots & Extracts, and All Other Articles Manufactured by the Society. [n.p., n.d.]. Broadside. 39 X 14 cm.
A list of 55 varieties of seeds, mostly vegetable, which appear to represent the contents of Shaker compartmentalized display seed boxes handled by storekeepers. The total of the papers is 160.
N, OClWHi*.

443 ———— Orders addressed to Philip Smith, Shakers, N.Y., . . . [n.p., n.d.]. Broadside. 39 X 14 cm.

A list of 53 slightly different varieties of seeds than the foregoing list. The total number of the papers is 160.
N, OClWHi*.

WHITEWATER, O. Seeds

444 Catalogue of Garden Seeds Raised by the United Society of Shakers. At Whitewater Village, Hamilton Co., O. [n.p., n.d.]. Broadside. 31 X 15 cm.
A list of 65 varieties of seed, mostly vegetable, printed on yellow paper. The Whitewater seed industry is poorly represented by this single item. J. P. MacLean states that this community "started on a successful career of raising garden seeds for the market" in 1847, and that in 1857 this enterprise earned $5074. It was abandoned in 1873 because "our seeds did not take, as they were put up in a brown colored paper and a plain stained box. It was conclusive we must keep up with the times or step down and out, which we did," "Watervliet, Ohio, Shaker Community," in his *Shakers of Ohio* (no. **2410**), p. 257.
OClWHi*.

445 Certificate of Membership of the Universal Peace Union. [Philadelphia: 1889]. Broadside. 30 X 24 cm.
Membership blank made out for Robert Aiken, Elder of South Family, Enfield, Conn., and signed by Alfred H. Love, President.
OClWHi*.

446 CHANDLER, LLOYD HORWITZ. A visit to the Shakers of East Canterbury, N.H. East Canterbury, N.H.: [Printed by the Shakers, 1894]. Cover title. 11 pp. illus. ports. 23 cm.
"The author has been greatly aided by the valuable work of Mr. Charles E. Robinson, as well as by writings of many prominent Shakers," p. 11. "A Glimpse into the Inner Circle." by Agatha B. E. Chandler, pp. 9-11. The same text appeared in the *Granite Monthly* (Concord, N.H.), 16 (Apr., May 1894), 255-66, 321-23, under the title, "The Followers of Ann Lee: History, Customs, and Beliefs of the Shakers," where it was followed in the next issue by "A Glimpse . . . ," pp. 323-38. *See also* nos. **3122-3124.**

MacLean 186. DLC, MPB, MWiW*, NBuG, NN, NSyU, Nh, OClWHi.

447 CHANDLER, OLIVE F. Wonder in Heaven —Rev. XII. "A woman clothed with the sun, moon under her feet!" [n.p., n.d.]. Broadside. 10 × 7 cm.
OClWHi*.

448 CHAPMAN, MRS. EUNICE (HAWLEY). An Account of the Conduct of the People Called Shakers: in the Case of Eunice Chapman and Her Children, Since Her Husband Became Acquainted with that People, and Joined Their Society. Written by Herself .... Albany [N.Y.]: Printed for the Authoress, at 95 State-street, 1817. Cover title. 60 pp. 17½ cm.
P. 13, misnumbered 31; p. 33, misnumbered 53; "Errata," 1 line, foot p. 60. Eunice Chapman's three-year campaign to dissolve her marriage and gain custody of her children was a *cause célèbre* which grew out of Shaker tenets on marriage, and resulted in the only divorce ever voted by the New York Legislature. James Chapman abandoned his family and later joined the Shakers at Watervliet, N.Y., October 1812. Subsequently, he surreptitiously removed the three children from their home in Durham, N.Y., and placed them with the Watervliet Shakers. Eunice spent some time with these Shakers, but could not accept their faith and was told by Elder Wells that she must leave. With the aid of relatives, several attempts had been made to recover the children when she was told that the children had been removed to Enfield, N.H., and that James considered their marriage dissolved. On February 7, 1815, she first petitioned the New York Legislature for divorce. The case attracted wide publicity and bills were introduced, amended and passed by the legislature, and vetoed by the Council of Revision before she was finally successful. This account is her side of the story written to sway public opinion on her behalf. It includes depositions and the favorable Report of the Committee on the Petition of Eunice Chapman, in Senate, Apr. 12, 1816, which was lost by a close vote. *See also* nos. **1015, 1402.**
MacLean 487. Sabin 11975. Shaw 40444. DeWint, MB, MHi, MPB, MWA, MWiW*,

MiU–C, NHi, PPAmP, PPPrHi, PPULC.

449 —— No. 2 Being the Additional Account of the Conduct of the Shakers, in the Case of Eunice Chapman and Her Children with Their Religious Creed. Written by Herself. Also, a Refutation of the Shakers Remonstrance to the Proceedings of the Legislature of 1817. By Thomas Brown. Also, the Deposition of Mary Dyer, Who Petitioned the Legislature of the State of New Hampshire for the Relief in a Similar Case. Also, Affidavits from Different Persons Who Have Been Members of the Shaker Society ... Albany, N.Y.: Printed by I. W. Clark for the Authoress, 1818. 82 pp. 21 cm.
Several friends of Eunice Chapman "put up the money to have her story printed in pamphlet form for distribution to every senator and assemblyman," N. M. Blake, "Eunice Against the Shakers" (no. **3088**), p. 368. The bill which dissolved the Chapman marriage was finally passed by the N.Y. Legislature, March 14, 1818, over the veto of the Council of Revision. *See also* nos. **1015, 1380,** and **2303.**
MacLean 488. Sabin 11976. Shaw 43576. MB, MBAt, MH–L, MWA, N, NHi, OClWHi*, PPPrHi, PPULC.

450 Characteristics of Thirty-one of the United States of North America. [Canterbury], Shaker Village, Mer. Co., N.H.: 1861. Broadside. 22 × 14½ cm.
Short rhymed descriptions of the states for school children, intended to aid the memory. At end: School district, No. 8.; Shaker Village, Mer. Co., N.H.
DLC, OClWHi*.

451 —— School District No. 8. [Canterbury] Shaker Village, Mer. Co., N.H. [n.p., n.d.]. Broadside. 20½ × 12½ cm.
Printed on yellow paper from a different setting of type.
OClWHi*.

452 Christmas Hymn. [n.p., 185–]. Broadside. 10 × 16 cm.
Three numbered stanzas without music printed within an ornamental type border on pink paper. The Williams College copy has

been pasted inside a Shaker box as a lining paper. Last line reads: And life eternal given. MWiW*.

453 ———— [n.p., 1858?]. Broadside. 10 X 16 cm. Identical with the foregoing, except that the last line reads: And life eternal gain, and the date, March 29, 1858, follows. This version lines the opposite end of the box referred to in no. 452.
MWIW*.

454 Christ's Suffering. Shaker Village [Canterbury], Mer. Co., N.H.: [186-?]. Broadside. music. 25 X 16 cm.
Hymn of 6 stanzas with the music written in Shaker letter notation. This hymn was also printed as Canterbury sheet music with the music written in conventional notation, no. 1043.
OClWHi*.

455 The Church of Christ, unto a People in Kentucky & the Adjacent States, Sendeth Greeting. [n.p., n.d.]. Caption title. 3 pp. 15 cm.
"Written in the Church at New Lebanon, in the town of Canaan, County of Columbia and state of New York. Dec. 31, 1804. Signed on behalf of the Church, — David Meacham, Amos Hammond, Ebenezer Cooly," p. 3. This greeting was carried by the Shaker Missionaries, John Meacham, Issachar Bates, and Benjamin Seth Youngs, who planted Shakerism in the West. It was first read to Richard McNemar's congregation at Turtle Creek (Union Village), Ky., Sunday, March 24, 1805. The date of this printed greeting differs from the date given by Julia Neal, "written Dec. 26, 1804," By Their Fruits (no. 2499), pp. 20-21, where Stephen Markham is also given as one of the signers. This appears to have been printed by R. McNemar in the 1830's (Watervliet, O.?). It is also found in some copies of [R. McNemar], A Review of the Most Important Events (no. 950), pp. 6-9.
Shaw 6834. MWiW*, ODa, OClWHi.

456 Circular. [n.p., 1838?]. Broadside. 22½ X 16½ cm.
Begins: You are aware that it has recently

been discovered that the recently Revised Statutes abolished the Trust law, under which the Shaker's property has been held, and rendered it subject to division among all who have been or now are members of the Society, when those members who were Trustees at the time the law was passed (1830) shall be out of office ... The group of apostate propagators of this circular claim that they are acting with legal advice, and that "A suit will be commenced." Further, that "the Legislature had special reference to the property held by the Shakers when they abolished the Trust Law," and that "The greater part, if not the whole [Shaker] property, is now liable to division." The recipient is directed to "Notify all in your region," and is informed where claims should be sent. The circular shows animus and also evidence that this group of agitators intended to inflict crucial damage upon the Society. "Now is the time for all who desire to leave the society to do so, and claim a portion of the property as their just right, and compensation for their services, and remain in servitude no longer." The Shakers recognized the threat. "It was found that some who had left the Society, had taken advantage of this deficiency in our deeds [i.e., abolition of Trust Law]. We learned that they congratulated each other on the present good opportunity to seize upon the consecrated property and thus dissolve the society," "History of the Church at Mt. Lebanon, No. 17," The Manifesto, 20 (November 1890), 242. See also nos. 1078, 1381, and 3511.
OClWHi*.

457 Circular. [n.p., 1870]. Broadside. 25½ X 20 cm.
Dated: Washington, D.C., April 5th, 1870. Signed: We are, in true Gospel love, Your Brethren. Benjamin Gates, Ezra T. Leggett. Begins: "In order to promote greater uniformity, and a more exact observance of the requirements of law, in making returns of income tax by our societies ...". Gates and Leggett had made a trip to Washington to secure relief against "the adverse ruling of Commissioner Delano," July 10, 1869. They are informing Shaker societies that they must modify income tax returns for 1868 and

1869 "to make them conform to the amended act we seek to have passed." Instructions for listing categories of income and deductions follow. *See also* nos. **1400** and **1411**. OClWHi.

458 Circular. Further Directions Concerning the Distribution of the Sacred Roll and Book ... Extract from the Roll by the Holy and Mighty Angel. New Lebanon, N.Y.: 1843. Broadside. 43½ X 14 cm.

"The foregoing directions are to be kept close by the Ministry and Elders in every society, for the information of Believers only; and are by no means to go into any book to be sent abroad." Dated: New Lebanon, N.Y., Nov. 11, 1843, *see* no. **1340**. MacLean 282. MWiW*, OClWHi.

459 Circular. To the Leading Authority in All the Branches of Zion on Earth. New Lebanon [N.Y.]: 1843. Broadside in two columns. 46½ X 26 cm.

Concerns the publication and distribution of Philemon Stewart's, *A Holy, Sacred and Divine Roll and Book*. This was "written and circulated by the unanimous request of the Ministry, Elders and Deacons, New Lebanon N.Y. Oct. 4, 1843," who had decided not "to circulate to the world, at present, the testimonies &c, which are appended to the Sacred Roll; therefore, the work has been divided into two parts; and the five hundred copies which are for the world, contain only the Sacred Roll and Book; the second part of which is to be preserved and bound by itself; but those for Believers, contain the additional testimonies, and may be bound both parts in one." "The order of distribution as arranged at New Lebanon," follows and specifies the number of copies that each Society is to present to the world. Four copies are to be sent to the President of the U.S., and one to the Pope, *see* no. **1340**. MWiW*, OClWHi.

460 Circular Concerning the Dress of Believers. To Our Dear Gospel Brethren and Sisters, Greeting. [Mt. Lebanon, N.Y.: 1866]. 12 pp. 23 cm.
Contents: Resolutions, p. 3; Observations, p. 7; Uniformity of hats, p. 9; Concerning bonnets, p. 10. The pamphlet is subscribed

by the Ministry, Mount Lebanon, N.Y. Authorship has sometimes been attributed to Giles B. Avery. MacLean 381 (attributed to Giles B. Avery). DLC*, MPB, NN, OClWHi.

461 Circular Epistle. [From the Ministry and Elders at New Lebanon, September 1, 1829]. [n.p., n.d.]. [73]-80 pp.

Copy in the Western Reserve Historical Society, a separate in wrappers, not bound with [Richard McNemar], comp., *Constitution* ... (no. **911**), where it is generally found. This communication concerning the "faithful examination of our state as a people" offers several instructions to the western societies where there existed a reluctance about accepting the 1829 revised Covenant. "Hence it becomes indispensibly necessary, that our temporal interest be secured in the hands of trustees, and that all our transactions, in thus arranging matters be legal and supportable in courts of justice and equity .... Mutual agreements in things lawful is, therefore, our only resource for the defense of our civil rights. Hence arises the necessity of a written covenant and a particular statement of the general principles of our church-order & form of government." pp. 77-78. MWiW*, OClWHi.

462 CLAPP, CHARLES. An Appeal. To One and All — for All are Concerned, to All the Clergy and Laymen of Every Sect, to Reformers of Every Grade and Class: [n.p., 1886?]. [4] pp. 22 cm.

On p. [2], signed: *Charles Clapp. Union Village, Warren Co., O., July 4, 1886*. Contains also: "Communism and Communists" and "Christianized Christianity," signed: *A.* (from *The Manifesto*, 16 (February 1886), 43-44). Clapp's *Appeal* is a circular letter to the "world" to restore "the heaven-born principles" embodied in Christ's testimony and life. MacLean 490 (title: *Circular Letter*). CtY, MSaE*, OHi.

463 [——], *comp.* The Present Truth, for the Honest Enquirer. Shaker Post Office, Warren County, Ohio. Miamisburg, O.: Bulletin Steam Presses, 1885. Cover title. 16 pp. 22 cm.

MacLean credits Charles Clapp with this compilation. Contents: "Marriage" by Daniel Frazer (from *The Manifesto* 14 (January 1884), 1-2); "Purity" by Martha J. Anderson (from *The Manifesto* 14 (January 1884), 2-4); "Christian Communists (vulgarly called Shakers)" by Charles Clapp (from *The Manifesto* 15 (October 1885), 223-24); "The Life in Common" by R. Heber Newton, p. 5. MacLean 187. CSmH, ICN, MPB, MWiW*, N, NBuG, NN, NOC, NjPT, OClWHi, OHi, WHi.

464 [——] ——— 2d ed. . . . Cincinnati: Elm Street Printing Co., 1887. 20 pp. 23 cm. NN, NOC*.

465 CLOUGH, HENRY TERRY, *comp.* A Classified List of American and Foreign Newspapers and Magazines with Subscription Prices at which they are Supplied Post-paid. Mount Lebanon, N.Y.: Subscription Agency Department. [n.d.]. 27 pp. 22 cm. OClWHi*.

C.M.S. *See* Skinner, Charles Montgomery, nos. 1313 and 2766.

466 A Collection of Harmonies and Melodies, Adapted to Sacred Worship . . . Canterbury, N.H.: Published and Printed at Shaker Village, 1878. [4], [blank leaf], 40, [60] pp. music. 23 X 20½ cm.

Cover title: Harmonies and Melodies. In two parts: Part I, pp. 1-40; Part II, pp. [1-60]. Hymns with the music written in conventional notation—4-part harmony, single-line melodies. Laid in Western Reserve Historical Society (Cleveland, O.) copy, Shaker sheet music: "A Prayer," following p. 40; "The Beacon," following No. 12 (nos. 1055, 104). MacLean 188. OClWHi*, NSyU (Pt. II, Nos. 1-12 missing).

467 A Collection of Millennial Hymns; Adapted to the Present Order of the Church . . . Canterbury, N.H.: [n.d.]. 8 pp. 16½ cm.

Words without music. The preface refers to the increased size of the work and the new system of numbering the hymns for greater ease in consulting them. This 8-page gathering is a fragment of the 24-page *Collection,* no.

468. The same hymns, pp. 3-8 (in the same sequence), appear in both items: No. 1, "The Final Decision"; No. 2, "Deceitfulness of Earthly Joy"; No. 3, "Who shall Stand?"; No. 4, "Celestial Blessing"; No. 5, "The Church of God." MacLean 189. DLC*.

468 ——— Canterbury, N.H.: [n.d.]. 24 pp. (i.e., 28 pp.; pp. 11-14 repeat). 17 cm.

Words without music. This collection was replaced by the 1847 *Collection of Millennial Hymns,* which included all but 3 of the hymns. Several sentences in the unsigned preface are identical with the 1847 preface; the sequence of hymns 1-10 is the same. The type size varies throughout. The gatherings are stabbed and laced into the binding with silk cords which are long enough to allow for additions. The Williams College copy may be incomplete because the cords could accommodate many more gatherings. MacLean 189 (same title and imprint, but only 8 pp.). MWiW*.

469 ——— Canterbury, N.H.: Printed in the United Society, 1847. 200 pp. 14 X 10 cm.

Words without music. Preface, signed: *Printer (H. C. Blinn).* "The first form of this book having been found by experience, to be somewhat imperfect, it was considered advisable to make some alteration. The near resemblance, and even identity of one [hymn] title to another, render it necessary to adopt some other method of designating the hymns; therefore, in addition to titles, figures will be used," p. 2. The printer explains that he has had many difficulties because "the printing of this work has been done at different times," and he begs indulgence for whatever errors may be found. Blinn states in his "Autobiographical Notes," in *In Memoriam* (no. 830), p. 31, "We also printed in 1844, a small book entitled 'Millennial Hymns.' It was a work of some four hundred pages." This appears to be a mistaken recollection; no such title has been located. Blinn must have referred to the work recorded here. The title, "Millennial Hymns," precedes the first hymn, "1. The Final Decision," but the book has only 200 pages. The Williams College (Williamstown, Mass.) copy

has 2 leaves (1 fold, 3 hymns) tipped in following the title page. One leaf, "Christmas Hymn. March 29, 1858," is tipped in following p. 194, *see also* nos. 452–453.
MacLean 13. CtY, DeWint, IU, MH, MPB, MWiW*, NBuG, NN, NNC, NOC, NSyU, NjPT, OClWHi, OHi, RPB, WHi.

470 ——— (Reprint). Communal Societies in America, 2d Series. New York: AMS Press, Inc., 1973.

471 [COLLINS, SARAH], *comp.* Memorial of Sister Polly C. Lewis. [Mt. Lebanon, N.Y.: 1899]. Cover title. [8] pp. 17½ cm.
Four poems, two of which are unsigned, "Kindly Dedicated ... Polly C. Lewis," and "Polly C. Lewis. One of Christ's Elect Ladies," pp. [1–4]. "In Fond Remembrance of Our Sister," pp. [5–6], signed: *Genevieve Delgram;* "Passing of the Ancients," pp. [7–8], signed: *Cecelia Devere* (printed in *The Manifesto,* 29 (March 1899), 37).
MacLean 376 (attributed to Sarah Collins). MPB, MWA, MWiW*, NN, NSyU, OClWHi.

472 [——] Memories. [n.p., n.d.]. Broadside. 32½ × 11½ cm.
Autograph of Sarah Collins appears at the end of the poem.
NOC*.

473 Commendation. [Mt. Lebanon, N.Y.: 1896]. [4] pp. 13 cm.
Letters of commendation for A. G. Hollister's *Pearly Gate,* from Margaret Egglson, Harvard, Mass., Dec. 30, 1895; Abraham Perkins, East Canterbury, Oct. 8th, 1894; and others. *See also* no. 1365. "*Morning Star Bible Lessons* was stampt on the cover of the first edition. *Pearly Gate* is the permanent title, and is stampt on the cover of the second edition," p. [4].
MacLean 112. DLC, MPB, MWiW*, NBuG, OClWHi.

474 The Conflagration at Shaker Village. Lebanon Springs [sic], Feb. 8th, 1875. Mount Lebanon, N.Y.: 1875. Broadside. 30 × 13 cm.
Catastrophic fire which destroyed Mt. Lebanon, N.Y., Church family dwelling, and eight other buildings with loss valued at $125,000–$150,000. Written by an eyewitness and published in *The Bennington [Vt.] Banner* of Feb. 17, 1875. Signed: *Edward Fowler, Benjamin Gates, Trustees.* A. White and L. Taylor, *Shakerism* (no. 1447), pp. 209–12, describe this and several other destructive fires in Shaker communities.
MacLean 203 (attributed to F. W. Evans). MPB, OClWHi*.

475 The Constitution or Covenant of the United Society of Believers Called Shakers, in the United States of America .... Louisville, Ky.: Printed by John P. Morton and Company, 1883. [1], 33, [1], [52] pp., incl. record blanks for signatures of witnesses and signers. 29 × 23 cm.
"A brief illustration of the principles on which the United Society is founded," pp. [3]–7. Text of this covenant varies considerably from that in no. 1279. "This is the Covenant written by Elder Harvey L. Eads in 1883, at a time when numerous thoughtful leaders and members were agitating some revision of the one adopted in 1830 as the Church Covenant." Manuscript note, signed: *M. C.*[atherine] *Allen, Sept. 1912,* in the copy at Western Reserve Historical Society, Cleveland, Ohio. "Church, in its broadest sense, signifies all possessing one faith. In a restricted sense, in this Covenant, it includes only the Covenant members; and in a still more restricted sense, it means and includes only the Covenant members of each Bishopric or separate Society ..." Note, p. [8].
CtY, DLC, MWiW*, OC, OClWHi.

476 Contents of Music in "The Shaker and Shakeress," "The Shaker," and "The Manifesto." [Canterbury, N.H.: 1889]. 4 pp. 22½ cm.
A title index to the hymns with music published, 1872–1888, no. 980 ff.
MWiW*, OClWHi.

477 COOLBROTH, [EUGENIA M.]. A Concise Answer to the Many Questions Asked by the Public. Sister Gennie M. Coolbroth, Shaker Village. Sabbathday Lake, Maine: [1933]. 1 p.l., 6 pp. 21 cm.
Sometimes cited, "Facts about Shakers," from

the cover title. "This pamphlet was printed
by Brother Earl Campbell on an historic
Shaker press placed in the community by
Eldress Josephine Wilson of Canterbury,
New Hampshire. It was upon this press that
many major Shaker works, including the
Shaker monthly '*The Manifesto,*' were
printed at the East Canterbury society," T. E.
Johnson, "Random Notes," Maine Library
Association *Bulletin,* 22 (February 1961), 20.
MWA, MWiW*, NOC.

478 —— ———— 2d ed. [Sabbathday Lake,
Me.: 1941].
 T. E. Johnson states that this was the last
publication printed at Sabbathday Lake, Me.,
"Random Notes," Maine Library Association
Bulletin, 22 (February 1961), 18–20. No
copy has been located.

479 Could'st Thou Not Watch One Hour?
Printed at Shaker Village, Mer. Co., N.H.: [n.d.].
Broadside. 24½ × 8 cm.
 Poem, 12 stanzas, reprinted from *Sabbath
Recorder.*
 OClWHi*.

480 The Covenant or Constitution of the
Church at ————— . [n.p., n.d.]. 17 pp.
20 cm.
 This covenant appears to have been printed
during the latter half of the 19th century for
the general use of individual Shaker societies.
Blank spaces are provided for the location of
the society and the date.
 MWA, N, NOC, OClWHi*.

481 [CRESSON, WARDER]. Babylon the
Great is Falling! The Morning Star, or Light
from on High. Written in Defence of the Rights
of the Poor and Oppressed. Philadelphia: Garden
and Thompson, 1830. 67 [1] 3 pp. 18½ cm.
 Preface signed: *Warder Cresson.* "Letter to a
Universalist" by W. Cresson, 3 pp. at end.
Some discussion of Hicksite and Shaker
beliefs, with an excerpt from B. J. Youngs'
Testimony of Christ's Second Appearing
(no. 1470). *See also* nos. 2455 and 3219.
MH, OClWHi*, PPeSchw, PSC–Hi.

482 CROSMAN, CHARLES F. The Gardener's

Manual; Containing Plain and Practical Directions for the Cultivation and Management of
Some of the Most Useful Culinary Vegetables;
To Which is Prefixed a Catalogue of the Various
Kinds of Garden Seeds Raised in the United
Society at New Lebanon, Pittsfield and Watervliet, with a Few General Remarks on the Management of a Kitchen Garden. By Charles F. Crosman, New Lebanon, Columbia Co., N.Y. Albany:
Printed by Hoffman and White, 1835. Cover
title. 24 pp. 18 cm.
 The cover title and verso were reprinted with
the appropriate corrections for those copies
sold to Earl Jepherson and distributed by the
Enfield, Conn., Shakers. "Catalogue of Garden
Seeds . . ." Enfield, Conn., was printed on p.
[3], cf. no. 483. J. P. MacLean did not acquire
this manual until after his *Bibliography* had
been published, a.l.s. MacLean to H. M. Lydenberg, Franklin, Ohio, May 28, 1905, New York
Public Library, Rare Book Room. The author's
name is also found spelled "Crossman."
NOC, OClWHi*.

483 —— ———— To Which Is Prefixed a
Catalogue of the Various Kinds of Garden Seeds
Raised in the United Society at Enfield, Conn.;
With a Few General Remarks on the Management
of a Kitchen Garden. By Charles F. Crosman.
Published for Earl Jepherson, Enfield, Hartford
Co., Conn. Albany [N.Y.]: Printed by Hoffman
and White, 1835. Cover title. 24 pp. 18 cm.
 "To Gardeners and Dealers in Garden Seeds,"
p. [2], is signed: *C. F. C.* (Charles F. Crosman).
*For Earl Jepherson, Enfield, August 29th,
1835.* "Catalogue of Garden Seeds, Raised by
the United Society of Shakers, Enfield, Hartford Co., Conn. Orders Addressed to Earl
Jepherson," p. [3]. "A Few General Remarks
on the Management of a Kitchen Garden," p.
[4]. "Directions for Making the Hot Bed," p.
[5]. "Practical Directions for the Cultivation of
Vegetables," pp. [6]-24, contains directions for
cultivating and cooking 25 vegetables. "The
French and Spanish names of the various vegetables are added . . . for the information of
foreigners who purchase our seeds," p. [6] n.
"Price 6¢" at foot of cover title. Cf. no. 261.
DLC, MWiW*, MiU-C, NOC, OClWHi.

484 —— ———— To Which is Prefixed a

Catalogue of the Various Kinds of Garden Seeds Raised in the United Society at New Lebanon with a Few General Remarks on the Management of a Kitchen Garden. By Charles F. Crosman. Albany [N.Y.]: Printed by Hoffman and White on the Power Press, 1836. 23[1] pp. 18 cm.

E. D. Andrews states that 16,000 copies were printed and that 3000 copies were sold to Jefferson White of the Enfield, Conn. Shakers, *Community Industries of the Shakers* (no. 1759), pp. 72-73, 271-72, n. 27. No copy has been found which has been appropriately corrected to apply to Enfield, but *see* no. 483. Andrews had not seen the 1835 *Catalogue* when he identified this as "the first attempt of the Shakers at New Lebanon to advertise their seed business," *op. cit.*, and no. 482.
OClWHi*.

485 [——] The Gardener's Manual Containing Plain Instructions for the Selection, Preparation, and Management of a Kitchen Garden: with Practical Directions for the Cultivation and Management of Some of the Most Useful Culinary Vegetables. Published by the United Society, New Lebanon, Columbia Co., N.Y. New York: Printed by J. W. Kelley, Printer, 1843. 24 pp. 17½ cm.

Introduction signed: *The Publishers.* Charles F. Crosman had seceded in May 8, 1840, very likely to join a seed firm in Rochester, N.Y., according to M. F. Sommer, *Shaker Seed Industry* (no. 2790), p. 40, n. 23. This manual differs somewhat from the earlier ones. Instructions for selecting the garden location and implements, preparing the ground, cultivation, making a hot-bed, and eliminating injurious insects, pp. [5]-12. "Catalogue of Garden Seeds Raised ... New Lebanon ...," pp. 12-13. "Particular Treatment of Different Varieties of Culinary Vegetables," pp. 13-24, has been shortened (pp. 6-24 in the 1835 *Manual*).
DLC, DeWint, MPH*, NSyU.

486 [——] —————— Facsimile Reprint. [Hastings-on-Hudson, N.Y.: Morgan & Morgan, Inc., 1972].

The new cover which was not part of the

original publication contains information (front cover, verso; back cover, recto) about the Shakers, signed *Amy Bess Miller, Hancock Shaker Village.* MPH, MWiW.

487 [——] The Gardener's Manual: Containing Plain and Practical Directions for the Cultivation and Management of some of the Most Useful Culinary Vegetables: to which is Prefixed a Catalogue of the Various Kinds of Garden Seeds Raised in the United Society of Shakers at Enfield, Ct. First Established in 1802 ... With a Few General Remarks on the Management of a Kitchen Garden. By Jefferson White ... Thompsonville, Conn. Rev. & Imp. Ed. Hartford [Conn.] : Elihu Geer, Stationer and Steam Printer, [185-]. Cover title. 26 pp. 19 cm.

"To Gardener's," signed *Jefferson White.* This is essentially the same as the C. F. Crosman *Manual* (1835). "Directions for Making the Hot Bed" has been added, p. 8. "A Catalogue of the Garden Seeds ... Raised ... Enfield, Conn.," pp. 3-5. For later publications based upon *The Gardener's Manuals, see Mt. Lebanon, N.Y. Catalogs, etc.,* Gardening and Seeds.
OClWHi*.

488 CUMINGS, HENRY. What Shall I Do to Be a Shaker? [Enfield, N.H.?: 1879]. Broadside. 39 × 20 cm.

Cumings was an Elder at Enfield, N.H., "who left the Shakers in 1881 to get married." M. Melcher, *Shaker Adventure* (no. 2451), p. 211. This was probably reprinted after its appearance in the *Shaker Manifesto*, 9 (March 1879), 56-58. *See also* no. 103.
MacLean 204. MPB, NBuG, NN, OClWHi*.

489 CUMMINGS, ADA S. The Crucible. [n.p., 1909]. Broadside. 21½ × 14 cm.
Poem of six stanzas. Dated at end: Jan. 19, 1909.
OClWHi*.

490 [——], *comp.* In Memoriam, Sister Aurelia G. Mace 1835-1910. [Portland, Me.: George Loring, 1910]. 100 pp. illus. 20 cm.
MWiW*, NOC, OClWHi.

491 CUSHMAN, CHARLOTTE. Lines ...

Suggested by a Visit to the Shaker Settlement, near Albany. [poem]. [Printed at Shaker Village, Mer. Co., N.H.: 188-?]. Caption title. [4] pp. 28 cm.

    At head of title: "From the Knickerbocker [9 (January 1837) 46–47]." Includes also "Answer to 'Lines by Charlotte Cushman' from *The Knickerbocker* (no. 3159). From the Russellville, Kentucky, Advertiser,"

unsigned, written at South Union. This poem is by H. L. Eads, cf. his *Shaker Sermons* (1884), p. 268, no. **546.** Both poems were reprinted in *The Shaker,* 1 (January 1871), 7–8, where "Answer" is signed: S. [ally] *E.* [ads]. Later, Eads identified himself (and not his mother) as author. MWiW, O, OClWHi*, ODa.

D

492 D., A. B. A Poem: For the Dedication of the New House, Oct. 25, 1868. [n.p., Lowe's Cylinder Press Print., n.d.] [2] pp. 23 cm. (trimmed?).

    The Shaker community is not identified. OClWHi*.

493 DAVIS, A. B. ... True Love: What It Is, and What It Is Not. With an Appendix .... Shirley, Mass.: Published for the Author, 1869. Cover title. 27 pp. 15½ cm. (Shaker tracts for the times, No. 1.).

    Written "partly to meet a general demand for the views of 'a peculiar people'."

    "Errata," p. 27.

    MHarF, MWA, MWiW*, NBuG, OClWHi.

494 *Day-Star.* Cincinnati, O., etc., Vols. 1–13, no. 3; 1841–July 1847. Vols. 1–4, no. 13, as *Western Midnight Cry.* 13 vols. music. 33 cm.

    The *Day-Star* was a Second Adventist publication that became a Shaker organ in the aftermath of disillusion caused by the failure of William Miller's prophecy that the end of the world would occur in 1843, and also his second prophecy which set the date ahead to 1844. Enoch Jacobs, editor and publisher of the *Day-Star,* became seriously interested in Shakerism and printed excerpts from Shaker publications and articles, letters, and poetry by Shakers. Several pieces of Shaker music written in alphabetic notation appeared with explanatory notes signed: *H. L. E.* [ads]. Jacobs became a member and worked actively with the Shakers among the disaffected Adventists in the West and they

were successful in attracting more than 200 persons to Shakerism. In the summer of 1846 his proselytizing activities were extended during an eastern tour. In this period the *Day-Star* appeared irregularly "only as often as the occasion demanded." Volume 11, Nos. 5–7 (August 8 and 25, 1846), were published in New York. Thirteen hundred copies of Vol. 11, No. 8 (Sept. 19, 1846), were published at Shaker Village, Canterbury, N.H., the Shakers assisting with typesetting and presswork, and also contributing $20.00 toward expenses. Publication of the *Day-Star* at Union Village, Ohio, began with Vol. 11, No. 9 (Nov. 7, 1846), after Jacobs went to live in the Shaker community there. "It is probable" that it was printed on McNemar's press, according to J. P. MacLean, *Life* (no. 2411), p. 61, n. The masthead was changed to indicate official Shaker sponsorship, Vol. 13, No. 1 (May 26, 1847): "The *Day-Star* will be published semi-monthly by the United Society of Believers (called Shakers), at Union Village, Warren Co., Ohio." Publication ceased abruptly, however, after No. 3 (July 1, 1847) because of financial difficulties and also because of Jacobs' disenchantment with Shakerism. J. P. MacLean, *Bibliography* (no. 2407), pp. 19–20, states that Jacobs withdrew declaring that he would "rather go to hell with Electra his wife than to live among the Shakers without her." *See* his "Letter" to Elder Eads and Elder Blinn's favorable comment, *The Manifesto,* 21 (November 1891), 250–51.

MWiW*, OHi, OCHP, OClWHi, ODa.

495 Debt Collecting. [Mount Lebanon, N.Y.?: n.d.]. Broadside. 22 × 8 cm.

Reprint of an editorial from the *Albany Evening Journal,* commenting on Frederick Evans' letter to the *Sun. See also* no. **591.** OClWHi*.

496 A Declaration of the Society of People (Commonly Called Shakers) Shewing Their Reasons for Refusing to Aid or Abet the Cause of War and Bloodshed, by Bearing Arms, Paying Fines, Hiring Substitutes, or Rendering Any Equivalent for Military Services. Albany: Printed by E. & E. Hosford, 1815. Cover title. 20 pp. 24½ cm.

Signed: *David Meacham* [and 23 others] *Mt. Lebanon, Feb. 2, 1815.* This eloquent pacifist declaration of principles was presented to the New York Legislature after several Shakers had been "drafted in the war service" in 1813 and 1814. "History of the Church of Mt. Lebanon, N.Y., No. 17," *The Manifesto,* 20 (November 1890), 241. "Our objections are founded on a sense of duty to God, to ourselves and to our fellow-creatures; and are supported first, by divine revelation; second, by the natural rights of man; third, by the Constitution and fundamental laws of our country," p. [3]. Harassment by the military continued, and on February 13, 1816, the Shakers followed this declaration with *The Memorial* (1816), no. **1019,** to the New York Legislature. MacLean 206 (200 pp.!), where the authorship is attributed to Calvin Green and Seth Y. Wells. Sabin 79702. Shaw 35908 and 34545. CSmH, Ct, CtY, DLC, ICJ, ICN, KyU, MB, MBC, MH, MHarF, MPB, MWA, MeB, MeHi, MiU–C, N, NN, NBuG, NHi, NNUT, NOC, NjPT, OClWHi*, PPULC, PPAmP, WHi.

497 ―――― Hartford, Conn.: Printed by Hudson and Goodwin, 1815. Cover title. 23 pp. 23 cm.

Signed: *Nathan Tiffany* [and 10 others] *Enfield* [Conn.], *May 8th, 1815.* Excerpts from the New Hampshire and Massachusetts laws which exempt Shakers from military service, pp. 21–23. Slightly different text. Sabin 79702. Shaw 35909. CtHT–W, CtHi,

CtY, DLC, KyBgW, MB, MBA, MBC, MH, MWA, MWiW*, NHi, OClWHi.

498 ―――― Lenox, Mass.: Walter Wilson Publishing Associates, [n.d.]. [2] 20 [6] pp.

A facsimile reprint preceded by an explanatory statement. The unnumbered pages at the end include "Resolutions Adopted at the Peace Convention of the Shakers of Mount Lebanon, held at Mt. Lebanon, N.Y., August 3, 1905." MPH, NOC*.

499 Declaration of Trust. [n.p., n.d.]. Broadside. 25½ × 20 cm.

Trustee's declaration of the acceptance of trust according to "the provisions of the Covenant or Constitution," of the Church and Society called Shakers. This form specifies the "State of New Hampshire," consequently, it could be used for either Enfield or Canterbury. Private collection.

500 ―――― (Identical text).

Different type setting, and the "State of Maine" substituted for "New Hampshire." Typewritten certificates of the appointment of Trustees by the Ministry in the 20th century have not been included. Private collection.

501 Description of the Person and Character of Jesus Christ, as It Was Found in an Ancient Manuscript, Sent by Publius Lentulus, President of Judea, to the Senate of Rome. [n.p., n.d.]. Broadside. 20½ × 16 cm.

Reprint of a purported letter to the Roman Senate from one Lentulus, who has been variously identified as a Roman official in Judea, Governor of Judea, or President of Judea. The description reflects medieval ideas of Christ's appearance and is generally considered to be unauthentic. This copy was found in a Union Village Journal, 1805–1840 (No. 287), in the Library of Congress, Manuscript Division. There is nothing to indicate that it is a Shaker publication except its typography and the ornamental type border which is found on other items printed at Canterbury, N.H., by the Shakers. DLC*.

502 DEVERE, MARGARET CECELIA. ...
Monopoly! Mount Lebanon, N.Y.: The Leba-
non Press, [n.d.]. Cover title. 4 pp. 13½ cm.
(Lebanon Leaves. Stir Up Series, No. 2.)
> Contains two poems, "The Larger Theft"
> [by Cecelia Devere?], and "Love Near Its
> Own" by Charlotte P. Stetson.
> MacLean 208. CtY, DLC, MPB, MPH, MWA,
> MWiW*, NBuG, NN, OClWHi.

503 —— Open Letter to Catholic Priests. A
Shaker Sister's Appeal to Ireland. [n.p., n.d.].
Broadside. 23 X 8½ cm.
> Signed: *Margaret Cecelia Devyr* [!], *Mt.
> Lebanon, N.Y.* Later the name Cecelia
> Devere was used exclusively.
> MacLean 209. MPB, MWiW*, OClWHi.

504 —— A Shaker Chieftain Crowned. Presented to Elder Frederick Evans, of Mt. Lebanon, 1893. Broadside.
> Poem. No copy located. Entry taken from
> MacLean 210.

[——] Table Monitor. *See* Table Monitor,
no. 1357. Cf. 119-123.

505 [DE VOE, WALTER]. A Healing Prayer
from Healing Currents. [Chicago, Ill.: Vita Publishing Co., 1915]. [4] pp. 13½ cm.
> This entry is taken from *Shaker Literature
> in the Rare Book Room of the Buffalo and
> Erie Public Library*, revised by J. S. Ellett,
> no. 2947.
> NBuG*.

506 *The Dew Drop.* Nos. 1, 4-5, October 1876-
[1877-78?]. Shaker Village [Canterbury], Mer.
Co., N.H.: Published by the Shakers, 1876-
[1877-78]. Caption title. 14½ cm.
> Each issue has 4 unnumbered pages. Contains
> *Notice to Visitors,* poems, Juvenile (column),
> and miscellanea. Advertisements, No. 5, for
> Canterbury sheet music and Shaker washing
> machine, including the medal awarded at the
> Centennial Exposition, Philadelphia, 1876.
> Three paragraphs were reprinted in *The
> Shaker,* 7 (March 1877), 28, where the *Dew
> Drop* is described as "a beautiful little sheet,
> published at Shaker Village, N.H. As it is the
> only rival *The Shaker* has, we are happier for

thus noticing it. It is printed anonymously, a
favorite of the people there ..."
> DLC (no. 4), MWiW* (no. 1), OClWHi (no. 5),
> WHi (no. 5).

507 DIBBLE, CHANCEY. United Inheritance.
Canterbury, N.H.: [Printed at Shaker Village,
Mer. Co., N.H., 1888?]. Cover title. 16 pp.
11 cm.
> Contains also: "An Open Vision" by Amelia
> J. Calver; "Visions" by Elder J. G. Russell;
> "Love" [poem] by Mary Whitcher; "A Kind
> Word" [poem] by Jessie Evans. The selec-
> tions in this pamphlet were printed in *The
> Manifesto*, vol. 18, June 1888. The author's
> given name is found spelled both Chancy and
> Chancey. The spelling here is found in the
> death notice, *The Manifesto*, 12:89.
> MacLean 211. DLC, MWA, MWiW*, MiU-C,
> N, NBuG, NSyU, OClWHi.

508 The Difference. Printed at Shaker Village,
Mer. Co., N.H.: [Canterbury, n.d.]. Broadside.
17½ X 9 cm.
> Biblical and other quotations on war and pacifism.
> OClWHi.

509 DOOLITTLE, MARY ANTOINETTE.
Autobiography of Mary Antoinette Doolittle
Containing a Brief History of Early Life Prior to
Becoming a Member of the Shaker Community,
also an Outline of Life & Experience Among
the Shakers. Mt. Lebanon, Columbia County,
N.Y.: 1880. 48 pp. 17 cm.
> "The first edition of this little work was only
> designed as a brief narrative of the author's
> recollections, anterior to entering the Shaker
> Society. It has been suggested, through the
> public press, and by numerous correspondents,
> that the work be extended, giving the writer's
> experience after entering the Community," p.
> [5]. The statement about the author's having
> spent 55 years with the Shakers remains un-
> changed, p. 48, cf. no. 510.
> MacLean 214. CtY, MPB, MWiW*, MeHi, N,
> NBuG, NN, NjPT, OClWHi, OHi, WHi.

510 —— —— Doolittle Prior to Becoming
a Member of the Shaker Community at New
Lebanon, N.Y., in the Year 1824. [Mt. Lebanon, N.Y.: 1880]. 27 pp. 17 cm.

On title page in place of imprint: Enquirers address F. W. Evans, Mt. Lebanon, Columbia Co., N.Y. The date 1880 appears on cover title, and in the "Conclusion," p. 27, the author states, "Fifty-five years of my life have been spent among the Shakers." CtY, IaU, ICN, MB, MH, MHarF, MPH, MWiW*, MiU-C, N, NN, NOC, NSyU, OClWHi, OHi.

511 —— Conflict between Right and Wrong. [n.p., n.d.]. Broadside. 25 X 8 cm.
Signed: *Antoinette Doolittle, Mt. Lebanon, N.Y.*
MWiW*.

512 —— A Shakeress on American Institutions. Mt. Lebanon, [N.Y.]: [n.d.] Broadside. 30 X 8 cm.
A plea for women's rights. "A change must and will come in this respect. Women possess latent powers that need to be brought into action, both for her own benefit and the good of the community." This was printed in two different issues of the *Shaker Manifesto*, 11 (November 1881), 250-52, and 12 (February 1882), 32-33. In both printings it carried the subtitle: Where They are Defective and the Remedy, and both were addressed: To the Editor of the *Brooklyn Eagle*. MacLean 215. OClWHi*. WHi.

513 —— Thoughts Concerning Deity. [Mt. Lebanon, N.Y.: n.d.]. Caption title. 4 pp. 18 X 9 cm.
MacLean 216. DLC, MH-AH, MPB, MWA, MWiW*, NN, NOC, NjPT, OClWHi, WHi.

514 —— War Positively Unchristian. [Mt. Lebanon, N.Y.: 1879?]. Caption title. 6 pp. 13½ cm.
Reprinted from the *Shaker Manifesto*, 9 (January 1879), 3-4. Contains also: "The Religion of the Future," G. A. Lomas. MacLean 217 (2 pp.). DLC, MPB, MWiW*, N, NBuG, NN, OClWHi.

515 DOWE, ARTHUR W. The Day of Judgment as Taught by the Millennial Church (Shakers) with a Few Rays of Light Gathered from Scriptures and Other Sources. S.[an] F.[rancisco]: Rembaugh, Printer, 1896. 24 pp. 12½ cm.

A blank leaf precedes title page. Dowe was attempting to organize a Shaker community in San Francisco. His letter to Jennie H. Fish, East Canterbury, N.H., April 29, 1894, states that he has "circulated most of the [Shaker] literature" sent to him, *The Manifesto*, 24 (July 1894), 157-59; the letter is signed: *Your Brother in the Gospel, Arthur W. Dowe.* "We have received leaflets from our Brother Arthur W. Dowe, 948 Mission St., San Francisco, Cal., dealing with the much discussed and long expected 'Day of Judgment.' The subject is well handled and an intelligent view taken of that important event ..." North Family, Mt. Lebanon, N.Y., "Notes," signed: *Hamilton DeGraw, The Manifesto*, 26 (October 1896), 164-65. *See also* no. 1350. MacLean 218. CtY, DLC, MH, MPB, MWiW*, N, NN, NSyU, OClWHi, WHi.

516 [DREW, IRA T.]. Legal Decisions of Common Law of the United States. [n.p., 1865]. Caption title. 4 pp. 22 cm.
On p. 4, signed: *Ira T. Drew*. Dated at Alfred, Me.: Sept. 30, 1865. The letter, addressed to Elder Otis Sawyer, Alfred, Me., submitted "suggestions and replies" in response to his inquiry concerning the legal liabilities of the Society of Believers for actions taken by Trustees. A clarification of the Society's liabilities was particularly important at this time. In 1863, after the murder of Caleb Dyer, Trustee of the Enfield, N.H., Shaker community, A. Conant and Company initiated a suit against the Shakers, who fought the claim for 20 years but finally had to pay $20,000. *See* M. F. Melcher, *Shaker Adventure* (no. 2451), pp. 232-33. MacLean 219. MPB, MWA, MWiW*, MeB, N, NN, NBuG, OClWHi.

517 DUNLAVY, JOHN. The Manifesto, or A Declaration of the Doctrines and Practice of the Church of Christ .... Pleasant Hill, Ky.: P. Bertrand, Printer, 1818. vi, [blank leaf] 520 pp. 21 cm.
This work is considered by many to be the definitive treatise on Shaker theology. One of the earliest converts to Shakerism in the West, Dunlavy was chief minister at Pleasant Hill for 20 years. This book was printed by Shakers,

on Shaker-made paper, and bound in full sheep by Shakers, cf. E. D. Andrews, *People Called Shakers* (no. 1767), p. 319, n. 143, and D. M. Hutton, *Old Shakertown* (no. 2302), p. 60. Extracts from this standard treatise on Shaker doctrine were used in Dunlavy's later publications, nos. 520 and 522. "The substance of a letter to Barton W. Stone," pp. [439]-520.
MacLean 15. Sabin 21310. Shaw 43894. CSmH, CtY, DeWint, DLC, ICJ, InHi, InI, KyBgW, KyLoF, KyLxCB, KyLxT, KySP, KyU, KyWAT, MHi, MPB, MPH, MWA, MWiW*, MiU-C, MoU, N, NBuG, NHi, NN, NNG, NNUT, NOC, O, OCHP, OClWHi, ODa, OHi, OLeWHi, OO, PPPrHi.

518 —— ———— ... Printed at Pleasant-Hill, Ky. MDCCCXVIII. New-York: Reprinted by Edward O. Jenkins, 1847. viii, 486 pp. 23 cm.

The "Advertisement," p. [iii], states that this is not intended to be a revised edition, but that slight textual changes have been made in accordance with the author's request made before his decease. "The substance of a letter to Barton W. Stone," pp. [411]-486. Excerpts from Dunlavy's *Manifesto* were printed in *The Circular* (Oneida Community, N.Y.), no. 1649.
MacLean 16. Sabin 21310. CSmH, CtY, DeWint, DLC, ICU, KyBgW, KyHi, KyLxT, KyU, KyWAT, LU, MB, MBAt, MH, MHi, MPB, MPH, MWA, MWiW*, MeB, MiU-C, N, NHi, NN, NOC, NRCR, NSyU, NhD, NjPT, O, OC, OCl, OClWHi, ODa, OHi, OKentU, OLeWHi, OO, PPL, PPULC, WHi.

519 —— ———— (Reprint). New York: AMS Press, Inc., 1972.

520 —— The Nature and Character of the True Church of Christ Proved by Plain Evidences, and Showing Whereby it May Be Known and Distinguished from All Others. Being Extracts from the Writings [i.e., *The Manifesto*] of John Dunlavy ... New York: Printed by George W. Wood, 1847. 93 pp. 19½ cm.

Originally published with the title: *Plain Evidences*, no. 522. Slight textual changes occur, and "Extracts from a Letter Addressed

to Barton W. Stone," pp. [105]-119, and his "Poem" are omitted.
MacLean 220. CtY, DLC, ICN, In, KyBgW, MB, MBAt, MPB, MWA, MWiW*, MeB, MiU-C, N, NBuG, NHi, NN, NOC, NSyU, NhD, O, OClWHi, ODa, OO, OOxM, PPC, PPDrop, PPPrHi, TxU, WHi.

521 —— ———— 1850. 93 pp. 19 cm.
At head of title: For circulation gratis.
MPB, MWA, MWiW*, MSaE, MeB, NN, OHi, NOC, NRCR, OClWHi, PPL.

522 —— Plain Evidences, by which the Nature and Character of the True Church of Christ May Be Known and Distinguished from All Others. Taken from a Work Entitled "The Manifesto, or A Declaration of the Doctrines and Practice of the Church of Christ:" Published at Pleasant Hill, Kentucky, 1818 .... Albany [N.Y.]: Printed by Hoffman and White, 1834. 120 pp. 18½ cm.

"Errata," verso, back cover. "The most clear and conclusive parts" of Dunlavy's *Manifesto* (no. 517) were chosen by Calvin Green and Seth Y. Wells for inclusion in this work, C. Green's "Biographic Memoir," p. 641; "Extracts from a letter addressed to Barton W. Stone," pp. [105]-119; "Poem" [by John Dunlavy], p. 120. "Extracts ..." was reprinted in the *Day-Star*, 11 (June 13, 1846), 6-7, under the title, "Present Truth."
MacLean 17, Sabin 79717. CtHi, CtY, DLC, MH, MPB, MPH, MWA, MWiW*, MeHi, MiU-C, N, NBuG, NN, NOC, NRCR, NjPT, OClWHi, OHi, OWoC.

523 [——] Public Discourses, Delivered (in Substance) at Union Village, August, 1823, and Prepared for Publication. By Order of the Ministry. A Few Paragraphs and Explanatory Notes Have Been Added. [Union Village, O.: 1823?]. Caption title. 35 [1] pp. 18 cm.

"A clear distinction between the law and the gospel: and consequently between the state of those under the law and of those in the gospel." "Hymn," verso, page 35. This is sometimes attributed to Richard McNemar. MacLean, *Life* (no. 2411), p. 64, states that this "should be credited to Richard McNemar," but on p. 67 identifies McNemar as assistant editor. It is likely that McNemar wrote the explanatory notes.

MacLean 418. Shaw 12407. ICJ, MPB, MWA, MWiW*, NBuG, NN, NOC, OC, OClWHi, WHi.

524 DURKEE, JAMES M. The Spirit Life. [Mt. Lebanon, N.Y.: 1886]. Caption title. 4 pp. 13½ cm.

A letter dated at Pittsfield, Mass., May 14, 1886, addressed to Elder Evans, concerning a conversation between the author and Isaac Auger of the Hancock Shaker Village. Reprinted from *The Manifesto*, 16 (October 1886), 234-35.

MacLean 221. DLC, MWiW*, OClWHi.

525 DYER, JOSEPH. A Compendious Narrative, Elucidating the Character, Disposition and Conduct of Mary Dyer, from the Time of her Marriage, in 1799, till she Left the Society called Shakers, in 1815. With a few Remarks upon Certain Charges which she has since Published Against the Society. Together with Sundry Depositions. By her Husband Joseph Dyer. To Which is Annexed, A Remonstrance Against the Testimony and Application of the said Mary, for Legislative Interference. Concord [N.H.]: Printed by Isaac Hill, For the Author, 1818. Cover title. 88 pp. 17 cm.

Written to refute the accusations in Mary Dyer's *Brief Statement*, no. 530. The "Remonstrance" referred to in the title is reprinted on pp. [80]-87, *see* no. 1235. Dyer's *Compendious Narrative* is reprinted in R. McNemar's *The Other Side of the Question* (no. 946), pp. 40-114, with the omission of the "Remonstrance."

MacLean 222. Shaw 43899. CtY, MHi, MPB, MWA, MWiW*, MiU-C, N, NN, OClWHi, RPB.

526 —— ———— Concord [N.H.]: Printed by Isaac Hill for the Author, 1819. 88 pp. 17½ cm.

Cover title: Dyer's Narrative. Printed from the same typesetting but the date has been changed to 1819. Sabin 21591 (With "Shakers" in the title misprinted "Quakers," and an incorrect reference to "Tuke's Biographic Notices; Vol. II, p. 45," which con-

cerns the Mary Dyer who was an early New England Quaker martyr.

Shaw 47864. CtHT, DLC, MB, MBAU, MH, MHarF, MHi, MWA, MWiW*, MiU, N, NN, Nh, NhD, NhHi, OClWHi.

527 —— ———— ... till she Left the Society, Called Quakers [sic] in 1815. Compiled by her Husband ... Concord [N.H.]: 1824. 88 pp.

This entry has been taken from Shaw. Both Sabin 21591 and Shaw 16027 record this edition, and Shaw shows holdings for DLC, MH, MiU, MWA, and MWiW. Such an edition is found neither in the *National Union Catalog* nor the *Library of Congress Catalog*. Shaw mistakenly credits Williams College with a copy. No copy has been located.

528 —— ———— Concord [N.H.]: Printed by Isaac Hill, For the Author, 1826. 88 pp.

Shaw 24389 mistakenly credits OClWHi with this edition. No copy has been located.

529 —— ———— Second edition. Pittsfield [Mass.]: Printed by J. M. Beckwith, at the Office of the Berkshire American, 1826. Cover title. 80 pp. 23½ cm.

The text of *A Compendious Narrative* ... is the same as the first edition (Concord, N.H., 1818), no. 525, with new material added. "To the Reader" by J. Dyer explains that this is republished to rebut Mary Dyer's *Reply to the Shakers' Statements* (Concord, N.H., 1824), no. 534, and also to circulate his side of the dispute "in the neighborhood of her late rambles." Mary Dyer had visited New Lebanon, N.Y., in 1825-26 and had issued two "slanderous productions against the Shakers there," (nos. 537 and 538). The Appendix, pp. 67-80, contains some additional depositions supporting the Shakers. Pages 75-80 contain James Farnham's second refutation of the charges in Mary Dyer's New Lebanon handbills, and contains the notarized denials by Amy Russell and Harriet Sellick of Mary Dyer's false accusations that Farnham "stood on the shore [of Whiting's Pond] while the women went naked into the water." The women state that they wore long garments "suitable for the purpose," and that

Phebe Smith, who was in ill health, did not "go into the water at all." Moreover, they went into the water "to find some leeches for her use." *See also* no. **690**.
MacLean 223. Sabin 21591. Shaw 24390. CSmH, CtY, DLC, MH, MPB, MWA, MWiW*, NBuG, NNC, NNNAM, NhD, OClWHi, WHi.

530 DYER, MARY MARSHALL. A Brief Statement of the Sufferings of Mary Dyer, Occasioned by the Society Called Shakers. Written by Herself. To Which Is Added, Affidavits and Certificates. Also, a Declaration from Their Own Publication . . . Concord, N.H.: Printed by Joseph C. Spear, 1818. Cover title. 35 pp. 19 cm.

"To the Honorable Senate, and House of Representatives of the State of New-Hampshire, in General Court Convened . . ." p. [3], precedes the text, and is signed: *Mary Dyer, Enfield, June 6, 1818*. "To the Honourable Senate and the Honourable House of Representatives in General Court convened. The Petition of Mary Dyer . . ." pp. 32-34, signed: *Mary Dyer, Concord, June, 1818*. The petition is followed by a statement, Enfield, May 28, 1818, addressed to the House and Senate, signed by 47 inhabitants. They assert that they have been visited by women whose "husbands, their property, and children are with said Society of Shakers, and the women deprived of every earthly enjoyment," pp. 34-35, cf. no. **1235**. This is the first work publicizing Mary Dyer's protracted dispute with the Shakers. She left the Enfield, N.H., Shaker community, but her husband remained and consigned their children, aged 3-14, to the Shakers. Mary Dyer lost her case, but, as late as 1847, continued to publish her attacks on the Shakers.
Shaw 44696. CtY, DLC, MB, MMHi, MPB, MWiW*, NhD, VtMiM.

531 —— —————— Boston: Published by William S. Spear, 1818. 35 pp. 19½ cm.

The type has been reset, but the text is unchanged. Priority of publication has not been established. It seems likely, however, that the Concord, New Hampshire edition should have preceded the Boston edition.
MacLean 493. Sabin 21594. Shaw 44695.

CSmH, CSt, CtHT-W, DLC, MBAt, MBC, MHi, MWA, MWiW*, N, NN, NHi, NNUT, NhHi, NjPT, OClWHi.

532 —— A Portraiture of Shakerism, Exhibiting a General View of Their Character and Conduct, from the First Appearance of Ann Lee in New-England, Down to the Present Time. And Certified by Many Respectable Authorities. Drawn up by Mary M. Dyer . . . The Author has Endeavored, while Exposing to the World the Dark Side of the Picture, to Give it No Deeper Shade Than the Light of Truth Will Warrant . . . . [Haverhill, N.H.:], Printed for the Author [by Sylvester T. Goss], 1822 [c. 1821]. 446 pp. 18 cm.

Concord, N.H., is usually given as the place of printing, but in her *Reply to the Shakers* (Concord, 1824), no. **534**, p. 28, Sylvester T. Goss, Haverhill, N.H., certified that he was the printer of *The Portraiture* . . . Some copies have an errata slip pasted on the end leaf following p. 446. This work is a miscellany of new material, new and reprinted affidavits; large sections are reprinted from other works, etc. For example, Reuben Rathbun's *Reasons Offered for Leaving the Shakers* (Pittsfield, Mass., 1800) no. **1215**, pp. 43-90; "Extract from Eunice Chapman's History," pp. 229-68; "Answer to the Shakers' Remonstrances against Eunice Chapman by Thomas Brown," pp. 268-75; "An Act for the Relief of Eunice Chapman . . ." (no. **1080**), pp. 288-91; "A Letter from Abram Van Vleet," Lebanon, Ohio, requesting "all the information on the subject you can [send], the proceedings of the Legislature [N.H.] in particular," pp. 306-307; James Smith's *Remarkable Occurences lately Discovered among the People called Shakers* (no. **1316**), pp. 308-28. Mary Dyer's *A Brief Statement* (Concord, N.H., 1818), no. **530**, pp. 339-66 *passim*, is a revision. *See also* no. **1242**.
MacLean 494 (Concord, N.H., 466 pp.). Sabin 21595. Shaw 9366. CSmH, Ct, CtHi, CtY, DLC, DeWint, KyU, M, MB, MBAt, MBC, MHarF, MH, MHi, N, NBuG, NCH, NN, NNC, NNUT, NOC, Nh, NhD, NhM, O, OClW, OClWHi, ODa, OHi, PPPrHi.

533 —— —————— (Reprint). Communal

Societies in America, 1st Series. New York: AMS Press, 1972.

534 —— Reply to the Shakers' Statements, Called a "Review of the Portraiture of Shakerism," with an Account of the Sickness and Death of Betsy Dyer; a Sketch of the Journey of the Author: and Testimonies from Several Persons ... Concord [N.H.]: Printed for the Author, 1824. Cover title. 112 pp. 18 cm.

In addition to the Shaker refutation (no. 1235) of the validity of the affidavits supporting Mary Dyer's cause, the Concord *Patriot* printed letters which charged falsehood and deception in the gathering and taking of the affidavits published in *The Portraiture*, (no. 532). A letter, pp. 28–29, from Obadiah Mooney, the Justice of the Peace who certified these affidavits, addressed to Isaac Hill, editor of the *Patriot*, vigorously affirms the correctness and authenticity of these affidavits. The Williams College copy is an autograph presentation copy from Isaiah Thomas to the American Antiquarian Society (blind stamped "Duplicate Sold"), October 1st, 1825. Isaiah Thomas' autograph note, p. 28, states that "After the receptial [sic] of this letter, the Editor would publish no more for the Shakers," cf. no. 3280 ff. Betsy Dyer, daughter of the author, died Jan. 14, 1824, at the Shaker Community, Enfield, N.H. MacLean 495. MH, MHarF, MHi, MWA, MWiW*, N, NhD.

535 —— The Rise and Progress of the Serpent from the Garden of Eden, to the Present Day: with a Disclosure of Shakerism, Exhibiting a General View of Their Real Character and Conduct from the Appearance of Ann Lee. Also, the Life and Sufferings of the Author, Who was Mary M. Dyer, but is now Mary Marshall. Concord, N.H.: Printed for the Author, 1847. 268 pp. port. 18½ cm.

Binder's title: Shakerism Exposed. Much of the text is reprinted from Mary Dyer's earlier publications, along with additional depositions and some new material. This revival of her dispute with the Shakers was intended to strengthen the petitions, including her own, that were being presented to

the New Hampshire Legislature at this time, *see* nos. **1071** and **3772**. After the Legislature granted her divorce, November 1829, Mary Dyer successfully petitioned the Legislature for legal permission to use her maiden name, Mary Marshall, as indicated on the title page. By this time, however, the name Mary Dyer had become indelibly fixed because of her publications and the wide notoriety attending her longstanding dispute with the Shakers. The name, Mary Marshall Dyer, is used in this bibliography.
MacLean 18. Sabin 21597. CSmH, CtY, DLC, MBC, MH, MHarF, MHi, MPB, MWA, MWiW*, MeHi, N, NHi, NBuG, NN, NOC, NRCR, NSyU, NhD, OClWHi, OHi, WHi.

536 —— Shakerism Exposed: By Mary M. Dyer. Hanover [N.H.]: Dartmouth Press, [n.d.]. Cover title. 32 pp. 23 cm.

This title, *Shakerism Exposed,* is often confused with the binder's title of M. Dyer's *Rise and Progress* (no. 535), Statement, p. [2], "An abridgment of Shakerism Exposed: [i.e., *Rise and Progress of the Serpent,* no. 535] with an explanation on a book called *Dyer's Narrative* [no. 525], which is a malignant work of abuse on a Shaker husband's wife. The following work is published for the benefit of helpless wives and children, who are bound down by the Shakers." Recapitulation of the "incident" at New Lebanon and James Farnham's *Handbill*, pp. 11–12. *See* nos. **690** and **538**. The British Museum *Catalogue* dates this publication [1850?].
Sabin 21598 (Concord, 1855). MPB*, NhD.

537 —— ... To the Elders and Principals of the Shaker Societies. [n.p., 1825]. Caption title. [2] pp. (1 fold, facing pages printed). 24½ X 20 cm.

Dated at head of title: New-Lebanon, (N.Y.) July 5, 1825. "To the Elders," p. [1], signed: *Mary Dyer;* "Depositions," p. [2], signed: *Silas Churchill.* Mary Dyer's long invective is intended only for Shakers who hold office. "Your subjects are honest, and their honesty you impose on." She repeats damaging rumors circulated earlier about Ann Lee's behaviour, and charges that a "recent transaction at ...

Whiting's Pond, in Canaan, near New-Lebanon ... James Farnam, one of your principal Ministers or speakers stood upon the shore while women went naked into the water and there exercised themselves in his presence," .... and that "documents from the first characters in your vicinity ... will be found lodged at the Rev. Mr. Churchill's, and are to be preserved with the Town Records." At the end she states, "Give me my children, I ask no more." *See* nos. **690** and **538**. A strongly worded communication published in the Pittsfield, Mass., *Sun*, Aug. 25, 1825, signed by local Shaker Elders and leaders, Nathaniel Deming, Daniel Goodrich, and Asa Patten, challenges the veracity of Mary Dyer's accusations.
MH, NjMD*.

538 —— To the Public. [New-Lebanon, N.Y.: 1826]. [4] pp. 23½ cm.

This is a refutation, dated March 25, 1826, of "a Circular signed *James Farnham* [no. **690**], who is a Shaker leader in New-Lebanon, N.Y., which contains an outrageous and wanton attack, not only on my character, but many venerable persons ...." It is notarized by those involved in the "Whiting's Pond transaction" and a supporting affidavit signed by 32 inhabitants of New Lebanon follows. At end, p. [4]: "I intend soon to publish an improved edition of the *Portraiture of Shakerism* [no. **532**]." No such edition has been located. Reprinted in Mary Dyer's *Rise and Progress of the Serpent from the Garden of Eden*, pp. 261-65 (no. **535**).
MHarF*, MWA.

E

E. H. W. *See* Wright, Eleanor Hayes, nos. **1466** and **1467**.

539 [EADS, HARVEY LAUDERDALE]. ... Answer. To "Lines by Charlotte Cushman," from the New-York Knickerbocker for January [1837]. [n.p., n.d.]. Broadside. 25 X 11½ cm.

"From the Russellville, Ky., Advertiser." Poem of 81 lines. *See also* no. **491**. The author's name is sometimes spelled "Eades" and his Christian name is also found spelled "Hervey."
OClWHi*.

540 [——] Condition of Society: And Its Only Hope, in Obeying the Everlasting Gospel, as Now Developing among Believers in Christ's Second Appearing ... Union Village, O.: Printed and Published at the "Day-Star" Office, 1847. 120 pp. 15 cm.

Offprint from the *Day-Star*, 12 (Mar. 20, Apr. 12, 21, May 5, 1847), 32-36, 40-41, 46-48, 50-53. Editor's note, *Day-Star*, 12 (Feb. 13, 1847), 17, proposes "soon to issue a pamphlet embodying the substance of most of the arguments that have been put forth during the last year, and perhaps some new articles calculated to throw light upon the minds of the present class of enquirers [i.e., Adventists]." This was probably printed on McNemar's press, and was available either in sheets or bound; 1000 copies were published, *Day-Star*, 12 (Apr. 12, 1847), 37. Eads' autograph presentation copy in the Kentucky Library (Bowling Green, Ky.) has note, "Friend Calvert—I do not expect to convert you with this little book which I published in Ohio some years since nor do I approve *all* its arguments—but I think it is in the main *true*—and all of us ought to be willing to hear, read and receive *truth* no odds from what quarter it may come—you can hand it to your neighbor when you are through with it—, Your friend, H. L. Eads." J. P. MacLean's a.l.s. to H. M. Lydenberg dated at Franklin, O., May 28, 1905, gives H. L. Eads as the author. Contains also: "Extract from a Sermon" by Robert Atkins of Liverpool, Eng., printed in the *Day-Star*, 12 (Mar. 20, Apr. 12, 1847), 31-32, 38-39; "Resurrection," a letter addressed: Dear Bro. Enoch Jacobs, and signed: *Joseph M. Myrick*, dated: Harvard, Mass., Feb. 8, 1847, printed in the *Day-Star*, 12 (Apr. 12, 1847), 39-40; "Praise the Lord"

[poem] by Samuel Hooser is printed on the verso of the back cover.

MacLean 202. Sabin 79701. CSmH, CtY, DLC, ICJ, KyBgW, MPB, MWA, MWiW*, MiU-C, N, NBuG, NN, NNC, NOC, NRCR, O, OClWHi, OHi, OOxM, PPC.

541 —— Discourses on Religion, Science, and Education. Published by Request. South Union, Ky.: 1884. 20 pp. 22½ cm.

"Religion and Science," pp. 3-8, reprinted (with slight changes) from *The Manifesto*, 14 (March 1884), 51-52, 79-81. Reprinted in his *Shaker Sermons* (1884), no. **547**, and in later editions. "Education," pp. 9-20, was reprinted in *Shaker Sermons* (1887 and 1889), nos. **548** and **549**.

MacLean 224. MH, MPB, MWA, MWiW*, MiU-C, N, NBuG, NN, NOC, NSyU, NhD, NjPT, OClWHi.

542 —— Expression of Faith. A Discursive Letter, by H. L. Eades, South Union, Ky., October 1875. Orange, N.J.: Printed for the Author at the Chronicle Book & Job Printing Office, 1875. 44 pp. 18½ cm.

Cover title: Discursive Letter. Reply to a letter from Elder Evans which "abounds in important questions as well as some mistakes," p. [6]. Letter signed: *H. L. Eads;* addressed: My brother B. Williams College (Williamstown, Mass.) copy is the author's autograph presentation copy to Elder D. Boler. Copies of this letter which contain only 36 pp. lack the Supplement, pp. 37-44.

MacLean 19. DLC*, KyBgW, KyLxCB, MWA, MWiW (36 pp.), MiU-C, N, NN, NOC, NjPT, OC, OCl, OClWHi.

543 —— From a Sermon, by Elder H. L. Eads of South Union, Kentucky, Sept. 1877. [Printed at Shaker Village, Mer. Co., N.H.: n.d.]. Caption title. 4 pp. 25 cm.

Contains also: "Our Petition" [poem] by Mary Whitcher; "Reflection" [poem] by Sophia M. Lowd.

MWiW*.

544 —— A Shaker Letter. [Shaker Village, Canterbury, N.H.: Printed by the Canterbury Shakers, 1880]. Caption title. 8 pp. 17 cm.

Letter addressed: Mrs. E. D. S., and dated: South Union, Ky., Mar. 1880. Written in response to her inquiries regarding passages in his *Shaker Sermons*. Also printed in the *Shaker Manifesto*, 10 (April 1880), 83-86, under the title, "A Very Plain Shaker Letter," and addressed: Elmina D. Slenker: Respected Friend.

MacLean 225. CtY, DLC, MPB, MPH, MWiW*, NBuG, OClWHi.

545 —— Shaker Sermons: Scripto-rational. Containing the Substance of Shaker Theology. Together with Replies and Criticisms Logically and Clearly Set Forth .... Shakers [Watervliet], N.Y., The Shaker Manifesto [Albany, N.Y.: Printed by Weed, Parsons & Co.], 1879. 3 p.l., 222 pp. port. 23½ cm.

Cover title: Shaker Theology. Eads, born at South Union, Ky., was presiding Bishop of the Kentucky Societies for two decades. The unsigned preface by the editor [G. A. Lomas] describes this as "the first book ever written for publication, by an individual whose whole life has been consecratedly devoted to and guided by the principles of Shakerism. The sermons embrace nearly or quite nearly every feature of Shaker polity ..." *See also* Lomas' review, "If on reading his book he appears to be bigoted, charge this to his enthusiasm and deep sincerity," *Shaker Manifesto*, 9 (September 1879), 212-13; also Eads' "An Open Letter — Book and Portrait," where he makes an apologetic explanation for the inclusion of his portrait which was "a departure from common usage and sense of society," and defends his book, "It cannot be expected that *all* of any profession will be able to see eye to eye in speculative theology," *ibid.*, 9 (November 1879), 245-46. Extracts and many of the sermons had appeared originally in the *Shaker Manifesto* and its precursors. The sermons are described in *Socialism and American Life*, no. **2081**, II: 182, as "The most sophisticated treatment of Shaker theology."

MacLean 20. CtY, DLC, ICN, ICRL, IU, KHi, KyBgW, KyHi, KyLxCB, KySP, KyU, MB, MBC, MBrZ, MH, MPB, MSaE, MWA, MWiW*, MeB, MeHi, MiD, MiU-C, N, NBuG, NHi, NIC, NN, NNC, NOC, MSaE, NSyU, Nh, NjMD, NjPT, OCl, OClWHi, OGK,

OFH, OHi, OO, PPL, RHi, TxU, WHi.

546 —— ———— New ed. Rev. and enl. Shakers [Watervliet], N.Y.: 1884. iv, [1], 271 pp. port. 23½ cm.

Binder's title: Shaker Theology. Printed from the plates of the 1st edition with new material added, and slight revisions. These plates were used for subsequent editions. "Two Poems," pp. [268]–271, include "Lines Suggested by a Visit to the Shakers, near Albany. By Charlotte Cushman," and "Answer: — To Lines by Charlotte Cushman." The author of the latter is identified, p. 268, as H. L. Eads, and not his mother, Sally Eads, or "Shaker Girl." MacLean, *Bibliography*, p. 25, notes that "This edition was ordered burned by the Mount Lebanon Ministry." No verification for this information has been found. A difference of opinion among the Shakers is implied, however, in the annotation following the 1879 edition, no. **545**. General acceptance by Shakers would seem to be evident, however, by the earlier appearance of so much of the contents in the *Shaker Manifesto*, etc., and would seem also to invalidate MacLean's statement. Why didn't the Ministry proscribe publication of the book, and thus avoid the order to burn? It may be significant that all later editions were published at South Union, Ky., where Eads was Bishop. The answer may lie in the longstanding differences between Eads, who represented the conservative concept of Shaker doctrine, and Elder Evans, who vigorously advocated liberalization of doctrine. For a discussion of these differences, *see* E. D. Andrews, *The People Called Shakers* (no. **1767**), pp. 231–36. MacLean 21. DLC, ICJ, KyBgW, KyU, MU, MWA, MWiW*, MiU–C, N, NBuG, NN, NSyU, OCl, OO, PPD, PU, WHi.

547 —— ———— Third ed. Rev. and enl. South Union, Kentucky: 1884. iv, 287 pp. port. 23½ cm.

Binder's title: Shaker Theology. New material (not included in the Table of Contents) has been added following p. 271; otherwise this is a reprint of the Shakers [Watervliet] N.Y., 1884 edition. Was the publication of

a second edition within one year occasioned by the destruction of the earlier 1884 edition? *See annotation* no. **546**. MacLean 22. CtY, DeWint, DLC, KyBgW, KyU, MH–AH, MPB, MSaE, MWiW*, N, NBLiHi, NBuG, NSyU, NhD, NjPT, O, OClWHi, OHi, TxFTC.

548 —— ———— Fourth ed. Rev. and enl. South Union, Kentucky: 1887. vi, 320 pp. port. 23½ cm.

Cover title: "The Faith Once Delivered to the Saints." Binder's title: Shaker Theology. Preface by the editor signed: *G. A. L.* [omas]. Slight revisions which do not interfere with use of the same plates. Some rearrangement of the text, with most of the new material added after p. 272. Recently, a stereotyped title-page plate dated 1886 was discovered at South Union. Printing delays caused another plate dated 1887 to be made. An advertisement in *The Manifesto*, January 1888, describes the *Sermons* as "containing the substance of Shaker Theology; together with replies and criticisms, logically set forth." MacLean 23. CtY, DLC, IU, KyLxCB, KySP, MPB, MWA, MWiW*, MiU–C, N, NN, NOC, NjPT, OC, OCl, OClWHi, ODa, OHi, OOxM, WHi.

549 —— ———— Fifth edition. Rev. and enl. South Union, Kentucky: 1889. vi, 366 pp. port. 23½ cm.

Cover title: The Faith Once Delivered to the Saints. Binder's title: Shaker Theology. Preface by the editor signed: *G. A. L* [omas]. Most of the new material follows p. 314. "True theology," pp. 315–30, appeared in *The Manifesto*, 18 (February, April, May 1888), 27–29, 77–80, 100–105. MacLean 24. CtY, DLC, KySP, MBC, MH–AH, MPB, MWA, MWiW, MiU–C, N, NN, NSyU, Nh, NjPT, OClWHi*, OHi, OLeWHi, WHi.

550 —— The Tailor's Division System, Founded upon, and Combined with Actual Measurements: Containing Thirty Diagrams and Designs, Reduced to Mathematical Principles. Union Village, O.: [A. F. Becker's Lith, Cincinnati], 1849. [23] l., XVIII (i.e., XVII), [3] pls. illus. 55 cm.

While he was living at Union Village, Ohio, Eads wrote and published this system of

designs for cutting out various articles of Shaker brethren's uniform dress. Plates and text alternate. Plates I–XVIII, three unnumbered diagrams, and the accompanying leaves of explanatory text are bound perpendicular to the binding edge and face the fore-edge, but leaves [1–2] (t.p. and "Preface and Introduction") face the binding edge. The 3 leaves of text which accompany the unnumbered diagrams are headed "Appendix," and contain "The Plumb & Square Rule" by Isaac N. Youngs. Patterns and a tailor's rule have been laid in the back fly leaves of the Western Reserve Historical Society's copy. All copies examined lack Plate XVII and accompanying text.
MacLean 25. DeWint, MHarF, NjPT, OClWHi*, OHi.

551 —— Types of Christ, and Manner of His Second Appearing . . . . South Union, Ky.: 1878. 20 pp. 19 cm.
 Reprinted from the *Shaker Manifesto*, 8 (August 1878), 200–208.
 MacLean 226. CSmH, CtY, DLC, ICN, KyBgW, KySP, MHi, MPB, MSaE, MWA, MWiW*, MiU-C, N, NBuG, NN, NOC, NSyU, NjPT, O, OClWHi.

552 The Ear. What Fine Organ Gives More Pleasure than the Perfect Human Ear . . . Shaker Village [Canterbury], Mer. Co., N.H.: [186–?]. Broadside. music. 25 × 15 cm.
 Song of 3 stanzas with the music written in Shaker letter notation. At end: School District, No. 8.
 OClWHi*.

553 EDWARDS, MATILDA C. Walking with the World [poem]. [East Canterbury, N.H.: Printed at Shaker Village, Mer. Co., N.H., n.d.]. 4 pp. 23 cm.
 Cut of beehive, foot of p. 4. "Reprinted from Baltimore Christian Advocate."
 OClWHi*.

554 ELAM, AIDA and MIRIAM WALL. History of the Shakers. Education and Recreation. A Brief History. Canterbury, N.H. [Penacook, N.H.: Hazen Printing Co., 1963]. Cover title. [11], [1 p. blank], [13–20] pp. 20½ cm.

A paper delivered at a seminar, Canterbury, N.H., 1961 and 1962.
MWA, MWiW*, NOC, NSyU, WHi.

555 Elder Evans's Millennium. [Hudson, N.Y.: 1888]. Broadside. 16 × 7½ cm.
 In response to a letter from F. W. Evans wherein he stated that he expects to live another decade and proceeds to make prophecies that will be completed in 1898, when he will be 90 years of age.
 OClWHi*.

556 Elementary Lessons in Arithmetic. Comprising the Rules of Notation, Numeration, Addition, Subtraction, Multiplication, and Division; also the Tables of Weights, Measures, Time, &c. Burnham's and Smith's Arithmetics. Shaker Village, Canterbury, N.H.: [n.d.]. 32 pp. 13 cm.
 MacLean 227. DLC*.

ELKING, WILLIAM. Eleven Years Among the Shakers at Enfield. By William Elking. Hanover: Dartmouth Press, 1853. 136 pp.
 Described in Sabin 22198. No other record of this title has been found, and no copy has been located. Cf. no. 558.

557 ELKINS, HERVEY. A Discourse on Modern Spiritualism, Delivered at Burlington, Vt., March 17, 1858. Burlington [Vt.]: Stacy, 1858. 32 pp. 22 cm.
 MB*, NN.

558 —— Fifteen Years in the Senior Order of the Shakers: A Narration of the Facts, Concerning That Singular People . . . Hanover, N.H.: Dartmouth Press, 1853. 136 pp. 23 cm.
 Elkins was a member of the Enfield, N.H. community from his childhood to about 1850. This sympathetic account has been used extensively by later writers on the Shakers. Contains also: "Lines" [poem] by Charlotte Cushman. Suggested by a visit to the Shaker settlement near Albany, N.Y. [i.e., Watervliet], pp. [5]–6; "Answer to Lines by Charlotte Cushman" by a Shaker Girl [i.e. Hervey L. Eads], "in one of the Kentucky societies," pp. [7]–8, *see* no. 491. "Errata": p. 136.
 MacLean 228. Sabin 22197 (incl. an 1852

imprint mistakenly credited to MBAt. No copy located.). CtY, DLC, KyBgW, MB, MBAt, MH, MWA, MWiW*, MiU, N, NN, NBLiHi, NN, NOC, NSyU, NhD, NhDo, OClWHi, OHi, OU, PPB.

559 —— ———— (Reprint). New York: AMS Press, 1972.

560 Enfield, New Hampshire. Annual Report ... for the Year Ending January 31, 1940. [Enfield, N.H.: 1940] [47] pp. illus.
"Shaker Bridge, 1849–1938," photograph on back cover. New Hampshire Highway Department's description of damage done to the bridge during the 1938 hurricane, pp. [1–2].
Private collection.

561 Enfield, N.H. Society of Believers. One Hundredth Anniversary of the Organization of the Shaker Church, Enfield, N.H., October 18, 1893. Enfield, N.H.: Abbott's Power Print., 1893. 36 [1] pp. 19 cm.
"Opening remarks," p. 5, and "Historical Address," pp. 12–16, by Abraham Perkins; "Historic Notes," pp. 17–23, by H. C. Blinn. Remarks, poems, etc., by representatives of other Shaker Societies. Errata slip tipped in following p. 36.
MacLean 391 (attributed to Abraham Perkins). CtY, DLC, MPB, MPH, MWA, MWiW*, MiU-C, N, NBuG, NHi, NN, NOC, NSyU, NjPT, OClWHi, OHi.

562 [ENNIS, JOHN E.]. The Home and Sanitarium. As Corporation from June, 1906 until Transferred to State of Florida, August 1st, 1909. [Kissimmee, Florida: 1909]. Broadside. 29½ X 19½ cm.
Reprinted from Kissimmee, Fla., *Valley Gazette*, August 13, 1909. Signed: *Jno. E. Ennis, M.D. Late resident physician the Narcoossee Sanitarium. Eliz. A. Sears, Vice-president of the Shaker family.*
OClWHi*.

563 Entertainment. Aug. 18, 1897. Programme [East Canterbury, N.H.: 1897]. Broadside. 20½ X 13 cm.
The program consists of music, reading,

"Joseph and his Brethren" in seven scenes, etc.
OClWHi*.

564 ESTABROOK, FIDELLA E. Berkshire Wildflowers. [advertising circular]. [n.p.: 1902]. Broadside. 15 X 9 cm.
"This book is especially designed for invalids and shut-ins, but may be found a . . . ." joy to others.
OClWHi*.

565 —— Berkshire Wild Flowers [poems]. New York: The Abbey Press, [c1902]. 89 pp. 19 cm.
MacLean 26. DLC, MPB, MWiW*, OClWHi.

566 —— Consecration Prayer for the Royal, True Blues [A Group of Young Shaker Sisters of the Hancock, Mass., community]. [Pittsfield?: 1900?]. Broadside. 19 X 7½ cm.
Poem of 7 stanzas.
NSyU*.

EVANS, F. W. Spiritualism on Trial; Containing the Arguments of Rev. F. W. Evans in the Debate on Spiritualism between Him and Mr. A. J. Fishback held in Osceola, Iowa, Commencing Nov. 18 and Closing Nov. 28, 1874. Cincinnati [O.]: Printed by Hitchcock & Walden, 1875. 432 pp.
The Rev. F. W. Evans named in the title of this work is identified on p. 104 as the "editor of the Ottumwa [Iowa] *Democrat*." Attribution of the authorship of *Spiritualism on Trial* is often mistakenly made to Shaker Elder Frederick William Evans; the Library of Congress makes this wrong attribution explicit by including Shaker Elder Evans' birth and death dates (1808–1893) in the entry. During part of the time these debates were held, Shaker Evans was one of a delegation of sixteen Shakers attending a meeting at Steinway Hall in New York, *see Shaker and Shakeress*, 5 (Jan. 1875), 4. This non-Shaker work has been included here to clarify authorship.

567 EVANS, FREDERICK WILLIAM. "Address" [on Shakerism]. In *Proceedings, Free Convention Held at Rutland, Vt., July 25th, 26th, 27th, 1858* (Boston: J. B.

Yerrington and Son, 1858. 186 pp.), pp. 151-59.
OClWHi*.

568 —— "Although We Are a Small People ..."
[n.p., 188-]. Broadside. 14½ × 8 cm.
Title from the first line of text. Reprinted
from the *Albany Evening Journal,* Oct. 23,
[188-].
CtY, MPB, MWiW*, OClWHi.

569 —— American Shakers. [Mt. Lebanon,
N.Y.: 1887?]. Broadside in 2 columns. 27 ×
14½ cm.
At head of text: Elder Evans in London,
England, *Food Reform Magazine* for June
[1887?]. At end of text: "Done at North
Family, Mt. Lebanon, Columbia Co., New
York."
MacLean 229. CtY, ICN, MPB, MWiW*,
NBuG, NN, OHi, OClWHi.

570 —— Ann Lee (Founder of the Shakers),
a Biography with Memoirs of William Lee,
James Whittaker, J. Hocknell, J. Meacham, and
Lucy Wright; Also a Compendium of the Origin,
History, Principles, Rules and Regulations,
Government, and Doctrines of the United Society of Believers in Christ's Second Appearing.
4th ed. [?]. London: J. Burns; Mt. Lebanon,
N.Y.: F. W. Evans, [1871]. 187 [3] pp. 17 cm.
Printed from the plates of his *Shakers. Compendium* ... (N.Y., 1859), except that the
title page has been reset and unpaged advertising matter added at the end. Cf.
MacLean, *Bibliography,* p. 25. "Fourth Edition" on the title page was inadvertently
included, and "Charles Van Benthuysen &
Sons, Printers" was not removed from the
verso of the title page. *Ann Lee* ... is usually
cited with the publication date, 1858. Apparently, the date of copyright, 1858, on the
verso of the title page has been used in place
of the publication date. This copyright
notice was carried in all so-called editions
of *Shakers. Compendium* ..., nos. **646, 648,**
and **649** below. MacLean does not give a
publication date; Library of Congress assigns
the date [1869?]. The publication date assigned here, [1871], is found in the advertising matter at the end, and coincides with
Evans' presence in London.

MacLean 30 (and 31 in paper covers). CtY,
DLC, ICJ, KyBgW, MB, MPB, MH, MHarF,
MWA, MWiW*, MiU-C, N, NBuG, NHi, NN,
NNC, NOC, NSyU, NjPT, O, OClWHi, OHi,
PHi, PPL, WHi.

571 —— —— (Reprint). New York:
AMS Press, Inc. Publication announced 1972–
1973.

572 —— Atlantic Cable and Materialization.
[n.p., 1880?]. Broadside in 2 columns. 18½ ×
16½ cm.
Reprinted from *The American Socialist*
(Oneida Community, N.Y.), 4 (Jan. 23,
1879), 27. The text is the same as *Elder
Evans on Materialization,* no. **593,** below.
MacLean 230. ICJ, MPB, MWiW*, NN,
OClWHi, OHi.

573 —— —— Broadside. 39 × 7 cm.
Type has been reset.
MHarF, MPB, OClWHi*.

574 [——] Autobiography of a Shaker, and
Revelation of the Apocalypse. With an Ap-
pendix ... Mt. Lebanon, N.Y.: F. W. Evans
[Albany, N.Y.: Charles Van Benthuysen &
Sons, Printers], 1869. 162 pp. 21 cm.
The first part, under the same title, ap-
peared in the *Atlantic Monthly,* April and
May 1869, *see* no. **1540.** The "Appendix,"
pp. [151]-62, consists of extracts from J. M.
Peebles, *The Seers of the Ages* (2d ed.,
Boston, 1869).
MacLean 27. DLC, ICJ, IEG, IaU, KyU, MB,
MPB, MWA, MWiW*, MiU-C, N, NHi, NIC,
NN, OC, OCl, OClWHi, OHi, OOxM, PBa,
PHC, PHi, PPPrHi, WHi.

575 [——] —— New York: American
News Company, [1869]. 162 pp. 21 cm.
Title page reset with new imprint, otherwise
identical with no. **574.**
MacLean 28. DLC, ICarbS, KEmT, KyBgW,
KyU, MB, MHarF, MPB, MWA, MWiW*, N,
NBuG, NN, NOC, NSyU, NhD, NjMD,
OClWHi, OHi.

576 [——] —— New and enlarged ed.
Glasgow, Scotland: United Publishing Company;

New York American News Co., 1888. xvi, 271 pp. port. 19½ cm.

The text of the *Autobiography*, pp. 1–119, remains unchanged. Excerpts from several of Evans' earlier works have been added: *Shaker Communism* (1871), pp. 132–89; *Ann Lee* ... ([1871]), pp. 189–92; *Religious Communism* (1871), pp. 193–219; "Shakers as Farmers," reprinted from the *Shaker Manifesto*, 13 (October 1863), 233–35, etc. Also included: J. M. Peebles, "Shaker Mission to Scotland and England" (1877), pp. 241–47; C. Rowley, "Mount Lebanon" (1887), pp. 259–64; Hester M. Poole, "Shakers and Shakerism" (1887), pp. 264–71, etc.
MacLean 29. CtY, DLC, ICJ, MB, MHarF, MPB, MWiW*, N, NN, NOC, NSyU, NcD, OClWHi, OHi, PSC-Hi.

577 —— ———— (Reprint). Philadelphia: Porcupine Press, Inc., 1972.

578 —— ———— (Reprint). New York: AMS Press, Inc., 1973.

Under Evans' "influence, the Shakers underwent a pronounced shift toward the 'outside world.' This work is of great importance for the study of the latter phase of Shaker history," advertisement.

579 —— The Battle of the Gods. An Open Letter to Col. Ingersoll ... [n.p., 1892]. Broadside. 21 × 13 cm.

Dated: Mt. Lebanon, Columbia Co., N.Y., March 20, 1892.
MacLean 231. MPB, MWiW*, MiU-C, OClWHi.

—— Brief and Useful Moral Instructions for the Young. *See* [Tillinghast, Joseph], no. 1371.

580 —— Capital and Labor. What is in a Name? Wail of a Striker. [Mt. Lebanon, N.Y.: 1886]. Cover title, 11 pp. 13½ cm.

Three separate articles. "What is in a Name?" (appeared in *The Manifesto*, 16 (May 1886), 120), pp. 10–11. Here Evans states, p. 10, that if he expresses "doctrinal views differing from, or at variance with the present theology," as published in *The Manifesto* (no.

990), etc., he desires his readers "to consider them as either heretical, or as expressing the *increasing light* of the church, just as they feel impressed." Alonzo Hollister expressed another viewpoint, "Some articles writ [!] by Elder F. W. Evans for the newspapers, of which he often had extra copies printed on slips or in booklets for his own correspondence ... I deem most of them comparatively unimportant. *Some* of them, at least, embodying only the personal viewpoint of the writer," a.l.s. to Wm. W. Ward, Dec. 27, 1909, Williams College Library, Williamstown, Mass. "Wail of a Striker" has the same text as no. 677.
MacLean 232. ICN, MPB, MWA, MWiW*, N, NBuG, NN, NSyU, OClWHi, OHi.

581 —— Carnivorous Parrots. Elder Evans' Theory of the Wonders of Animal Life. [Mt. Lebanon, N.Y.: 1882]. Broadside. 27½ × 7 cm.

Reprint of a letter addressed "To the Editor of the *Berkshire Eagle*" (Pittsfield, Mass.) dated: Mt. Lebanon, Feb. 20, 1882. Reprinted in *The Shaker Manifesto*, 12 (July 1882), 157.
MacLean 233. CtY, MPB, MWiW*, NBuG, NN, OClWHi, OHi.

582 —— Celibacy, from the Shaker Standpoint. New York: Davies & Kent, Printers, 1866. 12 pp. 15½ cm.

Letter addressed to: "Friend Wells," [i.e., Samuel Roberts Wells, editor of the *American Phrenological Journal*] in reply to an article by William Clark in that journal, no. 1541.
MacLean 234. DLC, MB, MWiW*, OClWHi, PHi.

583 —— Christ. [Mt. Lebanon, N.Y.: 1883]. Broadside. 24 × 14 cm.

Reprint of a letter to the *Berkshire County Eagle* (Pittsfield, Mass.). Appeared in *The Manifesto*, 13 (March 1883), 51–52.
MacLean 235. CtY, ICN, MHarF, MPB, NBuG, NN, OClWHi, OHi.

584 —— The Conditions of Peace. Mt. Lebanon, N.Y.: 1890. 1 p.l., 6 pp. 14 cm.

Letter addressed to: "Dear fried [sic], Alfred Love." Dated: Nov. 26, 1890. Love was

president of the Universal Peace Union.
MacLean 236. CSmH, CtY, DLC, MHarF,
MPB, MWA, MWiW*, MiU–C, N, NBuG,
NBuU, NN, NOC, NSyU, OClWHi, OHi, WHi.

585 —— Confession of Sin. [Mt. Lebanon,
N.Y.: n.d.]. Caption title. 4 pp. 14 cm.
Signed: *F. W. Evans, Mt. Lebanon Columbia
County, N.Y.*
MacLean 237. DLC, MPB, MWA, MWiW*,
MiU–C, N, NBuG, NN, OClWHi, OHi, WHi.

586 —— Correspondence. [n.p., 1890?].
Broadside in 2 columns. 30 × 17½ cm.
Letter from J. W. ——, concerning J. W.'s
return to Mt. Lebanon, dated: Carlinville,
Ill., Sept. [21] 1890. Evans' reply dated:
Mt. Lebanon, N.Y., Sept. 1890. Offprint
from *The Manifesto*, 20 (November 1890),
243–45.
MacLean 239. CtY, MPB, MWiW*, NN,
OClWHi, OHi.

587 —— The Country: A New Earth and New
Heavens. Mt. Lebanon, N.Y.: [n.d.]. Cover title.
8 pp. 13½ cm.
MacLean 238. CtY, DLC, ICN, MHarF,
MPB, MWA, MWiW*, NN, NOC, OClWHi,
OHi.

588 [——] Cruelty to Birds. [Mt. Lebanon,
N.Y.: 1888]. Caption title. [2] pp. 21½ cm.
Signed: *F. W. Evans, Mt. Lebanon, N.Y.,
Jan. 18, 1888.* Printed two columns to the
page. Contains also: "Elder Evans' Platform;
a Test Case at Lebanon." *Cruelty to Birds*
reprinted in *The Manifesto*, 18 (June 1888),
140–41. "Test Case at Lebanon" reprinted
in *The Manifesto*, 18 (February 1888), 35–
36. Elder Evans joins the crusade against
"feathered songsters" in the 1880's, protests
the wearing of feathers by women, and also
urges woman suffrage. "Test case" concerns
a Shaker refusal to admit a 64-year-old
woman who has asked to join the Shakers.
MWiW*, MiU–C, OClWHi.

589 [——] —— [n.p., n.d.]. Broadside.
22½ × 7½ cm.
OClWHi*.

590 —— Egyptian Sphinx. [Mt. Lebanon,

N.Y.: n.d.]. Caption title. 8 pp. 14½ cm.
Subheading, p. 2, "Riddle" is misprinted
"Eiddle." At end of text: Address F. W.
Evans, Mount Lebanon, Col. Co., N.Y. Con-
tains also: "Victor Hugo's Prophecy;" "To
the Sphinx" [poem] by L. L. [i.e., J. L.
Stoddard].
MacLean 240. DLC, MHarF, MPB, MWiW*,
MiU–C, NN, NSyU, OClWHi, OHi, WHi.

591 —— Elder Evans on Collecting Debts.
[Mt. Lebanon, N.Y.: 1883]. Broadside. 15 ×
10 cm.
Reprint of a letter to the New York *Tribune*,
14 October 1883.
MacLean 241. CtY, MHarF, MPB, MWiW*,
NBuG, NN, OClWHi, OHi, WHi.

592 —— —— [n.p., n.d.]. Broadside.
14½ × 8½ cm.
Letter address: To the Editor of the *Albany
Evening Journal,* signed: *F. W. Evans. Mount
Lebanon, N.Y., Nov. 8, 1883.* Reprinted in the
Shaker Manifesto, 13 (December 1883), 284–
85. Editorial printed the following week on this
article states that it "has attracted wide attention." Also that Henry George is popularizing
propositions under a new name, "but which Elder Evans elaborated before George was born."
MWiW*, OClWHi, OHi.

593 —— Elder Evans on Materialization. [n.p.,
n.d.]. Broadside, 28 × 11 cm.
At head of title: From the *Brooklyn Eagle.*
Text is the same as his *Atlantic Cable and
Materialization,* no. 572.
MPB, NjPT, OClWHi*.

594 —— Elder Evans' Reply. [Mt. Lebanon,
N.Y.: 1884]. Broadside in 2 columns. 21½ ×
15 cm.
This is a reply to the letter from W. Baker,
Sr., Otago, New Zealand (no. 62), dated at
Mt. Lebanon, March 7, 1884. Comments on
Shakerism, hopes for its growth, and the low
mortality among the Shakers. Reprinted in
The Manifesto, 14 (October 1884), 229–30.
OClWHi*.

595 —— Elder Evans to Henry George. [Mt.
Lebanon, N.Y.: 1886]. Caption title, 3 pp. 13½ cm.

Undated letter addressed to: Dear Friend. A note preceding the letter states, "Elder F. W. Evans, the amiable Shaker has written the following letter to Henry George." Evans congratulates George on his "good fight," and urges him to continue working to organize laborers, etc. Written after George's defeat for the office of Mayor of New York City.
MacLean 242 (broadside). DLC, MPB, MWA, MWiW*, NBuG, OClWHi, OHi.

596 ―― English Sparrows. [Mt. Lebanon, N.Y.: 1884]. Broadside. 26 × 7 cm.
Evans' defense of the benefits these birds offer. Includes a letter to the Editor of the N.Y. *Tribune* signed: *Grateful Philadelphian, Nov. 4, 1884.*
MacLean 243. MPB, NN, OClWHi*, OHi.

597 ―― Ensilage. [n.p., 1884]. Broadside. 23½ × 6 cm.
Letter in response to J. B. Brown's request (Mar. 1, 1884) for the latest views on ensilage, in connection with Report of 3d Ensilage Congress. Reprinted in Evans' *Autobiography* (no. 576), pp. 230–31.
OClWHi*.

598 ―― God is God. [Mt. Lebanon, N.Y.: 1892]. Caption title. 13 pp. 14 cm.
Contains also: "Physical and Spiritual Light" by Anna White (from *The Manifesto*, 22 (July 1892), 151–53); "Confession of Sin" by Martha J. Anderson (from *The Manifesto*, 22 (July 1892), 149–51); "Religious Sentiment" by M. J. Anderson (from the *Shaker Manifesto*, 11 (May 1881), 102–03); "Our Parentage" by M. J. Anderson (from the *Shaker Manifesto*, 11 (December 1881), 278), *God is God* appeared in the *Shaker Manifesto*, 10 (April 1880), 78–79.
MacLean 244. CtY, DLC, MHarF, MPB, MWA, MWiW*, N, NN, NSyU, OClWHi, OHi.

599 [――] Good Bread. [n.p., n.d.]. Broadside. 12½ × 8½ cm.
Addressed: To the Editor of *The Eagle* [Berkshire County Eagle, Pittsfield, Mass.?]. Appeared unsigned in the *Shaker Manifesto*, 12 (October 1882), 235.

MacLean 245. CtY, MPB, MWiW*, NBuG, NN, OClWHi, OHi.

600 ―― Good Manners. Mt. Lebanon, N.Y.: 1890. Cover title. 3 pp. 14½ cm.
Objects to name-calling by ministers. Appeared in *The Manifesto*, 20 (April 1890), 81–82.
MPB, MWA, MWiW*, N, OCl, WHi.

601 ―― "A Great White Throne." Chatham, N.Y.: Courier Printing and Publishing House, 1889. Cover title. 8 pp. 12½ cm.
MacLean 246 (1869 [sic]). DLC, MPB, MWiW*, MiU-C, N, NN, NSyU, OClWHi, OHi, WHi.

602 ―― ―――― Pittsfield, Mass.: Press of *Berkshire County Eagle*, 1889. Cover title. 8 pp. 15 cm.
MPB, MWiW*, NBuG, OClWHi.

603 ―― Interesting Correspondence. [n.p., 1884]. Broadside. 29 × 8 cm.
Unsigned letter inquiring if Shaker services are open to the public, dated: Lake Shore Farm, Stockbridge, Mass., Aug. 16, 1884. Evans' reply includes a long protest against the mistreatment of Mormons in Tennessee, dated: Mt. Lebanon, Aug. 21, 1884.
MacLean 247. MHarF, MPB, MWiW*, NBuG, OClWHi, OHi.

604 ―― Land Limitation. [Mt. Lebanon, N.Y.?: 1884]. Broadside in 2 columns. 24 × 15 cm.
Letter addressed: To the Editor of the *Sun* (Pittsfield, Mass.), Feb. 11, 1884, enclosing a letter from James Marlin, dated: Bloomington, Ind., Jan. 26, 1884. Evans' article, "Land Limitation," was printed in *The Shaker*, 7 (October 1877), 74–75. James Marlin's letter which also appeared in *The Manifesto*, 14 (April 1884), refers to an Evans' article, "Land Limitation," printed in the New York *Tribune*, Jan. 23, 1884. Marlin's letter in *The Manifesto* is preceded, however, on p. 90 by an Evans' article, "Land Limitation Law," no. 605.
MacLean 248. ICN, MPB, OClWHi*, OO.

605 ―― Land Limitation Law. [n.p., 1884]. Broadside. 28 × 8 cm.

Appeared in *The Manifesto*, 14 (April 1884),
90.
CtY, MWiW, MiU–C, NBuG, OClWHi*.

606 —— Lecture, Delivered in Taylor's Hall,
Amenia, N.Y. [Amenia, N.Y.: n.d.]. Caption
title. 4 pp. 18 cm.
 At end of text: Amenia Times — Extra.
 MacLean 288. MHarF, MPB, MWA, MWiW*,
 NBuG, OClWHi, OHi.

607 —— [Letter about Spiritualism, to H. S.
Olcott, Dec. 1st, 1874]. In H. S. Olcott, *People
from the Other World* (no. 2536), pp. 397–40.

608 —— Letter to Victoria C. Woodhull, Tennie
[i.e. Tennessee] Claflin and George Francis Train.
Mt. Lebanon, [N.Y.]: 1873. Broadside.
 No copy located. This entry is taken from
 MacLean's *Bibliography*, no. 249. Apparently
 the *Letter* concerns Victoria Woodhull's
 accounts of the unproven affair of Henry
 Ward Beecher and the wife of an associate,
 Theodore Tilton, published in *Woodhull and
 Claflin's Weekly*. *See* Evans' article, "The
 Impending Crisis. 'Caesarism in the U.S.',",
 Shaker and Shakeress, 3 (September 1873),
 67–68.

609 —— Liberalism, Spiritualism and Shaker-
ism. An Address . . . [Mt. Lebanon, N.Y.: 1880?].
Caption title. 8 pp. 15 cm.
 Appeared in the *Shaker Manifesto*, 10 (Oc-
 tober 1880), 221–24.
 MacLean 250. CtY, DLC, MHarF, MPB,
 MWA, MWiW*, N, NN, NSyU, OClWHi, OHi,
 WHi.

610 —— Liberty of Conscience. [Mt. Lebanon,
N.Y.: 1890]. Caption title. 4 pp. 14½ cm.
 Letter addressed to: "Friend Eagle" [*Berk-
 shire County Eagle?*], dated: Mt. Lebanon,
 N.Y., March 11, 1890.
 MacLean 251. CtY, DLC, MHarF, MPB,
 MWA, MWiW*, MiU–C, NBuG, NN, NOC,
 NSyU, NjPT, OClWHi, OHi, WHi.

611 [——] The New Earth. [n.p., n.d.]. Broadside in 2 columns. 24½ × 14½ cm.
 Signed: *F. W. Evans.*

MacLean 252. ICN, MPB, MWiW*, NBuG,
NN, OClWHi.

612 —— New England Witchcraft and Spiritual-
ism. [Mt. Lebanon, N.Y.: 1881]. Caption title.
8 pp. 13½ cm.
 An essay on intolerance and spiritualism. At
 end of text: "I have drawn liberally from
 Allen Putnam's *New England Witchcraft*."
 Appeared in *Shaker Manifesto*, 11 (February
 1881), 25–28.
 MacLean 253. CtY, DLC, ICN, MHarF, MPB,
 MWiW*, MiU–C, N, NBuG, NOC, NSyU,
 OClWHi, OHi, WHi.

613 —— Nobodies. [n.p., n.d.]. Broadside.
15 × 11 cm.
 Evans protests the use of his name "as one of
 [the] Community's prominent men," which
 leaves "some sixty communities of Shakers"
 as nobodies. Written in reply to an article,
 "Socialist Democracy," in the *American
 Socialist*, Vol. 3, no. 7 (1878).
 MacLean 254. MHarF, MPB, NBuG, NN,
 OClWHi*.

614 —— Obituary. Death of a Prominent
Shaker [Giles B. Avery] in the Community at
Watervliet, N.Y. [n.p., 1891]. Caption title. 4 pp.
19 cm.
 Signed: *F. W. Evans*. Also included in Giles
 Avery, *Autobiography* . . . no. 51, pp. 20–21.
 MacLean 255. MPB, MWA, MWiW*, NBuG,
 NN, NOC, OClWHi, OHi.

615 —— Obituary. Rufus Crossman, By Elder
F. W. Evens [sic]. Why am I a Christian? by
Walter Shepherd. Mt. Lebanon, N.Y.: 1891.
Cover title. 5 pp. 14 cm.
 Obituary . . . appeared in *The Manifesto*, 21
 (March 1891), 67–68. "Why am I a Christian?"
 was reprinted in *The Manifesto*, 23 (April
 1893), 89–90.
 MacLean 256. CtY, DLC, MHarF, MPB,
 MWA, MWiW*, MiU–C, NN, NSyU, NjPT,
 OClWHi, OHi, WHi.

616 —— An Open Letter. [n.p., 1892]. Broadside in 2 columns. 15 × 14½ cm.
 Addressed to: Alonzo T. Jones, Editor of

American Sentinel, dated: Mt. Lebanon, Oct. 1892, and signed: *F. W. Evans.* "Sabbaths," an article for publication was enclosed; probably no. **628**. Appeared in *The Manifesto,* 22 (December 1892), 267.
MacLean 257. CtY–D, DLC, ICN, MWiW*, MiU–C, NBuG, NN, OClWHi.

617 —— The Origin and Object of Spiritualism. Mt. Lebanon, [N.Y.]: [n.d.]. Broadside.
No copy located. Entry from MacLean's *Bibliography,* no. 259.

618 —— Original Ideas. [Mt. Lebanon, N.Y.: 1889]. Caption title. 4 pp. 14 cm.
An article on Shaker theology and spiritualism which appeared in *The Manifesto,* 19 (July 1889), 156–58. *See also* no. **660**.
MacLean 258. CtY, DLC, ICN, KyBgW, MH, MHarF, MPB, MWiW*, MiDW, MiU–C, NBuG, NN, NSyU, NjPT, OClWHi, OHi, WHi.

619 —— Our Centennial. The Other Side [of the Question]. Second Centennial . . . . Chatham, N.Y.: Press of The Chatham Courier, 1889. Cover title. 8 pp. 11 cm.
"The Other Side" originally appeared in the *Chatham Courier,* July 23, 1889.
MacLean 260. DLC, MHarF, MPB, MWA, MWiW*, N, NN, NOC, NSyU, OClWHi, OHi, WHi.

620 —— Peace Convention at Salt Point, Dutchess Co., N.Y. Delegation of Eight Shakers Attend. [Mt. Lebanon, N.Y.?: 1881]. Broadside. 23½ × 15 cm.
The convention was attended by eleven (not eight) Shaker brethren and sisters of the North Family, Mt. Lebanon, N.Y., August 26–27, 1882, who presented a statement urging action on a land limitation law, woman's suffrage, etc., *Shaker Manifesto,* 12 (October 1882), 234. Evans was vice-president of the Universal Peace Union for many years.
OClWHi*.

621 —— Proposed Memorial to the Late Rev. Henry Ward Beecher. [Mt. Lebanon, N.Y.: 1887]. Cover title. 21 pp. 14 cm.
Includes a letter from Edward W. Bok, dated

March 24, 1887, requesting a literary contribution for the memorial; Evans' reply and his contribution, *Beecher versus Shakers.* Evans' contribution was cut and printed with title, "Sympathy with the Shakers," no. **668**. "Appendix" of historical items is by Alonzo Hollister.
MacLean 261. DLC, MHarF, MPB, MWA, MWiW*, N, NBuG, NN, NOC, NSyU, O, OClWHi, ODa.

622 —— Religious Communism. A Lecture by F. W. Evans, (Shaker) of Mount Lebanon, Columbia Co., New York, U.S.A., Delivered in St. George's Hall, London, Sunday evening, August 6th, 1871; With Introductory Remarks by the Chairman of the Meeting, Mr. Hepworth Dixon (*see* no. **2055**). Also some Account of the Extent of Shaker Communities, and a Narrative of the Visit of Elder Evans to England. An Abstract of a Lecture by Rev. J. M. Peebles, and his Testimony in Regard to the Shakers. London: J. Burns, [1871]. 32 pp. 18 cm.
Reprinted with slight changes in Evans' *Autobiography* (no. **576**), pp. 193–219.
MacLean 263. CSmH, CtY, DLC, ICJ, ICN, MB, MH, MHarF, MPB, MWiW*, N, NBuG, NHi, NIC, NN, NNC, NOC, NSyU, NjPT, OClWHi.

623 —— —————— Glasgow: United Publishing Co., 1888. 40 pp. 21 cm.
Reprinted from the London ed. of 1871.
OClWHi*.

624 —— Resurrection. [Mt. Lebanon, N.Y.: 1890]. Cover title. 7 pp. 15 cm.
Appeared in the *Shaker Manifesto,* 20 (September 1890) 195–97; also printed in *World's Advance Thought* (no. **1544**).
MacLean 264. DLC, MWiW*, NBuG, NN, OClWHi, OHi, WHi.

625 —— Robert G. Ingersoll for 1892. Mt. Lebanon, N.Y.: [189–]. Cover title. 4 pp. 14½ cm.
Addressed: "To the Editor of the Fagle [sic]," [*Berkshire County Eagle,* Pittsfield, Mass.] nominating Ingersoll for President.
MacLean 265. DLC, MHarF, MPB, MWA, MWiW*, MiU–C, N, NN, NOC, NSyU, OClWHi, WHi.

626 —— Russian Famine. A Shaker Protest against Closing the World's Fair on Sunday. Mt. Lebanon, Columbia County, N.Y.: 1891. Cover title. 6 pp. 15 cm.
> MacLean 266. MHarF, MPB, MWA, MWiW*, N, NBuG, NN, OClWHi, OHi, WHi.

627 —— Sabbath. [Mt. Lebanon, N.Y.?: 1886]. Cover title. 7 pp. 14 cm.
> Protest against a fixed day of the week as the Sabbath. Addressed: For the *Eagle* [*Berkshire County Eagle*, Pittsfield, Mass.], signed: *F. W. Evans, Mount Lebanon, N.Y., March 19, 1886.*
> MacLean 267. DLC, MWA, MWiW*, N, NBuG, NN, OClWHi, OHi, WHi.

628 —— Sabbaths vs. the People. Shaker Address to the American People, Male and Female. Pittsfield, Mass.: Press Eagle Publishing Company, 1892. Cover title. 8 pp. 15 cm.
> Plea to keep the World's Fair open seven days a week.
> MacLean 268. CSmH, CtY, DLC, MHarF, MPB, MWiW*, MiU-C, N, NBuG, NN, NOC, NSyU, OClWHi, OHi, WHi.

629 —— Shaker Communism; Or, Tests of Divine Inspiration. The Second Christian or Gentile Pentecostal Church, as Exemplified by Seventy Communities of Shakers in America ... London: James Burns, 1871. vii [1], 120 pp. 18½ cm.
> "Appendix" contains: "Shakerism," an extract from Horace Greeley's *Hints toward Reforms* (New York, 1850), pp. 278–80. Shaker advertisements, pp. 119–20. Published earlier under the title: *Tests of Divine Inspiration*, no. 670. Reprinted with slight changes in his *Autobiography* ... (1888), no. 576, pp. 132–89.
> MacLean 37. CtY, DLC, ICJ, IaU, KyU, MB, MHarF, MPB, MWA, MWiW*, NN, NOC, NSyU, Nj, OClWHi, PPL, PPPrHi, WHi.

630 —— ———— (Reprint). New York: AMS Press, 1972.

631 —— Shaker Essay. [Mt. Lebanon, N.Y.: 1880?]. Caption title. 7 pp. 13 cm.
> At end of text: F. W. Evans. Mt. Lebanon, Columbia Co., N.Y. Written for the Ladies Club (Boston), "where they have been discussing the subject of Shakerism for some weeks." Autograph presentation copy, F. W. Evans to J.[ames] S. P.[rescott] 1880, owned by Shaker Historical Society, Cleveland, O.
> MacLean 269. DLC, MHarF, MPB, MWiW*, MiU-C, N, NN, NSyU, OClWHi, OHi, WHi.

632 —— Shaker Evans. [Manchester, England: 1886]. Broadside in 2 columns. 28½ × 14½ cm.
> Reprinted from the *Manchester Guardian*. A short introduction is followed by Evans' letter to a friend in Lancashire, England. This letter was reprinted in *The Manifesto*, 17 (February 1887), 30–32, where the editor's note gives the date, October 1886.
> MacLean 440. MWiW*, NN, OClWHi, OHi.

633 —— Shaker Land Limitation Laws. Why the Shakers are Decreasing ... [n.p., 1887]. Broadside in 3 columns. 15½ × 20½ cm.
> A statement followed by Evans' undated open letter to Henry George in which he states that his brother, George Henry Evans, was "the originator of the land reform movement 50 years ago [and] is materialized in Henry George," cf. no. 592. Evans comments that the Shakers have acquired too much land and that "The reason that Shakers are decreasing in numbers is that their best energies have been devoted to cultivating their lands and advancing their material prosperity." Evans' letter is reprinted with some changes in *The Manifesto*, 17 (March 1887), 67–68, *see also* no. 595.
> MacLean 270. MPB, MWiW, OClWHi*.

634 —— A Shaker on Political and Social Reform. [Mt. Lebanon, N.Y.: n.d.]. Broadside. No copy located. Entry taken from MacLean's *Bibliography*, no. 272.

635 [——] Shaker Pentecost. Mt. Lebanon, N.Y.: 1874. Caption title. 3 pp. 24 cm.
> At end of text: F. W. Evans. Religious information and the requirements for joining the Shakers, written in response to 135 letters of application or inquiry answering Shaker advertisements in the *New York World* and the *New York Sun*, "men, women,

and children can find a comfortable home
for life ... where want never comes with the
Shakers." Reprinted from *Shaker and
Shakeress*, 4 (February 1874), 9-10.
MacLean 273. DLC, MPB, MWA, MWiW*,
NN, OClWHi, OHi, WHi.

636 —— Shaker Reconstruction of the Ameri-
can Government. Hudson, N.Y.: Office of Regis-
ter and Gazette, 1888. Cover title. 8 pp. 12½ cm.
  Letter addressed: To the Editor of the
  Hudson [*N.Y.*] *Daily Register* criticizing the
  New York *Tribune* for its opposition to the
  woman suffrage bill, and suggesting many
  governmental reforms.
  MacLean 274. DLC, ICN, MH, MHarF, MPB,
  MWA, MWiW*, N, NBuG, NN, NOC, NSyU,
  OClWHi, OHi, WHi.

637 —— Shaker Sermon. "He is Not Here."
[Mt. Lebanon, N.Y.: 1886]. Caption title. 15
pp. 15 cm.
  "Delivered, Sept. 12, 1886, at the funeral of
  John Greaves of the North Family, Mt. Leba-
  non, Col. Co., N.Y." Contains also: "Elder
  Bushnell's Testimony" [concerning burial
  grounds]; "Funeral Reform."
  MacLean 280. CtY, DLC, MH, MHarF, MPB,
  MWiW*, MiU-C, N, NBuG, NN, NSyU,
  OClWHi, OHi.

638 —— The Shaker System and a Lecture
Delivered at Randolph, Cattaraugus Co., N.Y.,
Dec. 9, 1877. Albany, N.Y.: Weed, Parsons and
Company, 1877. Cover title. 19 pp. 12½ cm.
  The title of the lecture was "Pure vs. Adulter-
  ated Christianity," pp. 9-19. *The Shaker
  System* was reprinted in the *Shaker Mani-
  festo*, 8 (April 1878), 78-80, and a short ex-
  tract is included in his *Autobiography* ...
  (No. 576), pp. 223-25.
  MacLean 282. DLC, MH, MHarF, MPB,
  MWiW*, MeHi, NBuG, NN, OClWHi, OHi,
  WHi.

639 —— Shaker Travail. An Essay ... Written
Over Thirty Years Ago. Mt. Lebanon, N.Y.:
1891. Cover title. 13 pp. 14½ cm.
  Addressed to: "Beloved Elder William and
  Brother Alpheus," and dated Feb. 27, 1858.

MacLean 283. DLC, ICN, MPB, MWiW*, NN,
OClWHi, OHi, WHi.

640 —— Shaker Views and Reviews. [Mt.
Lebanon, N.Y.: 188-]. Caption title. 6 pp.
14 cm.
  Discussion of the problems of the late 1880's,
  written after Henry George was defeated in
  the New York City mayorality election of
  1886.
  MacLean 284. DLC, MHarF, MPB, MWiW*,
  NBuG, OClWHi, OHi, WHi.

641 —— Shaker-Russian Correspondence, between Count Leo Tolstoi and Elder F. W. Evans.
Mt. Lebanon, N.Y.: 1891. Cover title, 7 pp.
14 cm.
  Contains also "Whole Wheat," reprinted
  from *Hall's Journal of Health*. Tolstoi's letter dated: Tula, Yasnaya Poliana, Russia,
  February 15, 1891; Evans' reply dated: Mt.
  Lebanon, N.Y., U.S.A., March 6, 1891.
  Tolstoi acknowledges the receipt of "the
  tracts" Evans had sent him, and writes that
  he has read them "not only with interest,
  but with profit; and cannot criticize them,
  because I agree with everything that is said
  in them," and makes an inquiry about Shaker
  non-resistance. Evans replies with a long dissertation on non-resistance and invites Tolstoi
  to come to Lebanon and join the Society,
  "Then, return, and found the order in Russia,
  with the consent of the Government, which
  the Shaker Order can and will obtain for you."
  This letter is reprinted in [Anna White],
  comp., Affectionately Inscribed (no. 1434),
  pp. 116-20; the *Peg Board*, 4 (June 1936),
  75-76; and in H. Desroche, *Les Shakers
  Américains* (no. 2050) along with Tolstoi's
  letter, pp. 270, 272-75, and in J. Savacool's
  English translation (no. 2048), pp. 280, 282-
  85. *See also* nos. **882, 1588, 1663, 1664,
  2849** and **2861.**
  MacLean 275. DLC, ICN, MHarF, MWA,
  MWiW*, N, NBuG, NN, NSyU, OClWHi,
  OHi, WHi.

642 —— Shakerism, [n.p., 1886]. Caption title.
4 pp. 13½ cm.
  At end of text: *Albany Argus.* Contains also:

"Land Limitation" [Evans' letter addressed: "Dear Friend," dated: Mt. Lebanon, May 26, 1886]; "The Solution of the Labor Problem," by Daniel Fraser (from *The Manifesto*, 16 (September 1886), 211. *Shakerism* appeared in *The Manifesto*, 16 (September 1886), 231.
MacLean 287. CtY, MPB, MWiW*, NBuG, NN, OClWHi, OHi.

643 —— Shakerism in London. Addresses by Frederick W. Evans ... Dr. Peebles, J. Burns, and Others at Claremont Hall, Penton St., London N. Sunday evening, July 3, 1887. London: [1887]. Cover title, 8 pp. 18½ cm.
Reprinted from the *Medium and Daybreak*. Evans' Address reprinted in his *Autobiography* (no. 576), pp. 219–23.
MacLean 289. CSmH, CtY, DLC, ICN, MH, MHarF, MPB, MWiW*, MiU–C, N, NBuG, NN, NOC, NSyU, OClWHi, OHi, WHi.

644 [——] "Shakers," *The American Cyclopaedia*, Edited by George Ripley and Charles A. Dana (New York, 1883), XIV:809–12.
F. W. Evans is identified as the author in "Among the Contributors," p. v. An account of Shaker history and organization with a very full explanation of Shaker beliefs. Concluding remarks on the Shakers as spritualists, explain that "The spirits predicted that after performing a certain work in the world, they would return to the Shakers, and replenish their numbers from the ranks of the spiritualists."

645 —— The Shakers. Manchester, England: [1871?]. Broadside.
No copy located. Entry taken from MacLeans's *Bibliography*, no. 276.

646 —— and Others. Shakers. Compendium of the Origin, History, Principles, Rules and Regulations, Government, and Doctrines of the United Society of Believers in Christ's Second Appearing. With Biographies of Ann Lee, William Lee, Jas. Whittaker, J. Hocknell, J. Meacham, and Lucy Wright ... New York: D. Appleton and Company, 1859. 189 pp. 18½ cm.
Binder's title: Ann Lee. Shakers and Shaker-

ism. Information on Shakers and Shakerism "now spread through five or six volumes" is concentrated here by "the author and compiler, in union with, and aided by his Gospel friends." "To the reader," p. [iii] is signed: *F. W. Evans, Calvin Green, Giles Avery, Committee of Revision, August 1858.* Calvin Green states in his "Biographic Memoir," pp. 636–37, that when the Ministry "agreed to have the work done ... it was thought proper for Elder Giles and I to assist," and that Evans "employed William Offord to prepare it for the printer." With the exception of a reset title page, and pp. [185]–89 (advertising matter), the plates were used later for the so-called 3d Ed. (New Lebanon, N.Y., 1859), and 4th Ed. (New Lebanon, N.Y., 1867), and his *Ann Lee* ... (London, 1871), nos. 570, 648 and 649.
MacLean 32 (and 33 in paper covers). Sabin 23152. CtHC, CtY, DLC, GU, ICarbS, ICU, IEN, In, KyU, MB, MBAt, MBC, MBrZ, MH, MHarF, MHi, MPB, MWA, MWiW*, MU, MdBP, MeB, MeHi, MiD, MiU, MiU–C, N, NBuG, NBuU, NHi, NIC, NN, NOC, NSyU, NjMD, O, OC, OCl, OClWHi, OCHP, ODa, OHi, OO, OU, PHatU, PHi, PPL, PPPrHi, PSC-Hi, TxU, WHi, WaU.

647 —— —— (Reprint). New York: Burt Franklin, Publisher, 1972. (Philosophy and Religious Monographs, 101).

648 —— —— 3d ed. New Lebanon, N.Y.: Auchampaugh Brothers, 1859. 192 pp. 17½ cm.
At head of title: Third Edition. Binder's title: Shakers and Shakerism.
MacLean 34. CSmH, CU, DLC, DeWint, ICarbS, MPB, MWA, MWiW*, MiU–C, N, NHi, NN, NcD, OClWHi.

649 —— —— 4th ed. New Lebanon, N.Y.: [Charles Van Benthuysen & Sons, Printer], 1867. 192 pp. 17½ cm.
At head of title: Fourth Edition. Published in London with the title: *Ann Lee (the Founder of the Shakers)* ... no. 570.
CtY, DLC, DeWint, KyBgW, MB, MBC, MH, MPB, MWA, MWiW*, MiU–C, N, NBuG, NHi, NN, NOC, NSyU, OClWHi, OO, PU, Wa.

650 —— The Shakers. Interesting Correspondence. [n.p., 1885]. Broadside in 2 columns. 24½ X 13½ cm.

Undated letter from Frederick G. Obermain, and Evans' reply dated: Mt. Lebanon, Jan. 19, 1885. Appeared in *The Manifesto*, 15 (December 1885), 276–77. Contains also "An American on English Politics" [excerpt from an Evans' letter] reprinted from the *Manchester Guardian*, January 31 [1885]. CtY, DLC, MPB, MWiW*, OClWHi, OHi.

651 [——] The Shakers. [Who They Are and What They Believe]. [Mt. Lebanon, N.Y.: 1885]. Caption title. 12 pp. 14 cm.

Short introduction by Sherman P. Hand followed by an abstract of his letter to Elder Evans dated: Natick [Mass.], August 31, 1885, and Evans' undated reply. Reprinted from the *Natick Bulletin*. MacLean 286. DLC, MPB, MPH, MWA, MWiW*, MiU-C, N, NBuG, NN, NSyU, OClWHi, OHi.

652 —— Shakers and Koreshans Uniting. Mt. Lebanon, Columbia, N.Y.: [1892]. Cover title, 8 pp. 13 cm.

Reprint of letter addressed: Office of the Guiding Star Publishing House, 3619 Cottage Grove Avenue; dated: Chicago, June 26, 1892; signed: *Frederick W. Evans, Daniel Offord, Anna White, Martha J. Anderson*. p. [3], states, "We hereby declare our confirmation of the acceptance of Victoria [Mrs. Annie G. Ordway], into our body as a member of the North Family of Shakers at Mt. Lebanon, N.Y., and our approval of her election to the office, Shepherdess of the Gynecato of the Koreshan Unity, and we do hereby commission her to publish the Gospel of Sexual Holiness as ordained in the body of Christian Believers, called Shakers, and as in the same manner taught by the Koreshan Unity." F. W. Evans' letter addressed: Dearly Beloved Cyrus [R. Teed, i.e. Koresh]; dated: Mt. Lebanon, N.Y., July 3, 1892, pp. 4–8, is reprinted in *The Manifesto*, 22 (October 1892), 220–22. *See* editorial, pp. 229–31, clarifying the Koreshan and Shaker relationship. *See also* no. 1578 for Shaker disagreement. MWiW*, N, NOC, NSyU, OClWHi.

653 —— The Shakers and Their Belief. [London: 1888]. Caption title. [2] pp. 21 cm.

At end of text: From the *London Weekly Times and Echo*. Letter signed: *F. W. Evans, Elder. Mount Lebanon, Columbia Co., N.Y., June 4, 1888*, in reply to a letter of A. Gottschling which appeared in the same periodical, March 25, 1883 [!]. MacLean 277. DLC, MPB, MWiW*, NBuG, OClWHi, OHi.

—— Shakers as Farmers. A Visit to the North Family, at Mount Lebanon. *See Shakers as Farmers*, no. 1306.

654 [——] A Shaker's Ideas. [n.p., 1885]. Broadside in 2 columns. 18 X 14½ cm.

Evans' undated letter on the occasion of Grant's funeral, but primarily devoted to peace and the need for a land limitation law. Reprinted from the *Albany Journal*. MacLean 443. MPB, MWiW*, NBuG, OClWHi.

655 [——] ——— [n.p., n.d.]. Broadside. 29 X 8 cm.

Printed in smaller type than no. 654. MWiW*, OHi, OClWHi.

656 —— A Shaker's Look into the Future. [Mt. Lebanon, N.Y.: 1885]. Caption title. [4] pp. 15 cm.

Text is the same as *What the Future Will Be*, no. 679 below. Reprinted in *The Manifesto*, 15 (June 1885), 122–24. DLC, MPB, MWiW*, N, NBuG, OClWHi.

657 —— The Shakers of Mt. Lebanon. Mt. Lebanon, [N.Y.]. Broadside.

No copy located. Entry taken from MacLean's *Bibliography*, no. 278.

658 —— Shakers' Sabbath, Composed of Seven Days. "The Sabbath Made for Man, not Man Made for the Sabbath." Mt. Lebanon, N.Y.: [1891]. Cover title. 7 pp. 14½ cm.

A plea to keep the World's Fair [i.e., Columbian Exposition] open on Sundays, addressed to: Editor of *The Republican*, Oct. 5, 1891. CtY, MHarF, MPB, MWA, MWiW*, NOC, NSyU, NjPT, O, OClWHi.

659 —— ———— [Mt. Lebanon, N.Y.: 1892].
Caption title. 4 pp. 14½ cm.

An open letter to John McCabe about his
article published in the *Albany Evening
Journal.* Appeared in *The Manifesto*, 22
(July 1892), 154–55. About liberty of con-
science, and at end the "World's Fair." This
work differs from no. **658.**
MacLean 279. MPB, MWiW*, N, NBuG, NN,
O, ODa, OHi.

660 —— Shakers Shaking the Old Creation.
The "First Heavens and First Earth." . . . Hudson, N.Y.: Press of M. Parker Williams, 1889.
16 pp. 12 cm.

Reprint of Evans' letter addressed: To the
Editor of the *Hudson Daily Register*, published April 9, 1889. Reprinted in *The Manifesto*, 19 (May 1889), 101–103, under the
title, "Shaking the Old Creation." Contains
also: "Original Ideas," no. **618.**
MacLean 281. CSmH, DLC, ICN, MH,
MHarF, MPB, MWiW*, N, NBuG, NN, NOC,
NSyU, NjPT, OClWHi, OH, OHi, WHi.

661 —— A Shaker's Views on the Land Limitation Scheme and Land Monopoly, and Mormon Prosecution. [Mt. Lebanon, N.Y.: 1887?].
Cover title. 8 pp. 13 cm.

"A Shaker's Views . . ." addressed to: Editor
Berkshire County Eagle (Pittsfield, Mass.).
". . . Mormon Prosecution," addressed: To
the Editor of the *Sun* (New York?).
MacLean 285. CtY, DLC, ICN, MH, MPB,
MWA, MWiW*, MiU–C, NBuG, NSyU,
OClWHi, OHi, WHi.

662 —— Shaving. [n.p., 1885]. Broadside in
2 columns. 15 × 13 cm.

Reprint of an extract signed: *Dr. Wm.
MacDonald*, from the New York *Tribune*,
with a long introduction by F. W. Evans
signed: *Mt. Lebanon, Dec. 3, 1885.*
MPB, OClWHi*, OHi.

663 —— A Short Treatise on the Second
Appearing of Christ, in and through the Order
of the Female. Boston: Bazin & Chandler,
Printers, 1853. 24 pp. 19 cm.

Described in "To the Reader," p. [2] ". . .
as a succinct illustration of our real views

which we hold to be synonymous with *true,
genuine Christianity."* Pages 21–24 reprinted
in the *Shaker Manifesto*, 8 (June 1878), 137–
38, under the title, "Christ in the Order of
Male and Female."
MacLean 292. CSmH, CtHC, CtHi, CtY, DLC,
ICN, KyBgW, KyU, MB, MHarF, MHi, MPB,
MPH, MSaE, MWA, MWiW*, MiDW, MiU–C,
N, NBLiHi, NN, NNUT, NOC, NSyU, Nh,
NjPT, OClWHi, OCU, OHi, OOxM, OLeWHi,
PHi, PPL, PPPrHi, RPB, WHi.

664 —— The Sign in the Heavens. The Relation of President Garfield's Death to the Fulfillment of Prophecy. [Mt. Lebanon, N.Y.: 1881].
Broadside. 26½ × 7½ cm.

Reprint of a letter to the New York *Tribune*
signed: *F. W. Evans, Mt. Lebanon, September
26, 1881.*
MacLean 293. MHarF, MPB, MWiW*, NN,
OClWHi, OHi.

665 [——] Spirits the Shakers Saw. Wm.
Eddy's Work at Mt. Lebanon — Marvelous
Materializations. [Pittsfield, Mass.: 1878].
Broadside. 35 × 21 cm.

"From the *Berkshire County Eagle* (Pittsfield, Mass.), July 4, 1878." Reprinted with
additional material in his *Autobiography*
(no. **576**), pp. 232–39. MacLean attributes
authorship to F. W. Evans, but the possibility
of A. G. Hollister's authorship is shown in
the copy in Western Reserve Historical Society (Cleveland, O.), a.n.s., A. G. H.[ollister],
"I may not have put this together exactly as
spoken, but it was all spoken nearly word
for word."
MacLean 448. MPB, MiU–C*, NN, OHi, WHi.

666 —— Spiritual Materialization: Elder Evans,
of the Shaker Community, Sets Forth the Signif-
icance of Manna that Fed the Israelites. [n.p.,
n.d.]. Broadside. 32½ × 7½ cm.

"From the *Brooklyn Daily Eagle.*"
MacLean 295. MHarF, MPB, MWiW*, NBuG,
NN.

667 —— A Suggestion. [Mt. Lebanon, N.Y.:
188–]. Caption title. 4 pp. 15 cm.

The suggestion would exchange women for
men legislators, and send "into the legislative

halls none but intellectual celibates." Contains also: "Education" by Richard Bushnell, which appeared in *The Manifesto*, 17 (August 1887), 175-76; "Truth" by Richard Bushnell, which appeared in *The Manifesto*, 17 (May 1887), 108.
MacLean 296. CtY, DLC, MHarF, MPB, MWiW*, MiU-C, NBuG, NN, NjPT.

668 —— "Sympathy with the Shakers," In *Beecher Memorial; Contemporaneous Tributes to the Memory of Henry Ward Beecher*, comp. and ed., by Edward W. Bok (Brooklyn, Privately Printed [The Devinne Press]: 1887), pp. 100-102.
See also no. 621.

669 —— Testimony of Jesus; "Marriage, Jesus and the Shakers." 12 pp.
MacLean 455. No copy located.

670 —— Tests of Divine Inspiration; Or, The Rudimental Principles by which True and False Revelation, in all Eras of the World, can be Unerringly Discriminated .... New Lebanon, N.Y.: Published by the United Society Called Shakers, 1853. 127 pp. 19 cm.
"To the Reader" signed: *F. W. Evans; Calvin Green.* In his "Biographic Memoir," p. 638, Calvin Green states that this book is made up of selections of his own writings on true and false revelation and the writings of Frederick Evans. He does not, however, explain why his name does not occur on the title page. Published with slight changes under the title: *Shaker Communism ...*, no. 629. "Shakerism," pp. 278-80, is an excerpt from Horace Greeley's *Hints toward Reforms*, no. 2183.
MacLean 35 (and 36 in paper covers). CSmH, CtHC, CtY-D, DLC, InI, KEmT, KyBgW, MB, MH, MHarF, MPB, MWA, MWiW*, MiU-C, N, NBuG, NN, NOC, NSyU, NhD, NjPT, O, OClWHi, ODa, OHi, OO, OOxM, PHi, PPC, PU, WHi.

671 —— "They Sang the Song of Moses the Servant of God, and the Song of the Lamb," [Mt. Lebanon, N.Y.: 1888]. Broadside. 27½ × 7½ cm.
Short sermon "From the *Pittsfield Sun* [Mass.]," Aug. 23, 1888.

MacLean 297. MPB, MWiW*, OClWHi, OHi.

672 —— Treatise on Shaker Theology. [Mt. Lebanon, N.Y.: 186-]. Cover title. 17 pp. 17 cm.
Reprinted in *The Manifesto*, 17 (October, November, December 1887), 219-22, 244-47, 270-71. Contains also: "Note" by Richard Bushnell. Some copies have cover title with Mt. Lebanon, Columbia Co., N.Y.
MacLean 298. DLC, ICN, MHarF, MPB, MWiW*, MeHi, MiU-C, N, NNG, NOC, NSyU, OClWHi, OHi, WHi.

673 —— Two Orders: Shakerism and Republicanism. The American Church and American Civil Government, Coequal and Separate. The New Heavens and Earth. Pittsfield [Mass.]: Press of the Sun Printing Company, 1890. Cover title. 12 pp. 13 cm.
MWA, MWiW*, N, NBuG, OClWHi.

674 —— Union Belt. Views of a Shaker Regarding Garfield's Death. [n.p., 1881]. Broadside. 25 × 6½ cm.
"To the Editor of the Brooklyn Eagle." OClWHi*.

675 —— The Universal Church. Shakers [Watervliet] N.Y.: 1872. 16 pp. 14 cm.
"The Universal Church was first printed in *The Shaker* 1872"* (i.e., 2 (March 1872), 17-18), Catherine Allen to W. H. Cathcart, undated a.l.s., Western Reserve Historical Society, Cleveland, O.
MacLean 299. DLC, MWA, OClWHi*, PPL.

676 —— The Universal Republic. A Shaker Pronunciamento. [Mt. Lebanon, N.Y.: n.d.]. Broadside in 2 columns. 28½ × 15 cm.
Reprinted from the *World's Advance Thought*. MacLean 300. CtY, DLC, MHarF, MPB, MWiW*, NBuG, NN, OClWHi, OHi, PPL.

—— Wail of a Shaker. Mt. Lebanon, N.Y.: [n.d.]. Broadside.
No copy located. Entry from MacLean's *Bibliography*, no. 301, which appears to be a misprint of *Wail of a Striker*, no. 677. *See also* no. 580.

677 —— Wail of a Striker. Mt. Lebanon,

N.Y.: [n.d.]. Broadside. 15 × 8½ cm.
A protest against the handling of the great
strikes in Chicago, 1886. The text is the
same as no. 580, pp. 10–11.
MWiW*.

678 —— A Welcome to Whitelaw Reid. New
Lebanon, [N.Y.]: [n.d.]. Caption title. 4 pp.
15 cm.
OClWHi*.

679 —— What the Future Will Be. A Shaker's
Long Look Ahead. [n.p., n.d.]. Broadside in
2 columns. 25½ × 14 cm.
Appeared in *The Manifesto*, 15 (1885), 122–
24, under the title, "A Shaker's Look into
the Future." Text is the same as no. 656.
MacLean 302. CtY, MPB, MWiW*, NBuG,
NN, OClWHi, WHi.

680 —— White Cross Celibacy. [n.p., n.d.].
Broadside in 2 columns. 24 × 16 cm.
Appeared in *The Manifesto*, 18 (1888),
163–64.
MacLean 303. MWiW, NN, OClWHi*, OHi.

681 —— Who is Ann Lee? What Evidence is
There that She is the Second Messiah? Mt. Leba-
non, N.Y.: 1889. Cover title. 13 pp. 14 cm.
Letter from John H. Lane dated: West Stock-
bridge, Mass., Jan. 30, 1889; Evans' reply
dated: Mt. Lebanon, N.Y., Feb. 16, 1889.
The Williams College copy has 11 lines of
Evans' autograph additions at the end of text.
MacLean 304. CtY, DLC, InU, MHarF, MPB,
MWiW*, N, NBuG, NOC, NSyU, NjPT,
OClWHi, OHi, WHi.

682 —— ... The World's Fair. [Mt. Lebanon,
N.Y.: 1881]. Broadside. 21½ × 8 cm.
Letter addressed: To the Editor of the
Tribune. Evans' letter dated: Mt. Lebanon,
N.Y., Jan. 17, 1881, is preceded by the New
York *Tribune's* comment that Evans "writes
a characteristic letter protesting far in ad-

vance, against the closing of the New-York
World's Fair on Sunday ..."
MWiW*, NBuG, OClWHi.

683 —— The World's Fair! Shall it be Closed
One Day in the Week to Please a Certain Sect?
Pittsfield, Mass.: Press Eagle Publishing Company, 1891. Cover title. 5 pp. 11½ cm.
Appeared in *The Manifesto*, 22 (March 1892),
55–56, under the title, "Closing the World's
Fair," i.e., the Columbian Exposition, Chicago. Evans does not identify "a certain sect,"
but repeats a statement "that fifty thousand
gospel Ministers have been served with blank
petitions for their respective flocks to sign;
praying Congress to enact unconstitutional
'religious legislation' to close the World's
Fair upon the Constantine — Heathen —
Sabbath."
MacLean 305. ICN, MPB, MWiW*, N, NN,
NSyU, OClWHi, OHi, WHi.

684 [EVANS, JESSIE] The Story of Shakerism, by One Who Knows [*pseud.*]. East Canterbury, N.H.: Shakers, 1907. Cover title. 16 pp.
illus. 18½ cm.
History of the Shakers, pp. [3]–11; description of the buildings at East Canterbury,
N.H., pp. 11–14.
MWA, MWiW*, NBuG, NN, NOC, OClWHi.

685 [——] ———— 1910. Cover title. 16 pp.
illus. 18 cm.
MHarF, MPB, MWiW*, NhD, NjPT, OClWHi.

686 [——] ———— [Concord, N.H.: Evans
Printing Co.], 1936. 14 pp. 18½ cm.
Some changes in the text.
MWiW*, NOC.

687 [——] ———— 1939. Cover title. 15 [1]
pp. illus. 18½ cm.
Photographs of "Main Office Building. Built
in 1831," p. [2]; "Shaker Church Built in
1792," p. [1] at end.
MHarF, MWiW*, NN, NOC.

F

688 Facts About the Shakers, 1794-1941.
Sabbathday Lake, Me.: [194-]. Cover title.
[6] pp. 19 cm.
  MHarF, MPH*.

689 FAIRBANKS, MARILA. A Bond of Love
and Word of Comfort Written by Mother Ann,
on a Leaf on the Bough of Peace for Me Pretty
Yea Meritorious Little Daughter Marila. Read
to the Mortal Writer by One of Her Reading
Angels April 30th 1842. [Pittsfield, Mass.:
Shaker Village Work Group. 1964]. Caption
title. [17] pp. 16 cm.
  Cover title: A Handwritten Shaker Spirit
  Message. Facsimile of an original manuscript.
  "Everlasting Comfort," words and music
  written in Shaker letter notation, pp. [13-
  16].
  MPB, MPH, MWiW*, NOC.

690 FARNHAM, JAMES. To the Public.
Having Lately Seen a Scandalous Handbill in
Circulation, Published by Mary Dyer, Contain-
ing, Among Other Malicious Falsehoods, a
Slanderous Charge Against Me. . . . [n.p., 1825].
Caption title. [2] pp. (1 fold, facing pages
printed). 25½ cm.
  Dated at end: October 14, 1825. Farnham's
  refutation of Mary Dyer's handbill, no. 537,
  which accuses him of scandalous conduct at
  Whiting's Pond, near New Lebanon. See
  Joseph Dyer's *A Compendious Narrative*, no.
  529, pp. 75-80, for a later refutation, July
  18th, 1826, and notarized denials by Amy
  Russell and Harriet Sellick.
  Shaw 20488. OClWHi*.

691 Favorite Shaker Recipes. Compiled and
Tested by the Canterbury Shakers. Canterbury,
N.H.: [1970?]. 21 pp. 14 cm.
  Cover title: Gourmet's Delight. Cover photo-
  graph shows Eldress Marguerite Frost and
  5 Shaker sisters dining at the Canterbury
  community.
  MPH, MWiW*, NOC.

692 [FELLENBERG, FREDERICK] Speaking
Shakerism. [Mt. Lebanon, N.Y.: 1891]. Cover
title. 7 pp. 15 cm.
  Letter from Frederick Fellenberg, Zolliken,
  Zurich, Switzerland, dated: August 7th, 1891.
  Concerns a new community proposed by some
  young men in Switzerland. Evans' reply dated:
  Mt. Lebanon, N.Y., U.S.A., Sept. 11, 1891.
  Reprinted from *The Manifesto*, 21 (December
  1891), 272-75.
  MacLean 294. CtY, DLC, MHarF, MPB, MWA,
  MWiW*, N, NN, NSyU, OClWHi, OHi, WHi.

693 The First Covenant of the Church of Christ
(Shaker) in New Lebanon, N.Y. 1795. [Pitts-
field, Mass.:] Privately Printed for Edward D.
Andrews [by Donald P. Gerst], 1935. Cover title.
11 pp. 19½ cm.
  The first written Shaker Covenant was pre-
  ceded by an oral Covenant. This edition with
  Prefatory Note by the editor E. D. Andrews
  "is printed from the original manuscript in
  the library of the Andrews Collection . . .
  Authorship is credited to 'Father' Joseph
  Meacham . . . It is possible, however, that the
  first exposition of the doctrine of joint inter-
  est, or united inheritance, was the work of
  David Darrow." This Covenant was signed by
  43 brethren and sisters. Back cover verso:
  Gerst fecit.
  DLC, MPB, MPH, MWA, N, NBuG, NN*,
  OClWHi.

694 [FLETCHER, RICHARD] Broken Glass,
— Not a Bit Blue, [Mt. Lebanon, N.Y.: 188-?].
Broadside in 3 columns. 19½ X 29½ cm.
  A manuscript note on verso, *Written by
  Richard Fletcher Mt. Lebanon, N.Y. Medi-
  cine business was booming somewhere in the
  1880's.* This is a facetious treatment of the
  medicine industry at Mount Lebanon and of
  the workers.
  OClWHi*.

695 The Following Lines, Said to Be Written by

a Quaker, Contain the True Philosophy of Life.
Printed at Shaker Village, Mer. Co., N.H.: [n.d.].
Broadside. 9½ × 13½ cm.
    N*.

696 ——— ... Selected by Eliza Ann Taylor.
Printed at East Canterbury, Mer. Co., N.H.:
[n.d.]. Broadside. 11 × 13½ cm.
    OClWHi*.

697 The Following Report of a Public Meeting
Recently Held by the Shirley Shakers We Copy
from the *Public Spirit* [Ayer, Mass.]. [Ayer:
1873]. Broadside in 2 columns. 33 × 15½ cm.
    Signed: *Reporter*. A public service attended
    by Elders Otis Sawyer and John B. Vance
    of Alfred, Me., along with some members of
    the Harvard Society.
    OClWHi*.

698 For Enquiring Friends We Have Prepared
the Following Brief Summary. Shakers, E.
Canterbury, N.H.: [n.d.]. Broadside in 2 columns.
23 × 15 cm.
    Answers to ten questions commonly asked
    by outsiders. No. 5 specifies, "No believing
    husband or wife is allowed to separate from
    an unbelieving partner, except by mutual
    or legal agreement ..."
    OClWHi*.

Form of a Certificate of Residence in Another
State. *See Albany County, to Wit* ... no. 7.

699 $400 Reward. The Seed Store of the Sub-
scribers Was Broken Open, at Hancock Shaker
Village, on Saturday night, the 16th inst. and
Property to the Amount of from One Thousand
to Two Thousand Dollars Stolen Therefrom ...
Hancock, Feb. 18, 1839. [n.p., n.d.]. Broadside.
29 × 23 cm.
    Signed: *Joseph Patten, Joseph Wicker*. Trustees
    of the United Society of Shakers. $200 was to
    be paid upon conviction of the thief or thieves,
    and $200 paid upon recovery of stolen property.
    MPH, OClWHi*.

700 Fragrance from the Altar of Incense. Shaker
Contributions to the *Flaming Sword*. [Mt.
Lebanon, N.Y.: 1892]. Cover title. 23 pp.
20½ cm.

The contributions were made by various
members of the North Family, Mt. Lebanon.
The *Flaming Sword* was the organ of the
Koreshan Unity.
MacLean 306. DLC, MPB, MWA, MWiW, N,
NBuG, NN, NSyU, OClWHi*.

701 FRASER, DANIEL. Analysis of Human
Society. Declaring the Law Which Creates and
Sustains a Community Having Goods in Common. [Mt. Lebanon, N.Y.: 188-?]. Caption
title. 8 pp. 13½ cm.
    Reprinted from *The Manifesto*, 14 (Novem-
    ber, December, 1884), 247-49, 265-68,
    where it is reprinted from *The Shaker*, 7
    (March, June, 1877), 18-19, 44.
    MacLean 307. DLC, MHarF, MPB, MWiW*,
    NN, OClWHi, OHi.

702 [———] The Divine Afflatus: A Force in
History. Published by the United Society,
Shirley, Mass. Boston: Press of Rand, Avery,
& Co.: 1875. 46 [1] pp. 18½ cm.
    Preface signed: *John Whiteley. Daniel Fraser*.
    This work is generally attributed, however,
    to Daniel Fraser; *see* C. Allen, *Biographical
    Sketch of Daniel Fraser*, (no. 9), pp. 22-23;
    A. White and L. Taylor, *Shakerism*, (no.
    1447), p. 326. This is a socialist's exposition
    on the idea of progress.
    MacLean 212. CtY, DLC, DeWint, ICN,
    KyBgW, MB, MH-AH, MHarF, MHi, MPB,
    MPH, MSaE, MWA, MWiW*, N, NBuG, NN,
    NOC, NRCR, NSyU, NjPT, OClWHi, OHi,
    PCC, PPL.

703 ——— The Divine Procedure in the Affairs of
Men. [Canterbury, N.H.: 1888?]. Caption title.
4 pp. 24 cm.
    Reprinted from *The Manifesto*, 18 (October
    1888), 217-21.
    MacLean 308 (broadside). DLC, MPB, MPH,
    MWiW*, NBuG, NN, OClWHi.

704 [———] The Divinity of Humanity the Corner-
Stone of the Temple of the Future. Boston: Rand,
Avery & Co., Printers, 1874. Cover title. 8 pp.
16 cm.
    At end of text: Address, Daniel Fraser, Shir-
    ley Village, Mass. "Shakers."
    MacLean 213. CtY, MB, MHarF, MHi, MPB,

MSaE, MWA, MWiW*, MiU-C, N, NBuG, NN, NOC, NjPT, O, OClWHi, WHi.

705 [——] The Labor Question. The Millionaire and the Republic. [n.p., 1878?]. Broadside. 26 X 18 cm.

"The existence, and rapid rise of so many millionaires in our midst, is anomalous with the logic of the republic; in the nature of things they are the offspring of wrong conditions, and are clothed with power not compatible with the general good." Also printed in the *Shaker Manifesto*, 8 (September 1878), 217-19, where Daniel Fraser is given as author. This is often attributed to F. W. Evans.
MacLean 352 (attributed to F. W. Evans). DLC, MPB, MiU-C, NN, OClWHi*, OHi, WHi.

706 —— [Letter. Dated at Mt. Lebanon, N.Y., Oct. 1, 1885]. [Mt. Lebanon, N.Y.: 1885?]. Broadside in 3 columns. 32½ X 20 cm.

Addressed: Respected Friend. To Joseph Chamberlain M.P., with a discussion of his position on the Irish question. Fraser offers advice based upon Shaker ideals. Reprinted in *The Manifesto*, 15 (December 1885), 274-76.
NN, OClWHi*.

707 —— A Letter, Touching Important Principles [of Shakerism]. [Mt. Lebanon, N.Y.: n.d.]. Caption title. 7 pp. 13½ cm.

MacLean 309. CtY, DLC, MPB, MWA, MWiW*, MeHi, N, NBuG, NN, OClWHi, OHi, WHi.

708 [——] The Music of the Spheres .... Dedicated to the Consideration of Robert G. Ingersoll, and to Others Like-minded. Albany: Weed, Parsons and Company, Printers, 1887. 75 pp. 17½ cm.

Signed: *Daniel Fraser. Mount Lebanon, N.Y.* Most of this exposition of Fraser's religious, political, economic, etc., beliefs was printed earlier in *The Manifesto* (or, its precursors). The title article is reprinted from *The Manifesto*, 15 (May, June 1885), 103-105, 129-132.
MacLean 310. CtY, DLC, ICN, MH, MPB,

MWiW*, N, NBuG, NN, NOC, NSyU, NjPT, OClWHi, OHi, WHi.

709 —— Shaker Hygiene. The Dietetic Troubles of the First and Nineteenth Centuries Contrasted. [Mt. Lebanon, N.Y.?: 188-]. Cover title. 7 pp. 17 cm.

"P.S.," pp. 6-7, signed: *F. W. Evans.*
MacLean 311. CtY, DLC, MB, MPB, MWA, MWiW*, MeHi, N, NBuG, NOC, NN, OClWHi, WHi.

710 [——] Shaker Support for Henry George. [Mt. Lebanon, N.Y.?: 1886]. Caption title. 3 pp. 13½ cm.

A letter to the editor of the *Tribune* (N.Y.), signed: *D. Fraser, Mt. Lebanon, Col. Co., N.Y., Dec. 23, 1886,* supporting Henry George in the New York City mayoralty election.
MacLean 312. CtY, DLC, MPB, MWiW*, NN, OClWHi, OHi, WHi.

711 [——] Shaker Theology. Facts for Christendom. [Shaker Village, New Lebanon, N.Y.: n.d.]. Caption title. 3 pp. 15½ cm.

Other sects are compared under 17 items.
MacLean 444 attributes this to Daniel Fraser, about 1850.
DLC, MPB, MWA, N, NBuG, NN, NjPT, OClWHi*.

712 —— Witness of Daniel Fraser. [Mt. Lebanon: 1901]. Caption title. 16 pp. 14½ cm.

"Witness" is autobiographical and is signed: *Daniel Fraser, Dec. 21st, 1843.* Ascended from earth, Oct. 10th, 1889. Contains also: "Theocratic Government is Self Government," Daniel Fraser, 1877, pp. 7-9; "Government," A. G. Hollister 1894-1901, pp. 10-16. "Government" is reprinted from *The Manifesto*, 24 (October 1894), 227-30.
MacLean 313. CtY, MH, MPB, MPH, MWA, MWiW*, MiU-C, N, NBuG, NN, OClWHi, WHi.

713 A Friend to Justice, *pseud.* Shakers. [n.p., 1861]. 2 pp. 20 cm.
OHi*.

714 From the Canterbury Shakers. [Canterbury, N.H.: 188-?]. Caption title. [4] pp. 18 cm. illus.

A brief summary "In order to meet the many inquiries that are made in regard to the principles and regulations of our religious home." OClWHi*.

715 From the Shakers, Enfield, N.H. [East Canterbury, N.H.: 189–?]. Caption title. 4 pp. 17 cm.

Information on Shakerism listed under 17 numbered items. "Letters of inquiry may be addressed to Hiram C. Baker, Abraham Perkins, Wm. Wilson, Isabella Russell, Rosetta Cumings, or Charlotte Hart," p. 3. "No Surrender," a poem of 4 stanzas, p. 4. W. H. Cathcart's a.l.s. to Eldress Catherine Allen, Sept. 26, 1913 (Western Reserve Historical Society, Cleveland, O.) states that Dr. Mac-Lean has "erroneously described" this item as a broadside. See MacLean no. 314, p. 50, where the authorship is attributed to Blinn. MacLean 314 (?). MWiW*, OClWHi.

716 FROST, LILY MARGUERITE. About the Shakers. Canterbury, N.H.: [1958]. [8] pp. 23 cm.

MPH, MWiW*, NOC.

717 —— The Shaker Story ... Canterbury, N.H. [Penacook, N.H.: Hazen Printing Co., 1963]. Cover title. [22] pp. 22 cm.

A paper delivered at a seminar, Canterbury, N.H., 1961, 1962. A somewhat expanded version of her "Prose and Poetry of Shakerism," *Philadelphia Museum Bulletin*, 57 (Spring 1962), 67–82.

MPH, MWA*, MWiW, NOC, NSyU.

718 A Funeral Commemoration. [n.p., n.d.]. Broadside. 24 × 11 cm.

Poem of 9 numbered stanzas — type ornament — and two additional stanzas. This appears to be Richard McNemar's printing. OClWHi*.

G

719 General Annual Report of Business Conditions at .... for 18 .... [n.p., n.d.]. Broadside. 25½ × 14½ cm.

This form used at the Whitewater, O., Society of Shakers includes farm products and livestock, income from sales, outlays for materials, livestock, etc., as well as losses and liabilities, with a blank space for the signature of the business agent. OClWHi*.

720 General Rules of the United Society, and Summary Articles of Mutual Agreement and Release: Ratified and Confirmed, by the Society at Watervliet, Montgomery County, Ohio, January, 1833 ... [Watervliet? O.:] Union-office, 1833. 1 p.l., 9 pp. 17½ cm.

List of members at end. DLC, OClWHi*.

721 Gentle Manners a Guide to Good Morals .... Third Edition. East Canterbury, N.Y.: [1899]. xiii, [4] (blank), 79 pp. 18 cm.

Includes: "Preface to first edition"; "Preface to second edition"; and "Preface to third edition," signed: *Henry C. Blinn, March 1899*. According to H. C. Blinn, the 1st ed. was *A Juvenile Monitor* (1823), no. 848; 2d ed. was *A Juvenile Guide* (1844), no. 847; and this, therefore, is the 3d ed. Actually, this work is based upon *A Juvenile Guide*, but also includes long quotations from *Brief and Useful Moral Instruction* (1858), no. 1371, which are identified only by quotation marks. No mention is made of [G. K. Lawrence] *A Short Treatise* (1823), no. 859, which might be considered equally with *A Juvenile Monitor* (1823) which is identified as the "first edition." *See also* No. 1371, for "Gen. George Washington's Rules for Civility and Decent Behavior, as published by Prof. Sparks," pp. 34–41.

MacLean 55. Sabin 106199. CtY, DLC, ICN, InU, MH, MHarF, MPB, MPH, MWiW*, MiU–C, N, NBuG, NN, NPV, NSyU, NhD, NjPT, OHi, OClWHi, ODa.

722 GILLESPIE, MARY ANN and POLLY J. REED. The Gospel Grange and Order Originating from the Visit of the Shakers to the Spiritualist's Camp-meeting, at Lake Pleasant, Montague Co., Mass. Addressed to every Individual Member of the Shaker Fraternity Wherever Located, by Mary Ann Gillespie, Polly J. Reed. Printed at Union Vilage [sic], [O.]: N[orth] F[amily], [1880]. Cover title. [1], 8, [1] pp. 16 cm.

Preface signed: *Polly Reed, Mt. Lebanon, N.Y. Oct. 30, 1880.* "God's Wisdom," hymn by O. C. Hampton, Union Village, with music in Shaker notation, p. [1], at end. Proposal to establish an order that would not be confined to Shaker membership with the Mt. Lebanon Ministry acting as the spiritual and temporal lead of the Gospel Grange, p. 3. "Every penny given for admittance to the Lodge must be appropriated to the erection of a *New Dwelling House,* for our needy Brethren and Sisters in the Church Family, at New Gloucester, Maine. These consecrated and devoted people have suffered deprivation and loss of property for many years, through the selfishness and perfidy of some false hearted Trustees who left the society long ago and took with them its consecrated property to the amount of many thousands of dollars .... The dwelling they now occupy is the poorest habitable tenement in all our Shaker Societies," p. 5. Alonzo Hollister's ms. note in his correspondence with W. W. Wight (Williams College Library, Williamstown, Mass.) states that "consecrated members had no money to give and it soon dropt."
MacLean 316 (title differs slightly). DLC, MWiW*, OCHP, OClWHi.

723 GODDARD, CALVIN LUTHER. On the Birth of the Lord ... [n.p., n.d.]. Caption title. 12 pp. 13 cm.
CtY*.

724 —— The Revelations of the Lord our God on His Coming. [Worcester, Mass.: n.d.]. Cover title. 42 pp. 14 cm.
NNUT*.

725 The Good of Evil. [n.p., n.d.]. Broadside. 23½ X 9½ cm.
Poem of 8 stanzas.
OClWHi*.

726 The Gospel Monitor. A Little Book of Mother Ann's Word to Those Who are Placed as Instructors & Care-takers of Children; Written by Mother Lucy Wright, and Brought by Her to the Elders of the First Order, on the Holy Mount, March 1, 1841. Copies by Inspiration at Mother Ann's Desire, March 2, 1841. Printed at Canterbury, N.H.: 1843. 47 [1] pp. 16½ cm.

It is claimed that Lucy Wright, who died in 1821, took these instructions from Ann Lee (d. Sept. 8, 1784), and in turn communicated them spiritually to the "instrument" (medium) who copied them. The identity of the inspired instrument is not given. MacLean states that this book was "kept by the Elders." "The first part of the book contains an interesting interview of the instrument (writer) with Mother Ann, March 1, 1841. The second, is Mother's word to the care-takers; third, to the children; and the fourth, to the Elders," Note, p. [2]. "Errata," p. [1] at end.
MacLean 38. DLC, KySP, MHarF, MPB, MWA, MWiW*, MiU-C, N, NOC, NSyU, NhD, NjPT, OCl, OClWHi.

727 Grand Shaker Convention, in Steinway Hall, Nov. 22 [1874] ... Forenoon Meeting. Addresses Delivered by Elder Albert Loomis, Eldress Harriet Bullard, Thomas Smith, and Elder Evans. Afternoon Meeting. By Elder John B. Vance, Eldress Antoinette Doolittle, Elder Evans and Others ... [n.p., n.d.]. [2] pp. 20 X 14 cm.

A Shaker choir of twelve singers sang at the opening, between lectures, and at the close of the meeting. Includes a list of "Topics of Discussion." See *The Shaker,* 5 (January 1875), 4.
NOC*.

728 Great Moral Curiosity. Shaker Concert. The Celebrated and Far-famed Chase Family, from Canterbury, N.H. Who Have Performed for Seven Consecutive Weeks to Overflowing Houses at the American Museum, New York ... A

Grand Levee at —— Hall, On —— Evening
—— 184-. [playbill]. Ogdensburgh, N.Y.:
Sentinel Power Press, 184-? Broadside. 37 X
15 cm. illus. Woodcut depicting dancing and
Shaker costumes follows the title.

"Mr. N. E. Chase, who together with his
coadjutors, has lived many years among the
sect called Shakers .... In conclusion will
be introduced the remarkable Young Lady,
Miss. L. A. Chase ... with unheard of bodily
powers ... will execute Astonishing Shaker
Gyrations ... whirl round like a top, fifteen
hundred times .... The Company will
appear in real Shaker Costume." When the
"Chase Family" performed at the Apollo
Rooms in September 1848, an advertisement
in the New York *Herald* gave the names of
this group of Shaker seceders — Miss Willard,
Miss A. Foster, Mrs. Tripure, Mr. Otis, Dr.
Tripure, and Mr. Partridge, G. C. D. Odell,
Annals of the New York Stage (no. 2535),
V:311. These same Shaker seceders testified
or were mentioned in the New Hampshire
legislative investigation of the Shakers in
1848, *see* no. 1071. James M. Otis, formerly
a Trustee and Elder at Canterbury, N.H.,
initiated one of the petitions to the legislature and following his testimony was cross-
examined by Gen. Franklin Pierce, *see* no.
3772. After being shown a handbill which
showed his name as one of the performers,
Otis stated, "I have performed upon the
stage to represent the Shakerism. I was hired
to give exhibitions of Shakerism; had nothing to do with getting up the bill," p. 26.
See also nos. 729, 857, and 1617.
NHi (Film negative. Location of the original
not known. Probably ca. 37 X 15 cm.).

729 Great Moral Curiosity! Shaker Concert!
The Shaker Family, from the Society of Shakers,
in New Gloucester, Maine, Will Give a Concert
in This Place on —— Evening, —— 1848.
At —— Hall, —— Who have been Performing in New York, and most of the New England
States the Past Season with Unrivalled Success.
They will Appear in Shaker Costume. Lecture
by Mr. Wm. Palmer, who, together with his
Coadjutors, has Lived for many Years among
the Strange Sect Styled Shakers .... The Remarkable Young lady Miss L. A. Palmer, as the

Miraculous Shaker Teetotum ... will Execute
Astounding Shaker Gyrations! Poughkeepsie
[N.Y.]: "The America Peace" Press, [1848].
Broadside. 58 X 17 cm.

Friday, October 20th and *E. Myers Hall*
have been supplied in manuscript in the
spaces indicated above. A manuscript note
on the verso reads: This program probably
given in Lancaster or Amanda, Ohio. Shaker
records at Western Reserve Historical Society
list William Palmer and Love Ann Palmer as
members who had left the New Gloucester
Society. Mr. J. Adams, listed as dancing to
several of the songs, probably had been a
member of the Canterbury, N.H., Society.
The wording of this playbill is sometimes
identical with others, *see* nos. 728 and 857,
but the program of songs is entirely different,
and a new offering, "The Shaker Bible with
Illustrations," is followed by the note, "This
is no Burlesque upon the Shakers, for there
is not a more neat and industrious people in
the world."
OHi*.

730 GREEN, BENJAMIN. ... Biographical
Account of the Life of Benjamin Green, in
Which Are Set Forth His Pretensions to the
Throne. Written by Himself. Concord [N.H.]:
Published by the Author, 1848. 48 pp. 22 cm.

At head of title: Intellectual Fireworks.
Cover title: A Short Account of the Life of
Benjamin Green: A Man who Started in
Pursuit of a Theory of the Connexion between God and Man and Found It. Autobiography with a critical account of his life
with the Shakers at Enfield, N.H., where he
lived 7 years, but he does not state that he
signed the covenant, Chap. IX. "The Shakers
— Their Overseers — Temptations Resisted,"
pp. 26-31, 44. Green claims that when he
left the Shakers he was given $1.50 and some
clothes.
MPB*, NN.

731 —— The True Believer's Vademecum, or
Shakerism Exposed: Together with an Account
of the Life of the Author, from His Birth, to
the Period of His Joining and Leaving the Society of People Called Shakers, Who Have Excited the Astonishment and Wonder of the

Community of This Vastly Extended Empire. Also, a Fair Exhibition of the Way in Which Real Unmingled Happiness May Be Obtained, without Being Exposed to the Shackles of Superstition. Concord [N.H.]: Printed for the Author, 1831. 68 pp. 17½ cm.

The author was a member of the Shaker community at Enfield, N.H., for seven years. Sabin 28509. DLC, MB, MPB, MWA, MWiW*, NHi, NSyU.

732 [GREEN, CALVIN?] In Answer to Frequent Inquiries, the Following Scriptural Evidences Are Given in Favor of Dancing in the Worship and Praises of God. [Mt. Lebanon, N.Y.: n.d.]. Broadside (part in 2 columns). 32 × 15½ cm.

Title from the first line of text. MWiW, N, OClWHi*.

733 —— The Law of Life . . . . Extract from a Writing Received in the Name of the Prophet Joel, at Mt. Lebanon, N.Y., January, 1841. Calvin Green, Amanuensis. [Mt. Lebanon, N.Y.: 1901]. Caption title. 16 pp. 15 cm.

Contains also: "Appeal to Loyal Workers, Having Ears to Hear the Message of Christ," signed: *A. G. Hollister . . . 1901*, pp. 5–16. Hollister edited this work for publication. MacLean 317. CtY, MHarF, MPB, MPH, MWiW*, N, NBuG, NN, NOC, NSyU, NjPT, OClWHi, OCH, WHi.

734 [GREEN, CALVIN and SETH Y. WELLS] A Brief Exposition of the Established Principles and Regulations of the United Society Called Shakers . . . . Albany, [N.Y.]: Printed by Packard and Van Benthuysen, 1830. 23 pp. 18 cm.

"Published in behalf of the Society, by Calvin Green and Seth Y. Wells, Committee of Publication. New-Lebanon, March 15th, 1830," p. 21. "The Exposition, in its first form, was hastily written for the purpose of obviating a defamatory bill presented to the legislature of New York. Introductory statement, Watervliet, O., 1832 edition (no. 735), p. 3. Enemies had succeeded in having a bill introduced which would have seriously damaged the Shakers, *see* no. 1082. *A Brief Exposition* was written, and distributed in the Legislature, to correct "erroneous

opinions and false impressions" about Shakerism, and to demonstrate that it was "compatible with the free agency of man" and "consistent with truth, justice, reason and all civil and religious rights of man," p. 4. MacLean 481. Sabin 79695. Shaw 3457. DLC, MB, MH, MWA, MWiW*, MiU–C, MnU, N, NN, OCHP, OClWHi, ODa, OOxM, PPL.

Dow, E. F. *Portrait of the Millennial Church* (Orono, Me., 1931), p. 47, lists a Poughkeepsie, N.Y., 1822 edition of *A Brief Exposition* . . . No copy or other reference to this edition has been located. May be a misprint for 1832.

735 [——] ———— Printed at Albany, in the Year 1830; And Now Reprinted with Sundry Improvements Suggested by the Author . . . . Watervliet, O.: 1832. 36 pp. 19 cm.

"Edited by Richard M'Namer [!] and David Spinning," p. 36, but the statement from the 1830 edition is included, "Published in behalf of the Society, by Calvin Green and Seth Y. Wells, Cmmittee [sic] of Publication. New-Lebanon, March 15th, 1830," p. 14. The title is identical. "A Brief Exposition" is abridged, pp. 3–14; "The Exposition Continued," pp. 15–31, is written by David Spinning; "Form of a Revisal & Ratification of the Church Covenant" with blank spaces to be filled in, pp. 32–36. Advertisements on recto of back cover. This pamphlet was the first publication issued from the press presented to Richard McNemar by the Watervliet Society, *MacLean, Life . . .* (no. 2411), p. 46. Some copies include other publications which are paged to continue *A Brief Exposition* . . . The Buffalo and Erie County Public Library copy includes "An Improved Edition of the Church Covenant," pp. 37–48, no. 911(3); Western Reserve Historical Society Library copy includes, "A Brief Exposition of Certain Points of Doctrine – by Request. No. 4, October 1, 1832," pp. 37–48, no. 890. Copies of this edition (complete with title page) were also bound with *The Constitution of the United Societies* . . . no. 911(2).

MacLean 150. Sabin 79696. CSmH, CtY, ICJ, ICU, KyBgW, KyU, MB, MH, MHarF, MPB, MWA, MWiW, NBuG, NHi, NN, NOC, O, OC,

OCHP, OClWHi*, ODa, OFH, OHi, OO, PLC, PPULC.

736 [——] ———— of the United Society of Believers, Called Shakers. Improved Edition .... Albany [N.Y.]: Printed by Hoffman and White, 1834. Cover title. 36 pp. 18½ cm.

Follows the 1832 edition, but is corrected and amended. "Extracts from the Church Covenant," pp. 33-34, and "A Few Reflections on the Nature of the Church Covenant," pp. 34-36, are substituted for "Form of a Revisal ..." in the earlier edition. "Published in behalf of the Society, by Calvin Green and Seth Y. Wells, Committee of Publication, New-Lebanon, March 15th, 1830," p. 15. This statement is found unchanged in all editions until the 1851 New York edition, no. 740. This version of *A Brief Exposition ...* was reprinted in the *Day-Star*, 11 (June 13, 1846), 10-11, omitting only the introductory statement and the signatures at the end. Printed in [R. R. Hinman] *comp., Blue Laws of New Haven Colony* (no. 776), pp. 261-95. MacLean 151. Sabin 79697. CtY, DLC, MH, MHarF, MPB, MSaE, MWA, MWiW*, MdBP, MiU-C, N, NBuG, NHi, NN, OClWHi.

737 [——] ———— Improved edition. Printed at Canterbury, N.H.: 1843. Cover title. 37 pp. 20½ cm.

Text is the same as the 1834 Albany edition. MacLean 482. Sabin 79697. DLC, MB, MWiW*, MeHi, MiU-C, NBLiHi, NHi, NN, Nh, NHi, OCHP, OClWHi, OHi, PHi, PPULC, PU.

738 [——] ———— Improved edition. New York: Printed by Edward O. Jenkins, 1846. Cover title. 36 pp. 19½ cm.

Text is the same as the 1834 Albany edition. MacLean 152. Sabin 79697 (Includes also a Hartford, 1846 edition. No Copy located). CtY, DLC, ICJ, MB, MH, MPB, MSaE, MWA, MWiW*, MiU-C, N, NHi, NN, NOC, NSyU, NhD, PPL.

739 [——] ———— Improved edition. Hartford: Press of Elihu Geer, 1850. Cover title. 36 pp. 19½ cm.

Text is the same as the 1834 Albany edition.

MacLean 153. Sabin 79697. CSmH, CtHi, CtY, DLC, ICJ, KyBgW, KySP, MHarF, MHi, MPB, MPH, MWA, MWiW*, MiU-C, NN, NOC, NSyU, OClWHi, OHi, OOxM, PPULC.

740 [——] ———— New York: Printed by Edward O. Jenkins, 1851. Cover title. 30 pp. 19½ cm.

"It is now revised for the press, with such corrections and additions as appear to be necessary ... by the surviving author [Calvin Green]," p. [2]. "Published in behalf of the Society by Calvin Green and Seth Y. Wells. Committee of publication, and now republished, New Lebanon, N.Y., Jan. 1, 1851," p. 22. "Exposition," pp. [3]-22; "Appendix," pp. [23]-29; "Location of Societies," pp. 29-30. "Exposition Continued," has been omitted. MacLean 154. Sabin 79697. CSmH, CtHi, CtY, DLC, MB, MBC, MBrZ, MH, MHi, MSaE, MWA, MWiW*, MiU, N, NBLiHi, NHi, NN, NOC, OCHP, OClWHi, OHi, OU, PHi, PPDrop, PU, RHi, WHi.

741 [——] ———— New York: E. S. Dodge Printing Co., 1879. Cover title. 32 pp. 20 cm.

Text and contents the same as New York, 1871 edition. "This little work upon our faith and principles has ever been acknowledged as STANDARD. The last editions having been exhausted, and in consideration of the great value of the work, the Society of Canterbury has undertaken the issue of a large edition ...." *Shaker Manifesto*, 9 (January 1879), 22. MacLean 155. CtHC, CtY, DLC, MB, MBC, MH, MHarF, MHi, MH-P, MPB, MWA, MWiW*, MSaE, MiU, N, NBuG, NN, NOC, NSyU, OCHP, OClWHi, OHi, PHi, WaU, WHi.

742 ——— A Brief Exposition of the Principls [!] and Regulations of the United Society of Believers. By Calvin Green and Seth Y. Wells .... Shaker Village, East Canterbury, N.H.: 1895. Cover title. 24 pp. 19 cm.

This is a complete revision of the text and the first time that the authors' names have appeared on the cover. Simplified spelling is used throughout the text, indicating that Alonzo Hollister may have edited this edition. A wood engraving, "Shaker Village, East Canterbury, N.H.," appears on the verso of the back cover. Variant cover titles are found with parts of the title reset in a different typeface. Some of these copies have a wood engraving, "Industry," (beehive) or a picture of East Canterbury, N.H. on the verso of the back cover; others have a blank back cover. MacLean 156. DLC, MWA (2 variants), MWiW* (all variants), MeB, MeHi, MiU, MiU-C, N, NN, NOC, NSyU, NhD, OClWHi, ODa, OHi, OO, PHi, PPULC.

743 [——] A Summary View of the Millennial Church, or United Society of Believers, (Commonly Called Shakers.) Comprising the Rise, Progress and Practical Order of the Society; Together with General Principles of Their Faith and Testimony. Published by Order of the Ministry, in Union with the Church ... Albany, N.Y.: Printed by Packard & Van Benthuysen, 1823. xvi, 320 pp. 19 cm.

Preface, pp. [iii]-xiv, signed: *Calvin Green, Seth Y. Wells, New Lebanon, May 12, 1823.* Later in the 1848 edition, no. 744, "Advertisement," p. [ii], it was explained that "the original design ... was to present to the public a small, cheap volume, comprising particular information concerning the United Society, adapted to the general class of readers, and calculated to answer the usual inquiries respecting their religious principles and moral economy." Six thousand copies were printed, according to Calvin Green's "Biographic Memoir."
MacLean 96. Sabin 79721. Shaw 14086 (for "compiling" in title, read "Comprising").
CSmH, Ct, CtHT-W, CtY, DLC, ICJ, ICN, ICU, KyBgW, MBAt, MBrZ, MH, MWA, MWiW*, MeBaT, N, NBuG, NIC, NN, NNUT, NOC, Nh, NjMD, NjP, OClWHi, OO, PHi, PPL, ViW, WHi (*see* Shaw for other holdings).

744 [——] —— 2d ed., rev. and impr. Republished by the United Society with the Approbation of the Ministry. Albany, N.Y.: Printed by C. Van Benthuysen, 1848. vii, [1], 384 pp. 19 cm.

The Preface has been shortened to pp. [iii]-iv, but it carries the May 12, 1823 date, and is signed by Green and Wells. "Errata," p. [1]. Green's "Biographic Memoir," p. 641,

states that Part 7, included in this edition, was omitted from the 1st edition "because of technical reasons." Also, that 7000 copies were printed to fill requests from societies plus a few for the printer's own use. "A few improvements ... and several important articles never before published have been added ... The whole has been attentively examined and revised, and the original principles and design have been carefully preserved." Advertisement, p. [ii], dated October 1847.
MacLean 97. Sabin 79722 and 258513.
CSmH, CtHC, CtY, DLC, In, KyBgW, KyU, MB, MBC, MH, MHarF, MPB, MPH, MWA, MWiW*, MeHi, MiD, N, NHi, NBLiHi, NN, NNC, NOC, NRCR, NSyU, NhD, NjPT, O, OC, OCHP, OCl, OClWHi, ODa, OHi, OO, OLeWHi, PHC, PHi, PPULC, WHi.

745 —— —— (Reprint). New York: AMS Press, 1973.

746 Greetings. To You, From the Society of American Shakers ... [Sabbathday Lake, Me.?:] 1937. Broadside. 18½ X 16 cm.

Claims the distinction that the Shakers have existed "longer than any other Communist order," and that communism has not survived "except when identified with some religious creed." Note at end: Please do not confuse with Soviet Communism.
MHarF, MWiW*, NSyU.

747 [GROSVENOR, LORENZO DOW] Address at the Dedication of the Shirley Mills, Shirley. [South Groton, Mass.?: 1851]. Caption title. [4] pp. 28 X 20½ cm.

Printed three columns to the page. This appears to be a vigorous, if belated, refutation of Edward Everett's review of Youngs' *Testimony of Christ's Second Appearing* ... (no. 1470), *North American Review*, 11 (January 1823), 76-102. Everett's name is not mentioned, nor is reference made to the Shirley Mills.
MacLean 318 (broadside). MPB, MWA, MWiW*, OClWHi.

748 —— —— By Lorenzo D. Grosvenor, Harvard. Caption title. [4] pp. 28 X 20 cm.

The same as no. 747 except for variant caption

title. Both contain "Post Office Address of the Society of Shakers," p. [4].
MHi, MWA*, MiU-C.

749 —— America, the "Land of Emanuel:" Constitutional Liberty a Refuge for the Gathering to Shiloh. By Lorenzo D. Grosvenor of Shaker Community, South Groton, Mass. [n.p., 186?]. Caption title. 8 pp. 19 cm.
    MacLean 319. Sabin 28591 (Boston, n.d.). DLC, MB, MHi, MWiW*, NN, NOC, OClWHi (23 cm.).

750 —— Circular Letter. [South Groton, Mass.: 1849]. Broadside in 2 columns. 47 X 25 cm.
    Addressed: Esteemed Friend; dated: Harvard, Mass., March 29th, 1849; signed: *Lorenzo D. Grosvenor.*
    MacLean 321. MWiW*, OClWHi.

751 [——] ——— [South Groton, Mass.: 1858]. Broadside in 3 columns. 43 X 19 cm.
    Addressed: Friend; dated: South Groton, Mass., April, 1858; signed: *Lorenzo D. Grosvenor.* The text has been rearranged with part in a postscript and there are minor omissions. Otherwise this is practically the same as no. 750.
    MWiW*.

752 —— Circular Letter in Defence of the United Society of Believers, Commonly Called Shakers; with a Reply to Correspondents. [South Groton, Mass.: 1849]. Caption title. 17 [1] pp. 15½ cm.
    A letter addressed: Esteemed Friend; dated: Harvard (South Groton P.O.) Mass., April 20th 1849; signed p. 14: *Lorenzo D. Grosvenor.* The letter is an exposition of Shaker theology. "Reply to correspondents," pp. 14-17, dated: South Groton, Mass. August 25, 1849; signed: *L. D. Grosvenor.* Advertisement for Shaker publications, p. [1] at end.
    MacLean 320. Sabin 79699. DLC, MHarF, MHi, MPB, MWA, MWiW*, MiU-C, NHi, NN, NOC, OClWHi.

—— A Concise Answer . . . *See* McNemar, Richard, nos. **908-910.**

753 —— Swear Not at All. South Groton, Mass.: [n.d.] Broadside. 13½ X 7½ cm.
    Poem (28 lines) printed on blue paper.
    OClWHi*.

754 [——] Swear Not at All. Agur's Prayer. Consecration — "Give Me Heart" [3 poems]. [n.p., n.d.]. [2] pp. 20½ cm.
    At end, p. [1]: Presented by A. H. Grosvenor (South Groton Shaker Village) Mass., p. [2]: "Boston Indian Medical Institute," with a description of medicine practiced and names of officers.
    MHarF*, OClWHi.

755 —— Testimony of Jesus Concerning Marriage. [Boston: 185?]. Caption title. [2] pp. (3 columns to each page). 63 X 23½ cm.
    Three poems, "Watch," "And Nehemiah said: 'Remember Me, oh, my God for these things'." and "Agur's Prayer," follow the text. This appears to be reprinted from the *National Union and Spirit of Seventy-six,* a weekly published in Boston. An advertisement of this journal appears at the end of the article.
    MWiW*, NN, OClWHi.

756 [——] ——— [n.p., n.d.]. Caption title. 12 pp. 23 cm.
    MacLean attributes this incorrectly to F. W. Evans. Grosvenor's name appears as author, no. 755. The word "poor," line 5, has been corrected here to read "pure," and therefore this is probably a later printing than no. 755. The poems at the end of the text have been omitted. A subtitle has been added: "Marriage, — Jesus and the Shakers. Is Marriage a Christian Institution? Read the Testimony . . ."
    MacLean 454. ICN, MPB, MWiW*, OClWHi, PPL.

GROSVENOR, ROXALANA L. *See The Shakers' Covenant . . .* , nos. **1003, 1307,** and **1698.**

H

757 HAMMOND, JOSEPH. "Account of the Shakers." In Spofford, Jeremiah, *A Gazetteer of Massachusetts* (Newburyport, Mass., 1828), pp. 211–12.

A letter addressed: Friend Spofford. is a description of the Harvard, Mass., Shaker community written by one of the members in response to Spofford's request. There is a brief mention of the Hancock Shaker community, p. 210. Hammond's account was reprinted with minor changes in Spofford's *A Historical and Statistical Gazetteer of Massachusetts* (2d. ed., Haverhill [Mass.], 1860), pp. 234, 236–37.

758 HAMPTON, OLIVER C. The Balance Wheel. Union Village [O.]: 1869. Caption title. 4 pp. 24 cm.

MacLean 325. MWA, OClWHi*.

759 —— The Holy Trinity. [n.p., n.d.]. Broadside in 2 columns. 35 X 26½ cm.

A poem of 144 lines, signed: *O. C. Hampton.* OClWHi*.

760 —— Home of the Oracle. [Union Village, O.: 189–?]. Broadside. 23½ X 11½ cm.

Poem of 7 stanzas, signed: *O. C. Hampton, Union Village, O.* Appeared in *The Manifesto,* 23 (March 1893), 58–59.

MacLean 326. DLC, ICJ, MPB, MWiW*, OClWHi.

761 —— In Memoriam. Elder William Reynolds, Departed This Life, at Union Village, Ohio, May 13, 1881, Aged 66 Years, 1 Mo., 9 Days. [n.p., 1881]. Broadside. 36 X 12½ cm.

Signed: *O. C. Hampton.* "Lines read at his funeral;" poem of 14 stanzas. OClWHi*.

762 —— Paraphrase [poem]. Union Village, Ohio: [n.d.]. Broadside.

J. P. MacLean, *Bibliography,* p. 12, states

that Hampton "published, without date," this poem.

MacLean 327. DLC*.

763 —— Religion, Science, Reason. [Union Village, O.: 187–?]. Broadside. 29 X 15 cm.

Signed: *O. C. Hampton.* Poem of 56 lines. First line, "This sacred trine — Religion, Science, Reason,"/

DLC, MPB, MWiW*, OClWHi.

764 —— A Short but Comprehensive Definition of Shakerism. [Union Village, O.: 190–?]. Broadside. 31½ X 20½ cm.

Signed: *O. C. Hampton.* CtHi, CtY-D, ICJ, MPB, MWiW, MiU-C, OClWHi*.

765 —— ———— [Union Village, O.: 1901]. Broadside. 31½ X 20½ cm.

Signed: *Elder O. C. Hampton, United Society of Shakers, Union Village, Warren County, Ohio.* Text has been reset.

KyBgW, MPH, MiU-C, N, NBuG, NSyU, NjPT, OClWHi*.

766 —— A Special Call and Invitation. Union Village, O.: 1891. [2] pp. 24 cm.

"An Appeal," by Charles Clapp, p. [2]. OHi*.

767 —— To Whomever It May Concern. Invitation to Visit and Join the Shakers. [Union Village, O.: 1884]. Broadside. 16 X 10 cm.

Dated: Shaker, April 15, 1884. Signed: *O. C. Hampton, Shaker P.O., Warren County, Ohio.*

MWiW*, OClWHi*.

768 Happy Release. [n.p., 1892]. Broadside. 18½ X 7½ cm.

An announcement that Daniel Offord has taken Elder Evans' place with "Walter Shepard by his side." Tipped in December

1892 issue of *The Manifesto* of the Williams College copy (Williamstown, Mass.). MWiW, OClWHi*.

769 HARTER, MRS. J. H. and [HARVEY L. EADS]. True Religion. A Poem, by Mrs. J. H. Harter, Auburn, N.Y. and Rhymes on Shakerism by Lizzie Morton [*pseud.*] [n.p., n.d.]. Caption title. 20 pp. 14½ cm.
OClWHi*.

770 HARVARD, MASS. SCHOOL COMMIT-TEE. Annual Report of the School Committee of the Town of Harvard, for the School Year, 1881-82. Ayer, Mass.: Printed at Public Spirit Office, 1882. 14 pp.
Shaker schools, pp. 9, 14. *See also* nos. 994 and 995.
M, MB, MH, MWiW*.

771 HASKELL, RUSSELL, *comp.* A Musical Expositor: Or, a Treatise on the Rules and Elements of Music; Adapted to the Most Approved Method of Musical Writing. New York: George W. Wood, Book and Music Printer, 1847. 82 [1] pp. music. 14 × 23 cm.
Devoted to instruction in Shaker music notation which is based upon the letters a–g. The Introduction (dated Enfield, Conn., April 1847) modestly explains that this treatise should be regarded as "little more than an introduction, or a basis on which ... Harmony might rest." It is recognized that more songs would have been desirable, but "had to be omitted for want of suitable music type." Some letter music type is printed, but many symbols and the music scores have been supplied by hand in ink. MacLean 39. CtY-D, ICRL, MH, MPB, MWiW*, NBuG, NN, OClWHi.

772 HASKETT, WILLIAM J. Shakerism Unmasked, or the History of the Shakers; Including a Form Politic of Their Government as Councils, Orders, Gifts, with an Exposition of the Five Orders of Shakerism, Ann Lee's Grand Foundation Vision, in Sealed Pages. With Some Extracts from Their Private Hymns Which Have Never Appeared before the Public. Pittsfield: Published by the Author, L. H. Walkley, Printer, 1828. 300 pp. 18½ cm.

The initials of the printer in the imprints are indistinct (over-inked) and are found identified as E.H., L.H., and B.H. Pages 232-33 are sealed with wafers and contain "Ann Lee's Grand Foundation Vision." The "Private Hymns," pp. [235]-94, are reprinted from *Millennial Praises,* no. 1415, with Haskett's comments. Haskett was an English sailor, who signed the covenant at Mt. Lebanon, N.Y. He is well acquainted with Shaker history, doctrine, and publications.
MacLean 40. Sabin 30803. Shaw 33495. CSmH, CtHi, CtY-D, DeWint, DLC, ICN, ICU, KyBgW, KyU, MB, MBC, MH, MHi, MHarF, MPB, MWA, MWiW*, MeHi, MiU-C, N, NBuG, NHi, NN, NNC, NOC, NRU, NSchU, NSyU, NcD, NhD, NjPT, O, OC, OClWHi, OCU, ODa, OO, PHi, PPPrHi, RPB.

773 HAWKINS, DANIEL J. and PHILEMON STEWART. "Statement [on a variety of native grape improved at New Lebanon]." U.S. Commissioner of Patents, *Report for the Year 1854, Vol. 4, Agriculture.* p. 315.
The merits of the Shaker-originated Early Northern Muscadine Grape are discussed, but Burton's Early August Grape is also recommended. Printed also as *U.S. 33d Cong., 2d sess., Senate Ex. Doc., No. 42* (Ser. No. 755), and *H. of R. Ex. Doc., No. 59* (Ser. No. 787). *See also* nos. 353, 354 and 2149.

774 He Leadeth Me. [n.p., n.d.]. Broadside. 14 × 9 cm.
Hymn. Eleven stanzas, printed on heavy stock.
OClWHi*.

775 Heavenly Path-way [hymn]. [East Canterbury, N.H.:] Printed at Shaker Village, [n.d.]. [4] pp. 13 cm.
Contains also: "Couldst Thou Not Watch One Hour?" "Scenes of Glory"; "A Prayer." OClWHi*.

776 [HINMAN, ROYAL RALPH], *comp.* Blue Laws of New Haven Colony, Usually Called Blue Laws of Connecticut ... and Other Interesting Antiquities. Compiled by an Antiquarian. Hartford: Printed by Case, Tiffany & Co., 1838. 336 pp.

[C. Green and S. Y. Wells], *A Brief Exposition of the Established Principles and Regulations of the United Society of Believers, Called Shakers* (1832) is reprinted with slight changes, pp. 261-95, see no. 735. The compiler states that these pages have been added at the request of Seth Y. Wells of New Lebanon, New York. Running title: Shaking Quakers. Binder's title, Blue Laws, Quaker Laws, and Witchcraft.

777 HOAR, GEORGE FRISBIE. A Pathetic Petition. Mt. Lebanon, N.Y.: The Lebanon Press, [n.d.]. Cover title. [4] pp. 13 cm. (Lebanon Leaves. Charity Series, No. 1).

A plea to the General Court of Massachusetts to save the birds of the state. Hoar was a U.S. Senator elected in 1877 and 4 times thereafter. MacLean 328. DLC, OClWHi*.

778 [HODGDON, CHARLES C.] Just Published, Hodgdon's Life and Manner of Living among the Shakers ... Concord, N.H.: Published by the Author, 1838. 31 pp. 17 cm.

"These lines I have written for the purpose of giving the world a fair and just conception of this much abused and slandered Society." This is an account of Shaker beliefs and conduct during the three years the author lived with the Shakers at Canterbury, N.H. He seceded to marry a young Shaker sister, also a seceder. On p. 30, signed: *C. C. Hodgdon.* "To Mary [Dyer] as a Slanderer [poem]," p. 31, and verso of the back wrapper. MHarF*.

779 HOLLISTER, ALONZO GILES. Annunciation of the Way and Work of Christ's Manifestation and the New Day of His Visitation. [Mt. Lebanon, N.Y.: n.d.]. Caption title. 34 pp. 15 cm.
N*.

780 [——], *ed.* Calvin's Confession a Communication Given in the Name of John Calvin, the Geneva Reformer, in the Shaker Community, Shakers, Albany Co., N.Y. in 1842. Medium, J. LaFume. Reprinted from the *Progressive Thinker*, with Additions from the Original, Aug. 1904 ... Lebanon Shakers, N.Y.: [1904?]. Cover title. 26 pp. 14 cm.

"The Free Woman" [from the *World's Advance Thought*] by A. G. Hollister, pp. [17]-26; "Comradeship" [poem], p. 26.
MacLean 353. CtY, MHarF, MPB, MPH, MWiW*, NBuG, NN, NOC, NSyU, OClWHi.

781 —— Christ the Harvester. [Mt. Lebanon, N.Y.?: 189-]. Caption title. [4] pp. 18 cm.

Appeared in *The Manifesto*, 19 (November 1889), 244-46.
MacLean 329. CtY, DLC, MHarF, MPB, MPH, MWA, MWiW*, MiU-C, N, NN, OClWHi, WHi.

782 [——] Christ the Way the Word of God Abides Forever. [Mt. Lebanon, N.Y.?: 1909?]. Caption title. [4] pp. 15 cm.

"From the *World's Advance Thought.*" Signed: *A. G. Hollister, Mt. Lebanon, N.Y., 1890-1909.* Alonzo Hollister states in an a.l.s. to William Ward Wight, Dec. 1909, that *Christ the Way* was published in Aug. 1890, under the title: *Another Witness.* No copy of this title has been located. Hollister must have referred to "Witness," *The Manifesto*, 20 (August 1890), 170-73.
CtY-D, M, MHarF, MPB, MWA, MWiW*, N, NjPT, OClWHi.

783 —— The Coming of Christ. [Mt. Lebanon, N.Y.?: 189-?]. Caption title. 8 pp. 13 cm.

Contains also, "St. Patrick's Cathedral" [by] Anna White. Reprinted from *The Manifesto*, 17 (November 1887), 250-53.
MacLean 330. DLC, MHarF, MPB, MWA, MWiW*, N, NN, OClWHi, WHi.

784 ——, *comp.* Divine Judgment, Justice and Mercy. A Revelation of the Great White Throne. Judgment is an Influx of Higher Truths; Their Influence is an Efflux, and Their Effects are Purifying and Uplifting. Mount Lebanon, Columbia Co., N.Y.: 1895. Cover title. 48 pp. 12½ cm.

"Unveiling," pp. [22]-26, signed: *A. G. H.*
"The Shechinah," pp. 27-32, signed: *C. Allen.*
"We are Seen" [poem], pp. 47-48, signed: *Garrett Keatin Lawrence, 1835.*
MacLean 331. CtY, DLC, ICN, MHarF, MPB, MWA, MWiW*, MiU-C, NBuG, NHi, N, NN, NOC, NSyU, OClWHi, WHi.

785 [——] Divine Motherhood. [Mt. Lebanon, N.Y.: 1887]. Caption title. [4] pp.
21½ cm.
> Signed: *Mount Lebanon, Col. Co., N.Y. June
> 1887. Alonzo Hollister.*
> MacLean 332. CtY, DLC, MPB, MPH,
> MWiW*, MiU, NBuG, NN, NOC, NSyU,
> NcD, NjPT, OClWHi, WHi.

786 —— Doing and Being. Acting and React-
ing. The Seen and Unseen. Cause and Effect.
The Vail of Death Destroyed .... Mt. Lebanon,
Columbia Co., N.Y.: 1910. Cover title. 37 [1]
pp. 15½ cm.
> An untitled poem is printed on the verso of
> back cover.
> CtY, DLC, KyU, MPB, MWiW*, N, NOC,
> NjPT, OClWHi.

787 —— Government. [n.p., n.d.]. Caption
title. [2] pp. 31½ × 24 cm.
> Printed with 3 columns to each page. p. [1],
> "Government"; verso, miscellaneous short
> notices; running head: The Circle of Light.
> OClWHi*.

788 —— Harmonizing Power of Truth. [n.p.,
n.d.]. Broadside. 32½ × 25½ cm. Excerpt from
the *World's Advance Thought.*
> ICN, OClWHi*.

789 [——] Heaven Anointed Woman. [Mt.
Lebanon, N.Y.?: 1887]. Caption title. [4] pp.
21½ cm.
> Signed: *Mount Lebanon, Col. Co., N.Y.
> August 1887. A. G. Hollister.*
> MacLean 333. CtY, DLC, ICN, MPB, MPH,
> MWiW*, N, NBuG, NN, NOC, OClWHi, WHi.

790 [——], *comp.* Important Rules Necessary
for Every One to Observe. [Mt. Lebanon, N.Y.:
189–?]. Broadside. 16½ × 9½ cm.
> A.n.s. on the verso, no. 791, signed: *Alonzo*
> [Hollister], gives the information that "The
> main part of these were copied from an old
> almanac, perhaps 1828, more than 50 years
> ago. I printed a few for home circulation
> [but in response to requests of visitors and
> tourists] I printed 4 or 500 copies." These
> are found printed on blue, yellow, or white

paper – some with a type ornament at the
end, and some without.
> MPB, MWiW*, OClWHi.

791 [——], *comp.* ——— [New Lebanon,
N.Y.: 190–?]. Broadside. 19 × 10 cm.
> A.n.s. on the verso of the Williams College
> copy (Williamstown, Mass.), signed: *Alonzo*
> [Hollister], states that "Since this century
> began, I altered 2 or 3 to improve and
> added one on chastity and temperance and
> had 1000 printed."
> MPB, MPH, MWiW*, NBuG, NjPT, OClWHi.

792 [——] "In the Day Thou Eatest." [Mt.
Lebanon, N.Y.?: 1905?]. Caption title. 7 pp.
14½ cm.
> Signed: *A. G. Hollister.* The Williams Col-
> lege copy has a proof copy attached with
> additions and corrections in Hollister's hand,
> marked "first edition." It appears to have
> been clipped from a periodical.
> CtY, DLC, MPB, MWA, MWiW*, NBuG,
> NSyU, NjPT, OClWHi.

793 [——] ——— Caption title. [Mt.
Lebanon, N.Y.?: 190–?] 8 pp. 13 cm.
> Printed from a different type setting.
> CtY, DLC, ICN, MWA, OClWHi*.

794 —— Interpreting Prophecy. Portland,
Oregon: The World's Advance Thought
Envelope Line [after 1887]. Cover title. 20 pp.
13 cm.
> Blank leaf follows p. 20. The date 1887 is
> found in an advertisement for "simultaneous
> soul-communion," verso, back cover.
> MacLean 334 (1880?). MPB, MWiW*,
> NBuG, NHi, NN, OClWHi, WHi.

795 —— Interpreting Prophecy and the
Appearing of Christ. Chicago, Ill.: Guiding Star
Publishing House, [1892]. Cover title. 41 pp.
16½ cm.
> On p. 41, signed: *Alonzo Hollister, Mount
> Lebanon, Columbia County, N.Y., 1892.* Pt. I,
> pp. [1]–16; Pt. II, pp. [17]–41 contains new
> material. Published by the Koreshan Unity
> which at this time had a close relationship
> with the Shakers, *see* nos. 652 and 1578.

Ct-D, DLC, MH, MPB, MPH, MWiW*,
MeHi, MiU-C, N, NOC, NSyU, NjPT,
OClWHi.

796 —— —— Third Edition .... Wash-
ington Heights, Ill.: Guiding Star Publishing
House, 1892. Cover title. [2] 41 [1] pp. 17 cm.
  Same as no. 795, with a few additions and
  corrections.
  MacLean 335. CtY, DLC, ICN, KySP, MB,
  MH, MPB, MPH, MWA, MWiW*, MiU-C, N,
  NBuG, NN, NOC, NSyU, NcD, OClWHi,
  OHi.

797 —— Introductory Address Delivered ...
before the Litchfield County Historical and
Antiquarian Society on the Occasion of Com-
pleting its Organization. Hartford: 1856.
  This reference was contributed without
  further information.
  NjPT*.

798 [——] Joyful Tidings. [Mt. Lebanon, N.Y.:
1886]. Caption title. [4] pp. 21 cm.
  Signed: *Mount Lebanon, Col. Co., N.Y.
  1886. A. G. Hollister.*
  MacLean 336. CtY, DLC, ICN, MH, MPB,
  MWA, MWiW*, NN, OClWHi, WHi.

—— *ed.* Law of Life ... *See* Green, Calvin, no.
733.

—— Life and Sufferings of Jesus ... *See*
Leonard, William, no. 862.

799 [——] Millennium Seen in a Dream
Vision by Julia Ward Howe. [New Lebanon,
N.Y.?: 1908]. Caption title. [4] pp. 14½ cm.
  "From Progressive Thinker, July 11, 1908."
  Comments on Mrs. Howe's vision, followed
  by her own description of what was revealed,
  are reprinted from the *Chicago Examiner*,
  pp. [1-2]. "The Truth is Marching On," pp.
  [2-4], is a discussion of vision and revelations
  which employ many Biblical quotations. A
  copy at Western Reserve Historical Society
  (Cleveland, O.) is signed by A. G. Hollister.
  CtY, MHarF, MPB, MWiW*, N, NBuG.

800 —— Mission of Alethian Believers, Called
Shakers .... Mt. Lebanon, Columbia County,

N.Y.: 1892-1899. Cover title. 28 pp. 15 cm.
  "Alethianism or Shakerism," pp. 1-4;
  "Testimonia," pp. 5-11; "Heavenly Love,"
  pp. 12-15; "Marriage" by John Kenworthy,
  pp. 16-28. Supplementary text on verso of
  front cover, and recto, back cover. Some-
  times found cited as "Alethianism or
  Shakerism."
  MacLean 337. CtY, DLC, ICN, KySP,
  MHarF, MPB, MWA, MWiW*, MeHi, MiU-C,
  N, NBuG, NHi, NN, NOC, NjPT, OClWHi,
  OHi, WHi.

801 [——] The New Revelation. [n.p., n.d.].
Caption title. [4] pp. 22 cm.
  In Western Reserve Historical Society copy,
  a note in Hollister's autograph states: My
  first tract printed by William Koch on home
  press. Hollister to Wm. W. Wight, Dec. 6,
  1909, "only 200 copies 1st ed." ... "of the
  last 250." A.l.s. Williams College, Williamstown, Mass.
  MacLean 387 (lists a copy of "2 p."). DLC,
  MPB, MPH, MWiW*, MeB, NBuG, NN,
  OClWHi.

802 [——] —— [Mt. Lebanon, N.Y.:
1909]. Caption title. 14 pp. 12½ cm.
  Signed: *A. G. Hollister, Mt. Lebanon, N.Y.
  1886-1909.*
  CtY, MWiW*, NBuG, NjPT, OClWHi.

803 ——, *comp.* Prophecy Unseald [!] by the
"Word of God Reveald [!] out of Whose Mouth
Goeth a Sharp Sword" .... Brief Sketch of Ann
Lee the First Anointed, Emancipated, New
Woman, as Seen by Those Who Knew Her ....
Mount Lebanon Shakers, N.Y.: 1905. Cover
title. 33 pp. 15 cm.
  Text extends through p. 33, the recto of
  back cover. "A Revelation," pp. 3-12, is
  "Abridged from a Book of Holy Wisdom
  (pp. 344-369). Printed at Canterbury, N.H.,
  1849," p. 3. *See* no. 67.
  CSmH, DLC, MH, MPB, MPH, MWA,
  MWiW*, MiU-C, N, NN, NOC, NSyU, OClWHi.

804 [——] The Reapers. [Mt. Lebanon, N.Y.?:
1886]. Caption title. [4] pp. 22 cm.
  Signed: *A. G. Hollister. Mount Lebanon, Col.
  Co., N.Y. 1886.*

MacLean 338. CtY, DLC, MPB, MWA, MWiW*, NN, OClWHi, WHi.

805 [——] —— [Mt. Lebanon, N.Y.?: 1898]. Caption title. 16 pp. 12 cm.
Signed: *A. G. Hollister, Mount Lebanon, Col. Co., N.Y. 1886-1898.*
MacLean 339. DLC, MH, MH-AH, MPB, MPH, MWA, MWiW*, N, NBuG, NN, NOC, OClWHi.

806 [——] The Reapers. The Reapers Are the Messengers—Jesus. [Mt. Lebanon, N.Y.?: 1909]. Caption title. 16 pp. 12½ cm.
Signed: *A. G. Hollister, Mt. Lebanon, Col. Co., N.Y. 1886-1898-1909.*
ICN, MWA, MWiW*, OClWHi.

807 [——] Shaker Testimony. The Gospel of Eternal (Aionion) Life, Proclaimed in the Season of Judgement. [Mt. Lebanon, N.Y.: 1891]. Caption title. [2] pp. 29 cm.
Printed 2 columns to the page. Signed: *Mount Lebanon, Col. Co., N.Y., July 1891. A. G. Hollister.*
MacLean 340. DLC, MPB, MWiW*, NBuG, NN, OClWHi, WHi.

808 —— Shaker View of Marriage. [Mt. Lebanon, N.Y.?: 1885?]. Caption title. 11 pp. 13½ cm.
Contains also: "Non-resistance" by Wm. Leonard (from *The Manifesto*, 14 (November 1884), 241-43); "The Government of Christ's Kingdom a Theocracy" by Abraham Perkins (from *The Manifesto*, 14 (February 1884), 27-28); "Christ's Kingdom—its Bed Rock Foundations" by Daniel Fraser (from *The Manifesto*, 15 (February 1885), 25-26); "Self-examination" by Martha J. Anderson (from *The Manifesto*, 12 (December 1882), 273-74). *Shaker View of Marriage* was printed in *The Manifesto*, 12 (January 1882), 9-12.
MacLean 341. DLC, MHarF, MPB, MWA, MWiW*, N, NN, OClWHi, OHi, WHi.

809 —— "Shakers," in *Columbia County at the End of the Century*, no. 1991, pp. 678-90.
A history of Mt. Lebanon and discussion of Shaker beliefs.

—— Spirits the Shakers Saw. *See* [Frederick William Evans], no. 665.

810 —— ... Synopsis of Doctrine Taught by Believers in Christ's Second Appearing .... [Mt. Lebanon, N.Y.?:] 1893. Cover title. 24 pp. 12½ cm.
ICN, MPB, MWiW*, NBuG, PPL.

811 —— —— Second ed. enl. [Mt. Lebanon, N.Y.?:] 1893. Cover title. 30 pp. 12½ cm.
MacLean 343. DLC, MB, MH, MHarF, MPB, MPH, MWiW*, MeHi, N, NN, NHi, OClWHi, WHi.

812 —— —— [Mt. Lebanon, N.Y.?:] 1893-1902. Cover title. 31 pp. 12½ cm.
"A Divine Promise," U.[nion] V.[illage], p. 31.
MacLean 342. CSmH, CtY, DLC, MPB, MPH, MWA, MWiW*, MiU-C, N, NHi, NOC, NSyU, OClWHi.

813 —— —— [Mt. Lebanon, N.Y.?:] 1893-1915. Cover title. 31 pp. 12½ cm.
At head of title: The Lamp of the Body is the Eye.
MPB, MWiW*, OClWHi.

814 HOLLISTER, ALONZO GILES and CALVIN GREEN. Pearly Gate of the True Life and Doctrine for Believers in Christ .... By A. G. Hollister and C. Green. Mount Lebanon, Columbia Co., N.Y.: 1894. iv, 296, [3] pp. 17½ cm.
Preface signed: *A. G. Hollister.* Cover title: Morning Star Bible Lessons. Part I.
MacLean 41 (incl. Pts. I-III). CtHC (Pt. I), CtY-D, DLC, ICJ, ICN, ICU, KySP, MB, MHarF, MPB, MWiW*, MiU-C, N, NBuG, NN, NOC, NSyU, Nh, NjPT, OClWHi, WHi.

815 —— —— Second edition improved and enlarged. Mount Lebanon, Columbia Co., N.Y.: 1896. iv, 255 pp. 17½ cm.
Preface signed: *A. G. Hollister.* Cover title: Pearly Gate Bible Lessons. Part I. "Errata" slip pasted on p. [ii]. Chap. XVII, "Christ Appearing in the Clouds of Heaven ...." [Discourse] Delivered at Harvard, Mass., Aug. 2, 1829 [by Richard McNemar].

Stenographically Reported, pp. 214–29, *see* no. 1324.
MacLean 42. CtY–D, DLC, MB, MH (Pt. I), MPB, MWiW*, MiU–C, NN, NOC, NSyU, NjMD, NjPT, OClWHi, ODa, WHi.

816 ——— ——— Part II .... Compiled by A. G. Hollister. Mount Lebanon, Columbia Co., N.Y.: 1900. 1 p.l., iii, 17 [1] pp. 17½ cm.

Cover title: Pearly Gate Bible Lessons, Part II. Contains "Introduction to Part II"; Chapter I. "The virgin life and character." "Part II may be continued from time to time indefinitely, if the means afford encouragement to do so," p. iii.
CtY, ICN, MH, MHarF, MPB, MPH, MWiW*, MiU–C, NN, NOC, NSyU, OClWHi.

817 ——— Pearly Gate Bible Lessons, Part II. [Mt. Lebanon, N.Y.: 1901]. Cover title. ii, 34 pp. 17½ cm.

Contains "Introduction to Chapter II," signed: *A. G. Hollister, 1901;* "Chapter II. Born again, and life hereafter."
MacLean 43. DLC, MPB, MWiW*, NBuG, NN, NNC, OClWHi, WHi.

818 ——— Pearly Gate. "Part III Baptism ...." Compiled with Notes by A. G. Hollister. Mount Lebanon, Columbia Co., N.Y.: 1904. Cover title. 32 pp. 14 cm.

MacLean 44. DLC, CtY, MHarF, MPB, MPH, MWA, MWiW*, N, NBuG, NN, NOC, NSyU, NjPT, OClWHi.

819 [HOLMES, JAMES] [Collection of Anthems Given by the Spirits, 1837–1848]. [Sabbathday Lake, Me.: Printed by James Holmes, 185–?]. 29 pp. 17½ cm.

The title page is lacking in all copies examined, and the assigned titles vary. The title above is taken from the "Errata" sheet laid in the Shaker Museum, Old Chatham, N.Y., *Catalogue of the Emma B. King Library* (no. 2719), where the title was taken as found in "the Sabbathday Lake [Me.] copy in Deacon James' handwritten note." This collection of anthems dates "from the period of most active spirit manifestations among the Shakers [and] may be found under a number of variant imprints," T. E.

Johnson, "Random Notes," Maine Library Association, *Bulletin,* 22 (February 1961), 19. Some variation in the contents has been found, but the contents of the Williams College copy and the Fruitlands Museums (Harvard, Mass.) copy are identical and are shown in the assigned title of the Fruitlands' copy: Anthems, Containing The Resurrection, Voice of Mother, Encouraging Promise, Anthem, A Request, Quick Tunes, Travelling Tunes, Mother's Pretty Path, Holy Love, Heavenly Mansion, True Peace, Gift of Comfort, Angels Encouragement, Voice of Truth, White Robe & Bright Crown, St. Luke's Welcome in Heaven, Angel of Peace, Ye are Remembered. Fragments found in several libraries under individual anthem title have not been recorded.
MacLean 458. MHarF, MPB, MWA, MWiW*, MeB, NBuG, NN, NOC, OClWHi.

820 [——], *comp.* [A Collection of Useful Hints for Farmers. and Many Valuable Recipes]. West Gloucester [Me.]: Apr. 1849. 21 [1] pp.

E. D. Andrews, *Community Industries of the Shakers,* no. 1759, p. 298, and MacLean 46, identify this as the 1st edition with title page lacking.
MacLean 46. NN, OClWHi*.

821 [——], *comp.* [———] [West Gloucester [Me.]: 1850]. 1 p.l., [2]–113, [2] 1 l., 84–87 pp., 1 l. 12½ cm.

Lacks title page. Preface signed: *James Holmes, West Gloucester, May 1850.* "The publisher an Octogenarian who has neither press nor fixtures for printing, the types excepted, but those of his own invention, begs leave to say, that, if the reader detects errors, either in typography or in the mechanical execution, he hopes the above assertion may be received as sufficient apology ..." Most of the items are reprinted from farm journals.
MacLean 45 (120 pp.). DLC, MPB, MeB, NBuG, NN, OClWHi*.

822 [——] [———] Variant. 79 [2] pp. 12½ cm.

Preface signed: *James Holmes, West Gloucester, May 1850.* Lacks title page. "... Deacon James printed the first of three collections of hints for farmers." "There are numerous variants of each edition of these Farmer's Books." T. E. Johnson, "Random Notes," *Maine Library Association, Bulletin,* 22 (February 1961), p. 18. OClWHi*.

823 ——, *comp.* The Farmer's Second Book. A Collection of Useful Hints for Farmers, and Many Valuable Recipes, Collected and Compiled. [West Gloucester, Me.: 1853]. 4 p.ll., 2-152 pp. 12½ cm.

MacLean 47. DLC*, MPB, MeB, NBuG, NN (with [4] pp. at end), NOC, OClWHi, ViU.

824 ——, *comp.* The Farmer's Third Book. A Collection of Useful Hints for Farmers and Gardeners. And Many Valuable Recipes. Collected end [sic] Compiled by J.[ames] H.[olmes]. [West Gloucester, Me.:] 1856. 1 p.l., 42, [2] pp. 12½ cm.

"Contents," [2] pp. at end.

MacLean 48. DLC, MPB, MWiW*, MeB, NBuG, NN, NOC, OClWHi, OHi, ViU.

825 HOOSER, SAMUEL. A View of the Church. Written by Samuel Hooser, Soon after He Believed. Jan. 1808. [n.p., n.d.]. Broadside. 17 × 10 cm.

A poem of 11 stanzas which is found in the early editions of R. McNemar, *Concise Answer* (no. 898 ff.). This broadside appears to have been printed by McNemar. DLC, MWiW, OClWHi*.

826 [HOPLEY, CATHERINE COOPER] Among the Shakers. [n.p., n.d.] Broadside. 40½ × 26½ cm.

Reprinted from *Leisure Hour* (London), 1871, *see* no. 3312. MacLean 125. NN*.

827 [Hymns] [Canterbury? N.H.: 1842?]. 176, 4, [16] pp. 14 cm.

Collection of hymns and poems without title page, preceded by the tunes (in manuscript) of 122 hymns (31 pp.). Music with staff notation, employing the letters a–g. The hymns are designated by title instead of number; the first is "The Conquest"; the last, "Good Employment." The title and the descriptive notes here have been taken from the Library of Congress card. This collection appears to be a variant of MacLean No. 7, where it is described, "Book of Hymns without title page, containing 195 pp., besides the music, in script of 176 hymns. The poems are largely Western. Elder Henry C. Blinn thinks that the book was published at Canterbury in 1842. The first piece is 'The Conquest,' taken from the *Investigator* ...; the next, 'The Garden,' and the last 'Good Employment.' A fragment of the first form (16 pp.) I was also fortunate to obtain." This collection is a forerunner of *Sacred Hymns for Spiritual Worship* ... (no. 1262) and very likely represents an experimental attempt. MacLean 7? DLC*, OClJC, OClWHi (16 pp.).

I

828 I Hereby Certify, that John Whiteley Was Appointed Trustee of the United Society of Harvard, Worcester County, Massachusetts, According to the Constitution of Said Society, March 7th, 1890. [n.p., 1890]. Broadside. 21 × 13 cm.

Signed: *Andrew D. Barrett, Clerk of Society.* Witnessed by Benjamin Gates. OClWHi*.

An Improved Edition of the Church Covenant,

or Constitution ... *See* [McNemar, Richard], *An Improved Edition of the Church Covenant* ... no. 925.

829 In Consequence of the Frequent Intrusions and Annoyances from Many of the Multitude Who Visit this Society for Recreation, We are Constrained by a Sense of Duty and Propriety, to Give the Following Notice: Watervliet [N.Y.]: August 6th, 1849. Broadside. 35 × 23 cm.

Hereafter, the movements of visitors about

the buildings and grounds can be made only with an "appointed guard." Seven items are enumerated defining good behavior, and the same for bad behavior.
OClWHi*.

830 In Memoriam Elder Henry C. Blinn 1824–1902. Concord, N.H.: Rumford Printing Co., 1905. 131 pp. port. 20 cm.

"Inscribed to the memory of our beloved 'Elder Henry' by the home circle of East Canterbury, New Hampshire," p. [2]. "Autobiographical notes" by Henry C. Blinn, pp. 3–38, cover events through July 8, 1893. His later life is described pp. 38–40, "Memorial Service," pp. 43–62, followed by tributes, etc.
DLC, MPB, MPH, MWA, MWiW*, N, NN, NOC, NSyU, NjPT, OClWHi, PPULC.

831 In Memoriam Eldress D.[orothy] A.[nn] Durgin, 1825–1898; Eldress J.[oanna] J. Kaime, 1826–1898. Concord, N.H.: The Rumford Press, 1899. 100 pp. port., music. 25 cm.

Tributes by Shakers and others, press notices, poems, and music. "As the special companion of Eldress Dorothy, Eldress Joanna's stewardship is so closely interwoven with hers, that it would be difficult to disassociate the two." p. [69].
MacLean 52. CoU, CtY, DLC, MPB, MPH, MWA, MWiW*, MiU-C, N, NOC, NSyU, NhD, NjPT, OClWHi, OHi, RPB.

832 In Memoriam. Mary Hazard. [Mt. Lebanon: 1899]. Cover title. [8] pp. 17 cm.

Contents, p. [2], "A letter addressed to Sister Mary Hazard after her flight from the terrestrial to the celestial clime, by Anna White; 'The Three Marys,' a poem by Grace Ada Brown; 'A Double Tribute, in Verse,' by Cecelia De Vere." Sometimes attributed to Anna White.
MacLean 348 (with first line of text as subtitle).
MPB, MWiW*, NN, NjPT, OClWHi.

833 In Memoriam. Sister Aurelia Mace, 1835–1910. [n.p., 191–?]. illus. 19½ cm.

Poems, letters, etc., in memory of Aurelia Mace of the Sabbathday Lake, Me., Society, who "passed nearly fourscore years" among the Shakers where she served as teacher, eldress, and trustee.
CtY-D, DLC, MWiW*, NN, NOC, NSyU, OClWHi.

834 ... In the Family ... [n.p., 18–]. Broadside. 13 × 12 cm.

At head of title: December 31, 18 . Signed: *Isaac N. Youngs*. Blank form, suitable for a Shaker family or society, for recording annual statistics of new members, transferred members, seceders, and those "Gone to the SPIRITLAND," etc.
Private collection.

INDENTURES

Many different legal forms (printed and manuscript) for the indenture of minor children to the various Shaker societies are found in practically all of the Shaker collections. For the most part these are completed forms, signed and sealed by the parents (or guardians) of the child, the child itself (often signed only with an "X"), elders and/or trustees of the particular society, and witnessed by elders or trustees (occasionally by a justice of the peace). Such forms are dated from 1799 into the twentieth century. It has not been considered practicable to include all of the variations of these indenture instruments in this bibliography. Two examples are given here; for others *see* nos. 6, 1375, 1377.

835 This Indenture [blank form for the indenture of a minor child]. [n.p., n.d.]. Broadside. 35½ × 20½ cm.

Three copies of this form have been filled out for the indenture of William Alexander Thomas, Mary Blanche Thomas, and Gertrude

Thomas, aged 11, 12, and 4 years, respectively, dated Mt. Lebanon, February 18, 1880. These copies are signed and sealed: *Robert M. Wagan, Mrs. M. C. Thomas* (the mother), and individually, *His X Mark* (for William A.), *Mary Blanche Thomas*, and *Her X Mark* (for

Gertrude). Witnessed by *Polly C. Lewis, Katie Boyle.* MPH*.

nessed by Uriah Edwards [Justice of the Peace]. MPH*.

---

836 This Indenture [blank form for the indenture of a minor child]. [n.p., n.d.]. Broadside. 38½ × 31½ cm.

    Filled in and dated, New Lebanon, August 1, 1838, for the indenture of Cornelia Douglas, aged 11 years, of Farnham, Lower Canada. Signed and sealed: *Jonathan Wood* (an uncle), *Her X Mark* (for Lydia Douglas), *Her X Mark* (for Cornelia Douglas). Wit-

837 Information for Inquirers. In Reference to the "United Society of Believers." [Canterbury, N.H.: 1885?]. Broadside. 23 × 15 cm.

    Paragraph 6: "Parents that enter a Society ..." 7: "In the order and government of the Society ..." A slightly different version was printed in *The Manifesto*, 15 (January 1885), 25. MacLean 347. MHarF, MPB, NBuG, NN, OClWHi*.

INVENTORIES

Inventory blank forms were sometimes printed for the use of specific families in a Shaker community, and also printed with spaces to be filled in for any family or community. In general the forms provide for annual statistical reports on the money out at interest, "Notes Considered Good," various types of debts owed, grain and livestock raised, stock slaughtered, etc.; also, provisions on hand including groceries, livestock, dairy products, garden seeds, herbs and extracts, brooms, the dollar value of salable items, etc. Spaces at the end provide for membership figures—brethren, sisters, and total membership. Only scattered examples of these inventories have been found. Inventories filled in for the Watervliet, N.Y., Shaker community at the New York State Library (Albany) are incomplete for the years 1870 to 1897-98, but comprise the most complete records that have been located. Examples of inventory forms are recorded below.

838 General Annual Report of Business Conditions At . . . . . for 18 . . . . . [Last line]: . . . . . Business Agents. [n.p., n.d.]. Broadside. 25½ × 15 cm.

    Blank inventory form for use in any Shaker Family or Society. Arranged in two main columns. Four general heads: Farm Products, Income from, Live stock, Outlay for ... OClWHi*.

839 Inventory of Stock, etc., Belonging to the . . . . . Reported . . . . . 18 . . . . . [n.p., n.d.]. Broadside. 53 × 28 cm.

    This form has been found filled in for Sonyea, N.Y., 1888 and 1890. MWiW, OClWHi*.

840 Inventory of Stock, &c., belonging to the Church Family, West Glocester, (Me.). January 1st 18 . [n.p., n.d.]. Broadside. 24½ × 23 cm.

    Private collection.

841 New Lebanon, N.Y. Inventory of Stock, etc., Belonging to the . . . . . Reported . . . . . 1st, 18 . [n.p., n.d.]. Broadside. 39 × 22½ cm.

    Private collection.

842 New Lebanon. Inventory of Stock, &c., Belonging to the Church Family, January 1st, 18 . [n.p., n.d.]. Broadside. 33 × 18 cm.

    OClWHi*.

843 Watervliet, N.Y. Inventory of Money, Stock &c. Belonging to the Church Family, January 1st, 18 . [n.p., n.d.]. Broadside. 25 × 18½ cm.

    NN, OClWHi*.

Investigator. *See* [McNemar, Richard], *comp. Investigator,* nos. 926, 927.

844 Investigator's Application. Lebanon, Ohio: Western Star Print., [n.d.]. Broadside. 27 × 21 cm.

At head of title: Form A 93. Preliminary application for admission to membership in the United Society of Believers, Union Village, O. Blank spaces provide for full particulars of

health (including "malformations"), religious faith of the applicant, names and addresses of references. *See also* nos. 1368, 1424, and 1425. MWiW*, NSyU.

J

845 JOHNS, URBAN E. [Communication, dated Dec. 28th, 1850]. In U.S. Commissioner of Patents, *Report for 1850, Pt. II, Agriculture.* (31st Cong., 2d Sess., House Exec. Doc. 32). pp. 277-78.

Written in response to a circular from the Patent Commissioner requesting agricultural information. Sheep and wool growing at the South Union, Ky., Shaker community are described.

CtY, DLC, KyU, MWA, MWiW*, N, NN, NhD, OC.

846 JOHNSON, THEODORE E. Life in the Christ Spirit: Observations on Shaker Theology. Sabbathday Lake, Me.: United Society, 1969. 12 pp. 21½ cm.

Reprinted from the *Shaker Quarterly*, 8 (Fall 1968), 67-76, no. **1586**.

847 A Juvenile Guide, or Manual of Good Manners. Consisting of Counsels, Instructions & Rules of Deportment, for the Young. By Lovers of Youth. In Two Parts . . . . Canterbury, N.H.: Printed in the United Society, 1844. [8], 131 pp. 14½ cm.

Second title page, p. [3] reads: Part I. Containing Rules of Deportment, and Instructions for the Youth. Part II. A Juvenile Monitor. Consisting of Rules of Conduct. For Youth and Children. New Lebanon, N.Y., 1844. After the favorable review of *Lo Here!* (no. **2815**), a copy was sent to the editor of *The Knickerbocker* who commented on it, Vol. 29 (March, April 1847), 281, 376. Preface to *Gentle Manners*, (1899), no. **721**,

identifies this as the "second edition" of *A Juvenile Monitor* (1823), no. **848**, "revised and enlarged by Elder Giles B. Avery." Actually, Part I is based on [Lawrence, G. K.], *A Short Treatise* (1823), no. **859**, and Part II is based on *A Juvenile Monitor* (1823), no. **848**. "In 1844, we received from New Lebanon, N.Y. the manuscripts of the 'Juvenile Guide, or Manual of Good Manners.' A thousand copies were printed and the printing and binding were under my direction," stated by Henry C. Blinn, *In Memorium* (no. **830**), pp. 30-31. The Library of Congress describes this work as, "Compiled by Rufus Bishop, Garrett Lawrence and Isaac Newton Youngs. Revised by Giles Avery." MacLean 54. Sabin 79712 (and 106199). CSmH, DLC, DeWint, KyBgW, KyU, MPB, MPH, MWA, MWiW*, MeHi, N, NBuG, NHi, NN, NOC, NSyU, NhD, NjMD, OClWHi, ODa, WHi.

848 A Juvenile Monitor: Containing Instructions for Youth and Children; Pointing Out Ill Manners, and Showing Them How To Behave in the Various Conditions of Childhood and Youth . . . . Printed at New-Lebanon [N.Y.]: February 1823. 20 pp. 13 cm.

"Written by the instructors of the school at New-Lebanon," "Preface" (unsigned), p. [2]. MacLean names Rufus Bishop, Garrett K. Lawrence, and Isaac N. Youngs as compilers. For a later form of this work, *see A Juvenile Guide*, Part II, no. **847**. MacLean 53. Sabin 106199. MPB, MWA, MWiW*, N, NBuG, NN, NOC, OClWHi.

K

849 KAIME, B. J. To Br. Levi Holmes, on the Day he Was 83 Years of Age, Jan. 4, 1863 by B. J. Kaime, Poland, Me. [n.p., 1863?]. Broadside in 2 columns.
>Poem of 5 stanzas of unequal length. Ornamental type border.
>Private collection.

850 KAIME, JOHN. The Travel of the Soul [poem]. Canterbury, N.H.: [n.d.]. Caption title. 4 pp. 21½ × 13 cm.
>DLC, MPB, MWA (14 cm.), MWiW*, NN, OClWHi.

851 —— ——— 4 pp. 24 × 15½ cm.
>Poem of 22 stanzas. This is printed from a different setting of type. Note at end: "John Kaime was a Deacon of the Baptist Church at Barnstead, N.H., and joined the Shakers in 1843."
>MacLean 350? (broadside, and "travel" in the title printed "travail.") MWiW*, OClWHi.

852 KEEFOVER, JAMES R. Question about Shakerism. [Mt. Lebanon, N.Y.?: 1888]. Caption title. [4] pp. 15 cm.
>Letter from Jas. R. Keefover, dated: Wilton Junction, Iowa, March 24th, 1888; Evans' reply dated: Mt. Lebanon, March 31, 1888. Both appeared in *The Manifesto*, 18 (August 1888), 177–79.
>MacLean 262. CtY, MHarF, MWiW*, N, NBuG, NN, OClWHi, OHi, WHi.

KENTUCKY. COURT OF APPEALS. *See* [McNemar, Richard], *ed.*, nos. 913 and 915.

853 KING, EMMA BELLE. A Shaker's Viewpoint, [by] Eldress Emma B. King. Old Chatham, N.Y.: Shaker Museum Foundation, 1957. Cover title. [8] pp. 14 cm.
>". . . Written by Eldress Emma B. King at East Canterbury, N.H., in the fall of 1956," p. [2].
>MPB, MPH, MWiW*, NSyU, OClWHi.

854 KNIGHT, JANE D. Brief Narrative of Events Touching Various Reforms, by Jane D. Knight, Who Was Reared in the Society of Friends, and United with the Shakers at Mt. Lebanon, Columbia Co., N.Y., in the Year 1826, in the Twenty-second Year of Her Age. Albany: Weed, Parsons and Co., 1880. 29 pp. 15 cm.
>An autobiographical account of her early life as a Quaker, and her conversion to Shakerism.
>MacLean 351. CtY, DLC, MB, MHarF, MPH, MWiW*, N, NBuG, NN, NOC, NSyU, OClWHi, WHi.

KORESH, *pseud. See* Teed, Cyrus R., no. 1361 ff.

L

LA FUME, J. Calvin's Confession. *See* [Hollister, Alonzo G.], *ed.*, no. 780.

855 LAMSON, DAVID RICH. Two Years Experience among the Shakers; Being a Description of the Manners and Customs of That People, the Nature and Policy of their Government, Their Marvellous Intercourse with the Spiritual World, the Object and Uses of Confession, Their Inquisition, in Short, a Condensed View of Shakerism as It Is. West Boylston [Mass.]: Published by the Author, 1848. 212 pp. incl. front. illus. 17½ cm.
>Lamson, formerly a Congregational minister, and an active member of Ballou's Hopedale Community (*see* no. 1811) took his family to live with the Shakers at Hancock, Mass., in March 1843. According to his account, he was a member of the community, although he was

not required to sign the Covenant. Lamson left the Shakers in 1845 because they had failed to provide that "little heaven below." He gives a full account of the period known as "Mother Ann's Work" when Shaker behavior was influenced by active spirit communications in all communities. The wood-engraved illustrations have been reproduced many times, and often without credit —"Mountain Meeting," frontispiece; "The Whirling Gift," p. 85; and "The Gift of Father and Son," p. 104.

MacLean 56 (and 57 in paper). Sabin 38777. CSmH, CtY, DLC, ICJ, KyU, MB, MBrZ, MH, MHarF, MPB, MWA, MWiW*, N, NBuG, NHi, NN, NOC, NSyU, NjMD, NjPT, O, OClWHi, ODa, OHi, PHi, PPPrHi, RHi.

856 —— ——— (Reprint). New York: AMS Press, 1972.

The announcement of this reprint gives the original place of publication incorrectly as West Boylston, Ohio.

857 Last Night! Great Moral Entertainment! By the Celebrated and Far-Famed Shaker Family from Canterbury, N.H. Who have Recently Performed for Seven Weeks to Overflowing Houses at the New York American Museum, and Have Received the Unqualified Commendation and Patronage of the People of Boston and Other Cities in New England ... Intend Giving a Grand Levee, at Washington Hall, Bradley-st. Tuesday Evening, March 21. ... [n.p., 1847?]. Broadside. 37 X 15 cm. illus.

The Shaker performers left Barnum's American Museum, Dec. 7, 1846, and returned May 31, 1847 (G. C. D. Odell, *Annals of the New York Stage* (no. 2535), Vol. 5, pp. 305, 306). Apparently this handbill was issued in the interval. Here Mr. Maloon and "his coadjutors" who have "lived many years among the sect called Shakers" at Canterbury, N.H. are performing, and Miss L. A. Chase is featured as "The Miraculous Shaker Tetotum." A woodcut depicting the dancing and costumes, and the program of Shaker songs and dances is identical with the playbill, no. 728. The program includes "The Reapers," "Come Life Shaker Life," and "Mothers Love," which are songs found

in Shaker hymnals. An awareness of Shaker songs and dances as potential stage entertainment was realized earlier than the American Museum performances. H. Nathan, *Dan Emmett* (no. 2496), p. 94, n. 87, quotes part of a playbill of the American Theatre (New York, Dec. 12, 1835), "A Lebanon Shaker will make his 1st appearance before the public, late from the people, resident of New Lebanon ... State of New York ... member of their community for 15 years— he will exhibit the following peculiarities of the Society: 1. Circular March. 2. Square Order. 3. Shuffling Manner. 4. Square Order Step Manner. 5. Square Order Square. 6. Square Hollow Dance. 7. Round Shuffling Manner. 8. Circle Quick Step." MWiW*.

858 [LAWRENCE, GARRETT KEATIN] Immortal Scenes; Acknowledgment and Prayer. Broadside.

J. P. MacLean, Franklin, Ohio, May 28, 1905, to H. M. Lydenberg attributes authorship to G. K. Lawrence, a.l.s. New York Public Library. W. H. Cathcart to Eldress Catherine Allen, Sept. 26, 1912. "I have never seen this," a.l.s. Western Reserve Historical Society, (Cleveland, O.). MacLean 346. No copy located.

[——] Remarks on the Militia System. *See* no. 1233.

859 [——] A Short Treatise: Containing Observations on the Duty of Believers, Suitable for the Consideration of Those Who Have but Just Arrived at the Age of Discretion and Understanding; and Necessary to be Regarded and Put into Practice by All Who Wish to Have their Lives Agreeable to Themselves & Others. Addressed to Youth .... New-Lebanon: February—1823. 36 pp. 13½ cm. (trimmed).

Preface signed: *Writer*. Cover title: A Short Treatise, Containing, Instructions and Observations Suitable for the Consideration of the Unexperienced Mind. Particularly Designed for the Benefit and Edification of Youth. Written by a Friend and Lover of Youth and Children ... Printed at New-Lebanon, 1823. Covers printed on both sides with supplementary material, with "Contents" on recto of back cover. MacLean attributes authorship to Garrett K. Lawrence and Isaac N. Youngs; Library of Congress accepts this attribution; Sabin, however, credits the work to Isaac N. Youngs. For a later form of this work, *see A Juvenile Guide*, Part I, no. 847.

MacLean 445. Sabin 106200. Shaw 13072. DLC, MPB, MWiW*, NN, OClWHi.

860 Lecture. A Visit to the Holy Land, to be Given in the Canterbury Baptist Church. By Rev. T. A. Dwyer, of Shaker Village, Thursday Evening, August 26, 1897. Singing by the Shaker quartette ... East Canterbury, N.H.: August 17, 1897. Broadside. 22 X 15 cm.

OClWHi*.

861 LEONARD, WILLIAM. A Disclosure on the Order and Propriety of Divine Inspiration and Revelation, Showing the Necessity Thereof, in All Ages, To Know the Will of God. Also, a Discourse on the Second Appearing of Christ, in and through the Order of the Female. And a Discourse on the Propriety and Necessity of a United Inheritance in All Things, in Order to Support a True Christian Community .... Harvard [Mass.]: Published by the United Society, 1853. 88 pp. 18½ cm.

Cover title: On Revelation and Divine Inheritance. "Contents" precedes the title page in some of the copies in wrappers. Bound copies have cover title: On Revelation and United Inheritance. According to Calvin Green's "Biographic Memoir," pp. 636-37, the manuscript was sent to New Lebanon for "alterations and corrections," which he made, and then the manuscript was arranged in 3 parts for publication. H. S. Nourse, *History of Harvard, Massachusetts, 1732-1893* (no. 2524), p. 473, states that the *Discourse* was one of the few items printed at the Harvard Shaker community.

MacLean 58. Sabin 79703. CSmH, CtY, DLC, KyU, MB, MHi, MHarF, MPB, MPH, MSaE, MWA, MWiW*, MeB, N, NBuG, NHi, NN, NNC, NOC, NRCR, NSyU, Nh, NhD, NjPT, O, OClWHi, OHi, WHi.

862 —— The Life and Sufferings of Jesus Anointed, Our Holy Savior and of Our Blessed Mother Ann ... In Two Parts. Written by Inspiration, [Evolved thru the Inner Consciousness of] William Leonard, in the Church at Harvard, Mass., October, 1841. Prepared for Publication, with Notes, and Appendix, by A. G. Hollister. Mount Lebanon, Col. Co., N.Y.: 1904. 86 pp. 15 cm.

Cover title: The Inner Life Reveald [!] of Jesus Anointed and of Ann the Word .... First printing of the ms. "Harvard Book," MacLean 60. Contains also A. G. Hollister's "Divine Motherhood," pp. [64]-72 (no. 785); and "Heaven Anointed Woman," pp. 73-86 (no. 789). Some copies were issued later with the date "1906" impressed on the front cover. Simplified spelling used in part.

DLC, MHarF, MPB, MPH, MWA, MWiW*, N, NHi, NN, NOC, OClWHi.

863 [——] Respect and Veneration Due from Youth to Age. New Bedford, Mass.: Printed for Joseph S. Tillinghast, 1870. Cover title. 15 pp. 14½ cm.

Reprinted in *The Manifesto*, 15 (June, August 1885), 132-34, 180-82, where William Leonard of the Harvard, Mass., Shakers is given as the author.

MWiW*, OClWHi.

864 LINDSAY, BERTHA and LILLIAN PHELPS. Industries and Inventions of the Shakers. Shaker Music ... Canterbury, N.H. [Penacook, N.H.: Hazen Printing Co., 1968]. Cover title. [7], [1 blank], [8-15] pp. 20½ cm.

Paper delivered at a seminar, Canterbury, N.H., 1961, 1962.

MPH, MWA, MWiW*, NOC, NSyU.

A List of Different Tribes of Indians and From the World of Spirits Who Came to Learn the Way to God, of Mother's Children on Earth. Wisdom's Valley (Watervliet), South House, Oct. 26, 1842.

Listed in Chas. Haywood, *A Bibliography of Folklore* ... (New York, 1951), p. 726. No copy has been located. Apparently this is a manuscript, but its location is not given.

865 List of Publications That May Be Obtained at the Community, East Canterbury, N.H. Address H. C. Blinn ... [n.p., n.d.].

Broadside in 2 columns. 19 X 23 cm.
  Sixteen Shaker publications are listed with
  price, including Chandler (no. **446**) and
  Robinson (no. **1249**).
  MacLean 170 (2pp.). OClWHi*.

866 LOMAS, GEORGE ALBERT. Decay of
Shaker Institutions; Letter from Editor G. A.
Lomas of the Shakers Replying to W. D.
Howells' article in the June *Atlantic*. Watervliet,
N.Y.: [1897]. Broadside in 2 columns. 24 X
13½ cm.
  A discussion of Howells' reference "to the
  decay of numbers, which the Shakers confess with so great regret." *See* no. **2286**.
  Lomas concluded that Howells' article "is
  good, perhaps too good, as it gives lustre that
  we, as a people, are not worthy of, and some
  of which might be dispelled by active associ-
  ations; but he appears honest and 'almost
  persuaded' and worthy of thanks from us
  and all interested." Reprint of a letter addressed: To the Editor of the *Albany
  Morning Express*, May 20, 1876. Reprinted
  in *The Shaker*, 6 (July 1876), 53, and in the
  American Socialist, 1 (June 1, 1876), 75–76
  (no. **1600**).
  MacLean 355. DLC, MeB, NBuG, OClWHi*.

867 —— [Letter, dated: May 9th, 1871, Office
of *The Shaker*, Shakers [Watervliet], Albany
Co., N.Y.]. In *Phrenological Miscellany* (New
York, Fowler & Wells, 1882), p. 385.
  This letter addressed: My Dear Wells [i.e.,
  S. R. Wells, editor of the *Phrenological
  Journal*] concerns a spurious wood-engraved
  portrait of Ann Lee published in that journal.
  Lomas explains that "The picture is a copy
  from a crayon purported to be psychometri-
  cally drawn by one Milleson of New York."
  A person named Trow took it to a "test
  medium or psychological expert," who de-
  clared that it was a likeness of Ann Lee.
  Lomas politely expresses grave doubts about
  its genuineness. *See also* nos. **2547** and **2574**.

868 —— ... The Life of Christ Is the End of
the World .... Shakers [Watervliet], Albany,
N.Y.: [C. Van Benthuysen and Sons Print.],
1869. 16 pp. 13½ cm. (Shaker Tract, No. 1).
  MacLean 356. DLC, CtY-D, MH, MHarF,

MPB, MWA, MWiW*, N, NBuG, NN, NNC,
NOC, NSyU, NjPT, O, OCl, OClWHi, OHi,
RHi, WHi.

869 —— —— Mt. Lebanon, N.Y.: [n.d.].
MacLean 357. No copy with this imprint
has been located. Apparently, it is the same
as no. **868**.

870 —— —— Address F. W. Evans,
Mount Lebanon, N.Y. London: J. Burns [C.
Benthuysen and Sons' Print.], 1869. Cover
title. 16 pp. 12 cm. (Shaker Tract, No. 1.).
  Same as no. **868**, except type is more closely
  set, and London imprint has been added at
  foot of title page.
  MacLean 358. CtY, MHarF, MWA, MWiW*,
  OClWHi.

871 —— "A Man Approved of God." [n.p.,
n.d.]. Caption title. 4 pp. 14 cm.
  Jesus was "a godly man set for our example
  ... Knowing Jesus as 'a man,' tempted and
  tried like ourselves, is evidence of the possibility and probability of our being 'approved
  of God' ..."
  MacLean 359. CtY, DLC, MPB, MWiW*,
  NBuG, NN, OClWHi, OHi, WHi.

872 —— Plain Talks upon Practical Religion.
Being Candid Answers to Earnest Inquirers ....
Albany [N.Y.]: Van Benthuysen Printing House,
1873. 24 pp. 19 cm.
  "Animadvertory" by Eldress Harriet M.
  Bullard, pp. 8–9; "Do Those Once Married
  Enjoy their Change to a Shaker Life?"
  signed: *Galen Richmond*, pp. 15–17; "Can
  We Live the Angel Life Here?" signed:
  Rosetta Hendrickson, p. 17; "Novitiate
  Elders" and "Novitiate Eldresses," a list
  with locations, p. 24. An earlier version of
  Plain Talks appeared in *The Shaker*, 1 (April–
  July 1871), 30–32, 37, 47, 53. "Are Shakers
  Spiritualists?," pp. 14–15, reprinted in *The
  Shaker*, 7 (May 1877), 38.
  MWiW*, NjPT, OClWHi, OHi.

873 —— "What Shall I Do To Be a Shaker?"
or, Plain Talks upon Practical Religion: Being Candid Answers to Earnest Inquiries
.... Shakers [Watervliet], N.Y.: Office

of the Shaker, 1877. 24 pp. 19 cm.

"Do Those Once Married Enjoy Their Change to a Shaker Life?," pp. 13–14, signed: *Galen Richmond:* "Animadvertory" by Eldress Harriet M. Bullard, pp. 23–24. List of Novitiate Elders and Eldresses and an advertisement for the *The Shaker,* verso of back cover. Described in the *Shaker Manifesto,* 7 (February 1877), 12, "This little work is intended to answer the hundreds of questions naturally arising about the Shakers; and thereby not only give in epitome their general theology, but details of Shaker life ... To be issued in February 1877." *The Shaker,* 7 (June 1877), 55, "*Plain Talks,*" pamphlet, a large edition of which was issued from this place [Watervliet], is entirely exhausted." *The Shaker,* 7 (November 1877), 87, "Another edition of *Plain Talks* is called for from several directions ... The second [1877?] edition is entirely exhausted ... and we have had calls for 250 copies which we could not supply." An edition of 1000 is called for.
DLC, ICN, KyBgW, MWiW*, OHi.

874 —— ... Plain Talks upon Practical Religion: Being Candid Answers to Earnest Inquirers, Including an Answer to the Inquiry "What Shall I Do to Be a Shaker?" .... Fourth edition. Shakers [Watervliet] N.Y.: Office of the *Shaker Manifesto,* 1878. 24 pp. 19 cm.

Head of title: "Invitation to Fellowship ..." is repeated on verso of back cover and is followed by a list of Novitiate Elders and Eldresses, with locations, and an advertisement for the *Shaker Manifesto.* "Do Those Once Married Enjoy Their Change to a Shaker Life?," pp. 13–14, signed: *Galen Richmond;* "Animadvertory" by Eldress Harriet M. Bullard, pp. 23–24. "Another edition of this little work has been necessitated; and through the generosity of Elder H. L. Eads, who has thoroughly revised same, it has become a stereotype work." *Shaker Manifesto,* 8 (October 1878), 248. An earlier version appeared in *The Shaker,* 1 (April–July 1871), 30–32, 37, 47, 53.
MacLean 361. CSmH, DLC, MB, MH, MWiW*, NOC, OClWHi.

875 [——] Plain Talks: upon Practical,

Christian Religion; Being Answers to Ever-recurring Questions Concerning the Shakers. Prominent among which is the Answer to "What Must an Individual Do to Become a Shaker?" The Life of Christ is the Only True Christian Religion. Shakers [Watervliet], N.Y.: Published by the Shakers, [1882?]. Cover title. 24 pp. 19 cm.

"Do Those Once Married Enjoy their Change to a Shaker Life?" signed: *Galen Richmond,* pp. 13–14. "Animadvertory" by Eldress Harriet M. Bullard, pp. 22–23. Novitiate Covenant, p. 24. This edition is sometimes identified as the earliest. An advertisement for the *Shaker Manifesto* on the back cover, verso, however, dates this publication either 1878 or 1882 because the address given for the *Shaker Manifesto* is Shaker Village (Canterbury), N.H. The *Shaker Manifesto* was first published at Shaker Village, N.H., in 1878. In 1879 publication was returned to Shakers (Watervliet), N.Y., and publication was not moved back to Shaker Village, N.H., until 1882. The title was changed to *The Manifesto* in 1883 with volume 13. The date of publication must have been 1882 because the date 1878 and "Fourth Edition" is printed on the cover title of no. 874. *See also* no. 2849.
MacLean 360. DLC, MH, MPB, MSaE, MWA, MWiW*, N, NBuG, NOC, NSyU, Nh, OCHP, OClWHi, RPB.

876 —— —— 24 pp. 19 cm.
Variant with slight differences in the text, and, except for the cover title, the covers are blank. Advertisements in the *Shaker Manifesto* and *The Manifesto* indicate that editions, other than those recorded here, may have been printed. "Br. Albert by request from several societies has just got out a new edition of *Plain Talks.* He offers them for $4.00 per 100 copies ... Every society and family ought to have on hand a few hundred copies," *The Manifesto,* 13 (June 1883), 139. Copies of *Plain Talks* were used as handouts to visitors at Sunday meetings, etc. At this period the Shakers were urgently seeking new converts. *See also* annotation, no. 2849.
Private collection.

877 LOVE, ALFRED. A Shaker Meeting. Alfred Love, Pres. of the Universalist Peace Union, Speaks at Mt. Lebanon. Mt. Lebanon, N.Y.: 1891. 9 pp. 15 cm.

President of the Universal Peace Union, Love delivered a speech at a Sunday Shaker meeting at Mt. Lebanon, N.Y., Aug. 23, 1891 which was printed in *The Manifesto*, 21 (October 1891), 221–25.
MacLean 362. DLC, MWA, N, NN, NSyU, OClWHi*, OHi.

878 LOWRY, R. How Can I Keep from Singing? [n.p., n.d.]. Broadside. 23½ × 15½ cm.

Poem of 3 stanzas.
Private collection.

879 [LUDLOW, WILLIAM] The Belief of the Rational Brethren of the West, or Rational Creed. Cincinnati: Printed for the Society, 1819. 128 pp. 17½ cm.

Authorship is attributed to William Ludlow by J. F. C. Harrison, *Quest for a New Moral World* (no. 2212), pp. 107, 168, and 321. Harrison states that Ludlow "had been resident at the Shaker community, New Lebanon, [N.Y.]," and that he became a member of the Owenite community at New Harmony, Ind., before projecting the community of Rational Brethren at Oxford, Ohio, p. 107. Ludlow states that "some have endeavored to excite a prejudice in the minds of the people, by declaring us Shakers." An unfavorable discussion of Shakerism follows, and he concludes, "Therefore when the bridegroom of truth makes his appearance, the [Shakers] will be left in the dark, or rejected, because they have no oil of their own, and are destitute of those mental qualifications, which are figuratively represented by a wedding garment," pp. 119–21. R. McNemar refutes Ludlow's statements about the Shakers in *The Other Side of the Question* (Cincinnati, 1819), no. 946, pp. 160–64. *See also* A. E. Bestor, *Backwoods Utopias* (no. 1859), pp. 207–209.
Shaw 49238. O, OClWHi*, PLT.

M

880 McBRIDE, JOHN. An Account of the Doctrines, Government, Manners and Customs of the Shakers. By John McBride, a Member for Twenty Years. With Remarks on Confession to Catholic Priests and Shaker Elders. Cincinnati: 1834. 27 pp. 18 cm.

The author, formerly a Presbyterian who joined the Shakers in the aftermath of the Kentucky revival, recounts his disappointments and tribulations as a Shaker, and his reasons for seceding. Many of his criticisms parallel those made by Whitbey (no. 1427), mainly the requirement of implicit obedience to the elders and their despotic behavior. "For the elders say they are the true tabernacle, and that God can be found nowhere else for salvation."
MacLean 498. OCIIP*.

881 [MACE, AURELIA GAY] The Aletheia: Spirit of Truth . . . [prospectus]. Farmington, Me.: Published by Knowlton, McLeary & Co. For Sale by the Author, Miss Aurelia G. Mace, Sabbathday Lake, Maine, [1899]. Caption title. [4] pp. port. 22 cm.

Includes: Frontispiece, "Contents," and p. 102 of the text.
MacLean 111. MPB, MWiW*, NBuG, NN, OClWHi, OHi.

882 [——] ——— A Series of Letters in which the Principles of the United Society Known as Shakers are Set Forth and Illustrated. By Aurelia [*pseud.*] . . . Farmington, Me.: Press of Knowlton, McLeary & Co., 1899. 135 pp. incl. front., 32 plates (incl. ports.). 23½ cm.

Half title: Aurelia's book. This is a collection of letters, most of which were published in *The Messenger* (Bangor, Me.), 1883–1884, communications and short articles reprinted from *The Manifesto*, etc. "Letter to Count Leo Tolstoi," pp. [84]–85, dated at Sabbathday Lake, Maine, February, 1891, compares the work of Ann Lee with that of Tolstoi, and informs him that "a home is prepared for those who desire to live pure lives." The letter was written after the author finished reading *The Kreutzer Sonata, see* no. **1663**. Appendix: Shaker Church Covenant or Constitution, pp. [119]-135.

MacLean 4. CtHC, CtY, DLC, FMU, MB, MH, MPB, MWA, MWiW*, MeB, MeHi, MiU-C, N, NBuG, NN, NOC, NSyU, NcD, NcU, NhD, OHi, PP.

883 ―― ―――― 2d ed. Farmington, Me.: Press of Knowlton, McLeary & Co., 1907. 146 pp. incl. front. 34 plates (incl. ports.). 23½ cm.

The author's name appears on the title page of this edition. Church Covenant is omitted and new material added.

DLC, ICJ, MBrZ, MPB, MWiW*, MeB, MeHi, N, NN, NOC, NSyU, WHi.

884 ―― ―――― (Reprint). New York: AMS Press, 1972.

885 ―― The Mission and Testimony of the Shakers of the Twentieth Century to the World. A Lecture Delivered at Greenacre, Eliot, Maine, July 19, 1904. By Aurelia G. Mace of the Shaker Society, Sabbathday Lake, Cumberland County, Maine. [n.p., 1904]. 17 pp. incl. port. 21½ cm.

Reprinted in her *Aletheia,* no. **883**, and in J. M. Todd, *A Sketch of the Life* (no. **2846**), pp. 192-95.

DLC, ICN, MH, MWiW*, NOC, OClWHi.

886 MACE, FAYETTE. Familiar Dialogues on Shakerism; in which the Principles of the United Society are Illustrated and Defended . . . Portland [Me.]: Charles Day and Co., Printers, 1837. 120 pp. 18 cm.

Imprint on cover title: Portland, Chs. Day & Co., Printers, 1838. "Approved by the church" on the title page has been cancelled with a stamp. Errata: p. 120.

MacLean 62 (and 63 in paper covers). CSmH, DLC, MPB, MWiW*, N, NBuG, NHi, NN, NOC, NSyU, Nh, NjPT, OClWHi, PHi, PPL.

887 ―― ―――― . . . Portland [Me.]: Charles Day and Co. Printers, 1838. 120 pp. 19 cm.

Imprint on cover title of some copies: Concord [N.H.], William White, Printer, 1838.

The title page has been reset, and "Approved by the church" is omitted. The text is identical with no. **886** above. Errata: p. 120. MacLean 64 (with imprint: Concord, N.H., 1838). CSmH, CtY-D, DLC, KyU, MH, MHarF, MWA, MWiW*, MeHi, MiU-C, NHi, NN, NOC, NSyU, NhD, O, OClWHi, ODa, OHi, OO, OOxM, PHC, PPL, RPB.

888 McKECHNIE, FREDERIC. Prof. Comstock's Experience which Turned the Professor from his Cruel Ways . . . [Mt. Lebanon?:] 1902. Cover title. 16 pp. 14½ cm.

A short story condemning vivisection. The author was a member of the North Family, Mt. Lebanon, N.Y.

MacLean 368. CtY, DLC, MHarF, MPB, MWA, MWiW*, NBuG, NOC, NRCR, OClWHi, PCC, WHi.

McNEMAR, RICHARD. Richard McNemar, formerly a Presbyterian leader, was a tireless enthusiast who devoted his very considerable talents to the establishment and success of Shakerism in the West. Very early he recognized the importance of preserving Western Shaker history, records, hymns, etc., and urged the acquisition of community printing presses for this purpose. Some of McNemar's printing was done at Watervliet, O., 1832-1835, where the Shakers presented him with types, cases, and a press. *See* J. P. MacLean, *Life* (no. **2411**), p. 46. Unfortunately, McNemar's own endeavors at printing these materials fall short of the generally high standard of Shaker craftsmanship. Apparently the many demands made upon him as preacher, adviser, harmonizer, and defender of the faith did not allow for the undivided attention demanded by good printing which brooks almost no interruption. The products of his press recorded here exhibit idiosyncrasies of printing and gatherings, dissimilar contents in copies of the same title, and other irregularities which have resulted in "a perplexing number of variants." Many publications appear to have been catchalls of leftover sheets. In his *Life of Richard McNemar,* p. 46, J. P. MacLean explains that McNemar "intended to comprehend many things in one large book, which, for some reason, now unknown, was abandoned." The lack of sequence and repetitions of page numbers, duplications and lacking parts of his publications suggest that McNemar may well have become so bewildered by the perplexities involved that he abandoned the attempt to combine coherent copies from the remnants on hand. The letterpress faults may have been due to inexperienced help. These remarks do not apply to McNemar's works which were produced by commercial printers. Full bibliographical description of McNemar's literary and printing endeavors awaits a full length treatment which neither space nor consistency allows in this bibliography. Enough details and enumeration of contents are given for identification and comparative purposes, and as an aid to the identification of fragments. W. J. Hamilton, formerly Director of the Dayton Public Library, spent several years in the 1950's in an attempt to record and clarify the many McNemar publications and variants. His unpublished "Tentative Bibliography ..." (16 typewritten leaves) was kindly made available to the compiler. It is not feasible, however, to include here details of the many variant copies which Hamilton examined. Unfortunately, he did not indicate ownership of most of the items. The assignment of Richard McNemar's name as author, editor, compiler, etc., follows Hamilton's findings, which parallel many of the attributions made by J. P. MacLean in his *Bibliography* (no. 2407) and his *Life* (no. 2411). More recently these attributions have been reinforced by documentary evidence in the Shaker manuscripts cited by F. G. Ham, "Shakerism in the Old West" (unpublished Ph.D. dissertation, U. of Ky., 1962). *See also A Memorial Remonstrating* ..., no. 1023, and Springfield (Ohio) Presbytery, no. 1328 ff. Richard McNemar's name is occasionally spelled M'Namer, and he wrote under the pseudonyms Eleazar Wright, Philos Harmoniae, and Perigrinus.

[McNEMAR, RICHARD] Address to the State of Ohio Protesting ... *See* Address to the State of Ohio Protesting ... no. 4.

[——] Athanasian Creed. *See his Orthodox Trinity*, no. 940.

889 ——— A.l.s. "Eleazar Wright" (Richard McNemar's church name). 5¾ pp., large 4to,

Watervliet [Ohio], 8 Oct. 1833. With integral address leaf postmarked "Canton, O., Oct. 25," To his son, Richard McNemar, in Urbana, Ohio. *In The Celebrated Collection of Americana Formed ... by Thomas Streeter ...* (N.Y., Parke-Burnet Galleries, Inc., 1966–1969. 7 vols.), Vol. 7, no. 4242.

A long annotation describes and quotes from McNemar's letter. Richard McNemar joined the Shakers in 1805 along with his wife and seven children. Richard, his namesake and the youngest, incurred an estrangement with his father when he seceded from the Shakers in 1828 at 23 years of age. Five years later when McNemar did not recognize the son at a gathering, "young McNemar apparently wrote a long detailed indictment wherein was set forth the elder's shortcomings as a father." McNemar's "long reply is a chilly item-by-item refutation ... written as a spiritual rather than a natural father ... 'Your claim to sonship cannot be based upon the mere circumstances of my being the reputed means of your animal existence'." The father concludes, "I confess I never was a catamite or Ganymede to lavish on my flesh-kin the inferior passions of a selfish nature, nor to make myself a jack-fellow with my pupils ... I do not, however, dispute your statements in any matter or thing disconnected from your concerns with Believers and the faith of the gospel; but when you approach that ground, you guess right when you suppose I give but little credit to what is said by an apostate." MWiW*.

890 [——] A Brief Exposition of Certain Points of Doctrine — by Request. No. 4, October 1, 1832. [37]–48 pp. 18 cm.

Bound with *A Brief Exposition of the Established Principles, and Regulations of the United Society of Believers* (Watervliet, O., 1832), no. 735, in the Western Reserve Historical Society copy (Cleveland, O.). OClWHi*.

891 [——] A Brief Memorial of Mother Ruth Farrington. [Watervliet, O.?: 183–?]. 4 ll. 15 cm.

This is found as a separate publication, and also as part of *A Review of the*

Most Important Events (no. 950), pp. 35–36. MPB*, NN.

892 ——, *trans.* Cebetis Tabula or a Map of the Various State [!] of Man as a Candidate for Happiness or Misery by Cebes an Ancient Phylosopher [!]. Translated from the original Greek by Richard McNemar. Lebanon, O.: 1839. 1 + 1 + 30 pp.

This entry is taken from W. J. Hamilton's "Tentative Bibliography," No. 17. The title of the 18-page copy in Western Reserve Historical Society (Cleveland) differs: "The Map of Cebes the Theban Explained [.] In Form of a Dialogue between an Aged Man and a Youth." This copy has running titles: Map of Cebes, and Cebetis Tabula. It is a moral sketch or picture of human life written in a pleasing and simple style by the Theban, Cebes, a disciple of Socrates, which was frequently translated for school use. OClWHi* (18 pp).

893 —— "Christ Appearing in the Clouds of Heaven" ... [discourse] "Delivered at Harvard, Mass., Aug. 2, 1829. Stenographically Reported." In Hollister, A. G. and Calvin Green, *Pearly Gate* ... 2d imp. and enl. ed. (1896), Chap. XVII, pp. 214–29, *see* nos. 815 and 1324.

894 —— Chronology. A Memorial of Deceases at Union-Village, Ohio. Since the Commenement [sic] of the Society ... [Union Village, O.: 1831]. pp. 25–34.

Fragment of *Western Review* No. 3. NN*.

895 [——], *comp.* [A Collection of 23 Hymns] Union Village: June 6, 1831. 18 pp. 16 cm.

Title page lacking. This is very likely a fragment of *A Selection of Hymns*, no. 952. The entry is taken from J. P. MacLean's letter, Franklin, O., May 28, 1905, to H. M. Lydenberg (a.l.s. New York Public Library). This letter included a supplementary list of Shaker items received by MacLean after his *Bibliography* was published. The entry is No. 1 in the list. No copy located.

896 [——] Colloquy or Children's Talk. Anna, Maria, and Emily. [Watervliet, O.:

1835?] Caption title. 43–54 pp. 15½ cm.

Lacks title page. Page 46 misnumb. 48; p. 50 printed 05; p. 52 numb. 5g; pp. 53–54 unnumb. Contents: "Colloquy," pp. 43–47; scattered excerpts from William Law, *Serious Call* (Boston, 1808), pp. 47–49; excerpt from Thomas á Kempis, *Imitation of Christ*, pp. 50–[52]. This work, intended for the edification of the young, is found in some copies of *A Little Selection*, no. 937, and in some copies of [*Hymns*], no. 922. J. P. MacLean's *Additional List of Books for Sale*, no. 2414, however, lists it as a 12-page separate with the date 1837; no copy of this separate has been located.

MPB, MWiW*, OClWHi.

897 [——], *comp.* A Compendium of English Grammar Selected from Wells, Kirkham, Murray, Perry, &c. ... Union Village, O.: 1831. [12] pp. 14 cm.

The work consists of a collection of rules similar to the following: "A comma is a pause of one syllable ..."; "He that would learn without good grammar rules,/ Is like a tradesman working without tools." Richard McNemar is established as the compiler in a clipping, "Two Tiny Books," in a Shaker scrapbook in the Williams College Library (Williamstown, Mass.). It describes MacNemar's ownership of "the smallest English Grammar and Arithmetic in existence" and identifies the grammar as "the handwork of Richard McNemar."

DLC, OClWHi*.

898 [——] A Concise Answer to the General Inquiry, Who, or What are the Shakers. Union Village [O.]: 1823. Cover title. 12 pp. 10 × 9 cm.

Contents: "Title," p. [1]; "Notice," p. 2; "A Concise Answer, &c.," pp. [3]–10, in verse; "A Hymn" [Composed by Samuel Hooser], pp. [11]–12. The title poem "originated in the year 1808, from the application of an individual in the state of Georgia ... requesting information concerning the people who, at that time, greatly excited the attention of the public, in different parts of the United States." The information was requested from the Shakers

and the *Concise Answer* is "deemed a suitable answer to a general inquiry."
MacLean 190. Sabin 79700 and 97883. Shaw
13184. CSmH, DLC, ICN, MWA, MiU-C,
NHi, OClWHi, ODa, WHi.

899 [——] ———— Union Village [Ohio]:
1825. Cover title. 8 pp. 13½ cm.
　　Contents: "Title," p. [1]; "Notice," p. [2];
　　"A Concise Answer, &c.," pp. [3]-7, in
　　verse; "A Hymn" by Samuel Hooser, pp.
　　7-8.
　　MacLean 191. Sabin 79700 and 97883.
　　Shaw 21288. CSmH, DLC, ICN, MHarF,
　　MSaE, MPB, MWA, MWiW*, NN, NOC,
　　OCHP, OClWHi, ODa, RPB.

900 [——] ———— First Printed at Union
Village, Ohio: 1823. Reprinted at Enfield, N.H.:
Albon Chase, Printer, 1825. Cover title. 14 pp.
9 cm.
　　Contents: "Title," p. [1]; "Notice," p. [2];
　　"A Concise Answer &c.," pp. [3]-9, in verse;
　　"A Hymn," pp. 9-14.
　　MacLean 192. Sabin 79700 and 97883. Shaw
　　21287. CSmH, DLC, MB, MH, MHi, MWiW*,
　　MeHi, NHi, NOC, NcU, Nh, NhD, NjPT,
　　OClWHi.

901 [——] ———— Printed at Stockbridge
[Mass.]: 1826. 16 pp. 9 cm.
　　Contents: "Title," p. [1]; "Notice," p. [2];
　　"A Concise Answer, &c.," pp. [3]-7; "A
　　Hymn," pp. 7-10; "Dialogue between the
　　Church and the Old Gentleman," pp. [11]-
　　16, in verse. "Dialogue" is followed by the
　　manuscript signature of Oliver Prentiss in
　　the Library of Congress copy.
　　MacLean 193. Sabin 79700. Shaw 25180.
　　Ct, DLC, KyBgW, MH, MPB, MWA, MWiW*,
　　MiU-C, NBuG, NN, NOC, NSyU, NjPT,
　　OO, RPB, WHi.

902 [——] ———— Variant. Stockbridge
[Mass.]: 1826. 8 pp. 14½ cm.
　　Contents: "Title," p. [1]; "Notice," p. [2];
　　"Concise Answer &c.," [3]-7; "A Hymn,"
　　pp. 7-8. The title and contents are the same
　　as no. 901, pp. 1-10, but the contents have
　　been reset throughout, with "A Hymn" set
　　in a smaller size type.

Shaw 25179. CSmH, CtY, ICN, MPH, MWA,
MWiW*, MiU-C, NHi, NOC, NjPT, RPB.

903 [——] ———— First printed at Union
Village, Ohio: 1823. Reprinted at Enfield, N.H.:
1825. And at St. Albans, Vermont: J. Spooner,
Printer, 1829. 16 pp. 10 cm.
　　Sabin 97883. Shaw 39376. NN, RPB*.

904 [——] ———— Hartford [Conn.]:
Review Offce [*sic*] Print., 1835. 17 pp. 15 cm.
　　MacLean 194. Sabin 79700. CtHi, CtY, DLC,
　　MWiW*, N.

905 [——] ———— North Union: 1841. 16 pp.
32°.
　　Entry taken from MacLean 195. No copy
　　located.

906 [——] ———— North Union: 1844. 16 pp.
32°.
　　Entry taken from MacLean 196. No copy
　　located. W. H. Cathcart wrote to Eldress
　　Catherine Allen, Sept. 26, 1912, about their
　　cooperative efforts to build, as nearly as pos-
　　sible, a complete Shaker collection at Western
　　Reserve Historical Society (Cleveland, O.).
　　"The list is narrowing as far as MacLean made
　　[i.e., his *Bibliography*] ... A few of them, like
　　[MacLean] Nos. 195 and 196, we will never
　　find."

907 [——] ———— Union Village, Ohio:
1868. Cover title. 8 pp. 13 cm.
　　Contains the title poem only.
　　DLC, ICN, MPB, MWA, MWiW*, MiU-C.

908 [——] A Concise Answer to the Inquiry,
Who or What are the Shakers? [South Groton,
Mass.: 1849]. Caption title. 17 [1] pp. 15½ cm.
　　McNemar's poem has been extended from
　　150 lines to 402 lines by Lorenzo D. Gros-
　　venor, according to MacLean *Life*, p. 42,
　　where it is stated that this poem was pub-
　　lished in 1849 in both pamphlet and circular
　　form. Contents: "A Concise Answer ..." pp.
　　[1]-12; "Thoughts Suggested by the Ques-
　　tion, —'What Induced you to Join the
　　Shakers?'," signed: *E. H. W.* [Eleanor Hayes
　　Wright] *South Groton, Sept. 1849*, pp. 12-16,
　　see also no. 1466; "Hymn.—By Samuel

Hooser," pp. 16–17; "Gratuitous," signed: *L. D. Grosvenor, South Groton, Mass.*, followed by instructions for visiting the Harvard Society, etc., [1] p. following p. 17.
MacLean 322. DLC, ICJ, IU, MHarF, MPH, MWA, MWiW*, N, NBuG, NHi, NN, O.

909 [——] ——— [South Groton, Mass.: 1849?]. Caption title. [2] pp. 29½ × 22 cm. Printed with 3 columns to the page. The title poem occupies 5½ columns, followed by "Gratuitous," signed: *L. D. Grosvenor, South Groton, Mass.* Post Office addresses of 18 Shaker Societies are listed near the end. The poem, "Thoughts Suggested ..." is omitted.
MacLean 323. MWiW*, NOC, O.

910 [——] ——— [Hartford, Conn.?: 1849?]. Broadside in 5 columns. 53 × 36 cm. At head of title: Saturday Courant—Extra. Also contains "Thoughts Suggested by the Question—What Induced you to Join the Shakers?" signed: *E. H. W.* [i.e., Eleanor Hays Wright] *South Groton, September 1849.*
DLC, NN, OClWHi*.

911 [——], *comp.* The Constitution of the United Societies of Believers (called Shakers) Containing Sundny [!] Covenants and Artcles [!] of Agrement [!], Definitive of the Legal Grounds of the Institution ... Watervliet, Ohio: 1833. [138], various pagings. 18 cm.

This erratically gathered collection of separate pamphlets compiled by Richard McNemar is described in the *British Museum Catalogue of Printed Books* as "A made-up volume." What the contents or the sequence of pamphlets was originally intended to be cannot be discerned. Examination of several copies has revealed only two copies which correspond, but these lacked some pamphlets contained in other copies. It has been suggested that the collection was intended to be arranged in two groups, one relating to Ohio and the other to Kentucky. The wide variety of contents and the varying sequences of the pamphlets does not, however, substantiate this conjecture. MacLean was apparently unaware of the many variations of the con-

tents of MacNemar's compilation since he enumerated the items without qualifications in his *Bibliography* (no. 2407), p. 14. In his *Life of Richard McNemar* (no. 2411), p. 46, however, in discussing the *Decision of the Court of Appeals* (Ky.), no. 915, he remarks, "From the pagination of this pamphlet and that used in his 'Constitutions,' it is evident that he intended to comprehend many things in one large book, which, for some reason, now unknown, was abandoned." The autograph inscription on the flyleaf of a Williams College copy (Williamstown, Mass.), *A present from E. Wright* [Richard McNemar] *to Rufus Bishop. 1834,* implies that the compiler considered this copy to be satisfactory. It is in good condition; is in the original binding—yellow boards with dark green backstrip, somewhat worn. It consists of 12 separate pamphlets bound together as follows:
1. The title page (1 leaf) precedes: Sundny [!] Covenants &c. Copy of the First Covenant in Ohio, Drafted by Elder Benjamin, and Executed in the Year 1810. [n.p., n.d.]. Caption title. [1]–2 pp. The "2" is inverted.
2. A Brief Exposition of the Established Principles, and Regulations of the United Society of Believers called Shakers. Printed at Albany, in the Year 1830; and now Reprinted, with Sundry Improvements Suggested by the Author .... Watervliet, Ohio: 1832. 36 pp. Also published separately, *see* no. 735.
3. An Improved Edition of the Church Covenant, or Constitution of the United Societies, called Shakers .... Dayton, Ohio: 1833. Cover title. 2 p.ll. [37]–48 pp. 4. The Covenant, or Constitution of the Church, at Union-Village, Ohio. [n.p., 1829?]. Caption title. [61]–72 pp. On p. 72, signed *Dec. 31, 1829.*
5. The Constitution, or Covenant of the Church, at Pleasant-Hill. Kentucky. [n.p., 1830?]. Caption title. [61]–72 pp.
6. Circular Epistle [from the Ministry and Elders at New-Lebanon, Sept. 1, 1829]. [n.p., 1829?]. Caption title. [73]–80 pp., p. 79 misnumbered 73.
7. The Church-Covenant, Executed at Union-Village, January 15th, 1812. The State of Ohio Warren County. [Watervliet, O.: 1829?]. Caption title. [81]–88, i.e.–86pp.

(p. 85 unnumb., p. 86 misnumb. 88).
"Public notice." Dec. 28, 1818, is attached
to these pp. [85]-88, i.e., 86. Sometimes
found attached to the Pleasant Hill covenant.
8. Duplicates no. 5 above.
9. The Church-Covenant, Executed at Water-
vliet December 7th 1818. State of Ohio
Montgomery County. [n.p., 1829?]. Caption
title. [89]-96 pp.
Includes: "A Covenant Hymn, dated U.V.,
Sep. 1813,"; "The Ordination of a Trustee,"
pp. 94-96.
10. General Rules of the United Society, and
Summary Articles of Mutual Agreement and
Release: Ratified and Confirmed by the
Society at Watervliet, Montgomery County,
Ohio, January, 1833. [Watervliet: 1833?].
Caption title. [3]-9 pp.
11. A Revision and Confirmation of the Social
Compact of the United Society called Shakers,
at Pleasant Hill, Kentucky .... Published by
Order of the Church. Harrodsburg, Ky.:
Printed by Randall and Jones, 1830. Cover
title. 12 pp. Also published separately, *see*
no. 951.
12. Investigator; or a Defense of the Order,
Government & Economy of the United So-
ciety Called Shakers, against Sundry Charges
& Legislative Proceedings. Addressed to the
Political World. By the Society of Believers
at Pleasant Hill, Ky. ... Lexington, K.: Printed
by Smith & Palmer, 1828. x, [11]-47 pp.
Also published separately, *see* no. 926. Laid
inside back cover: A Special Covenant of the
First Family of the Church dated 3rd Month
8th 1815. [n.p., n.d.]. [2] pp.
MacLean 14. Sabin 97886. CSmH, CtY, DLC,
ICJ, KU, MB, MPH, MWiW*, N, NN, OCHP,
OClWHi.

912 [——] Reprint. New York: AMS Press.
Announced for publication, but which combination of contents is not indicated.

913 [——], *ed.* Court of Appeals, The Shaker
Case. Gass & Banta vs. Wilhite & als (Owsley,
for Appellants; Crittenden, Haggin & Cunning-
ham for Appellees). Judge Nicholas Delivered the
Opinion of the Court, May 5, 1834. [Frankfort:
Published by O. Brown and A. G. Hodges, 1834?]
Caption title. [53]-62, 55, 58 pp. 17½ cm.

The last two page numbers misprinted (63
misnumb. 55; 64 misnumb. 58), but the
text runs consecutively. The contents and
the page numbering support Hamilton's
suggestion ("Tentative Bibliography," p. 3)
that these pages were purchased unbound
in Kentucky and were intended to be combined with *The Decision of the Court of
Appeals* ..., no. 915. Gass and Banta were
denied the property they sought, and the
Shakers were upheld. Banta is sometimes
spelled Bonta.
MWiW*, OClWHi.

914 [——] A Damper to the Spirit of Litiga-
tion. [n.p., n.d.]. pp. [189]-200. 18 cm.
Fragment of his *A Selection of Hymns and
Poems*, no. 952.
OClWHi*.

915 [——], *comp.* The Decision of the Court
of Appeals, (in Kentucky) in a Case of much
Interest to Religious Communities in General,
and to the Shakers in Particular. To which is
Prefixed A Brief Illustration of the Ground of
Action .... Dayton, Ohio. [Frankfort, Ky., O.:
Brown and A. G. Hodges], 1834. 66 pp. 19½
cm.
W. J. Hamilton, "Tentative Bibliography,"
p. 3, suggests that the "latter pages [were]
purchased unbound in Kentucky and com-
bined with his own [McNemar's] Dayton
'Prefix'—'Brief Illustration'; pp. 49-54?
with Dayton title page." Page numbers are
irregular, but at foot of p. 54 (64?) is found
"Frankfort. Published by O. Brown and
A. G. Hodges." Contains also brief and
judges' opinion in the case "Ballance and al.
Compl's ag'st the Shaker Society def'ts, Lincoln c't court," and no. 913.
MacLean 205. ICJ, MWiW, MHi, OCHP,
OClWHi*.

916 —— Dedication. [n.p., n.d.]. [4] pp. 14 cm.
Contents: "Dedication," "Good Believers Char-
acter," "A Request." *Dialogue between the
Church* ... Copies are also found attached to no. 917.
OClWHi, ODa.

917 [——] Dialogue Between the Church and the
Old Gentleman. [Watervliet, O.: n.d.] 12 pp. 14 cm.

Contents: "Dialogue," pp. 1–5; "Hireling Priests," pp. 6–8; "Thoughts on Seeing a Forlorn Looking Child in the Meetinghouse, May 14th, 1820," pp. 8–10; "Except a Man Deny Himself," pp. 10–12. Also contained in the Stockbridge, Mass., 1826 (no. 901), and later editions of *Concise Answer;* and *A Selection of Hymns and Poems* (Watervliet, O., 1833), pp. 166–68, no. 952. Sometimes cataloged under Oliver Prentiss. OClWHi*.

918 [——] ——— [n.p., n.d.]. [4] pp. 19 X 8½ cm.
This poem of 20 stanzas may have been composed by Oliver Prentiss. OClWHi*.

919 [——] Epistle Dedicatory of the Union Press. To the Respected Ministry and Eldership of the United Society. [Watervliet, O.: 1832]. Caption title. [4] pp. 14 cm.
Contents: "We Humbly Present this Brief *Epistle* as *Dedicatory* of the Little Printing Establishment ..." [3 paragraphs], p. [1]; four additional paragraphs signed: *The Editors, Watervliet, May 1, 1832,* p. [2]; "A New Explanation of the Revelation," signed: *"Reformer,"* pp. [3–4]. Found also attached to *Review of Most Important Events,* no. 950 and other McNemar publications. CSmH, DLC, MWiW, OCHP, OClWHi*, ODa.

920 [——] For a More Ample Illustration of the Parable, take the Following Poem, Written by a Young Believer about Twenty-Seven Years ago . . . . An Allegorical Detail of the Entrance of the Present Gospel in the West. [Watervliet, O.: 183–?]. [2] pp. 19 cm.
A poem of 18 stanzas, printed on heavy bluish-gray paper. This poem with somewhat different headings and type settings is also attached to the Williams College copy of *Western Review, No. VII,* no. 968, and on pp. 136–37, of *A Selection of Hymns and Poems,* no. 952. MWiW*, OClWHi.

—— A Friendly Letter to Alexander Mitchell ... *See Western Review, No. VII,* no. 968.

921 [——], *ed.* General Rules of the United Society, and Summary Articles of Mutual Agreement and Release: Ratified and Confirmed, by the Society at Watervliet, Montgomery County, Ohio, January, 1833 ... [Watervliet? O.:] Union-office, 1833. Caption title. pp. [3]–9. 18½ cm.
Copies are found both as separates (with collation 1 p.l., 6 pp.), and included in *The Constitution of the United Society, see* no. 911, No. 10.
Sabin 97887. DLC, MWiW*, OClWHi, ODa.

[——] How Precious is the Way of God. *See Let Names and Parties Accost my Ears no More,* no. 935.

922 [——], *comp.* [Hymns]. [Watervliet, O.: 1833?]. [80], [9]–32, [41]–64 pp. [i.e., 128 pp.] 16 cm.
Lacks title page. The typography indicates that this collection was printed in Ohio in the early 1830's. The first hymn is "The Second Part of Christ's Second Appearing"; the second hymn is "The True Gospel Light." All copies examined lack title pages, and the assigned titles vary in library card catalogs, which makes identification hazardous without a close comparison of copies. Variants contain different sequences of the same and different hymns, duplications of text, misnumbered and unnumbered pages, and also pages of varying sizes and different typography. Irregularities in Williams College copies (Williamstown, Mass.) are described below. *See also* nos. 952 and 956.
MWiW*, N (different variants).

923 [——] [———] Variant. [28], [9]–64, (61)–(64), (73)–(74), (79)–(80) pp. 17½ cm. (Leaves have been trimmed at different times; sizes vary from 16.2 to 17.4 cm. Typography differs with each cluster of page numbers.)
Lacks title page. Pages [7–10] of the first numbering repeat pp. [3–6]. The first hymn is "True Wisdom," pages (61)–(64) of the third numbering are from McNemar's *Selection of hymns and poems ...* (1833), no. 952. The final four pages are the first and last leaves (pp. [73]–74, 79–80) of "Circular

Epistle ..." (New Lebanon, 1829) which is contained in *Constitution of the United Societies*... (Watervliet, 1833), MacLean 14, and no. **911**(6) here.
MWiW*.

924 [——] [————] Variant. [8], [17]–64, [9], 10–16, [44] pp. [i.e. 116].
Lacks title page. The first hymn is "A Family Hymn"; the last hymn is "Spiritual Relation, Part 2d."
MWiW*.

925 [——], *ed.* An Improved Edition of the Church Covenant, or Constitution of the United Societies, called Shakers. Collated from the Several Copies which Have Been Duly Executed in the Sevral [!] Societies, Respectively; and Officially Sanctioned by the Several Ministries, for the Purposes Therein Contained. Dayton, Ohio: 1833. 2 p.ll. [37]–48 pp. (p. 45 misnumb. 43).
This is an earlier printing than no. **911**(3). The pages are set with fewer lines to the page, and at the end, p. 48, 3 lines of text are lacking and have been supplied in manuscript and pasted on recto of back cover. The 4-line footnote on p. 38 is lacking. Apparently, it was paged to continue *A Brief Exposition* (no. **735**), and is sometimes found bound with it.
Sabin 97888. MWiW*, NBuG, NN, OCHP, OClWHi.

926 [——], *comp.* Investigator, or A Defense of the Order, Government & Economy of the United Society called Shakers, Against Sundry Charges & Legislative Proceedings. Addressed to the Political World. By the Society of Believers at Pleasant Hill, Ky.... Lexington, Ky.: Printed by Smith & Palmer, 1828. 47 pp. 18 cm.
Although this compilation is usually credited to Richard McNemar, Green and Wells, *A Brief Exposition* (no. **735**), p. 15, refer to the committee of publication as having written part, particularly Elder David Spinning. Contents. – "Petition of John Whitbey and Others to the Legislature," pp. v–viii; "An Act to Regulate Civil Proceedings Against Certain Communities Having Property in Common," pp. viii–x; "Objections to

the Petition of J. Whitbey, &c.," pp. 11–12; "Objections to the Foregoing Act," pp. 13–18; "Statements of John Whitbey Concerning the Society; Extracted from his book Entitled – A Short Account of Shakerism [*sic*]" (no. **1427**), pp. 19–24; "Origin and Progress of the United Society at Pleasant Hill," pp. 24–30; "Court Decisions Affecting the Shakers," pp. 31–44; "Extract from Dr. Holley's Review of Professor Silliman's Journal. Western Review, vol. 3, p. 203," pp. 44–46; "Poetry," p. 47.
MacLean 349. Sabin 79710. Shaw 33962. CSmH, Ct, DLC, ICJ, ICN, KyBgW, MHi, MPB, MWA, MWiW*, MiU-C, NBuG, NN, Nh, OC, OClWHi, WHi.

927 [——] ———— Printed at Lexington, Ky.: 1828. Reprinted New-York: [Egbert, Hovey & King, Printers, 1846]. 84, 19 pp. 18½ cm.
Cover title: Account of Some of the Proceedings of the Legislatures of the States of Kentucky and New Hampshire, 1828 &c. in Relation to the People Called Shakers. The cover title is often used incorrectly in citations, and *not* the title as found on the title page. Lacks "Poetry," p. 47, in the 1828 edition. Includes "Speech of Robert Wickliffe in the Senate of Kentucky – Jan. 1831," pp. 57–84. "... Proceedings of the Legislature of New Hampshire" is appended (MacLean 502) 19 pp. at end, with caption title, "Some Account of the Proceedings of the Legislature of New Hampshire in Relation to the People Called Shakers in 1828."
MacLean 1 (and 2 in paper covers). Sabin 37486 (19 pp.) and 79711. CSmH, CtY, DLC, KyBgW, KyU, MH, MHarF, MPB, MWA, MWiW*, MiU-C, N, NBuG, NN, NHi, NNC, NRCR, NOC, Nh, NhD, NcD, NjPT, ODa, OClWHi, OHi, OOxM, PHi, WHi.

928 [——], *ed.* Journal of Peter Pease. [Union Village, O.: 1831?]. 19–22 pp.
This corresponds to pp. 19–22 (Dec. 6, 1806 to March 1810) of *A Review of the Most Important Events* (no. **950**), where a note, "End of Elder Peter's Journal," appears at the foot of p. 21. MacLean 371

mistakenly identifies this as "A fragment from the *Western Review.*"
MacLean 371. OClWHi*.

929 —— The Kentucky Revival, or, A Short History of the Late Extraordinary Out-Pouring of the Spirit of God, in the Western States of America, Agreeably to Scripture-Promises, and Prophecies concerning the Latter Day: with a Brief Account of the Entrance and Progress of What the World call Shakerism, Among the Subjects of the Late Revival in Ohio and Kentucky. Presented to the True Zion-traveller, as a Memorial of the Wilderness Journey. By Richard M'Nemar .... Cincinnati: From the Press of John W. Browne, 1807. 119 [1], 23 pp. 19 cm.

"Errata," verso p. 119. With this is bound as issued (23 pp., at end): *Observations on Church Government, by the Presbytery of Springfield [Ohio]* .... with special title page, separate paging, and non-consecutive signatures. *See also* no. 1333. This is a first-hand account by a leader of the Kentucky Revival, one of the first western Shaker converts, which has been quoted extensively by later authors. McNemar describes frontier revivals, the Presbyterian schism, beginnings of Shakerism in the West, and early Shaker relations with the Indians. It is the first bound book to be published by the Shakers.
MacLean 65. Sabin 43605. Shaw 12969. CtHC, CtY, DLC, ICU, KyBgW, KyLoF, MBC, MWA, MWiW*, NN, NOC, OC, OClWHi, PPPrHi, WHi.

930 —— ———— Cincinnati Printed: Albany: Reprinted by E. and E. Hosford, 1808. 119, 23 pp. 17½ cm.

"Errata" slip mounted on verso, p. 23. "A Letter from the Author, to a Friend in New-Lebanon ..." pp. [iii]–iv, is found only in this edition (reprinted MacLean *Bibliography*, p. 4 n.). Otherwise contents are the same as no. 929 above. In spite of the imprint, this edition was actually printed in Cincinnati, according to MacLean, *Bibliography* (no. 2407), pp. 4–5.
MacLean 66. Sabin 43605 and 43606 (*Observations*). Shaw 15477. CtHC, CtW, CtY, DLC, ICU, Ia–HA, IaU, KyBgW, KyU, MB,

MBC, MH, MHarF, MH–AH, MMeT, MNtcA, MPB, MWA, MWiW, MWiW*, MdBE, MeHi, MiU–C, N, NBuG, NN, NNG, NNUT, NOC, NSyU, NcD, OClWHi, OCo, ODa, OFH, OHi, OO, PHi, RHi, RPB, TxDaM, WHi.

931 —— ———— Pittsfield [Mass.]: Reprinted by Phinehas Allen, 1808. 148, 28 pp. 17 cm.

This appears to be a later edition than no. 930. The text is the same, except that "A Letter from the Author ..." has been omitted, and most of the errata have been corrected. A larger size type has increased the number of pages.
MacLean 67 (and 68 in paper covers). Sabin 43605. Shaw 15478 (148 pp.). Streeter 4228. CSmH, CtHT-W, CtY, DeWint, DLC, KyBgW, KyU, MBAt, MH, MHarF, MWA, MWiW*, N, NHi, NOC, NSyU, OCHP, OFH, TxU.

932 —— ———— Third edition [*sic*]. Cincinnati [O.]: Printed 1807. Albany reprinted: 1808. Union Village: 1837. 2 p.ll., [9]–119 pp. 17½ cm.

"McNemar prepared two copies for a reprint of what he called the 'Third Edition — Union Village, 1837,' and, the other copy: 'Union Village — Revised by the Author, 1837.' ... was never published owing to the want of money caused by the defalcation of Nathan Sharp in 1835, and the necessity for a new residence, which made strict economy imperative," MacLean, *Life*, p. 43. McNemar added "Apologetical, Sept. 29th, 1837," to the Union Village 1837 edition, and this is not found in any other editions, J. P. MacLean, *Bibliography*, p. 5.
MacLean 69. DLC* (imperfect, all after p. 86 wanting).

933 —— ———— New York: Reprinted by Edward O. Jenkins, 1846. 156 pp. 9 cm.

The words "Out-Pouring" and "Scripture-Promises" in the title are printed "outpouring" and "Scripture promises." "Observations on Church Government ..." pp. [133]–156. A few footnotes have been added. *The Kentucky Revival,* somewhat abridged and edited, was reprinted in *The Manifesto,*

Vols. 21–22 (January 1891–July 1892), *passim*.
MacLean 70. Sabin 43605. CtY, DLC, ICJ, In, InI, KyBgW, KyLxT, KyU, MB, MBC, MHarF, MHi, MPB, MWA, MWiW*, MeB, MiU, N, NHi, NN, NNC, NRCR, NSyU, Nh, NhD, NjPT, OC, OCl, ODa, OHi, OO, OOxM, PCC, PHC, PPL, ViW, WHi.

934 —— ———— (Reprint). New York: AMS Press, Inc. Publication announced 1972–1973.

935 [——] Let Names and Sects and Parties Accost my Ears No More; — How Precious is the Way of God [poems]. [Union Village: 1829?]. 2 pp. 18 cm.
Entry taken from MacLean's *Bibliography*, No. 386. MacLean, *Life*, p. 42, "Probably about this period [1829] his two poems ... were printed." The first poem of 16 stanzas is contained in two Williams College copies of a miscellaneous collection, [*Hymns*], nos. 923–924, pp. 33–36 under the title "The Pillar of Truth." Two different versions of "The Precious Way of God," contained in the same copies (12 and 13 stanzas), are printed from two different type settings.
MacLean 386. DLC.

936 —— The Life and Labors of Father David Darrow. Watervliet, Ohio: 1834. 12 pp.
Entry taken from MacLean's *Bibliography*, no. 370. This is pp. 3–12 of the *Western Review*, No. 1 (no. 965).
No separate publication located.

937 [——] A Little Selection of Choice Poetry New and Old, Doctrinal and Devotional. Submitted to the Patronage of the Pious, by E.[leazar] W.[right] [*pseud.*]. (C.S.) .... Watervliet, O.: 1835. Cover title. [2]–16 pp. 14½ cm.
Pages 9 and 13 lack page numbers. Three different sizes of type were used to print the poetry. Contents: Title, p. [1]; "Caution," p. [2]; "A Choice Selection &c.," pp. [3]–4; "II. Precious Way of God," pp. 5–7; "III. The Beauty of the Gospel," pp. 7–8; "IV. Woman's Seed," pp. 8–[9]; "God Moves in a Mysterious Way," p. 10; "VII.

Christmas, 1834," pp. 11–12; "VIII. My Reliance. —Xtn. B. 1835," p. 12; "Friendship, Love and Union," pp. [13]–16. "God Moves in a Mysterious Way," p. 10, changes lines 3–4 and adds two stanzas to William Cowper's hymn, "Light Shining Out of Darkness." *See* his *Olney Hymns* (London, W. Oliver, 1799), p. 328. Variant copies of this collection are found with different total paginations, i.e., 12, 16, 24, 32, 42 or 54 pp., and with different combinations of numbered and unnumbered and differently numbered pages. MacLean's *Life*, p. 65, and *Bibliography*, p. 18, lists a copy with 55 pp. The Library of Congress card gives total pagination as 55 pp., but with note: Imperfect: pp. 21–55 wanting. Sabin 97889 (56 pp.) and 105575 (20, 41–56 pp.). CSmH, DLC, MH–AH, MPB, MWiW*, NN, NcU, NjPT, OCHP, OClWHi, RPB.

938 [——] A Newyear's Gift; Jan. 1831. The Following are the Orders, Rules and Regulations which are to be Observed and Kept Throughout the Church. [n.p., 1831?]. [6] pp. 14 cm.
Twenty "contrary to order" rules that appear to have been printed by Richard McNemar, probably at Union Village. The rules are not so specific as those listed in Haskett's *Shakerism Unmasked* (no. 772), pp. 168–84, which are reprinted in E. D. Andrews, *People Called Shakers*, (no. 1767), pp. 244–47, and also pp. 249–89 for a later version. Published separately, but is also included in copies of *A Little Selection of Choice Poetry*, no. 937.
CSmH, DLC, OClWHi*, ODa.

[——], ed. Observations on Church Government. *See* his *Kentucky Revival*, no. 929 ff., and Springfield (Ohio) Presbytery, no. 1333 ff.

939 [——], ed. The Orthodox Incarnation, or Divine Humanity of Jesus Christ. [Watervliet, O.: 1835?]. 17–24 pp. 14 cm.
This is a fragment of the final section of *The Orthodox Trinity*, no. 940.
MPB*, NBuG, ODa.

940 [——], ed. The Orthodox Trinity, with a Few Remarks on Certain Doctrines Therewith Connected [4-line quotation]. [Watervliet, O.: 183–?]. Caption title. 24 pp. 14½ cm.

Wrong imposition of pages has resulted in a weird sequence of page numbers which occur in one Williams College copy as follows: [1], 4, 15, [14], 3, 2, 5, 8, 7, 6, 11, 10, 9, 12, 13, 16, [17], 18 [digits inverted], 15, 20, 21, 22, 23, 24. This results in a similar lack of sequence in the poems and text. (Different sequences occur in other copies.) Third line of the quotation in the title is printed: TO THE UNKNOWN GOD!!! "Paul" is omitted at the end of the quotation. Six lines of the third stanza of the title poem are printed on the first page. Correct contents and sequence. "Orthodox Trinity" [poem "said to have originated at Canterbury, N.H.," p. 13], pp. 1–13; "The Athanasian Creed," pp. 14–16; "Orthodox Incarnation," pp. 17–24. MPB, MWiW*, OClWHi.

941 [——] ——— Variant.
"TO THE UNKNOWN GOD!" is printed with one exclamation mark. "Paul" is omitted after the quotation. Only four lines of the third stanza of the title poem are printed on the first page. OClWHi*.

942 [——] ——— Variant.
In a Dayton Public Library incomplete copy, containing only 16 pages, "Paul" is printed after the quotation in the title, and "Watervliet, O., Mar. 1, 1835" occurs in a note on p. 16. Four lines of the third stanza of the title poem are printed on the first page. MacLean 395? ODa*.

943 [——] ——— with a Few Remarks Upon Certain Doctrines Connected Therewith. [5-line quotation]. [Watervliet, O.: 183–?]. Caption title. 16 pp. 13 cm.
Contains only the title poem. Type setting, paper, and line arrangement of the title are different. The words "Connected Therewith" in the title are reversed. It is probably a later edition. The printing is superior, and the page numbers run consecutively. Only eight lines of the first stanza of the title poem are printed on the first page. The word "invented" has been pasted over the original print, p. 15, line 19. "Erratum" notice occurs at end, p. 16.

MacLean 394. MPB, MWiW*, NBuG, NN, NjPT, OClWHi.

944 [——] ——— Variant line arrangement of title. Lacks "Erratum," errors corrected, and last line of quotation is printed in italics. ODa*.

945 [——] ——— 12 pp. 14 cm.
Same title, variant paper size and typography. ODa*.

946 [——] The Other Side of the Question. In Three Parts. I. An Explanation of the Proceedings of Eunice Chapman and the Legislature, against the United Society, called Shakers, in the State of New York. II. A Refutation of the False Statements of Mary Dyer against said Society, in the State of New Hampshire. III. An Account of the Proceedings of Abram Van Vleet, Esq. and his Associates, against the said United Society at Union Village, Ohio. Comprising a General Vindication of the Character of Mother and the Elders against the Attacks of Public Slander — The Edicts of a Prejudiced Party — and the Misguided Zeal of Lawless Mobs. Published by Order of the United Society at Union Village, Ohio . . . . Cincinnati: Looker, Reynolds & Co., 1819. 168, vii pp. 17½ cm.
"Signed in Behalf of said Society, Union Village, Aug. 10, 1819. Eleazar Wright [Richard McNemar], Calvin Morrell, Matthew Houston, Samuel Sering." This was published to counteract "evil reports and defamatory statements" circulated against the United Society in the *Western Star*, and *An Account of the Conduct of the Shakers* (Lebanon, O., Van Vleet & Camron, 1818), no. 1402. Pt. I, pp. [5]–37, and Pt. II, pp. [38]–114, reprint Shaker publications defending their actions in the cases of Eunice and James Chapman (New York), and Mary and Joseph Dyer (New Hampshire). Pt. III, pp. 115–59. A refutation of charges made by Van Vleet was written by Richard McNemar. Cf. J. P. MacLean, *Bibliography*, p. 11, and *Life*, p. 44, and R. L. Rusk, *Literature of the Middle Western Frontier* (N.Y., 1926. 2 vols.), II:226. "Appendix," pp. 160–64, is a refutation of William Ludlow's statements about the Shakers, *see* no. 879. "Errata," p. 164, and p. vii.

MacLean 76 (164 pp.). Sabin 57844. Shaw 48553. CSmH, DeWint, DLC, MHarF, MPB, MWiW*, N, NHi, NN, NOC, NhD, OClWHi, ODa, OHi, WHi.

—— Public Discourses ... *See* Dunlavy, John, Public Discourses ... no. 523.

947 [——] ... A Pure Church Anticipated. A Revival-Hymn in the Year 1801. [n.p., n.d.]. [2] pp. 15½ cm.

Contains a letter written by Richard McNemar, dated at Union Village, July 15, 1837.
OClWHi*.

948 [——], *ed.* A Record Relating to the Cogar Mob and Boon Suit. [By] Perigrinus [*pseud.*]. [n.p., 1831]. [10] pp. 11 cm.

"To the Public," pp. [3]–[6]. "Extract," [from a speech of the Honorable John Brethett, Lieut. Gov. of Kentucky], pp. [7]–[10], W. H. Cathcart manuscript note on the Western Reserve Historical Society copy (Cleveland, O.), *Only one other copy of this known to M.*[innie] *C.*[atherine] *A.*[llen]. This *Record* is McNemar's printing.
OClWHi*.

949 [——] Review. Of American Policy. July 1819. "I am not thine ASS on which Thou hast Ridden, ever since I was Thine." Numb. 22, 30. [Union Village: n.d.]. 8 pp. 14 cm.

Last paragraph, p. 8, "Whatever views Mary Dyer, Aquila Bolton and others may have had of spiritual marriage & conjugal love, certainly no true Believer ever set out with any other view but to 'Renounce the flesh forever': Therefore, care ought to be taken, that nothing be left in any of our important writings that would clash with the work of the present day." Also found cited: *Review.* R.[ichard] M.[cNemar] to I.[ssachar] B.[ates].
OClWHi*.

950 [——], *comp.* A Review of the Most Important Events Relating to the Rise and Progress of the United Society of Believers in the West; with Sundry other Documents Connected with the History of the Society. Collected from

Various Journals. By E. Wright [*pseud.*] ... Union Village, Ohio: [Union Press], 1831. 34 pp. [i.e., 42]. 15 cm.

"The following pages are intended only for the use of the Church & particularly of the Ministry and Eldership ..." Contents: Title, p. [1]; "Take Notice," p. [2]; "Review of Events Chapter I," pp. [3]–6; "The Church of Christ unto a People in Kentucky ....," pp. 6–9; "Chap. II," pp. 9–13; "Chapter III. The Formation of the Society," pp. 14–17; "Chapter IV. Foundation of the Church at Union Village ...," pp. 17–21; "Chapter V. Church-order Established," pp. 22–25; "Chapter VI. Memorial of Deceases, from the Year 1805, to 1831," pp. 25–33; "Supplement," p. 34. Pages 19–22 repeat twice in this copy. Pages 25–34 are identical with the corresponding pages in [*Western Review,* No. 3], *Chronology. A Memorial of Deceases at Union Village* ... no. 966, except for pp. 25–26 which are reset. Copies are found with both 34 pp. and with 56 pp. W. J. Hamilton, "Tentative Bibliography," notes that in some copies, "Pagination actually [1]–34, [33], 34–56, i.e., 58." MacLean 476 (34 pp.). Sabin 105576 (56, 43–54, 24 pp. "Epistle dedicatory of the Union Press" 1st preliminary leaf dates: Watervliet, May 1, 1832). DLC (2 p.ll., 3–34, [33]–34, [35]–56, 43–54, 24 pp. Pages 41–56 incorrectly numbered; a correct signature inserted at end.).
CSmH, DLC, MWiW*, N, NN, OClWHi (34 pp. and 56 pp.).

951 [——] A Revision and Confirmation of the Social Compact of the United Society called Shakers, at Pleasant Hill, Kentucky ... Published by Order of the Church. Harrodsburg, Ky.: Printed by Randall and Jones, 1830. 12 pp. 17½ cm.

Attested by: G. R. Runyon, J. R. Bryant, James Rankin [May 20, 1830]. The number of subscribers is given as 210. MacLean, *Bibliography* (no. 2407), pp. 11–12, attributes authorship to McNemar, as does Hamilton, "Tentative Bibliography," p. 10. *See also* no. 911(11).
MacLean 425. Sabin 97896. Shaw 2345. ICJ, KyBgW, MPB, MWA, MWiW*, NN,

NOC, OCHP, OClWHi, PHi, WHi.

952 [——] A Selection of Hymns and Poems;
for the Use of Believers. Collected from Sundry
Authors, by Philos Harmoniae [*pseud.*] ...
Watetvliet [*sic*], Ohio: 1833. 180 (i.e., 184),
[4] pp. 17½ cm.

At end, p. [4], signed: *Your devoted Servant
in the Gspel* [*sic*], *Eleazar.* Contents: Title,
p. [1]; [2] blank; "Preface," pp. [3]-4 (misnumb. 5); "A Selection of Hymns and
Poems," pp. [5]-72; "A Selection of Hymns
and Poems, Part II," pp. [73]-96; "Part III,"
pp. 97-116; "A Selection &c., Part IV," pp.
[117]-180; "Index," pp. [1-4]. "IX. Good
Feelings," p. 131, is signed: *South Union.
Feb. 1834. — H.*[arvey] *L. E.*[ads], which
is either a misprint, or casts doubt on the
accuracy of the 1833 imprint date on the
title page. The note, p. [4], at end, signed:
Eleazar [Eleazar Wright, *pseud.*] recognizes
the inconsistencies and typos throughout the
printing. "N.B. From the embarrassments,
under which this little work has been executed, sundry errata will be discovered in
some copies, and more or less in all." Pp. 4,
26, 61, 120, 121, 122, 123 are misnumbered
5, 29, 81, 119, 117, 138, 139; thereafter the
page numbers are in the correct sequence, but
are misnumbered 4 numerals less than the
actual count, i.e., 124-125 are misnumbered
120-121, etc. The numbers on several other
pages are so indistinct as to be illegible. Incorrect "Selection" numbers occur in the
text. Pp. 12, 21, 53-57, 95 lack page numbers.
The signatures are erratically signed and
gathered, but apparently the gatherings were
intended to be in sixes. Richard McNemar is
often credited with the authorship of most
of the hymns and poems. Four selections are
signed: *R. M.*, and sixteen are signed: *E. W.*
Words only.
MacLean 80. Sabin 79718 and 97897. CtY,
DeWint, DLC, KyBgW, MPB, MWA, MWiW*,
N, NN, NBuG, NOC, NjPT, OCHP, ODa, OHi,
OOxM, RPB. (Comparison of these copies
has not been made.)

953 [——] ———— By Philos Harmonia
[*pseud.*] ... Watetvliet [*sic*], Ohio: 1833. Cover

title, [3], 68-75, 79, 9-16 pp. (i.e., 20 pp.).
16 and 16½ cm.

Made up of cover title, "Preface," (verso
numb. 68), pp. 69-79 [i.e., 76] of the edition
above, and pp. 9-16 of a different work. "Harmoniae" is spelled "Harmonia" in cover title.
MWiW*.

954 [——] [A Selection of Shaker Literature.]
[1836?]. [78] pp. 18½ cm.

Entry taken from *Shaker Literature in the
Rare Book Room of the Buffalo and Erie
Public Library* (no. 2947), no. 190. Badly
mutilated. Contains miscellaneous material
including pages 29-40, 53-56, 69-72, 77-88,
169-172 of [McNemar, Richard]. *A Selection
of Hymns and Poems; for the Use of Believers.*
Watetvliet [*sic*], Ohio, 1833, no. 952.
NBuG*.

955 [——] A Series of Lectures on Orthodoxy
and Heterodoxy, in Allusion to the Testimony of
Christ's Second Appearing. Introduced by a
Rpely [*sic*] to Sundry Defamatory Letters writ-
ten by A. M. Bolton, late, a Catechuman in the
United Society at Union Village. Designed for the
Edification of Young Believers. By E. W. [Eleazar
Wright, *pseud.*] ... Dayton, O.: 1832. Cover title,
12 pp. 17½ cm.

Contents: Cover title, p. [1]; "Introduction,"
p. [2]; "Reply to Sundry Defamatory Letters
..." pp. [3]-11; "A Few Extracts from the
Whore of Babylon Unmasked," pp. 11-12, *see*
no. 105. The Library of Congress copy contains only "The Reply to Sundry Defamatory
Letters ..." and "A Few Extracts ..." The
Dayton Public Library copy has a peculiar
gathering and attached thereto *Western Review, or Memorial* (no. 965), and *Western Expositor, No. 4* (no. 964).
Sabin 105577. DLC, ODa, OClWHi*.

956 [——] [Shaker Hymn Book]. [1833?].
[1-9], 10-64, [65]-[100].

Entry taken from W. J. Hamilton's "Tenta-
tive Bibliography," p. 12. Lacks title page.
Another variant of no. 922.
DLC*.

957 [——], *ed.* The Shaker Society Adv-s Gass,

Banta, &c. Upon an Appeal from a Decree of the Lincoln Circuit Court. [n.p., 1834?]. 8 pp. 18½ cm.

> A brief, signed: *Ch. Cunningham*, followed by "Note. 'We have found by experience, that however learned or skillful lawyers may be; yet unless they are made fully acquainted with the principles of our institutions, they are but poorly qualified to manage a suit for us'," signed: *Seth Y. Wells*, p. 8. Also contained in [R. McNemar], *comp., Decision of the Court of Appeals*, no. 915. Both J. P. MacLean, *Bibliography*, pp. 41–42, and F. G. Ham, "Shakerism in the Old West," p. 153, ftn. 69, credit McNemar with this publication. MWiW*, OClWHi.

958 —— "Shakerism Detected, &c." [a pamphlet by Col. James Smith of Kentucky] Examined and Refuted, in Five Propositions ... Lexington, Ky.: Printed by Thomas Smith, 1811. 10, [1] pp. 20½ cm.

> "Postscript to the second edition," p. 10, implies that there was an earlier edition of McNemar's reply to Smith printed separately. Sabin, however, using information supplied by W. H. Cathcart, states that this was published in "Lebanon, Ohio in 1811, probably in the 'Western Star,' and separately at Lexington, 1811." Cf. J. P. MacLean, *Life*, p. 44. No copy of a Lebanon, O., 1811 edition has been located.
> Sabin 82770B. Shaw 23274. OClWHi*.

959 —— Shakerism Detected [a pamphlet published by Col. James Smith of Kentucky] Examined and Refuted in five Propositions; Published at Lebanon (O) and Lexington (K) in 1811, by Richard M'Namer [!] .... (Reprinted by Request). Water[v]liet, Ohio: May 8, 1833. Cover title. 12 pp. 18 cm.

> Contents: Title, p. [1]; "Introduction," p. 2; "Proposition," I–V, pp. 3–9; "Postscript to the Second Edition," dated at end: Lexington (K) April 20, 1811, p. 10; "A Brief Memorial, Supplementary to this Edition," p. 11; "Extract of a Poem," pp. 11–12. MacLean 372. Sabin 82770B. CSmH, DLC, KyU, MWA, MWiW*, OClWHi, ODa.

960 [——] A Special Covenant of the First Family of the Church [Union Village], dated 3rd Month 8th 1815. [Watervliet, O.?: n.d.]. [2] pp. 20 cm.

> This is not the Shaker Church covenant describing the organization of the society, disposition of property, etc., but it is a declaration of faith, rules of behavior, etc., which begins: "We believe it is high time that we should come to the light, and declare our faith openly to each other, and maintain, aboveboard, what we believe to be right, to the laying down of our lives," Signed: *Richard M'Namer, Calvin Morrell, Samuel Rollins, Ashbel Kitchell, William Sharp, James Smith, Amos Valentine, Abner Bedell,* and 21 others of the first order, or Center Family Brethren, Union Village, O. MPB*, MWiW.

[——] Speech of Robert Wickliffe. *See* Wickliffe, Robert, no. 1457, *and also* no. 927.

961 [——] [Statement of Henry Banta]. [n.p., n.d.]. [39]–42 pp. 14 cm.

> Signed: *Henry Banta*. "The Printer of the Kentucky Reporter. Please to insert the above in your paper. H. B." Followed by: "Copied from the original, VERBATIM, et LITERATIM, et PUNCTUATIM. — By E. W. [i.e., Richard McNemar]." OClWHi*.

962 —— A Thumb Paper and Captain Me Big. [Union Village, O.:] 1829. 9 pp. 8 X 9 cm.

> Poems for juveniles. "Thumb Paper," one stanza of 8 lines. "Captain Me Big," 6 stanzas of 12 lines each.
> MacLean 373. Shaw 39377. CSmH, DLC*, NN, RPB.

963 [——] Valuable Extracts from Sundry Writers (on Various Subjects) Congenial to the Faith of the Gospel, for the Refutation of Bigotry and Infidelity (W.V.). Dayton, Ohio: 1835. 2, [17]–20, [13]–30 (i.e., 24 pp.) pp. 13½ cm.

> Contents: Title, p. [1]; "Introduction," p. [2]; "Extract from Cicero 'De Senectute'," pp. [17]–20; "Cicero on Friendship," pp. [13]–28; "Review, Truth and Reality of Apparitions," pp. 28–30.
> DLC, N, OClWHi*, ODa.

964 [——] The Western Expositor. No. 4. A
Brief Exposition of Rev. 12, – Ezek. 17, &c.
Communicated to a Friend. [Watervliet?: 183–?].
Caption title. [50]-53 pp. 18 cm.

Denounces Aquila M. Bolton, a former
member at Union Village, O., referred to as
"the Eagle." *See also* no. **105**. The Dayton
Public Library copy has a manuscript note
on p. [50]: "Ministry Confidential, No. 2."
MPB, MWiW*, NBuG, ODa.

[——] *Western Review.* Richard McNemar was
"assigned to keep a journal of events relating to
the progress of Shakerism in the West. To preserve the more important facts he started the
Western Review ... [and] was projector, editor,
typesetter, and pressman" at the Watervliet
press, J. P. MacLean, *Bibliography*, p. 19. The
Western Review represents another of McNemar's
erratically printed and gathered combinations;
examination of several copies does not clarify
his original intention. There appears to be an
interrelationship with the *Review of the Most
Important Events*, no. **950**; parts of the contents are sometimes found in *A Little Selection*
... no. **937**; and MacLean 371 identifies *Journal
of Peter Pease*, no. **928**, as "a fragment from the
Western Review, 19-22 pp." The numbered
entries below under *Western Review* are found
so numbered, or reveal some interrelationship
which indicates that they were originally intended to be consecutive parts.

965 [——] *Western Review* Nos. [1]-2, or, A
Memorial of the Labors of our Parents and
Ministers, in Founding the Church in the West.
By Eleazar Wright [*pseud.*], Recorder. Water-
vliet, Ohio: 1834. 24 pp. 18 cm.

Contents: Title, p. [1]; "To the Reader,"
p. [2]; "The Life and Labors of Father
David Darrow Extracted from Records Kept
by Individuals," pp. 3-12; "Western Review,
No. 2. Nov. 1834," pp. [13]-24, contains an
untitled account of the last days of Father
David Darrow, January 1, 1823-June 25,
1825. A note at end, p. 24, is dated December 4, 1834. MacLean No. 370 describes
"The Life and Labors of Father David
Darrow" as a 12-page separate with the same
imprint. A manuscript note on the front
cover of the Williams College copy (Williams-

town, Mass.): No. 2 Western Review Eleazar.
R. G. [?] 19. 12. 1834.
MacLean 370. CSmH, DLC, MWiW (inc.),
NOC*, OClWHi, ODa.

966 [——] ———— [No. 3?]. Chronology.
A Memorial of Deceases at Union-Village, Ohio.
Since the Commenement [*sic*] of the Society.
[Watervliet, O.: 183–?]. Caption title. 25-34 pp.
16 cm.

The page numbers continue the *Western
Review*, No. 2, above. Except for pp. 25-26
which are reset, the pages are identical with
the corresponding pages in *Review of the
Most Important Events ...*, no. **950**. Contains a chronological list of deaths "for which
we are indebted chiefly to brother Daniel
Miller," p. 25, The earliest death recorded
is April 11, 1807; the latest death, June 2,
1831, is numbered 194, followed by two unnumbered entries, i.e. [195-196].
Sabin 97882. DLC, MWiW*, NN.

967 [——] ———— [No. 4?]. Deceases Continued, from 197. [Watervliet, O.: 1834?].
Caption title. [33]-56 pp. 14½ cm.

Page 54 is misnumbered 55. Contents: "...
Deceases continued, from 197," pp. [33]-34
(deaths recorded, Union Village, Oct. 1, 1831-
Oct. 5, 1834, numbered [198]-119 [i.e., 219].
Watervliet deaths numbered 1-36, Nov. 20,
1807-July 1, 1832); "A Brief Memorial of
Mother Ruth Farrington," pp. 35-36; "The
Western Review Continued," pp. 37-40;
"Review, Part II," Chaps. I-III, pp. [41]-56.
Chap. I, p. [41] begins: "We now resume our
memorandum of important events ... relating
to the establishment of the Chh. and terminat-
ing with a general list of deceases ..." Restricted use is indicated in a footnote, p. 40, and
also the implication that only enough copies
were printed to serve "official characters."
"N.B. It is to be hoped that any official character, who may be trusted with a copy of
this Review, will see that it fall not into improper hands, and that there be no evil sur-
misings concerning it." Sabin 105575 describes a copy of *A Little Selection*, no. **937**,
that (following p. 20) contains pp. 41-56 of
the *Western Review*, Pt. 2, Chap. I-III, 1834,
"evidently so issued by the author."

DLC, MPB, MWA (pp. 34–40), MWiW*, NN.

[——] ——— [Nos. 5–6]. No copy or record of publication has been located which would fill these lacunae. Among Watervliet and Union Village publications there are no reasonably likely candidates. The following item is, however, numbered "7" indicating that publication of No. 5–6 must have at least been contemplated.

968 —— ——— No. VII. A Friendly Letter to Alexander Mitchell a Solitary Christian of Eaton, Ohio: In Answer to his "Religious Circular" lately Presented to the Public. Dated June 1837. Written at his Request; and for the better Information of Him and Others, on Some Parts of his Said Letter. By Richard M'Namer Sen. [Union Village: 1837]. Caption title. 10 pp. 19 cm.

    Contents: Letter addressed: "Esteemed Friend & quondam Brother, in the Christian Faith," dated: Union Village, July 15, 1837," p. [1]; "Preliminary. — A Pure Church Anticipated. A Revival-hymn in the Year 1801," p. [2]; Letter addressed: "Friend Alexander," dated: July 30, 1837, pp. [3]–10. A printed leaf 18.7 cm. is attached to the Williams College copy following p. 10, "For a more Ample Illustration of the Parable of the Ship take the Following Allegory . . . ." A poem of 18 stanzas printed on heavy paper. MacLean, *Life*, p. 47, confuses the date of the first letter with the printing date. Footnote, p. 10, is dated: U. V. Aug. 12, 1837. MacLean 369 (describes a variant identified as a broadside, which is probably only the first leaf of this item).
    MPB, MWiW*, OClWHi.

McNEMAR, RICHARD. *See also* Springfield (Ohio) Presbytery, no. 1328 ff.

969 McNISH, JAMES. From the West Indies. Something about the Shakers There. [n.p., 1881]. Broadside in 2 columns. 26 X 15 cm.
    A letter to Elder Evans dated: Basseterre, St. Kitts, B. West Indies, Sept. 29, 1881. About the sect of Shakers or Quakers on the Island of Nevis. Reprinted from the *Berkshire County Eagle* (Pittsfield, Mass.). Reprinted in the

Shaker Manifesto, 12 (January 1882), 15–17. CtY, MPB, MWiW*, NBuG, OClWHi.

970 Maine. Board of Agriculture. Report of the Secretary, 1857. Augusta, Me.: 1858.
    Report on grapes, pp. 181–87, by Henry Little, includes the Northern Muscadine grape "brought to our notice by the Shakers of New Lebanon, N.Y., which is as good as any of its class, being a native fox grape," pp. 182–83. D. C. Smith, "William A. Drew and the Maine Shakers — A Note," *Shaker Quarterly*, 7 (Spring 1967), 28–32, describes the dispute in Maine concerning the quality of the Northern Muscadine grape, *see* nos. 258, 353 ff.
    MeHi*.

971 MAINE AUCTION SERVICE GALLERY, Porter, Me. Shaker Society, Sabbathday Lake, Me. Auction [at the Maine Auction Service Gallery, Porter, Maine]. June 20, 1972. [Kezar Falls, Me.: Maine Auction Service, 1972]. Cover title. 30 pp. illus. 22 cm.
    "All items in this Auction are from the Shaker Colony at Sabbathday Lake, Maine. Exceptions will be noted . . ." p. 3. Three hundred numbered items include Shaker furniture, stoves, boxes, buckets, baskets, tinware, woodenware, bottles, a variety of other small objects, about 60 printed items, etc. An inserted addenda sheet contains 12 items, mostly printed materials. Photographs of over 60 items are by Herschel Burt. Bibliographical descriptions are by Theodore Johnson. Proceeds of the auction are intended to augment the funds for the restoration of the herb house and "to finance construction of a fire proof library facility at the Sabbathday Lake Colony." A list of the auction prices was later available to purchasers of the catalog.
    MPH, MWiW*, NOC*.

972 A Man of Kindness, to his Beast is Kind . . . [n.p., 185–?]. Broadside. 25½ X 27½ cm.
    Originally this admonition, an 8-line verse, was posted in the New Jersey barns of Robert White, a Quaker who joined the Shakers at Hancock, Mass., in 1846. It was hung in many Shaker barns at his suggestion,

see E. D. Andrews, *People Called Shakers* (no. 1767), p. 322, no. 182.
MPB, OCIWHi*.

973 ———— 18 X 23 cm.
Wall card printed on heavy glazed stock with 2 holes punched at the top. A variant of this wall card which is in a private collection has the verse printed within a double rule border, reprinted by the Shaker Museum, Old Chatham, N.Y. Another variant in the New York State Library, Albany, has "Shaker Home" printed at the foot of the card. Another copy in a private collection is printed in heavy black sans serif typeface.
MPB, MPH, OCHP, OCIWHi*.

974 MANCHESTER (ENG.). The Constables' Accounts of the Manor of Manchester . . . from the Year 1612 to the Year 1647, and from the Year 1743 to the Year 1776 . . . Ed. by J. P. Earwaker. Manchester: H. Blacklock and Co., printers. 1892. 3 vols.
Vol. 3, "From the Year 1743–1776," Introduction, p. vii, the Shakers are referred to as "a body of religious fanatics led by John Lees and his daughter Ann Lees or Lee — which came into notoriety at this time (1772–1773)." Five Shakers were apprehended on Sunday and 24 persons paid 6d each for assisting in the arrest, p. 227, July 14, 1772. Three entries for expenses for the safekeeping of the Shakers, two of whom were committed to the House of Correction, ale for 24 persons who assisted in the Shakers' apprehension, and 1s 2d paid "for drink when the Shakers was [!] brought before the Justice," p. 228, July 15, 1772. Expense for the "Jurors Baillif on prosecuting John Lees and his daughter Ann," p. 229, July 23, 1772. "John Lees and Ann Stanley were sentenced for an assault, to be imprisoned one month." A footnote identifies Ann and her father as "founders of the sect of Shakers." Bill of expenses at the Mule when Justice Mainwaring attended to examine the Shakers," p. 230, July 30, 1772. Apprehended persons were frequently detained at the Sign of the Mule until brought before a Justice. Reimbursement to the widow Shepley "for Ironwork when the Shakers were apprehended," also "expences Quelling a Mob who were beginning to pull down the House of

John Townley a Shaker," p. 235, Oct. 3, 1772. "To repairs making good the breaches at Lee's in Toadlane in order to apprehend a gang of Shakers lock't up there," p. 241, Oct. 19, 1772. "To the like apprehending and detaining James Lees whilst he could find Sureties," *ibid.*, Oct. 20, 1772. "To Ann Lees a shaker apprended [*sic*] for disturbing the Congregation in the old Church detaining her in the Prison room two days 2s maintaining her with meat and drink and her attendant," p. 256, May 30, 1773. A footnote, p. 256, states that at the Manchester July Quarter Sessions "John Townley, John Jackson, Betty Lees, and Ann Lees (Shakers) for going into Christ Church in Manchester, and there willfully and contemptuously in the Time of Divine Service disturbing the Congregation then assembled at Morning Prayer in the said Church, were severally fined Twenty Pounds each." Expenses for "attending Ann Lees two whole nights," p. 265, July 28, 1773. The names John Lees, Betty Lees, James Lees, and Nancy Lees occur in other entries, but the name Lee or Lees was common in Lancashire and no accompanying information connects these Lees with those of the same name who are known to be early Manchester Shakers. Aside from the London dispatch printed in the Virginia Gazette, November 9, 1769, describing the Shakers and their conduct, this is the earliest reference to the Shakers that has been located.
CSmH, CtY*, DLC, MB, NcD, PPB, TxU.

THE MANIFESTO. Published monthly by the United Societies. Vols. 1–29 (1871–1899). illus., music. 22–37 cm. Strictly, this title, *The Manifesto*, refers *only* to Vols. 13–29 (1883–1899) of the monthly Shaker periodical, which appeared previously under various titles. It is customary, however, to refer to the whole sequence of volumes by its last title, *The Manifesto*. Earlier titles are given below. Publication ceased with Vol. 29 (1899). This Shaker monthly was to serve as a news medium among the various communities and to provide a forum where "interested and gifted individuals, might bear testimony, and manifest their convictions, experiences, revelations and Christian sympathies, in behalf of suffering humanity . . ." In addition, it was to serve as "our principal missionary." Although *The*

Manifesto was devoted primarily to Shaker religious beliefs, details about the diverse interests and activities of the Shakers, their domestic life, and their history are found scattered through the original articles, editorials, diaries, reprinted Shaker publications, historical accounts and contemporary news of communities, book notices, practical agricultural and household notes, advertisements of Shaker and other products for sale, death notices, etc. Shaker music and poetry were among the monthly's most popular features. Most of this material, however, is not easily accessible. The table of contents and annual indexes (Vols. 16–29, 1886–1899), are inadequate, and in accordance with Shaker custom, personal names are generally avoided even in the indexes. The AMS Press, New York, has reprinted the complete run of *The Manifesto*, 1973.

975 *The Shaker.* Vols. 1–2 (1871–1872). Published under the Direction of the Mt. Lebanon Bishopric at Shakers [Watervliet] N.Y. Editor: G. A. Lomas. Albany, N.Y.: Printed by Weed and Parsons, music. 33 cm.

The Shaker was advertised as "the most radically religious monthly in the world." Since wide circulation among the "world's people" was encouraged, it was recognized that Shaker music would have to be printed in a form in general use. The many difficulties involved in changing from the Shaker letter notation, written without staff, to conventional or modern notation were described by Elder Henry C. Blinn over 20 years later in *The Manifesto*, Vol. 25 (January 1895), 14–15. "Faith's Vision" was the only music in the first volume, a few pieces of music were printed in the second volume, and thereafter, Shaker hymns and songs were a monthly feature, *see* no. **476**.
MacLean 109. Ct, DLC, ICN, IU, MB, MHarF, MPH, MWiW*, N, NN, NOC, Nh, OClWHi, WHi.

976 —— Circular. [New Lebanon, N.Y.: 1870]. Caption title. [4] pp. 20 cm.

Letter addressed: Dearly Beloved and Gospel Friends, and signed: *The Ministry, New Lebanon, N.Y.* A Prospectus describing the new monthly periodical to be called *The Shaker,*

with a statement of policy and subscription terms. Subscriptions are solicited and a sample of the periodical is accompanied by an appeal for support. It is stated that "subscriptions ought soon to amount to *five* and even *ten* thousand copies ... Mt. Lebanon Bishopric proposes to subscribe to 2000 copies."
MacLean 379. DLC, MWiW*, OClWHi, OHi, RPB.

977 —— —— Extra. [Watervliet, N.Y.: 1872?]. 4 pp. 32 cm.

Printed in 3 columns. A dialogue, "The 'Orthodox' Deacon and the Shaker," pp. 1–3 (center column). Advertisements throughout with an explanation that the *Extra* is an experiment, with each advertiser described in one paragraph, p. 4.
OClWHi*.

978 —— —— Most Radically Religious Monthly in the World. Organ of the Societies of People, called Shakers .... Address G. A. Lomas. Shakers [Watervliet], N.Y.: [Albany, N.Y.:] 1871?]. Broadside. 19 X 14 cm.

Advertising handbill (29 lines) which includes a statement of Shaker doctrine and beliefs, and the price of the monthly.
N*.

979 —— "The Shaker" issued Monthly by the Shakers. Containing Expositions of Shaker Life and Principles; with their Arguments in Favor of their Unpopular, but Truly Christian Life ... G. A. Lomas, Resident Editor. Shakers, Albany, N.Y.: [1871?]. Broadside. 27 X 34½ cm.
OClWHi*.

980 *Shaker and Shakeress.* Vols. 3–5 (1873–1875). Published by the United Society at Mt. Lebanon, N.Y. Editor: F. W. Evans; Editress: Antoinette Doolittle. Publisher: G. A. Lomas. Shakers [Watervliet], N.Y. Albany, N.Y.: Printed by Weed and Parsons, 1873–1875. music. 33 cm.

An extra unnumbered issue, August 19, 1873, "Society Gathering of the Junior Order of Believers, of Mt. Lebanon, in the Pine Grove, Canaan, Columbia County, N.Y.," is included in Vol. 3. A devastating fire in the Watervliet, N.Y., Shaker community had caused Elder

George A. Lomas to withdraw as editor in order to direct the necessary rebuilding and repairs. The change in editorial policy is described: "Agreeable to our fundamental idea of a *duality* in the Divine government of the universe, and also in our Society organizations, *The Shaker* will henceforth contain a department edited by Eldress Antoinette Doolittle, open to contributions from the Sisterhood of our Order . . ." and to other females. Receipts and expenditures for 1873, 1874, 5:16.
MacLean 109. Ct, DLC, ICN, IU, MB, MHarF, MPH, MWiW*, N, NN, NOC, Nh, NjPT, OHi, OClWHi, WHi.

981 —— Extra. [Mt. Lebanon, N.Y.: 1873?]. [2] pp. 34 cm.
    Printed in 3 columns. "The Church and the Old Gentleman" (poem by Oliver Prentiss), center column. "This Extra is issued by the Editor at his discretion. Only [advertisements of] firms of undoubted merit accepted." For terms apply to F. W. Evans, Mt. Lebanon, N.Y., or G. A. Lomas, Shakers [Watervliet], N.Y."
    OClWHi*.

982 *The Shaker.* Vols. 6–7 (1876–1877). Official Monthly Published by the United Societies. Editor: G. A. Lomas, Shakers [Watervliet], N.Y. Publisher: N. A. Briggs, Shaker Village [Canterbury], N.H. Albany, N.Y.: Printed by Weed and Parsons, Vol. 6 (1876); Concord, N.H.: J. H. Pearsons, Vol. 7 (1877). music. 33–36 cm.
    Vol. 7, nos. 7–9, are misnumbered Vol. 6. A greeting to readers in the January 1876 issue explains that, "Though returning to its original title, it would be understood to amplify rather than detract dual principles in all things which the name *Shaker* could imply . . ." A proud note is found on p. 5 of the January 1877 issue: "The music . . . is the production of SHAKER SOULS; the typography the work of SHAKER hands; and we are proud to feel, that it will be appreciated the more, when the fact is known. We feel almost warranted in challenging better typography than is set by our dear Shaker sisters." With the approval of the Mount Lebanon Ministry, the editor and

publisher proposed "changing the present large-quarto form [to one] somewhat similar to the well-known *Harper's Monthly* and *American Phrenological Journal.*" It is explained that the change will prevent "wear and soiling" and that it will offer more "suitability for binding."
MacLean 109. Ct, DLC, ICN, IU, MB, MHarF, MPH, MWiW*, N, NN, NOC, Nh, NjPT, OHi, OClWHi, WHi.

983 —— Circular Letter. [Mt. Lebanon, N.Y.: 1876]. Caption title. [2] pp. 20½ cm.
    Addressed: Beloved Gospel Friends, and signed: *Ministry of Mt. Lebanon, N.Y.* "Partly owing to the default of some families, and especially of one entire Society in timely paying in their quota, per capita for the support of the paper, and some difficulties, attending the enterprise, our Canterbury Friends deem it best not to continue to print and publish it at that place." An award of a Groves & Baker Sewing Machine and $10.00 worth of attachments is offered to any Shaker group that sends in forty new subscriptions.
    OClWHi*.

984 —— ———— Shaker Village, Mer. Co., N.H.: 1876. Broadside in 2 columns. 31 × 21 cm.
    Signed: *N. A. Briggs, March 29, 1876.* "The Beloved Ministry now ask that we still continue the publication of the paper for the year to come, and also to assume the burdens of correspondence in relation to the same." Questions follow with a request for responses from each Society.
    OClWHi*.

985 —— ———— Shaker Village, N.H.: 1876. Broadside in 2 columns. 24 × 20 cm.
    Signed: *N. A. Briggs, July 26, 1876.* Response to the letter of March 29th is acknowledged "with real pleasure," and a compromise arrangement for the year 1877 is submitted for approval.
    OClWHi*.

986 —— Circular. Shaker Village, N.H.: 1877. Cover title. [4] pp. 23½ cm.
    "To Believers" signed: *G. A. Lomas, N. A.*

Briggs. "Circular Letter" signed: *Ministry of Mount Lebanon.* Both are dated: April 26, 1877. A hymn with words and music, "Praise the Lord," pp. [3-4]. The communications concern the change in the size of *The Shaker* with Vol. 8 (1878). This circular is a sample of the proposed size. Believers are requested to contribute 80¢ per member for every society or family, and the subscription terms for Believers are described.
MWA, OClWHi*.

987 —— [Financial Statement of *The Shaker,* 1876, 1877]. [East Canterbury, N.H.: 1878]. Broadside in 2 columns. 24 × 24 cm.

Shows the amounts spent for paper, printing, use of type, supplies, travel, postage, freight, etc. Receipts include "Cash from Believers as pro rata tax" in the amounts of $1640.20 for 1876, and $1137.85 for 1877.
MWiW*, OClWHi.

988 *The Shaker Manifesto.* Vols. 8-12 (1878-1882). Official Monthly Published by the United Societies. Editor: G. A. Lomas, Shakers [Watervliet], N.Y., Vols. 8-11 (1878-1881); H. C. Blinn, Shaker Village [Canterbury], N.H., Vol. 12 (1882). Publisher: N. A. Briggs, Shaker Village [Canterbury], N.H., Vol. 8 (1878); G. B. Avery, Shakers [Watervliet], N.Y., Vols. 9-11 (1879-1881); H. C. Blinn, Shaker Village [Canterbury], N.H., Vol. 12 (1882). Printed by J. H. Pearsons, Concord, N.H., Vol. 8 (1878); Weed and Parsons, Albany, N.Y., Vols. 9-11 (1879-1881); Sleeper and Evans, Concord, N.H., Vol. 12 (1882). illus. music. 22½ cm.

Throughout Volume 8 (1878) the front covers carry the statement, "Published and printed at Shaker Village, N.H." This statement is misleading and is at variance with Elder Blinn's account in *The Manifesto,* Vol. 25 (January 1895), 15, where he states, "In 1877-78 'The Shaker' was printed in the office of J. H. Pearsons of Concord. In 1878 the publication took the name of 'The Shaker Manifesto' ... The compositors were now the sisters of our home in Canterbury, while the printing continued to be done by the firm [J. H. Pearsons] in Concord." In view of this statement and Blinn's later statement about the necessity of installing the printing equip-

ment required to handle the monthly in 1887, it must be assumed that the type for Vol. 8 (1878) was set at Canterbury, N.H., by Shaker sisters, but that the actual printing was done by J. H. Pearsons in Concord. Printing the Shaker monthly was repeated in this manner for Vols. 12-13 (1882-1883). A printing press was being operated at Canterbury at this time, but in order to turn out several thousands of copies of the periodical each month, additional equipment would indeed have been necessary. *See also In Memoriam Elder Henry C. Blinn* (no. 830), pp. 33-35. During the three-year period (Vols. 9-11, 1879-1881) that the printing was done by Weed and Parsons in Albany, N.Y., the sisters at Mount Lebanon set the type for the music which appeared in every issue. This was noted in the *Shaker Manifesto,* 9 (February 1879), 46. The title of the monthly has been changed; the size has been reduced to octavo; the text has been increased to 24 pages, and additional pages have often been allowed for 8-10 pages of advertisements of Shaker products and "world" products which met Shaker approval. Views of various Shaker communities appeared on the front covers; portraits were not accepted.
MacLean 109. Ct, DLC, ICN, IU, MB, MHarF, MPH, MWiW*, N, NN, NOC, Nh, NjPT, OHi, OClWHi, WHi.

989 —— [Financial Statement]. For 1878 [Canterbury, N.H.: 1878]. Broadside in 2 columns. 24 × 24 cm.

A short financial statement for 1879 and 1880 was printed in the *Shaker Manifesto,* 10 (December 1880), 278.
OClWHi* (with explanatory manuscript notations by the editor).

990 *The Manifesto.* Vols. 13-29 (1883-1899). Published by the United Societies. Editor: H. C. Blinn, Shaker Village [Canterbury], N.H. Publisher: No name appears until A. Y. Cochran's Vol. 14 (October 1884) - 19 (June 1889), when the masthead directs that all communications be sent to H. C. Blinn. Printed by Sleeper and Evans, Concord, N.H., Vols. 13-16 (1883-1886); printed by the Shakers, Canterbury, N.H., Vols. 17-29 (1887-1899). illus., music. 23 cm.

The November and December issues of Vol.

17 are misnumbered Vol. 18. The former title, the *Shaker Manifesto*, appeared on the covers of Vol. 13 (1883), but *The Manifesto* appeared on the masthead. Annual indexes were provided for Vols. 16-29 (1886-1899). Elder Blinn, the editor, wrote in *The Manifesto*, 25 (January 1895), 15, "From 1882 till 1887 the types were arranged into pages and taken to the office of Sleeper and Evans in Concord, N.H. to be printed." All management activities were moved to Canterbury in 1887, and "the printing office was fitted up with the necessary machinery, and when 'The Manifesto' was ready for the mail, at the close of the month, we were much pleased with our own success." Thereafter all phases of the publication and printing of *The Manifesto* were carried out by the Shakers at Canterbury, N.H. The changeover from commercial printers was not noticeable. Shaker printing presented a professional appearance with good color and impressions. Views of various Shaker communities appeared among the text pages. A mild form of simplified spelling was introduced in Vol. 27 (1897). Consequently, words such as "wished," spelled "wisht," should not be mistaken for misprints. The only portrait which ever appeared in the monthly was that of Elder Joseph Slingerland, Union Village, O., in the October 1897 issue. A steadily decreasing number of advertisements were appearing in *The Manifesto*, the text was shortened to 16 pages, and no music appeared after Vol. 25 (1895). In early 1896 it was announced that *The Manifesto* would be discontinued, but publication continued until a later proposal to close publication after 1899 found a reluctant acceptance. MacLean 109. Ct, DLC, MB, MHarF, MPH, MWiW*, N, NN, NOC, Nh, NjPT, OClWHi, WHi.

991 —— Circular to Believers. [Mt. Lebanon, N.Y.: 1885]. Caption title. [2] pp. 26 X 17½ cm.
   Addressed: Beloved Brethren and Sisters. Signed and dated: *In kindest love to all our Zion, Ministry of New Lebanon, Columbia Co., N.Y., July 27th, 1885.* Reference is made to a "former circular, relative to the

continuance or discontinuance of our *'Manifesto'*." The consensus indicates that "the best means available ... of presenting the testimony of Christ's Second Appearing before the world is to continue the publication of the *'Manifesto'*."
MacLean 380. MWiW*, NN, OClWHi.

992 —— Circular Letter. [Mt. Lebanon, N.Y.: 1887]. Broadside. 23 X 16 cm.
   Addressed: Dearly Beloved Brethren and Sisters. Signed and dated: *Ministry of New Lebanon, Columbia Co., N.Y., Jan. 20th, 1887.* Concerns "the delinquency of some families and societies in forwarding their quota of assessment to the publisher" of *The Manifesto*, and suggestions for printing the paper more cheaply and lowering the assessment.
OClWHi*.

MARSHALL, MARY. *See* Dyer, Mary, no. 530 ff.
   After Mary Dyer's divorce from Joseph Dyer, she resumed her maiden name, Mary Marshall. Her notoriety was gained, however, and her books were published under the name Mary Dyer, the name by which she is still generally known.

993 MASSACHUSETTS (COLONY). Laws, Statutes, *etc.* The Acts and Resolves of the Province of Massachusetts Bay ... with Historical and Explanatory Notes ... Boston: Wright & Potter Printing Co., 1869-1922. 21 vols.
   A petition for a special order "to Chuse another Constable" from the Selectmen of the Town of Hancock, Mass., addressed to "The Honnourable [*sic*] Council and House of Representatives of the State of Massachusetts," Sept. 7, 1780. In March 1779, Hezekiah Osborn had been reappointed Treasurer and Constable by the Hancock Selectmen, but he "has of late fell into So gross a delusion: in Religious Matters with a number of others in this; and in New York State: that they Seem Totally to Deny all Civil Authority; and Rule: and Intirely refuse to give their Assistance in any Publick way whatever, we hauve had two Town Meetings on the Account." The committee of the House of Representatives

that considered the petition notes that "It is not unlikely that he [Hezekiah Osborn] had become a follower of Ann Lee, who about that time, had made many converts in that region." V:1441-42. Hezekiah Osborn was one of the earliest members of the Church Family at Hancock Shaker Village, Pittsfield, Mass.
M*.

994 MASSACHUSETTS (STATE). BOARD OF EDUCATION. Abstract of the Massachusetts School Returns, for 1840-41. Boston: Dutton and Wentworth, 1841. 328 pp. (Pt. II of the Annual Report, separately paged.)

The Shirley, Mass., School Committee reports that District 7, "wholly composed of Shakers," has refused to allow the customary teacher examination and the visit of the School Committee. The Shakers were warned that their determination "seemed to be an act of resistance ... against the laws of the Commonwealth, and that it might lead to consequences much more serious than they supposed. The [Shaker] answer was 'that the matter had been well considered,—that they had no complaint to make against the State, the town, or the committee; but they were a peculiar people, differing, in their notions and habits, from the rest of the world, and they wished their school to be separate and entirely under their own control'," pp. 70-71. See also no. 770. In the returns for Harvard, Mass., the School Committee reports that there has been no winter school under their superintendance in the district "entirely constituted of the Shaker family," and that Abel Jewett has informed the Committee that the Shaker School "would no longer be subject to the same regulations as other schools in the town." It is explained in a footnote that the Shakers "have a new 'gift' or, what is more probable, have received an edict from the 'higher powers' . . . This edict requires them to perpetuate a kind of educational nullification . . ." pp. 99-100.
M*, MB, MH, MHi.

995 —— Fifth Annual Report ... together with the Fifth Annual Report of the Secretary [Horace Mann] ... Boston: Dutton and Wentworth, 1842. 135 pp.

Horace Mann, who was largely responsible for the secularization of Massachusetts public schools, expresses concern over the withdrawal of the Harvard and Shirley Shaker communities from the provisions of the general school law (see no. 994), and the consequences inherent in weakening the "universal interest of education with those of particular religious sects." He discusses the special interests of other homogeneous groups and warns that "If a difference of opinion, on collateral subjects, were to lead to a secession, and to exclusive educational establishments among us, it is obvious that all multiplication of power which is now derived from union and concert of action would be lost." Pp. 66-69. See also no. 770.
M*, MB, MH, MHi.

996 MASSACHUSETTS. GENERAL COURT. HOUSE. Journal, Vol. 2 (May 1781-May 1782). Ms. Massachusetts State Library Archives.

"Sent up for concurrence. That Petition of James Whittaker and William Lees relative to the ill treatment the people called Shakers, have received, is read and Ordered that the Petitioners have leave to withdraw their Petition," entry for Feb. 22, 1782, p. 601. This is the first of many petitions and memorials presented by the Shakers to state legislatures requesting redress of grievances. Account of Shaker persecutions at this period have not recorded this petition which was undoubtedly intended to terminate the persecution of Ann Lee and her missionary companions who were active in the Harvard and Shirley areas at this time. Since little or no public sympathy for the Shakers existed, the petition would have received negligible support in the General Court. Consequently the petitioners were permitted to withdraw it, and thus avoid embarrassment. See no. 1804. The Massachusetts legislative journals for this period have not yet been printed.
M*.

997 —— Journal. Vol. 9 (May 1788-May 1789). Ms. Massachusetts State Archives.

A Petition from "Daniel Goodrich (Hancock, Mass.) and others of the religious Sect Called Shakers praying to be exempt from military duty to which they were conscientiously

opposed," November 10, 1788, p. 192. Read several times and passed to be engrossed, p. 216. This is the first of many Shaker petitions or memorials to various state legislatures asking exemption from military service on the grounds that their religious beliefs forbid such service.
M*.

998 MASSACHUSETTS. Laws, Statutes, etc. "An Act for Regulating, Governing, and Training the Militia of this Commonwealth," Mass. Stat. (1809) Ch. 108.

"Every person of the religious denominations of Quakers and Shakers, who shall, on or before the first Tuesday of May, annually, produce a certificate to the commanding officer of the company within whose bounds such Quaker or Shaker resides; such certificates, signed by two or more elders . . . and countersigned by the clerk of the society with which such Quaker or Shaker meets for religious worship" may be exempted from military duty. The form of the certificate follows," Sect. 1. "The certificate must conform with the statutory model, or exemption from military duty may not be granted." This statute, with slight changes, governed the exemption of Shakers from military duty in Massachusetts into the 20th century.
M*.

999 —— "An Act Respecting Public Worship and Religious Freedom," Mass. Stats. (1811) Ch. 6.

Specifies how membership in a religious society is to be certified (see also no. 1912), sec. 2. Provision for unincorporated religious societies to have power to manage gifts, to elect suitable trustees, to prosecute and sue for any right vested in such societies, sec. 3. Popularly known as the "Religious Freedom Act."
M*.

1000 —— Acts and Resolves Passed by the General Court in the year 1791-1792. Boston: Wright & Potter Printing Co., State Printers, 1801. 515 pp.

"Resolve on the Petition of Amos Buttrick,"

March 8, 1792, Chap. 150, pp. 523-34. Shaker Buttrick's petition was in the form of a letter addressed to the Governor, Senate, and House, dated at Shirley [Mass.], February 21st, 1792 (a.l.s. Massachusetts State Archives). He described his conscientious scruples about receiving a disability pension, 15 shillings per month, due to an injury and loss of the sight of his right eye in the battle of White Plains while serving in the Massachusetts Militia, "commanded by Eleazer Brook, Esq. in Captain Simon Hunt's Company in the year 1776." Because of his own personal conviction and Shaker practices, Buttrick expresses a profound desire to return to the state the pension payments he has already received, and that hereafter the pension "be ever null and void." It is an eloquent letter which refutes charges that the Shakers were pragmatic pacifists. Since the legislature had made no administrative provision for handling such highly unlikely requests, it was necessary that the General Court pass a special resolution to enable Amos Buttrick to return to the treasury pension payments already received. A Treasury Office receipt (No. 10496), Mar. 12, 1792, shows that Buttrick returned £82 7s 8d. See also A. White and L. Taylor, Shakerism (no. 1447), p. 178.
M*.

1001 —— Acts and Resolves of the Legislature of Massachusetts in the Years 1839, 1840, 1841, 1842. Boston: Dutton & Wentworth, 1842. 642 pp.

"Resolve on the Petition of Joseph Wicker and Joseph Patten," approved by the Governor, Jan. 27, 1841, Chap. 5, p. 412. As a result of their petition, Wicker and Patten, members of the Hancock Shaker community, were paid $275 from public moneys "for services rendered and expenses incurred by said Society [of Shakers], in arresting one Lewis Wheeler, charged with the crime of larceny."
M*.

1002 —— Extracts from the Revised Statutes of Massachusetts. Communicated from Seth Y. Wells of New Lebanon, N.Y. to a Friend at Union Village, O., Feb. 16,

1837. [n.p., n.d.]. [2] pp. 17½ cm.
Laws governing property held by religious
societies. This appears to have been printed
by R. McNemar.
OClWHi*.

1003 MASSACHUSETTS. SUPREME JUDI-
CIAL COURT, SUFFOLK SS. Roxalana L.
Grosvenor vs. United Society of Believers.
Mary F. Grosvenor vs. same. Plaintiff's brief.
[Boston: 1871]. [5] pp. 25½ cm.
Plaintiffs were expelled from the Harvard,
Mass., Society, July 26, 1865, and the writ is
dated July 10, 1871. *See* nos. 1307, 1698, 3795.
M, MH-L, MWiW*.

1004 [MATHERS, JENNIE], *comp.* Receipts
as Used by the Shaker Sisters. Sabbathday Lake,
Me.: [1933]. Cover title. 1 p.l. 33 pp. 17½ cm.
T. E. Johnson states that this was printed by
Earl Campbell (Sabbathday Lake, Me.) in
1933, and edited by Sister Jennie Mathers,
"Random Notes," Maine Library Association
Bulletin, 22 (February 1961), 20.
KyBgW, NOC*, NSyU.

1005 [——], *ed.* Shaker Poems. Printed at
Sabbathday Lake, Maine: [by Earl Campbell,
1933]. [11] leaves processed. 21 cm.
Stapled in blue paper cover (unfolded separate sheets). "Just a few poems written by
Shaker Sisters and put in this little booklet
so that you can have an inexpensive remembrance of the Shakers." Contains 10 poems,
ed. by Sister Jennie Mathers. Cf. T. E. Johnson, "Random Notes," Maine Library Association *Bulletin*, 22 (February 1961), 20.
CtY, MHarF*, MWA.

1006 [MEACHAM, JOSEPH] A Concise State-
ment of the Principles of the Only True Church,
according to the Gospel of the Present Appear-
ance of Christ. As Held to and Practiced upon
by the True Followers of the Living Saviour, at
New Lebanon, &c. Together with a Letter from
James Whittaker, Minister of the Gospel in this
Day of Christ's Second Appearing—to his
Natural Relations in England. Dated October 9th,
1785. Printed at Bennington, Vermont: By
Haswell & Russell, 1790. 24 pp. 12 cm.
This is considered to be the first printed

publication of The United Society, and the
first printed statement of Shaker theology.
The author's name does not appear in this
edition, but authorship of *A Concise Statement*, pp. [3]–17, has been generally attributed by the Shakers to Joseph Meacham.
James Whittaker's letter, pp. 17–24 is signed
on p. 24. *A Concise Statement* was reprinted
in 1812 from a ms. copy given by Benjamin
S. Youngs in late 1798 to Thomas Brown. He
later included it in his *Account of the People
Called Shakers* (no. 114), pp. 33–42, where
he refers to this work as "written by their
esteemed Elder Joseph Meacham," p. 32. *A
Concise Statement* was reprinted in *The
Shaker*, 1 (January, February 1871), 8, 16,
where at the end, it is signed: "*J. M., 1798*,"
and with the title "The Four Dispensations,"
followed by: Elder Joseph Meacham, *The
Manifesto*, 16 (January–February 1886),
1–3, 25–27. The New York Public Library
copy of *A Concise Statement* has ms. changes
marked by the Ministry. These were made to
be incorporated in the 1900 edition (no.
1010), and show the changes in Shaker doctrine over the intervening century.
MacLean 491. Evans 22664 and 23082.
Sabin 97884. McCorison 181. DeWint, DLC,
MPB (pp. 17–24), MWA, MWiW*, NN, NOC,
OClWHi.

1007 [——] ——— Principles of the/ Only
True Church, according to the Gospel of/ the
Present Appearance of Christ, as Held to/ and
Practised upon by the True Followers of/ the
Living Saviour, at New-Labanon, &c./ By James
Whittaker,/ Minister of the Gospel in this Day
of Christ's Second Appearance./ *Dated October
the 9th, 1785./* [n.p., n.d.]. Caption title. 8 pp.
21 × 13½ cm.
A unique copy of an unrecorded edition
acquired in 1972 by the Kentucky Library,
Western Kentucky University, Bowling Green,
Ky. The place of publication, printer's name,
and date of publication of this Shaker item
remain unidentified in spite of considerable
research and extensive inquiries. "By James
Whittaker" in the caption title appears to
identify him as the author of *A Concise Statement*. Aside from the statement in Thomas
Brown's *Account* (no. 114), p. 32, attribution

of authorship to Joseph Meacham was not
made in print until the 1847 Canterbury,
N.H., edition, 57 years after publication. The
New Gloucester, Me., edition also published
in 1847, omits any mention of Joseph
Meacham as author. Elder Meacham's authorship is, however, an almost certain attribution, but it has never been documented. Evans
19386 records an otherwise unknown edition
under Whittaker with the title precisely as it
appears here, including the misspelling "New-
Labanon," and supplies the imprint: [Wor-
cester: Printed by Isaiah Thomas? 1785], and
describes it as 18 pp. 12 mo. Clearly the
item recorded above is 8 pp. and 8 vo. It is
possible that still another edition of *A Concise Statement* which corresponds to Evans'
description remains to be discovered. The
American Antiquarian Society has not identified the printing of the edition recorded
here as that of Isaiah Thomas, but has reported that Thomas did not advertise *A
Concise Statement* in his *Massachusetts Spy.*
The date of printing has been identified as
"before 1800" and also "not after 1810" by
those who have examined photocopies of
this item. In this edition *A Concise Statement,*
pp. [1]-5, is followed by James Whittaker's
undated letter, pp. 6-8, although no reference
to the letter occurs in the title (cf. no. **1006**).
The letter, signed: *James Whittaker,* on p. 8,
is followed by a 14-line untitled poem. A
ms. notation occurs at the foot of the page:
*Chrischene Wait s book geven hur by an old
pedler in the yar* . The last word may have
been "yard." If it were intended to be "year"
the binder has probably cropped a date. The
paper does not contain a watermark.
KyBgW*.

1008 —— ———— Principles of the Only
True Church of Christ. By Joseph Meacham.
Together with a Letter from James Whittaker,
to his Natural Relations in England. Printed at
Bennington, Vt: By Haswell & Russell, 1790.
Reprinted in the United Society, Canterbury,
N.H.: 1847. Cover title. 23 pp. 10½ cm.
The first edition with Joseph Meacham's
name in the title. "Introduction," p. [2],
"A short information of what we believe of

the dispensations of God's grace to fallen
man."
MacLean 200. Sabin 79884. CSmH, MHarF,
MSaE, MWA, MWiW*, NN, NOC, OClWHi.

1009 [——] ———— Printed at Bennington,
Vermont: By Haswell & Russell, 1790. Reprinted in the United Society, New Gloucester,
Me.: 1847. Cover title. 26 pp. 16 cm.
Minor changes in title and text. "Advertisement to the second edition," p. [3], "In
republishing this little work it is the design
of the publishers to preserve a *true copy* of
the first printed publication, ever issued by
the United Society, very few of which copies
are now extant." "A Letter from James Whittaker," pp. 19-26. Erratum (note) pasted on
recto of blank page following p. 26. T. E.
Johnson, "Random Notes," Maine Library
Association *Bulletin*, 22 (February 1961), 18,
states that this was printed by Deacon James
Holmes.
MacLean 199. Sabin 97884. CSmH, DeWint,
MHi, MWA, MWiW*, MeB, NBuG, NN, NOC,
NjPT, NSyU, OClWHi.

1010 [——] ———— Reprinted 1900. [Mt.
Lebanon, N.Y.?:] Cover title. 16 pp. 14½ cm.
Title with minor changes is preceded by the
word "[Dispensations]." "Addenda, by A. G.
Hollister," pp. 15-16, contains brief biog-
raphies of Whittaker and Meacham. *See*
annotation no. **1007**.
MacLean 201. Sabin 97884. CtY, MH, MHi,
MPB, MWA, MWiW*, N, NBuG, NN, NOC.

1011 [——] ———— [Sabbathday Lake, Me.:
c 1963 by the United Society.] 14 pp. 21½ cm.
(Mother's work series, No. 2.)
Facsimile title page of the 1st edition, Bennington, Vt., 1790, follows p. 155. "First
Shaker Imprint," [Foreword], pp. [3]-4.
Reprinted from the *Shaker Quarterly*, 2
(Winter 1962), 144-55, where it is observed in the foreword that "The simplicity and openness of his [Meacham's]
approach is much more in the spirit of
the recorded utterances of Mother Ann,
Father William and Father James than is
that of his brother John, who with David

Darrow and Benjamin Seth Young[s], co-authored *Testimonies of Christ's Second Appearing* eighteen years later."
MPH, MWA, MWiW*, NOC.

1012 Meditation for the New-Year. 1834. Canterbury?: 1833]. Broadside. 12½ X 17½ cm.
Poem of 6 stanzas.
OClWHi*.

1013 ... Melbourn Nut [Registry No.] 18731. Bred by Robert Bonner, New York. Foaled June 15th, 1888. [Enfield, Conn.: 188–?] Broadside. 28 X 17 cm.
Pedigree describing four generations of horses in his ancestry. Present owner, R. H. Van Deusen, Shaker Station, Conn. *See also* no. 1094.
OClWHi*.

1014 Memorial. To the Honorable [blank space]. [n.p., 1863]. Caption title. 8 pp. 23 cm.
Begins: "The undersigned, in behalf of the Order of the United Society of Believers, or Shakers, composed of eighteen distinct communities and located in seven of the states of the Union, respectfully ask for exemption from service ... under the act entitled, An Act for Enrolling and Calling out the National Forces ...'" This Memorial is designed for general Shaker use. No community is indicated, blank space in the salutation allows for the appropriate name to be supplied, and blank space at the end, p. 8, provides for the addition of signatures, date, and place. Civil War draft legislation, approved Mar. 3, 1863, did not exempt Shakers. Here the petitioners give reasons, under 6 headings, why Shakers should be exempted from the draft. It is pointed out that the government has realized an aggregate sum of $439,733 because Shakers who served in the Revolution and the War of 1812 had not drawn their pensions or bounty lands. The facts are given in Schedule A (which did not accompany the copy described here). It is stated in a ms. note on the Shaker Museum (Old Chatham, N.Y.) copy that "this Memorial was drawn up and published by Lockwood Data, private secretary to Governor [Horatio] Seymour of N.Y. Gratuitous,

as he thought the conscription was wronging the Believers." The two introductory paragraphs of this Memorial are written almost verbatim in the ms. "Memorial" in the Lincoln papers (no. 1401), where it is signed: *F. W. Evans, Benjamin Gates.*
MacLean 374. MWA, MiU–C, NN, NOC*, OClWHi, WHi.

1015 The Memorial of James Chapman, to the Respectable Legislature of the State of New York, Now in Session. [Albany: 1817]. Caption title. 8 pp. 21½ cm.
Signed: *James Chapman, Albany, 24th March, 1817.* A refutation of the charges made by his wife, Eunice Chapman. *See* nos. 448 and 449. "The Shakers also circulated a memorial from James Chapman giving his side of the family quarrel (i.e., Eunice Chapman's efforts to recover her children and obtain a divorce), but this document proved something of a boomerang, since its appearance gave the lie to the Shaker claim that they did not know where James and the children were hiding," N. M. Blake, "Eunice Against the Shakers" (no. 3088), 368–69. Reprinted in R. McNemar, *The Other Side of the Question* (no. 946), pp. 22–29. Cf. no. 1380.
Shaw 40445. MB, MWA, OClWHi*.

1016 ... The Memorial of Stanton Buckingham, Stephen Wells, Justice Harwood, and Chauncey Copley, Trustees of the United Society of Believers Called Shakers, Residing at Watervliet in the County of Albany, most Respectfully Represents, on Behalf of the Society and by Their Direction ... [Albany: 1845]. Broadside. 33 X 20 cm.
At head of title: To the Senate of the State of New York: Dated at end: Watervliet, March 18, 1845. The Shakers' reply to accusations of immoral practices made against them on the occasion of the introduction of a bill which would have prevented the binding of minor children to the Society. The Shakers believed the proposed legislation had been provoked by the case of Sarah Ogden, whose mother, Margaret Ogden, brought suit for compensation for the services of her daughter during the time she remained with the Shakers. A brief history of the circumstances of their

guardianship of Sarah Ogden is included. DLC, MPB, N*, NjPT, OClWHi.

1017 The Memorial of the Society of People of Canterbury, in the County of Rockingham, and Enfield, in the County of Grafton, Commonly Called Shakers. [n.p., 1818]. Cover title. 13 pp. 18 cm.

Signed on behalf of the Society: *Francis Winkley, Nathaniel Draper* [and 7 others]. The New Hampshire law of 1808 exempted Shakers from military duty and all equivalents thereof. This Memorial objects to an amendment to a pending bill for regulating the militia which would require every Shaker and Quaker between the ages of 18 and 45 to pay an annual sum of $2.00. The Shakers plead their claim to exemption from military duty or any equivalent on the basis of their constitutional rights of conscience, and present a statement of the principles and reasons for their conscientious aversion to bearing arms, hiring substitutes, or paying fines. The statement, p. [1], "as this postponement has continued to the present session, June, 1818," indicates that the Memorial was printed in 1818. The Memorial was reprinted in Lillian Schlissel *ed., Conscience in America* (no. 2673), pp. 73-79. MacLean 375 (attributed to John Whitcher). Sabin 79714 and 47632. Shaw 45694 and 49403 (with note: Though credited by N.Y.P.L. cataloger to Enfield, N.H., it was likely printed at Andover, N.H. in 1819). DLC, MB, MHarF, MPB, MPH, MWA, MWiW*, NN, NNC, NOC, NhD, NHi, OCl, OClWHi, WHi.

The Memorial of the Society of People of New Lebanon, in the County of Columbia ... Commonly Called Shakers, to the Legislature of New York. New Lebanon: 1815. 20 pp. 8°.

No copy located. This publication is described in MacLean's *Bibliography*, no. 499, in the section, "Shaker Publications not owned by the Author," pp. 63-66, where the New York Historical Society is credited with owning a copy, but no copy has been located there. Since MacLean did not have the publication in hand, it appears that he wrote this description from memory with

the result that two contemporary Shaker publications became confused, and that his no. 499 is a ghost. *A Declaration ... Shewing Reasons for Refusing to Aid or Abet the Cause of War or Bloodshed ...* (Albany, E. & E. Hosford, 1815. 20 pp.), no. **496**, where the date and total number of pages are identical with MacLean's. *The Memorial of the Society of People of New-Lebanon, in the County of Columbia ... Commonly Called Shakers. To the Respectable Legislature of New-York* (Albany, Churchill & Abbey, 1816. 8 pp.), no. **1018**, whose title is identical with MacLean's, except for the word "Respectable." The same explanations and arguments contained in *A Declaration* were used later in the 1816 *Memorial.* Moreover, it is stated that "... A memorial was drawn up and laid before the [New York Senate] in 1816. This was the first address laid before the State Legislature," "History of the Church of Mt. Lebanon," *The Manifesto,* 20 (November 1890), 241. Sabin 97890 records the same publication but with the note, "Title taken from MacLean's Bibliography, no. 499," and again it is credited to the New York Historical Society. Shaw does not record this publication.

1018 The Memorial of the Society of People of New-Lebanon, in the County of Columbia, and Watervliet, in the County of Albany, Commonly Called Shakers. To the Respectable Legislature of the State of New-York. [Albany: Churchill & Abbey, Printers, 1816]. Caption title. 8 pp. 21 cm.

Signed: *Richard Spier, Morrell Baker* [and 3 other] *Trustees.* Dated: Watervliet, February 13, 1816. The Western Reserve Historical Society copy has a contemporary ms. notation, p. [1], "Printed February 1816." Printers' names and place follow the text. This Memorial was drawn up and laid before the New York Senate in 1816. In his "Biographic Memoir," pp. 143-51 (a section entitled, "Military Troubles") Calvin Green states that he wrote "a Memorial for the Legislature of the State of New York" which Wells prepared for the press, and that it was printed and received by the Senate Feb. 19, 1816. He also refers to Green's meetings with Martin Van Buren and states that the Shakers

paid him a fee at this time to represent them legally. Ms. copy, Library of Congress, Manuscripts Division. "This was the first address ever sent by Believers to the Legislature," "History of the Church of Mt. Lebanon," *The Manifesto*, 20 (November 1890), 241. It is a protest against the militia law of the State of New York and a plea for the exemption of Shakers from military duty and "from all fines and taxes in lieu thereof." *See also* nos. **496, 1019**, and **1120**. It might be noted that the earliest, and heretofore overlooked, Shaker legislative petition was presented to the House of the Massachusetts General Court, February 22, 1782 (no. **996**), by William Lee and James Whittaker "relative to the ill treatment of the Shakers," ms. Massachusetts State Archives, Boston. Another petition for exemption from military duty was presented to the Massachusetts General Court in 1788 by Daniel Goodrich and others, *see* no. **997**.
Sabin 97891 (and 47632? without place or date). Shaw 38919. DLC, MWA, NN, NHi, OClWHi*.

1019 ——— To the Respectable Legislature of the State of New-York. [Albany: 1816]. 5 pp. 29½ cm.

At head of title: In Senate, Feb. 19, 1816. On p. 4, signed: *Richard Spier, Morrell Baker* [and 3 other] *Trustees*. Dated: Watervliet, Feb. 13, 1816. Contains also, "The Memorial and Petition of the Undersigned, Inhabitants of the Towns of Canaan and Watervliet, and other Places in the State," pp. 4–5. This is signed by 120 (some copies have 160 signers) Shaker friends and acquaintances who urged the Legislature "to pass a law" exempting the Shakers from military duty or fines "in lieu thereof." Pages 1–4 are the counterpart of *The Memorial* (1816), no. **1018**, which was printed by the Shakers for presentation to the Legislature. This edition was printed for the use of members of the Legislature after the presentation. Closer setting of the text has resulted in fewer pages, but the texts are identical. *See* page 197, To the Honorable ... NOC*, NSyU, OClWHi.

1020 ... The Memorial of the United Society (Commonly Called Shakers), of New-Lebanon and Watervliet, Respectfully Sheweth. That whereas, in Consequence of the Ninth Section of the Act ... Passed April 23, 1823, and also ... [Albany?: 1825?]. Caption title. 5 pp. 32 cm.

At head of title: To the Legislature of the State of New York. Signed: *Stephen Munson, Morrell Baker, Peter Dodge, Joseph Hodgson, Seth Y. Wells, Calvin Green–Watervliet, Jan. 17th, 1825.* "An Act to Organize the Militia" passed April 23, 1823, ninth section, makes the Shakers liable to militia fines, or imprisonment. This Memorial is a statement of conscientious objections to the militia system as it affects the Society. It describes again the Shaker benefits which affect the public, such as their full support for their own poor (and through taxes support of public paupers) and the religious beliefs which have prevented Shaker acceptance of military pensions or bounty lands. The legislative committee reported favorably on this petition, but it was rejected by the House.
OClWHi*.

1021 ... The Memorial of the United Society (Commonly Called Shakers) of New-Lebanon and Watervliet. To the Legislature of the State of New York. [Albany: 1826]. Caption title. 6 pp. 33½ cm.

At head of title: In Senate, January 10, 1826. (Presented by Mr. Jordan.) Signed: *In behalf of the United Society of New-Lebanon and Watervliet, we subscribe ourselves the friends of justice, equity and peace. Calvin Green, Stephen Munson, Daniel J. Hawkins, Joseph Hodgson, Freegift Wells. New-Lebanon, January 2, 1826.* This Memorial is a petition for relief from "the ninth section of the act, entitled 'an act to organize the militia,' passed April 23d, 1823, and also an amendment of said act, passed April, 1824," which makes such Shakers as are liable subject to "militia fines, or a commutation thereof, or in default to suffer imprisonment." *See also* no. **1091**. Shaw 25550. DLC, MWiW*, N, NOC, OClWHi.

1022 ... The Memorial of the United Society of Believers (Commonly Called Shakers) of the Towns of New-Lebanon and Watervliet, Respectfully Sheweth ... [Albany: 1823]. Caption title. 5 pp. (plus one blank leaf). 20 cm.

At head of title: To the Legislature of the State of New York, now in Session. At end, p. 5: In behalf of the United Society, signed by Stephen Munson, Morrell Baker, Sen. of New-Lebanon. Peter Dodge, Luther Wells, of Watervliet. Dated: February 24, 1823. This Memorial charges that "by the fifth section of the seventh article of the New Constitution of this State [New York, 1821], it becomes the duty of the Legislature to enact laws respecting such persons as, from scruples of conscience, may be averse to bearing arms ... [and that] such laws may have a peculiar bearing upon the said United Society." The Shakers request a "candid consideration" of their situation and refer to the "liberal minded Legislature which in 1816 ... concurred with the general principles of civil and religious liberty established in our country, by exempting us from all military services, and from any equivalent whatever."

Shaw 14087. MPB (p. 5 not conjugate), MWA, N (pp. 3-4 not conjugate), OClWHi*.

1023 A Memorial Remonstrating Against a Certain Act of the Legislature of Kentucky, Entitled "An Act to Regulate Civil Proceedings against Certain Communities Having Property in Common"—and Declaring,—That it shall and may be Lawful to Commence and Prosecute Suits, Obtain Decrees and have Execution against any of the Communities of People called Shakers,—without Naming or Designating the Individuals, or Serving Process on them, Otherwise than by Fixing a Subpoena on the Door of their Meeting-house, &c. Approved Feb. 11, 1828 .... [Harrodsburg, Kentucky: Printed at the Union Office, 1830]. Caption title. 8 pp. 22 cm.

Signed, p. 7: *Pleasant Hill, South Union [Ky.]*. *"Officially Represented by their Responsible Agents, John R. Bryant, Eli McLean."* MacLean, *Life*, p. 36, states that the Memorial was presented to the Legislature between Dec. 2 and 9, 1830. Ham, "Shakerism in the Old West," p. 152, ftn. 66, states that this document "was actually written by Richard McNemar," and that it was also printed at South Union. No copy

printed at South Union has been located, but a statement quoted from McNemar's "Diaries," in MacLean, *Life*, p. 37, indicates that another printing was made at South Union, "At South Union matters [i.e., printing the remonstrance] were happily managed by means of a small press constructed by Elder Benjamin (Youngs)." The Memorial is a protest against the Kentucky law of 1828 which made it unnecessary to name individuals in legal suits against the Shakers, and which would have invalidated the Covenant. The law was instigated by "The Petition of John Whitbey and Others to the Legislature," printed in [R. McNemar], *comp., Investigator* (no. 926), pp. 6-9. Whitbey and his brother, Richeson, after leaving the Pleasant Hill Shaker community became members of Robert Owen's New Harmony Society, which accounts for that part of the Memorial devoted to the "High handed influence" of Owen's New Harmony. The aftermath of suits against the Shakers is described by Ham, pp. 150-57, 185-87. *See also* no. 1426.

Sabin 97892. Shaw 35157. CSmH, DLC, ICJ, In, InU, KyBgW, KyLO, KySP, KyU, MHarF, MPB, MWiW*, MWA, MiU-C, N, NN, NOC, NNUT, NjPT, OCHP, OClWHi.

1024 Memorial Services, at East Canterbury, Mer. Co., N.H. Jan. 9, 1890, in Memory of Sister, Mary Whitcher ... [East Canterbury, N.H.: 1890]. Caption title. 12 pp. music. 23 cm.

Cover title: Sister Mary.

MacLean 377. MWA, MWiW*, NN, NOC, NSyU, OClWHi.

1025 "Memorial to Congress by the Society of Shakers," [Feb. 5, 1816]. In C. E. Carter, ed., *Territorial Papers of the United States* (26 vols., 1934-62), "The Territory of Indiana 1810-1816," 8 (1939), 384-87.

Requests redress for losses at Bosseron Creek (West Union, Ind.) due to the damage committed by troops under Col. Russell and Gen. Hopkins, signed: *Adam Gallagher, Samuel Johnson, William Douglas, Trustees.* Includes an endorsement signed by ten neighbors that the Shakers are "an orderly, moral, and industrious body of people" who have suffered distress by their losses, and an itemized statement of losses, which total $4813.50.

1026 Memorial to the Eastern Elders. [Union Village, O.?: 1832?] Broadside?

No copy located. A memorial which concerned the acceptance of army pensions by Shakers. Ham, "Shakerism in the Old West," p. 149, ftn. 58, states that Richard McNemar printed *A Memorial to the Eastern Elders* on the pension dispute, and cites McNemar's "Journal," 74 (Library of Congress, Manuscripts Division, ms., no. 301, p. 74.)

A Memorial to the Legislature of 1817, Dated, Columbus [Ohio:] Dec. 8, 1817.

No copy located. This plea for the exemption of Shakers from military duty and the payment of equivalent fines was hurriedly prepared by Richard McNemar and Calvin Morrell for submission to the legislature. Very likely it was not printed. The contents are described by Ham, "Shakerism in the Old West," pp. 144-45, where he cites, ftn. 48, a copy in "[Fragments of a Journal kept by Richard McNemar]," Library of Congress, ms., no. 341b. *See also* no. 4.

A Memorial to the Ohio Legislature, 1837. Request for an Act that would "in Effect Recognize Shaker Real Estate as a Legal Perpetuity." Bill failed by a small margin. Cited by F. G. Ham, "Shakerism in the Old West," p. 160, ftn. 83, where he states that "a copy of this memorial is in E. Wright (i.e., Richard McNemar) to S. Y. Wells, May 1, 1837." Library of Congress, ms., no. 347b. He continues, "See also LC, No. 304 ([Richard McNemar], comp.), Ohio Legislature, 1834-37. Bills, petitions, etc. respecting the Shakers."

1027 Midsummer Entertainment at Shaker Village, East Canterbury, N.H., Aug. 18, 1897 ... [n.p., n.d.]. Broadside. 19 X 13½ cm.
OClWHi*.

1028 *Millennial Educator.* [Holy Hill, East Canterbury, N.H.: "Hebrew Press," 1895?]. Caption title. 35-38 pp. 21½ cm.

Contains a letter addressed: Eldress Dorothy [Durgin], dated: June 10, 1895, and signed: *Brother Daniel* [Milton]. Here Milton refers to having been rejected at Mt. Lebanon, where "Elder Giles Avery said to me, 'Your place is at Canterbury'." Much the same answer was given to him at Shirley, Mass., but Milton had troubles and asked Eldress Dorothy how he could keep his "Home in Peace," when he "saw four worldly men tearing down that comfortable broom house" that he had worked in. *See* nos. 1032-1036. MWiW*.

1029 Millennial Laws. Section IV. The Order of Christmas. [n.p., 1958]. Broadside. 23 X 15½ cm.

Printed excerpt from "Millennial Laws," a manuscript in the Andrews' collection. Faith and Edward Deming Andrews, Christmas 1958.
Private collection.

1030 Millennium. [Canterbury, N.H.?: n.d.]. [4] pp. 20 cm.

Title poem of 8 stanzas, pp. [1-2]; "Truth," poem, 14 stanzas, pp. [3-4].
OClWHi*.

1031 ——— Variant. 16½ cm.
More closely set and printed on different paper.
OClWHi*.

1032 [MILTON, DANIEL] Important Notice: Stop and Read. To the Public. Death & Co., Wholesale and Retail Dealers in Spirits, Wine and Malt Liquors, Tobacco, Snuff, and Cigars, Take this Opportunity of Informing their Friends that they Continue the Trade of making Drunkards, Bankrupts, Beggars, and Thieves ... Portsmouth, N.H.: Hebrew Press, [1896]. [2] pp. 25 cm.

The text is repeated on p. [2]. Contains: Letter to Shaker Ministry, Mount Lebanon, N.Y. Addressed at Portsmouth, N.H., August 14, 1885. Daniel Milton was a self-styled "Wandering Israelite," who from time to time published items identified as products of the "Hebrew Press." This may have been a peripatetic press, or more likely, an identification supplied by Milton himself. At one period he was a vigorous proponent of the doctrines of Joanna Southcott, an English prophetess, 1792-1814. It is clear that he lived among the Shakers in various com-

munities; it is not clear that he ever became a
member. Milton's published writing about his
role as a Christian Israelite and those concerned with Joanna Southcott's beliefs have
been omitted in this bibliography. *See also*
no. 1028.
OClWHi*.

1033 —— Spirit of Truth – the American
Shaker. 3d ed. [Portsmouth, N.H.: 1878].
Broadside. 24½ X 20½ cm.
   Signed: *Peace Ground, Harvard, Mass., May
   12, 1878.* A note at the end identifies the
   editions: "Published at the 'New Hampshire
   Gazette' Office, Portsmouth, N.H., in June
   1859; 2d edition, at the 'Portsmouth Journal'
   Office, in September 1862; 3d edition, at the
   Office of the 'New Hampshire Gazette,'
   Portsmouth, N.H., May 21, 1878."
   OClWHi*.

1034 —— ... Testimony of Daniel Milton
before the 'United Society of Believers in
Christ's Second Appearing' at East Canterbury,
on Sunday October 1895. [Holy Hill, East
Canterbury: Hebrew Press, 1895]. Caption title.
4 pp. (Millennial Educator, Vol. I, October 1895).
   OClWHi*.

1035 —— ... Theology of Daniel Milton, the
Promised Shiloh, Prophesied in the Writing of
Joanna Southcott, George Turner, and John
Wroe ... Wakefield [Eng.]: G. Horridge, Printer
and Stationer, 1861. Cover title. 8 pp. 18 cm.
   At head of title: Appearance of the Promised
   Shiloh. The peculiar theology of Milton, fol-
   lowed by a poem, "Sabbath of Rest," pp. 6–8.
   MWiW*.

1036 —— United Society. The Seventh Church
of Divine Revelation. Letter to Harvey L. Eads,
Bishop of South Union, Ky. [Ayer, Mass.:
Hebrew Press], 1881. Caption title. 4 pp. 21 cm.
   Letter dated: Harvard, Mass., December 12th,
   1881.
   OClWHi*.

1037 MONMOUTH, ELIZABETH HARPER.
Living on Half a Dime a Day. An Actual Experi-
ence. [n.p., n.d.]. 54 [1] pp. illus.
   Short stories and poems by the Minister (lay
   reader) of Worsted Church, Hillville, East
   Canterbury, N.H. The Shaker community
   originally printed for Mrs. Monmouth the
   pamphlets now reproduced as "a loving
   tribute by Alida Cogswell Hodges." Mrs.
   Monmouth sometimes used the pseudonym
   Effie Afton.
   NOC*.

1038 MOORE, J. HOWARD. ... A Race of
Somnambulists. Mount Lebanon, N.Y.: The
Lebanon Press, [n.d.]. Cover title. [4] pp. 15
cm. (Stir up series, No. 1.)
   A denunciation of cruelty to animals.
   MacLean 384. MWiW*, NOC, OClWHi.

1039 MOORE, NANCY ELY. The Journal of
Eldress Nancy, kept at the South Union, Ken-
tucky, Shaker colony, August 15, 1861–Septem-
ber 4, 1864. Edited with an Introduction and
Glossary by Mary Julia Neal. Nashville, Tenn.:
Sold by The Shaker Museum, Inc., Auburn,
Kentucky, [1963]. xii, 256 pp. plates. ports.
map. 23 cm.
   Map of South Union, Kentucky, 1860–65
   on end papers. "Bibliography," pp. 249–50.
   "Glossary," pp. 229–248, includes biograph-
   ical and local history items. Excerpts from
   Eldress Nancy's "Journal" were published in
   The Manifesto, 21 (December 1891), 275–
   77; 22 (January–April 1892), 20–21, 58–59,
   78–80.
   CtY, MB, MHarF, MPB, MWA, MWiW*,
   NOC.

MORTON, LIZZIE, *pseud. See* Harter, Mrs.
J. H. and Harvey L. Eads, no. 769.

1040 Mother's Gift. [n.p., n.d.]. Broadside.
21 X 9 cm.
   Poem, 5 stanzas, 8 lines each.
   OClWHi*.

MUSIC LEAFLETS

The Shaker music leaflets below were published by the Canterbury, N.H., Shakers during the 1870's,
with some few exceptions, three of which were published later at Sabbathday Lake, Me. Publication

of the periodical, *The Shaker,* in January 1871, provided the impetus for the changeover to conventional notation that could be read by "the world," and replaced the esoteric Shaker notation written without the staff and based upon the letters a–g. Elder Henry Blinn has described the reasons for the innovation, the necessity of instructing members to read the newly adopted conventional notation, and their resistance to the "hide and seek" notes. To the Shakers the innovation "was like a backward move of many years, and from their hearts the 'black heads' had no word of welcome," "The Incoming Year," *The Manifesto,* 25 (January 1895), 14–15. It is not surprising that Shaker music written in conventional notation did not appear in *The Shaker* until December 1871, when "True Love" was printed with simple music for the melody. This is the earliest Shaker music printed in conventional notation that can be dated definitely. In 1872 only four hymns with music were printed in *The Shaker,* but thereafter, music became a regular feature of the monthly issues with the music becoming increasingly sophisticated. Although the Shaker music leaflets recorded below are not dated, it is highly unlikely that any Canterbury music leaflets were published before 1873. Canterbury music leaflets may be dated safely from 1873–74 and on into the 1880's. By this time collections of hymns with the music printed in conventional notation were available for general use, namely, the 1875 *Shaker Music. Inspirational Hymns and Melodies* (no. 1293), published by the Mt. Lebanon, N.Y., Shakers and printed in Albany, and the 1876 *Selection of Devotional Melodies* (no. 1274), printed and published by the Canterbury, N.H., Shakers. Many more pieces of sheet music were published than are recorded below, as will be seen by the following hymn titles. An advertisement on the back cover, verso, of the undated (1874?) *Brief Account of Shakers and Shakerism* (no. 108), both printed and published at Canterbury, lists the following "Shaker Sheet Music" at 5¢ each, or 50¢ per dozen: "Star of Hope," "Morning Dawn [also *The Shaker,* 5 (1875), 32]," "More Love," "Jordan's Tides," "Soul Cheer," "Sure Promise," "True Inspiration," "Happy Land," "A Prayer [also *The Shaker,* 6 (May 1876), 33]," "The Higher Life," "Happy Change," and "Life." Another advertisement p. [4], *The Dew Drop,* No. 5 (1877?), lists the "Sheet Music" titles: " 'We are Marching On [also *The Manifesto* (September 1883), 215],' 'Pure Spirit,' 'Song of Praise [also *The Shaker,* 6 (January 1876), 8],' 'The Gospel Day, and other pieces in Harmony'," (no. 506). *See also* no. 108.

1041 The Beacon. [Canterbury, N.H.: n.d.]. Broadside. music. 22½ × 32 cm.
   OClWHi*.

1042 The Call. Printed in Shaker Village [Canterbury], Mer. Co., N.H.: [n.d.]. Broadside. music. 32 × 23 cm.
   MWiW*, OClWHi.

1043 Christ's Sufferings. Shaker Village [Canterbury], N.H.: [n.d.]. Broadside. music. 13 × 20½ cm.
   The hymn was included in the 1876 collection, *Selection of Devotional Melodies* (no. 1274), pp. 10–14, and was published in *The Shaker,* 7 (September 1877), 64. It was also printed as a broadside with the music written in Shaker letter notation, *see* no. 454.
   OClWHi*.

1044 Consecration. "Harvard, Mass." Published and printed at Shaker Village [Canterbury], Mer. Co., N.H.: [n.d.]. Broadside. music. 30 × 20½ cm.
   This hymn was printed in the *Shaker Manifesto,* 10 (April 1880), 95.
   OClWHi*.

1045 God's Blessing. Printed and Published by the Shakers [Canterbury], Mer. Co., N.H.: [n.d.]. Broadside. music. 19 × 17 cm.
   This hymn was printed in *The Shaker,* 7 (May 1877), 40.
   NOC*.

1046 Happy Land. Shaker Village [Canterbury], Mer. Co., N.H.: [n.d.]. Broadside. music. 14 × 21 cm.
   Included in the 1876 collection of hymns, *Selection of Devotional Melodies* (no. 1274), p. 7.
   OClWHi*.

1047 Holy Faith. [Canterbury, N.H.?: n.d.]. Broadside. music. 45½ X 15½ cm.
  This hymn was printed both on white paper and on yellow.
  OClWHi*.

1048 Joy and Peace. [Canterbury, N.H.: n.d.]. Broadside. music. 15 X 16 cm.
  Private collection.

1049 Life. Printed at Shaker Village [Canterbury], Mer. Co., N.H.: [n.d.]. Broadside. music. 23 X 25 cm.
  This hymn was printed in both editions of the undated (1874-75?) *Brief Account of Shakers and Shakerism* (nos. 108 and 109).
  MWiW*.

1050 MACE, AURELIA G. and ARVILLA MORRISON. Lebanon and Her Cedars. Words by Aurelia G. Mace. Music by Arvilla Morrison. Published at Shaker Village, Sabbathday Lake, Cumberland Co., Maine: [n.d.]. Broadside. music. 27½ X 17½ cm.
  OClWHi*.

1051 —— The Voice of God. Words by Aurelia G. Mace. Music by Arvilla Morrison. Published at Shaker Village, Sabbathday Lake, Cumberland Co., Maine: [n.d.]. Broadside. music. 27½ X 17½ cm.
  OClWHi*.

1052 —— Zion, O Zion, ... The Voice of God ... Words by Aurelia G. Mace and Music by Arvilla Morrison. Published at Shaker Village, Sabbathday Lake, Cumberland Co., Maine: [n.d.]. Broadside. music. 27 X 17½ cm.
  OClWHi*.

1053 More Love. Shaker Village [Canterbury], Mer. Co., N.H.: [n.d.]. Broadside. music. 15 X 19½ cm.
  Reproduced in E. D. Andrews, *The Gift to be Simple* (no. 1764), opp. p. 84. This hymn with music is also found in *Brief Account of Shakers and Shakerism* (no. 109), p. 4, and in the 1876 *Selection of Devotional Melodies* (no. 1274), pp. 14-15. No copy located.

1054 My Call. Printed at Shaker Village [Canterbury], Mer. Co., N.H.: Broadside. music. 24½ X 15½ cm.
  OClWHi*.

1055 A Prayer. Printed at Shaker Village [Canterbury], Mer. Co., N.H.: [n.d.]. Broadside. music. 21½ X 29 cm.
  OClWHi*.

1056 Purest Blessing. Published and Printed at Shaker Village [Canterbury], Mer. Co., N.H.: [n.d.]. Broadside. music. 37 X 24 cm.
  This hymn was printed in *The Manifesto*, 13 (July 1883), 167.
  MWiW*, OClWHi.

1057 SMITH, THOMAS. Spirit of Prophecy. Although a copy has not been located, presumably this hymn was printed and available as a broadside sheet with the music. "There is a beautiful piece of music attached to 'Spirit of Prophecy.' Believers desirous of obtaining the same may address our young and noble Prophet Elder, Thomas Smith, Canaan Corners, N.Y.," *The Shaker*, 2 (August 1872), 64, where "Spirit of Prophecy," is printed without the music.

1058 Song of Praise. Published and Printed at Shaker Village [Canterbury], Mer. Co., N.H.: [n.d.]. Broadside. music. 30 X 20½ cm.
  Printed in *The Shaker*, 6 (January 1876), 8.
  OClWHi*.

1059 Soul Cheer. Printed in Shaker Village [Canterbury], Mer. Co., N.H.: [n.d.]. Broadside. music. 23 X 25 cm.
  Included in the 1876 *Selection of Devotional Melodies* (no. 1274), p. 27.
  MWiW*.

1060 Sun of Righteousness. Published and Printed at Shaker Village [Canterbury], Mer. Co., N.H.: [n.d.]. Broadside. music. 30 X 23 cm.
  OClWHi*.

1061 Sure Promise. [Shaker Village, Canterbury, N.H.: n.d.]. Broadside. music. 30 X 23½ cm.
  This hymn was printed in *The Manifesto*, 14 (October 1884), 239.
  OClWHi*.

1062 That Beautiful City. "Glorious Things are Spoken of Thee, O City of God," Psalm LXXXVII. 3. Published at Shaker Village, East Canterbury, N.H.: [n.d.]. Broadside. music. 30 × 24 cm.

    Agnes Newton, East Canterbury, N.H., is given as author (lyrics?) by J. P. MacLean in a letter to H. M. Lydenburg, May 28, 1905. New York Public Library, a.l.s. Rare Book Room.

    MacLean 456. MPB, MWiW*, N, NN, OClWHi.

1063 Will Obey. Canterbury, N.H.: [n.d.]. Broadside. music. 13½ × 23½ cm.

    OClWHi*.

1064 The Musical Messenger. A Compilation of Hymns, Slow and Quick Marches, etc., Used in Worship by Believers. [Union Village, O.: Printed at the Shaker Printing Office, n.d.]. Cover title. 32 pp. music. 11 × 15½ cm.

    "The Bishopric of the western churches have advised the printing of a few hymns, songs, marches, etc., for general distribution among the western societies ..." Signed: *O. C. Hampton* (By Order of the Ministry.) — Preface. This is probably the printing referred to by MacLean, *Life*, p. 61, "Oliver C. Hampton printed on it [McNemar's press] his 'Musical Messenger' ..." The music is in Shaker letter notation.

    NN, OClWHi*.

1065 ———— Published by the United Society of Believers, Union Village, Ohio. Lebanon, Ohio: F. Estes, [18-?]. [3]-64, [5 leaves], [2] pp. music. 20½ cm.

    Words with music in Shaker letter notation, with the length of the notes indicated by printing the letters a-g in italic, roman, etc. After the first stanza the words of subsequent stanzas in 15 of the selections are printed inside 5-line staffs. "Index to First Lines," [2] pp., at end. In the Western Reserve Historical Society copy, 3 printed half leaves and 3 full leaves have been tipped in following p. 64. The 3 half leaves occur in some other copies, but are not always present.

    ICN, KyBgW, MPB, MWiW*, N, OClWHi.

1066 Mutual Insurance Blank. [n.p., 186-]. Broadside. 40 × 22 cm.

    "It is believed that the time has arrived for Believers to unite and form a compact by which a more equal division may be made among the different societies of Shakers ... as a contribution toward losses by fire" in excess of $400. The proportion each Society is to contribute is shown in percentages, but the Ministry at Mt. Lebanon, N.Y., may "change and rearrange the apportionment when proper equity indicates." Includes a list of communities and assigned percentages of responsibility, and a list of fire prevention rules. The date *1866* is supplied in ink in the copy described here. *See also* no. 1134.

    OClWHi*, NOC.

1067 MYRICK, ELIJAH. The Celibate Shaker Life. [Mt. Lebanon?: 1889?]. Caption title. 8 pp. 13½ cm.

    Contains also: "Shakerism. Is Celibacy Contrary to Natural and Revealed Law?" by Daniel Fraser (from *The Manifesto*, 19 (April 1889), 78-80). "Longevity of Virgin Celibates" (Written for the *Alpha*) by Giles Avery (from the *Shaker Manifesto*, 12 (October 1882), 217-19). *The Celibate Shaker Life* is reprinted from the *Shaker Manifesto*, 11 (December 1881), 266-67.

    MacLean 385. DLC, MHarF, MPB, MWA, MWiW*, NBuG, NN, OClWHi, WHi.

N

1068 NATIONAL COUNCIL OF WOMEN. Report of the 16th Annual Executive held Oct. 1, 2, 3 & 4, 1907 at Jamestown, Va. 108 pp.

Contains account of the part taken by M. Catherine Allen at this meeting.

    OClWHi*.

1069 NEALE, EMMA JANE. In Memory of
our Sister [poem]. [n.p., n.d.]. Broadside.
18½ × 12 cm.

> Signed: *Emma J. Neale.* The poem of 6 stan-
> zas does not identify in whose memory it is
> written. Begins: Angels ope the gates im-
> mortal,/ Our dear sister joins the blest . . . .
> MWiW*.

1070 NEW HAMPSHIRE. GEOLOGICAL
SURVEY, 1840-1844. Final Report on the
Geology and Mineralogy of the State of New
Hampshire, by Charles T. Jackson . . . Published
by Order of the Legislature. Concord, N.H.:
Carroll & Baker, State Printers, 1844. 376 pp.
illus. 23½ cm.

> Reference to the geology of Shaker Village
> at Canterbury, p. 85. Jackson's visit to
> "Shaker Farm," Canterbury, and his instruc-
> tions about the best method of peat compost
> and of reclaiming bogs, pp. 271-73. "Histori-
> cal Sketch of the Community of Shakers" is
> an account written by a Trustee, p. 355. Wil-
> liam Tripure's letter to Dr. Charles T. Jackson,
> Feb. 1, 1843, with a report on the reclamation
> of the bog and the resultant tremendous
> success of the quality and amount of farm
> products grown, trials with several vegetables,
> description of experiments with the compost
> heap, and sincere thanks for Jackson's
> advice, pp. 352-54.
> NhD*.

1071 NEW HAMPSHIRE. LEGISLATURE.
HOUSE. JUDICIARY COMMITTEE. Report of
the Examination of the Shakers of Canterbury
and Enfield before the New-Hampshire Legislature, at the November Session, 1848, Including
the Testimony at Length; Several Extracts from
Shaker Publications; The Bill which Passed the
House of Representatives; The Proceedings in
the Pillow case [N.Y.]; Together with the Letter
of James W. Spinney. From Notes Taken at the
Examination. Concord, N.H.: Printed by Ervin
B. Tripp, 1849. 100 pp. 22 cm.

> Cover title: Shaker examination before the
> New-Hampshire Legislature, November ses-
> sion, 1848. Dated at end of Preface, June 3,
> 1849. This account of the "examination"
> (i.e. hearing) held by the Judiciary Committee
> was made up from two sets of notes taken at

the time. It is anti-Shaker in tone and was
very likely published by some of the petitioners. In the unsigned Preface, it is stated
that it was hoped that "the correct report of
the Examination" would be published, but
that this report "has been suppressed." In
1848 a series of petitions, signed by several
hundred persons, requested "passage of a
law prohibiting the binding of minor children
to the Shakers, providing for the support of
the wife and children of husbands joining
that society [Shakers], and for the remunera-
tion of the services of persons leaving . . ."
The Shakers retained Franklin Pierce and
other distinguished counsel to defend them.
This bill passed the House, but was lost in the
Senate. A substitute bill which was enacted
amended the divorce laws and provided that
a spouse not joining the Shakers need wait
only 6 months (not 3 years) before filing for
a divorce from the spouse who had joined
the Shakers. *See also* no. 3772.
MacLean 422. Sabin 69858. CtY, DLC, MH,
MPB, MWA, MWiW*, MiU-C, N, NN,
NBLiHi, Nh, NhD, NjPT, OClWHi.

1072 ———— Report of the Minority of the
Judiciary Committee upon the Petition of
Franklin Munroe and Others, in Relation to the
Society of Christians Called Shakers. [Concord,
N.H.: 1849]. Broadside. 39 × 29 cm.

> The dissenting minority report on the anti-
> Shaker proposed "Act for the better Protec-
> tion of Married Women and Children." This
> report is reprinted in N. H. Leg. House,
> Judiciary Comm., *Report of the Examination*
> (no. 1071), pp. 84-85, and in R. F. Upton's
> "Franklin Pierce and the Shakers" (no.
> 3772), pp. 12-15; the majority report is
> reprinted, pp. 11-12.
> OClWHi*.

1073 NEW LEBANON, N.Y. To the Trustees
of the United Society of Shakers of New Lebanon, N.Y. [New Lebanon, N.Y.: 1899?]. Broadside card. 8½ × 14½ cm.

> "Resolved, That the Thanks of the Town of
> New Lebanon be and are hereby Tendered
> to the Society of Shakers, for the Great
> Liberality and Public Spirit Shown by
> Them in Donating the Right of Way

Amounting to about Sixteen Acres Through Their Lands."
MWiW*.

1074 New Lebanon Shaker School, District 12, Dept. no. 2, New Lebanon, N.Y. Attendance and Recitation of [blank space for pupil's name] Commencing [blank space for date] ... New Lebanon [N.Y.]: Church, First Order, Elisha Blakeman, Printer, 1858. Broadside. 27 X 16 cm.

> Report form covering a period of six weeks. It provides for a record of the pupil's grades in reading, spelling, geography, arithmetic, writing, variety, grammar, astronomy, physiology, philosophy, composition, conduct, and cleanliness. To be signed by the "Parent or Guardian."
> NSyU*.

1075 New Year, – 1842. [n.p., 1842?]. [4] pp. 14 X 8½ cm.

> Contains two poems (8 and 6 numbered stanzas) with the title given above.
> OClWHi*.

1076 New Year's Address 1836. [n.p., n.d.]. Broadside. 19½ X 11½ cm.

> Poem of 5 stanzas by Ben Noyes of the Poland Hill, Me., family. Signed in ink: *from Benjamin.*
> Private collection.

A Newyear's Gift; Jan. 1831. *See* [McNemar, Richard], *A Newyear's Gift; 1831,* no. 938.

1077 NEW YORK. COMMISSION FOR DETECTING AND DEFEATING CONSPIRACIES. Minutes of the Commissioners for Detecting and Defeating Conspiracies in the State of New York. Albany County Sessions, 1778–1781. Edited by Victor Hugo Paltsits ... Albany: Pub. by the State of New York [J. B. Lyon, State Printers], 1909–10. 3 vols. (paged continuously). illus.

> These *Minutes* constitute the official record of the arrest, imprisonment, and release of Shakers of Niskayuna (Watervliet) N.Y. for whatever cause during the Revolutionary period, beginning with the imprisonment of Zadock Wright, July 10, 1778 for loyalist military activities, to the release of Abel Bacon, "one of those infatuated People denominated Shaking Quakers." More than 20 "Shaking Quakers," including Ann Lee, appeared before the Commissioners in response to complaints about their refusal to bear arms, and also complaints about their pacifist activities "daily dissuading the friends of the American cause from taking up Arms in defence of their Liberties." Zadock Wright was summoned again July 7, 1780, for dissuading people from raising arms. David Darrow refused to recognize civil authority and also declared that his religious principles prevented his partaking in any kind of military duty. Complaints were also heard concerning a Shaker's having persuaded a negro slave "to go to the enemy," and the Shakers having "lately purchased Arms and Ammunition which was supposed to be done by them with a View to assist the Enemy should they come into the Country." Vol. I, pp. 43n, 167, 292, 312–13, 343–44; Vol. II, pp. 452, 456, 461, 469, 470–71, 478, 482, 504, 506–7, 524–25, 542, 555, 569–72, 573–74, 575, 592, 636, 677–78, 680, 723–24. *See also* nos. 1977 and 3056.
> MH, MWiW*, N, NNC.

1078 NEW YORK. *Laws, Statutes, etc.* ... An Act in Relation to Certain Trusts. Passed April 15, 1839 ... [Albany: 1839]. Broadside. 24 X 15 cm.

> At head of title: Albany Argus – Extra. Chapter 174. The privileges granted in this act apply exclusively to the United Society. Its passage secured Shaker deeds of trust "executed and delivered prior to the first day of January, eighteen hundred and thirty," but limited the Shaker annual income "after deducting necessary expenses," to $5,000 "on pain of forfeiture of the privileges conferred by this act." N.Y. Statutes. 62 sess. Chap. 174, p. 146. *See also* nos. 456, 1381, 2841.
> MWiW*, N, NNC.

1079 —— Laws of the State of New York Passed at the Sixty-second Session of the Legislature ... Albany: Printed by E. Croswell for Wm. and A. Gould & Co., etc., 1839. 433 pp. 22½ cm.

> "An Act in Relation to Certain Trusts," p. 146.

1080 NEW YORK. LEGISLATURE. ASSEM-
BLY. An Act for the Relief of Eunice Chapman,
and for Other Purposes. Whereas Eunice Chapman in the Year One Thousand and Eight
Hundred and Four .... [Albany: 1818]. Caption title. [2] pp. 33½ cm.

> At head of title: In Assembly, Feb. 10, 1818.
> Reprinted in *The Other Side of the Question*
> (no. 946), pp. [4–5]. *See also* no. 1085.
> OClWHi*.

1081 —— Amendments Offered by Mr. L. S.
Chatfield, in Committee of the Whole, on the
Engrossed Bill from the Senate, Entitled "An
Act in Relation to Certain Trusts." [Albany:
1839]. 4 ll. 32½ cm.

> At head of title: State of New York. No. 434.
> In Assembly, April 2, 1839. This bill was
> introduced as the result of the Shakers'
> efforts (no. 1381) to obtain legislation which
> would confirm their right of land ownership
> and deeds of trust. This official copy has
> each line of text numbered for easy reference.
> OClWHi*.

1082 —— ... Remonstrance of the United
Society, Called Shakers, Against the Passage of a
Certain Law. To the Honorable Legislature of
the State of New-York. The Memorial of the
Undersigned Committee ... Respectfully
Showeth. [Albany: 1830]. 10 pp. 21½ cm.

> At head of title: No. 300. In Assembly.
> March 20, 1830. Signed: *Calvin Green,*
> *Garrett K. Lawrence, Frederick S. Wicker ...*
> *New-Lebanon and Watervliet.* It is likely that
> the Shakers presented their own printed
> remonstrance to the legislature, but this
> legislative printing is the only copy located.
> A vigorous protest is argued under 3 headings
> which attack the principles implied in the
> bill before the legislature. Each part is refuted
> with "a plain statement of facts, and of the
> impressions we feel on the subject of these
> propositions." 1. Authorize seizure of Shaker
> property "on account of judgments and exe-
> cutions obtained against any person who may
> belong to this community." 2. Prohibit "the
> society from taking and appropriating to its
> use, all the property and effects of fanatical
> fathers; thus leaving their wives and children
> destitute of the means of support." 3. "Guard

> more effectively against the evasion of the
> militia laws by members of the society." *See*
> *also* C. Green and S. Y. Wells, *A Brief Exposi-*
> *tion* (no. 734) which was intended to cor-
> rect erroneous information being circulated
> about the Shakers at this time. *See also* no.
> 1233.
> MacLean 511. ICN, K, MPB, NOC,
> OClWHi*.

1083 NEW YORK. LEGISLATURE. ASSEM-
BLY. COMMITTEE ON THE JUDICIARY.
... Report of the Committee on the Judiciary
on the Petitions of John Black and William H.
Pillow, for a Divorce of the Marriage Contract,
and Bills Referred to Them on the Same Subject. [Albany: 1849]. 6 pp. 23 cm.

> At head of title: State of New York, No. 66.
> In Assembly, Jan. 30, 1849. The Committee
> points out that the New York Constitution
> (1846) Art. 1, sec. 10, provides "that no
> divorce shall be granted otherwise than by
> judicial proceedings." In considering the
> Black and Pillow petitions for divorce, how-
> ever, the Committee recommends extending
> the permissible grounds for divorce (incur-
> able insanity, etc.), and "to provide by law,
> that where a husband or wife, after marriage,
> joins a religious sect" whose teachings "are
> to the effect that marriage is in itself sinful ...
> and where the party proceeded against has
> been actually living for five years in the prac-
> tice of such principles, proceedings for a
> divorce may be instituted." "Divorce laws
> of the different States," pp. [5–6], *see also*
> nos. 1195, 1304 and 1384.
> OClWHi*.

1084 NEW YORK. LEGISLATURE. ASSEM-
BLY. SELECT COMMITTEE ON THE SHAKERS.
... Report of the Select Committee on the Subject of the Shakers. [Albany: 1849]. Caption
title. 13 pp. 24½ cm.

> At head of title: State of New-York. No. 198.
> In Assembly, April 2, 1849. "The Committee
> reports on a resolution, inquiring into the
> propriety of rescinding certain trusts held by
> the United Society ... under a law ... passed
> April 15, 1839 (*see* no. 1078); and several
> petitions on the same subject." This report is
> largely devoted to "the origin, progress, and

present position" of the Society and is obviously derived from Shaker sources. The
Committee concluded that in view of all of
the facts laid before it, "the matter presents
no cause for legislative interference," and
asked "to be discharged from further consideration of the subject." The discharge was
granted and the Assembly ordered that "five
times the usual number of the said report be
printed for the use of the Legislature." *See
also* no. **1089**.
MacLean 423. MPB, MWiW*, N, NN, NBuG,
NhD, NjPT, OClWHi*.

1085 NEW YORK. LEGISLATURE. SENATE.
... In Council of Revision, January 27, 1818.
Resolved, that it Appears Improper to the
Council that the Bill, Entitled "An Act for the
Relief of Eunice Chapman, and for Other Purposes," Should Become a Law of this State ....
[Albany: 1818]. Broadside. 33 X 21½ cm.
　　At head of title: In Senate, January 27, 1818.
The Council of Revision's veto was based
upon the Eunice Chapman act, "as being
inconsistent with the free exercise and enjoy-
ment of that religious profession or worship,
secured by the constitution," and for other
reasons. Signed: *Charles D. Cooper, Secretary.* Reprinted in [R. McNemar], *comp.,
The Other Side of the Question* (no. **946**),
pp. 7-12. *See also* no. **2818**.
OClWHi*.

1086 —— ... In Council of Revision. February
27, 1818. [Albany: 1818]. [2] pp. 25 cm.
　　At head of title: In Senate, February 28,
1818. The Council of Revisions' resolution,
Feb. 27, 1818, which again vetoed "An Act
for the Relief of Eunice Chapman, and for
Other Purposes." Signed: *Chas. D. Cooper,
Secretary.* "Regarding that Institution [Mar-
riage], therefore, as the Greatest of Earthly
Blessings, the Council Feel the Solemnity of
their Obligation to Guard it with Scrupulous
Fidelity." *See also* nos. **448** and **3088**. On
March 14, 1818, the Act for the Relief
passed, but most of its objectionable anti-
Shaker provisions had been eliminated.
N*.

1087 —— Introduced on Notice by Mr. Putnam

... An Act in Relation to Conveyances and
Devises of Personal and Real Property and Real
Estate for Religious Purposes. [n.p.] 1855. 3 pp.
33 cm. (No. 115).
　　At head of title: In Senate. January 25, 1855.
OClWHi*.

1088 —— Report of the Trustees of the United
Society of Shakers in the Town of New Lebanon, Columbia Co., N.Y. [Albany: 1850].
Caption title. 14 pp. 23½ cm.
　　At head of title: State of New York. In
Senate, Mar. 1850. "Report of the Trustees
of the United Society of Shakers in the Town
of Watervliet, Albany County," pp. 11-14.
The Report was submitted in compliance
with the requirements of the Senate Resolution passed Feb. 8th, 1850, which called for
an exact accounting of the real and personal
property owned by all branches of the society
in New York (properties held in 1839 and
also properties acquired since that date). It is
evident that the Shakers felt that they were
unable to comply with the exact requirements
of the Resolution. The report for New Lebanon is signed: *Jonathan Wood, Edward
Fowler, Trustees of the United Society of
New Lebanon.* This document contains a
detailed statement of the community's buildings, real estate purchased and sold since 15
April, 1839, moneys on hand, bonds, stocks,
mortgages held, etc. Total real estate, including additions during the 11 years since the
Trust Act (no. **1078**), amounted to 3,053
acres. The net value of additions during this
11-year period amounted to $17,278, but the
total value of all real estate is not given. The
Trustees state, p. 6, that a more strict
compliance with the terms of Section 4 of
the Resolution, that is *"the value of all personal property, of every description, now
owned or possessed by and for the society,"*
is "utterly beyond our ability." Moreover, if
the Legislature should appoint a committee
"whose abilities are equal to the task," all
assistance would be rendered "in the prosecution of their intricate labors." General statements follow about the society's livestock,
dwelling houses and their furnishings, shops
and their fittings and implements. The Watervliet community's report is signed: *Chauncey*

Copley, Stephen Wells, Joseph Goodhow,
Trustees of the United Society of Watervliet.
These Trustees state, "That having carefully
examined the resolution of your honorable
body in all its parts and bearings, we find it
utterly impossible for us to fulfill the obligations therein required; and this we think must
appear obvious to every candid mind who
will take the trouble to give it a thorough
investigation." Instead of following the form
recommended in the Resolution, they
"adopted a form as being more brief and
equally efficient." The land "does not
exceed" 2,547 acres "as taken from the
assessors roll of the past year," and is valued
at $46,900.
MacLean 424. (10 pp., lacks Watervliet
report). ICJ, ICN, MPB, MWiW*, N, NBuG,
NN, NSyU, OClWHi.

1089 —— Resolution Passed in Senate, N.Y.,
Feb. 8, 1850, Concerning Property in Trust in
U.[nited] S.[ociety]. [Albany?: 1850]. 2 ll.
25 cm.
    In Senate, No. 89. The trustees of every
    Shaker society in New York state are
    required to report to the Legislature "a full
    and true inventory and account" of all
    properties. A copy was transmitted to each
    Society by the Clerk of the Senate. This
    report was passed "pursuant to the act en-
    titled, 'An Act in Relation to Certain Trusts',"
    no. 1078.
    OClWHi*.

1090 —— COMMITTEE ON THE JUDICIARY.
... An Act to Authorize the Levying of a Tax
upon the Taxable Property of the Different
Counties and Towns in this State, to Repay
Moneys Borrowed for or Expended in, the Pay-
ments of Bounties to Volunteers, or for the
Expenses of their Enlistment, or for Aid to their
Families ... [n.p.], 1863. 8 pp. 33 cm. No. 73.
    At head of title: State of New York, No. 73.
    In Senate, February 5, 1863. Reported by
    Mr. Folger. Official copy with each line
    numbered.
    OClWHi*.

1091 —— COMMITTEE ON THE MILITIA.
... Report ... on the Memorial of Calvin Green

and Others. [Albany: 1826]. 2 pp. 34½ cm.
    At head of title: No. 193. In Senate, March
    10, 1826. The Committee reporting on the
    Shaker *Memorial* (1826), no. 1021, sees
    "no reason to doubt the facts" set forth
    regarding Shaker payment of taxes which in
    part support the state's poor, and the sup-
    port of their own poor, etc., but "cannot
    discover how this support can in any shape
    be considered a payment to the state of an
    equivalent in money for militia service."
    The Committee concludes that "Congress
    has the power to exempt the memorialists
    from militia service totally and absolutely,"
    that the Shakers can have no relief except
    from Congress, and recommends "That the
    memorialists have leave to withdraw their
    memorial."
    DLC, OClWHi*.

1092 NEW YORK. STATE BOARD OF
CHARITIES. Annual Report ... for the Year
1892. Transmitted to the Legislature January
26, 1893. [Albany: 1893]. 589 pp. illus.
(Assembly Doc. 6, 116th Sess., 1893).
    "Report of the State Board of Charities on the Se-
    lection of a Site for and the Organization of an
    Epileptic Colony," pp. 367–411. Includes engi-
    neers' reports on the water supply, and other re-
    ports on the conditions of the buildings, purity of
    the water, etc., of the former Shaker community
    "Sonyea," i.e., Groveland, N.Y. Frontispiece map
    shows the Shaker community buildings, wood-
    lands, etc. "Exhibit 9," p. [412] ff. contains
    photographs of 18 of the Shaker buildings.
    N*.

1093 The North Family Shakers, P.O. Shaker
Station, Conn. will Pasture Horses for $1.00
per Week, at Owner's Risk ... [n.p., 1889].
Broadside. 16 X 27½ cm.
    Signed: *R. H. Van Deusen. April 30th, 1889.*
    MWiW*, OClWHi.

1094 North Family Shakers, Shaker Station,
Conn. The Season of 1893. The Standard
Trotting Stallion, Melbourn Nut, 18731. [En-
field, Conn.: 1893]. Broadside. 21 X 43 cm.
    Melbourn Nut "is perfectly sound and a
    sure foal getter." "He will be allowed to
    cover a limited number of approved mares,

at the low price of twenty-five dollars."
Complete description of the horse and his
pedigree. Present owner is R. H. Van Deusen,
Shaker Station, Conn. *See also* no. **1013.**
Gives register of pedigree of Melbourn Nut
for four generations (Foaled June 15, 1888).
OClWHi*.

1095 The North Family of Shakers, Shaker
Station, Conn., will Keep Horses, on Winter
Feed, Hay and Grain, for $ per Week ...
[n.p., 1884]. Broadside. 18 X 27 cm.
  Signed: *R. H. Van Deusen, Agent. July 17th,
1884.*
  MPB, MWiW, N, NOC, OClWHi*.

1096 [NORWOOD, WESLEY C.] Materia
Medica and Therapeutics of Norwood's Tincture
of Veratrum Viride. Eleventh Edition. Robert
Halford, Agent, Mt. Lebanon, N.Y. [n.p.], 1904.
Cover title. 32 [2] pp. 21½ cm.
  This is a new title for no. **1102.** The text has
been changed but contains essentially the
same material.
  MacLean 185. DeWint, MPB, MWA, MWiW*,
NN, NOC, OClWHi.

1097 [——] ——— Twelfth edition. Mt.
Lebanon, N.Y.: United Society of Shakers,
1936. Cover title. 31 pp. 21½ cm.
  Text of the 11th ed. reset.
  DeWint, MWA, NOC*.

1098 [——] Therapeutical Powers and Proper-
ties of Veratrum Viride. Mt. Lebanon, N.Y.:
[n.d.]. Caption title. [4] pp. 13½ cm.
  At end: Manufactured by the Shaker Society,
Mount Lebanon, Columbia County, N.Y.
Printed in blue ink on stiff buff colored
paper.
  OClWHi*.

1099 [——] ——— Variant. Reset in differ-
ent type and printed on stiff blue paper. The
text is identical with no. **1098,** but at end:
Benjamin Gates, Manufacturer for Dr. W. C.
Norwood, Mount Lebanon, Columbia County,
N.Y.
  OClWHi*.

1100 —— ——— Fourth edition. Albany:

Van Benthuysen's Print, 1858. 24 pp. 23 cm.
  This medicine made from American hellebore
and manufactured by the Shakers of Mt.
Lebanon according to Norwood's original
formula was still being marketed in the
1930's. This is a discussion of its attributes
and indications for beneficial use. "The
Vegetable Extracts ... Manufactured by the
Shakers, New Lebanon, N.Y.," pp. 22-24,
includes a list of 70 "pure inspissated alco-
holic and hydro-alcoholic extracts"; list of
70 "Fluid Extracts," p. 23. All are listed
with prices for various amounts.
  KyBgW, MPH, MWA, NBuG*, NOC,
OClWHi.

1101 —— ——— 7th ed. New York: C. N.
Crittenton, [1899]. Cover title. 23 pp. 23 cm.
  OClWHi*.

1102 —— ——— Tenth edition. [New
York?: 1902?]. Cover title. 38 [2] pp. 21 cm.
  The text extends through both sides of the
back cover. Contents: "An introduction to
the eighth edition" by Willard H. Morse,
M.D.; "Norwood on the therapeutical powers
of veratrum viride"; Physicians' testimonials
and favorable quotations from medical
journals.
  MacLean 184. MWiW*, NN.

1103 —— Veratrum Viride. [n.p., n.d.].
Caption title. 4 pp. 21 cm.
  "Reprinted from 'Southern Clinic'." Description of this Shaker-made medicine, indications for its use in the treatment of disease,
and physicians' reports on its beneficial
effects.
  MPH*, OClWHi.

1104 Notice. A Horse and Sleigh was Left
Yesterday, in Care of Isaac Bailey, in Shaker
Village, in the South Part of Lancaster [Mass.]
by some Person Unknown. They Have Not Been
Called For ... Lancaster: Feb. 11, 1860. Broad-
side. 30 X 20½ cm.
  OClWHi*.

1105 Notice. For Certain Reasons we Omit
Inserting in Shaker Manifesto the Granger Contributions for the New Dwelling House at West

Gloucester. But True to Promise Publish on a Separate Slip. [Shaker Village, Canterbury, N.H.: 1881]. Broadside. 21 X 18 cm.

    Signed: *P. J. R.* (Polly J. Reed). "Grangers first contribution, three hundred and eleven dollars, was forwarded to the Treasurer, Elder Otis Sawyer, Dec. 30th, 1880 . . . for a universal New Years Gift." *See* no. 722.

OClWHi*.

NOTICES TO VISITORS, RULES OF BEHAVIOR, ETC.

MacLean 388 (*Notice. Rules for Visitors* (1840?). Broadside. f°.) lacks sufficient information to make identification certain. Consequently, this MacLean number is not assigned to any entry below. Similarly, lack of information (e.g., 1 sheet, 1 leaf, etc.) on the cards in the National Union Catalog does not allow the holdings in some libraries to be identified or credited. MacLean 427 gives the date: 1875. No copy printed with this date has been located. No copy has been located of MacLean 462 (United (The) Society of Believers, called Shakers. Notice to Writers; Friendly Advice. *Shaker Village, N.Y.* Broadside. f°.). W. H. Cathcart thought that MacLean has made a mistake in this entry: "There is a mistake in the way this is put down in the list. It should be 'Notice to Visitors' and not 'Notice to Writers'." W. H. Cathcart a.l.s. to Eldress Catherine Allen, Sept. 26, 1912, in the manuscript collection of the Western Reserve Historical Society. The arrangement below is alphabetical insofar as the entries permit, and is not intended to indicate priority of publication.

1106 Notice! For the Benefit of Friends who May Call upon Us, as well as for the Better Protection of Ourselves it has been Thought Advisable to Adopt the Following Rules for Visitors. [Canterbury, N.H.?: n.d.]. Broadside. 30 X 24 cm.

    Signed: *United Society.* Eight rules are listed: "1. As our Home is not open for public entertainment, our rules are such as would be adapted to the use of the private dwellings . . . . 8. For reasons that may be satisfactorily explained, we prefer that parents would not make protracted visits with children under our care." This appears to be the earliest of such "Notices." The text of apparently later rules was revised, and the 8th rule was omitted. MWiW*, OClWHi, OHi.

1107 Notice. In Consequence of the Amount of Company to which our Societies are at All Times Subject, We have been under the Necessity of Adopting the Following Rules for Visitors. [Union Village, O., n.d.]. Broadside. 38½ X 24½ cm.

    Signed: *The United Society of Union Village.* OClWHi*.

1108 Notice. In Consequence of the Increasing Amount of Company to which our Societies are at All Times Subject, we have been under the Necessity of Adopting the Following Rules for Visitors: Printed at New Lebanon, [n.d.]. Broadside. 24 X 19 cm.

    Signed: *United Society.* Minor differences in punctuation, but the rules are the same as those in nos. 1106 and 1107. OClWHi*.

1109 ———— to which we are at All Times Subject, it Becomes Necessary to Adopt the Following Rules for Visitors. [n.p., n.d.]. Broadside. 34½ X 29½ cm.

    Signed: *United Society.* Probably printed at Canterbury. Seven rules of conduct are given: "First. We wish it to be understood that we do not keep a public house . . . Seventh. Strangers calling for meals or lodgings are expected to pay if accommodated." This *Notice* has been reprinted by the Shaker Museum, Old Chatham, N.Y., from the Fruitlands Museums, Harvard, Mass., copy. MHarF, MWiW*, OClWHi.

1110 Notice. Parties who are Shown about the Premises will be Charged a Fee of Twenty Five Cents, as Compensation for Time and Trouble. [East Canterbury] Printed at Shaker Village, Mer. Co., N.H.: [n.d.]. Broadside. 28 X 37½ cm.

    MPH*, OClWHi.

1111 Notice to Visitors. [Canaan, N.Y.: n.d.]. Broadside. 33½ × 26½ cm.

Entirely different text from other "Notices" with the same title. The text gives directions for registering, name and address, price of meals, care of teams, etc. It is printed within an ornamental type border with "Berkshire Industrial Farm" printed at the bottom, outside of the border.
OClWHi*.

1112 ... Notice to Visitors. [Enfield, Conn.: *ca.* 1874]. Caption title. [2] pp. 22 cm.

At head of title: The United Society of Believers, called Shakers. With a notice of *Shaker and Shakeress* and subscription price is followed by "Address George Wilcox or Elder Stoughton H. Kellogg, Thompsonville, Conn.," p. [1]. "Rules for Behavior in Places Consecrated to Worship," p. [2], are numbered 1-11.
CHi, MWiW*, NN, OClWHi*, OHi.

1113 ... Notice to Visitors. [Shaker Village, Mer. Co., N.H.: 1873-75]. Caption title. [2] pp. 22 cm.

At head of title: The United Society of Believers, called Shakers. Begins with directions for traveling by train to Canterbury, N.H. At end, p. [1], is a notice of the *Shaker and Shakeress,* "a new monthly magazine," with subscription price, and "Address H. C. Blinn, Shaker Village, Mer. Co., N.H." "The United Society of Believers, called Shakers," caption title, p. [2], is a short description of Shakerism followed by "Our house of worship ... will be opened again ... in May 1874."
MWiW*, OClWHi.

1114 —— [Shaker Village, Mer. Co., N.H.: 1873-75]. Caption title. [2] pp. 22 cm.

At head of title: The United Society of Believers, called Shakers. The text and type setting, p. [1], is identical with p. [1], no. 1113. Begins with directions for traveling by train to Canterbury, N.H. At end, p. [1] notice of the *Shaker and Shakeress,* with the

subscription price, and "Address H. C. Blinn, Shaker Village, Mer. Co., N.H." "Friendly Advice to those who Contemplate Placing their children in Charge of the Society of Shakers," p. [2]. The rules which follow are numbered, 1-7.
DLC, MWiW*.

1115 —— Printed at Shaker Village, Mer. Co., N.H.: [18-?]. Broadside. 19½ × 13 cm.

At head of title: The United Society of Believers, Shakers. Text begins "Those who visit us as enquirers will be cordially entertained." Rules of behavior when visiting follow. At end, "Shaker Village is situated 12 miles NE from Concord, N.H."
OClWHi*.

1116 —— Printed at Shaker Village, Mer. Co., N.H.: [1873-75]. Caption title. [2] pp. 22 cm.

At head of title: Shakers. Unnumbered rules of behavior are followed by a notice of the *Shaker and Shakeress,* with the subscription price, and "Address H. C. Blinn, Mer. Co., N.H." At end, "Services are held ... from the first of May, to the first of Nov. each year." "The United Society of Believers," caption title, p. [2], is a short description of Shakerism.
DLC*.

1117 Rules for Behavior in Places Consecrated to Worship. Shaker Village [Canterbury], Mer. Co.: [n.d.]. Broadside. 25 × 20½ cm.
MPH*.

1118 —— (on verso) The United Society of Believers Called Shakers. Notice to Visitors. Shaker Village, N.H.: [1875]. Caption title. 2 pp. 22 cm.
MacLean 428(?). OClWHi*.

1119 Rules for Behavior in the House of Worship. Printed at Shaker Village, N.H.: [n.d.]. Broadside. 21½ × 14 cm.

Rules numbered 1-10 within ruled border.
OClWHi*.

NOVITIATE COVENANTS

Individual novitiate covenants for probationary membership in the various Shaker societies are found in bound volumes which contain both filled and blank covenants. *The Catalogue of the Emma B. King Library* (Shaker Museum, Old Chatham, N.Y.), no. 2719, records 13 such volumes which represent covenants of 6 societies and cover the years 1857–1934; similar items are found in other collections. Adaptations of these covenants by individual Shaker communities result in some variation of wording, but all contain essentially the same provisos. This document is an agreement for probationary membership in a particular Shaker society in which the prospective member agrees to conform to all rules and orders of the society, and not to create dissatisfaction or "disharmony" within the family. Lack of such compliance is sufficient to cause the person to be requested to withdraw peaceably from the society. This covenant provides further that any account, claim, or demand against the society or any member(s) will never be made for the use of any money or property brought into the society, and the same applies to any labor or service performed. It is stipulated that a probationary member is free to withdraw, and that after proper notice has been given all money or property will be returned. "The Shaker Novitiate Covenant," drawn up by Elder Harvey L. Eads, is printed in the *Shaker Manifesto*, 8 (June 1878), 136–37. Cf. nos. 1307 and 1279. Novitiate Covenants have not been recorded here, but see nos. 844, 1368, 1424, and 1425.

1120 Observations on the Natural and Constitutional Rights of Conscience, in Relation to Military Requisitions on the People Called Shakers. [Albany, N.Y.: E. & E. Hosford, Printers, 1816]. Cover title. 24 pp. 21 cm.

On p. [2], signed: *In behalf of the Society, Richard Spier, Peter Dodge, Morrell Baker, Calvin Green, Seth Y. Wells, Watervliet, Feb. 20th, 1816.* When the *Observations* were prepared for the information of particular members of the N.Y. Legislature, there was no intention of printing them. The members who received them, however, advised that the *Observations* be printed for the information of all members. This is a plea to the legislature "to take measures to secure [Shaker] ... religious and constitutional rights," and supplements the Shaker *Memorial*, addressed to the New York Legislature, Feb. 19, 1816. *See* no. 1019. It supports "the reasonableness, the constitutionality, the justice, and the sincerity" of the Shakers in claiming "exemption from the operation of the present militia laws of this State, which so materially affect our religious rights," p. [3]. "Supplementary Observations," pp. 21–24.
MacLean 501. Sabin 79715. Shaw 38920.
CSmH, DLC, ICN, MB, MH, MWiW*, N,

NHi, NOC, OClWHi, OWoC, RPB.

1121 OFFORD, DANIEL. "The Doctrine and Life of the Shakers." In John Henry Barrows, ed., *The World's Parliament of Religions; An Illustrated and Popular Story of the World's First Parliament of Religions,* Held in Chicago in Connection with the Columbian Exposition of 1893 (Chicago: 1893. 2 vols.), Vol. 2, p. 1380.

1122 —— Happy Release. [n.p., 1892]. Broadside. 18½ × 7½ cm.

Announcing Frederick Evans' resignation as Elder of the North Family, Mt. Lebanon. Succeeded by Walter Shepard. This notice is tipped in *The Manifesto*, 22 (December 1892), preceding p. [265], in the Williams College copy (Williamstown, Mass.).
MWiW*, OClWHi.

1123 —— Letter from Daniel Offord, with Reply by Koresh. [Chicago?: 1893]. Caption title. 12 pp. 17 cm.

An inquiry about the "interior meaning" in an article on Shaker celibacy in the *Flaming Sword*, Sept. 10, 1892. Koresh (Cyrus R. Teed), the editor, had been certified as a Shaker, *see* no. 652. "Our Babylon" [poem]

by James R. Clark, pp. 11–12 (from *The Manifesto*, 23 (March 1893), 67); "Conquering Legions" [poem] by Martha J. Anderson, p. 12.
MacLean 389. CtY, MPB, MPH*, MWA, MWiW, N, NBuG, NN, OClWHi.

1124 —— Seven Travails of the Shaker Church. Mt. Lebanon, N.Y.: [1889]. Cover title. 8 pp. 14½ cm.
  Signed: *Daniel Offord. Mt. Lebanon, N.Y., Sept. 26th 1889.* Reprinted in *The Manifesto*, 20 (January 1890), 5–9.
  MacLean 390. CtY, DLC, MHarF, MPB, MWA, MWiW*, N, NBuG, NN, O, OClWHi, ODa, WHi.

1125 [——] and Others. Original Shaker Music Published by the North Family. Of Mt. Lebanon, Col. Co., N.Y. .... New York: Wm. A. Pond & Company [F. H. Gilson, Music Typographer, Boston], 1893. 271 pp. music. 21½ cm.
  Cover title: Original Shaker Music. Volume II (i.e., of Shaker Music (1884), no. **1126**). MacLean attributes this compilation to Daniel Offord, Lucy Bowers, and Martha J. Anderson. Leila Taylor, *A Memorial to Anna White* (no. **1359**), p. 69, states that Anna White "devoted much time and effort to this work." Intended as a "befitting companion" to Vol. I, issued in 1884. It is announced in the Home Notes of the North Family, *The Manifesto*, 23 (November 1893), 262, that 1000 copies have been printed. "To those who have not had experience in this line, we would say that it costs considerable time and money ... and a scarcely conceivable amount of careful, exhausting work to publish a music book .... It is issued at bare cost." Conventional notation, 4-part harmony.
  MacLean 75. DLC, DeWint, ICN, MPB, MWiW*, MiU-C, N, NBuG, NN, NOC, NSyU, NjPT, OClWHi, ODa, OHi, OLeWHi, RPB, WHi.

1126 [——] and Others. Shaker Music. Original Inspirational Hymns and Songs Illustrative of the Resurrection Life and Testimony of the Shakers .... New York: Published for the North Family, Mt. Lebanon, N.Y., by William A. Pond & Co. [F. H. Gilson, Music Typographer, Boston, 1884]. 250 pp. music. 20½ cm.
  Cover title: Original Shaker Music. Inspirational. At foot of title page: Copyright 1884, by Daniel Offord. Daniel Offord has been credited as compiler, *see Shaker Quarterly*, 3 (Winter, 1963), 131. Frederick Evans has also been credited as compiler. Leila Taylor, *A Memorial to Anna White* (no. **1359**), p. 69, states that Anna White composed the 6-line verse used as the motto on the title page. This compilation is a revision and enlargement of *Shaker Music. Inspirational Hymns* (no. **1293**); parts of the preface are identical, and although not so indicated it is generally considered to be Vol. I of no. **1125**. Conventional notation with mostly 4-part harmony; a few single-line melodies.
  MacLean 92. CtHC, CtY, DLC, DeWint, ICN, KyBgW, MHarF, MPB, MPH, MWA, MWiW*, MeHi, MiU, MiU-C, N, NN, NOC, NjPT, OClWHi, ODa, OO, OU.

1127 OHIO. *Laws, Statutes, etc.* An Act for the Relief and Support of Women Who may be Abandoned by Their Husbands, and for Other Purposes, Jan. 11, 1811. Ohio Laws (1811) IX, 13–16.
  This act followed Thomas Freeman's proposal for legal remedies for disuniting families (no. **3221**). It relates specifically to the Shakers, who "inculcate and enjoin upon all who become attached to them, that they must lead a life of *celibacy*, in consequence of which women have been abandoned ... robbed of their children and left destitute of the means of support." The act provides that any man who renounces the marriage covenant by joining the Shakers shall lose authority over his children, that the court will decree what portion of his property will become the woman's, that property previously given to the Shakers may be recovered by the injured party, and that anyone causing a renunciation of the marriage covenant is liable for a fine of $500. Reprinted in J. P. MacLean's *Shakers of Ohio* (no. **2410**), pp. 15–17. Thomas Freeman's proposal was printed in a series of articles in the Lebanon, O., *Western Star*, Nos. IV, V, Sept. 29, Oct. 13, 1810, Ham, "Shakerism in the Old West," p. 134, ftn. 24. Ham also states here that two memorials were presented to the legislature and cites, ftn. 25,

Ohio Senate Journal, pp. 71, 77, 89, 105, 106, 224 and equivalent references in the *Ohio House Journal*.
O, OClWHi*.

1128 The Old Man Adam [poem]. [n.p., n.d.]. 4 pp. 13 cm.
OClWHi*.

1129 On the Shakers. Composed by Caleb Munson, Sodus, N.Y., June 10, 1826. Putneyville [N.Y.]: Commercial Press, [1826]. Broadside. 26 × 17½ cm.
A poem of 16 stanzas.
Private collection.

1130 100 Years of Shaker Life. Centennial of a Communism of Peace. [n.p., 1874?]. Caption title. 8 pp. 13½ × 17½ cm.
Reprinted from the [New York?] *World*, Dec. 27 [1884?]. Authorship is often attributed to F. W. Evans, but several places in the text make this attribution doubtful. Moreover, a statement on p. 8, "when the writer visited it [Mt. Lebanon] a few days ago," indicates other authorship.
MacLean 392 (attributed to Evans). CtY, DLC, ICN, MPB, MWA, MWiW*, MiU-C, N, NBuG, NN, NjPT, OClWHi.

1131 ONE THAT WAS PRESENT, *pseud.* Father Tillinghast's Labors. Interesting Services at the Anniversary of the Allen Street Methodist Sabbath School, New Bedford, Mass., Holden on the 2d inst. New Bedford: Feb. 10, 1862. Broadside in 2 columns. 25 × 19½ cm.
Third annual report by F. Tillinghast about hundreds of visits to Sabbath Schools and his other efforts among children to further their religious education. *See no.* 1371.
OClWHi*.

ONE WHO KNOWS, *pseud. See* Evans, Jessie, no. 684 ff.

1132 Opinions of the Press. The Following Extracts from Different Papers, here and elsewhere, Show the Favorable Opinions of the Press Wherever this Group has Been ... [New York?: 1846]. Broadside. 38 × 21 cm.
Seven laudatory reviews of the exhibition performed by six Shaker seceders from the Canterbury, N.H., community are reprinted from the New York *Sun*, New York *Tribune*, Albany *Herald*, Troy *Post*, Troy *Budget*, the Newark *Daily Advertiser*, and a circular, *To the Citizens of Poughkeepsie*, signed by eight prominent citizens. All are dated in 1846; the latest is Sept. 24, 1846. It was stated that "The vocal powers are of the highest order," while Miss Willard's "whirling" 1000–1500 times without stopping drew rave notices. The respectability of the group is emphasized; "One was a celebrated Doctor [Wm. Tripure], another an Elder [James M. Otis]... the ladies were in high standing." Their secession "was owing entirely to a disbelief in the doctrines of the Shakers, which resulted from a long and patient investigation thereof." *See also* nos. 728, 2496 and 2535. Prudence Morell reported that "We still keep hearing from Tripure & Company. The people in the country do not appear to have any fellowship with their conduct. The Cincinnatians say they hope the Ohio turn-offs [seceders] will never act in this manner." "Account of a Journey to the West in the year 1847," no. 1617, pp. 54–55.
MHarF (photo copy)*, NHi.

1133 Our Title Deeds. [n.p., n.d.]. Broadside in 2 columns. 31 × 17½ cm.
From the *Belfast Star*, Ireland. Concerns a tablet in Westminster Abbey memorializing Judge Theophilus Harrington of Vermont because in a court of justice he would not recognize a certain slaveholder's title of ownership of a runaway slave since there was "no deed of sale from God Almighty," with extrapolation and application to landlords' titles to land.
MacLean 396. MHarF, MPB, OClWHi*.

P

1134 PARKER, DAVID and JAMES S. KAIME. [Circular] Letter. Shaker Village (Canterbury), N.H.: [June 23, 1866]. Broadside. 23½ × 20 cm.

A proposal suggesting the advisability of all Shaker communities cooperating in setting up a mutual fire insurance company to cover Shaker properties, submitted by David Parker and countersigned in ink by James S. Kaime. This letter was sent at the request of the Ministry at Mt. Lebanon, N.Y., and a response is requested within 30 days. Refers to accompanying circular, no. 1066.
OClWHi*, NOC.

PATENTS

The fertile ingenuity of the Shakers as shown in their inventions and labor-saving devices has been commented upon time and again in the accounts written by visitors to the various Shaker communities. Moreover, there is abundant evidence that the inhabitants of the vicinities surrounding Shaker communities looked upon these people, sometimes enviously, as highly successful in the utilization of mechanical means in the efficient operation of the routines of their daily lives and in their agricultural and industrial productions. Shaker ingenuity and inventions were responsible for many improvements upon the customary ways of the time. However, more Shaker inventions were originated and are credited in Shaker and other sources than are shown in the Shaker patents here, particularly inventions claimed in the early 19th century. *See* D. A. Buckingham, *The Shaker*, 7 (misnumb. 6), (August, October, 1877), 59, 77; A. White and L. Taylor, *Shakerism, Its Meaning and Message* (Columbus, O., 1904), pp. 310–16; E. D. Andrews, *Community Industries of the Shakers* (Albany, N.Y., 1932), pp. 39–45; M. Melcher, *The Shaker Adventure* (Cleveland, O., 1960), pp. 134–35, 282–83. With some exceptions these references enumerate undocumented claims of Shaker inventions for which, in the absence of patent rights, priority has not been established. The discrepancy between such claims and the list below is accounted for in part by Shaker beliefs which opposed in principle the monopolistic and exploitation features which patent rights generated among the "world's people." *See* A. White and L. Taylor, *ibid.*, p. 310, where it is stated that "patent money savors of monopoly, the opposite of the Golden Rule." Whatever the Shaker "invents is for the use of the whole world"; quoted in F. G. Ham, "Shakerism in the Old West," p. 221, where other quotations concerning patent rights and exploitation of Shaker inventions are given. These quotations are taken from an exchange of letters between the Union Village, O., and the Mt. Lebanon, Ministries. While the Shaker attitude discouraged applications for patent rights, the patents below reflect an increasing relaxation of opposition. The available ms. records of Shaker membership are dispersed and are incomplete. All of the patentees below, however, have been identified as Shakers either in published death lists or in the extensive file of Shaker membership at the Western Reserve Historical Society (Cleveland, O.). Nearly one hundred other patents described in the patent records appear to have been granted for Shaker inventions, but they have been omitted here because it has not been possible to establish the patentee's Shaker connection. Another source of confusion about Shaker patents is that many of the mechanical contrivances used and produced by the Shakers, and in consequence considered to be Shaker inventions, were in fact the result of negotiations with non-Shaker patentees for concessions or even outright purchases of patents. A partial list of such negotiations is found in E. D. Andrews, *ibid.*, p. 45. *See also* nos. 3126, 3283, 3286, and 3446.

U.S. letters patent have been issued since 1790, but the Patent Office was not established until 1836, at which time it was provided that a list of patents and patentees be included in the Annual

Report of the U.S. Patent Commissioner. Patent information before 1837 is sketchy and patent numbers are often lacking. From 1837 to 1872, lists of patents and patentees may be found in the Patent Commissioner's *Annual Report* covering the year in which the patent was granted. Details of the contents of these *Reports* and peculiarities of the patent information they contain are described in the *Checklist of United States Public Documents 1789-1909*, comp. under the Direction of the Superintendent of Documents (Washington, D.C., 1911), pp. 511-17, where the various indexes to U.S. patents will also be found. After 1872, abstracts of patent specifications and drawings are found in the U.S. Patent Office *Official Patent Gazette* for the week in which the patent was granted.

1135 ADAIR, WILLIAM, Pleasant Hill, Ky. Truss for Hernia. Patent granted Feb. 17, 1836. Patent number lacking.

1136 ANNIS, H. K., Enfield, N.H. Assignor to Jason Kidder and Hiram C. Baker. Improvement in Water-Wheel (with Controlling Gate). Patent granted Nov. 15, 1864. Patent No. 45114.
An abstract of this patent is found also in the *Scientific American*, n.s. 11 (Nov. 26, 1864), 349.

1137 BAIRD, DANIEL N. (Daniel W.?), Warrensville, O. (i.e., North Union). Assignor to Nathaniel Potter. Improved Brace. Patent granted Aug. 26, 1856. Patent No. 15632.

1138 BENNETT, NICHOLAS, New Lebanon, N.Y. Assignor to David Parker, Shaker Village (Canterbury), N.H. Improved Washing Machine. Patent granted Jan. 26, 1858. Patent No. 19181.
This patent is usually credited to David Parker, Canterbury, N.H., but patent records identify Parker as the assignee. The patent abstract does not, however, give the date that application for this patent was filed. Shaker records show that Nicholas Bennett (or Bennet) died at New Lebanon, N.Y., October 15, 1857, over 3 months before the patent was granted, R. Cottrell, "Shaker Death Records," *New England Historical and Genealogical Register*, 115 (Jan. 1961), 37. According to E. D. Andrews, *Community Industries of the Shakers* (no. 1759), pp. 269-70, n. 15, the Bennett patent is likely an improvement on Patent No. 1193, granted to Sylvester Noble, Hoosick, N.Y., Feb. 1, 1810. Noble sold to Nathan Kendall, a Shaker at New Lebanon, N.Y., for $1.00, the right to use the machine or to make improvements upon it. *See also* no. 1141. The Shaker Washing Machine, or Wash Mill, exhibited at the Centennial Exposition in Philadelphia, 1876, was awarded a gold medal.

1139 BLAKEMAN, ELISHA D., New Lebanon, N.Y. Assignor to Jacob J. and Levi Auchampaugh of New Lebanon. Improved Fly-Trap. Patent granted Mar. 29, 1859. Patent No. 23422.

1140 —— New Lebanon, N.Y. Piano-Violin. Patent granted May 9, 1871. Patent No. 114520.
This is a keyed violin-like instrument for setting the pitch, and was generally referred to as a "toneometer" or a "modeometer."

1141 BRIGGS, NICHOLAS A. and ELIJAH H. KNOWLES, Shaker Village, N.H. Assignors to said Briggs. Improved Washing-Machine. Patent granted Aug. 7, 1877. Patent No. 193802.

1142 CHANDLER, HEWITT, New Gloucester (Sabbathday Lake), Me. Harvesting Machine. Patent granted August 22, 1865. Patent No. 49501.
"One of the first mowing machines ever invented was built at the Shaker Mill [Sabbathday Lake, Me.] and sold to farmers throughout the state. As many as a hundred a year were built for sale. They were made in the north room of the mill which contained engine lathes, planers for ironwork, drill punches and every facility for dressing iron and making repairs to machinery. One peculiarity of these mowing machines was that the cutter bar ran at the rear of the right front wheel instead of in front." Elsie McCool, "A Brief History of the Shaker Mills, Sabbathday Lake, Maine," *Shaker Quarterly*, 3 (Fall 1963), 100-101. J. S. Kouwenhoven, *Made in America* (no. 2355), p. 119, refers to this mower.

1143 CHASE, NELSON, Enfield, N.H. Folding Stereoscope. Patent granted July 16, 1872. Patent No. 129100.

"The staff of the instrument is jointed, the eye-piece and hood folding upon it." Elder Henry Blinn, "Journey to Kentucky in the Year 1873," *Shaker Quarterly*, 5 (Spring 1965), 11–12, describes the reaction to his efforts to sell this stereoscope. "Its neatness, compactness—and general appearance was highly commended by all, but the price was thought to exceed propriety. The retail price of this one was to be $15.00... The majority of inspectors thought Springfield [Mass.] would be a poor market for such an expensive article."

1144 COPLEY, LUTHER, New Lebanon, N.Y. Wheel Mill, or Machine, and Applying Water, Wind or Steam thereto. Patent granted May 15, 1834. Patent No. lacking.

1145 DONNELL, GEORGE O., New Lebanon, N.Y. Improvement in Chairs. Patent granted Mar. 2, 1832. Patent No. 8771.

"A new and improved mode of preventing the wear and tear of carpets and the marring of floors caused by the corners of the back posts of chairs as they take their natural motion of rocking backward and forward." The improvement consists of a metallic ferrule, ball, and foot piece applied to the back posts. It is often called a "tilter." In a broadside, *Price List of Shaker Chairs*, (185–?), twenty-five cents extra is charged for chairs with "Button joint Tilts," *see* no. 249. E. D. Andrews, *Community Industries of the Shakers* (no. 1759), p. 239, states that this improvement was "based upon an earlier invention in wood," and that "apparently not many of these chairs with patent feet were made," p. 291, no. 102.

1146 DYER, CALEB M. and D. M. CUMMINGS, Enfield, N.H. Improved Shingle Machine. Patent granted Mar. 20, 1860. Patent No. 27534.

1147 GROSVENOR, LORENZO D., Shaker Village (Harvard), Mass. Improvement in Machines for Sorting Broom Corn. Patent granted Jan. 1, 1851. Patent No. 7872.

1148 —— South Groton (i.e., Harvard), Mass. Machine for Stripping Seed from Broom Corn. Patent granted Sept. 23, 1851. Patent No. 8375.

1149 HARTFORD, BENJAMIN and W. B. TILTON, Enfield, N.H. Loom-Heddle and Harness. Patent granted Dec. 29, 1837. Patent No. 544.

1150 HURLBUT, SAMUEL G., Cleveland (North Union), O. Cider-Mill. Patent granted Sept. 6, 1864. Patent No. 44096.

1151 MYRICK, ELIJAH, Harvard, Mass. Chimney Caps. Patent granted May 25, 1869. Patent No. 90380.

1152 —— Another invention of Elijah Myrick's is described in *The Shaker Manifesto*, 11 (August 1881), 184, as "a novelty in top carriages. An ingenious device to protect the curtains when rolled up. They are placed in a pocket, made by means of the connection between the posts and top of the carriage, requiring no strap or buckle ... It is now at the carriage manufactory of Brigham, McRay & Co., where it can be seen, and by whom it was made. We understand they are to make one to exhibit in the New England Mechanics fair ... A patent has been applied for ..." No patent located.

1153 OSBORNE, DAVID, Berkshire County (Hancock), Mass. Churn. Patent granted Jan. 8, 1810. Patent No. lacking.

1154 PARKER, DAVID, Shaker Village (Canterbury), N.H. Method of Preserving and Drying Green Corn on the Cob. Patent granted Apr. 10, 1866. Patent No. 53861.

1155 PENNEBAKER, FRANCIS M. and WILLIAM F. PENNEBAKER, Pleasant Hill, Ky. Improvement in Dumping Wagons. Patent granted Oct. 3, 1876. Patent No. 182955.

"A farm utility wagon which had high rear wheels and very low wheels in front. A box mounted on a frame could be shifted back and forth by use of ropes and pulleys, and could be dumped with ease by the driver from his seat. The low front wheels permitted short turns ... Models of this wagon were actually built and demonstrated, but the Shakers were unable to manufacture it cheaply enough to be sold competitively," T. D. Clark and F. G. Ham, *Pleasant Hill and its Shakers* (no. 1969), pp. 77–78.

1156 POTTER, WILLIAM J., Mount Lebanon, N.Y. Assignor to himself and Robert M. Wagen (i.e., Wagan), same place. Improvement in Green-Corn Cutters. Patent granted Feb. 23, 1875. Patent No. 160119.

The green-corn cutter was exhibited at the Centennial Exposition in Philadelphia, 1876. This machine was intended primarily for preparing the corn for drying.

1157 PRICE, GEORGE BELLAMY, Watervliet, N.Y. Pea-Sheller. Patent granted Aug. 16, 1864. Patent No. 43864.

This patent abstract is found also in the *Scientific American*, n.s., 11 (Aug. 27, 1864), 140.

1158 PRICE, THOMAS J., South Union, Ky. Grain Separator. Patent granted May 1, 1866. Patent No. 54403.

1159 —— Auburn (South Union), Ky. Combined Seeder and Cultivator. Patent granted Aug. 14, 1866. Patent No. 57185.

1160 RANDLETTE, TIMOTHY, Enfield, N.H. Improvement in Mop-Heads. Patent granted Nov. 15, 1853. Patent No. 10237.

1161 RIEDEL, JULIUS, Pleasant Hill, Ky. Improvement in Cartridges. Patent granted Sept. 9, 1856. Patent No. 15707.

1162 RODMAN, J. M., South Union, Ky. Plough. Patent granted Feb. 26, 1861. Patent No. 31559.

1163 RUSSELL, SANFORD J., Greensburg, Indiana. Cord-Clamp for Windows. Patent granted July 16, 1872. Patent No. 129367.

The non-Shaker residence given in Russell's patent application is due to his having seceded

from Union Village, Sept. 2, 1861. There is, however, evidence that he was at South Union, Ky., in 1873, and that he rejoined the Shakers in 1880. He died at Union Village, O., Nov. 10, 1890. The "Shaker Sash Balance" was advertised repeatedly in the *Shaker Manifesto*. Russell is credited with having improved and perfected this invention, but no later patent is recorded in the *Official Gazette* of the U.S. Patent Office.

1164 SHEPARD, ROBERT. Shaker Village (Canterbury), N.H. Improved Land-Leveller. Patent granted Apr. 1, 1862. Patent No. 34851.

1165 SLOSS, L. L., South Union, Ky. Double Shovel Plow. Patent granted Aug. 27, 1867. Patent No. 68247.

1166 STEWART, AMOS, Mount Lebanon, N.Y. Water Wheel. Patent granted Nov. 22, 1864. Patent No. 45191.

This invention is concerned with the peculiar shape of the water buckets and the manner in which water is applied to the wheel. The patent abstract of this invention was also printed in the *Scientific American*, n.s., 11 (Dec. 3, 1864), 365.

1167 STEWART, PHILEMON, New Lebanon, N.Y. Assignor to Auchampaugh Bros. of said New Lebanon. Cast Iron Fence Post. Patent granted Mar. 1, 1859. Patent No. 23140.

1168 THOMAS, MARKWELL, Alfred, Me. Winnowing, Cleaning and Separating Machine. Patent granted May 30, 1837. Patent No. 213.

1169 TRULL, NEHEMIAH, Shaker Village (Canterbury), N.H. Wind Wheel. Patent granted Oct. 4, 1864. Patent No. 44564.

1170 WHITE, JOHN, South Union, Ky. Washing Machine and Churn. Patent granted Apr. 11, 1831. Patent No. lacking.

1171 The Peace Resolutions. [n.p., 1905]. Broadside. 23 X 7½ cm.

About the resolutions adopted at the Peace Congress held at Mt. Lebanon, N.Y., reprinted

from "St. Clair McKelway in Brooklyn Eagle, Oct. 19, 1905." States that the resolutions adopted will be sent to Congress for endorsement.
MWiW*, N, OClWHi.

1172 PEEBLES, JAMES MARTIN. "Can any Good Come out of Nazareth? Abstract of [a] Lecture, July 30 [1871]," in F. W. Evans, Religious Communism (no. 622), pp. 30-32.
Peebles is referred to as "that associate Shaker" in *Shakerism, Its Meaning and Message* (Columbia, O., [1904]), by Anna White and Leila S. Taylor, p. 215. In non-Shaker publications, he has been described as "a First Order Member."

1173 —— Immortality, and our Employments Hereafter. With what a Hundred Spirits, Good and Evil, Say of Their Dwelling Places. Boston: Colby and Rich, 1880. 296 pp. 23½ cm.
"The Friends and Shakers in Spirit Life," pp. 159-69. "A Beautiful Vision," *Shaker Manifesto*, 10 (October 1880), 219-20, reprinted a vision of Sister Eunice Bathrick from pp. 168-69 of this work.
DLC, MPH*, MiU, NN, OCl, PU.

1174 —— Jesus: Myth, Man, or God . . . London: J. Burns. Progressive Library, 1870. iv, 108 pp. 21½ cm.
Letter written by Frederick Evans replying to critical comment in the *Springfield Republican* (Mass.), pp. 101-102.
ICN, MPH, NN, OClWHi*, PU.

1175 —— Nihilism — Socialism — Shakerism — Which? [Mt. Lebanon, N.Y.?: 1880?]. Caption title. 7 pp. 13 cm.
A letter addressed: Ed. *Shaker Manifesto*. Signed: *J. M. Peebles, Hammonton, N.J.* Appeared in the *Shaker Manifesto*, 10 (April 1880), 86-89.
MacLean 398. DLC, MPB, MWiW*, N, NN, NSyU, OClWHi, OHi, WHi.

1176 —— Oriental Spiritualism. From the Spirit of Mother Ann Lee to J. M. Peebles. [Mt. Lebanon: 1877]. Cover title. 13 pp. 13½ cm.
A letter to F. W. Evans from Point de Galle,

Isle of Ceylon, Aug. 2, 1877. Contains also: Letter from Elder Evans, "Look behind the Curtains of Shakerism," addressed to the Editor of the Hudson Register; "Selfish Property. A Dream" by one of the Sisters on the night of Nov. 9, 1877. Signed: *F. W. Evans.*
MacLean 399. CtY, DLC, MPB, MPH, MWA, MWiW*, N, NBuG, NN, NSyU, OClWHi, OHi, WHi.

1177 —— Seers of the Ages; Embracing Spiritualism, Past and Present. Doctrines Stated and Moral Tendencies Defined . . . 3d ed. Boston: William White and Co., 1870. 376 pp. 22 cm.
Shakers, pp. 182-84, Lecture V, "Churchal Spiritualism," cites F. W. Evans' personal statements and quotes William H. Dixon. Later editions were published by the Banner of Light Publishing Co., Boston.
DLC*, MB, NN, PU.

1178 —— A Shaker Mission. Results of Elder Evans' Visit to England . . . [Mt. Lebanon, N.Y.?: n.d.]. Broadside in 3 columns. 27 X 26 cm.
"From the New York Tribune August 8." Includes "The Other Side" by F. W. Evans.
MacLean 271. MH, MHarF, MPB, NN, NSyU, OClWHi*, OHi.

1179 —— The Shaker Mission to England. Letters from J. M. Peebles M.D. [Mt. Lebanon, N.Y.?: 1887?]. Caption title. [4] pp. 22½ cm.
Peebles' letter dated August 5th, 1887, is addressed: To the Elders and Eldresses and Believers at Mt. Lebanon. Contains also: "The Other Side" by Frederick Evans, which was reprinted in his *Autobiography*, no. 576 above, pp. 248-49.
MHarF, MPB, MWA, MWiW*, OClWHi.

PELHAM, RICHARD W., *ed.,* Shakers; A Correspondence . . . *See* [Carr], Mary Frances, no. 144.

1180 PELHAM, RICHARD W. The Shaker's Answer to a Letter, from an Inquirer. Union Village, Ohio: 1868. Cover title. 23 pp. 15 cm.
A letter addressed to E.—— W.——.
MacLean 400. DLC, MB, MPB, MWA, MWiW*, NBuG, NN, NOC, OClWHi, OHi.

1181 —— ——— Second edition. Union
Village, Ohio. Cincinnati: Jos. B. Boyd, Printer,
1868. Cover title. 32 pp. 14½ cm.
   A larger size type increases the number of
   pages, but text is the same.
   MacLean 401. DLC, ICN, MH, MHarF, MPB,
   MPH, MWA, MWiW*, MeHi, N, O, OClWHi.

1182 [——] ——— ... The Higher Law of
Spiritual Progression .... Albany, N.Y.: Printing
House of Van Benthuysen & Sons, 1868. 32 pp.
14 cm. (Shaker tracts, No. 2.).
   A new title, but the text is identical with
   Pelham's *The Shaker Answer*. This is an
   exact reprint, including caption title, of the
   2d ed. (Cincinnati, 1868), no. 1181.
   MacLean 408. MB, MPB, MWiW*, N, NN,
   NOC, NhD, OClWHi.

1183 [——] A Shaker's Answer to the Oft-
Repeated Question, "What Would Become of
the World if All Should Become Shakers?"
Stereotyped edition. Orders supplied by John
Whiteley, Shirley, Mass. Boston: Press of Rand,
Avery & Co., 1874. 31 [1] pp. 17 cm.
   Extended title, but the text remains the same,
   except that in earlier editions the person
   addressed was E.—— W.——, but is now
   reversed to W.—— E.——. Post office
   addresses of the societies, p. [1], at end.
   "Publications of the United Society of
   Believers," verso of back cover. This cover
   is blank on some copies. *See also* no. 2849.
   MacLean 402. CSmH, CtY-D, DLC, ICJ,
   ICN, MB, MBC, MH, MHarF, MPH, MWA,
   MWiW*, N, NBuG, NN, NNC, NOC, NSyU,
   NjPT, O, OClWHi, ODa, OHi.

1184 [——] ——— (Facsimile reprint). [Pitts-
field, Mass.: Shaker Village Work Group, 1964].
NOC*.

1185 [——] ——— Orders Supplied at East
Canterbury, N.H.: [188-]. 17 [1] pp. 20½ cm.
   "For further information, as follows," p. [1],
   at end. An advertisement for *The Manifesto*
   dates this 1883 or later. Pelham's *A Shaker's
   Answer* was reprinted in Avery's *Sketches of
   "Shakers and Shakerism,"* nos. 56 and 57.
   MacLean 404. CtY, DLC, MH, MPB, MWA,
   MWiW*, NBuG, NSyU, OClWHi.

1186 —— To the Memory of David Spinning.
North Union: [1841?]. 2 pp. 15 cm.
   Introduction and poem of 39 lines. J. P.
   MacLean, *Bibliography*, p. 13, attributes this
   to Richard W. Pelham, "The poem was probab-
   ly written in 1841, and soon after printed."
   MacLean 409. DLC*.

1187 The People of the State of New York, by
the Grace of God Free and Independent: To
Mary A. Ayres and Clarissa Shoefelt as Deacon-
esses of the South Family of Shakers of Watervliet ... [n.p., n.d.]. Broadside. 17½ × 14 cm.
   Signed: *Francis H. Woods, Surrogate.*
   OClWHi*.

PERIGRINUS, *pseud. See* [McNemar, Richard],
ed., no. 948.

1188 PERKINS, ABRAHAM. Autobiography
of Elder Abraham Perkins and In Memoriam.
Concord, N.H.: The Rumford Press, 1901. 22 pp.
front. (port.) 18 cm.
   The *Autobiography*, pp. 9–22, was written
   when Perkins was eighty-six years of age "to
   satisfy the feelings of many dear friends who
   have solicited me to have some notes of the
   experiences of my life." It is preceded by a
   memorial poem and extract from the *Granite
   State Free Press*, pp. 3–8. Includes one hymn
   by the author, and "Tribute to [his] Memory
   [in verse]" by A. C. Stickney.
   MacLean 410. DLC, MPB, MPH, MWiW*,
   N, NBuG, NOC, NRCR, NSyU, OClWHi, OHi.

1189 Perseverance [and other poems]. [Water-
vliet, O.: 183-?]. [4] pp. 15½ cm.
   The title hymn is signed: *J. M. 1831;* "Poem,"
   beginning "The Pure Way of Self Denial," is
   signed: *Tyringham 1829;* "Happy Choice" is
   signed: *H. P. 1831;* "The Way of God is Lovely"
   is signed: *Alpheds Ruje* [i.e., Alpheus Rude]
   of N. Lebanon in his 80th year 1829. This
   hymn is also printed in Richard McNemar's
   A Selection of Hymns (no. 952), p. 142, in
   the Williams College copy (Williamstown,
   Mass.). The [4]-page item described here is
   McNemar's printing.
   OClWHi*.

1190 "Petition to Congress by the Society of

Shakers," [1812]. In C. E. Carter, ed., *Territorial Papers of the United States* (26 vols., 1934-62), "The Territory of Indiana, 1810-1816," 8 (1939), 166-67.

> A petition to enter with the Register of the Public Land Office "a quantity of land, not exceeding 200 acres as near as circumstances will admit to a four hundred Acre survey we now own on Burrow's Creek." Signed: *David Edie, Wm. Davis, Robt. Houston, Trustees for the Society. See* no. **8**.
> CtY, DLC, KyU, MH, MWiW*, NN.

1191 PHELPS, BERTHA LILLIAN. Shaker Music, a Brief History. [Canterbury, N.H.: Penacook, N.H., Hazen Printing Co., 196-]. Cover title. [8] pp. 20½ cm.
> MPH, MWA, MWiW*, NOC, NSyU.

1192 —— Who are the Shakers? [East Canterbury Shakers, Printed in Penacook, N.H.:], 1959. Cover title. [4] pp. 14 cm.
> The author has spent many, many happy years as a Shaker.
> MPH, MWiW*, NOC.

PHILANTHROPOS, *pseud. See* Wells, Seth Youngs, no. **1413**.

PHILOS HARMONIAE, *pseud. See* McNemar, Richard, nos. **952** and **953**.

1193 PILATE, PONTIUS, [*purported author*]. An Interesting Narrative of our Saviour Jesus Christ. By Pontius Pilate. Translated from the Latin by M. Swan. Canterbury, N.H.: 1849. Cover title. 16 pp. 13½ cm.
> One of the apocryphal accounts of the innocence of Pontius Pilate. It is a purported confession made by Pilate to his old friend, Fabricius Albinus. The chronicle "was extracted from an old Latin manuscript, found in a monastery near Vienne."
> MacLean 411. DLC, MWA, OClWHi*.

1194 —— Pilate's Narrative, of our Saviour, Jesus Christ. Canterbury, N.H.: Shakers' Press, [1851?]. Caption title. 16 pp. 14½ cm.
> "Pontius Pilate at Vienne. Translated and Abridged from the 'Courier des États Unis'."
> MWiW*.

1195 PILLOW, WILLIAM H. [Letters to Rachel G. C. Patten, Dec. 6, 1846; James Pilcher, Dec. 15, 1847; and Susannah Myrick, Jan. 6, 1847]. [New Lebanon, N.Y.: 1848?]. 13-18 pp. 19 cm.
> MacLean 412 gives the collation as 6 pp. This item is, in fact, pp. 13-18 of the 18-page *Shakers' Reply* to Luther Lee's attack published in the *True Wesleyan, see* nos. **1238, 1304, 1384.**
> NN*.

1196 POMEROY, MARCUS MILLS. Visit to the Shakers. [Canterbury, N.H.: 1883?]. Caption title. 11 pp. 13 cm.
> The visit to the Canterbury Shakers, pp. 1-10, appeared in *The Manifesto*, 13 (May, June 1883), 117-19, 134-36, where it was reprinted from *Pomeroy's Democrat*. "Would you," pp. 9-11, describes the "demands of Shakerism ... and ultimate consequences."
> MacLean 413. DLC, MPB, MWA, MWiW, N, NN, NSyU, OClWHi*.

1197 POOL, JASON BLAKELEY. A New Theory of Life and Species, Published by J. B. Pool, West Pittsfield, Mass.; Nantucket [Mass.]: Hussey & Robinson, Printers, 1878. 48 pp. 15 cm.
> Published earlier with title: *The Origin of Life and Species*, no. **1198**. Links the Darwinian theory with spiritualism.
> DLC, MB, MPB, MWiW*, OClWHi.

1198 [——] The Origin of Life and Species. A New Theory. Published at West Pittsfield, Mass.: W. H. Phillips Steam Print., 1875. 18 pp. 14 cm.
> Later issued as: *A New Theory of Life and Species*.
> MacLean 393. MPB*, NBuG, NN, OClWHi.

1199 POOLE, CYRUS O. ... Spiritualism as Organized by the Shakers. [Mt. Lebanon, N.Y.?]: 1887. Caption title. 16 pp. 14 cm.
> "From the Banner of Light .... Delivered before the Brooklyn, N.Y. Progressive Conference, Oct. 1st, 1887."
> MacLean 414. DLC, MPB, MWA, MWiW*, N, NN, NSyU, OClWHi, OHi.

POOR MAN'S SON, *pseud. See* Remarks on the Militia System, no. **1233**.

1200 Post Office Addresses of the Several Communities. [Canterbury, N.H.: 188–]. Broadside. 25 × 16 cm.
> Addresses for 17 communities are listed.
> N*, OClWHi.

1201 Precepts and Prohibitions. [Canterbury, N.H.?: n.d.]. Broadside. 19½ × 17 cm.
> Printed on blue paper. *See also* no. **1360** for publication as part of *Teacher's Testimonial.* OClWHi*.

1202 PRESCOTT, JAMES SULLIVAN. The Social Evil. North Union, O.: 1870. 14 pp. 16 cm. (Tract No. 1).
> Reprinted in *The Shaker,* 1 (May 1871), 34–35.
> MacLean 416. DLC, NN, OClWHi*.

1203 PRETER, CARL JULIUS, *trans.* and *comp.* Eine kurze Beschreibung des Glaubens und Praktischen Lebens der Verein. Gesellschaft Gläubiger in Christi Zweiter Erscheinung, gewöhnlich genannt "Shakers." Das Leben Christi ist die einzige Wahre Christliche Religion. Carl Julius Preter, Verfasser. Union Village, O.: 1888. 32 pp. 22 cm.
> Although Preter is given as author on the title page, he has adapted selections from various Shaker works and interspersed Biblical references among them. Based in part on G. B. Avery's *Sketches of "Shakers and Shakerism."* "Purity, Reinheit" by Martha J. Anderson was printed in English in *The Manifesto,* 14 (January 1884), 2–4. Preter was a member of the Union Village, O., Community.
> CtY, DLC, KyBgW, MHarF, MPB, MWiW*, MiU–C, N, NBuG, NN, NOC, NSyU, NjPT, OClWHi, OHi, OLeWHi, OOxM, Vi.

1204 Primaries. [n.p., n.d.]. 10 pp. 19 cm.
> Relates to the basic principles of Shakerism.
> MacLean 417. MPB*.

1205 Private School for Girls, from Eight to Twelve Years of Age, under the Auspices of the Alethian (Shaker) Church, at Mt. Lebanon, New York. Proposed to be Opened October 1, 1897. [Mt. Lebanon?: 1897]. Cover title. [3] pp. 16 cm.
> Inquiries to be addressed to: Eldress Anna White, North Family, Mount Lebanon, N.Y. The text of this circular was used in advertisements carried in *The Manifesto,* September 1897 and later.
> MWiW*, OClWHi.

Proceedings of the New Hampshire Legislature (*in re*) Shakers in 1828. *See* [R. McNemar], comp., *Investigator . . .* 1846, no. **927**.

1206 Proceedings of the Ninetieth Birthday Celebration and Banquet to J. M. Peebles . . . Los Angeles: Peebles Publishing Co., 1912. 31 pp.
> Greetings from Catherine Allen and Belle Bush, Shakers, pp. 22, 27.
> OClWHi*.

1207 Programme of Family Union Circle Tuesday [blank] 188–. [n.p., n.d.]. 19 × 14 cm.
> Eight blank lines follow, apparently for writing the program, within an ornamental type border.
> OClWHi*.

1208 Prophecy in 1008. Translated from the German by Goff. [n.p., n.d.]. 57–58 pp. 14 cm.
> Miscellaneous prophesies expressed symbolically, particularly in regard to Daniel's prophecy. This appears to have been printed by Richard McNemar.
> OClWHi*.

1209 [PROUTY, LORENZO D.] [Poem]. Shirley, [Mass.]: March 1876. Broadside. 19½ × 10½ cm.
> An acrostic poem of 3 stanzas. First line: L-and of light and endless glory. The first letters of the first words of two stanzas form the name "Lorenzo D. Prouty." First letters of the last stanza form the word "Shirley."
> OClWHi*.

1210 —— The Sabbath. Groton Junction, Mass.: Printed by John H. Turner, [n.d.]. Broadside. 18 × 11 cm.
> An acrostic poem. The initial letters of the lines form "Lorenzo Prouty, Shirley, Mass."
> OClWHi*.

1211 Public Notice. The Public are hereby Informed that a Change has been made in the Management of the United Society, Shirley, Mass., by which John Whitely will Officiate as First Trustee of said Society; Leander Persons being Released from the Duties and Responsibilities thereof ... Per Order of the Ministry, Elders and Trustees. Shirley Village, Mass.: January 28th, 1884. Broadside. 21 X 13 cm.

> Persons holding "accounts against the Society, or against Leander A. Persons as Trustee" are requested to submit accounts for examination. OClWHi*.

1212 PURINGTON, C., comp. On the Second Coming of Christ; not Personal, but Spiritual and Gradual; Progressive, like the Rising of the Sun. Compiled from The Millennial Church ... Sherbrook, E. T. [Canada]: J. S. Walton, Printer, 1843. 72 pp.

> The compiler claims "no merit for originality in the following work; as it is almost wholly copied from the writings of Green and Wells, authors of 'The Millennial Church'." Signed: C. P., Farnham [Quebec], August, 1843, p. 3. See no. 743. OClWHi*.

R

1213 R., H. Purity of Heart. [n.p., n.d.]. [2] pp. 17 X 9 cm.

> Poem. OClWHi*.

1214 RATHBUN, DANIEL. A Letter from Daniel Rathbun, of Richmond in the County of Berkshire, to James Whittacor, Chief Elder of the Church, called Shakers. Springfield [Mass.]: Printed at the Printing-Office near the Great Ferry, 1785. xi, [1], [13]-128 pp. 17 cm.

> Preface signed: V[alentine]. R[athbun]. This letter, intended to justify Rathbun's apostacy, is a strong attack upon the Shakers and relates scandalous incidents among them. See also "Reasons offered for leaving the Shaker Society," M. Dyer, Portraiture (no. 532), pp. 43-90, signed: Daniel Rothbun, where it is identified as "an extract of a pamphlet by Mr. D. Rothbun [sic]." (Not to be confused with the almost identical title, no. 1215.) Rathbun was intimately acquainted with the early Shakers. He journeyed with Ann Lee, and also later with James Whittaker to gather proselytes. MacLean 503. Evans 19212. Sabin 67949. CtY, DLC, MHi, MWA*, N, OClWHi, PPRF.

1215 RATHBUN, REUBEN. Reasons Offered for Leaving the Shakers. Pittsfield, Mass.: Printed by Chester Smith, 1800. 28 pp. 20½ cm.

> Reuben Rathbun, a Shaker convert in 1780 and intimately acquainted with the English founders, became an Elder in the Hancock, Mass., Shaker community. He describes the contentions among the founders and reaffirms the charges of drunkenness made earlier by others. This is a straightforward but restrained presentation of his dissatisfactions which finally caused him to secede in 1799. Afterward he married a former Shaker sister who had followed him into the world. Gross (no. 3255), p. 461, n. 12, thinks that Reuben suggests the figure of Josiah in Hawthorne's Canterbury Pilgrims (no. 2222). MacLean 504. Evans 38359. CtHi, DLC, MPB*.

1216 RATHBUN, VALENTINE WIGHTMAN. An Account of the Matter, Form, and Manner of a New and Strange Religion, Taught and Propagated by a Number of Europeans, Living in a Place called Nisqueunia, in the State of New-York. Written by Valentine Rathbun, Minister of the Gospel. Providence [Rhode-Island]: Printed and Sold by Bennett Wheeler, 1781. 23 pp. 20 cm.

> This is the first of many published anti-Shaker attacks to be made by Shaker apostates. Valentine Rathbun visited the first Shaker settlement at Niskayuna, N.Y., and joined in 1780, but after only 3 months seceded and became an inveterate enemy of Shakerism. He was not only a founder and

pastor of the Baptist Church in Pittsfield, Mass., but was a prominent citizen who had been entrusted with civic responsibilities as a member of the Massachusetts General Court and was also an advocate of liberal reforms within the Baptist Church organization. Some local accounts suggest that his zealous patriotism in the Revolutionary cause led to an emotional over-involvement which was evident in other causes. In any case, his relentless anti-Shakerism damaged the Shaker missionary efforts and must have been in some degree responsible for Shaker persecution during 1781–1783. "There are few people in this land no doubt but what have heard of the contents of Valentine Rathbun's Narrative," Amos Taylor, *A Narrative* ... 1782 (no. 1358), p. 4. It is of interest that in December 1909 William W. Wight sent a list of wanted Shaker items to Elder Alonzo G. Hollister who wrote alongside the Rathbun items (MacLean, nos. 503–510), "I never saw ... these items & I know nothing about them." ms. Williams College, Williamstown, Mass. It is stated in *The Month at Goodspeed's*, 9 (May 1938), 277, that this is the first of the works "devoted to uncomplimentary observations" about the Shakers. The author, Valentine Wightman Rathbun, is not to be confused with an older Baptist relative of the same name, active in Bellingham, Massachusetts.
Evans 17318. Sabin 67954. DLC, MBC, RHi, RPB*.

1217 —— —— Halifax, [N.S.]: Reprinted and Sold by Anthony Henry. 1781, 20 pp. 21 cm.
NjPT*.

1218 —— A Brief Account of a Religious Scheme, Taught and Propagated by a Number of Europeans, who Lately Lived in a Place called Nisquenunia, in the State of New-York, but now Residing in Harvard, Commonwealth of Massachusetts, Commonly Called Shaking Quakers. To which is added A Dialogue between George the Third of Great-Britain, and his Ministers; Giving an Account of the Late London Mob, in the Original of the Sect Called Shakers. The Whole Being a Discovery of the

Wicked Machinations of the Principal Enemies of America. Worcester: 1782. 36 pp. 17 cm.
Second title page: A Dialogue between George the Third ... London, Printed. Worcester: Reprinted, 1782. pp. 27–36. MacLean 507. (MacLean 505 records a Boston, 1781 edition. No copy has been located.) Evans 17681. Sabin 67955. DLC, MHi, MWA*, N, NjPT, PMA (28 pp.).

1219 —— Some Brief Hints of a Religious Scheme, Taught and Propagated by a Number of Europeans, Living in a Place Called Nisqueunia, in the State of New York ... Hartford Printed. Boston: Re-printed by Benjamin Edes & Sons, 1781. 24 pp. 17½ cm.
Evans 17320. Sabin 67956. MWA*, N, NHi.

1220 —— —— Norwich, [Conn.]: Printed by John Trumbull, 1781. 24 pp. 18 cm.
Evans 17321. CtHi, CtY, KyBgW, MWA*, NHi.

1221 —— —— Hartford [Conn.]: Printed and Sold in the Year, MDCCLXXXI [1781]. Cover title. 27 pp. 17½ cm.
OClWHi*.

1222 —— —— Second Edition. Hartford: Printed by Hudson and Goodwin? 1781. 27 pp.
"The only recorded copy of this ed. was sold at the Brinley sale," C. K. Shipton and J. E. Mooney, *National Index of American Imprints through 1800* (2 vols., Worcester, Mass., 1969), II:714, from which this entry is taken. MacLean 506? (24 pp.). Evans 17319. Sabin 67956.

1223 —— —— Boston: Reprinted and Sold by Benjamin Edes and Sons, 1782. 24 pp. 17½ cm.
MacLean 509. Evans 17682. Sabin 69757. CSmH, MHi, MWA*, NNC, OClWHi*, RPB.

1224 —— —— Salem: Re-printed and Sold by S. Hall. 1782. 23 pp. 18½ cm.
MacLean 508. Evans 17683. Sabin 67956. MB, MHi, MWA*, N.

1225 —— —— New-York: Printed in the Year 1783. 36 pp. 18 cm.

MacLean 510. Evans 18145. Sabin 67957.
MWA, NN, NNC, OClWHi*, RPB.

1226 RAYMOND, WILLIAM GOULD. Life,
Sketches and Faith Work of Elder W. G. Ray-
mond. Written by Himself. Boston: Geo. E.
Crosby & Co., Printers, 1891. ii, 304 pp. illus.
24 cm.
  "He Changes Never [hymn]. Dedicated to
  Eld. W. G. Raymond" (with music): p. 286.
  DLC, NOC*.

1227 Reading from the Best Authors. [n.p.,
n.d.]. [8] pp. 17 cm.
  Poetry made up of excerpts from various
  authors. "The Brook," pp. 6-7; "Bugle
  Song," p. [8].
  OClWHi*.

1228 Received of . . . . . Trustees of the Shaker
Society at East Canterbury, N.H. . . . . . Dollars,
to my Full Satisfaction. [n.p., n.d.]. Broadside.
18 X 11½ cm.
  Receipt of payment to a member withdrawing from the Society which releases and dis-
  charges "the Trustees of the Society from
  any further obligations, claims or demands of
  any kind."
  Private collection.

1229 REED, CALVIN G. O my Father, my
Father. Jan. 31, 1897. [n.p., n.d.]. Broadside in
2 columns. 18 X 19½ cm.
  Poem of 76 lines, signed: *Jan. 31, 1897.*
  Calvin G. Reed.
  OClWHi*.

1230 Religions-Register, oder Kurz-Beschreibung
der Glaubenslehre und Gottesdienstliche Ver-
richtungen der sogenannten Schäking-Quäkers,
in dem Staat Ohio; aus dem Englischen genau
übersetzt. Nebst eine kurze Erinnerung an den
Leser. Newmarket (Virg.): gedruckt und zu
haben bei Ambrosius Henkel, 1809. 28 pp. 12
cm.
  This is addressed to the editor of the *Western
  Calendar (see* no. 1908), and is intended to
  correct and to amplify the information about
  the Shakers in a paragraph dated: 28 July
  1807. The author, who appears to be a Shaker,
  claims that he has a personal and exact

knowledge of these people, who have not
bothered to propagate their beliefs by "paper
and ink," (i.e., printed works), but operate
only from the heart. He describes the missionary labors of Elders B. S. Youngs,
Issachar Bates, and John Meacham in Ohio,
where several "households" have been established in the faith: 30-40 at Turtle Creek,
20-30 at Eagle Creek, and 6 at Beaver Creek;
in Kentucky 6 or 7 have been established in
Mercer County, with a few in Butler and
Selby counties. These converts were drawn
mostly from the Presbyterians.
Shaw 18489. DLC, MWA*, NcD, ViU, ViW.

1231 A Remarkable Old Man. Elder Evans at
the Age of 80 still Bent on Reforming the World.
[n.p., 1888]. Caption title. 14 pp. 15 cm.
  An interview reprinted from the *New York Sun.*
  MacLean 419. CtY, DLC, MPB, MWA, MWiW*,
  N, NN, NBuG, OClWHi, OHi.

1232 ———— 8 pp. 13 cm.
  At end of text: *N.Y. Sun.*
  MWiW*, OClWHi.

1233 Remarks on the Militia System by a Poor
Man's Son. New York: Published by the American Peace Society, 1831. 8 pp. 13 cm.
  "The following remarks were published in the
  Albany Evening Journal during the last session
  of the New York Legislature, while our Militia
  laws were under consideration. But as no alterations have been made in those laws, the writer
  has thought proper to offer these remarks to
  the public in the present form . . ." Signed:
  P.M.S. E. D. Andrews, *People Called Shakers*
  (no. 1767), p. 216, credits Garrett Lawrence,
  herbalist at New Lebanon, as author. Garrett
  K. Lawrence was one of the signers of the 1830
  Remonstrance (no. 1082) which included a
  protest against the N.Y. Militia Law. His
  authorship of *Remarks* has not been documented. *See also* nos. 1413 and Add. 1614a.
  Sabin 69474. ICN, ICU, MWA, NN, OClWHi*.

1234 Remember Me. [n.p., n.d.]. Broadside.
19 X 9½ cm.
  Poem of 3 stanzas that appears to be a fragment of Richard McNemar's printing.
  OClWHi*.

[Remonstrance, to the Legislature of the State of Ohio.] [n.p., 1817].

No copy located. "On December 3d [1817], Richard McNemar and Calvin Morrell went to Columbus to present a remonstrance to the Legislature against Van Vleet and Cameron ... and others on account of persecutions," J. P. MacLean, "Mobbing the Shakers of Union Village" (no. 2410), p. 380. Ham, "Shakerism in the Old West," p. 144, ftn. 46, states that "There is no bibliographic record of this pamphlet but McNemar said he put the document 'into the hands of the state printer' for him to give 'to the legislature and the public'," and cites: McNemar to M. Houston, Dec. 29, 1817, Union Village Letters, ms. Western Reserve Historical Society, Cleveland, O.

1235 A Remonstrance Against the Testimony and Application of Mary Dyer, Requesting Legislative Interference Against the United Society Commonly Called Shakers. Together with some Affidavits and Certificates, Showing the Falsity of her Statements. Concord [N.H.]: Printed by Isaac Hill, 1818. 23 pp. 17½ cm.

Addressed: to the Honorable, the Legislature of New Hampshire, now in session. Signed: *In behalf of the said United Society. June 17, 1818. Nathaniel Draper* [and 5 other] *Overseers ... Enfield. Francis Winkley* [and 5 other] *Overseers ... Canterbury.* A refutation of Mary Dyer's and other charges against the Shakers, and the statement that compulsory legislation would be "an abridgment of our inherent rights." The Shakers suggest that a committee of examination "search out secret causes of complaint," and that inspection of their institution and conduct would be freely laid open at any time. Reprinted in Joseph Dyer, *Compendious Narrative*, nos. 525 and 526, pp. [80]-87, and no. 529, pp. [60]-65. MacLean 420. Sabin 21596 and 97894 (where reference is made to Concord, 1818, as a "second issue"). Shaw 45697. CSmH, CtY, MB, MPB, MWA, Nh, OClWHi*.

1236 A Remonstrance ... Tggether [*sic*] with some Affidavits and Certificates, Showing the Falsity of Her Statements. Boston: Printed for N. Coverly, 1818. 24 pp. 17 cm.

Sabin 21596 and 97894. Shaw 45695. CSmH, MSaE*.

1237 ——— Boston: Printed for N. Coverly, 1818. 24 pp. 20½ cm.
Shaw 45696. MWA*.

1238 Remonstrance of the United Society Called Shakers, Against the Passage of a Certain Law. To the Honorable the Legislature of the State of New-York: The Memorial of the Undersigned, Committee of the United Society, Called Shakers, Respectfully Showeth. [Albany: 1849]. Broadside. 25 X 19 cm.

Dated: New-Lebanon, Feb. 26th 1849. Signed: *Richard Bushnell, Frederick W. Evans — New-Lebanon. Issachar Bates, Richard Dean — Watervliet.* Submitted in protest against the Assembly Report of the Judiciary Committee, no. 1083, and the "Bill accompanying it" which would deprive persons of marital and parental rights, if they should become members "of any religious sect teaching certain doctrines and tenets [i.e., celibacy, etc.]." The proposed legislation grew out of William Pillow's and other petitions for divorce.
N*, NOC, OClWHi.

1239 A Repository of Music, containing Elementary and Advanced Lessons, Selected from the Works of Able Teachers .... Canterbury, N.H.: Printed at Shaker Village, 1880. Cover title. xxviii, 73 pp. music. 22½ cm.

MacLean attributes this to H. C. Blinn, who may have been the compiler, but the title and contents indicate other than Shaker authorship. It is a peculiar work for the Shakers to have printed. There is no mention of the Shakers, their music, hymns, etc. No. 1 of the lessons following the exercises is "Stabat Mater," with words and music.
MacLean 84. MPH, MWiW*, MiU-C, NOC, NSyU, OClWHi.

1240 Resolutions Adopted at the Peace Convention of the Shakers of Mount Lebanon, Held at Mount Lebanon, N.Y. August 31, 1905. [Mt. Lebanon, N.Y.: 1905?]. Broadside in 2 columns. 27 X 21½ cm.

The resolutions proposed by Leila S. Taylor

and the Rev. Henry S. Chubb. Signed: *Henry Nichols, Moderator.*
MPB, MWiW, N*, NjPT, OClWHi.

1241 ———— Broadside. 33 X 8 cm.
Includes the resolutions proposed by
Catherine Allen.
MWiW, OClWHi*.

1242 A review of Mary Dyer's Publication,
Entitled "A Portraiture of Shakerism"; Together
with Sundry Affidavits, Disproving the Truth of
her Assertions. Concord [N.H.]: Printed by J. B.
Moore, For the Society, 1824. 70 pp. 19½ cm.
"To the Reader," pp. [5]-15, signed by
Francis Winkley [and three other] Trustees
of the United Society at Canterbury and
Enfield, N.H., June 7, 1824, is followed by
affidavits and statements refuting Mary
Dyer's charges against the Shakers.
MacLean 421. Sabin 21595 and 97895.
Shaw 17943. DLC*, MH, MHi, MWA,
MWiW, MiU-C, N, NN, Nh, NhD, NhHi,
OCHP, OClWHi, RPB.

1243 Reward of Merit. North Union [O.]:
1852. Broadside. 21 X 17½ cm.
"A reward for good behavior in school, and
diligent attention to study." On verso: Poem
to Sister Margaritta, in ms., signed: *Arabella,
Apr. 19, 1852.*
OClWHi*.

1244 RICHMOND, DAVID. Created Order: A
Lecture to "The Spiritual Brotherhood."
Keighley, December 28, 1873. Darlington [Eng.]:
D. Richmond, 1874. 28 pp. 17 cm.
Shakerism, pp. 10-13.
OClWHi*.

1245 ———— The Divine Order: An Address to
"The Spiritual Brotherhood." Keighley, Nov. 2,
1873. Darlington [Eng.]: D. Richmond, [1873?].
11 pp. 17 cm.
Father-Mother God and Shakerism referred
to throughout, especially pp. 4, 8, 9, 10.
OClWHi*.

1246 ———— An Explanatory Address and Testimony of Light and Truth. To the United Society
of Believers or Shakers, in the United States of

America, and to Whom it may Concern. Darling-
ton, [Eng.]; [Glasgow: Hay, Nisbet & Co.,
Printers], 1879. 40 pp. 18 cm.
A discussion of the author's interpretation
of Scripture and spiritualism in which he
takes exception to Shaker beliefs.
MacLean 426. DeWint, DLC, NBuG, OClWHi*,
PPL.

1247 [ROBERTSON, JAMES] Dr. Peebles and
Elder Evans in Glasgow. Farewell Meetings. [Mt.
Lebanon?: 1887]. Caption title. 6 pp. 14 cm.
"From the London, Eng. *Medium and Day-
break*, July 29, 1887." Signed: *Jas. Robertson,
Glasgow, July 23, 1887.* Reprinted in *The
Manifesto*, 17 (October 1887), 234-36.
CtY, MPB, MWiW*.

1248 [——] ———— Cover title. [2] pp.
22½ cm.
Signed: *Jas. Robertson. Glasgow, July 23,
1887.* Text identical with no. 1247.
MacLean 397. MHarF, MWA, MWiW*,
OClWHi, OHi.

1249 ROBINSON, CHARLES EDSON. A
Concise History of the United Society of
Believers Called Shakers. East Canterbury, N.H.:
[Printed at Shaker Village, c1893]. ix, 1 l., 134
pp. 25 illus. incl. ports. 24 cm.
Preface by the publisher is signed: *H. C. Blinn.*
Cover title: The Shakers and their Homes. A
variant cover title: The Shakers, has a dif-
ferent cover design. Originally published as
part of a series of articles on communism
written under the pseudonym, "C. R. Edson,"
see no. 3581.
MacLean 86 (and 87 in paper covers). CHi,
CSmH, CU-SB, CtY, DLC, ICN, InU, KyBgW,
MB, MBC, MBrZ, MPB, MPH, MWA, MWiW*,
MiU, N, NBuG, NHi, NN, NRCR, NSyU,
NcD, NjMD, O, OCl, OClWHi, OHi, PU,
WaU, WHi.

1250 [ROBINSON, MARY ANN] Adam's Good
Ale. [n.p., n.d.]. Broadside. 23½ X 12½ cm.
Poem of six stanzas followed by a note about
the author.
OClWHi*.

1251 Roxalana L. Grosvenor *vs.* United Society

of Believers. Maria F. Grosvenor *vs.* Same. In Massachusetts. Supreme Court. *Reports* ... June–October 1875, John Lathrop, Reporter. Boston: Houghton, 1876. pp. 78–91. (118 Mass. 78, June 23, 1875).

> The Court upheld the Shakers in their refusal to support members who had been expelled from the Society. "Covenant or Constitution" runs concurrently with the text, pp. 79–85. *See* annotation no. 1307 and nos. 1252 and 1698.
> MWiW*, OClWHi.

1252 Roxelana [*sic*] L. Grosvenor *vs.* United Society of Believers. Mary F. Grosvenor *vs.* Same. Plaintiff's Brief. [Boston: 1875]. [4] pp. 25½ cm.

> At head of title: Supreme Judicial Court, Suffolk [County, Massachusetts]. C. S. Lincoln, Geo. W. Morse, Counsel for the Plaintiffs.
> OClWHi*.

Rules for Behavior ... *See* Notices to Visitors, Rules of Behavior, Etc., *see* p. 162 f.

1253 Rules for Deportment. Printed at Shaker Village [East Canterbury], Mer. Co., N.H.: [n.d.]. Broadside. 15 × 11 cm.

> Signed: *H. C. Blinn.* Printed on yellow paper.
> OClWHi*.

1254 Rules for Doing Good. [Mt. Lebanon, N.Y.: n.d.]. Wall card punched at the top. 23 × 18½ cm.

> Identified as "John Wesley's Rule," J. Bartlett, *Familiar Quotations* (14th ed., rev. & enl. Boston, 1968), p. 421.
> MPB, MHarF, MPH, N, OClWHi*.

1255 ——— (Reprint). Old Chatham, N.Y.: Shaker Museum. 196–?
NOC*.

1256 Rules for Workmen Employed by the

United Society, Alfred, Maine. [n.p., n.d.]. Broadside. 33½ × 21 cm.

> Six rules concerning the time of rising in the morning, restriction of movement in the community, temperance, gambling, smoking, food, and lodging. Signed: *Hiram Tarbox, James H. Pender, Trustees.*
> OClWHi*.

1257 RUNYON, GEORGE R. Shakers and Shakerism. Private Property Possession, Real or Personal, Inconsistent with the True Character of the Church of Christ, First and Last, etc. Pleasant Hill, Mercer County, Ky.: November 1, 1875. Broadside in 2 columns. 35½ × 14 cm.

> Signed: *G. B. Runyon.* An excerpt printed in *The Shaker,* 6 (January 1876), 11, where this is identified as an address to "the people of Nicholasville, Ky.," and as "plain, blunt, wholesome, southern testimony."
> MacLean 429. DLC*, OCHP.

1258 —— ——— The Two Adams. Their Respective Posterities and Positions. Pleasant Hill, Ky.: Sept. 17, 1877. Broadside. 40 × 17½ cm.

> MacLean 513. DLC*, OCHP.

1259 RUPE, NANCY. A Poem Dedicated to Pleasant Hill. [n.p., n.d.]. Broadside. 30 × 15 cm.

> A poem of 18 stanzas. Last line: To waning Pleasant Hill. Ms. note on the Pleasant Hill, Ky., copy reads "Presented to Frank E. Cooley by the author at Pleasant Hill, Ky., Aug. 22, 1904."
> MacLean 430. KySP, MWiW, OClWHi*.

1260 Rural Health Home, Ayer, Mass. [n.p., n.d.]. Cover title. 14 [1] pp. illus. 18½ cm.

> A prospectus which emphasizes the availability and high quality of water from the Shaker Medicinal Spring.
> OClWHi*.

S

S., C. M. *See* Skinner, Charles Montgomery, nos. 1313 and 2766.

1261 Sacred Hymns for Spiritual Worship of Believers in Christ's Second Appearing .... Canterbury, N.H.: 1845. 1 leaf (verso blank), [16] pp. (lettered A–P), 180 pp. music. 13½ X 8½ cm.

The music written in Shaker letter notation is printed for 2 hymns, "True Thankfulness," p. 39, and "Youth's Invitation," p. 61. The first hymn in the section which has the pages designated by letters is "A Scene of Time," p. A; the last, "A Sinless Life," p. P. "The Conquest. From the Investigator, 1829," p. 1; "Peace and Purity," p. 176; "Index of First Lines," pp. [177]–80. The size of type varies throughout, but individual hymns are printed in one size type. The hymns are unnumbered, and designated by title only. Elder H. C. Blinn states in his "Autobiographical Notes" in *In Memoriam* (no. 830), p. 31, "We also printed in 1844, a small book entitled, 'Millennial Hymns.' It was a work of some four hundred pages." This seems to be a mistaken recollection. No copy of this title has been located. Blinn may have referred to the 1845 hymnal described here, possibly to the 1847 *Collection of Millennial Hymns* (no. 469), but neither is 400 pages. *See also* [Hymns], no. 827.

DLC, MWiW*, NNUT, NOC, OClWHi.

1262 The Sacred, Solemn and Sealed Roll, Open[ed] and Read by the Mighty Angel. To the Inspired Writer, Philemon Stewart. [n.p., 1844?]. Broadside. 28 X 21 cm.

At end: Information in relation to this Holy Book, can be obtained by addressing me, at Rochester, New York. Signed: *Edward U. Blake.* The text reprints excerpts from pages 11–15 of the *Sacred Roll*, including the introduction dated: New Lebanon, Feb. 2d, 1843. The only copy located was found pasted to the cover of a ms. account book of the Groveland community, Vol. 7 of financial records, Container 1, Western Reserve Historical Society. *See no.* 1340.

OClWHi*.

1263 SAMPSON, JOSEPH ADAM HALL. Remains of Joseph A. H. Sampson, who Died at New-Lebanon, 12 mo. 14, 1825, Aged 20 Years. Published by the Request of his Friends, for the Benefit of Youth .... Rochester, N.Y.: Printed by E. F. Marshall, For Procter Sampson, of New-Lebanon, 1827. 59, [1] pp. 13 cm.

"Preface by His Father," signed: *P. Sampson.* Portbay, Wayne Co., N.Y. 1st mo. 20th, 1827. "The pieces [poems] are mere juvenile productions ..." "Short Account of the Death of Polly Lawrence," pp. [49]–56.
MacLean 81 (82 in paper covers). Sabin 75939. CSmH, CtY, DeWint, DLC, ICU, IU, MPB, MPH, MWA, MWiW*, NBuG, NHi, NN, NOC, NRHi, NSyU, NjPT, OClWHi, OU, RPB.

1264 —— —— Born at Marshfield, 10th month, 20th, 1805; Died at New-Lebanon, 12th month, 14th, 1825. Aged 20 years. Published for the Benefit of Youth .... Albany [N.Y.]: Printed by Hoffman and White, For Procter Sampson of New-Lebanon, 1834. 35 [1] pp. 14½ cm.

Text of "Advertisement" has been changed. Lacks preface; only the poems are included in this edition.
MacLean 83. Sabin 75939. CtY, ICN, MH, MHarF, MPB, MPH, MWA, MWiW*, NBuG, NjPT, OClWHi.

1265 SAWYER, OTIS. "Shaker Village [New Gloucester]," In *History of Cumberland County, Maine* (Philadelphia, 1880), (no. 1972), pp. 328–30. *See also* no. 1973 for his account of the Alfred, Me., Shaker community.

MeHi*, MWA.

1266 —— "The United Society of Shakers. May Their Numbers Never be Less," Response ... In *The New Gloucester Centennial*, September 7, 1874, by T. H. Haskell. Revel Small, stenographer. (Portland, Me.: Hoyt, Fogg & Donham, 1875), pp. 100–109.

Early Shaker history and a description of Shaker accomplishments in the New Gloucester (Sabbathday Lake, Me.) community.
MeHi*, NSyU.

1267 Scientific and Practical. Printed at Shaker Village, Mer. Co., N.H.: [n.d.]. Broadside. 25½ X 16 cm.

Instructions for care and protection of children's eyesight printed on yellow paper. Reprinted from *Popular Science Monthly*.
OClWHi*.

1268 SEARS, CHAUNCY EDWARD. Shakers. Duality of the Deity; Or, God as Father and

Mother .... Rochester, N.Y.: Daily Democrat Steam Printing House, 1867. Cover title. 7 pp. 14½ cm.

The author's given name is sometimes spelled "Chancy"; "C. E. Sears, Mount Morris, N.Y.," occurs frequently. MacLean 432. CtHi, CtY, InU, MB, MHarF, MHi, MPB, MWA, MWiW*, NBuG, NN, OClWHi, PU.

1269 ——— Shakers. A Short Treatise on Christian Love. Rochester, N.Y.: Daily Democrat Steam Printing House, 1867. Cover title. 10 [1] pp. 15 cm.

MacLean 433. CtY, DLC, DeWint, MHi, MPB*, MWA, NBuG, NOC, OClWHi.

1270 ——— Shakers. A Short Treatise on Marriage. By C. E. Sears, Mount Morris, N.Y. ... Rochester, N.Y.: Daily Democrat Steam Printing House, 1867. 13 [1] pp. 15 cm.

"Standard Works by Shakers," p. [1], at end. Williams College copy (Williamstown, Mass.) has ms. notes, quotation on title page has been pasted on p. 3, and 3 lines of additional printed text are pasted over the author's signature at end. MacLean 434? (1869). CtY, DLC, InU, MB, MHarF, MPB, MWiW*, N, NBuG, NN, NjPT, O, OClWHi.

1271 ——— ——— Lebanon, Ohio: Patriot Print, 1884. 11, [1] pp. 15 cm.

"Standard Works by Shakers," p. [1], at end. MacLean 435. DLC, MWiW*, OClWHi.

1272 ——— Shakers. A Treatise on the Second Coming of Christ .... Rochester, N.Y.: Daily Democrat Steam Printing House, 1867. Cover title. 25 pp. 14½ cm.

"Standard Works by Shakers," p. 25. MacLean 436. DLC, InU, MB, MWA, MWiW*, O, OClWHi.

1273 SEARS, CLARA ENDICOTT, comp. Gleanings from Old Shaker Journals ... Boston: Houghton Mifflin, 1916. xiii, 298 pp. front., illus. (incl. facsims., music), plates, ports. 20 cm.

History and description of the Harvard, Mass., Society, with liberal quotations from Shaker printed works and manuscript journals which are not always identified, by one who was intimately acquainted with this community. InU, MB, MBC, MBrZ, MHarF, MPB, MPH, MWA, MWiW*, MeHi, NN, NOC*, NSyU, NcD, NjPT, OClWHi, ODa, PHC, PP, PPL, PSC-Hi, PU, RPB, ViU.

1274 Selection of Devotional Melodies; Simple in Arrangement, yet, — Inspirational ... Canterbury, N.H.: Published and Printed in Shaker Village, 1876. 2 p. ll. 44 pp. music. 14 X 19 cm.

A collection of 38 hymns, one of the three earliest Shaker publications to have the music written in conventional notation, see nos. 107-109, 1292. Some 4-part harmony, but contains mostly single-line melodies. "Index of First Lines," second preliminary leaf, verso. "First piece of music set to block notes [i.e., conventional notation] in Shaker Village [Canterbury] N.H.," autograph notes signed: H. C. Blinn. Pasted to the fly leaf of the Shaker Museum Library's copy (Old Chatham, N.Y.). At least 8 of the hymns were also published as sheet music (see information note under Music Leaflets, p. 152 ff.): "Happy Change," "Happy Land," "Jordan's Tide," "More Love," "Morning Dawn," "A Prayer," "Soul Cheer," and "Star of Hope." Others were printed in The Shaker, "Hour of Worship," 2 (May 1, 1872), 39: "Our Zion Home," 2 (December 1872), 88: "Christ's Sufferings," 6 (August 1877), 64: "Morning Dawn" was printed in The Shaker and Shakeress, 5 (April 1875), 32. MacLean 437. ICN, MWiW*, NBuG, NN, NOC, NjPT, OClWHi.

1275 $75 reward! Stolen from the Shaker Settlement, in Watervliet [N.Y.] on Monday Night, 21st. inst. A Bay Horse ... Watervliet, [N.Y.]: September 22, 1846. Broadside. 16½ X 24 cm.

Signed: Stanton Buckingham, Chauncey Copeley. "Postmasters are requested to post this bill." OClWHi*.

The Shaker. See The Manifesto, pp. 138-139, and nos. 975-979, 982-987.

Shaker and Shakeress. See The Manifesto, pp. 138-139, and nos. 980-981.

1276 Shaker Anthems and Hymns, Arranged for Divine Worship. Shaker Village, N.H.: 1883. Cover title. 16 pp. music. 23½ cm.

Words and music for 14 unnumbered hymns and anthems, all but 4 of which are identified as Canterbury, N.H., compositions. The music is written in conventional notation for 4-part harmony. "Fourteen choice gems, words and music original, each one worth the price of the whole collection. The words are beautiful, the music sweet," advertisement, *The Manifesto*, 13 (August 1883). opp. p. [169].
MacLean 438. DLC, MPB, MWiW*, N, NBuG, NN, OClWHi.

1277 Shaker Anthems and Hymns, Arranged for Divine Worship. Shaker Village, N.H.: Printed at Canterbury, 1887. Cover title. 40 pp. music. 23½ cm.

Thirty-eight unnumbered Shaker hymns and anthems, with music written in conventional notation. Contains 4-part harmony, almost no 1-line melodies.
OClWHi*.

1278 Shaker Child's Prayer. Presented by G. A. Lomas. [Watervliet, N.Y.: 187-?]. Broadside. 7½ × 10 cm.

First line, "Good Spirit, Hear my Prayer"/. "To our surprise two editions of . . . are exhausted," *The Shaker*, 7 (May 1877), 34. "It is beautifully printed in blue on cards," *The Shaker* (May 1877), 21. "It is a short easily-learned poem, non-sectarian and universally practicable." "Address Shakers, N.Y. 5¢, *Shaker Manifesto*, 9 (March 1879), 69. The The price indicates that the *Prayer* was printed for sale as well as for presentation by G. A. Lomas.
OClWHi*.

1279 Shaker Church Covenant . . . [Canterbury] Shaker Village, N.H.: 1889. Cover title. 12, [2] pp. 23 cm.

Back cover, recto: Gläubige im zweiten Erscheinen Christi. Belehrung für Fragesteller. Back cover, verso: Information for Inquirers, which was previously printed in *The Manifesto*, 19 (January 1889), 3-12, and in *The Shaker*, 7 (October, November 1877), 75-76,

85-86. "The covenant was a growth. The last revision, 1830, was made by Seth Y. Wells," J. P. MacLean, *Bibliography* (no. 2407), p. 60, No. 441. "This work sets forth the form of appointment, the qualifications and powers of the several orders of offices in the Community: of the privileges and obligations of all the Members, and of the dedication and consecration of persons and property." This *Covenant* is reprinted from *The Manifesto*, 19 (January 1889), [3]-12. Advertisement, back cover, verso, *The Manifesto*, August 1889. *See* M. Melcher, *Shaker Adventure* (no. 2451), pp. 88-94 for a discussion of the *Covenant*.
MacLean 441. KU, MHarF, MPB, MPH, MWA, MWiW*, MeHi, MnU, N, NBuG, NN, NOC, NSyU, OClWHi, ODa.

1280 ———— East Canterbury, N.H.: 1906. Cover title. 13 [1] pp. 22 cm.
CU, ICU, MB, MWA, NOC, NhD, NhHi, OClWHi*.

1281 ———— East Canterbury, N.H.: [Shakers, 1910?]. 16 pp.
Entry from the *Catalogue of the Emma B. King Library of the Shaker Museum*, Old Chatham, N.Y., No. 47.
NOC*.

1282 Shaker Concert. For the Benefit of Miss L. A. Chase. The Shaker Teetotum! [n.p., 184-?]. Broadside. 41 × 15 cm. illus.

Playbill for a program of Shaker songs and dances performed by a group of seceders from Canterbury, N.H., in "Real Shaker Costume." The name and location of the theater is not given, and the only performers who are identified are Mr. N. E. Chase and Miss L. A. Chase. "The secession of the Chase family . . . is in perfect accordance with the rules of the sect." A poorly executed unsigned woodcut, following the title, depicts a Shaker sister and brother holding hands. *See also* no. 728.
NHi*.

1283 The Shaker Conference. [n.p., 1905]. Broadside. 25 × 7½ cm.

Reprinted from the *Pittsfield Eagle*. Concerns

the Peace Convention at Mt. Lebanon, Aug.
31, 1905. Contains also: "The Shakers are
for Peace" [reprinted from the *Syracuse
Post-Standard.*]
MWiW*, OCIWHi (30 X 7½ cm.).

1284 Shaker Hymnal by the Canterbury Shakers
.... East Canterbury, N.H., The Canterbury
Shakers [Boston: Stanhope Press, Gilson Com-
pany], 1908. [3], blank page, 273 pp. music.
23½ cm.
"The following repository of hymns and
anthems has existed as a temporary volume
for local use," Preface. Contains nearly 250
selections with music, written in conventional notation for mixed voices. Contains
4-part harmony and a few melodies. All but
18 originated in the Canterbury society.
IaU, KyU, MWiW*, MeHi, MiU, N, NN,
NRCR, OCIWHi, OU, PPULC, RPB.

1285 ———— Reprinted in 1961 by the Shaker
Savings Association with the express permission
of the Shaker Society.
Preface signed: *Alexander Mintz*, President
Shaker Savings Association, Shaker Heights,
Ohio. Feb. 15, 1961.
MWiW, OCIWHi*.

1286 . . . A Shaker Invention. Poland Spring,
Maine: Sabbathday Lake Shaker Society, 1963.
Cover title. [2] pp. 10½ X 13½ cm.
At head of title: 1817. Printed as one sheet on
card stock and folded horizontally. It is stated
the Shakers invented the metal pen nib at New
Lebanon, N.Y., about 1817, and about 1819
"invented plate rolling machinery for working
the [silver] metal into sheets, and *invented* special shears for cutting the sheets, and then shaping the nibs." At Watervliet, N.Y., in November
1824, Robert Owen's party was "shown some
silver pens of their own [i.e., Shakers'] making
which slide upon black handles, and some of
which are in silver cases." Before departing they
purchased 2 silver pens. William Owen,
"Diary," (no. 3510), pp. 10, 13.
NOC*.

1287 Shaker Lecture & Concert at Tweeddle
Hall [Albany, N.Y.] on Tuesday Evening, Nov.
1, 1870. Elder F. W. Evans . . . will Deliver a

Lecture on The Existing Relations of Shakerism
as a System and a Republican Form of Government. [Albany: 1870]. Broadside. 24 X 15½ cm.
A handbill advertising the lecture which will
include "30 Sisters and Brethren who will
sing several of their spiritual songs, thus form-
ing ... an Entertainment at once pleasing and
instructive." Excerpts "from the Sunday
Morning Press, Oct. 16th, 1870" are reprinted.
N*.

1288 Shaker Literature. Books — Old and New.
North Family, Mount Lebanon, Columbia
County, New York. [Mt. Lebanon: 1904].
Cover title. [4] pp. 19 cm.
Lists 57 Shaker publications with prices.
Grace Ada Brown's *Song and Story* (no. 112)
is described as "in preparation" to be issued
in the fall and winter of 1902–3; advertise-
ment describing the contents of White and
Taylor's *Shakerism, Its Meaning and
Message,* pp. [2–3].
MacLean 113. ICN, MWiW*, N, NN, NSyU,
OCIWHi.

The Shaker Manifesto. See The Manifesto, pp.
138–139, and nos. 988 and 989.

1289 The Shaker Manifesto. Some Plain
Answers. [n.p., n.d.]. Broadside. 68½ X 10½
cm.
"From many plain questions concerning the
Shakers received by us."
OCIWHi*.

1290 A Shaker Meeting. Alfred Love, President
of the Universalist Peace Union, Speaks at Mt.
Lebanon. Mt. Lebanon, N.Y.: 1891. Cover title.
9 pp. 14½ cm.
Minutes of the meeting, Sunday, Aug. 23,
1891, of which Love's speech is the largest
part. Reprinted in *The Manifesto,* 21 (October
1891), 221–24.
MacLean 362. DeWint, MPB, MWA, MWiW*,
OCIWHi, OHi.

1291 Shaker Museum. Founded 1931. Sabbath-
day Lake, Poland Spring, Maine. Exhibits
Housed in 1794 Meetinghouse of America's
Oldest Religious Community. Shaker Furniture,
Tin and Woodenware, Folk Art, Textiles, Early

American Farm Tools and Farm Implements. [n.p., n.d.]. Broadside. 28 X 21½ cm.
    Poster with cut of 1794 meetinghouse.
    Private collection.

1292 Shaker Music. [Canterbury, N.H.?: 1875–1906?]. Cover title. [10], 388 pp. music. 22–27 cm.
    With words and the music written in conventional notation for 1-line melodies and for 4-part harmony. "Contents to Shaker Music. Titles in Capitals.—First Line in Roman," [10] pp. preceding musical selections. The selections are numbered 1–102 and 1–302, but in the second sequence many hymns are unnumbered. Some hymns are dated; the latest date in the copy described here is 1888. This is a made-up volume of pages of varying sizes, and obviously printed at different times. Copies are usually bound in black or brown Shaker cloth with cover label: Shaker Music. Some selections are headed "Class No. 1" and "Class No. 2," indicating that this compilation may have been used in training the distinguished Shaker singing groups at Canterbury, N.H. Many hymns were printed as music leaflets and many also appeared in *The Shaker* (no. 975) and its successors. All copies examined showed irregularities of contents, total number and size of pages. A close comparison of the contents was not made. One Winterthur (Wilmington, Del.) copy is loose-leaf and contains 492 pp. A manuscript note on the Shaker Museum copy (Old Chatham, N.Y.) explains that *This book is reserved as a copy containing a full number of the pages as printed between 1875 and 1906. In March 1906, 28 strikes are removed from this Hymn book*, signed: *J.*[osephine] *E. Wilson.* This copy contains 500 pp. Western Reserve Historical Society (Cleveland, O.) has one copy of 504 pp. Whatever the original purpose of these compilations, they appear to be accumulations for and antecedents of the *Shaker Hymnal*, published by the Canterbury Shakers in 1908, no. 1284.
    CtY, DeWint, MWiW*, NOC, OClWHi.

1293 Shaker Music. Inspirational Hymns and Melodies Illlustrative [*sic*] of the Resurrection

Life and Testimony of the Shakers .... Albany, N.Y.: Weed, Parsons and Company, Publishers, 1875. [2], 2 p. ll., 5–67, [1] pp. music. 20 X 24 cm.
    Words with music written in conventional notation. Contains 4-part harmony and some 1-line melodies. MacLean attributes this compilation to Daniel Offord and Martha J. Anderson. It is attributed to F. W. Evans by the Library of Congress and *Shaker Quarterly*, 3 (Winter 1963), 131. "Copyright" by Weed, Parsons and Company. "The Dependence of the Singing or Speaking Form of the Larynx upon the Respiratory Effort" by John Howard, pp. 65–67. "Errata," p. [1], at end. Copies are found with blank leaves bound in, pp. 69–152, at end. "For the use of schools among Believers. Contains all the pieces that have appeared in the *Shaker and Shakeress*, and some forty new songs. A beautiful book," advertisement, *Shaker and Shakeress*, 5 (March 1875), 24 (no. 980).
    MacLean 91. CtY, DLC, MB, MPB, MWiW*, MiU–C, N, NBuG, NN, NNC, NOC, NSyU, NjPT, OClWHi, OO, OOxM, RPB, WHi.

1294 ——— (Reprint). New York: AMS Press, 1973.

1295 ——— Variant. [2], 67 pp. music. 20 X 24 cm.
    The errata (except title page) have been corrected; the preliminary blank pages have been eliminated and utilized for additional songs; "Gladsome Sound" replaces "Christmas Offering" as the first selection. Table of contents reflects the changes.
    MPB, MWiW*.

1296 Shaker Orders. [n.p., n.d.]. Broadside card. 15½ X 9½ cm.
    At end: St. Paul. The 12 orders, printed within an ornamental border, differ from the Millennial Laws and appear to have been intended only for young people, and may even be a parody on them. "9th. The Boys and Girls must not kiss one an other. 10th. The Boys are forbid winking across the big dinning-room [*sic*] table at the Girls."
    MPH*.

1297 The Shaker Peace Convention Recently Held at Mount Lebanon, N.Y. Adopted Strong Resolutions in Favor of International Arbitration ... [n.p., 1905]. Broadside. 9½ X 8 cm.
Title from first lines of text. Reprinted from the *Springfield Republican.*
MWiW*.

1298 Shaker Publications. For Sale by the Several Societies. [Canterbury, N.H.: 189–?]. Caption title. 3 pp. 23 cm.
"As enquiry is constantly being made in regard to our publications, it was suggested that we ascertain what books might be obtained, the price, and the Society that could furnish them. We accordingly wrote to the Elders of the several Societies and have obtained that desired information." The publications are listed under the name of the Society that has them for sale.
MWiW*, OClWHi, OHi.

1299 *Shaker Quarterly*, Vol. I, no. 1, Spring, 1961–to date. Sabbathday Lake, Poland Spring, Me.: Published by the United Society [Portland, Me., Anthoensen Press], 1961–date. 22 cm. illus. ports.
It is recognized in the first issue of this Shaker periodical that "many changes have been wrought both in the Society and in the world," since publication of the last issue of *The Manifesto* in 1899. "Despite the vicissitudes which time has worked upon us the divine truths upon which Shakerism has rested for nearly two hundred years are unchanged and unchangeable. It is the desire to serve these same truths that has resulted in the 'wave of enthusiasm' which Elder Henry C. Blinn long ago hoped would some day once again draw Believers into the world of periodical literature." The new *Quarterly* is devoted to all historical aspects of Shaker interest and contemporary interpretations of Shaker theology including original articles by Shakers and non-Shakers, historical articles on former communities and industries, music, biographical sketches of Shakers, book reviews, and Shaker writings heretofore available only in manuscript. "News and Notes," a regular feature, provides news of the two remaining Shaker communities at Sabbathday Lake,

Me., and Canterbury, N.H. Edited by Theodore E. Johnson.
CtHC, CtY–D, DLC, KyBgW, MBAt, MHarF, MPH, MWiW*, NNUT, NOC, NSyU, NhD, NhU, NjPT, OClWHi.

1300 Shaker School for Girls at Mount Lebanon, New York. [Mt. Lebanon: 1897?]. Cover title. [4] pp. 19 cm.
Curriculum, dress, tuition ($200 annually), etc. Inquiries are to be addressed to: Eldress Anna White, North Family, Mount Lebanon, N.Y.
MacLean 114. CtY, DLC, MPB, MWiW*, MeHi, NN, NOC, NSyU, OClWHi.

1301 Shaker Tract. Christ Church. Harrison, Ohio: North Family Shakers, [n.d.]. Cover title. 4 pp. 22 cm.
An unsigned manuscript note in the Berkshire Athenaeum copy (Pittsfield, Mass.) states that Elder Peter Stephen is the author.
MH–AH, MPB, MWiW*, OClWHi.

1302 Shaker Village, Inc. Canterbury, New Hampshire. A Restored Shaker Village. [Concord, N.H.: The Village Press, 1972]. Cover title, [4] pp. illus., map. 21½ cm.
This non-profit organization was founded in 1969. Canterbury Shaker properties were transferred to Shaker Village, Inc. and corporators were appointed in 1973. This farsighted action assures that buildings will continue to be restored and that the sisters will continue to live in the buildings now occupied. An aerial view shows clearly more than twenty buildings clustered in the Shaker manner. "Starting as a one building museum in 1959, each year more buildings and more displays will be open to the public."
MPB, MWiW*, NOC.

1303 The Shakers. [Concord, N.H.: 1828]. [2] pp. 45 cm.
"From the New Hampshire Patriot." The petition of James Wallace and 124 others "praying legislative aid for the wives and children of such as join the Shakers" was presented to the New Hampshire House, June 1828, and action was postponed. At the November 1828 session similarly worded

petitions were presented by Amasa Sargent and 56 others, and Lemuel Dow and others. The Amasa Sargent petition is printed here and also the Shaker remonstrance refuting the petitions, along with the House Selective Committee Report, Dec. 16, 1828, which resolved "that the petitioners and remonstrants have leave to withdraw their respective papers." This account is appended to the 1846 edition of [R. McNemar], *comp.*, *Investigator* (no. 927), 19 pp. at end. OClWHi*.

1304 Shakers. [New Lebanon, N.Y.: 1848?] Caption title. 18 pp. 19 cm.

Contents: "Whereas there appeared in the True Wesleyan." Shakers [reply to Luther Lee's attack in the *True Wesleyan*, Oct. 1847 (no. 1384), concerning the Pillow case] by Richard Bushnell, pp. 1–4; Shakers to the Public, p. 4; The Shakers. The Legislature of New Hampshire and their Constitution [from the Boston *Courier*], signed: *Junius Americus*, pp. 4–7; Minority Report of the Judiciary Committee [N.H. Legislature] upon the Petition of Franklin Munroe and Others in Relation to the Society of Christians called Shakers (no. 1072), pp. 7–12; [Three letters from William H. Pillow] To Rachel G. C. Patten, James Pilcher, Susannah Myrick, pp. 13–18. *See also* no. 1384 and entry under Pillow, William H. Copies of this complete 18-page item have been located at MWiW* and OClWHi. Other copies located are incomplete and correspond to MacLean's division: MacLean 442 (12 pp.). MH–AH, MHarF, MPB, MWA, N, NBuG, NN, NjPT, OClWHi. (MacLean 412. 6 pp., i.e., numb. 13–18). MPB, NBuG*, NNC.

1305 "Shakers, or The United Society of Believers." In J. Hayward, *The Book of Religions* (Boston, 1842), no. 2225, pp. 75–85.

A letter written by the Enfield, N.H., trustees in response to a circular requesting information about Shakerism for inclusion in the forthcoming book.

1306 Shakers as Farmers. Chatham, N.Y.: Chatham Courier, [n.d.]. Broadside. 35 X 15 cm.

Reprinted from the Chatham [N.Y.] *Courier*. Reprinted in *The Manifesto*, 13 (October 1883), 233–34, with the subtitle, "A Visit to the North Family at Mt. Lebanon." The writer states that his visit was "on the invitation of Elder F. W. Evans" and he thanks Evans for "favors extended" as host. Reprinted in Evans' *Autobiography* (no. 576), pp. 225–30.
MacLean 439 (attributed to F. W. Evans). MHarF, NN, OClWHi*, OHi.

1307 The Shakers' Covenant (Never before Published,) with a Brief Outline of Shaker History by Roxalana L. Grosvenor, Author of "Reminiscences of Life among the Shakers; Historical and Biographical Sketches," Entered according to Act of Congress April 16, 1873, by Roxalana L. Grosvenor, in the Office of the Librarian of Congress at Washington. Boston: W. C. Allen, Printer, 1873. 1 p.l. ii, 12 pp. 22½ cm.

"Covenant or Constitution," pp. 1–8; "A Brief Outline of Shaker History," pp. 9–12. Roxalana L. Grosvenor had been an eldress at the Harvard, Mass., Shaker community and also a member of the bishopric of that area. She and her sister, Mary F. Grosvenor, were placed in the Society as young children and signed the covenant when they were twenty-one years of age. They "were expelled for having entertained and expressed a difference of opinion from that taught by the Ministry, in regard to certain matters," *Oneida Circular*, Oct. 11, 1875, p. 2. Each received $50 at the time of expulsion, and brought suit for recovery of compensation for their many years of services in the society. The case went to the Supreme Court (Mass., June 3, 1875), which upheld the Shakers in their refusal to support members who had been expelled from the society, *see* nos. 693, 1251 and 1698. "Shaker Church Covenant," was published somewhat later in *The Shaker*, 7 (October, November 1877), 75–76, 85–86. *See also* no. 693. An advertisement on the back cover of this publication identifies Mary F. Grosvenor as a "magnetic physician" in Boston.
MacLean 324. DLC, ICN, MB, MHarF, MiD, NBuG, NOC, OClWHi*.

1308 The Shakers of Mount Lebanon Extend to You an Invitation to Attend a Peace Convention in the Interest of Universal Peace, to be Held at Mount Lebanon, N.Y., August 31, 1905. [Mt. Lebanon: 1905]. Broadside. 22 X 19 cm.

Printed on blue paper.

MPB, MWiW*, OClWHi.

1309 ———— Mount Lebanon Invite You to Attend a Peace Convention in the Interest of Universal Peace, to be Held at Mount Lebanon, N.Y., Thursday, Aug. 31, 1905. [Mt. Lebanon: 1905]. Broadside. 23 X 19 cm.

Printed on blue paper. The text differs from no. **1308**. A list of the speakers is given: Joseph Holden, Harriet Bullard, August Stone, Daniel Offord, Anna White, Sarah Burger.

MWiW*.

1310 Shakers Work For Peace. [n.p., 1905]. Broadside. 19 X 7½ cm.

Reprinted from the *Albany Evening Journal*, August 9, 1905. Concerns the Peace Conference held at New Lebanon, N.Y., and the Shakers' consistent pacifist beliefs.

MPB, MWiW*, OClWHi.

1311 Shakertown at South Union, Kentucky. Divided into Small Farms and will be Sold at Public Auction Beginning Tuesday, September 26 at 10 o'clock A.M. Smith & McClanan, Agents. Home office: Springfield, Tennessee. Branches at Russellville, Kentucky, South Union, Ky. [n.p., 1922.]. Cover title, 20 pp. 24½ cm. illus.

The sale included livestock, implements, etc. Former Shaker lands were subdivided into 60 farms of 25-150 acres, and some parcels included Shaker buildings. This brochure gives full descriptions and is illustrated with 12 photographs.

KyBgW*.

1312 ... Shiloh's United States Spiritual Magazine ... New York: Christian Israelite Press. May 1865. Cover title. 12, 8, [2] pp. 22 cm.

At head of title: Hebrew Dispensation. "Perfect Gospel Advocate,—5," p. [1]. Contains two parts: Judgment of Daniel Milton, the promised Shiloh! and Stone from the Moun-

tain!; and The True Explanation of the Bible, Revealed by Divine Communications to Joanna Southcott. "Catalogue of the Books that contain her [Joanna Southcott's] *'Sacred Writings'*," pp. 9-10. "Millenial [*sic*] Church. 'United Society of Believers.' 1792," back cover, recto, lists Shaker societies with their locations. *See also* nos. **1032-1036**.

MWiW*.

1313 [SKINNER, CHARLES MONTGOMERY] Among the Shakers. Successful Communism at Mount Lebanon — Interview with Elder Evans — A Lunch — Principles of Faith and Practice — Spiritual Guidance — Modes of Life — Practical Religion. [n.p., 1886?]. Broadside in 4 columns. 40 X 26 cm.

Signed: *C. M. S.* Account of visits to the Hancock, Mass., and Mt. Lebanon, N.Y., Shaker communities. Charles Montgomery Skinner, brother of Otis, was on the staff of the *Brooklyn Eagle*, where this account was probably printed originally. This broadside appears to have been printed from newspaper galleys. Not indicated in the long title is Skinner's interview with Daniel Fraser, or his description of the 25¢ luncheon at Hancock, Mass., where "the cooking is worthy of Delmonico's though the habitués of that restaurant might regard it as limited in scope." Appeared in *The Manifesto*, 16 (March, April, 1886), 62-63, 90-92. J. S. Ellett, ... *Buffalo and Erie County Public Library* (no. 2947), No. 5, records another edition reprinted from *Leisure Hour* (London), 1871, signed: *C. M. S.* MacLean 431. CtY, MHarF, MPB, MWiW*, NBuG, OClWHi.

1314 SMITH, HILRIE SHELTON and ROBERT T. HANDY and LEFFERTS A. LOETSCHER. American Christianity; An Historical Interpretation with Representative Documents. New York: Charles Scribner's Sons, 1960-63. 2 vols. illus.

Shakers, I:563-64; "The Last Will and Testament of Springfield Presbytery," (reprinted from *Observations on Church Government*, no. **1333** with discussion), I:576-78. "By-Product of Revival: Growth of the Shakers," I:586-96 includes most of the text of *The Peculiarities of the Shakers*, which is here attributed to Benjamin Silliman. Cf. no. **1828**.

1315 SMITH, JAMES. An Account of the Remarkable Occurrences in the Life and Travels of Col. James Smith During his Captivity with the Indians, in the years 1755, '56, '57, '58 & '59. With an Appendix of Illustrative Notes. By Wm. M. Darlington ... Cincinnati: R. Clarke & Co., 1870. xii, 190 pp. 24 cm. (Ohio Valley Historical Series, no. 5).

This is a reprint of the Lexington 1799 edition. Because his son had joined the Shakers at Union Village, Smith lived there for a short time "to see what sort of people they were." His active disapproval of the Shakers was engendered by his son's behavior which is described by Robert Clarke, pp. vii–xi of the "Prefatory," in this edition.
CSmH, DLC, ICN, MWA, OCl, OClWHi*, OCU, OU, PHi, PPD, PPiU, PPL, PPPrHi, PWcHi.

1316 —— Remarkable Occurrences Lately Discovered among the People Called Shakers; Of a Treasonous and Barbarous Nature, or Shakerism Developed. Carthage [Tenn.]: Printed by William Moore, 1810. 22 pp.

The first of Smith's charges against the Shakers which led to the controversy that resulted in the mob attack on Union Village, O., see no. 1474. Reprinted in M. Dyer, *Portraiture* (no. 532 ff.), pp. 308–28.
Sabin 82769. Shaw 21362. KyBgW, OClWHi*.

1317 —— ———— Paris [Ky.]: Printed by Joel R. Lyle, [1810]. 24 pp.
MacLean 514. Sabin 82768. Shaw 21363. NN*.

1318 —— ———— Abington [Va.]: Printed by John G. Ustick, 1811. Cover title. 23 pp. 21 X 14 cm.
Sabin 82770A. Shaw 23945. NHi*.

1319 —— ———— Lynchburg, Virginia: Printed by Jacob Haas, 1811. 20 pp. 16½ cm.
Caption title: "An Attempt to Develop Shakerism."
MWA*.

1320 —— Shakerism Detected, their Erroneous and Treasonous Proceedings, and False Publications, Contained in Different Newspapers, Exposed to Public View, by the Depositions of Ten Different Persons Living in Various Parts of the States of Kentucky and Ohio, Accompanied with Remarks. Paris, Kentucky: Printed by Joel R. Lyle, 1810. 44 pp. 24½ X 15 cm.

Copyright notice on the last page is dated: November 21, 1810. Smith's reply to McNemar's newspaper attacks, with depositions which accuse the Shakers of inciting the Indians. For McNemar's reply, see no. 958.
MacLean 515. Sabin 82770B. Shaw 21364. Streeter 4230. DLC, KyU, NHi*, NN, PPiU.

1321 SMITH, WALTER C. Self-worship [poem]. [n.p., n.d.] Broadside in 3 columns. 25 X 19½ cm.

Includes "The Motherhood of God" by Rev. John Pulsford, D.D. of Edinburgh.
MPB, MWiW*, NBuG, OClWHi.

1322 Solid Extracts of Truth. [n.p., n.d.]. Broadside. 20 X 13 cm.

Beginning: Beautiful manners spring from self-control and a kind heart .... End: Our prayers are *prophets:* but there must be *consistency* and *constancy* in the petitioners. Hands to work and hearts to God. — Ann Lee.
OClWHi*.

1323 Solomon Rankin. "Happy are They Who Die for the Lord" [eulogy]. South Union, Ky.: Jan. 23, '83. Broadside. 29 X 14 cm.
Signed: *H. H. H.*
OClWHi*.

Some Account of the Proceedings of the Legislature of New Hampshire in Relation to the People called Shakers in 1828. See [R. McNemar], *comp., Investigator* ... (1846), nos. 926 and 1071.

1324 *Something New.* Exeter, N.H.; Boston: 1830–1832. 13 issues.

An almost unknown magazine published by Michael H. Barton, February 1830 through October 1832 (No. 1; s. 2, Nos. 1–12) and printed by Brother Simon Blanchard of the Harvard, Mass., Shaker community, February–October 1832 (s. 2, Nos. 5–12). It was devoted to improving and perfecting "the orthography of the English language by substituting an alphabet, in place of the present one, which shall contain thirty-nine letters, each representing one of the distinct articulate sounds used in our language." A note by Barton (s. 2, No. 5, p. 49) states that publication would have ceased with the last issue, but "a friend of mine at Harvard, Mass., on learning of this kindly offered to erect a printing press and give me all needful aid to go through with it." "Printed by S. Blanchard, Harvard, Mass.," appears at the foot of p. 179 (s. 2, No. 12). H. S. Nourse, *History of the Town of Harvard, Massachusetts* (no. 2524), p. 473, states that this magazine was printed at Harvard, Mass., beginning February 1832, by Simon Blanchard, and that the type "somewhat resembled" shorthand writing. Actually most of the text cannot be read by anyone unacquainted with Barton's unique alphabet of 39 characters. Excerpts from Dunlavy's *Manifesto* were reprinted in several issues, but could not be identified by the compiler. *See also* nos. 1563 and 1669. The magazine ceased publication with s. 2, No. 12 (October 1832). MB, MH, MHarF*, MHi, NN.

1325 Sonnet. Mt. Lebanon: Christmas Day, 1874. Broadside. 7 × 7 cm.
   Printed on gold colored paper.
   OClWHi*.

1326 Souvenir Folder of the Shakers, East Canterbury. Published by the Shakers, East Canterbury, N.H. [Tilton, N.H.: The Atkinson News Co., 1939?]. 9 × 14 cm.
   The folder contains 18 colored postal card views of the buildings, grounds, dining room, washing mill, etc. The cards are attached and folded accordian style, so that they may be viewed vertically.
   N*.

1327 A Special Covenant of the First Family of the Church, Dated 3rd Month 8th 1815. [n.p., n.d.]. [2] pp. 20 × 12 cm.
   "We believe it is high time that we should come to the light, and declare faith openly to each other, and maintain, aboveboard, what we believe to be right, to the laying down of our lives ... What follows is a declaration of faith and rules of behavior." Union Village?

Signed: *Richard McNemar, Calvin Morell, Samuel Rollins, Ashbel Kitchel, William Sharp, James Smith, Amos Valentine, Abner Bedell,* and 21 other brethren.
MPB, MWiW* (pasted inside back cover of *The Constitution*, no. 911), 17 × 10 cm. (trimmed).

1328 SPRINGFIELD (Ohio) PRESBYTERY. An Apology for Renouncing the Jurisdiction of the Synod of Kentucky ... Lexington [Ky.]: Printed by Joseph Charles, January 31, 1804. 144 pp.
   The Presbytery of Springfield was formed by the leading Presbyterian preachers Richard McNemar, John Dunlavy, Barton Stone, and John Thompson because of disagreements with the Lexington, Ky., Synod about the interpretation of the Westminster Confession, conduct of the Kentucky Revival, etc. The *Apology* recounts the background and the reasons for their withdrawal. An account of McNemar's differences with the Presbyterian hierarchy is found in J. P. MacLean, *Life* (no. 2411), pp. 6–15. This entry is taken from Shaw.
   Shaw 5716. NcMHi.

1329 —— An Apology for Renouncing the Jurisdiction of the Synod of Kentucky. To which is added, A Compendious View of the Gospel, and a few Remarks on the Confession of Faith. By the Presbytery of Springfield ... Lexington, Ky.: Printed by Carlisle. Re-printed by G. Kline, 1805. 116 pp.
   This entry is taken from Shaw.
   Shaw 9190. ICU.

1330 —— ———— Philadelphia: Printed by S. Engels, 1805.
   Sabin 65137. Shaw 9191. No copy located.

1331 —— A Compendious View of the Gospel, and a few Remarks on the Confession of Faith, of the Synod of Kentucky ... Windsor [Vt.]: Reprinted by Alden Spooner, 1808. 72 pp. 19 cm.
   McCorison 1024. Shaw 16173. MWA, VtHi.

1332 —— The Last Will and Testament of the Presbyter [!]. From a Copy Reprinted in Albany.

1808. [n.p., 1808?] [4] pp. (last page numb. 22). 18 cm.

Signed: *Springfield Presbytery, June 28th 1804.* (L.S.) *Robert Marshall, John Marshall, John Dunlavy, Richard M'Nemar, B. W. Stone, John Thompson, David Purviance, Witnesses.* " 'The Last Will' was published in 1804. No known copy," F. G. Ham, "Shakerism in the Old West," p. 24, ftn. 52. Copies of "The Last Will" were included in *Observations on Church Government* which were appended to various editions of R. McNemar, *The Kentucky Revival,* nos. 929–933. The Williams College copy (Williamstown, Mass.) is bound with the separate publication, *Observations on Church Government* (Cincinnati, From the Press of John W. Browne, 1807), no. 1333, but the typography differs, and the printing appears to be McNemar's. *See also* no. 1314.
Shaw 16174. KyBgW, MWA, MWiW*, NNUT, OClWHi.

1333 —— Observations on Church Government, by the Presbytery of Springfield, To which is added, the Last Will and Testament of that Reverend Body: With a Preface and Notes, by the Editor ... Cincinnati: From the Press of John W. Browne, 1807. 23 pp. 18½ cm.

With as issued, Richard McNemar, *Kentucky Revival* (Cincinnati, 1807), no. 929. Signed: *The Editor* [i.e., Richard McNemar], "Preface," p. 5, and followed by the note, "For further information respecting this publication, those who have opportunity may enquire of Matthew Huston [i.e., Houston], John Dunlavy, or Richard M'Nemar. Turtle Creek, June 15, 1807."
Sabin 43606. Shaw 13571. DLC*, ICU, KyLoF, MWiW, NN, NRAB, OClWHi, PPPrHi.

1334 —— —— Cincinnati–Printed. Albany [N.Y.]: Reprinted by E. and E. Hosford, 1808. 23 pp. 16½ cm.

Appended to Richard McNemar, *Kentucky Revival* (Albany, N.Y., 1808), no. 930. Separately paged and separate signatures. "Errata" mounted on blank leaf at end. Text is the same as the 1807 edition above. "Last Will and Testament," pp. [19]–23.
Sabin 43606. Shaw 16175. DLC, IaU, MMeT,

MWA, MWiW*, NBuG, NN, NNG, NNUT, OClWHi, ODa, PPULC, WHi.

1335 —— —— Pittsfield [Mass.] : Reprinted by Phinehas Allen, 1808. 28 pp. 16½ cm. MWiW, N, OClWHi*.
Revival (Pittsfield, Mass., 1808), no. 931, separately paged, but the signatures run consecutively through both works. The text is unchanged, but the number of pages has been increased by the use of a larger size of type. "Last Will and Testament," pp. 23–28.
Shaw 16176. CSmH, DLC, MMeT, MWA, MWiW*, OClWHi.

1336 STEPHENS, A. ROSETTA and MARTHA J. ANDERSON. Song of the Dell (for the Children), by A. Rosetta Stephens. Song of the Rain (for the Children), words by M. J. Anderson; music by A. Rosetta Stephens. [n.p., 19-]. Broadside. music. 28 X 42 cm.

The words and music for 2 songs printed as parallel pages. At end: A "20th Century" Release, North Hollywood, Calif.
NOC*.

1337 STETSON, Mrs. CHARLOTTE PERKINS. ... A Clarion Call to Redeem the Race: The Burden of Mothers [poem]. Mt. Lebanon, N.Y.: The Shaker Press, [189-?]. Cover title. 4 pp. 13 cm. (Lebanon leaves. Stir up series, No. 3.).

The author married George H. Gilman in 1900, and thereafter was known as Charlotte Perkins Gilman.
MacLean 449. MWA, MWiW*, NBuG, NN, NSyU, OClWHi.

1338 STEWART, PHILEMON. ... Closing Roll from Holy and Eternal Wisdom, Mother Ann, Father William and Father James, to the Children of Zion. Part II. A Sacred Covenant of Our Heavenly Parents, sent forth upon Earth to Their Children, at the Close of Their Late Manifestation, (on the Holy Mount of God,) for the Purification of Zion and the Inhabitants Thereof. Given by Inspiration, in the Church of the Holy Mount of God at New Lebanon, December 31, 1841. To be Kept Sacred by All Zion's Children. Printed at Canterbury, N.H.: 1843. Cover title. 39 [1] pp. 21 cm.

These inspired messages are generally attributed

to Philemon Stewart. At end of Covenant, p. 29, "Approval of the Ministry on the Holy Mount," signed: *Ruth Lindon. Asenath Clark. Ebenezer Bishop. Rufus Bishop.* MacLean 11. MPB, MWA, MWiW*, MiU-C, N, NN, NOC, OClWHi.

1339 [——] Extract, Taken from a Roll Written by the Holy and Mighty Angel, October, 1843, Copied November 11, 1843. New Lebanon, N.Y.: [n.d.]. Broadside. 22 × 14½ cm.
     Signed: *Inspired writer, Philemon Stewart.* The angel's admonition, "Let there be no caviling or disputing upon my word, or upon any of the sacred givings that have been sent forth from Heaven unto you." MWiW*, OClWHi.

1340 [——] A Holy, Sacred and Divine Roll and Book; From the Lord God of Heaven, to the Inhabitants of Earth: Revealed in the United Society at New Lebanon, County of Columbia, State of New-York ... Read and Understand all Ye in Mortal Clay. In Two Parts. Received by the Church of this Communion, and Published in Union with the Same. Canterbury, N.H.: Printed in the United Society, 1843. 2 pts. in 1 vol., paged continuously, vii, 222, [8], 223-402, [3] pp. 21½ cm.
     Title page, Part II (p. [5] following p. 222) reads: Part II. Being a Sequel or Appendix to the Sacred Roll and Book, to the Nations of the Earth; Containing the Testifying Seals of Some of the Ancient Prophets and Holy Angels, with the Testimonies of Living Witnesses, of the Marvelous Work of God, in his Zion on Earth. Canterbury, N.H., Printed in the United Society, 1843. The writer is identified as "a mortal instrument in the hands of Holy Angels, in writing the foregoing sacred pages," p. 219; signed: *Philemon Stewart*, p. 222, *see also* Add. no. 1206a. This book is a product of the most intense spiritual manifestations among the Shakers, and its contents were believed to be a new revelation of the will of God. Later, when the Ministry decided that it did not represent a true revelation, the book was withdrawn from circulation. Its affinity to the Book of Mormon (1830) has often been noticed. "As this is the first printed book ever issued by

the United Society at Canterbury, among whom there is no regular printer, the mechanical execution may not be perfect in all respects," Advertisement, p. [iii]. The books were bound by the Harvard Shakers. A journal entry records Jan. 15, 1845, "William Leonard finishes binding the Sacred Roll." C. E. Sears, comp., *Gleanings from Old Shaker Journals* (no. 1273), pp. 211, 241, 246. Following p. 222, "Notice to all who may read the foregoing sacred pages," p. [1]; "To printers. Explanations, amendments, and corrections," pp. [2-3]; p. [4] blank; title page, Part II, p. [5]; p. [6] blank; "Preface," p. [7]; p. [8] blank. "Errata to Part II," p. 402; "Corrections," i.e., 2 unnumbered pages of corrections are found tipped in (or bound in with stub) following p. 402; "Contents to Part II," pp. [1-3], at end. Chaps. 21, 23, 25 reprinted in the *Day-Star*, 11 (Dec. 27, 1846), 50-51; 12 (Feb. 13, 1847), 14 (no. 494). *See also* nos. 458-459. MacLean 93. Sabin 79708. CSmH, CtY, DLC, DeWint, KyBgW, MB, MBC, MPB, MPH, MSaE, MWA, MWiW*, MeB, MeHi, MiD, N, NBuG, NHi, NN, NOC, NRCR, NSyU, NhD, NjMD, OC, OClWHi, ODa, OHi, WHi.

1341 [——] ——— Part I .... 222 [3] pp. 21½ cm.
     Parts I and II were also published separately. The 500 copies distributed "to the world" consisted only of Part I, bound separately. *See* no. **459**. MacLean 94. Sabin 79706. DeWint, MH, MHarF, MPH, MSaE, MWiW*, NOC, NSyU, OClWHi.

1342 [——] ——— Part II. Being a Sequel or Appendix .... with the Testimonies of Living Witnesses ... Canterbury, N.H.: Printed in the United Society, 1843. vi, 223-402 [2] pp. 21½ cm.
     Some copies have a cover label which reads: Testimonies to the Sacred Roll. "Corrections," [2] pp. at end. Part II was circulated only among Believers, who might have it bound with Part I, if desired. *See* no. **459**. MacLean 95. Sabin 79707. MHi, MSaE, MWA, MWiW*, MeB, N, NOC, OClWHi, OLeWHi.

1343 —— To the Inhabitants of Zion. A Short Roll of the Word of the Lord to the Inhabitants of Zion, Concerning the Holy and Sacred Pages, that are Sent Abroad into the World Among the Children of Men, Showing in what Manner and Spirit to Answer All Questions that They May Be Asked Relative to the Same, from Those Without. New Lebanon, N.Y.: 1843. Broadside. 43½ × 14 cm.

These instructions concern his *A Holy, Sacred and Divine Roll and Book.* Dated: New Lebanon, N.Y., April 18, 1843. Signed: *Inspired Writer, Philemon Stewart.* "N.B. The above is intended for circulation among Believers generally; but not to go out of the Society."
MWiW*, N, OClWHi.

1344 [STOFFEL, MARGARETHA] Remarkable Prophecy. [Translated from the German by Elias Schnider.] [Canterbury, Mer. Co., N.H.: Shaker Press, 1852]. Cover title. 13 pp. 14 cm.

Reprinted from the *Kennebec Journal* (Augusta, Me.), March 8, 1852. The prophecy "was made on Christmas day, 1847, by Margaretha Stoffel of Ehrenthiel in Tyrol. The whole is to be fulfilled between 1847 and 1856. ... It was reduced to writing by Edward Brann ..." p. [3]. "Afterward it was published in Philadelphia by L. A. Wollenweber [who] ... had received a copy of it from Germany in the month of Feb. 1848," p. 4. The prophecy included the prediction that "a woman will arise who shall preach the true religion and all nations will be converted unto the doctrines of this new messenger of God ..." p. 13. Apparently the Shakers believed this woman to be Ann Lee.
DLC, MWiW*, OClWHi.

1345 —— ———— [New Gloucester, Me.: Printed by James Holmes, 1854]. Caption title. 18 pp. 12½ cm.

T. E. Johnson, "Random notes," Maine Library Association *Bulletin,* 22 (February 1961), 19, describes this as "Another of Deacon James productions is the curious little pamphlet ..."
OClWHi*.

1346 STONE, HENRY M. and JULIA ANN STONE. To the Public. [n.p., 1847]. Caption title. 4 pp. 22½ cm.

Individually signed statements of two members (brother and sister) of the New Lebanon community giving the circumstances and reasons for their joining the Shakers. Excerpts from these statements were reprinted in *The Knickerbocker,* 29 (March 1847), 277-78, where the authors are identified as "brother and sister of the author of the [anti-Shaker] pamphlet entitled *'Lo Here! and Lo There!'*" This is their denial of the charges made by their brother, Horatio Stone, identified here as "a physician in New York." *See* no. 2815.
MWiW*, OClWHi.

1347 STOUT, HOSEA. Autobiography ... 1810-1844, ed. by Reed A. Stout. [Salt Lake City: Utah Historical Society], 1962. 88 pp. illus.

A vivid account of the author's childhood with the Shakers at Pleasant Hill, Ky., where he lived for 4 years, 1814-1818, pp. 10-18. Stout later became a prominent Mormon and attorney for Brigham Young. His sister Rebecca became a deaconess at Pleasant Hill. Reprinted from the *Utah Historical Quarterly,* Vol. 30 (1962).
KyLoF*.

1348 STROUD, THOMAS. The Spiritual Teacher. Why the Shakers are Entitled to a Candid Hearing. [Canterbury, N.H.: 1891]. Caption title. [2] pp. 22 cm.

Thomas Stroud was a member of the Enfield, Conn., community. Reprinted from *The Manifesto,* 21 (September 1891), 196-98, with slight changes and the omission of the last 2 sentences.
MacLean 450 (identified as broadside).
MPB, MWiW*, N, NBuG, NN, OClWHi.

1349 —— ———— [Enfield, Conn.: 1891]. Caption title. [2] pp. 24 cm.

At head of title: "From the Medium and Daybreak Apr. 17, 1891." Signed: *Thos. J. Stroud, Enfield, Conn.* "Editorial from the *Medium and Daybreak*" at end, p. [2].
DLC, MHarF, MPB, N, NN, NOC, OClWHi*.

1350 Sun Spots and their Ominous Meaning to

Man and the Planet. A Divine Revelation by a Shaker. [New Monterey, Calif.: The Shaker Mystics, copyright by R. A. Benninghoven, 1907]. Cover title. XXXIV pp. 15 cm.

There is no evidence that this is a Shaker publication, but it is the product of a group organized somewhat on the Shaker pattern and practicing similarities of doctrine. Here it is claimed that the leader predicted the San Francisco earthquake, 1905. It is likely that the group is associated with or part of the group in San Francisco gathered by Brother Arthur W. Dowe, *see* no. 515. MPH*.

1351 Sunday Service. Shaker Village, Mer. Co., N.H. May 6–Oct. 27, 1877. [Canterbury, N.H.: 1877]. Caption title. 24 nos. (each 4 pp.). 15½ cm.

Almost entirely hymns, words only. Libraries holding a few scattered or single issues of the Canterbury *Sunday Service* are not indicated here or below. OClWHi* (lacks July 15).

1352 —— —— June 2–Oct. 27, 1878. [Canterbury, N.H., 1878]. Caption title. 88 pp. (24 nos., each 4 pp.). 15½ cm.

Almost entirely hymns. "Public Service Closes for the Winter after Oct. 27." MWA (lacks July 28; Aug. 18, 24; Oct. 20, 28), MWiW* (lacks Sept. 1), MiU–C (lacks Oct. 27), NOC*, OClWHi (lacks July 28, Sept. 1, Oct. 27).

1353 —— —— May 11–Oct. 26, 1879. [Canterbury, N.H.: 1879]. Caption title. 96 pp. (25 nos., each 4 pp.). 15½ cm.
NOC*, OClWHi.

1354 —— —— June 6–Oct. 24, 1880. [Canterbury, N.H.: 1880]. Caption title. 88 pp. (24 nos., each 4 pp.). 17 cm.

A sermon or exposition in nearly every issue.
MacLean 451. (MacLean 452. "Sept. 4 to Oct. 2, 1880," duplicates issues included in MacLean 451.) DLC, MWiW (lacks Sept. 26), NOC*, OClWHi.

1355 —— —— July 31–Oct. 16, 1881. [Canterbury, N.H.: 1881]. Caption title. 12 nos. (each 4 pp.). 17–19 cm.

A more complete set of *Sunday Service* for 1881 has not been located.
OClWHi*.

1356 Supplementary Rules of the Shaker Community. These are Published to Encourage the Spirit of Carefulness. Mount Lebanon, N.Y.: [Printed at Canterbury, N.H.?], 1894. Cover title. 4 pp. 17½ cm.

J. P. MacLean a.l.s. Franklin, O., May 28, 1905, to H. M. Lydenberg, New York Public Library "arranged and printed by H. C. Blinn," *see also* no. 50.
CtY, DLC, KyBgW, MH, MHarF, MPB, MWA, MWiW*, MiU–C, N, NBuG, NN, NOC, NSyU, NjPT, O, OClWHi, ODa, OHi.

T

1357 Table Monitor. [n.p., n.d.]. 20 × 30 cm.
A poem of only twelve lines with an entirely different text from *Table Monitor* by Hannah Brownson, *see* nos. 119–125. Authorship of this short poem is sometimes attributed to Cecelia Devere. First line: I stood amid a bounteous banquet hall. Last line: I will not mock with selfish wastefulness. MWiW, N, OClWHi*.

1358 TAYLOR, AMOS. A Narrative of the

Strange Principles, Conduct and Character of the People Known by the Name of Shakers: Whose Errors Have Spread in Several Parts of North-America, but are Beginning to Diminish, and Ought to Be Guarded Against. In Two Numbers. By Amos Taylor. Late of Their Number and Acquainted with Them in Five Different Governments for Ten Months. Number I. Wherein Their Whole Constitution is Laid Open, more Particularly the Method Used by That People in Making Their Proselytes. Worcester

(Massachusetts): Printed for the Author [by Isaiah Thomas], 1782. 23 pp. 16½ cm.

> Dated at end: Harvard [Mass.] April 15, 1782. "General Advertisement, intended to promote Printing, and the Manufacture of Paper in the United States of America," is appended, pp. 18-23. The title and references in the text indicate that a second number is anticipated, but no copy has been located. Valentine Rathbun's *Account* (no. **1216**) pointed out "some gross absurdities in point of doctrine and worship," but Taylor feels that the public should "be able to judge for themselves what the power is, and from what it proceeds." Taylor, "an itinerant teacher, poet, publisher, and bookseller," states that he had been a member of the Harvard, Mass., Shaker community, and considers the Shakers to be "artful, designing men, especially their leaders," *see* M. A. McCorison, "Amos Taylor, A Sketch and Bibliography," American Antiquarian Society, *Proceedings*, 69 (April 15, 1959), 39-41 (no. **3392**), where a bibliography of Taylor's later works is included.
> MacLean 516. Evans 17735. Sabin 94439. KyBgW, MHarF, MPB, MWA*, N, OClWHi, PPL.

1359 TAYLOR, LEILA SARAH, *ed.* A Memorial to Eldress Anna White, and Elder Daniel Offord. Mount Lebanon, N.Y.: North Family of Shakers, 1912. 2 p. 1l., 182 pp. ports. 18 cm.

> Tributes, including poems from various communities and friends, and biographical information.
> MB, MPH, MWA, MWiW*, N, NHi, NN, NOC, NSyU, NjPT, OClWHi, OO, RPB.

1360 Teacher's Testimonial ... Precepts and Prohibitions. [Canterbury, N.H.?: n.d.]. Broadside. 27½ × 18 cm.

> The testimonial has blanks to be filled in with pupil's name, etc. "The Precepts and Prohibitions are given to strengthen and encourage" practice of these virtuous principles. *See* no. **1201** for separately published *Precepts.*
> OClWHi* (blue paper).

1361 [TEED, CYRUS REED]. From Thence is the Shepherd the Stone of Israel. The Lord Comes through the Posterity of People. By Koresh [*pseud.*]. Chicago: 1892. 23 pp. 17 cm.

> For a time Teed enjoyed a special relationship with the Shakers at Mt. Lebanon, N.Y., *see* no. **652**. Teed's works appeared as late as 1927, but only those works published during his association with the Shakers are included here.
> OClWHi*.

1362 [——] Judgement. By Koresh [*pseud.*] Chicago, 1892. 16 pp. 16½ cm. (Women's Mission Tract, No. 4).

> OClWHi*.

1363 [——] The Law of God Delivered on Sinai is the Basis of the Koreshan System. By Koresh [*pseud.*] [n.p., n.d.]. 8 pp. 17 cm.

> Private collection.

1364 —— Re-incarnation, or the Resurrection of the Dead. [Chicago, Ill.: Guiding Star, 189-]. 44 pp. 15½ cm.

> Shakers and celibacy, pp. 39, 40.
> OClWHi*.

1365 [Testimonials Advertising the 2d Edition of A. G. Hollister's *Pearly Gate*]. [n.p., 1896]. [2] pp. 18 cm.

> Letters from Hon. Hiel Hollister, Granville, N.Y., Oct. 29, 1894; Eldress Ann Taylor, Mt. Lebanon, N.Y., 1894; and others.
> MacLean 112? MWiW*, OClWHi.

1366 Testimony of Words. [n.p., n.d.]. Broadside in 2 columns.

> Poem of 6 stanzas. J. P. MacLean to H. M. Lydenberg, dated: Franklin, O., May 28, 1905, suggests that the author is Seth Y. Wells (a.l.s. New York Public Library).
> MacLean 455. No copy located.

1367 This Agreement Made This ..... [n.p., n.d.]. Broadside. 35 × 23 cm.

> An instrument of manumission for three slaves, a family named Joseph, Chloe, and George, by their owner Thomas MacLean who was required to free the slaves before

he could join the Shakers at South Union, Ky. Signed and witnessed, and filled in for July 31, 1819.
KyBgW, OClWHi*.

1368 This Agreement, made this —— day of —— one thousand eight hundred and —— between —— of —— County of —— and State of —— of the first part, and —— —— of the —— Family of the Society of Shakers in said —— of the second part: Witnesseth ... [n.p., n.d.]. Broadside. 32½ × 20½ cm.

Blank membership agreement form for use between a new member and the United Society. "In consideration of the benefits and privileges covenanted by the party of the second part" agrees he (or she) will give his "time and services for the use and benefit of the family or society," and will keep orders, rules, and regulations as a faithful member and agrees that if he should "ever leave" the Society, no charge or demand for wages and/or compensation for any service performed will be made. To be signed and sealed in the presence of witnesses. *See also* no. 844.
MPB, OClWHi*.

1369 This Too Helps. [n.p., 1905]. Broadside. 22½ × 7½ cm.

Reprinted from the *Albany Journal.* Concerns the resolutions adopted at the Peace Convention held at Mt. Lebanon, Aug. 31, 1905.
MWiW*, OClWHi.

1370 THOMASON, JEAN HEALAN. Shaker Manuscript Hymnals from South Union, Kentucky. With Comment on Musical Notation by Fann R. Herndon, and Introduction by Julia Neal. Bowling Green, Kentucky Folklore Society, 1967. 56 pp. music. (Kentucky folklore series no. 3.).

Description and discussion of 15 Shaker manuscript hymnals in the Kentucky Library, Western Kentucky University, Bowling Green, Ky.
ICN, InU, KyBgW, MHarF, MPH, NOC*, NcU, OU, ViU.

1371 [TILLINGHAST, JOSEPH] Brief and Useful Instructions for the Young. By a Friend of Youth and Children. Worcester [Mass.]: Printed by Chas. Hamilton, 1858. 39 pp. 15½ cm.

Signed, p. 39: *The Giver.* The precepts accord with Shaker practices, but the text strongly suggests other authorship. Western Reserve Historical Society's attribution of authorship to Tillinghast depends upon information supplied by Eldress Catherine Allen, whose autograph note on the fly leaf of the Society's copy reads, "Joseph Tillinghast was a Quaker who was thoroughly in accord with the ideals and motives of the Shakers *and* was recognized as a brother of the outer court often lecturing at the different communities of the Shakers." Library of Congress attributes authorship to Frederick William Evans, but without documentation. "A Friend of Youth and Children" is identified as Frederick White Evans in William Cushing, *Initials and Pseudonyms,* 1st Ser. (N.Y. 1885), p. 107. This work furnished much of the material for *Gentle Manners,* no. 721, *see also* nos. 859 and 1131.
DLC, MWA, MWiW*, NBuG, NN, OClWHi, OHi.

1372 Time Table for Public Meetings, Canterbury, N.H. 1881. Broadside. 27 × 21½ cm.

A schedule of weekly union meetings, choir rehearsals, prayer services, etc., for 1881 at Canterbury Shaker Village, N.H. "The signal bell is to be rung ten minutes before every public gathering."
OClWHi*.

1373 —— Canterbury, N.H.: 1882. Broadside. 25 × 20½ cm.
OClWHi*.

1374 "To." An Anthem. Oct. 10, 1868. [n.p., n.d.]. Broadside. 8 × 13 cm.
OClWHi*.

1375 To All People Who Shall See These Presents. Know ye, that whereas my Child has been Placed by me in the Society of Shakers, (United Society), in Shirley, Massachusetts, Middlesex County, Mass., with the Intent that

———— Shall Remain with the same Society, and be Subject to the Rules and Government thereof, so long as ———— Shall so Conduct ———— as to Satisfy the Authorities of Said Society, and no Longer.... [n.p., n.d.]. Broadside. 26 X 18 cm.

> Indenture blank for minor children being placed with the Shakers, *see also* nos. 6, 835-836, and 1377.
> MWiW*, OClWHi.

1376 To All Whom It May Concern ... [form to be filled in for a member who is withdrawing from the United Society]. [n.p., n.d.]. Broadside. 23 X 14½ cm.

> Specifies that the member is withdrawing voluntarily, refuses to be governed by the rules and regulations any longer, and releases the "Trustees, Society, Church, and every member from all claims," and further that he has no valid claim for labor or services. To be signed and witnessed.
> OClWHi*.

1377 To All Whom It May Concern. In Consequence of the Many Applications to the Society to Receive Minors, and in Order for Those Who Place Them There to Gain a More Correct Understanding of the Terms upon which They Are Received, it has been Thought Advisable to Adopt the Following Rules and Regulations .... [n.p., n.d.]. Broadside. 31 X 20 cm.

> Specifies complete care of the child including "education, government, and management" which are "surrendered to the Society." Parents, relatives, or guardians must apply to the Trustees' Office for permission to visit the child, and visits are "not to be prolonged ... nor repeated too often." *See also* nos. 6, 835-836, and 1375.
> Private collection.

1378 To Believers in Christ's Mission, to Mankind in his Second Appearing. [Mt. Lebanon, N.Y.: 1887]. Broadside. 21½ X 17½ cm.

> Signed: *Ministry of Mount Lebanon, Aug. 19th, 1887.* "The call for 'A world's soul communion,' — A universal prayer meeting, by 'The World's Advance Thought' of Salem, Oregon ... If this call is sincerely regarded, we believe angel messengers will fly through-

out the world, bearing messages of *light, truth, the wisdom and love of God, a knowledge of his will, way and work to mankind ....* ms. note: *Meeting for August is on 30th Inst. succeeding months on 29th of each. At 3:15 for New York.*
> MacLean 378. MWiW*, N, NN, OClWHi*.

To the Honorable Legislature of the State of New-York. The Memorial and Petition of the Undersigned, Inhabitants of the Towns of Canaan and Watervliet, and other Places in said State, Respectfully Sheweth ...

> This title has been described as a separate publication with imprint date: [1816]. No such copy has been located. This "Memorial" with identical title is found, however, as part of ... *The Memorial* ... [Albany, 1816], no. 1019, pp. 4-5, where it begins, p. 4: That your memorialists are, and for a long time have been, well acquainted with the society of people commonly called Shakers ... P. 5 begins: "Your memorialists beg leave ..." and it is signed by 120 Shaker friends and acquaintances, who are petitioning the Legislature "to pass a law" which would exempt the Shakers from military duty and also from the payment of "money in lieu thereof." The Shakers are described as a "peaceable, industrious, charitable and moral people," and that "whatever property they possess is dedicated solely to acts of benevolence and charity." *See also* no. 1022.

1379 To the Honorable the Legislature of the State of New York. [n.p., 1852]. 3 pp. 30 cm.

> A strong protest made by the freeholders of New Lebanon, N.Y., against a bill before the New York Legislature in 1852 which would extend Shaker special privileges. It is signed by John Kendall, Chairman, and Andrew R. Clark, Secretary, and 36 inhabitants. The bill would allow the local Shakers an increase in their annual income, from the $5,000 stipulated in the 1839 "Trust Act," to $25,000. The group claimed that numerous Shaker purchases of local farms had encroached upon the community, and that the community has no legal protection. Consequently, it is requested that a Legislative

committee visit the community and make a
thorough investigation.
OClWHi*.

[To the Honorable, the Legislature of the State
of Ohio. n.p., 1817].
   It is possible that this citizens' petition was
   printed separately for presentation to the
   Legislature, but no copy has been located.
   Ham, "Shakerism in the Old West," p. 143,
   ftn. 45, cites a copy printed in the newspaper,
   Western Star (Lebanon, O.), October 22,
   1817. The attacks on the Shakers by the
   editor (Van Vleet) and others, printed in the
   Western Star in 1817, culminated in this
   citizens' petition calling for legislative interference to curb the evils of Shakerism. *See*
   MacLean's *Life of Richard McNemar* (no.
   2411), pp. 29-30, and no. 1402.

"To the Honourable, the Legislature of the
State of Ohio [1819]." In [R. McNemar],
comp., The Other Side of the Question (no.
946), pp. 130-36.
   Signed: *Malcham* [!] *Worley, Francis Bedle,
   Amos Valentine, John Miller, Samuel Sering,
   Union Village, 9th September 1819.* An
   explanatory paragraph states that this is "a
   petition which was intended to have been
   presented to the Legislature." It is a refutation of "misstatements" about the Shakers,
   particularly that the properties of Union
   Village were fraudulently acquired. The
   signers certify that their properties were
   consecrated "to the pious and charitable
   uses of the Gospel," and that they were
   "never to be recalled." No copy located.

1380 To the Legislature of the State of New-
York. [n.p., 1817]. Caption title. 8 pp. 21½ cm.
   Signed: *In behalf of the Society, Peter Dodge,
   Seth Y. Wells, Joseph Hodgson, Watervliet,
   March 20th, 1817.* This statement is intended
   as a protest and refutation of the "false and
   libellous statements and gross misrepresenta-
   tions concerning the character and conduct"
   of the Shakers made by Eunice Chapman,
   "with the intention of inducing the Legislature to pass a law injurious to the Society."
   A Select Committee of the New York Senate
   had reported favorably on a bill which would

"strip a man entirely of all property, and
divest him of the right of citizenship, of all
government over his family, and all right of
ever receiving property during life." For
Thomas Jefferson's comments on this bill,
see no. 2320. *See also* nos. 1015 and 1597.
Reprinted in [R. McNemar], *The Other Side
of the Question* (no. 946), pp. 30-37, and
pp. 19-20 for Mary Dyer's threatening letter
to the three Shakers who signed this protest.
Shaw 40686, 42097, and 42098. MB, MPB,
MWA*, N, NOC, OClWHi.

1381 To the Legislature of the State of New-
York: [Albany: 1839]. Broadside. 34½ X 21
cm.
   Begins: The communities of Christians residing in New Lebanon in the county of Columbia, and in Watervliet in the county of Albany,
   associated under the name of the United
   Society, and commonly called Shakers ...
   To represent the injurious operation to their
   societies, of the present laws of the state,
   respecting conveyances of lands, and to ask
   a remedy adapted to their peculiar situation
   ... The Western Reserve Historical Society
   copy is accompanied by a blank leaf presumably intended to provide for the signatures
   of the brothers and sisters. This leaf carries
   a ms. note, "Document XY. A petition or
   memorial presented 1839 Jan. 7." A bill,
   which had been drafted at the request of the
   Shakers, was submitted along with this address which requested that the Legislature
   pass the bill, "or one similar in principle,"
   which would exempt the Shakers "from the
   laws concerning trusts." The N.Y. Revised
   Statutes had abolished the Trust Law, and
   thus jeopardized the Shaker right to land
   ownership, if in fact, this right was not invalidated by the law. The committee reported
   favorably on the bill, but the session ad-
   journed before acting upon it. *See* nos. 456
   and 1078.
   Shaw 38922 (entry mistakenly dated [1816?]).
   N, OClWHi*, WHi.

1382 To the Legislature of the State of New-
York in Senate and Assembly Convened: [n.p.,
1838?]. Broadside. 32 X 20 cm.
   Begins: "The subscribers respectfully represent,

that they have been informed that the United Societies of Shakers at Lebanon and Watervliet, are about to present a memorial to your honorable body, praying for such alteration in the laws concerning trusts in lands, as will enable them to retain their communities and their property in a manner consistent with their faith ... Ms. notation on the New York State Library copy reads, "Petition of our neighbors 1839." This petition, or memorial, is signed by Jonas C. Heartt and 45 others, including Thurlow Weed, John A. Dix, Erastus Corning, etc. This group testified to the "peaceful, sober, industrious, and charitable qualities of the Shakers" as well as their proverbial honesty and morality. Also that the Shakers had brought "agriculture to the highest pitch of perfection known in this region, and [that] their horticulture excites universal admiration."
OClWHi*.

To the Public. [Harrodsburg, Ky.?: 1825?]. Broadside?

No copy located. This is described as a defense which reflects a changing attitude toward the Western Shakers, and a protest against the violation of the constitutional rights of a religious minority, Ham, "Shakerism in the Old West," p. 133, where it is identified, ftn. 20, "Handbill: 'To the Public,' signed: *The Printer*, reprinted in the Lexington *Kentucky Gazette*, June 16, 1825, and the Lexington *Kentucky Reporter*, June 13, 1825." The sane reaction of "The Printer" was also evident in the notice of the "violent outrage" recently committed upon the Shakers at Pleasant Hill, Ky., reported in *Niles' Weekly Register*, July 9, 1825, no. 3683. *See also* no. 1426.

1383 [TREAT, RICHARD]. "Kitchen Gardening," In *The New-England Almanac ... 1830* (New-London, Conn., Printed and Sold by Samuel Green, [1829]), pp. [18–20].

Instructions for cultivating vegetables for the common kitchen garden "received from Richard Treat, the oldest gardener at the Shaker Village, in New-Lebanon, Columbia Co., N.Y."
MWA*.

1384 Trial of the Shakers for Attempt to Restrain the Wife and Three Children of William H. Pillow; an Exposure of their Deceptions, and Her Final Release. By a Writ of Habeas Corpus. Extracted from the *True Wesleyan*. October, 1847. [n.p., n.d.]. 22 pp. 19 cm.

Includes the Writ, statement by Mrs. Pillow, Wm. H. Pillow's "Reply to the Return," "Reply to the Further Return," and testimony of witnesses. *See also* nos. 1083 and 1304.
MacLean 517. OClWHi*, PHi.

1385 $200 Reward. Stolen! From the Stable at Union Village on Sunday Night, 6th inst., a Pair of Matched Horses! Union Village, Warren County, O., May 7, 1866. Broadside. 20½ X 34½ cm.

Signed: *Stephen Easton.*
OClWHi*.

1386 TYNER, PAUL. The Christ Ideal in Shakerism. [East Canterbury, N.H.: 1896]. Cover title. 10 pp. 22½ cm.

"Published in *The Humanitarian* of January 1896, and republished by permission," Editor's note, p. 1. Note at end signed: *H. C. Blinn.* Also printed in *The Manifesto*, 26 (June–August 1896), 95–97, 108–12, 124–27.
MacLean 459. MB, MBC, MPB, MWiW*, NBuG, NN, O, OClWHi.

U

1387 Union Plums [poem]. North Union: 1834. Broadside. 21 X 15 cm.

"The origin of this poem arose from the sugar plums which the North Union Believers sent to the Shakers at Groveland and Water-

vliet [N.Y.] to be eaten on Christmas, 1834," MacLean, *Bibliography*, p. 13.
MacLean 460. OClWHi*, OHi.

1388 The United Society of Believers. Blessed

are the Peacemakers .... [Printed at Shaker Village, N.H.: n.d.]. Caption title. [2] pp. 17½ cm.

> Quotations, mostly from the Bible.
> MacLean 461? MWiW*, NN, OClWHi.

United Society of Believers. Notice to Visitors. *See Notice to Visitors*, nos. 1111-1116.

1389 The United Society of Believers, Called Shakers. [Canterbury, N.H.: 19-]. Caption title. [3] pp. 19½ cm.

> A brief summary of information "to meet the many inquiries." "Letters of inquiry may be addressed to Elder Benjamin H. Smith, or Eldress Harriet March, Sarah Libbey, or Elder Henry C. Blinn." Cf. no. 715. MWiW*, NHi.

1390 ... The United Society of Believers, Called Shakers. Answers to Inquirers. [Canterbury, N.H.: n.d.]. Caption title. [2] pp. 19 cm.

> At head of title: No. 2.
> MacLean 463. MWiW*, OHi.

1391 The United Society of Believers, Called Shakers. [Questions and Answers about the Shakers.] Printed at Shaker Village, Mer. Co., N.H.: [n.d.]. Caption title. [2] pp. 20½ X 14 cm.

> OClWHi*.

1392 U.S. Bureau of the Census. Religious Bodies 1916. Washington, D.C.: Gov't. Print. Off., 1919. 2 vols.

> "United Society of Believers (Shakers)," Pt. 2, pp. 230-32, includes an account of Shaker history, doctrine, polity, statistics of membership, etc., and a comparative summary of the statistics for 1916 and 1906. *See also* "Explanation of Terms," pp. 4-5.

1393 —— Religious Bodies: 1926. Washington, D.C.: Gov't. Print. Off., 1929. 2 vols.

> "United Society of Believers (Shakers)," Vol. II, pp. 441-45, includes an account of Shaker history, doctrine, organization, and work, which is "substantially the same" as that published in the 1916 census, but "has been revised by Walter Shepherd, trustee of the United Society ... and approved by him

in its present form." Tables of statistics include comparative data from the available statistics for the censuses of 1926, 1916, 1906, and 1890. This census lists the Shakers and Amana Society in a section, "Communistic Societies," which was reprinted as a 13-page pamphlet (1928); the general statement and Shaker statistics are on pp. 9-13.

1394 —— Religious Bodies: 1936. Washington, D.C.: Gov't. Print. Off., 1941. 2 vols. in 3.

> "United Society of Believers (Shakers)," Vol. II, Pt. 2, pp. 1261-64, with an account of Shaker history, doctrine, organization, and work, which is reprinted from the 1926 census, and "approved in its present form by Irving Greenwood, trustee of the United Society ... East Canterbury, N.H." The statistical tables include a comparative summary of data for the census years, 1936, 1926, 1916, and 1906. Shaker information and statistics were also included in the 1941 separate publication ... *Miscellaneous Denominations* (U.S. Bureau of the Census, Bulletin 76, 41 pp.).

1395 —— Report on Statistics of Churches in the United States at the Eleventh Census: 1890. Henry K. Carroll, Special Agent. Washington, D.C.: Gov't. Print. Off., 1894. 812 pp.

> "Society of Shakers," pp. 323-24, includes a brief description of Shaker history and beliefs and a statistical summary of membership by states and counties, value of church property, etc.

1396 —— Special Reports. Religious bodies: 1906. Washington, D.C.: Gov't. Print. Off., 1910. 2 vols.

> "United Society of Believers (Shakers)," Pt. 2, pp. 220-23, includes an account of Shaker history, doctrine, polity, work, and statistics of membership, value of church property, debt, etc. Statistics of the religious affiliations of the population were analyzed for the first time in this census.

1397 —— The Statistics of the Population of the United States ... Compiled from the Original Returns of the Ninth Census (June 1, 1870) ... Washington, D.C.: Gov't. Print. Off., 1872. 3 vols.

"Shakers," Vol. I, p. 521. Comparative data for 1850, 1860, and 1870 census. Statistics of the religious affiliations of the population were not included in the census before 1850. The validity of the U.S. census statistics of Shaker membership is discussed by H. Desroche, *The American Shakers*, no. 2048, along with tables and comparisons of other available statistics of membership, pp. 126-38.

1398 U.S. Congress. Annals of Congress ... 18th Congress, 1st Session. Washington, D.C.: Printed and Published by Gales and Seaton, 1856. 2 vols.

House — Vol. I, col. 1586 — Feb. 18, 1824. "Mr. Williams of North Carolina, from the Committee of Claims, made an unfavorable report on the petition of the trustees in behalf of the United Society, commonly called Shakers, residing at West Union, in Indiana"; which was laid on the table, *see* no. 1025. This reference is also found in the House *Journal*, Feb. 19, 1824, p. 245. Available in any large library.

1399 —— ————

Senate — Vol. I, col. 315 — March 3, 1824. "Mr. Van Buren presented the memorial of the United Society, called Shakers, of New York, praying to be exempted from the performance of military duty, being conscientiously opposed to bearing arms; which was read, and referred to the Committee on Militia." No printed copy of this memorial has been located. A manuscript copy in the National Archives is identified as Rg. no. 46, stack area 8E-4, row 5, Sen. 18A-G8, Committee on the Militia. It is signed by Ebenezer Bishop, Rufus Bishop, and 39 others. Vol. I, col. 499 — April 7, 1824. "On motion of Mr. Chandler, the Committee on Militia were discharged from the consideration of the memorial of the Society of Shakers in New York and on motion by Mr. Mills was ordered to lie on the table." *See also* no. 2880.

1400 U.S. CONGRESS. HOUSE. Shaker Association at New Lebanon, N.Y. Letter from the Commissioner of Internal Revenue in Reply to a Resolution of the House of the 12th ultimo, Relative to the Mode of Taxing the Shaker Association of New Lebanon, N.Y. [Washington, D.C.: Gov't. Print. Off., 1867]. 2 pp. 24½ cm. (U.S. Cong. 40th, 2d sess., H. Exec. Doc., No. 82).

A communication dated December 21, 1867, transmitting an earlier ruling of the Commissioner of Internal Revenue interpreting the provisions of the Income Tax Law of 1862 (Civil War Tax) as they applied to the Shakers. The ruling, contained in a letter dated June 1, 1863, was addressed to James Macklin of the 12th district of New York. It informed him that in regard to the Shaker societies, the statutory allowance of $600 for each covenanting male member was to be effective in the tax assessment. The decision applied to all Shaker societies, and the Commissioner stated that as far as he knew it was being carried out. *See also* nos. 457 and 1411. The House Resolution directed the Commissioner to inform the House, "whether under the peculiar arrangements of the Shaker institution at New Lebanon, N.Y." the statutory allowance was being made. It was introduced by Charles A. Eldridge, Representative from Wisconsin, *Congressional Globe*, 40th Cong., 2d sess., 1 (Doc. 12, 1867), 162.

1401 U.S. LIBRARY OF CONGRESS. MANUSCRIPT DIVISION. Index to the Abraham Lincoln Papers. Washington, D.C., Library of Congress, 1960. 124 pp.

A finding list for the Lincoln papers available on microfilm that is essentially a name index. Page 95, under "Shakers — United Society to AL — 1863," the symbol, Ag 1-25267-Memonote-docket, refers to a ms. "Memorial" addressed: To his Excellency the President of the United States, and signed: *F. W. Evans, Benjamin Gates.* It is dated: Aug. 1, 1863 (in a different hand), and is a petition for the exemption of Shakers from the draft, cf. no. 1014. This Memorial is printed in A. White and L. Taylor, *Shakerism* ... (no. 1447), pp. 182-83, with somewhat different paragraph arrangement. This is accompanied by an unaddressed statement dated: August 1, 1863, which may be in Gates' autograph. It concerns "some 12 or 15 of our Members" who have been drafted, and the plea "to change the decision of the Provost Marshall to imprisonment during the Draft. As we would prefer suffering the Extreme Penalty of the Law rather than violate our *Nonresistant Principle*," signed: *Benjamin Gates, Frederick W. Evans.* Another entry on p. 95, "Shakers — FR*AL-1864-Ag8-2-42981-3 Wise 1864

Ag 17 refers to Lincoln's letter dated: Executive Mansion, Washington, August 8, 1864, addressed: My good friends. This refers to John Hay's first draft of a letter that Lincoln sent to the Shakers, thanking them cordially "for the very comfortable chair." *See* no. 2381.

V

1402 [VAN VLEET, ABRAM], *comp.* An Account of the Conduct of the Shakers, in the Case of Eunice Chapman & Her Children, Written by Herself. Also, a Refutation of the Shakers' Remonstrance to the Proceedings of the Legislature of New-York, in 1817, by Thomas Brown. To Which are Added, the Deposition of Mary Dyer, Who Petitioned the Legislature of the State of New-Hampshire, for Relief in a Similar Case. Also, Depositions of Others Who Have Been Members of the Shaker Society. Also, the Proceedings of the Legislature of the State of New-York in the Case of Eunice Chapman. Lebanon, O.: Printed by Van Vleet & Camron, 1818. v, [7]–105 pp. 18 cm.

This is a compilation of anti-Shaker materials to which Van Vleet has added depositions about the Shakers at Union Village, O., and other information. Van Vleet, editor of the *Western Star*, Lebanon, O., was responsible for the anti-Shaker news items printed in his paper, and has often been labeled a Shaker baiter. In a letter to Mary Dyer printed in her *Portraiture* (Haverhill, N.H. 1817), no. 532, pp. 306–07, Van Vleet states that he had paid little attention to the nearby Shakers at Union Village, O., until a case was brought before him as Justice of the Peace, Lebanon, O. The case involved a boy who had escaped from the Shakers, and after five days was forcibly returned to the Shaker village. A complaint was filed, and five Shakers were arrested and bound over to the court to answer. As a result of the testimony and other information brought out in this case, Van Vleet writes that he saw it as his "duty to arouse the attention of the public, that some measure should be taken to check if

possible, the abominable practices which appear to exist in the society." He continues that he has recently received Eunice Chapman's first and second publications (nos. 448 and 449) along with her "very lengthy and interesting letter," written upon her return from Enfield, N.H., where she had gone to recover her children. His letter to Mary Dyer is a request for "all of the information" that she can send him about the proceedings of the New Hampshire legislature in her own case against the Shakers to recover her children. Two letters from Mary Dyer, pp. 50–52; Thomas Brown's "refutation," pp. 52–57; Mary Dyer's deposition, pp. 65–73; "Shaker Tenets: the Riligious [*sic*] Sentiments of the Shakers . . . Disclosed in a Poem," pp. 101–5, *see also The Other Side of the Question*, no. 946, which was published to refute the charges in Van Vleet's compilation, "An Account of the Judicial Proceedings of Abram Van Vleet, Esq. . . ." pp. 115–29.
Sabin 11975. Shaw 46629 and 43575? DLC*.

1403 VANCE, JOHN B. Address of Elder John B. Vance, of Shaker Village [Alfred, Me.] Delivered in Oxford Street Chapel, Lynn, on Sunday Evening, June 1, 1874. [n.p., 1874]. Caption title. 20 pp. 15 cm.

T. E. Johnson states that this was issued by the Alfred Society, "Random notes," Maine Library Association *Bulletin*, 22 (February 1961), 19.
MacLean 464 (Lynn, Mass.). DLC, MPB, MWA, MWiW*, MeHi, NBuG, NN, OClWHi.

1404 —— —— Reported expressly for the Record [Lynn, Mass.: 1874].

Excerpt: *Lynn Record.* Elder Vance and Shakers from Shirley and Harvard, Massachusetts, and Alfred, Maine, held a series of meetings at the Oxford Street Chapel, at the invitation of J. M. Peebles.
MPB*.

1405 —— An Unusual Real Estate Opportunity ... A Comparative Statement of the Analysis of the Poland Mineral Spring Water ... with Remarks by Prof. H. T. Cummings ... [West Gloucester, Maine?: 1893]. Caption title. 16 pp. 9 X 15 cm.
> Signed: *Elder John B. Vance, West Gloucester, or Alfred, Me.* Advertising the sale of "Upper Shaker Village," South Poland, Maine. "The removal of the Shaker family from the 'Upper Shaker Village' South Poland, Me. throws on the market one of the most desirable estates in New England."
> MacLean 115. MPB, MWiW*, NBuG, NN, OClWHi.

1406 Views of North Family Shakers at Mt. Lebanon, New York. [New Lebanon, N.Y.: n.d.]. Broadside. 14 X 13 cm.
> Twenty-nine photographs are listed. "Address Anna White, Mt. Lebanon, N.Y." The photographs are by J. E. West.
> MWiW*.

1407 VINCENT, HENRY. Henry Vincent's Visit to Mt. Lebanon, Columbia County, N.Y. Albany: Printing House of Charles Van Benthuysen & Sons. 1868, 12 pp. 19 cm. (Shaker Tracts, No. 1).
> "The following account ... was written to the London [*Morning*] *Star* by Henry Vincent .... It was sent to us by Elder Frederick W. Evans ... with the request that we would republish it in *The Methodist*," p. [3].
> MacLean 465. DLC, MB, MHarF, MPB, MWiW*, N, NBuG, NSyU, Nh, OHi, PHC, PHi.

1408 "A Visit to the North Family, at Mount Lebanon." [Chatham, N.Y.: n.d.]. Broadside. 29 X 12 cm.
> Description of the great stone barn, ensilage, dairy cattle, stock, creamery, and poultry yards, kitchen gardens, etc. Reprinted from the Chatham [N.Y.] *Courier.*
> OClWHi*.

1409 Voice of Mother. [Sabbathday Lake, Me.: 1840]. Broadside. 20½ X 15 cm.
> This anthem is found in [James Holmes], *comp.* [*Collection of Anthems*], no. 819. The date assigned here has been taken from an entry in the *Shaker Quarterly*, 3 (Winter, 1963), 132.
> NN, OClWHi*.

W

W., E. H. *See* Wright, Eleanor Hayes, nos. **1466** and **1467.**

1410 W., J. The Way to Mend. Shirley, Mass.: Jan. 9, 1899. Broadside. 20 X 8½ cm.
> Poem of 5 stanzas, signed: *J. W.*
> OClWHi*.

1411 WARD, DURBIN (i.e., Jessie Durbin). Shaker Income Tax. Application to Commissioner Delano. Brief of Durbin Ward for Applicants. Albany: J. Munsell, 1869. Cover title. 21 pp. 22 cm.
> The Commissioner of Internal Revenue, Columbus Delano, had ruled that the whole Shaker Society be treated as one person in the composition of income tax under the Internal Revenue Act of 1867. Counsel for the Shakers outlined their religious tenets, the rights and responsibilities of the Ministry and Elders, and the rights and obligations of members as defined in the Covenant (Schedule A, not included with the copy described here), and argued that the ruling worked a great injustice upon the Shakers. The Shakers did not ask that their income tax be remitted, but only that they "be taxed equally with their neighbors, though their income is so largely devoted to charitable uses," *see also* nos. **457** and **1400.**

MacLean 466. CtY, DLC, MWiW*, NN, NSyU, OCIWHi, WHi.

1412 [WEBSTER, NOAH]. Rules of Punctuation from Webster's Dictionary. Quarto Edition, of 1828. Canterbury, N.H.: 1833. 12 pp. 14 cm.
Excerpts for use in the Shaker School, Canterbury, N.H.
OCIWHi*.

1413 [WELLS, SETH YOUNGS] A Brief Illustration of the Principles of War and Peace, Showing the Ruinous Policy of the Former, and the Superior Efficacy of the Latter, for National Protection and Defence; Clearly Manifested by their Practical Operations and Opposite Effects on Nations, Kingdoms and People. By Philanthropos [*pseud.*] ... Albany [N.Y.]: Printed by Packard and Van Benthuysen, 1831. 112 pp. 19 cm.
Both S. Y. Wells and William Ladd used the pseudonym "Philanthropos." Merle E. Curti attributes this work to Ladd, *Dictionary of American Biography*, Vol. 10, pp. 527-28, as does the Library of Congress, and Wm. Cushing, *Initials and Pseudonyms* (N.Y., 1885), p. 231. The Library of the American Peace Society, founded by Ladd, doubted this attribution and ascribed it to Wells. Sabin 38522 credits Ladd, but later in Vol. 28, p. 43 (unnumbered item) states that the work is incorrectly attributed to Ladd, and quotes Richard McNemar's letter to Seth Y. Wells, dated: Union Village [O.], May 10, 1831, "I am much pleased to hear that your treatise on war is published and hope you will favor me with a copy." E. D. Andrews, *People Called Shakers* (N.Y., 1963), p. 216, states that Wells "composed an historical argument against war as an instrument of national policy. Subsequently, at the request of *The Harbinger of Peace* ... Wells expanded his thesis including suggestions on enforcement curiously anticipatory of modern proposals and sanctions," and p. 333, n. 296, credits Wells as author of *Brief Illustration*. The work contains a series of essays on the effect of war from the earliest ages to the present time, "Preface," p. iv. *See also* nos. **1082** and **1233**.
MacLean 78 (and 79 in paper covers). Sabin

38522. DLC, MH-AH, MHarF, MPB, MPH, MWA, MWiW*, N, NBuG, NN, NOC, NSyU, O, OCIWHi, OHi, WHi.

1414 —— [Letter to Michael H. Barton, dated: Mt. Lebanon, N.Y., June 4, 1832]. *See* Michael H. Barton's *Something New* (no. 1324), pp.113-14.
Enthusiastic approval of a new system of shorthand.
MB, MH, MHarF*, MHi, NN.

1415 [——] *comp.* Millennial Praises, Containing a Collection of Gospel Hymns, in Four Parts; Adapted to the Day of Christ's Second Appearing. Composed for the Use of His People. Hancock [Mass.]: Josiah Tallcott, Jr., 1812. viii, 288, [4] pp. 17 cm.
Words only. This compilation is generally attributed to Seth Y. Wells. This first Shaker hymn book was published for circulation and use among Believers exclusively. Parts 1-2 and 3-4 were issued separately according to the cover on the Berkshire Athenaeum copy (Pittsfield, Mass.).
MacLean 71 (incl. No. 73). Sabin 97893. Shaw 27517. CtHT-W, CtY, DLC, IU, KyBgW, KyU, MH, MPB, MWA, MiU, N, NNUT, NSyU, OCIWHi*, OHi, OOxM, PCC, WHi.

1416 —— —— Printed by Josiah Tallcott, Junior, 1813. viii, 288, [4] pp. 17½ cm.
"The object of this publication is to furnish Believers with a collection of hymns, which have been composed by the Believers of different places, and which have met the general approbation of the Ministry and Elders of the Church," Preface. MacLean, *Bibliography* (no. **2407**), p. 6, states that the collection is "largely composed of Western hymns." "Errata," p. [4] at end.
MacLean 72 (incl. No. 73). Sabin 79719 and 97893. Shaw 30511. CSmH, CSt, Ct, CtHC, DLC, DeWint, ICN, KySP, KyU, M, MHi, MBrZ, MH-AH, MPB, MWA, MWiW*, MeHi, MiU, NBuG, N, NN, NOC, NSyU, NRCR, NjMD, NjPT, OCIWHi, OCo, OHi, PU, RPB, WHi.

1417 —— The Shakers, or United Society of Believers ... [n.p., 186-?]. Caption title. 4 pp. 17 cm.

Printed in double columns.
NN*.

1418 —— Thomas Brown and his Pretended
History of Shakers. [Mt. Lebanon?: 1848?].
Caption title. 8 pp. 16 cm.

    Published after the death of Seth Y. Wells,
October 30, 1847. This correspondence
between Seth Youngs Wells and Professor
Benjamin Silliman of Yale College, New
Haven, occurred in November 1823 and concerns Silliman's use of Brown's *Account*
for his discussion of the Shakers in his
Remarks on a Short Tour, no. 2761. Wells
states "Brown has lately issued proposals for
printing by subscription a new edition of his
History (i.e., *Account of the People Called
Shakers*) ..." This edition was never pub-
lished. The correspondence is preceded by a
brief biography of Seth Y. Wells, signed
A.[lonzo] *G. H.*[ollister]. *See also* nos. 114
and Add. 115a-e.
MHarF, MPB, MWiW*, N, NBuG, NN, NOC,
NjPT, OClWHi.

1419 WELLS, SETH YOUNGS and CALVIN
GREEN. "History of the United Society of
Believers," In *History of all the Religious
Denominations in the United States* ... (Harris-
burg, Pa., Winebrenner, 1848), pp. 567-78 (no.
2251).

1420 —— "The Shakers, or United Society of
Believers," In *Cyclopedia of Religious Denominations containing Authentic Accounts of the
Different Creeds and Systems Prevailing throughout the World* ... (London and Glasgow, 1853),
pp. 279-82 (no. 2020).

1421 [——] *eds.* Testimonies Concerning the
Character and Ministry of Mother Ann Lee and
the First Witnesses of the Gospel of Christ's
Second Appearing; Given by Some of the Aged
Brethren and Sisters of the United Society,
Including a Few Sketches of Their Own Religious
Experience: Approved by the Church .... Albany,
N.Y.: Printed by Packard & Van Benthuysen,
1827. 178 pp. 19 cm.

    "To the reader" signed: *Seth Y. Wells.* Con-
tains similar but different testimonies than
those edited by Rufus Bishop in 1816, no.

80. Owing to the false reports "scandalizing
the character of our Blessed Mother & first
Gospel parents, the aged Brethren & Sisters
felt it to be their duty to give each, their
respective Testimonies ... That which their
own eyes had seen & their own ears had
heard ... Several of them requested me to
write their communication, which ... I freely
did, exactly as they stated the facts. A sufficient number of these, selected from the
best acquainted were ... compiled by Br.
Seth & I into a small volume," Calvin Green,
"Biographic Memoir," p. 641. "It is a simple,
strong story by eye and ear witnesses of her
words and deeds, told by her associates and
spiritual children," A. White and L. Taylor,
Shakerism (no. 1447), p. 323.
MacLean 98. Sabin 102603. Shaw 30577.
CSmH, CtHC, CtHi, CtY, DLC, ICN, In,
KyBgW, KySP, KyU, MB, MHarF, MPB,
MSaE, MWA, MWiW*, MeHi, MiD, MiU-C,
N, NBuG, NHi, NN, NOC, NSyU, NhD,
NjPT, NjR, O, OC, OClWHi, OHi, OLeWHi,
OOxM, PPL, PHi, PPULC, WHi.

1422 WEST, BENJAMIN. Scriptural Cautions
Against Embracing a Religious Scheme, Taught
by a Number of Europeans, who Came from
England to America, in the Year 1776, and
Stile [!] Themselves the Church, &c. &c. By
Benjamin West, who had been Deluded by Them,
to the Great Injury of Himself and Family ....
Hartford: Printed and sold by Bavil Webster,
1783. 15 pp. 17½ cm.

    An early seceder's account. "With sorrow and
grief I must confess I have been much capti-
vated with and deeply involved in this new
and strange scheme, to the admiration of
many of my former acquaintances, and was
extremely zealous, being persuaded, it was
the only way to perfection out of all sin; but
alas, the great deception in this, to be ever
going on in a way that never comes to the
knowledge of the truth." p. 11.
Evans 18310. Sabin 102714. Streeter 4224.
CtHi*, NjPT.

1423 What Are We Without Salvation?/
Wand'ring Stars through Sorrows Gloom./
[n.p., n.d.]. Broadside. 18½ × 12½
cm.

Title from first two lines of the poem of
three stanzas.
OClWHi*.

1424 Whereas: ——— Lately of ——— has
Applied for Admission into the United Society
of Shakers, in Canterbury, County of Merrimack,
and State of New Hampshire, and it is Desirable
for said ——— to more Fully Investigate the
Faith and Principles of the Society, and also to
Demonstrate his Sincerity, Competency, and
Eligibility to Membership . . . may be Permitted
a Temporary Residence . . . [n.p., n.d.]. Broadside. 27½ X 21½ cm.
   A disclaimer for any wages or compensation
   for labor is included in this form which was
   used for taking provisional members into the
   Canterbury Society. *See also* nos. 1368 and
   844.
   Private collection.

1425 Whereas, I, the Undersigned, have this
Day Attached Myself as Probationary Member
to the United Society of Believers at . . . .
[n.p., n.d.]. Broadside. 26 X 19½ cm.
   The blank portions of this form provide for
   its use by any Shaker society. It is an agreement to observe "the rules, regulations,
   moral and religious instructions" and "never
   prefer any account, claim, nor demand
   against the said Society, or any member."
   See also no. 1368.
   MPH*.

1426 Whereas in the Year 1828, an Act of the
Legislature of this State [Kentucky] was Passed
for the Purpose of Regulating Civil Proceedings
Against the Shakers . . . South Union [Ky.]:
1830. Broadside. 16½ X 19½ cm.
   A petition of citizens of Mercer and Logan
   Counties, Ky. which supports the Shaker
   Memorial (no. 1023) and requests that the
   law of Feb. 11, 1828, be revised or repealed
   by the General Assembly, so that it will be
   "just and proper." "An Act to Regulate Civil
   Proceedings" was printed in [R. McNemar],
   comp., Investigator (no. 926), pp. viii–x.
   OClWHi*.

1427 WHITBEY, JOHN. Beauties of Priestcraft;
Or, a Short Account of Shakerism. New Har-

mony [Ind.]: Printed for the Author at the
Office of New Harmony Gazette, 1826. 70 pp.
22 cm.
   Whitbey lived over seven years in the "young
   order" at Pleasant Hill, Ky., at a time of crisis
   and confusion in this Shaker community. He
   held warm feelings towards the Shakers whom
   he found to be clean, decent, industrious,
   cheerful and affable, and declares that he still
   feels "a kind of tender respect for them." His
   quarrel was with the elders whom he criticized
   for their deception in order to win new members, their coercive measures to hold members,
   and their government of the community which
   he described as a "hierarchical monarchy." A
   thoughtful man, sympathetic to the ideas of
   Robert Owen, he could not accept some Shaker
   practices and beliefs, provoked discussions
   about his doubts, and asked embarrassing
   questions. It is not surprising that he was
   ordered to leave the community — "placed out
   of union." He joined the Owenite community
   at New Harmony, Ind., where he published
   his criticism of Shakerism as he had found it.
   After dissolution of New Harmony, Whitbey
   returned to Kentucky where with 17 other
   disaffected former Shakers, he petitioned the
   legislature for some plan whereby their
   grievances might be redressed. The resulting
   "Act to Regulate Civil Proceedings against
   certain Communities" caused great consterna-
   tion among the western Shakers. *See The
   Investigator* (no. 926), particularly pp. 6–9,
   23–27, which contain the petition and excerpts from this work, presumably chosen by
   Richard McNemar. The fullest account of this
   period and Whitbey's activities is found in
   F. Ham, "Shakerism in the Old West."
   Whitbey's work is rare and little known. The
   copy at the Cincinnati Historical Society is
   the only copy located.
   MacLean 521. Sabin 103329. OCHP*.

1428 WHITCHER, MARY. Mary Whitcher's
Shaker House-Keeper. Boston: Weeks & Potter,
[c1882]. Caption title. 32 pp. 18 cm.
   Contains Shaker recipes and menus, inter-
   spersed with household hints, testimonials for
   Corbett's Sarsaparilla, and other medicines.
   DLC, MPB, MPH, MWA, MWiW*, NSyU, Nh,
   OClWHi.

1429 ——— ————— Variant with cover title: Mary Whitcher's Cook Book [printed above the portrait and signature of Mary Whitcher]. From Wm. Richards & Co., Wood Block, Natick, Mass.: "Patent Medicine Depot." [copyright by Weeks & Potter, A.D.1882].
N*.

1430 ——— ————— (Facsimile Reprint). [Hastings-on-Hudson, N.Y.: Morgan & Morgan, Inc., 1972].
The new cover, which was not part of the original publication, contains information about the Shakers, signed: *Amy Bess Miller, Hancock Shaker Village, Hancock, Massachusetts.*

1431 ——— ... Our Thought. East Canterbury: Printed at Shaker Village, Mer. Co., N.H., [n.d.]. Caption title. 4 pp. 26 cm.
The title poem is an answer to Charlotte Cushman's "Lines," reprinted here from the *Knickerbocker* (no. 3159). "Answer" [by Harvey L. Eads, South Union, Ky.], pp. 3-4, is reprinted from the Russellville, Ky., *Advertiser, see* 539.
OClWHi*.

1432 ——— Our Thought [poem]. Canterbury [N.H.]: Printed at Shaker Village, Mer. Co., N.H., [n.d.]. Broadside. 20 X 11½ cm.
Poem of 7 stanzas.
MWiW*.

1433 [WHITE, ANNA], *comp.* Affectionately Inscribed to the Memory of Elder Frederick W. Evans, by his Loving and Devoted Gospel Friends ... Pittsfield, Mass.: Press of the Eagle Publishing Co., 1893. 129 pp. port. 18 cm.
Cover title: Immortalized; Elder Frederick W. Evans. "Obituary," [5]-11, reprinted from the *Berkshire County Eagle* (Pittsfield, Mass.), was also published in *The Manifesto*, 23 (May 1893), 105-110, where it is signed: *Anna White.* "Gleanings," pp. [103]-129, contains excerpts from Evans' published works. MacLean attributes this compilation to Anna White.
MacLean 3. CtY, DLC, ICJ, MHarF, MPB, MPH, MWiW*, MiU-C, N, NB, NN, NOC, NSyU, NcD, NjPT, OClWHi, OHi.

1434 [———] *comp.* Affectionately Inscribed to the Memory of Eldress Antoinette Doolittle, by her Loving and Devoted Gospel Friends ... Albany: Weed, Parsons, and Company, Printers, 1887. 32 pp. port. 17 cm.
"The following articles composed by different members of the North Family, Mt. Lebanon ..." p. [3]. The tribute by Anna White, "The heavenly transition," pp. [5]-7, appeared in *The Manifesto*, 17 (February 1887), 44-45. L. Taylor, *A Memorial* (no. 1359), pp. 70-71, describes this collection as "gracefully written and the gathered flowers of memory tastefully arranged."
MacLean 117. IU, MHarF, MPB, MWA, MWiW*, N, NN, NOC, NRCR, NSyU, O, OClWHi, ODa, OHi.

1435 ——— Dedicated to the Memory of Sister Polly Lewis. The King's Daughter. [Mt. Lebanon, N.Y.?: 1899]. Cover title. 7 pp. 13½ cm.
Contains also: "In Love's Bond" [poem] by Cecelia Devere, which was printed in *The Manifesto*, 29 (March 1899), 37, under the title, "Passing Away of the Ancients." Often cited by the subtitle: *The King's Daughter.*
MacLean 468. CtY, DLC, MPB, MWiW*, NN, OClWHi, RPB.

1436 [———] The Motherhood of God. [Canaan Four Corners, N.Y.: Press of the Berkshire Industrial Farm, 1903]. Cover title. 27 pp. 12 cm.
Miscellaneous writings of Anna White, e.g., A paper read "at the meeting of the Equal Rights Club of Hartford, Conn., on February sixth," 1903, remarks and a poem, "Maternal Spirit," pp. 26-27, reprinted from *The Manifesto*, 13 (March 1888), 51.
MacLean 469. CtY, DLC, MHarF, MPB, MPH, MWA, MWiW*, NBuG, NN, NOC, NSyU, NcD, NjPT, O, OClWHi, OHi.

1437 [———] *comp.* Mount Lebanon Cedar Boughs. Original Poems by the North Family of Shakers .... Buffalo [N.Y.]: The Peter Paul Book Company, 1895. 316, [4] pp. 19½ cm.
A collection of poems written by the North Family Sisters that appeared earlier in *The Manifesto*, etc. Four unnumbered pages at end contain "List of Publications," "Post Office Addresses of the Several Communities,"

and "A Brief Citation of the Regulations
Governing the Society of Shakers."
MacLean 74. CSmH, CtY, DLC, KyBgW,
MB, MH, MPB, MWiW*, MeHi, N, NBuG, NN,
NOC, NSyU, OClWHi, OHi, RPB, WHi.

1438 [——] Present Day Shakerism. Mount
Lebanon, N.Y.: North Family, [1906?]. 39 pp.
12 cm.
   Leila S. Taylor, *A Memorial to Anna White*
   (no. 1359), p. 70, gives Anna White as author,
   but incorrectly refers to this as a reprint of
   Concise Statements, no. 106. The texts are
   entirely different. An article by the same
   title, signed: *Philo*, appeared in *The Light of
   Truth*, Sept. 2, 1905, but this text also differs. "Principal Publications" with prices, p.
   38. A list of Shaker societies includes the
   society at Ashland, Osceola County, Florida.
   ICN, InU, MWA, NjPT, OClWHi*.

1439 [——] *comp.* To Our Well Beloved
Mother in Israel. Eldress, Eliza Ann Taylor
whose Spirit Passed "within the Vail" November
28, 1897, in the 87th Year of her Age ....
Mount Lebanon, N.Y.: 1897. 43 pp. 23 cm.
   Cover title: Only Arisen. Eldress Eliza Ann
   Taylor. Sister, Martha J. Anderson. In Affec-
   tionate Memory of our Dear Sister, Martha
   J. Anderson, pp. [23]-43. Includes tributes
   and poems by several authors from various
   communities. Leila S. Taylor, *A Memorial
   to Anna White* (no. 1359), p. 71, describes
   this as Anna White's "most tender and touching [tribute] of all, a white flower of
   memory laid sacredly aside, and rarely mentioned." Attributed by MacLean to Amelia
   J. Calver and Anna White.
   MacLean 457. MHarF, MPB, MPH, MWiW*,
   NN, NOC, NSyU, OClWHi.

1440 —— True Source of Happiness. [Mt.
Lebanon?: n.d.]. Caption title. 6 pp. 13½ cm.
   Contains also: "Labor" by Annie R. Stephens,
   which appeared in *The Manifesto*, 19 (No-
   vember 1889), 247-48.
   MacLean 470. CtY, DLC (2 pp.), MPB,
   MWiW*, N, NN, NSyU.

1441 [——] Vegetarianism among the Shakers.
Republished from "The Counsellor." Mount

Lebanon, North Family, [n.d.]. Cover title. 16
pp. 12½ cm.
   "Eldress Anna White has authorized or written
   this at our request," the editor [of the *Counsellor*], pp. 2-3. It is based on Martha J. Anderson's *Social Life and Vegetarianism*, no. 41.
   "Some Shaker Recipes," pp. 11-16.
   DLC, DeWint, MPB, MPH, MWiW*, N,
   OClWHi.

1442 [——] Voices from Mount Lebanon.
[Canaan 4 Corners, N.Y.: Berkshire Industrial
Farm, Print., 1899]. 15 pp. 13 cm.
   "A paper read at the Universal Peace Meeting,
   Mystic, Conn., Aug. 23, 1899, by Eldress
   Anna White." Contains also "The American
   Flag" [poem] by Cecelia Devere.
   MacLean 471. CtY, DLC, MHarF, MPB, MWA,
   MWiW*, N, NN, NSyU, OClWHi.

1443 —— Woman's Mission. [Mt. Lebanon,
N.Y.?: 1891?]. Caption title. 6 pp. 13½ cm.
   Appeared in *The Manifesto*, 21 (January
   1891), 3-4. Contains also: "Maternal Spirit"
   [poem] by Anna White.
   MPB, MWiW*, OClWHi.

1444 [WHITE, ANNA, and LEILA SARAH
TAYLOR] The First Authoritive [*sic*] and
Comprehensive History of the Sect. Shakerism,
its Meaning and Message by Anna White and
Leila S. Taylor [n.p., 1904?]. Caption title.
[4] pp. 18½ cm.
   Promotion leaflet with testimonial for the
   book and excerpts from published reviews.
   OClWHi*.

1445 [——] Shakerism, Its Meaning and Message ... [Prospectus]. [n.p., 1904?]. Caption
title. [4] pp. 15 cm.
   The third page is in the form of a typed letter
   from Anna White. "... Three years have been
   spent in its production. For revision, correction and criticism, the ms. was placed in the
   hands of different persons, and such suggestions as were offered received careful attention."
   OClWHi*.

1446 —— Shakerism, Its Meaning and Message
... [publisher's announcement]. Columbus, O.:

Fred J. Heer, Publisher, 1904. Caption title.
[4] pp. 19 cm.

> "The book in ms. was carefully read by Dr.
> J. P. MacLean." Page [4] is an order blank
> for the book.
> MWA, MWiW*, OClWHi.

1447 —— Shakerism, Its Meaning and Message;
Embracing an Historical Account, Statement of
Belief and Spiritual Experience of the Church
from its Rise to the Present Day. Columbus, O.:
Press of Fred J. Heer, [c1904]. 417 pp. 32
plates (incl. front. ports.). 20 cm.

> This work does not carry a statement of
> official approval, but it is generally consid-
> ered to be an official account of the religious
> beliefs, history and literature of the Shakers,
> written from the Shaker standpoint. It is not
> documented. Anna White was associated
> with Frederick Evans in the Eldership of the
> North Family of Mt. Lebanon for 27 years.
> Leila Sarah Taylor, *Memorial to Anna White*,
> no. 1359, p. 70, writes that when the book
> was finished Anna White felt that "the whole
> truth had not been told. The cause of its
> [Shakerism's] temporary failures had not
> been portrayed. She seized pen in hand and
> in a trenchant, but terrible indictment,
> declared the tale of unfaithfulness, blight,
> mistake, and wrong. These passages, the
> strongest in the book, embodied in the last
> chapter can be readily recognized." Alonzo
> Hollister states that "While Eld. Anna and
> Leila were rewriting their book, he [J. P.
> MacLean] remained at the North [Family]
> several weeks & read all the manuscript,
> making suggestions for correction and amend-
> ment." Also that MacLean arranged with
> F. J. Heer for the publication of "Eld. Anna's
> book, on much better terms than were
> offered by Funk & Wagnalls," a.l.s., A. G.
> Hollister to Brother Harlan, Feb. 3, 1908,
> Berkshire Atheneum, Pittsfield, Mass.
> CSmH, CtHC, CtY-D, KyU, MH, MWiW*,
> MiU, N, NBuG, NN, NOC, NRCR, NSyU,
> NjPT, OClWHi, OCU, OHi, OLeWHi, OO,
> WaU.

1448 —— —— (Reprint). New York:
AMS Press, [1972].

1449 —— —— [c1905].

> The copyright notice has been changed to
> 1905, but the Preface is still dated: Mount
> Lebanon, N.Y., June 28, 1904. The book is
> otherwise identical with no. 1447 above.
> MacLean 107. CSmH, MB, MPB, MWiW*,
> N, NOC, NjMD, O, OClWHi, ODa.

1450 WHITSON, ROBLEY EDWARD, *comp.*
Shaker Theological Sources; An Introductory
Selection. Bethlehem, Conn.: United Institute,
1969. ix, 52 ll.

> Reprinted excerpts of basic Shaker works.
> "This compilation is intended to serve as a
> theological 'sampler' indicative of the wide
> range of religious thought and concern en-
> compassed within the more than two cen-
> turies of the development of the Shaker Tra-
> dition." Introduction, ll., i–v, by R. E.
> Whitson.
> MPH, MWiW*, NOC, OClWHi.

1451 WHITTAKER, JAMES. The Shaker
Shaken; Or, God's Warning to Josiah Talcott,
as Denounced in a Letter from James Whittaker,
One of the United Society of Believers in Christ's
Second Appearing, (Vulgarly Known as Shakers).
From an Original Manuscript [in the possession
of E. D. Andrews]. New-Haven: Printed at the
Bibliographical Press, 1938. 16 [1] pp. front.
17 cm.

> "To the reader" signed: *E. D. A.* The letter is
> undated, but Andrews dates it February 1782,
> pp. 8–9. Father James' letter scolding Talcott
> for his slothfulness and neglect of his farm,
> "The View of Shakers Dancing was engraved
> by the late Mr. Barber," *see* no. **1819**. *See
> also* nos. **1006** and **2882**.
> DLC, MB, MH, MPB, MWA, MWiW*, NN.

1452 [WHITTIER, JOHN GREENLEAF]
Hymn. Written for the Opening of the Interna-
tional Exhibition, Philadelphia, May 10th, 1876.
Printed at Shaker Village, Mer. Co., N.H.: [1876].
Broadside. 25½ × 13½ cm.

> Poem, six stanzas, printed on pale green
> paper.
> OClWHi*.

1453 Who Leads Us Back to Paradise? [n.p.,

n.d.]. Caption title. Broadside in 2 columns. 24 × 19 cm.

    Hymn of 8 stanzas printed as 2 parallel pages.
    MWiW*.

1454 WICKERSHAM, GEORGE M. How I Came to Be a Shaker. Mount Lebanon, N.Y., [Printed at East Canterbury, N.H.: 1891]. Cover title. 15 pp. 14½ cm.
    Appeared in *The Manifesto*, 21 (June 1891), 123-28.
    MacLean 472. DLC, MB, MHarF, MPB, MPH, MWiW*, NBuG, NOC, NSyU, NhD, NjPT, O, OCl, OClWHi, OHi, WHi.

1455 —— —— By George W. [*sic*] Wickersham ... [n.p., n.d.]. Cover title. 16 pp. 14½ cm.
    Contains also: "Our Shaker Number," pp. 15-16.
    MPB, MWA, MWiW*, OClWHi, OHi.

1456 —— —— [Mt. Lebanon, N.Y.: Shaker Village Work Camp, c1952]. Cover title. 17 pp. 15 cm.
    "Preface" signed: *Jerome Count.*
    MPH, MWiW*.

1457 WICKLIFFE, ROBERT. Speech of Robert Wickliffe, in the Senate of Kentucky, on a Bill to Repeal an Act of the General Assembly of the State of Kentucky, entitle [*sic*] "An act to regulate civil proceedings against certain communities having property in common." [Lebanon, O.: Star Office, 1831]. 16 pp. 22½ cm.
    This speech defending the Pleasant Hill, Ky., Shaker community against charges brought by seceders has been attributed to Richard McNemar, MacLean, *Bibliography* (no. 2407), p. 11 and his no. 473, and *Life* (no. 2411), p. 45; M. F. Melcher, *The Shaker Adventure* (no. 2451), p. 272. Includes "Extract from a Speech of the Honorable John Brethett, Lieut. Gov. of Kentucky," pp. 15-16.
    MacLean 473. Sabin 103874 (under Mc-Nemar). DLC, MH-AH, MWA, MWiW*, NN, O, OCHP, OClWHi, WHi.

1458 [——] The Shakers. Speech of Robert Wickliffe. In the Senate of Kentucky—Jan. 1831. On a Bill to Repeal an Act of the General Assembly of the State of Kentucky, entitled, "An Act to Regulate Civil Proceedings against Certain Communities having Property in Common." [Frankfort, Ky.: A. G. Hodges, Printer, 1832]. Caption title. 32 pp. 18½ × 11 cm.
    Reprinted with slightly different paragraph arrangement in [R. McNemar], *comp., Investigator*, no. 927, pp. 57-84.
    MacLean 474. Sabin 103870. CSmH, MPB, MPH*, MWA, MWiW, N, NBuG, NHi, NN, OClWHi, OHi, WHi.

1459 WILCOX, ELLA WHEELER. Clear away the Rubbish [poem]. Mount Lebanon, N.Y.: The Lebanon Press, [n.d.]. Cover title. [4] pp. (Lebanon leaves. Hope Series, No. 1.)
    MacLean 475. DLC, KyBgW, NOC, OClWHi*.

1460 "William Wells to the Secretary of War [Henry Dearborn], 14 July 1807." In C. E. Carter, ed., *Territorial Papers of the United States* (26 vols., 1934-62), "The Territory of Indiana, 1800-1810," 7 (1938), 465.
    "The Indians are religiously mad," and the Shawnee prophet [Tenskwatawa, brother of Tecumseh] plans a meeting of 2000 Indians in a month. "He is supported by a society of white people called Shaking Quakers — whos[!] Head Quarters appear to be on the Little Miamie State of Ohio." Wells, Indian Agent at Fort Wayne, was discharged early in 1809.

1461 WINGATE, CHARLES F. Shaker Sanitation. [Mt. Lebanon, N.Y.?: 1880?]. Broadside. 40 × 11 cm.
    Reprinted from the *Sanitary Engineer*, 3 (September 1880), 397. Relates to the North Family, Mt. Lebanon, N.Y. *See also* no. 3816.
    DLC, MPB*, OClWHi, OHi.

1462 WINKLEY, FRANCIS and ISRAEL SANBORN. "Short Account of the Faith and Discipline of the Shakers, East Canterbury." In E. Merrill and P. Merrill, *A Gazetteer of the State of New Hampshire* (no. 2461), pp. 91-92.

1463 WOODS, JOHN. Shakerism Unmasked, Or, A Narrative Shewing the Entrance of the Shakers into the Western Country, Their Stratagems and Devices, Discipline and Economy; Together with What May Seem Necessary to Exhibit the True State of That People. By John Woods: Who Lived with Them Seventeen Years ... Paris K[y.]: Printed at the Office of the Western Observer, 1826. 84 pp. 17½ cm.

> An unfriendly attack by a former schoolmaster at Union Village, Ohio. Reprinted in Burton A. Carr, *Gleanings of Religion* (no. 139), pp. 212-70.
> MacLean 522. Sabin 105124. Shaw 27696. DLC, MH, N, NN*, NhD.

1464 WOODS, JOSEPH. The Christian. Canterbury, N.H.: [1888?]. Cover title. 16 pp. 11½ cm.

> Appeared in *The Manifesto*, 18 (March 1888), 54-56. Contains also: "Maternal Spirit" [poem] by Anna White; Information for Inquirers in Reference to the United Society of Believers. Advertisement, p. 16.
> MHarF, MPB, MWA, MWiW*, OClWHi.

1465 Word of Jacob to the World of Mankind with an Appendix Reviewing the Faith and Principles of "the United Society of Believers, or Shakers," as Published by the Society. Volume first. [n.p.], 1857. 110 pp. 23 cm.

> Hollister to WWW, Jan. 4, 1910. "As to the [MacLean] No. 523, the word of Jacob to the world of mankind, I don't remember taking notice of it till you called my attention to it in your last letter. I have no such work in my possession. If I ever saw it, it must have been a borrowed copy — & nothing that Shakers ever approved. They had one Thomas Richmond at Enfield [Conn.], awhile, an Englishman & profest spiritualist,

that they finally had to dismiss for his oddities. He profest Shaker faith after he was sent away — went back to England wrote considerable, I think he claimed under spirit control, & got it printed — returned to Enfield. I think he still claimed union, as he wrote in Believer's favor, tho Believers never owned the writings as emanating from them. I saw some but do not remember this title. At any rate I have no knolej [!] of such a writing. Where MacLean saw it, I don't know." a.l.s. Williams College. This has been attributed also to David Richmond.
> MacLean 523. MiU*.

1466 [WRIGHT, ELEANOR HAYES]. Thoughts Suggested by the Question, What Induced You to Become a Shaker? South Groton, Mass.: 1849. 4 pp. 18 cm.

> Poem of 18 stanzas, signed: *E. H. W.* During Marianne Finch's visit to the U.S., she spent an evening in Boston with the author, and later reprinted most of this poem in her *An Englishwoman's Experience in America* (no. 2119), pp. 154-56. *See also* nos. 908 and 910.
> OClWHi*.

1467 [——] ———— [n.p., n.d.]. Broadside in 3 columns. 27 X 20 cm.

> Autograph of Eleanor Hayes follows the text.
> MHarF, MPH*, NOC, OClWHi.

WRIGHT, ELEAZER. *pseud. See* McNemar, Richard, nos. **889, 937, 946, 950, 955, 965** and **969.**

1468 [WYETH, EUNICE]. The Holy Shepherd; — The Rising Youth [poems]. [n.p., n.d.]. [2] pp. 15 cm.

> MacLean 344. OClWHi*.

Y

1469 [YOUNGS, BENJAMIN SETH] The Testimony of Christ's Second Appearing Containing a General Statement of All Things Pertaining to the Faith and Practice of the Church of God in This Latter-day. Published in Union. By Order of the Ministry .... Lebanon, State

Ohio: From the Press of John M'Clean, Office of the Western Star, 1808. 600, [2] (poem) pp. 1 l. 19 cm.

> Following the text, "A Poem, Containing a Short Abridgment of the Foregoing Testimony [by Richard McNemar?]," [2] pp.;

"Errata," 1 leaf at end. Preface signed: *David Darrow, John Meacham, Benjamin S. Youngs.* "The two first-named ... signed their names not as authors, but as counsellors, and as sanctioning the work," Note, p. xiv, 4th ed. ([Albany, 1856]), no. 1472. F. G. Ham, "Shakerism in the Old West," p. 81, states that the writing was done with the "assistance of John Meacham, John Dunlavy, Matthew Houston, and especially Richard McNemar." In a long discussion of this work in Calvin Green's "Biographic Memoir," pp. 67–70, he states that Seth Y. Wells was selected "as the one best qualified to write *The Testimony*, and that Father David Darrow assisted "in inducing sound Gospel principles." Further, that "This primary publication of the faith and principles of Believers" was printed to provide true information "respecting this new and strange system," and that it "would also be of great importance to Believers to harmonize the sense, and especially to instruct the minds of young Believers." Green continues, "The spiritual and moral progress of the work of God in the world is figuratively like the growth of all living productions of the soil, successively developed from one degree to another, into higher and higher more perfect orders," and that any ambiguities will be clarified by "successive revelations" and "spiritual travel." This authoritative statement of Shaker theology became known in "the world" as the "Shaker Bible," but *see also* nos. 1487 and 1497. It is a "correct statement of their faith," sanctioned by the Society, and was written to correct slanderous and prejudiced information being circulated about the sect and its practices. Cf. "Preface," pp. 5–12. "To the Reader," p. [iii], 3d ed. (Union Village, O., 1823), explains that a number of copies were bound and circulated; but through the inattention of the bookbinder, a great part remained in sheets for several years, till finally, one whole sheet was missing; and with this deficiency, the books had to be finished (bound) by another hand. "This, together with the various stratagems of the enemies of the cross of Christ to prevent the circulation of the books, rendered the first edition quite deficient in

answering the demand of the public, or even affording the Believers a competent supply." The "whole sheet" missing, occurs in signature Ee (Ee 3–6), pp. 327–34. MacLean, *Life* (no. 2411), pp. 44–45 gives the edition as 1500 printed copies, from information he found in McNemar's ms. diary, but in his *Bibliography* he describes the edition as "small."
MacLean 101. Sabin 79723. Shaw 16776 (602 pp.). Streeter 4229. (Shaw 5632 incorrectly describes a Lebanon, O., 1803 edition of 202 pp. as belonging to the Chapin Library, Williams College. The Chapin copy is the 1808 edition described here, but lacks the [2] pp. and 1 leaf at end.) C, CSmH, CtHi, CtY, DeWint, DLC, ICN, KyLx, MB, MHarF, MWA, MWiW (lacks pp. 327–34), MeB, MiU, N, NHi, NN, NOC, NjPT, OCHP, OClWHi*, ODa, OHi, PPULC, WHi.

Sabin 79724 describes an edition with imprint, Albany, N.Y., Published by the United Society Called Shakers, 1808, 12 mo., 620 pp. No other record of such an edition has been found, and no such copy has been located.

1470 [——] ———— Second Edition, Corrected and Improved. Albany: Printed by E. and E. Hosford, 1810. xxxviii, 620, [2] pp. 18 cm.
Slight punctuation changes in title. In 1809, "preparation was made, by the parent society, at New-Lebanon, state of New-York, for a second edition: accordingly, a copy was forwarded to brother Seth Y. Wells, as principal editor, with suitable corrections and improvements by the authors .... Between two and three thousand copies [i.e. 2500] were struck." "To the reader," p. [iii], 3d ed. (Union Village, 1823), no. 1471. Calvin Green's "Biographic Memoir," pp. 672–73, gives a factual account of the preparation of this edition of 2500 copies. He describes working closely with Seth Y. Wells to make additions and corrections for further elucidation. These were sent to Benjamin Seth Youngs at Union Village, and final amendments were incorporated "with his union." Errata have been corrected and the changes necessary "to render the sense more clear, plain and familiar to the understanding of common capacities," Adver-

tisement, p. [iv]. This edition was reviewed critically and at length by Edward Everett, *North American Review*, 16 (January 1823), 76-102 (no. 3199); Timothy Dwight's unsympathetic attention occupies several pages in his *Travels* (no. 2071), III:149 ff. MacLean 102. Sabin 79729. Shaw 22127 (622 pp.). CSmH, CtHC, CtHi, CtY, DeWint, DLC, KyBgW, MB, MBAt, MBC, MH, MHarF, MHi, MPB, MPH, MSaE, MWA, MWiW*, MeB, MeHi, MiD, MiU, N, NHi, NBuG, NN, NNG, NOC, NRCR, NSyU, NjPT, OCHP, OClWHi, ODa, OHi, OO.

1471 [——] —— Third Edition, Corrected and Improved. Union Village, Ohio: B. Fisher and A. Burnett, Printers, 1823. xxxv, [1], 573, [3] pp. 19 cm.

"Index," p. [1] at end, enumerates changes in the text; "A Poem," pp. [2-3] at end. MacLean attributes the editorship of this edition to Benjamin Seth Youngs and Richard McNemar. Changes in the text were necessary because the second edition (1810) "was originally adapted to the infant state of believers as well as to the state of a dark world, and had as yet, been improved only in proportion, as the light increased ... The present edition might be the last under the special oversight of the principal and primary author." This is the first printing done by Shakers at Union Village. The press and types were obtained in Cincinnati, and Andrew Burnett, a printer living in the Pleasant Hill, Kentucky, Society, went to Union Village, to direct the project, "To the Reader," p. [iii]. J. P. MacLean, *Life* (no. 2411), p. 45, states that 3000 copies were printed, and that Richard McNemar kept "a minute of all who received [gift] copies and that Thomas Jefferson was among the recipients." A. White and L. Taylor, *Shakerism, Its Meaning and Message* (no. 1447), p. 321, quote Thomas Jefferson's appraisal of *The Testimony*, without identifying the edition or documenting the source. "I have read it through three times, and I pronounce it the best Church History that was ever written, and if its exegesis of Christian principles is maintained and sustained by a practical life, it is destined eventually to overthrow all religions." In the attempt to document this quotation an inquiry was addressed to Julian Boyd, editor of *The Thomas Jefferson Papers* currently being published by the Princeton University Press. He courteously replied, January 28, 1970, "We have not been able to find any comment on Benjamin Seth Youngs' *Testimony of Christ's Second Appearing*, nor have we found any evidence that he [Jefferson] owned the book," cf. no. 114. Some copies were issued with pages [xix]-xxxv[1] lacking, which comprise the "Introduction," and "Poem to the Introduction. A Memorial to Mother Ann." MacLean 103. Sabin 79726. Shaw 15003. CSmH, CtHC, CtY, DeWint, DLC, ICN, ICU, IU, KyBgW, KyLoF, KyU, MB, MBAt, MH, MHarF, MPB, MWA, MWiW*, MeB, MiU-C, MnU, N, NBuG, NHi, NN, NOC, NRCR, NcD, NjPT, O, OC, OClWHi, ODa, OFH, OHi, OLeWHi, OO, PPL, PPPrHi, PPULC, WHi.

1472 [——] Testimony of Christ's Second Appearing, Exemplified by the Principles and Practice of the True Church of Christ. History of the Progressive Work of God, Extending from the Creation of Man to the "Harvest." — Comprising the Four Great Dispensations Now Consummating in the Millennial Church .... Antichrist's Kingdom, or Churches, Contrasted with the Church of Christ's First and Second Appearing, the Kingdom of the God of Heaven .... Fourth edition. [Albany, N.Y.:] Published by the United Society, Called Shakers [Van Benthuysen, Printer, 1856]. xxiv, 631, [1] pp. 23 cm.

"Preface to the Fourth Edition," signed: *Benjamin S. Youngs, Calvin Green.* The preparation of this edition of 5000 is described by Calvin Green in his "Biographic Memoir," pp. 674-77. In spite of advancing years and severe illness, Youngs worked on the amendments, explanations, and additions with Green, both at New Lebanon and Watervliet, N.Y., 1853-1855. The final draft was approved with his "full satisfaction." Youngs died March 24, 1855, before the book was published. The title has been changed. Numerous changes have been made in the text of "Preface to the First Edition." The poem which occurs at the end in earlier editions is

omitted, and "Locations of the Society" has been added, p. [1] at end. Other changes are explained on pp. v-vi. ". . . During the year 1838, a most wonderful manifestation of Divine revelation and heavenly light and power, simultaneously commenced in the two central societies, and in a few months visited every branch and family of the people called Shakers, throughout the land . . . . Therefore it has been judged expedient to issue the present edition, with such further illustrations and improvements as to us appear adapted to the present order of the work of God, both within and without this Society; it therefore has been prepared in accordance with the increasing Divine light brought forht [sic] among us by those in-spired manifestations and our experience." This edition was still being advertised in January 1888 (The Manifesto, back cover, verso).
MacLean 104. Sabin 79727. CtHC, CtY, DLC, DeWint, InI, KyBgW, KySP, KyU, MB, MBAt, MBC, MH, MHarF, MHi, MPB, MPH, MSaE, MWA, MWiW*, N, NBLiHi, NBuG, NHi, NN, NNC, NNG, NOC, NSyU, NhD, NjPT, O, OC, OCH, OCl, OClWHi, ODa, OHi, OLeWHi, PPL, PPULC, RHi, WHi.

1473 —— ——— (Reprint). Communal Societies in America, 2d series, New York: AMS Press. 1972.

1474 [——] Transactions of the Ohio Mob, Called in the Public Papers "An Expedition Against the Shakers," [Albany, N.Y.: E. & E. Hosford?, 1810?]. Caption title. 11 pp. 18 cm.
Signed: Benjamin Seth Youngs. Miami Country, State of Ohio, August 31, 1810, p. 11. Describes an unsuccessful mob action of 500 armed men at the Union Village, O., Shaker community to demand the release of children, who, it was claimed, were being held against their wishes by the Shakers. Other demands included the departure of the Shakers from the area. Reprinted with title, "An Expedition Against the Shakers," Ohio Archaeological and Historical Quarterly, 21 (October 1912), 403-415, nos. 1677 and 3300. See also no. 3498.
MacLean 477. Sabin 10697. Shaw 22128.

Streeter 4231. CSmH, CtY, DLC, DeWint, KyBgW, MH, MPB, MWA, MWiW*, NBuG, NHi, NN, NOC, NSyU, O, OC, OClWHi, ODa, OLeWHi, WHi.

1475 [——] ——— [Albany, N.Y.: E. & E. Hosford?, 1810?]. Caption title. 12 pp. 19 cm.
Signed: Benjamin Seth Youngs. Miami Country, State of Ohio, August 31, 1810, p. 11. Contains also: "Lines Written on the Preced-ing [poem], by Richard McNemar," pp. 11-12. Otherwise, the text is the same as no. 1474. The caption titles are identical, but this text has been reset more closely, and begin-ning page 10, line 5, a smaller size type is used. This change may well have been made during an interruption in the printing in order to accommodate McNemar's poem and to utilize the blank page [12] of no. 1474. Shaker frugality did not favor wasteful blank pages. Priority has not been established for either the 11 pp., or the 12 pp. edition of Youngs' Transactions.
Sabin 106197 (dated [1850?], but with ref-erence to it as the first edition). Streeter 4230. CSmH, MH, MPB, MPH*, MWA, N, NOC, NjPT, OClWHi, WHi.

1476 YOUNGS, ISAAC NEWTON. "Clock Makers Journal with Remarks and Observations. Experiments etc. Beginning in 1815." Western Reserve Historical Society ms., reprinted in E. D. and Faith Andrews' Shaker Furniture (no. 1772), pp. 112-114.

1477 [——] Dedication [sung at the dedication of the New Lebanon meeting house]. [n.p., n.d.]. [4] pp. 15½ cm.
Contents: "Dedication," pp. [1-3]; "Good Believers Character," pp. [3-4]; "A Request," p. [4].
MacLean 207. Sabin 106198. OClWHi*.

1478 [——] My Prayer [poem]. [n.p., 1824]. [4] pp. 18 cm.
Contains also: "Heavenly Joys," [by Garrett Keatin Lawrence]; "Mother's Gospel," and "New Years Thoughts," [by Youngs]. OClWHi*.

—— On Entering the Dairy . . . See Shaker

Community, Inc., Hancock Village Keepsake
No. 2, no. 2697.

1479 —— A Short Abridgment of the Rules
of Music. With Lessons for Exercise, and a Few
Observations; for New Beginners. Printed at New
Lebanon: 1843. 40 pp. 12½ X 20½ cm.

The first printed use of the unique Shaker
notation, variously identified as letteral,
phonetic, alphabetic, etc. The notation,
based on the first seven letters of the alphabet (a–g), was used exclusively by the Shakers
until about 1871. The music for a few simple
songs is included. Type is lacking for some
of the symbols and has been supplied in
manuscript. Youngs, who wrote the text,
cut the music type, set the type, printed and
bound this work, describes the difficulties
of this one-man operation. "These last two
weeks I have been chief of the time engaged
at my music types & preparing the printing
furniture, press &c. Besides having many
little jobs & calls that hinders me much of
my time. It requires much perseverance, in
my situation to go on with such an undertaking, having but little experience in writing,
having but little experience in printing — &
a poor press — poor supply of common types
..." Isaac N. Youngs, "Journal, Sept. 1839 –
1858," ms. Western Reserve Historical Society, pp. 14–15. Other references, p. 16, refer
to cutting the music types and p. 18, where
Youngs states that he printed and bound
100 copies.
MacLean 105. CSmH, DLC, DeWint,

MPB, MWiW*, NN, NOC, NSyU, OClWHi.

1480 [——] —— Printed at New-Lebanon:
1843. Reprinted in 1846. 40 pp. 12½ X 20½
cm.

Introduction, signed: *Isaac N. Youngs*, credits
the introduction of "the use of letters for
notes" to the Harvard Society. Although the
title page identifies this as a reprint, it is
actually a second edition, with changes and
additions. Type has been used for all of the
symbols, and the printing is greatly improved.
MacLean 106. CtY, DLC, KyBgW, MPB,
MWiW*, NN, NOC, NSyU, OCl, WHi.

Your Memorialists Beg Leave Respectfully to
State, That they are Strongly Impressed with a
Belief, that, by the Constitution of the United
States and of this State, the Society of People
Called Shakers ... Ought to be Totally and Un-
conditionally Exempted from Military Duty,
and from the Payment of All Fines or Sums of
Money in Lieu Thereof ... [n.p., n.d.]. Broad-
side. 30 X 17½ cm.

Title from first lines of text. This so-called
broadside is in fact, p. 5 of ... *The Memorial
...*, no. 1019. Page 5 was printed as a single
page (leaf not conjugate; verso, blank) and
consequently, easily separated from pp. 1–4.
It contains two short paragraphs of text, followed by 160 signatures of petitioners, and
is the conclusion of "... The Memorial and
Petition of the Undersigned, Inhabitants of
the Towns of Canaan and Watervliet ..."
which begins on p. 4.

Periodical Articles

References in this section include articles written by Shakers for both Shaker and non-Shaker periodicals and also the first printing of Shaker manuscripts as periodical articles. The representation of articles by Shakers published in non-Shaker periodicals might have been expanded. For the most part these articles appeared in inaccessible 19th century periodicals—*Hall's Journal of Health, Light of Truth, Human Nature, Voice of Angels, Mind and Matter, Witness*, etc. This class of periodical is not included in indexes to periodical literature. Complete sets are rarely encountered, and searches of broken sets have seldom been rewarding.

Enough articles by Shakers which appeared in the *Day-Star* (no. 494) have been included here to reflect the extent of Shaker contributions to this little-known Adventist publication which shortly before its demise in 1846 became in fact a Shaker publication. *Something New* (no. 1324) was not published by the Shakers, but was printed in the Shaker community at Harvard, Mass., February 1830–October 1832, and included a few Shaker contributions.

Indexes were not issued for the precursors of *The Manifesto*, nor for *The Manifesto* before Volume 16, 1886 (see no. 990). The indexes to the individual volumes, 1886–1899 (vols. 16–29), are inadequate for 20th century needs, and moreover, are generally lacking in library sets. Consequently, the contents of this important 30-volume source of Shaker primary materials remain largely unknown. It has not been the intention, however, in this bibliography to provide an index, but it has been considered proper to provide the user with a generous sampling of the contents. In addition to numerous references to articles in *The Manifesto* and its forerunners that are to be found in the preceding section in the appropriate annotations, references to important Shaker manuscripts, histories of various Shaker communities, and a few articles of special interest printed in *The Manifesto* are included here.

In the absence of an index to *The Shaker Quarterly* (no. 1299) currently published by the United Society, Sabbathday Lake (Poland Spring, Me.), death lists of Shakers of various communities and some Shaker manuscripts printed in the *Shaker Quarterly* have been included to increase their availability to researchers. Also included are 20th century articles written by Shakers about the Shaker spirit and beliefs, an area which is generally neglected in non-Shaker publications.

A

1481 AITKEN, ROBERT. "Shaker and Vegetarian. Autobiographical Sketch ..." *Independent Vegetarian Advocate* (London), No. 6 (January 1891), 21–22, port.

This autobiographical article is followed by an account of Aitken's remarks at a reception held by J. Burns, and also "Further particulars about the Shakers," an interview with the editor. Aitken was "one of the delegates from the Shaker Societies of America to the Vegetarian Congress in London in September last [1890]." *See also* his letter describing this long visit in England and Scotland with his companion, John Whiteley, *The Manifesto*, 20 (November 1890), 246–49.

MWiW*.

1482 ALBATROSS, *pseud.* "Letter from a Shaker," *American Socialist* (Oneida Community, N.Y.), 2 (February 1, 1877), 37–38.

Albatross is a Novitiate Elder according to the editor's note, *The Shaker*, 7 (January 1877), 4. An article, "What Shall I Do to Be a Shaker? No. 2," and 2 letters are signed "Albatross" in the February issue of *The Shaker*. The letters are dated at Shakers, N.Y. (i.e. Watervliet). The writer may be Galen Richmond who was a Novitiate Elder at Watervliet in 1877.

DLC, ICJ, MH, MWA*, NIC, NN, NhD, WHi.

1483 AMERY, GEORGE B. "Religious Communism," *American Socialist* (Oneida Community, N.Y.), 3 (August 29, 1878), 274.
DLC, ICJ, MH, MWA*, NIC, NN, NhD, WHi.

1484 ANDERSON, MARTHA JANE. "History of Dietetic Reform as Practiced at North Family, Mt. Lebanon, Col. Co., N.Y.," *Food, Home, and Garden* (Philadelphia), 6 (January 1894), 6–7.
MB*.

1485 ANSTATT, ISAAC. "Notes from Florida," *The Manifesto*, 25 (April 1895), 92–93.
Letter addressed: Beloved Elder Henry [Blinn], and dated: March, 1895. Gives a description of the land bought by the Shakers 17 miles from Kissimmee. He cautions that "it might be well to test all locations and hold fast to the best. All things should be well considered and the only way to find out is to try on a small scale, before a rush is made." The brethren are building a house 20 X 30 for present convenience." Anstatt obviously anticipated a much larger Shaker community than ever developed in Florida.
Ct, DLC, ICN, IU, MB, MHarF, MPH, MWA, MWiW*, Nh, NhD, NjPT, OClWHi, WHi.

1486 AVERY, GILES BUSHNELL. "A Defense of the Shaker Friends," *Mind and Matter*, January 3, 1880.
A communication dated at Shakers [Watervliet], Albany Co., N.Y., November 18, 1879, which takes exception to an article in the August 9th issue, "The American Shakers and their Spiritualism" by Julia Johnson, who was raised by the Shakers at Tyringham, Mass., (*see* no. 1584). The charge that young people are not permitted to read "the news of the day and age" is answered and the author lists the newspapers and periodicals available at Mt. Lebanon, and states that "the school rooms are well equipped and that a good curriculum is pursued." Charges of censorship, the slavery of Shaker life, and special privileges of the elders and eldresses are answered. The reasons why young people leave the Shakers are discussed, *see also* no. 1610.
MB*, MWiW.

1487 —— "The Mythical Shaker Bible," *The Manifesto*, 13 (June 1883), 121–23.
Refutation of part of a speech, January 28, 1883, by Annie T. Anderson, "The Sect of Shakers have Mother Ann's Bible," reprinted in *Mind and Matter*. Elder Giles states that the Shakers "never had any different Bible from that of all other professed Jewish and Christian denominations,–the translation of the King James!" *The Testimony of Christ's Second Appearing* (nos. 1469–1473) is a "general review of all church history, with quotations and criticisms, together with a statement of the principles of religious light and faith which have been revealed to, and accepted by the people called Shakers at that time." It is not a Bible any more than the writings of John Calvin, Martin Luther, George Fox, John Wesley, or George Whitfield, "may be called Bibles." It is not a creed, but is "a fixed boundary of religious ideas and supposed revelations of truth beyond which there is no revelation of light, truth, and duty. But the Shakers believe in a continuous revelation of Divine light and truth."
Ct, DLC, ICN, IU, MB, MHarF, MPH, MWA, MWiW*, Nh, NhD, NjPT, OClWHi, WHi.

1488 —— "The Shakers. Spirit Manifestations Among Them. A Sketch of Their History," *Harbinger of Light* (Melbourne, Australia), April 1, 1891.
This article has been found only in a scrapbook at Western Reserve Historical Society. A manuscript note gives the information that "Elder Frederick [Evans] and Eldress Anna [White] thought this an unusually good and historically important article."
OClWHi*.

1489 —— "Spirit Manifestations," *Progressive Thinker* (Chicago), November 25, 1890, pp. 64–76.
In F. W. Evans' obituary of Giles Avery (no. 614) it is stated in a note, p. 3, that "all editors and publishers should possess [this article]." "Therein it is shown that spiritualism is not a religion, but a science, like astronomy—an important distinction; and that it

passed through all sixty families of Shakers, from its commencement, eleven years before the 'Rochester rappings' occurred."
No copy located.

1490 —— "To the Honorable Rutherford B. Hayes, President of the United States of North America," *Truthseeker* (New York), 7 (October 1879).
Long letter, dated: Mt. Lebanon, N.Y., September 29, 1879, vigorously protesting the unfair trial and imprisonment of D. M. Bennett and defending the constitutional rights of freedom of conscience, liberty of free speech, protection of the press, and the sanctity of the mails. Reprinted in the *Shaker Manifesto*, 9 (December 1879), 278–80,

where it is identified as a "petition." The flippant writings of the freethinking editor of *The Truthseeker*, D. M. Bennett, had offended orthodox churchmen and provoked that "Roundsman of the Lord," Anthony B. Comstock, whose efforts finally brought Bennett's conviction for sending so-called indecent matter (*Cupid's Yokes*) through the mails, resulting in 13 months' imprisonment (Sing Sing) and a $300 fine. Bennett was reared in the Shaker community at New Lebanon and became physician there. He seceded with his sister and others in September 1846 and the next month married Mary Wicks, another seceder, *see also* no. 74.
DLC, MWA*, NN, WHi.

B

1491 B., W. H. "Visiting the Shirley Shakers," *The Manifesto*, 19 (November 1889), 257–58.
A letter, signed: *W. H. B.*, dated at Milford Springs, N.H., Aug. 1889. The writer appears to be associated with the Christian Union, Boston. Includes some history of the Shirley community and biographical details about Elder John Whiteley.
Ct, DLC, ICN, IU, MB, MHarF, MPH, MWA, MWiW*, Nh, NhD, NjPT, OClWHi, WHi.

1492 BARKER, RUTH MILDRED. "The Gift to be Simple," *Good Work*, 28 (Autumn 1965), 113–14. illus.
Response on behalf of the United Society called Shakers upon the occasion of the presentation of the Catholic Art Association's medal.
MPH, MWiW*, NOC, NSyU.

1493 —— "A History of 'Holy Land'—Alfred, Maine," *Shaker Quarterly*, 3 (Fall, Winter 1963), 75–95, 107–27.
A full account of the early history, growth, and industries of the Shaker community at Alfred, Me., with 13 historical photographs.
CtHC, CtY-D, DLC, MBAt, MHarF, MPH,

MWiW*, NNUT, NOC, NhD, NhU, NjPT, OClWHi.

1494 —— "History of Union Branch, Gorham, Maine, 1784-1819," *Shaker Quarterly*, 7 (Summer 1967), 64–82. illus.
Early history of the Shaker community at Gorham, Me., including entries from a journal of 1807 and 1808, with some details of the lives of Elders Joseph Brackett, Sr., and Joseph Brackett, Jr. Appendix A, "Gorham Covenants," 1804, 1810, with the subscribers. Appendix B, "The Holy Fountain," a hymn written in Shaker letter notation, and a portrait of Elder Joseph Brackett, Jr., composer of "The Gift to be Simple."
CtHC, CtY-D, DLC, MBAt, MHarF, MPH, MWiW*, NNUT, NOC, NhD, NhU, NjPT, OClWHi.

1495 —— "Our Mother in the New Creation," *Shaker Quarterly*, 1 (Spring 1960), 10–15.
An account of the early life of Ann Lee and her revelation during imprisonment in Manchester. Comparison of Christ's baptism with water and Ann Lee's baptism of the Holy Spirit. Through Ann Lee's spiritual elevation

she "paved the way for all women to accept their rightful place of equality with men." Ann Lee's forgiving spirit toward her persecutors is described.
CtHC, CtY-D, DLC, MBAt, MHarF, MPH, MWiW*, NNUT, NOC, NhD, NhU, NjPT, OClWHi.

1496 —— "Revelation: A Shaker Viewpoint," *Shaker Quarterly*, 3 (Spring 1963), 7–17.
A review of Shaker history and beliefs in which the author concludes, "A new age demands new intellectual growth, new revelation of truth and understanding and yet must return to the testimony and understanding upon which the principles were founded."
CtHC, CtY-D, DLC, MBAt, MHarF, MPH, MWiW*, NNUT, NOC, NhD, NhU, NjPT, OClWHi.

1497 —— "A Shaker Viewpoint on the Authority of the Bible," *Shaker Quarterly*, 1 (Winter 1961), 140–44.
"The Word of God is too vast and eternal to be confined within the pages of any book or books." Too often the Bible is used for justification or condemnation of an individual belief—the Spirit is neglected. Although the Scriptures are the result of many inspired authors, "The Bible is neither a complete nor the only revelation of the Word of God. In no part of the Scriptures is the least intimation given that revelation of the Divine and Holy Spirit to man will ever cease." God's "law is endless growth and through the advent of Mother's ministry we [the Shakers] have found continued revelation of divine truth and light."
CtHC, CtY-D, DLC, MBAt, MHarF, MPH, MWiW*, NNUT, NOC, NhD, NhU, NjPT, OClWHi.

1498 —— "Simplicity: God's Christmas Gift to Man," *Shaker Quarterly*, 10 (Winter 1970), 107–115.
Jesus Christ "considered simplicity to be a prime requisite for His church. His gospel was spelled out in simple language for all to hear and understand. Here, then, is the root from which grew the Gift to be Simple as taught by Mother Ann." "As with the teach-

ings of Jesus it was the simplicity of her gospel which gave it its greatest force."
CtHC, CtY-D, DLC, MBAt, MHarF, MPH, MWiW*, NNUT, NOC, NhD, NhU, NjPT, OClWHi.

1499 BASTING, LOUIS. "The Believers of Indiana in 1811," *The Manifesto*, 20 (January 1890), 11–14.
Subtitle: "The Great Revival at Busro [West Union] at the Community of Shakers. The Indian War. The Peace Principles of the Believers. The Kindness of Col. Boyd. The Work of Gen. Wm. H. Harrison in Favor of the Shakers."
Ct, DLC, ICN, IU, MB, MHarF, MPH, MWA, MWiW*, Nh, NhD, NjPT, OClWHi, WHi.

1500 BATES, ISSACHAR. "A Ballad by Elder Issachar Bates," with an Introduction by Daniel W. Patterson, *Shaker Quarterly*, 2 (Summer 1962), 60–66. music.
This ballad relates the circumstances of the historic journey of Issachar Bates, Benjamin Youngs, and Richard McNemar to Busro, Indiana (*see also* no. 65) in 1809. The first of the 16 stanzas is printed with the melody scored.
CtHC, CtY-D, DLC, MBAt, MHarF, MPH, MWiW*, NNUT, NOC, NhD, NhU, NjPT, OClWHi.

1501 —— "Issachar Bates," Nos. 1–8, ed. by Henry Blinn, *The Manifesto*, 14 (August–December 1884), 183–84, 200–01, 227–28, 252–53, 277–78; 15 (January–March 1885), 14–15, 38–39, 60–61.
A note explains that much of this account "was taken from the writings left by Elder Issachar."
Ct, DLC, ICN, IU, MB, MHarF, MPH, MWA, MWiW*, Nh, NhD, NjPT, OClWHi, WHi.

1502 —— "On the First of the Month in Eighteen Hundred Five," [ballad]. First printed in D. W. Patterson's article, "Turtle Creek to Busro," *North Carolina Folklore Journal*, December 1955, pp. 33–36.
First stanza with music.
DLC, MH, NN*, NcD, NcU, KyU, OCl, PU.

1503 —— "A Sketch of the Life and Experience of Issachar Bates," with an Introduction by Theodore E. Johnson, *Shaker Quarterly*, 1 (Fall, Winter 1961), 98–118, 145–63; 2 (Spring 1962), 18–35.

> From a copy of a Bates' autobiographical manuscript in the library at Sabbathday Lake, Me., written in 1833 when Elder Issachar was 75 years of age. This version is complete and preserves the original spelling and punctuation. *See also* nos. 66 and **1501**.
>
> CtHC, CtY-D, DLC, MBAt, MHarF, MPH, MWiW*, NNUT, NOC, NhD, NhU, NjPT, OClWHi.

1504 BEAR, HENRY B. "Letter from Brother Bear," *Day-Star*, 10 (May 16, 1846), 46.

> Letter dated at Whitewater Village, O., May 11, 1846, which was written in response to the editor's request for clarification of some aspects of Shaker belief.
>
> MWA, MWiW*, OClWHi, OCHP.

1505 BERNE, JOSEPH L. "A Visit to White Water Village, and to Union Village, Ohio, in the Autumn of 1887, by One who was a Shaker Boy." *The Manifesto*, 18 (January 1888), 11–13.

> Describes a visit to the Shaker community and conversations with old friends after 23 years' absence and a later visit to Union Village.
>
> Ct, DLC, ICN, IU, MB, MHarF, MPH, MWA, MWiW*, Nh, NhD, NjPT, OClWHi, WHi.

1506 BLAKEMAN, ELISHA D'ALEMBERT. "Elisha Blakeman's Journal," *Peg Board*, (Darrow School, New Lebanon, N.Y.), 4 (June 1936), 80–81.

> Excerpts from the manuscript "Journal" recently discovered by Sister Emma J. Neale include a 19-line poem never before published. "Brother Blakeman had charge of the boys in the Church Family and directed them in their work outside of school." *See also* no. 84.
>
> MHarF, MPB, MPH*, NOC, OClWHi.

1507 BLINN, HENRY C. "Florida," *The Manifesto*, 25 (March 1895), 69–70.

> Report of the purchase of 4,400 acres of land in Osceola County, Fla., by the Shaker Societies of Mt. Lebanon and Watervliet, N.Y., and information about the agricultural conditions there.

Ct, DLC, ICN, IU, MB, MHarF, MPH, MWA, MWiW*, Nh, NhD, NjPT, OClWHi, WHi.

1508 —— "From Our Diary," *The Manifesto*, 19 (November 1889), 248–53.

> A warm account of a distinguished Shaker Elder's visits to the Hancock, Mass., and Mt. Lebanon, N.Y., Shaker communities, October 1–9, 1889.
>
> Ct, DLC, ICN, IU, MB, MHarF, MPH, MWA, MWiW*, Nh, NhD, NjPT, OClWHi, WHi.

1509 —— "A Journey to Kentucky in the Year 1873. Parts I–IX," with an Introduction by Theodore E. Johnson, *Shaker Quarterly*, 5 (1965), 3–19, 37–55, 69–79, 107–33; 6 (1966), 22–30, 53–72, 93–102, 135–44; 7 (Spring 1967), 13–23.

> The original manuscript, "Notes by the Way while on a Journey to the State of Kentucky in the Year 1873," in the Shaker Museum, Old Chatham, N.Y., was transcribed by Mrs. Muriel Collins to be published in 9 instalments here. Elder Henry visited 12 societies on his two-month journey. "The detailed picture it gives of the order's social, economic, and religious life during the post-Civil War era places it among the important Shaker manuscript records of the period," p. 5.
>
> CtHC, CtY-D, DLC, MBAt, MHarF, MPH, MWiW*, NNUT, NOC, NhD, NhU, NjPT, OClWHi.

1510 BRIGGS, NICHOLAS A. "Forty Years a Shaker," *Granite Monthly* (Concord, N.H.), 52 (1920), 463–74; 53 (January, February, March 1921), 19–32, 56–65, 113–21.

> A former Shaker's description of his life among the Shakers, Canterbury, N.H., from the time he "was a boy of ten years and all the way up through youth and manhood to the mature age of fifty-three." Somewhat critical, but the author reveals affection for many Shaker friends and aspects of his life among them.
>
> DLC, MB, MH, MeB, N, NN, NhD*, NjP, OCl, PP, WHi.

1511 —— "The Origin of the Shakers," *Granite Monthly* (Concord, N.H.), 53 (April 1921), 150–55. port.

The English background of the Shakers and
their early history in the U.S.
DLC, MB, MH, MeB, N, NN, NhD*, NjP,
OCl, PP, WHi.

1512 BUCKINGHAM, DAVID AUSTIN.
"Epitomic History of the Watervliet [N.Y.]
Shakers," *The Shaker*, 7 (May–November 1877),
37, 41–42, 49–50, 59, 66–67, 76–77, 85, *see
also* p. 86.

The destitute condition of the Shaker settlers
and the earliest converts at Watervliet, clear-
ing the land, business matters, growth of the
seed industry, broomcorn and broom making,
agricultural improvements including agricultural machinery, and Shaker inventions are
covered in Nos. 1–5. Education and the difficulties of educating children sent to the
Shakers, Shaker abstinence from alcohol,
swine flesh, and tobacco, Shaker dress and
uniformity of appearance are discussed in Nos.
6–7. The author states that the motive for
writing this series of articles was the attempt
to refute current reports that misrepresented
the Shakers.
Ct, DLC, ICN, IU, MB, MHarF, MPH, MWA,

MWiW*, Nh, NhD, NjPT, OClWHi, WHi.

BULLARD, SISTER MARCIA. *See* Marcia,
Sister, p. 236 and no. **1609** ff.

1513 BUNTING, R. G. "To Adventist Believers
Throughout the Land," *Day-Star*, 12 (January
16, 1847), 2–3.

An elaborate invitation to Adventists to join
the Shakers.
MWA, MWiW*, OClWHi, OCHP.

1514 BURGHALDER, CHRISTIAN. "Spiritualism," *The Regenerator* (Fruit Hills, O.), n.s. 2
(December 13, 1847), 278–79.

Letter addressed: "Friend Murray," [Editor],
and dated: New Orleans, La., November 20,
1847. In an attempt to describe instances of
"genuine spiritualism" the writer refers to the
Shaker controversy about dogs, and criticizes
the Shakers on the grounds that they do not
open their minds to one another. Burghalder
claims "fifteen years abode with the Shakers."
He was a member of the South Union community.
OClWHi*.

C

**1515 CARR, FRANCES A. and THEODORE
E. JOHNSON**, *comps.* "An Index of Deaths
Listed in Shaker Periodical Literature 1871–
1899," *Shaker Quarterly*, 3 (Winter 1963), 133–
48; 4 (Spring, Summer 1964), 15–37, 64–80.

Death notices of over 1,000 Shakers which
appeared originally in *The Manifesto* and its
precursors have been extracted and arranged
alphabetically by personal names, with reference to volume and page number of the
original notice.
CtHC, CtY-D, DLC, MBAt, MHarF, MPH,
MWiW*, NNUT, NOC, NhD, NhU, NjPT,
OClWHi.

1516 "The Confession of Sin," *Day-Star*, 11
(December 27, 1846), 46–48. Reprints Pt. VI,
Chap. 4, pp. 290–302, of C. Green, *Summary*

View of the Millennial Church (Albany, N.Y.,
1823), no. 743.
MWA, MWiW*, OClWHi, OCHP.

1517 [CORBETT, THOMAS?] "The Produc-
tion and Management of Bees," by Apiarius
Medicus [*pseud.*], *Boston Medical and Surgical
Journal*, 50 (February 1, 1854), 15–17.

A ms. note on the front cover of the Shaker
Museum, Old Chatham, N.Y., copy reads,
"The King Bee, by Thos. Corbett, 1854."
Another ms. note at head of title reads,
"Thomas Corbett's bee piece." After long
observation the author concludes, "I have
at last come to the satisfactory and unerring
conclusion, that the bee universally called
queen is male and that the drones are females
which produce all the young swarms."

MU, MWA, MeB, N, NOC*.

1518 "The Cost of Communal Living," *American Socialist* (Oneida Community, N.Y.), 4 (February 13, 1879), 52.

> Contains a comparison of budgets of the Oneida community and that of the Shakers, using figures supplied by Elder Wm. Reynolds of Union Village.
> DLC, ICJ, MH, MWA*, NIC, NN, NhD, WHi.

1519 COUNT, JEROME. "Teen-agers and the Shakers," *Shaker Quarterly*, 1 (Summer 1961), 80-87.

> A discussion of the attraction of Shakerism for teen-agers as evidenced by the large numbers of adolescents among the early converts, and Shakers' warm relations with young people. Also a description of the activities of modern teen-agers, the members of the Shaker Village Work Group, who spend their summers at the former South Family of the Mt. Lebanon Shaker community.
> CtHC, CtY-D, DLC, MBAt, MHarF, MPH, MWiW*, NNUT, NOC, NhD, NhU, NjPT, OClWHi.

1520 CRESSON, WARDER. "Vindication of the Shaker Doctrine: in Reply to Robert Dale Owen's Observations in No. 16 of the Present Volume," *Free Enquirer* (New York), s. 2, 3, (April 2, 1831), 186-87.

> A defensive refutation (*see* no. 3509) which Owen, an editor, characterizes as "somewhat long," giving the opinions of "a very curious (in my view), a very interesting, however mistaken sect." Further, Owen states in a footnote, "I admit the full force of the argument drawn from the fact that of all sects the Shakers, take them as a body, do appear the most contented and comfortable; but I see, in their domestic economy, causes fully adequate to produce this effect without tracing it (as they strangely do) to their favorite abnegation [celibacy]."
> DLC, NN, OClWHi, PU.

1521 CROSSMAN, ABIGAIL. "Prophetic," *Day-Star*, 11 (December 27, 1846), 51.

> The author recounts her visions which she states "may appear to some, as phantoms of a disordered brain, but to the candid and unprejudiced, must stand in their true light, unalterable truths ..."
> MWA, MWiW*, OClWHi*, OCHP.

D

1522 "Death List of the United Society of Believers, North Union, Cuyahoga County, Ohio, 1827-1888. Obituary Copied from the Original Manuscript Amended and Improved ..." *Shaker Quarterly*, 2 (Winter 1962), 119-40.

> Preface signed: *J. S. P.* (James Prescott). Contains a death list of 138 North Union Believers, October 4, 1827-September 19, 1888, supplemented by the death dates for 21 Believers (October 2, 1889-1916), who moved to Union Village or Watervliet, Ohio, upon the dissolution of North Union. The location of the manuscript is not indicated.
> CtHC, CtY-D, DLC, MBAt, MHarF, MPH, MWiW*, NNUT, NOC, NhD, NhU, NjPT, OClWHi.

1523 DEGRAW, GEORGE HAMILTON. "The Higher Life," *World's Advance Thought* (Portland, Ore.), n.s. Vol. 5, no. 8 (1891), 117.
> OClWHi*.

1524 ——— "International Arbitration," *The World's Advance Thought* (Portland, Ore.), n.s. Vol. 6, no. 6 (March 1892), 95.
> OClWHi*.

1525 ——— "Obsession," *The Sower* (New York), 3 (December 1891), 354-55.
> On spiritualism, "written expressly for *The Sower*."
> KySP*.

1526 ——— "Our Mother, We Greet Thee," *The*

World's Advance Thought (Portland, Ore.), n.s.
5, no. 8 (1891), 104.
 OClWHi*.

1527 [DOOLITTLE, MARY ANTOINETTE]
"The March of Events," *Woodhull and Claflin's
Weekly,* 1872.
 Note in *The Shaker,* 2 (April 1872), 32. "In
 a late number of *Woodhull and Claflin's
 Weekly,* we read with pleasure *The March of
 Events,* accredited to a Quaker Lady; but we
 soon substituted, By a Shaker Sister—A.
 Doolittle."
 DLC, MWA*, NN, PPL.

1528 [DUNLAVY, BENJAMIN B.] "Extract
of a Letter [to Beloved Brother Hervey]," *Day-
Star,* 12 (March 4, 1847), 27-28.
 Discussion of the lack of results of Enoch's
 [Jacobs] and Br. Charles' [Clapp] labors in
 the vicinity of Pleasant Hill, Ky. (*See also* no.
 1583). "From present appearances, it would
 seem that a display of divine power would be
 requisite to humble the pride of Kentuckians,
 before many of them will be willing to abandon their worldly pursuits . . . ."
 MWA, MWiW*, OClWHi, OCHP.

1529 [DUNLAVY, JOHN] "The Shakers. The
Nature and Character of the True Church of
Christ, Proved by Plain Evidences and Showing
Whereby it may be Known from All Others.
Being an Extract from the Writings of John Dun-

lavy (New York, 1847)," *The Nineteenth Century* (Philadelphia), April 1848, pp. 350-53.
 DLC, MWA*.

1530 DURGIN, ELIZABETH CONVERSE.
"Twentieth Century Shakers," *Banner of Light,*
September 10, 17, 1904.
 Summary of Shaker history and beliefs, including the period of manifestations. "Our
 forms of worship follow the advancing ever-
 involving life of God in humanity." The
 author describes the improvement in Shaker
 music since the period of *Millennial Praises*
 (no. 1415), Henry Blinn's great contribution
 to Shakerism, current Shaker industries,
 education of the young, and Shaker activity
 in the cause of peace and vivisection with
 poems of Grace Ada Brown's, "Bobolink"
 and "America."
 DLC, MH, MWA, MWiW*.

1531 DYER, CALEB M. "Improved Berkshire
Swine," *Farmer's Monthly Visitor* (Concord,
N.H.), 2 (May 30, 1840), 65.
 Letter addressed to Isaac Hill [editor], and
 dated: May 11th, 1840. Discusses the advan-
 tages of this breed and warns buyers to be-
 ware of frauds. "All our Berkshires are from
 Lossing's stock, or from the Society at
 Watervliet, or from late importations." *See
 also* no. 3386.
 Ct, DNAL, MU, Nh, NhD*.

E

1532 [EADS, HARVEY LAUDERDALE] "Ann
Lee," *Day-Star,* 11 (December 27, 1846), 49.
 Refutation of letter from J. B. Cooke on the
 impiety of Ann Lee published in the *Day-Star,*
 11 (October 21, 1846). Signed: *E. See also* no.
 3145.
 MWA, MWiW*, OClWHi, OCHP.

1533 —— "The 'Day-Dawn,'" *Day-Star,* 11
(November 7, 1846), 33-34.
 Refutation of an article, "The Principal Seat
 of Human Depravity," which was published in

the *Day-Dawn,* a competitor of the *Day-Star.*
 MWA, MWiW*, OClWHi, OCHP.

1534 —— "The Shaker Problem, No. 2"
Phrenological Journal, August 1873, pp. 111-
15.
 Answers to the questions propounded in no.
 3651. *See also* nos. 1535 and 1604.
 DLC*, DNLM, MB, NN, OCl.

1535 —— "The Shaker Problem, No. 3,"
Phrenological Journal, March 1874, pp. 194-96.

More answers to the questions in no. 3651.
See also nos. 1534 and 1604.
DLC*, DNLM, MB, NN, OCl.

1536 —— "Up Stairs and Down Stairs: A
Shaker View of the Situation," *American
Socialist* (Oneida Community, N.Y.), 2 (January
18, 1877), 21.
　　Complaint, addressed to J. H. Noyes, that
　　Hinds' series on visits to Shaker communities
　　is too secular-minded.
　　DLC, ICJ, MH, MWA*, NIC, NN, NhD, WHi.

EADS, HARVEY L. *See also* "God and the
Bible in Court," no. 1560.

1537 "Elder Frederick's Criticisms," *American
Socialist* (Oneida Community, N.Y.), 3 (March
21, 1878), 92.
　　Evans had visited Oneida and criticized the
　　community for not composing its own songs
　　and not grinding its own flour.
　　DLC, ICJ, MH, MWA*, NIC, NN, NhD, WHi.

1538 EVANS, FREDERICK WILLIAM. "American Vegetarianism," *Independent Vegetarian Advocate* (London), No. 6 (January 1891), 22–23.
　　"A paper sent by Elder Evans to the Vege-
　　tarian Congress . . . He sent us a copy . . . with
　　the desire that we might give it publicity." A
　　short resumé of vegetarianism in the United
　　States, where it had failed with the exception
　　of the North Family of Shakers at Mt. Leba-
　　non, N.Y. "It succeeds amongst the Shakers
　　because it has a theological, scientific, and
　　religious basis in the *Shaker system*" as is the
　　case with all true reforms.
　　MWiW*.

1539 —— "Atlantic Cable and Materialization,"
American Socialist (Oneida Community, N.Y.),
4 (January 23, 1890), 27.
　　Reprinted as a broadside, no. 572.
　　DLC, ICJ, MH, MWA*, NIC, NN, NhD, WHi.

1540 —— "Autobiography of a Shaker,"
Atlantic Monthly, 23 (April, May 1869), 415–
26, 593–605.
　　In a foreword Frederick Evans writes that as
　　"a consequence of the Shakers' having held a

convention in Boston on November 11th and
12th, 1868," he received a note from James
T. Fields suggesting that he write an article
for the *Atlantic Monthly*, "which should be
an autobiographical account of your experience as a seeker after truth, and should give
the 'reason and hope that is in you,' that
people may understand precisely the meaning of a sect which has lately been brought
into notoriety by the writings of [William
Hepworth] Dixon and [Henry] Vincent."
Evans' reaction is that "he can see *great importance* in a *principle*, very little in an
individual. Not of myself should I write *of*
myself; but in the hope that others may be
advantaged thereby." *See also* nos. 574,
1407, and 2055.
CtY, ICU, MB, MH, MPB, MWiW*, MeB, N,
NN, Nh, NhD, NjP, OCl, RPB, WHi.

1541 —— "Celibacy. Letter from a Shaker."
American Phrenological Journal, 43 (June 1866),
177–78.
　　Reply to William Clark, *see* no. 582. It would
　　be wrong for the race to cease to exist. Mar-
　　ried persons might indulge in sexual inter-
　　course every 3 or 4 years for the purpose of
　　generation, but for the higher order holiness
　　to the Lord should precede all things.
　　DLC, DNLM, MB, NN*, OCl.

1542 "Letter," *Day-Star*, 12 (March 20, 1847),
36.
　　Report of a Conference of Believers and
　　Adventists, February 18, 1847, Enfield,
　　Conn., which was attended by the writer,
　　Isaac Youngs, and Giles Avery. The editor
　　notes that since the Conference, about 20
　　Adventists have joined the Shakers.
　　MWA, MWiW*, OClWHi, OCHP.

1543 [——] "Religious Communities," *Phalan-
sterian Record* (Moore's Hill, Ind.), 1 (April
1858), 17–20.
　　Lead article is a letter from Evans correcting
　　a statement concerning the divinity of Ann
　　Lee, and the *Record's* reply.
　　MB, MWiW*.

1544 —— "Resurrection," *World's Advance*

Thought (Portland, Ore.), n.s. 4, no. 11 (1870), 168.

NN*, OCIWHi.

1545 —— "Shaker Burials," *American Socialist* (Oneida Community, N.Y.), 2 (February 22, 1877), 60.

In Evans' "Rational Funerals," *Shaker Manifesto*, 8 (June 1878), 130-31, he discusses this article "published a year or two ago ..." in the *American Socialist*. "It has been going the rounds of the press ever since. A few weeks ago the *New York Times* had a cleverly written burlesque of the same two columns." DLC, ICJ, MH, MWA*, NIC, NN, NhD, WHi.

1546 —— "The Shaker Outlook," *American Socialist* (Oneida Community, N.Y.), 2 (August 1877), 251.

Reprint of a letter (July 26, 1877) to the *New York Tribune* about "how a Shaker regards the contest between the railroads and their employees." DLC, ICJ, MH, MWA*, NIC, NN, NhD, WHi.

1547 —— "The Shaker Remedy," *American Socialist* (Oneida Community, N.Y.), 2 (October 18, 1877), 331.

Letter to the *Albany Morning Express* concerning the political disease which threatens the life of the nation. Reprinted in *The Shaker*, 7 (December 1871), 91. DLC, ICJ, MH, MWA*, NIC, NN, NhD, WHi.

1548 —— "Shakerism and Spiritualism in Their Moral Aspects," *Human Nature* (London), No. 53 (August 1, 1871), 401-06.

Reprinted from *The Shaker*, 1 (July 1871), 49-51. IaU, MH*, PU.

1549 —— [Shakers and Girlingites], *American Socialist* (Oneida Community, N.Y.), 3 (October 3, 1878), 313.

Quotations from Evans' letter to the *Brooklyn Eagle* concerning the followers of Mrs. Mary Ann Girling who were often called Shakers. Frederick W. Evans wrote earlier that he had "corresponded with the Girling woman ever since they were organized. James Hasse, a leading member of Mother Girling's household, received faith in Shakerism and came over from England. This led to the Girlingites being called Shakers in England. They had no right to the name." *See* "Mother Girling," *The Shaker*, 6 (October 1876), 78; *see also* letter by Giles B. Avery, "Shakers vs. Girlingites," *Shaker Manifesto*, 8 (November 1878), 274. DLC, ICJ, MH, MWA*, NIC, NN, NhD, WHi.

1550 —— "The Shakers on the Crusade," *American Socialist* (Oneida Community, N.Y.), 4 (February 27, 1879), 67.

Letter enclosing a communication from Oliver Prentiss with editorial comment, *see* no. 1628. DLC, ICJ, MH, MWA*, NIC, NN, NhD, WHi.

1551 —— "What is the Shaker System?" *American Socialist* (Oneida Community, N.Y.), 2 (November 8, 1877), 35.

Reprint of a letter to *Albany Morning Express*. DLC, ICJ, MH, MWA*, NIC, NN, NhD, WHi.

1552 —— "William Oxley and Shakerism," *Medium and Daybreak* (London), August 10, 1888.

Evans' reply to "Oxley on Shakerism" which appeared in the May 18th issue of *Medium and Daybreak. See* no. 2547. MnU, OClWHi*.

1553 "Extracts from the Journal of a Shaker Journey 1856," edited by Robert G. Newman, *New England Galaxy* (Old Sturbridge Village, Mass.), 4 (Summer 1962), 20-28. illus.

Journey through the states of Connecticut, Massachusetts, Vermont, New Hampshire, and Maine made by Benjamin Gates, Dwight Hinckley, Sally Bushnell, Leah Taylor, Mary Hazard, and Jane Blanchard. MPB*, MPH, RP.

F

1554 "Fifteen Years a Shakeress," *Galaxy* (New York), 13 (January–April 1872), 29–38, 191–201, 337–46, 460–70.

An anonymous melodramatic narrative of a young girl's life among the Shakers at Watervliet, N.Y. This series of articles was recognized in *The Shaker*, 2 (May 1872), 40, with the declaration, "We pronounce some truth founded on fiction."

CtY, DLC, ICU, KyHi, MWiW*, NBuU, NN, Nh, NhD, NjPT, OC, PPL, WHi.

1555 FRASER, DANIEL. "Brook-Farm Community," *Shaker Manifesto*, 11 (July 1881), 146–48.

In part, Fraser's reaction to an article in the London *Standard.* An informed and thoughtful article which concludes, "All honor to the Brook Farm Communists whether in the land of souls or still in the body. They honored themselves, Massachusetts and humanity. Happy day, when men and women will fulfill all righteousness, while doing 'that which is right in their own eyes'."

Ct, DLC, ICN, IU, MB, MHarF, MPH, MWA, MWiW*, Nh, NhD, NjPT, OClWHi, WHi.

1556 —— "Visit to and Observations upon a

Forty Acre Fruit Farm," *Shaker Manifesto*, 10 (May 1880), 110–11.

Discussion of the cultivation of raspberries, strawberries, and blackberries, and their ready market. The Wachusett blackberry "bears abundantly, berries of good size, and of good quality. The canes are remarkably *free of thorns* ... The Wachusett was presented to the public by the Shakers at Shirley, Mass., by Leander Persons."

Ct, DLC, IU, MB, MHarF, MPH, MWA, MWiW*, Nh, NhD, NjPT, OClWHi, WHi.

1557 FROST, MARGUERITE. "Notes on Shaker Herbs and Herbalists," *Herb Grower Magazine* (Falls Village, Conn.), 5 (Spring 1951), 86–94.

An account of the Shaker herb gardens at Canterbury, N.H.

DLC, MPH*, OCl.

1558 —— "The Prose and Poetry of Shakerism," *Philadelphia Museum Bulletin*, 57 (Spring 1962), 67–82. illus.

Résumé of Shaker history and activities by a member of the Canterbury, N.H., society.

CtY, ICU, MPH, MWA, MWiW*, N, NN, NhD, PP.

G

1559 G., T. C. [Condition of the Society at South Union]. *American Socialist* (Oneida Community, N.Y.), 3 (March 21, 1878), 94.

Novitiate letter signed: G. T. C., and dated: South Union, March 15, 1878.

DLC, ICJ, MH, MWA*, NIC, NN, NhD, WHi.

1560 "God and the Bible in Court," *Religio-Philosophical Journal* (Chicago), March 17, 1888.

Verbatim account of a mock court proceeding with A. E. Tisdall as counsel for the plaintiff and H. L. Eads, counsel for the defendant.

ICN, MB*.

1561 GREEN, CALVIN. "Biographical Account of the Life, Character & Ministry of Father Joseph Meacham ... 1827," edited with a Foreword by Theodore E. Johnson, *Shaker Quarterly*,

10 (Spring, Summer, Fall 1970), 20–32, 58–68, 92–102.

From an 84-page manuscript copy, dated July 15, 1859, in the Shaker Library, Sabbathday Lake, Me. "This is the only serious attempt by a Believer at a full-length treatment of Shakerism's first American-born leader."
CtHC, CtY-D, DLC, MBAt, MHarF, MPH, MWiW*, NNUT, NOC, NhD, NhU, NjPT, OClWHi.

1562 GROSVENOR, LORENZO DOW. [Letter], *Day-Star*, 11 (November 7, 1846), 35–36.

Short letter submitting a copy of a letter written by Mary M. Wood, an Adventist recently converted to Shakerism. The letter was written to the sisters at Harvard, Mass., and is dated from Shaker Village, N.H., September 22, 1846.
MWA, MWiW*, OClWHi, OCHP.

1563 —— [Letter to Michael H. Barton, dated: May 12, 1832], *Something New* (Harvard, Mass.), n.s. 2, No. 8 (May 1832), 199–200.

On combining Barton's "pronouncing alphabet" with stenography, i.e., shorthand writing, *see* no. 1324.
MHarF, MB*, MH, MWA, NN.

H

1564 "History of the Church of Mt. Lebanon, N.Y.," Nos. 1–17, *The Manifesto*, 19 (July–December 1889), 145–48, 169–71, 193–96, 217–20, 241–43, 265–67; 20 (January–November 1890), 3–4, 25–28, 49–51, 73–75, 97–100, 121–23, 145–47, 169–70, 193–95, 217–18, 241–42.

A full treatment of the early history and organization of the Mt. Lebanon community, the changes in worship, and the period of manifestations, Nos. 1–7. Describes dietary regime, farming and gardening, music, education, and various industries, Nos. 8–16. "Believers before the Legislature" gives the history of Shaker memorials, petitions to the New York State Legislature, No. 17.
Ct, DLC, ICN, IU, MB, MHarF, MPH, MWA, MWiW*, Nh, NhD, NjPT, OClWHi, WHi.

1565 HOLLAWAY, JOANNA, "Corruptions of Shakerism," *Voice of Truth* (Rochester, N.Y.), April 7, 1847.

A bitter communication involving incidents at the Whitewater and Union Village Shaker communities in Ohio. The author, a seceder, states that she was a Shaker for twenty-seven years. Reprinted in M. Dyer, *Rise and Progress* ... (Concord, N.H., 1847, no. 535), pp. 130–35.
MWA*.

1566 —— [Letter], *Voice of Truth* (Rochester, N.Y.), May 1847.

A follow-up to her earlier communication recounting a purported misdeed of a Shaker Elder at Union Village. Reprinted in M. Dyer, *Rise and Progress* ... (Concord, N.H.: 1847), no. 535, pp. 150–52.
MWA*.

1567 HOLLISTER, ALONZO GILES. "Concerning God," *World's Advance Thought* (Portland, Ore.), n.s. 5 (June 1893).
OClWHi*.

1568 —— "Confession of Sins," *Flaming Sword* (Chicago), 4 (July 2, 1892), 11–12.
DLC, MH, MiU, NN, OClWHi*, WHi.

1569 —— "The Final Harvest," *World's Advance Thought* (Portland, Ore.), n.s. 5, no. 7 (1891), 301 (i.e. 103), 119.
OC1WHi*.

1570 —— "From a Shaker Standpoint," *Flaming Sword* (Koreshan Unity, Entero, Fla.), Sept. 8, 1911.

Reference is made to an earlier article, "Lawlessness in Georgia," signed: *A. E. M.* Concerns the death by euthanasia of Sister Sadie L. Marchant which actually occurred

in the Florida Shaker colony, Narcoossee, Aug. 22, 1911. Sister Eliza Sears and Brother Egbert B. Gillette were arrested, but the charges were dropped.
DLC, MH, MiU, NN, OClWHi*, WHi.

1571 ——— "A Kind Letter from a Prominent Shaker," *The Sower* (New York), 3 (December 1891), 358-59.
A response to an article about Ann Lee in the June 1891 issue, and description of a spirit visit from John Calvin.
KySP*.

1572 ——— "Liberalism," *World's Advance Thought* (Portland, Ore.), n.s. 5, no. 5 (1891), 96 (i.e., 69).
On the figurative and symbolic use of language in dealing with spiritual ideas, and the lack of liberalism in applying literal interpretations. Reprinted in *The Manifesto*, 23 (April 1893), 85-87.
OClWHi*.

1573 ——— "Life's Exchanges—a Lesson from Experience," *World's Advance Thought* (Portland, Ore.), n.s. 4 (August 1890).
OClWHi*.

1574 ——— "Modern Revelations," *A Fountain of Light*, 1 (January 19, 1881), 230-31.
MPH*.

1575 ——— "Natural and Spiritual Man," *World's Advance Thought* (Portland, Ore.), n.s. 4, pt. 11 (1890), 166-67.
OClWHi*.

1576 ——— "Remarkable Phenomena among the Shakers in 1850; A Spiritual Manifestation and Revelation among the Alethians of Shakers at Mt. Lebanon, N.Y.," *Banner of Light*, Vol. 96, August 27; September 3, 10, 1904.
August 27th article is an announcement of forthcoming articles on Shaker spiritualism. The September 3rd and 10th articles are long "Records of Visits while Entranced to a Spiritual Telegraph Office by Sister Adah Zilla Potter, of the First Family, [who] was Accompanied by Spirit Brother Seth Youngs Wells, who passed away in 1850." Many spirits and friends were seen, including George Washington, Lafayette, Benjamin Franklin, Isaac Newton, etc., all distinguished souls now "Mother's Children." Also an account of the visit of Elder Bushnell, Antoinette Doolittle, and Jane Knight to Dr. Phelps' home in Stratford, Conn., where communications were received about the questions asked Sister Potter in her first interview.
DLC, MH, MWA, MWiW*.

1577 ——— "True Judgment Liberates," *World's Advance Thought* (Portland, Ore.), n.s. 5, no. 10 (July 1892), 148.
OClWHi*.

I

1578 "Immortalized," *Flaming Sword* (Koreshan Unity, Esterao, Fla.), 6 (July 15, 1893), 24.
The article was criticized as being "singularly narrow and unspiritual." Exception was taken to the conclusions concerning Mother Ann in an editorial, "Comments on 'Immortalized,'" *The Manifesto*, 23 (September 1893), 204-06; in the same issue Daniel Offord adds further criticism, "Immortalized," pp. 207-08. He refers to the Shakers having extended union and fellowship to the Koreshan leaders, and also having accepted them as members of the North Family, Mt. Lebanon, but this is not to imply endorsement of "theological statements and ideas set forth in the *Flaming Sword*."
DLC, MiU, NN, OClWHi*, WHi.

1579 "Immortalized," *Flaming Sword* (Koreshan Unity, Estero, Fla.), 6 (September 2, 1893), 132-34.

This article refers disparagingly to the comments in *The Manifesto* (no. 1578) and quotes

from both the editorial and the Offord article. DLC, MiU, NN, OClWHi*, WHi.

J

1580 [Jacobs, Enoch] "The Body of Christ," *Day-Star*, 11 (June 13, 1846), 9, 12.
A plea to Second Adventists who, the author asserts, had been expecting external means of salvation, when they should have sought "a faithful cross against the flesh and its lusts"— the Shaker way.
MWA, MWiW*, OClWHi, OCHP.

1581 [——] "Eastern Tour," *Day-Star*, 11 (August 8, 25; September 19, 1846), 23–24, 27–28, 31.
A full account of the author's visits to the eastern Shaker communities and to the Adventist Camp Meeting, Enfield, Conn., which was also attended by Shaker elders. Includes an account of a proselytizing visit to Philadelphia in company with Brothers Frederick Evans and George Wickersham, and Sisters Antoinette Doolittle and Phebe Ann Jones.
MWA, MWiW*, OClWHi, OCHP.

1582 [——] "Northern Tour," *Day-Star*, 13 (June 15, 1847), 12–13.
Description of a missionary tour in company with Charles Clapp to "gather" disillusioned Adventists in Northern Ohio.
MWA, MWiW*, OClWHi, OCHP.

1583 [——] "A Visit in Kentucky and Indiana," *Day-Star*, 12 (January 16, 1847), 5.
Description of a six-weeks' missionary tour among the Adventists with Brother Charles Clapp. They were joined at times by other Shakers.
MWA, MWiW*, OClWHi, OCHP.

1584 JOHNSON, JULIA H. "Among the Shakers: Some Peculiar Spirit Manifestations," *Progressive Thinker*, n.d.
This article is contained in a Shaker scrapbook at Williams College. A manuscript note

states that Julia Johnson was brought up at Tyringham, Mass., and left "our community after she was 50 years of age or thereabouts." The author describes the spinning [whirling] and trance states she has witnessed, and refers to the effects of suggestion and warming up by the leader. Various examples of strange behavior are given. She states that she had heard from an eldress that they had seen occasion "to burn many of the writings of that early time [period of manifestations, 1837–1845]," and that the Bible contains many passages unfit for the young.
MWiW*.

1585 JOHNSON, THEODORE E., *comp.* "A Complete Register of Deaths which have Occurred in the United Society of Believers, Alfred, Maine 1790–1931," *Shaker Quarterly*, 1 (Winter 1961), 168–78.
The death dates of 242 Believers at Alfred, Me., are based upon records kept by Elder Otis Sawyer supplemented by 2 lesser manuscript records. Birth dates are included for most entries. The list is arranged alphabetically by personal names under Church, Second, and Third Families.
CtHC, CtY-D, DLC, MBAt, MHarF, MPH, MWiW*, NNUT, NOC, NhD, NhU, NjPT, OClWHi.

1586 —— "Life in the Christ Spirit: Observations on Shaker Theology," *Shaker Quarterly*, 8 (Fall 1968), 67–76.
"Being in Substance Remarks Delivered at the Shaker Conference, Hancock, Massachusetts, September 7, 1968." A discussion of "the major theological emphases—unity and simplicity," and the misunderstandings concerning the Shaker conception of the dual nature of God, Shaker Christology, and other beliefs concerning the sacraments, revelation, the afterlife, worship, and Holy Scripture.

Interpretations are supported by quotations from Mother Ann and the words of Elders Benjamin Seth Youngs and Rufus Bishop. The author concludes that "The potentiality within Shakerism to play a role in the future of the universal church is great, for the seeds of divine truth inherent within the basic theological concepts represent the best of both the ethos and ideal of the Christian community. Shakerism still holds within itself a germ of that indwelling spirit which if nourished has the power to influence our day." Reprinted as a separate, no. 846.
CtHC, CtY-D, DLC, MBAt, MHarF, MPH, MWiW*, NNUT, NOC, NhD, NhU, NjPT, OClWHi.

K

1587 KAIME, JOHN. "New Year's Hymn for 1847," *Day-Star*, 12 (April 12, 1847), 43.
MWA, MWiW*, OCHP, OClWHi.

1588 [The *Kreutzer Sonata*], *The Manifesto*, 20 (October 1890), 238.

A short critical notice reprinted from *World's Advance Thought* on the censorship of Tolstoi's *Kreutzer Sonata* in Russia, and the ban on its circulation through the mails in the U.S., with editorial comment. *See* no. 882 and no. 1163 for follow-up.

L

1589 LAMSON, DAVID. "Communities," *Practical Christian* (Milford, Mass.), 2 (August 21, 1841), 30.
Announces the formation of the "Fraternal Community, No. 1," founded on Christian love, and where ministers will receive no more than laborers. At this time Lamson was a member of Ballou's Hopedale Community, but later with his family moved to the Shaker community at Hancock, Mass., *see* no. 855.
MWA*, WHi.

1590 LANE, CHARLES. "Charles Lane and the Shakers," *The Regenerator*, n.s. 1 (February 8, 1847), 358.
Answer to David Richmond (no. 1637), dated at Alcott House, Ham, England, January 2, 1847. Lane reasserts that his son was articled to the Shakers within 24 hours after arriving at Harvard, Mass. village, denies that he ever made any promise to be silent about the Shakers, and suggests that "Perhaps, it would be more prudent as well as more valiant for some 'Old Believer' to speak the mind of the Society . . . rather than for the inexperienced to take up so combative a position as that of general champion." Richmond was a young man who had lately joined the Shakers at Enfield, Conn.
OClWHi*.

1591 —— "The Consociate Family Life," *New Age and Concordium Gazette* (London), 1 (November 1, 1843), 116–20.
Reprints Lane's letter to the *New York Weekly Tribune*, September 2, 1843. The letter is dated at Harvard, Mass., August 1843. He describes the plans and philosophy underlying the establishment of Bronson Alcott's Fruitlands community. On the question of "family," Lane discusses the success of the Shaker system and states that the Shakers are entitled to greater consideration than has been accorded to them.
CtY, MH, NN, NNC, OClWHi*.

1592 [——] "A Day with the Shakers," *The Dial* (Boston), 4 (October 1843), 165–73.
Signed: C.[harles] L.[ane]. Lane, an Englishman, and Bronson Alcott visited the Harvard, Mass., Shaker village to purchase seeds and

stayed to observe the community and talk with the Shakers. Lane was highly impressed, read several of their publications, and discusses *A Summary View of the Millennial Church* (no. 743). When Fruitlands, a nearby transcendentalist consociate family failed, Charles Lane who had financed the quixotic experiment in communal living, moved to the Harvard Shakers along with his young son. He stayed several months, but articled the boy to the Shakers where his son stayed four years. Cf. C. E. Sears, *Gleanings* (no. 1273), pp. 262–70, and nos. 1594 and 1637. CtY, DLC, MB*, MeB, N, NN, NIC, NjP, OC1.

1593 [——] [Developments at Fruitlands, Mass.], *New Age and Concordium Gazette* (London), 1 (August 1, 1843), 75–76.

Includes a long quotation from information received by the editor, surely a letter from Lane. In the last paragraph a visit to the Shakers at Harvard is described. "You would approve of many of their plans and practices, I am sure. The order, cleanliness, and quiet of the place and people are extremely attractive .... There is much sympathy between us [Fruitlands], especially towards me." The writer has bought Shaker publications and suggests that a copy of *A Summary View of the Millennial Church* (no. 743) be obtained and read. A longer account of this visit is found in Lane's article in *The Dial*, no. 1592. CtY, MH, NN, NNC, OClWHi*.

1594 —— "Letter from Charles Lane—The Shakers—Community &c.," *The Regenerator* (Fruit Hills, O.), n.s. 1 (October 19, 1846), 239.

The letter, dated: New York, September 7, 1846, is a formal leave-taking after four years in the United States. The Fruitlands experiment has failed "from causes for which no one is to be blamed." "During the summer I had become much attracted by the Shaker Community in the same town [Harvard, Mass.], and as many of my sentiments coincided with theirs the attraction was mutual. I resolved therefore on trying if their outward order and worldly success were founded on the true basis. In January 1844, I and my boy removed thither, and I was so unfortunate as to article

him to them within twenty-four hours, as they requested, before I became acquainted with their principles ... I still do, as I did then, disbelieve much of the slander publicly banded about against them, though it is not without foundation." He refers to "the system of spiritual despotism which does not allow a man to think for himself," and continues, "Among them are some honest men and more honest and intelligent women, but the mistaken notions on education lead to such a general contraction of the soul as might make one weep ... After a patient investigation of seventeen months I was conscience-compelled to give up the pursuit ..." These sentiments are at some variance with Lane's earlier published statements and were the cause of an acrimonious exchange of letters with David Richmond of the Enfield, Conn., community, *see* nos. 1637 and 1638. OClWHi*.

1595 [——] "Millennial Church," *The Dial*, 4 (April 1844), 537–40.

A review and commentary of *A Holy, Sacred, and Divine Roll and Book* by P. Stewart (no. 1340), in which it is advised that "A perusal of the work should be delayed until the reader is in a state to appreciate it with fairness and candor." Lane is identified as the author in R. W. Emerson, *Letters* (no. 2091), III, 243.
CtY, DLC, MB*, MeB, N, NN, NIC, NjP, OCl.

1596 "Legislature of Kentucky, Jan. 10 [1812]. Report of the Committee of Religion," *Niles' Weekly Register* (Baltimore, Md.), 2 (March 21, 1812), 33.

Reprints, without comment, the report of the legislative Committee of Religion on "the petitions of sundry persons respecting the people called *Shakers*." In spite of the conclusion, "The Committee leave the Shakers and all other sects to pursue uninterruptedly the dictates of their own consciences—leaving their religious creed to the approbation or disapprobation of themselves and their God." An act concerning alimony and separate maintenance of wives and children abandoned by husbands and fathers who joined the Shakers was approved.

CtY, DLC, KyBgW, KyU, M, MB, MWA,
MWiW*, Me, MeP, NBuG, NIC, NN, Nh,
NhD, OC, OCl, OClWHi, PU, WHi.

1597 "Legislature of New York," *Niles' Weekly Register,* 12 (March 29, 1817), 74-75.

"In Senate, March 10. An Act Concerning the Shakers," which is headed "a curiosity well worth the preservation." The act is printed without comment. This act would have dissolved the marriage contract between Eunice and James Chapman. Among the other provisions it stipulated that married persons "attaching themselves to the Shakers" would become "civilly dead" and forfeit real and property rights, and that the custody of the children could be awarded by the chancellor or a judge. The somewhat amended bill passed both Houses on April 7, 1817, but was vetoed by the Council of Revision, January 27, 1818. *See also,* nos. 2320 and 3088, and entries under Eunice Chapman and James Chapman.
CtY, DLC, KyBgW, KyU, M, MB, MWA, MWiW*, Me, MeP, NBuG, NIC, NN, Nh, NhD, OC, OCl, OClWHi, PU, WHi.

1598 "Letter from Shaker Village, Merrimack County, N.H.," *Farmer's Monthly Visitor* (Concord), 2 (January 1840), 4.

Addressed to Isaac Hill, and dated: December 18, 1839, and signed: *Francis Winkley, Israel Sanborn, William Willard.* Expresses satisfaction with the first volume of *Farmer's Monthly Visitor* and the opinion that the journal would serve as a text in the Shaker school and concludes with an order for 26 copies of the first volume.
Ct, DNAL, ICJ, MU, Nh, NhD*.

1599 LINDSAY, BERTHA. "The Canterbury Shakers: 1792-1967," *Shaker Quarterly,* 7 (Fall 1967), 87-95.

Early history and the establishment of the Shaker community at Canterbury, N.H., with short biographies of Father Job Bishop, Benjamin Whitcher, Mary Whitcher, Hannah Goodrich, Micajah Tucker, John Wadleigh, James Daniels, Francis Winkley, and Peter Ayers.
CtHC, CtY-D, DLC, MBAt, MHarF, MPB,

MWiW*, NNUT, NOC, NhD, NhU, NjPT, OClWHi.

1600 LOMAS, GEORGE ALBERT. "Decay of Shaker Institutions," *American Socialist* (Oneida Community, N.Y.), 1 (June 1, 1876), 75-76.

Reprint of a letter to the *Albany Morning Express* replying to W. D. Howells' "A Shaker Village," *Atlantic Monthly,* 37 (June 1876), 699-710. Lomas declares that "Shakerism is not dependent upon a steady increase in numbers." Also reprinted in *The Shaker,* 6 (July 1876), 53, along with a confirming letter from Daniel Fraser. *See* no. 3319.
DLC, ICJ, MH, MWA*, NIC, NN, NhD, WHi.

1601 —— "Early Manufacturer of Steel Pens," *Scientific American,* 39 (November 23, 1878), 325.

Letter of inquiry addressed to the editor about the priority of the manufacture of metal pens. "I am almost persuaded that my people [the Shakers]—were the originators of metal pens." The answer was that "We find no record of the manufacture of metal pens in this country as early as 1820," and refers to barrel steel pens, "made by a Mr. Wise in England," as early as 1803. Reprinted in the *Shaker Manifesto,* 9 (January 1879), 20.
CtY, DLC, MB, ICJ, MiU, OClWHi*, PPL, RP.

1602 —— [Letter], *Phrenological Journal,* June 1872.

Reprinted in *The Shaker,* 2 (July 1872), 55. Addressed to Samuel R. Wells, part owner of the *Journal,* answering a charge about Shaker celibacy which had appeared earlier.
DLC, DNLM, MB, NN*, OCl.

1603 —— "Shaker Criticism," *Oneida Circular,* n.s. 6 (February 21, 1870), 389.

Letter explaining why the chapter on the Shakers in Noyes' *American Socialisms* is "not a fair representation of them at the present time." *See* no. 2527.
DLC, MH, MWA*, NN, WHi.

1604 —— "The Shaker Problem, No. 1,"

Phrenological Journal, July, 1873, pp. 42–44.
A defense of Ann Lee and Shaker beliefs, particularly celibacy, intended as an answer to no. **3651.** *See also* nos. **1534** and **1535.**
DLC, DNLM, MB, NN*, OCl.

1605 —— "The Shaker View," *American Socialist* (Oneida Community, N.Y.), 3 (November 21, 1878), 373.
Reply to a communication signed: *Communist,* and dated: October 26, 1878, New Garden, Chester Co., Pa., which asks for "more light" on Shaker life "upstairs," i.e., celibacy.

DLC, ICJ, MH, MWA*, NIC, NN, NhD, WHi.

1606 LUDLOW, WILLIAM. "Lecture," *New Harmony Gazette,* 1 (February 8, March 8, 1826), 156–57, 186–87.
Ludlow, formerly resident at the New Lebanon, N.Y., Shaker community, had joined Owen's New Harmony community in Indiana. Here he discusses the "established means by which our happiness is consummated" and the advantages and rewards of communal living in the face of the present arrangement of society which encourages insincerity and deception. *See* no. **879.**
CtY, DLC, MBAt, NN*, PU, WHi.

M

1607 MC CLELLAND, SAMUEL S. "Busro," Nos. 1–5, *The Manifesto,* 15 (May–September 1885), 110–12, 139–41, 164–66, 183–85, 205–07.
After a brief introduction this is taken from a "Memorandum of Events" or journal written by McClelland between May 20, 1811, and March 30, 1826.
Ct, DLC, ICN, IU, MB, MHarF, MPH, MWA, MWiW*, Nh, NhD, NjPT, OClWHi, WHi.

1608 MC COOL, ELSIE, *comp.* "Gleanings from Sabbathday Lake Journals, 1872–1884," with an Introduction by Theodore E. Johnson, *Shaker Quarterly,* 6 (Fall, Winter 1966), 103–12, 124–34.
The selections are taken from the journals of the Church Family, kept by Elder Otis Sawyer and Eldress Mary Ann Gillespie. The first entry is dated January 1, 1872; the last is dated November 27, 1884, on Thanksgiving Day when the first meal was served in the New Dwelling House.
CtHC, CtY-D, DLC, MBAt, MHarF, MPH, MWiW*, NNUT, NOC, NhD, NhU, NjPT, OClWHi.

The following six articles were published under the name, Sister Marcia, and are sometimes attributed to Sister Marcia Bullard. Confirma-

tion for such attribution has not been located, but if this attribution be correct, the articles were published posthumously. Marcia Bullard died May 7, 1899, at Ayer (Harvard), Mass.

1609 MARCIA, SISTER. "How the Shakers Kept Christmas," *The Housekeeper* (Minneapolis), 29 (December 1905), 30. illus.
DLC*.

1610 —— "Recollections of My Childhood," *Good Housekeeping,* 43 (August 1906), 126–29. illus.
Illustrations signed: *Phillips Ward.* A Shakeress's delightful account of life in the children's order, Mt. Lebanon, N.Y.
MB, MNF*, NBP, OCl.

1611 —— "Shaker Industries," *Good Housekeeping,* 43 (July 1906), 33–37. illus.
Sister Marcia describes the herbs grown and packaged by the Mt. Lebanon, N.Y., Shakers and writes that "On the whole there was no pleasanter work than that in the 'Medical Garden' and 'Herb Shop'."
MB, MNF*, NBP, OCl.

1612 —— "The Shakers' Christmas Fast," *Good Housekeeping,* 43 (December 1906), 613.
MB, MNF*, NBP, OCl.

1613 —— "The Shakers' Fine Cookery," *Good Housekeeping*, 41 (August 1905), 202-05.
MB, MNF*, NBP, OCl.

1614 —— "Thanksgiving in a Shaker Village," *Good Housekeeping*, 41 (November 1905), 560-61.
MB, MNF*, NBP, OCl.

1615 "The 'Millennial Laws' of 1821," edited with an Introduction by Theodore E. Johnson, *Shaker Quarterly*, 7 (Summer 1967), 35-58. illus.
The text is preceded by a facsimile of the title page, "Order and Rules of the Church at New Lebanon, August 7th 1821 ..." in the autograph of Elder John Coffin, and also p. 33 of the manuscript. "These 'laws' of 1821 which appeared with full approbation of the Ministry and Elders of New Lebanon, seem to have been given fairly wide circulation and we may assume that there was at least one manuscript copy in each community."
CtHC, CtY-D, DLC, MBAt, MHarF, MPH, MWiW*, NNUT, NOC, NhD, NhU, NjPT, OClWHi.

1616 MONROE, JAMES. "The Shakers as Communists," *The Altruist*, 11 (May 1891), 41.
The masthead identifies the author as Farm Manager of the Altruist Community, St. Louis, Mo. He is further identified in a note as having been a "working member" at the Watervliet, N.Y., Shakers "during the past year."
DLC, NNC, OClWHi*, WHi.

1617 MORRELL, PRUDENCE. "Account of a Journey to the West in the Year 1847," edited with a Foreword by Theodore E. Johnson, *Shaker Quarterly*, 8 (Summer, Fall 1968), 37-60, 82-96.
A vivid description of the pleasures and difficulties of early western travel which is also a social document of considerable interest and a well-rounded picture of life in the Shaker communities visited during a trip of more than 4 months. Taken from a manuscript in the Shaker Library, Sabbathday Lake, Me. Two references are made, July 9th

and July 23d, to the Canterbury apostates who are performing in Ohio. *See* no. 728.
CtHC, CtY-D, DLC, MBAt, MHarF, MPB, MWiW*, NNUT, NOC, NhD, NhU, NjPT, OClWHi.

1618 "Mother Lucy's Sayings Spoken at Different Times and under Various Circumstances," edited and with an Introduction by Francis A. Carr, *Shaker Quarterly*, 8 (Winter 1968), 99-106.
Mother Lucy Wright, an early convert to Shakerism who had enjoyed the trust and friendship of Mother Ann Lee, was appointed by Joseph Meacham "as the female head of the church to work with him in the first formally ordered Ministry." Her wise sayings, compiled after her death, circulated freely in manuscript among Believers. Printed from an 1887 manuscript copy in the Shaker Library, Sabbathday Lake, Me. *See also* "Remarks of Mother Lucy Wright," Nos. 1-4, *The Manifesto*, 26 (April, July, November 1896), 65-66, 113-14, 169-70; 27 (January 1897), 5-6.
CtHC, CtY-D, DLC, MBAt, MHarF, MPH, MWiW*, NNUT, NOC, NhD, NhU, NjPT, OClWHi.

1619 MYRICK, ELISHA. "Letter from a Shaker," *American Socialist* (Oneida Community, N.Y.), 2 (February 22, 1877), 37-38.
Addressed to W. A. H. [William A. Hinds], and dated: Ayer, Mass., February 12, 1877.
DLC, ICJ, MH, MWA*, NIC, NN, NhD, WHi.

1620 —— "A Shaker Herb Department Taken from the Journal Kept by Elisha Myrick at Harvard, Massachusetts ..." *Herb Grower Magazine*, 4 (October 1950), (Falls Village, Conn.), 218-26.
The manuscript Journal is in the collection of Mr. and Mrs. E. D. Andrews. Facsimile of the title page, p. 219.
DLC, DNAL, MHarF*, MPH, NOC, OCl.

1621 MYRICK, JOSEPH M. "The Resurrection," *Day-Star*, 12 (April 12, 1847), 39-40.
A clarification of his views about Christ's resurrection to reassure Adventists who doubt the Shaker interpretation.
MWA, MWiW*, OClWHi, OCHP.

N

1622 "New Lebanon," *The Manifesto*, 22 (May 1892), 101–03.

Printed at the request of M. J. A. (Martha J. Anderson). An account of early converts to Shakerism at New Lebanon, New Canaan, and Hancock, with some account of their activities during the Revolutionary War. Ct, DLC, ICN, IU, MB, MHarF, MPH, MWA, MWiW*, Nh, NhD, NjPT, OClWHi, WHi.

1623 "Notes about Home," *The Manifesto*, 25 (March 1895), 63.

Timothy Rayson of the Center Family, Mt. Lebanon, N.Y., reports, "Next Thursday morning two Brethren of the fraternity, Henry G. Hollister of Watervliet, and Andrew Barrett of Mt. Lebanon leave for Florida to make some initial preparations for a home for those who wish to migrate." Thereafter, communications in "Notes about Home," a regular feature of *The Manifesto*, provide one of the few sources of information about the Florida Shaker settlement, *see* no. 3005. For example, it will be learned from the "Notes," 28 (April 1898), 58, that "Feb. 14, Elder Joseph Holden, Eldress Harriet Bullard, and Sister Emma Jane Neale started for Florida to visit Olive Branch to judge of its future prospects . . . and will stop in Georgia to view a part of the 46 square miles that the Union Village [Ohio] community have purchast [!] there."
Ct, DLC, ICN, IU, MB, MHarF, MPH, MWA, MWiW*, Nh, NhD, NjPT, OClWHi, WHi.

O

1624 OFFORD, WILLIAM. " 'Cause and Cure of Evil.'—A Shaker's View," *Spiritual Telegraph* (New York), 7 (November 14, 20, 1858), 283–85, 291–93. NN*.

P

1625 PEAVEY, G. W. "Letter," *Day-Star*, 12 (January 16, 1847), 6–7.

A report of a "tour of the escaping remnant" of Adventists in New York State, who have not joined the Shakers. Before his conversion to Shakerism, Peavey questioned Shaker belief in several scaptical letter to the *Day-Star*. MWA, MWiW*, OClWHi, OCHP.

1626 PELHAM, RICHARD. "A Sketch of the Life and Religious Experience . . ." edited with an Introduction by Theodore E. Johnson, *Shaker Quarterly*, 9 (Spring, Summer, Fall 1969), 18–32, 53–64, 69–96.

This autobiography is taken without change from a manuscript copy made by Mary P. Vance of Alfred, Me., now in the Shaker Library, Sabbathday Lake, Me. This account written in 1844 by Pelham who was "a gifted preacher, and successful missionary . . . a skilled tailor, herbalist, horticulturalist, and woodsman, as well as a schoolmaster." He was also instrumental in establishing the North Union and Whitewater, Ohio, and Sodus Bay, N.Y., Shaker communities. CtHC, CtY-D, DLC, MBAt, MHarF, MPH, MWiW*, NNUT, NOC, NhD, NhU, NjPT, OClWHi.

1627 PERKINS, ABRAHAM. "Enfield [N.H.]," *The Manifesto*, 14 (October 1884), 224–25.

Very brief history and description of the

Shaker community by an elder, with a view of Enfield.
Ct, DLC, ICN, IU, MB, MHarF, MPH, MWA, MWiW*, Nh, NhD, NjPT, OClWHi, WHi.

1628 PRENTISS, OLIVER. "New Earth and New Heavens," *American Socialist* (Oneida Community, N.Y.), 4 (April 3, 1879), 107.
Faint praise of the Oneida Community.
DLC, ICJ, MH, MWA*, NIC, NN, NhD, WHi.

1629 —— "A Shaker Heard From," *American Socialist* (Oneida Community, N.Y.), 4 (February 27, 1879), 67.
Reprint of communication to *Albany Evening Post* with editorial comment supporting Oneida Community.
DLC, ICJ, MH, MWA*, NIC, NN, NhD, WHi.

1630 —— "The Title Wave," *American Socialist* (Oneida Community, N.Y.), 3 (April 25, 1878), 133.

Communication dated: Mt. Lebanon, April 14, 1878.
DLC, ICJ, MH, MWA*, NIC, NN, NhD, WHi.

1631 —— "What the Shakers Expect," *American Socialist* (Oneida Community, N.Y.), 4 (September 4, 1879), 286.
Communication about whether the Shakers expect the whole world to become Shakers.
DLC, ICJ, MH, MWA*, NIC, NN, NhD, WHi.

1632 "Present Truth," *Day-Star*, 11 (June 13, 1846), 6-9.
Extract of an unsigned letter from John Dunlavy to Barton Stone. *See also* no. 522.
MWA, MWiW*, OCHP, OClWHi.

1633 "Principal Seat of Human Depravity," *Day-Star*, 11 (August 8, 1846), 17-18.
Reprints Pt. I, Chap. 6, pp. 41-47, of *The Testimony of Christ's Second Appearing* (Union Village, O., 1823), no. **1471**.
MWA, MWiW*, OCHP, OClWHi.

R

1634 RANKIN, JOHN N. and HARVEY LAUDERDALE EADS. "To the Honorable Abraham Lincoln, President of the U.S. Kind friend;—Strike, but Hear," *The Manifesto*, 25 (March 1895), 50-52.
An undated letter (dated by the editor, August 16, 1863) signed: *John N. Rankin, H. L. Eads, Leaders of the Society of Shakers at So. Union, Ky.* Contains a vivid description of the Civil War damage suffered at South Union. "The armies of the south, like a great prairie fire swept over this part of Ky. in the fall and winter of 1861, licking up the substance of the land." The young men of the community are not only pledged to nonresistance, but are also the main support of 150 women, children, and invalids. A plea is made that Lincoln arrange for their exemptions from the draft for the U.S. Army. Parole was granted December 30, 1863. Reprinted in White and Taylor, *Shakerism*, no. **1447**, and Julia Neal, *By Their Fruits*, no.

2499. *See also* nos. **1014** and **1401**.
Ct, DLC, ICN, IU, MB, MHarF, MPH, MWA, MWiW*, Nh, NhD, NjPT, OClWHi, WHi.

1635 "Recruiting the Shakers," *American Socialist* (Oneida Community, N.Y.), 3 (July 4, 1878), 213.
Includes comments by F. W. Evans and G. B. Avery.
DLC, ICJ, MH, MWA*, NIC, NN, NhD, WHi.

1636 REYNOLDS, WILLIAM. "From a Shaker Elder," *American Socialist* (Oneida Community, N.Y.), 3 (August 8, 1878), 251.
Takes exception to the views expressed by J. G. Truman, no. **1666**, "a novitiate member of but a few months standing."
DLC, ICJ, MH, MWA*, NIC, NN, NhD, WHi.

1637 RICHMOND, DAVID. "Charles Lane and the Shakers," *The Regenerator* (Fruit Hills, O.), n.s. 1 (November 30, 1846), 278-79.

A long letter refuting Lane's statements about his experience with the Shakers (no. 1594), dated at Ballard Vale, Andover, Mass., November 10th, 1846. With William White, Richmond, a young Believer, has visited the Harvard, Mass., Society and "made the strictest inquiry," and states that Lane "promised without the least hint or request from the Shakers, that he would not write or speak anything against them." He states that the son was not articled to the Shakers until after 12 days, discusses each of Lane's dissatisfactions with the object of bringing "Charles home again to the truth, and to remove the effects on, and injustice to, an unoffending people," and asks Lane to answer him. The "Form of Article or Indenture" is reprinted. OClWHi*.

1638 —— "Charles Lane and the Shakers," *The Regenerator* (Fruit Hills, O.), n.s. 2 (April 5, 1847), 6–7.

A long answer to Lane's letter (no. 1590), dated at Andover, Mass., March 10th, 1847, taking further issue with Lane's statements and calling upon him "to substantiate the serious charges he prefers against the 'Believers'," particularly what Lane referred to as the Shakers' "mistaken notions on education." The Editor, Orson S. Murray, adds a note of criticism stating that Richmond's "pursuit of brother Lane in the case savors too much of wrangling and accusatoriness," and continues, "The exceeding sensitiveness you manifest in behalf of Shakerism, does anything but commend Shakerism to the discerning. What have the 'seven thousand' to fear from the one." A postscript by the Editor advises that "If the Shakers have any further defense in the case, I ask Brother Richmond to try the New York Tribune a while." OClWHi*.

1639 —— "Communication from David Richmond," *The Regenerator* (Fruit Hills, O.), n.s. 2 (June 14, 1847), 91.

A reply to the Editor's addendum (no. 1638), dated at Andover, Mass., May 26th, 1847. Richmond writes that the Editor "very much mistook the spirit of my letter," and that although he is not personally acquainted with Lane, he holds "high esteem" for him and "justly appreciates him," and that "What he [Lane] states of the Shakers was from a very unhappy state of mind." OClWHi*.

1640 RICHMOND, DAVID and WILLIAM WHITE. "Letter," *Day-Star*, 11 (November 7, 1846), 35.

An order for copies of the *Day-Star*, accompanied by a recital of their "journey through the Infidel school, commencing with Socialism ... through all the phases of gross unbelief, up to Ham Commonism, or 'Concordism,' *alias* refined unbelief, which was the last steppingstone to our present position," when they became Shakers at Enfield, Conn. MWA, MWiW*, OCHP, OClWHi.

1641 "Rules and Orders for the Church of Christ's Second Appearing. Established by the Ministry and Elders of the Church, Revised and Reestablished by the Same, New Lebanon, New York, May, 1860," edited and with an Introduction by Theodore E. Johnson, *Shaker Quarterly*, 11 (Winter 1971), 139–65.

The Introduction, pp. 139–43, clarifies an unfortunate misunderstanding regarding the "Millennial Laws" of 1845, *see* no. 1766. These laws should not be considered as the model for communal rules and behaviour throughout Shaker history; they "were a product of that era of spiritual ferment [spirit manifestations] and searching in which they were written," and were shortlived. They were replaced by the "Rules and Orders" of 1860 "which remained in effect for over twenty-seven years" and which "marked a steady return to those communal rules and orders of the past which were more deeply rooted in tradition and common sense." *See also* "The 'Millennial Laws' of 1821," no. 1615. CtHC, CtY-D, DLC, MBAt, MHarF, MPH, MWiW*, NNUT, NOC, NhD, NhU, NjPT, OClWHi.

1642 RUNDELLE, COURTNEY. "White Oak, Ga.," *The Manifesto*, 19 (October 1899), 160.

A communication in the regular section, "Notes about Home." "Today the first brick of our enlarged Southern home was laid by a son of Ham ... Ten months ago a small company from Union Village and White Water, Ohio, accompanied the beloved Western Ministry to this location, close to the town of White Oak, in the extreme south east county of Georgia to found another center [10,000 acres] of spiritual life and light as understood and enjoyed by 'the people called Shakers.' Elder Charles Faraday or Eldress Laura Fridger will gladly give any further information desired." Subsequent "Notes" reveal very little information about the progress of the Georgia Shaker settlement. *See* no. 3004.

Ct, DLC, ICN, IU, MB, MHarF, MPH, MWA, MWiW*, Nh, NhD, NjPT, OClWHi, WHi.

S

1643 SAWYER, OTIS. "Alfred, Me.," Nos. 1-5, *The Manifesto*, 15 (January–May 1885), 9, 11–12, 33–34, 58–59, 79–81, 105–07.

Considerable detail is given about the early history of the Shakers in Maine, including Gorham and New Gloucester, as well as Alfred, by a beloved Shaker Elder. Includes New Light Baptist activities, voyage of "The Snark," two visits of Father James Whittaker, and the founding of the Alfred Society. Concludes essentially with the visit of Mother Lucy Wright to Alfred in 1810. Brief references at the end to industries.

Ct, DLC, ICN, IU, MB, MHarF, MPH, MWA, MWiW*, Nh, NhD, NjPT, OClWHi, WHi.

1644 —— "... 'A Complete Register of all the Deaths that have Occurred in the United Societies of Gorham and New Gloucester, Maine,'" edited by Theodore E. Johnson, *Shaker Quarterly*, 1 (Spring 1961), 32–42.

Taken from Elder Otis Sawyer's manuscript records in the Shaker Library, Sabbathday Lake, Me. The list contains death dates for 144 Believers. Many of the entries give pertinent information about the causes of death.

CtHC, CtY-D, DLC, MBAt, MHarF, MPH, MWiW*, NNUT, NOC, NhD, NhU, NjPT, OClWHi.

1645 —— "Introduction to the Christmas Meeting of Dec. 25th 1845 on Chosen Land," with a Foreword by Theodore E. Johnson, *Shaker Quarterly*, 7 (Winter 1967), 119–31.

First printing of a manuscript account in the Sabbathday Lake Library written by Elder Otis Sawyer. "As we read the following account in which the worshipers were open to a very great variety of spirit operations it is well that we accept the happenings at face value."

CtHC, CtY-D, DLC, MBAt, MHarF, MPH, MWiW*, NN, NNUT, NOC, NhD, NhU, NjPT, OClWHi.

1646 —— "Letter," *Day-Star*, 12 (April 12, 1847), 37.

Praises the missionary efforts of Enoch Jacobs in bringing Adventists to Shakerism. Dated at Alfred, York Co., Me., March 29, 1847.

MWA, MWiW*, OCHP, OClWHi.

1647 "Shaker Depletion," *American Socialist* (Oneida Community, N.Y.), 4 (January 30, 1879), 35.

A communication about declining membership from a New Lebanon Shaker, "an obscure individual for whose act the community is not responsible," signed: *O. P.* (Oliver Prentiss?). Suggests that Frederick Evans may be the explanation of Shaker decline.

DLC, ICJ, MH, MWA*, NIC, NN, NhD, WHi.

1648 "Shaker Inventions," *American Socialist* (Oneida Community, N.Y.), 2 (August 20, November 15, 1877), 246, 365.

Reprinted from D. A. Buckingham, "Epitomic history of the Watervliet Shakers," *The Shaker*, 7 (August 1877),

59, no. 1512.
DLC, ICJ, MH, MWA*, NIC, NN, NhD, WHi.

1649 "A Shaker Theologian," *Oneida Circular,*
n.s. 2 (July 10, 1865), 129–30.
  Excerpts from Dunlavy's *Manifesto.*
  CtY, DLC, ICJ, MH, MWA*, NhD, WHi.

1650 "The Shakers," *Niles' Register,* 24 (May
17, 1823), 167–68.
  Verbatim declaration of pacifist Shakers who
  have recently been members of the New
  Lebanon, N.Y., community announcing that
  they have taken residence at the Hancock,
  Mass., Shaker community to avoid being subject to the militia laws of New York State.
  We "publicly declare that we consider the
  present militia laws of the state of New York
  as Oppressive and as infringement upon our
  religious and civil rights." Signed by 23
  Shakers, who state that they "are not required
  by law to bow down, nor subscribe to the
  lofty image of military despotism"; certified
  by William Porter, Presiding Elder, and Joseph
  Allen, Trustee, Hancock, Mass. Reprinted
  from the Albany, N.Y. *Daily Advertiser. See
  also* no. 7.
  CtY, DLC, KyBgW, KyU, M, MB, MWA,
  MWiW*, Me, MeP, NBuG, NIC, NN, Nh,
  NhD, OC, OCl, OClWHi, PU, WHi.

1651 "Shakers and Quakers," *New Moral
World* (London), 3d s., 6, no. 34 (February 15,
1845), 267–68.
  Contains a long excerpt from Elder Myrick's
  letter to William Oldham on the distinguishing
  doctrine of the Shakers-celibacy. He attributes
  the evils of society to its nonenforcement.
  This is intended to distinguish, in part, the
  differences between Shakers and an Irish sect
  of Quakers who "are eloquent in defence of
  matrimony."
  DLC, ICN, NNC*, NcD.

1652 SHEPHERD, WALTER. "A Different
Kind of Fundamentalists," *Christian Century,*
39 (November 30, 1922), 1494–95.
  A letter from Mt. Lebanon, signed: *Walter
  Shepherd.* It was written in reply to an
  earlier anonymous article, pp. 1383–84.

CtY–D, DLC*, MH–AH, NRCR, ODa, PSt.

1653 "The Shirley Shakers," *The Manifesto,*
23 (December 1893), 273–76.
  From the Fitchburg, Mass., *Daily Sentinel* on
  the 100th anniversary of the founding of the
  Shaker community: "The People, their Society,
  Home and Modes of Life," with biographical
  details of the life of Elder John Whiteley.
  Ct, DLC, ICN, IU, MB, MHarF, MPH, MWA,
  MWiW*, Nh, NhD, NjPT, OClWHi, WHi.

1654 "Socialistic Notes," *American Socialist*
(Oneida Community, N.Y.), 3 (October 10,
1878), 321.
  Quotations from a letter written by a Shaker
  who suggests that the published criticism of
  "contemporaneous communists be shared"
  with the Shakers because it would spread
  information about the sect.
  DLC, ICJ, MH, MWA*, NIC, NN, NhD, WHi.

1655 "South Union," Nos. 1–18. *The Manifesto,*
23 (November–December 1893), 249–50, 276–
79; 24 (1894), 3–6, 25–28, 53–56, 77–81, 101–
04, 125–27, 149–51, 173–76, 197–99, 221–25,
245–48, 269–71; 25 (January–April 1895), 3–5,
25–28, 49–52, 73–77.
  Revival in Kentucky, establishment of Shakerism, organization of South Union Society,
  October 17, 1811, early hardships, illness,
  slavery, and legal actions against the Shakers
  are covered. Civil War hardships and incidents
  at South Union are described in some detail.
  Ct, DLC, ICN, IU, MB, MHarF, MPH, MWA,
  MWiW*, Nh, NhD, NjPT, OClWHi, WHi.

1656 STEPHENS, ANNIE ROSETTA. "The
Social Gathering," *Peg Board* (Darrow School,
New Lebanon, N.Y.), 4 (June 1936), 57–58.
  Description of the annual festival and picnic
  held on a hill near Lake Queechy, *see also*
  no. 43.
  MHarF, MPB, MPH, MWiW*, NOC.

1657 STEWART, EZRA J. "Cassava and
Arrowroot," *St. Cloud Tribune* (Osceola County,
Fla.), 1 (December 23, 1909), 1, 4.
  Starch-producing plants which promise great
  profits. Stewart's newspaper accounts have

been included here because they provide scarce firsthand information about the Shaker Florida settlement at Narcoossee, *see also* no. 1623.
OClWHi*.

1658 —— "Citrus Groves in Florida," *St. Cloud Tribune* (Osceola County, Fla.), 1 (November 18, 1909), 1–2. illus.

Practical information on planting, cultivating, gathering, and marketing oranges, with photograph of Stewart picking oranges at the Shaker farm.
OClWHi*.

1659 —— "Hunting and Fishing, South Florida, a Paradise for Hunters and Fisherman," *St. Cloud Tribune* (Osceola County, Fla.), 1 (November 11, 1909), 1–2.
OClWHi*.

1660 —— "Stop the Seining," *St. Cloud Tribune* (Osceola County, Fla.), 1 (October 21, 1909), 3.

A plea not to deplete lakes of fish, written by a member of the "Shaker Colony."
OClWHi*.

1661 —— "Yule-tide Meditations," *St. Cloud Tribune* (Osceola County, Fla.), 1 (December 23, 1909), 2.

Signed: *Ezra J. Stewart, Shaker Colony.*
OClWHi*.

T

1662 TAYLOR, LEILA S. "A Remarkable Statement," *Christian Science Journal*, 75 (December 1907), 543–49.

A description of Anna White's interest in Christian Science, especially her illness in the summer of 1907 when her life was saved by the treatments of two practitioners. "Eldress Anna is a thorough convert and is constantly studying and demonstrating the truth as given in 'Science and Health with Key to the Scriptures,' by Mrs. Eddy. Others in the family are with her ..." Among early Shaker leaders the gift of spiritual healing was one of the apostolic gifts, and "The real thought and teachings of the leaders in primitive Shakerism are almost identical with Christian Science, sometimes even to identical expressions and turns of phrase ..." "Corroboration, by, Anna White, North Family of Shakers," pp. 548–49. *See also* L. Taylor's *A Memorial,* no. 1359, pp. 81–82, where Anna White's cure is described, and her letter to Mary Baker Eddy is included testifying to the cure; also p. 158, where the acceptance of Christian Science teachings by Elder Daniel Offord is described. "He never gave up the study of *Science and Health.*"

DLC, MB, MH, MWiW*, NN, NNUT, PP, WHi.

1663 TOLSTOI, LEV NĬKOLAEVĬCH, Graf. "Conscience the Guide," *The Manifesto,* 20 (October–November 1890), 227–29, 250–52.

"Reprinted from the *Philadelphia Press.* Translated from Count Tolstoi's manuscript." This is an explanatory statement intended to answer critics of the *Kreutzer Sonata, see* no. 1588. It is a condensed version of "An Afterword to the *Kreutzer Sonata,*" contained in his *Essays and Letters,* trans. by A. Maude (London, H. Frowde, 1903), pp. 36–52, including many verbatim excerpts. The editor has headed the article: "Christians Should Not Marry. Count Tolstoy Declares That Marriage Was Not Instituted by Christ. The Author of the 'Kreutzer Sonata' Advances a Startling Theory That Celibacy is Right and Marriage Wrong." It was scarcely a startling theory to the Shakers who had long employed the same justification for their practice of celibacy. Undoubtedly, Tolstoi's reading of Shaker doctrinal works in 1889 had an influence on his thinking and writing at this time, *see also* Desroche (no.

2050), pp. 275–278. In dialogue deleted from the final version of the *Kreutzer Sonata,* "the hero supported his argument for celibacy by mentioning the example of the Shakers, which, he declared, was based on the fact that Christ never married," E. J. Simmons, *Leo Tolstoy* (no. 2763), p. 128. This hitherto unpublished version is included in Vol. 26 of the Jubilee Edition of Tolstoi's works, available only in Russian (no. 2849). Three editions of the *Kreutzer Sonata* were published in the U.S. in 1890.
Ct, DLC, ICN, IU, MB, MHarF, MPH, MWA, MWiW*, Nh, NhD, NjPT, OClWHi, WHi.

1664 —— "A Letter from Tolstoi, the Russian Reformer, in Reply to a Letter Commending Tolstoi's 'Answer to his Critics,'" *The Manifesto,* 20 (December 1890), 271.
The letter is addressed to A. G. Hollister and dated: September 8, 1890. Tolstoi acknowledges receipt of Hollister's letter and continues, "I knew that my ideas about marriage would be approved by your Community. Your books and tracts, especially 'What Would Become of the World if all were Shakers,' corroborated my views and helped me very much to a clear understanding of the question. I am very much astonished how a Christian cannot approve your and my view of marriage . . . . It was very painful to me to read in your letter the account of the influx of spirits from heaven and so on," *see also* no. 2861. Hollister is admonished to put

aside such superstitions: "Put them away, and your Shaker faith, with your chaste and spiritual life, your humility, charity, and principles of moderation and manual work, will conquer the world." The Tolstoi-Hollister correspondence, 1889–1891, antedates the Tolstoi-Evans correspondence which has received so much attention, *see* H. Desroche, *Les Shakers Americains* (no. 2050), 269–77, and nos. 641, 882, 2116, and 3760.
Ct, DLC, ICN, IU, MB, MHarF, MPH, MWA, MWiW*, Nh, NhD, NjPT, OClWHi, WHi.

1665 TRIPURE, WILLIAM. "[Letter Accompanying Samples of Soil Taken at Shaker Village, N.H.]," *Farmer's Monthly Visitor* (Concord), 3 (November 30, 1841), 165.
This letter was also printed in the *Final Report on the Geology and Mineralogy of the State of New Hampshire* by C. T. Jackson. *See* no. 1070.
Ct, DNAL, ICJ, MU, MWA, MeU, N, NN, Nh, NhD*, OCHP, RPB, WHi.

1666 TRUMAN, J. G. "Shakerism," *American Socialist* (Oneida Community, N.Y.), 3 (July 18, 1878), 227–28.
A novitiate member of North Union, Ohio, suggests that "Scientific propagation of men is no more incompatible with their religion [Shakerism] than is the scientific breeding of horses and cattle which they now practice."
DLC, ICJ, MH, MWA*, NIC, NN, NhD, WHi.

U

1667 "United Society of Believers," *Day-Star,* 10 (June 13, 1846), 10–11.

Extracts from *A Brief Exposition of Established Principles,* no. 737.
MWA, MWiW*, OCHP, OClWHi.

V

1668 VON EUW, RUTH E. and MARGOT MAYO. "A Beginning List of Shakers of Enfield,

Conn.," *Shaker Quarterly,* 10 (Fall 1970), 71–84.

Death dates of 380 Believers compiled from various sources, arranged alphabetically by personal name, with source indicated.

CtHC, CtY-D, DLC, MABt, MHarF, MPH, MWiW*, NNUT, NOC, NhD, NhU, NjPT, OClWHi.

W

1669 WELLS, SETH YOUNGS. "[Letter to Michael H. Barton, Dated: June 4, 1832]," *Something New* (Harvard, Mass.), s. 2, No. 9 (June 1832), 105–06.

Expresses full approval of the system of orthography advocated by Barton, *see* no. 1324.
MB, MH, MHarF*, MHi.

1670 [——] "The Shakers," *Christian Spectator* (New Haven, Conn.), 6 (July 1824), 351–59.

A foreword explains that this account of Shaker religious beliefs was prepared "by two intelligent members" at Benjamin Silliman's request because "some members at New-Lebanon and Watervliet" had objected to statements in his *Remarks* . . . (no. 2761) derived from Thomas Brown's *Account* . . . (no. 114). Richard Bushnell and another member objected during a visit to Silliman in 1822, as did Seth Wells in a long letter, November 24, 1823 (no. 1418). This article was intended for insertation in the 1824 edition of Silliman's *Remarks* . . . The manuscript arrived, however, after the book was in press and Silliman recommended its publication in this journal of "extensive circulation."
CtY, DLC, ICN, MB, MH, MWA, MWiW*, MeB, N, NNC, Nh, NhD, OClW, PP.

1671 WEST, ARTHUR T. "Reminiscences of Life in a Shaker Village," *New England Quarterly*, 9 (June 1938), 343–60.

In his boyhood West lived in the Harvard, Mass., Shaker community and later taught in the Shaker school there. His recollections of life with the Shakers are graphic and sympathetic.
Ct, DLC, ICU, MB, MH, MWiW*, MeB, N, NN, Nh, NhD, NjP, OCl.

1672 WHITCHER, JOHN. "Reasons. For

Believing in the Second Coming of Christ in Mother Ann Lee," *Day-Star*, 12 (February 13, 1847), 18.

A long poem extending through 2 columns, dated at Canterbury, N.H., January 1847.
MWA, MWiW*, OCHP, OClWHi.

1673 [WHITE, ROBERT] [Letter], *The Knickerbocker*, 29 (February 1847), 180–81.

Communication to the editor, George Gaylord Clark, protesting his favorable review of the attack on the Shakers, *Lo Here! Lo There!* (no. 2815), and inviting him to visit New Lebanon, "Come then, I repeat; leave thy prepossessions behind." The letter is signed: *R --- W --- Jr.* Robert White was a prominent Quaker who joined the Shakers at Hancock, Mass., in 1846. He was the father of Anna White. *See also* nos. 2908, 3129, and 3130.
CtY, DLC, ICN, MWiW*, MeB, N, NN, Nh, NjP, OCl, PU, RPB.

1674 WILSON, DELMER. "The Diary of a Maine Boy: Delmer Wilson—1887," with Notes and an Introduction by Theodore E. Johnson, *Shaker Quarterly*, 8 (Spring 1968), 3–22.

Written when the author was 13 years of age, this diary covers the period, January 1– August 13, 1887, and "paints for us a unique picture of life in a relatively isolated Shaker community." Taken from a manuscript in the Shaker Library, Sabbathday Lake, Me.
CtHC, CtY-D, DLC, MBAt, MHarF, MPH, MWiW*, NN, NNUT, NOC, NhD, NhU, NjPT, OClWHi.

1675 [WINKLEY, FRANCIS, ISRAEL SANBORN, and DAVID PARKER] "[The Village of the United Society of Shakers, in Canterbury, N.H.]," *American Magazine of*

Useful and Entertaining Knowledge (Boston), 2 (November 1835), 133-35. illus.

Usually cited by the title above, which is actually the caption for the wood engraving of Canterbury Shaker Village. Following a description of the Society, the editor explains, "As many false impressions and erroneous opinions are entertained, concerning the people known by the name of Shakers, in compliance with the request of its friends, we publish the following sketch of their religious tenets, furnished by one of the Society, which we have reason to believe correct," and that "every sect should be heard in its own defense." Signed: *In behalf of the Society: Francis Winkley, Israel Sanborn, David Parker, Trustees for and in behalf of the Society.*

CtY, DLC, IU, MB, MWA, MWiW*, MeB, N, Nh, NjP, OClWHi, RPB.

1676 "The Worship of God," *Day-Star*, 11 (November 21, December 5, 1846), 37-38, 41-42.

The origin, practice, and reasonableness of dancing as an act of divine worship, reprinted from Pt. II, Chap. 5, pp. 77-89, of C. Green, *Summary View of the Millennial Church* (Albany, N.Y., 1823), no. 743.

MWA, MWiW*, OCHP, OClWHi.

Y

1677 YOUNGS, BENJAMIN SETH. "An Expedition against the Shakers," edited by J. P. MacLean, *Ohio Archaeological and Historical Society Publications*, 21 (1912), 403-15.

See no. 1474 for the 1810? edition and annotation.

Ct, DLC, KyBgW, MB, MWA, MWiW, MeB, Nh, NhD, OU, OClWHi*, PU.

An Annotated Bibliography of the Reported Decisions of the Courts . . . Relating to the Shakers

Compiled & Edited by Gerard C. Wertkin

Because this section represents a departure both in content and manner of presentation from the other material in this bibliography, a brief introductory note may be useful. The aim here is to direct the researcher to reported court decisions, *as decisions,* and not as printed works. Hence, the usual bibliographic paraphernalia are absent, and the relatively simple form of legal citation is used. These citations follow generally the suggestions contained in *A Uniform System of Citation* (better known as the "Harvard Blue Book") published by the Harvard Law Review Association (10th ed. 1962), with a number of technical variations thought to be advisable. The researcher who is unfamiliar with legal citations is directed to that reference work for any required clarification.

By necessity, the annotations are brief. In keeping with the general purposes of this bibliography, they are designed primarily to direct the researcher to those specific areas of Shaker interest with which the cases may be concerned. Thus, an attempt has been made to place the cases within the context of Shaker history, where possible, and in so doing, to identify the communities and personalities involved. Because the legal issues or specific holdings of the court are often of a highly technical nature, however, it was thought inadvisable within the context of a bibliography to attempt to delineate all of the issues or holdings.

The researcher is cautioned to keep in mind that only a small portion of the litigation in which the Shakers were involved is included in this compilation. As with litigation in general, many cases initiated by or against the United Society were disposed of prior to trial. Of those that were tried, only a small number may be assumed ever to have reached the higher appellate levels, where a printed report of the court decision is likely. Nevertheless, it is clear that these cases may be considered representative of the kinds of legal problems which the Shakers faced.

With only one or two exceptions, the reporters containing all of these decisions will be found in the leading law libraries of each state. Accordingly, it was thought unnecessary to include references to library collections as was done with the other material in this bibliography. In compiling these legal materials, the facilities of the law libraries of the Association of the Bar of the City of New York and New York University School of Law have been used.

1678 ADAMS V. BOHON, 176 Ky. 66, 195 S.W. 156 (1917).

The conveyance in 1910 of the lands of the Pleasant Hill community to George Bohon, a non-Shaker, by the remaining members of the Society prompts this action to determine whether this property had escheated to the common schools of Mercer County, Kentucky. The report is especially rich in historical data, with particular emphasis on the final days of the community. *See also* no. 1691.

1679 ANDERSON V. BROCK, 3 Me. (3 Greenl.) 243 (1825).

The issues before the Court in this action in trespass brought by John Anderson and Isaac Brackett, as "deacons and overseers" of the Alfred Society, are the capacity of the Shakers to take and hold lands in succession and the competence of members of the community to act as witnesses in an action instituted by the deacons.

1680 BOARD OF PARENT MINISTRY V. BOHON, 192 Ky. 285, 233 S.W. 721 (1921).

The Mount Lebanon (N.Y.) Ministry seeks possession of the Pleasant Hill (Ky.) properties.

1681 CHURCH OF THE UNITED SOCIETY IN CANTERBURY V. WINKLEY, 73 Mass. (7 Gray) 460 (1856).

The Canterbury (N.H.) Shakers, by David Parker, Trustee, bring an action on four promissory notes.

1682 CINCINNATI SOUTHERN RY. CO.'S TRUSTEES V. SOCIETY OF SHAKERS' TRUSTEES, 25 Ky.L.Rep. 1339, 78 S.W. 130 (1904).

Two acres of land near High Bridge, Kentucky, are the subject of this action against the Pleasant Hill Society.

1683 CURTIS V. CURTIS, 71 Mass. (5 Gray) 535 (1855).

Habeas corpus proceeding instituted by Joseph Fairbank, a trustee of the Enfield, Connecticut community, against Jane Curtis, who had placed her daughter Emily with the Shakers under an indenture of apprenticeship in 1851. Emily was later seized by her mother and brothers while on a day trip with members of the Shaker family to Springfield, Massachusetts.

1684 DAVIS V. BRADFORD, 58 N.H. 476 (1878).

Another aspect of the Shaker Mills litigation, *see* nos. **1685–1688**.

1685 DAVIS V. DYER, 54 N.H. 146 (1873).

The famous "Shaker Mills Case." This action was commenced against Orville Dyer and John Bradford, as trustees of the Church Family, Enfield, New Hampshire, by the surviving partner of the Shaker Mills Company. *See* no. **77.**

1686 DAVIS V. DYER, 56 N.H. 143 (1875).

Another aspect of the foregoing case.

1687 DAVIS V. DYER, 60 N.H. 400 (1880).

The same case, no. **1685.**

1688 DAVIS V. DYER, 62 N.H. 231 (1881).

The same case, no. **1685.**

1689 DYER V. DYER, 5 N.H. 271 (1830).

Action brought by Mary Dyer against her husband Joseph, a member of the Enfield, New Hampshire, community for a divorce under the Statute of December 21, 1821. *See also* nos. **525, 530, 532, 534,** and **535.**

1690 DYER V. HUNT, 5 N.H. 401 (1831).

The validity of an indenture of apprenticeship under which the overseer of the poor of Norwich, Vermont, had bound a boy to Joseph Dyer, as trustee of the Enfield, New Hampshire, Shakers is decided by the Court.

1691 EASUM V. BOHON, 180 Ky. 451. 202 S.W. 901. L.R.A. 1918D, 1144 (1918).

Another attempt to obtain control of the Pleasant Hill properties, this time by the descendents of John Shain, one of the founding members of the Society and a signatory of the Covenant of 1814. *See also* no. **1678.**

1692 FEINER V. REISS, 98 App. Div. 40, 90 N.Y. Supp. 568 (1st Dept. 1904).

The marketability of title to property in New York City which was owned by the Mount Lebanon Shakers from 1885 to 1890 is the issue before the Court.

1693 FITTS V. FITTS, 46 N.H. 184 (1865).

When Eliza A. Fitts refuses to join her husband Edward in leaving the Canterbury Shaker community, he sues her for divorce.

1694 FOWLER V. HOLLENBECK, 9 Barb. 309 (N.Y. Sup. Ct. 1850).

Edward Fowler, a trustee of the New Lebanon Shakers, brings this action against the Sheriff of Columbia County, New York, and William H. Pillow for removing Pillow's sons, who had been legally bound to Fowler as apprentices, from the community. *See also* nos. **1071, 1083, 1195,** and **1384.**

1695 GASS V. WILHITE, 32 Ky. (2 Dana) 170, 26 Am. Dec. 446 (1834).

This significant case was instituted by two seceding members of the Pleasant Hill Society, Gass and Bonta [i.e., Banta], for the purpose of obtaining a division of the Society's property and having their shares allotted to them. Contains extensive extracts and legal analysis of undated Covenant, the validity of which is upheld by the Court. *See also* no. **913.**

1696 GOODRICH V. WALKER, 1 Johns. Cas. 251 (N.Y. Sup. Ct. 1800).

Plaintiff, a member of the New Lebanon Society until 1796, sues for the value of his work, labor, and services. The issues before the Court are the validity of a release signed by the Plaintiff when he left the community and the competence of members of the community to testify as witnesses in the Society's behalf.

1697 GRACE V. UNITED SOCIETY CALLED SHAKERS, 203 Mass. 355, 89 N.E. 552 (1909).
An employee of the Hancock Shakers sues to recover damages for personal injuries sustained while assisting in the operation of a "cylinder planer."

1698 GROSVENOR V. UNITED SOCIETY, 118 Mass. 78 (1875).
Companion actions brought by Roxalana L. Grosvenor and Maria F. Grosvenor, who had been expelled from the Harvard community in 1869, for services rendered while members of the community and for damages sustained as a result of the failure of the Society to support them after their expulsion. In dismissing their claims, the Court held that the rights of the two sisters must be determined by the Shaker Covenant, an undated copy of which is set out in the report. Ironically, Roxalana was defeated by the very instrument which she revealed to the world in 1873, *see* nos. **1003, 1307, and 3795.**

1699 HAMILTON V. PEASE, 38 Conn. 115 (1871).
Motion to set aside the verdict in an action commenced against Omar Pease, as Trustee of the North Family, Enfield, Connecticut, for diversion of a stream of water, on ground that a member of the jury having been given a copy of *Shakerism Unveiled* (no. 2739) was prejudiced against Shakers. Plaintiff is alleged to have purchased 1,000 copies of the pamphlet from "one Munger" with whom he cooperated in having it printed in 1869.

1700 JOHNSON V. UNITED SOCIETY OF SHAKERS, 6 Ky. Opin. 139 (1872).
The ownership of land in Logan County, Kentucky, conveyed in 1836 to George Rankin and Eli MacLean, as Trustees of the South Union Society, is the subject of this action.

1701 LAWRENCE V. FLETCHER, 49 Mass. (8 Metc.) 153 (1844).
In suing to redeem land in Littleton, Massachusetts, the plaintiff argues that the Harvard Shakers lacked the capacity to take an assignment of a mortgage affecting the land. Reviewing the history of the organization of the community and the succession of its trustees, the Court holds that the Shakers formed an unincorporated religious society entitled to receive grants of land.

1702 LAWRENCE V. FLETCHER, 51 Mass. (10 Metc.) 344 (1845).
Another decision arising out of the foregoing case. This report is limited to a discussion of the issue of waiver of foreclosure.

1703 In re M'DOWLE, 8 Johns. 328 (N.Y. Sup. Ct. 1811).
This early case involving the custody of children placed with the Shakers was commenced by the issuance of writs of habeas corpus directing Nathan Spier and Nathan Slosson of the Watervliet, New York, community to produce two boys, Hugh and John M'Dowle, who had been apprenticed to the Shakers in 1808 by their father Matthew. Although the Court held the indentures of apprenticeship were not binding upon the boys, a footnote to the report indicates that they chose to return to the Shakers.

1704 MERRIFIELD V. THE SHAKERS, 30 Ky. 496 (1832).
Rebecca Merrifield's suit to recover the value of personal property brought with her when she entered the South Union (the report erroneously says "West Union") Society is dismissed on a technicality.

1705 PATTERSON V. PEASE, 5 Ohio 190 (1831).
Land conveyed in 1811 by John Patterson, prior to joining the Shakers, is sought in this action by his son.

1706 PEASE V. PEASE, 35 Conn. 131, 95 Am. Dec. 225 (1868).

Action against Omar Pease, as Trustee of the East Family, Enfield, Connecticut, on promissory notes executed by Zelotes Terry, a former trustee, in connection with the purchase of land in Massachusetts. Report includes dates of establishment and identity of trustees of the several Enfield families.

1707 PENNEBAKER V. PENNEBAKER HOME FOR GIRLS, 291 Ky. 12, 163 S.W. 2d 53, 143 A.L.R. 389 (1942).

Litigation instituted by collateral kinsmen and heirs of Dr. Pennebaker claiming property of Pennebaker Home for Girls (formerly part of the Pleasant Hill Shaker community) on ground that the purposes for which the trust had been established had failed because of the alleged mismanagement of the Home. Pennebaker's will set out in full in report.

1708 PENNEBAKER V. PENNEBAKER HOME FOR GIRLS, 297 Ky 670, 181 S.W. 2d 49 (1944).

The trustee of the Pennebaker trust seeks to sell the property of the Pennebaker Home for Girls and to invest the proceeds to carry out the purposes of the trust. *See* foregoing case.

1709 PENNEBAKER BROS. V. BELL CITY MFG. CO., 130 Ky. 592, 113 S.W. 829 (1908).

Action to cancel notes for the purchase of a threshing machine.

1710 PENNEBAKER HOME FOR GIRLS V. BOARD OF DIRECTORS, 250 Ky. 44, 61 S.W. 2d 883 (1938).

The will of Dr. W. F. Pennebaker of Pleasant Hill, under which former Shaker property conveyed to him in 1913 by George Bohon (*see* no. **1678**) was left for the creation of a school for young girls, is construed by the Court.

1711 PEOPLE EX REL. BARBOUR V. GATES, 43 N.Y. 40 (1870).

The Court of Appeals reverses the decision

below and dismisses the habeas corpus. Report contains revealing cross-examination on the basic tenets of the Shaker religion.

1712 PEOPLE EX REL. BARBOUR V. GATES, 57 Barb. 291 39 How. Prac. 74 (N.Y. Sup. Ct. 1869).

Proceeding upon habeas corpus instituted by Sarah Ann Barbour, for several years a member of the Mount Lebanon community, to obtain custody of her daughter Marion, whom she had bound to Benjamin Gates, a trustee of the Society, under an indenture of apprenticeship in 1866. Relying on technical deficiencies in the indenture, the Court grants custody of the child to her mother.

1713 RAYBOURNE V. SOCIETY OF SHAKERS, 17 Ky. L. Rep. 143, 30 S.W. 622 (1895).

The Shakers of Pleasant Hill sue to recover possession of a horse.

1714 RICHARDSON V. FREEMAN, 6 Me. (6 Greenl.) 57 (1829).

The competence of members of the community to act as witnesses in the absence of a release is the question before the Court in this action founded on a promissory note endorsed by the deacons of the Alfred Society as sureties.

1715 SOCIETY OF SHAKERS V. WATSON, 68 Fed. 730 (6th Cir. 1895).

Suit against the Pleasant Hill, Kentucky, Society to subject the property of the Society to a charge for the payment of a promissory note.

1716 SOCIETY OF SHAKERS V. WATSON, 77 Fed. 512 (6th Cir. 1896).

Another aspect of the foregoing case. Some interesting evidence of relationship between Shakers and Rappites.

1717 SOCIETY OF SHAKERS V. WATSON 163 U.S. 704, 16 S.Ct. 1206, 41 L.Ed. 313 (1895).

The foregoing case. Certiorari denied.

1718 SPENCER V. SOCIETY OF SHAKERS, 23 Ky. L. Rep. 854, 64 S.W. 468 (1901).
Action against the Pleasant Hill Society on promissory note signed in 1896 by James W. Shelton and M. Jane Sutton, Trustees.

1719 STATE EX REL. BALL V. HAND, 5 W.L.J. 361, 1 Ohio D. Repr. 238 (Super. Ct. 1848).
Stephen Ball attempts to obtain custody of his two daughters from their maternal grandmother with whom they have resided since he entered the Shakers.

1720 STATE EX REL. SHARP V. TRUSTEES, 2 Ohio 108 (1825).
The distribution of proceeds reserved for "ministerial purposes" is sought by the Union Village Society in this mandamus proceeding against the Trustees of Township 4, Range 3, Warren County, Ohio.

1721 UNITED SOCIETY, CALLED SHAKERS V. BROOKS, 145 Mass. 410, 14 N.E. 622 (1888).
Action on a contract for the sale to defendant of timber standing on the Hancock, Mass., Society's land in Stamford, Vermont.

1722 UNITED SOCIETY OF SHAKERS V. UNDERWOOD, 72 Ky. (9 Bush) 609, 15 Am. Rep. 731 (1873).
The South Union Shakers sue the officers of the Bank of Bowling Green, Kentucky, alleging conversion of bonds deposited by Urban Johns, a trustee of the community.

1723 UNITED SOCIETY OF SHAKERS V. UNDERWOOD, 74 Ky. (11 Bush) 265, 21 Am. Rep. 214 (1875).
Another decision arising out of the foregoing case.

1724 WAITE V. MERRILL, 4 Me. (4 Greenl.) 102, 16 Am. Dec. 238 (1826).
Of great importance, this decision upholds the validity of the Shaker Covenant, the Court dismissing the claims of a seceder from the Society at Sabbathday Lake for compensation for services performed while a member of the community. The Covenant of January 31, 1814, is fully set out in the introduction to the report. *See also* nos. 926 and 927.

1725 WELLS V. LANE, 8 Johns. 462 (N.Y. Sup. Ct. 1811).
The plaintiff seeks a penalty from the Watervliet, N.Y., Shakers, who are accused of harboring his slave Betty.

1726 WHITE V. M'BRIDE, 7 Ky. (4 Bibb) 61 (1815).
This important early case involving Shaker pacifism was instituted by the Pleasant Hill Shakers against the deputy sheriff of Mercer County, Kentucky, to obtain possession of property taken to satisfy fines assessed against members of the community for not attending military musters. The Court, reviewing the applicable constitutional principles, holds that persons conscientiously opposed to bearing arms cannot be fined by a court martial for failure to attend musters.

1727 WHITE V. MILLER, 71 N.Y. 118, 27 Am. Rep. 13 (1877).
Informative decision involving the seed business conducted by the Watervliet, New York, Shakers. This decision reversed White v. Miller, 7 Hun 427. *See also* White v. Trustees of the Shakers, 2 N.Y. Wkly. Dig. 368 (Sup. Ct. 3d Dept. 1876), and White v. Miller, 78 N.Y. 393 (1879).